Computer Science

AN INSTRUCTIONAL MANUAL

C. S. FRENCH, B.Sc.(Hons), M.Sc., Grad.Cert.Ed., AFIMA, MBCS

Carl French *is employed as a Senior Lecturer at The Hatfield Polytechnic. He has spent a number of years teaching on a wide variety of computer courses in colleges in Hendon, Uxbridge and Cambridgeshire.*

2nd Edition

Grahame Smith

DP PUBLICATIONS Ltd.
12 Romsey Road, Eastleigh
Hants. SO5 4AL
1985

ACKNOWLEDGEMENTS

I wish to express my thanks to the following:

Messrs E. C. Oliver and R. J. Chapman for their permission to use material from their book "Data Processing".

To Mr. J. A. Moffat of Uxbridge Technical College, Mr. I. P. Page of The University of Texas and Mr. D. W. B. Bale of Dorset Institute of Higher Education all of whom read and checked the first edition at various stages and who made numerous helpful comments and suggestions.

Mr. P. Harrison of Hendon College of Further Education who read and checked the second edition and also made numerous helpful comments and suggestions.

IBM UK Ltd for permission to use illustrations at Fig. 2.5, Fig. 2.8, Fig. 2.11, Fig. 5.6, Fig. 19.14, Fig. 19.6 and appendix 2.1(a), and for permission to use a number of photographs within the text. (Separate acknowledgements are given with each of the photographs within the text.)

CalComp Ltd. and Rediffusion Computers Ltd. for permission to reproduce photographs of their products.

Mr. J. Beasley of The Hatfield Polytechnic for permission to reproduce sample outputs from the Spider and Bezlib graphics package.

The Associated Examining Board (AEB), The British Computer Society (BCS), The University of Cambridge Local Examinations Syndicate (Cambridge), The Joint Matriculation Board (JMB), The University of London University Entrance and School Examination Council (London), The University of Oxford Delegacy of Local Examinations (OLE) and The Welsh Joint Education Committee (Welsh) for permission to reproduce past examination questions.

Carl French 1984

First Edition 1980
Reprinted 1981
Reprinted 1982
2nd Edition 1984
Reprinted 1985

British Library Cataloguing in Publication Data

French, C.S.
Computer Science. – 2nd ed.
1. Electronic data processing 2. Computers
I. Title
001.64 QA76

ISBN 0-905435-38-9

Printed by The Guernsey Press Company Ltd
Braye Road, Vale,
Guernsey, Channel Islands.

Preface

AIMS OF THE MANUAL.

1. The primary aim of this manual is to provide a simplified approach to the understanding of Computer Science, which is the study of computers and the ways and methods of using computers. The manual assumes a minimum of prior knowledge which enables the early chapters in the text to be used to introduce or reappraise basic methods and ideas according to the reader's needs.

2. The text is intended to suit a number of courses including those leading to these examinations:

a. G.C.E. 'A' Level Computer Science. Many questions set within the text are taken from examination papers set by the various boards.

b. B.C.S. Part 1. The manual should serve as a general introductory text. Some questions set within the text are taken from past examination papers.

c. First year University and Polytechnic examinations in Computer Science.

d. Computer Options in BTEC, Higher National Courses.

e. Many City and Guilds examination subjects, including 746, 747 and 748.

f. I.D.P.M. parts I and II.

g. BTEC National and Higher National awards in Computer Studies.

APPROACH.

3. The manual has been designed for use in independent study or as a text to be used in conjunction with tuition at school, college etc.

END OF CHAPTER.

4. At the end of chapters is found:

a. Summary of chapter.

b. Points to note. These are used for purposes of emphasis or clarification.

c. Questions. (see below)

QUESTIONS.

5. In order to satisfy a variety of uses; as an instructional manual, course text book, revision text, etc., the following types of questions have been included:

a. **Student self test questions** at the end of each chapter. These questions enable the reader to test his or her understanding of the material covered. The reader is advised to attempt all these questions. Answers are provided in appendix 1.

b. **Questions without answers** at the end of most chapters. These are mostly questions appropriate for use as homework exercises but also include questions which do not require answers. Teachers and Lecturers may obtain a free copy of answers to these questions if they send a written request to the publishers using school or college headed stationery.

c. **Revision test questions** at the end of the text. Answers are given in appendix 1.

APPENDICES.

6. Use has been made of appendices and the reader should note carefully the purpose of each.

a. Appendix 1 contains answers to the Student Self test questions set at the end of each chapter and contains answers to revision test questions too.

b. Appendix 2 contains details which have been excluded from the text in the interests of clarity.

c. Appendix 3 contains notes on projects, coursework and other study.

HOW TO USE THE MANUAL.

7. Students are advised to read the manual chapter by chapter since subsequent work often builds on topics covered earlier.

8. The layout of the chapters has been standardised so as to present information in a simple form which is easy to assimilate. However, in some chapters the emphasis is on principles and applications while other chapters emphasise methods and procedures. These differences reflect the fact that students will be expected to answer examination questions which require both written answers and problem solving. The study of methods and procedures should be combined with practical coursework whenever possible.

9. Students are advised to attempt questions as they come to them, and to check their answers in the appendix before reading further.

10. A minimum of prior mathematical knowledge is assumed. When post O level Mathematics does occur, as in chapter 49, the student is warned in advanced and may avoid it. Most students taking this subject have the necessary mathematical skills and the mathematical topics are generally popular with students.

NOTATION AND TERMINOLOGY.

11. The terminology used within this manual is consistent with the more widely accepted definitions, and in particular, it is consistent with the booklet containing "A glossary of computer terms" published by the BCS. Where other equivalent terms are also in common use in examinations they have been mentioned. Notation is defined as it is introduced.

OTHER READING.

12. The reader should find that this text provides the appropriate coverage of the material needed for those examinations for which the text is intended as a preparation. However, the reader might like to know that much of the more elementary material in this text is covered in more detail in Computer Studies by C.S. French. Greater detail of some aspects of data processing are provided in Data

Processing by E.C. Oliver and R.J. Chapman, (the text has some material in common with Computer Science) and a Practice and Revision Manual by W.D. Nash covers some Computer Science topics in more detail. All these texts are published by DP Publications.

SUGGESTIONS AND CRITICISM.

13. The author would welcome any suggestions or criticism from students or lecturers.

CSF

Note to the 2nd Edition.

1. In order to give readers a full and up to date account of Computer Science the material has been **extensively** revised for this edition. The contents have also been revised so as to reflect the revision of examination syllabuses by established examinations boards and the introduction of new syllabuses by other examination boards.

2. As part of the revision the opportunity has been taken to respond to the suggestions and criticisms received by the author. For example, the appendices have been rationalised, and where appropriate, material has been incorporated into the main body of the text. Far more material has been introduced in order to provide the necessary coverage of software, programming and file processing. I would like to take this opportunity to thank all those who have written to me with their comments and suggestions.

CSF.

Contents

COMPUTERS IN CONTEXT

Foundation Topics

1. The first three chapters contain introductory material which will be developed in later chapters. Students with prior knowledge are advised to read these chapters as a revision exercise.

1 Basic Ideas and Terms

INTRODUCTION.

1. This chapter introduces some basic terminology and gives an overview of the elements from which computers are made.

2. Data.
'Data' is the name given to basic *facts* eg the number of items sold by a business, or the numerical values used in mathematical formulae.

3. Computer.
A computer is a device which accepts data in one form and *processes* it to produce data in another form. A more precise definition will be given later.

4. Program.
A program is a *set of instructions* which is written in the language of the computer. A program is used to make the computer perform a specific task such as producing a payroll. (Note the spelling program **not** programme.)

5. Information.
A distinction is sometimes made between *data* and *information.* When data is converted into a *more useful or intelligible form* then it is said to be processed into information.

6. Hardware and software.

a. **Hardware** is the general term used to describe *all* the electronic and mechanical elements of the computer, together with those devices used with the computer.

b. **Software** is a general term used to describe *all* the various programs which may be used on a computer system together with their associated documentation.

COMPUTER TYPES.

7. There are several methods of classifying computers. The main distinction between digital and analog devices is given first, followed by classification by purpose, classification by age of technology and lastly some further classifications.

BASIC TYPES.

8. a. **Digital.** So called because they process data which is represented in the form of discrete values (eg 0, 1, 2, 3 .....) by operating on it in steps. Discrete values occur at each step in the operation. Counting on ones fingers is probably the simplest *digital operation* we all know.

b. **Analog** computers are akin to measuring instruments such as thermometers and voltmeters. They process data in the form of electrical voltages which are variable like the variable positions of a pointer on a dial. The output from analog computers is often in the form of smooth graphs from which information can be read.

c. **Hybrid** computers, as their name suggests, are computers which have the combined features of digital and analog computers.

This book is mainly concerned with digital computers, which are by far the most widely used type.

PURPOSE.

9. a. **Special purpose.** These, as their name suggests, are computers designed for a particular job only; to solve problems of a restricted nature. Examples are computers designed for air traffic control or weapons guidance systems.

b. **General purpose.** Computers designed to solve a wide variety of problems are called general purpose machines. Within the limitations imposed by their particular design capabilities, they can be adapted to perform particular tasks or solve problems by means of specially written programs.

NB. This distriction is not as sharp as it first appears because a general purpose computer can temporarily become special purpose through adaptation.

COMPUTER GENERATIONS

10. The first *electronic* computers were produced in the 1940s. Since then a series of radical breakthroughs in electronics has occured. With each major breakthrough, the computers based upon the older form of electronics have been replaced by a new **"generation"** of computers based upon the newer form of electronics. These "generations" are classified as follows:-

a **First Generation.** Early computers using electronic valves. (Circa 1940s). Examples were EDSAC, EDVAC, LEO and UNIVAC1.

b. **Second Generation.** More reliable computers using transistors which replaced the first generation. (Circa 1950s). Examples were LEO mark III, ATLAS and the IBM 7000 series.

c. **Third Generation.** More powerful, reliable and compact computers using simple integrated circuits (**ICs**). (Circa 1960s and early 1970s). Examples were the ICL 1900 series and the IBM 360 series.

d. **Fourth Generation.** The computers in use today and which contain more sophisticated microelectronic devices such as complex integrated circuits which are classified as "Large Scale Integration" (**LSI**) or "Very Large Scale Integration" (**VLSI**).

e. **Fifth Generation.** There are many predictions that by the end of the century computers will have been developed which will be able to converse with people in a human like manner and which will also be able to mimic human senses, manual skills and intelligence. The term "Fifth Generation" is often used to describe such computer systems.

FURTHER CLASSIFICATION.

11. a. **Mainframe.** Large general purpose computers with extensive processing, storage and input/output capabilities.

b. **Minicomputer.** Physically smaller computers compared with mainframes. They are used for special purposes or smaller scale general purpose work. Examples DEC's PDP11 and VAX range.

c. **Microcomputers.** These represent a further step in miniaturisation in which the various integrated circuits and elements of a computer are replaced by a single integrated circuit, called a 'chip'. Their low cost, matchbox size, and rapid technological development is having a revolutionary effect on the whole computer industry. Examples are the Commodore Pet, the Apple, the IBM PC, ACT Sirius and BBC microcomputer.

d. A **visible record computer** uses a special form of storage – a *magnetic stripe ledger card* which has the data both printed (and so intelligible to the user) and encoded on the magnetic tape (so that the card is also intelligible to the machine).

e. A **Word Processor** is a *special purpose* computer used in the production of office documents, letters, contracts, etc.

NB. A general purpose computer can run a Word Processing program and hence temporarily become special purpose.

SOFTWARE.

12. In the preceding paragraphs the emphasis was on differences in hardware. We will now look at the general classification of the software applicable to all machines, before we go on to consider the elements of the computer.

13. Types of Software.

The two main classes are

a. **Applications programs.** These are programs which do specific jobs for the user, such as solving equations or producing a payroll.

b. **Systems programs.** These are programs which control the performance of the computer. They do a variety of jobs to ensure the proper, orderly and efficient use of hardware by user programs, as well as performing many standard tasks. Most applications programs can only work when used in conjunction with the appropriate systems programs.

BASIC ELEMENTS (FUNCTIONS) OF A COMPUTER SYSTEM.

14. The basic elements which make up a computer system are as follows:–

a. Input.

b. Storage.

c. Control.

d. Computing/Processing.

e. Output.

15. Brief description of each element.

a. **Input.** Most computers cannot accept data in forms customary to human communication such as speech or hand written documents. It is necessary therefore, to present data to the computer in a way which provides easy conversion into its own electronic pulse based forms. This is commonly achieved by typing the data into keyboard devices which convert it into *machine-sensible* forms. In some cases machine readable documents or, media are produced as part of the input process. Data finally enters *Storage.*

b. **Storage.** Data and instructions enter *main* storage, and are held until needed to be worked on. The *instructions* dictate action to be taken on the *data.* Results of action will be held until they are required for output. Main storage is supplemented by less costly *auxiliary* or backing storage (eg. disks – see later) for mass storage purposes. Backing Storage serves an important role in holding 'maintained data' ie. data held by the computer so that it can provide information to the user when required to do so.

c. **Control.** Each computer has a control unit which fetches instructions from main storage, *interprets* them, and issues the necessary *signals* to the components making up the system. It directs all *hardware* operations necessary in obeying instructions.

d. **Computer/processing.** Instructions are obeyed and the necessary arithmetic operations etc are carried out on the data. The section that does this is called the Arithmetic-Logical Unit (ALU). In addition to arithmetic it also performs so-called "logical" operations. These operations take place at incredibly high speeds eg. 1 million numbers may be totalled in one second.

e. **Output.** Results are taken from main storage and fed to an output *device.* This can be a Printer, in which case the information is automatically converted to a *printed form.*

16. The elements are produced in chart form in Fig. 1.1. The chart shows what is often referred to as 'the Logical Structure' of the computer. Notice particularly the following points:–

a. Data normally flows from input devices or backing storage into *main storage* and from main storage to output devices or backing storage.

b. The processor performs operations on data from main storage and returns the results of processing to main storage.

c. In some cases, which will be discussed in later chapters, data flows directly between the processor and input or output devices rather than as described in (a).

d. The arithmetic-logical unit, control unit, and main storage combine to form the CENTRAL PROCESSOR or CENTRAL PROCESSING UNIT (CPU).

In recent years, because of changes in computer design and construction, it has become common to use the term CPU to refer to the ALU and control unit combined, *excluding* main memory. To avoid confusion in this book "CPU" will mean ALU + control unit + main memory and "Processor" will mean just ALU + control unit.

e. The difference between the data lines and command/signal lines.

f. Data held on backing storage may be input to main memory during processing, used and bought up to date using newly input data, and then returned to backing storage.

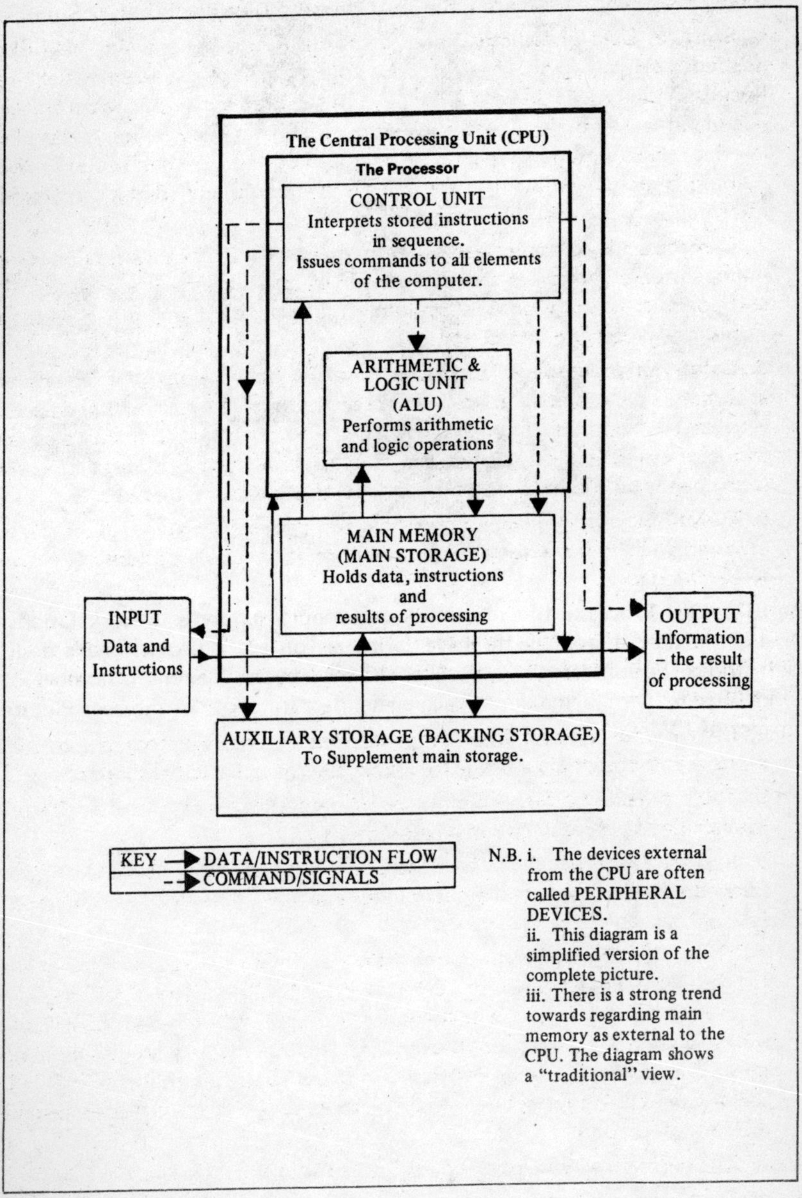

Fig. 1.1. The elements of a Computer System showing its "Logical Structure"

The IBM 4361 Processor has the ability to support hundreds of workstations, the 4361 makes it possible to have terminals on every professional's desk. Main storage options are 2, 4, 6, 8 or 12 megabytes. Maximum number of channels is 6, with a maximum aggregate data rate of 10 mb/sec. Picture courtesy of IBM.

SUMMARY.

17. a. This manual is mainly concerned with general purpose digital computers.

b. The basic elements of a computer system are:

i. Input
ii. Storage
iii. Control
vi. Arithmetic
v. Output

c. Two main classes of software are **applications programs** and **systems programs.**

POINTS TO NOTE

18. a. The Central Processor is sometimes called the Central Processing Unit (CPU).

b. The hardware devices external from the CPU are often called PERIPHERAL DEVICES.

c. The term "processor" is used within this book to mean the ALU + Control Unit and "CPU" is used to mean the processor + main storage.

d. The material covered in this chapter now allows a more precise definition than that given originally. **We now define a computer as a device which works under the control of a stored program, automatically accepting and processing data to produce information which is the result of that processing.**

STUDENT SELF TESTING QUESTIONS (answers begin page 679)

1. Distinguish between the terms 'data' and 'information'.

2. Identify the elements of a computer system and give a brief description of each.

QUESTIONS WITHOUT ANSWERS

3. Find out whether the place where you are studying Computer Science has a mainframe, minicomputer or microcomputer and make a list of the hardware.

2 Data Representation and Transmission

INTRODUCTION.

1. Ideally we would like to communicate with computers in the spoken or written form of everyday language. In practice we have to convert data to forms more readily acceptable to a machine. This chapter describes the basic methods of representing and transmitting data, and takes commonly used methods as examples.

CHARACTERS.

2. Sets of letters, digits and other symbols (see Fig. 3.1) are frequently used to represent data items such as names prices etc. Such a set of symbols is called a **character set.** Keyboard devices, including ordinary typewriters, each have their own character sets which are commonly engraved onto the keys. Keyboard devices are frequently used to input data into computers. A character set, comprised of 96 characters is shown in fig. 2.1.

s
p
a !"#$%&´()*+,–./0123456789:;<=>?@ABCDEFGHIJKLMNO
c
e

PQRSTUVWXYZ[\]^_`abcdefghijklmnopqrstuvwxyz{¦}"

Fig. 2.1. A character set of 96 characters.

CHARACTER TRANSMISSION.

3. When a key on the keyboard of a computer input device is pressed the device produces an electrical signal which represents the key's character and which the device transmits to the computer. The transmission passes through a cable from the device to the computer and the signal for each individual character is a series of electrical pulses called a **pulse train.** (see Fig. 2.2)

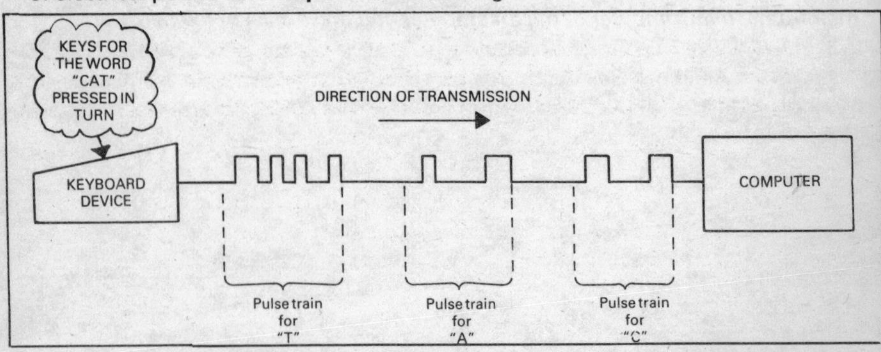

Fig 2.2. A simplified view of data being transmitted from a keyboard device to a computer

CODE TRANSMISSION DETAILS.

4. We will now look at pulse trains in more detail. As you read the next few paragraphs you may find it useful to refer to fig. 2.3 which gives a detailed illustration of the pulse code for "T" shown in figure 2.2.

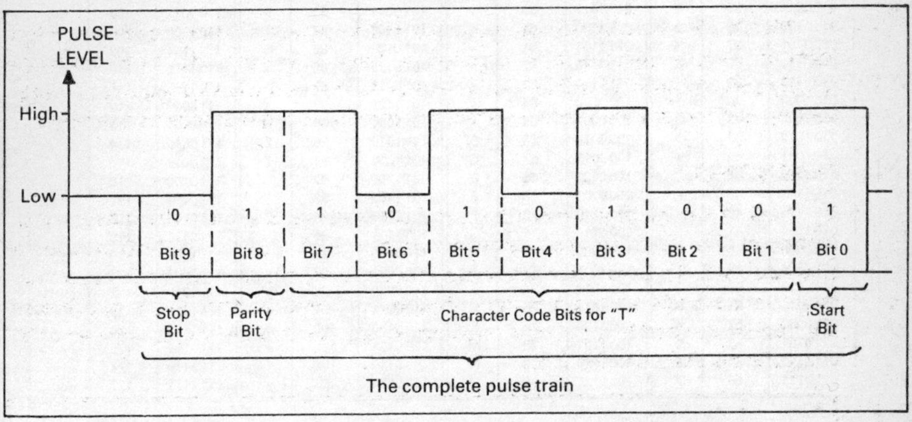

Fig. 2.3. Details of an asynchronous transmission of the ASCII character "T"

5. The complete pulse train by Fig. 2.2 is comprised of ten pulses in sequence which are each either at a high level or at a low level. These two levels are represented by 1's and 0's respectively.

6. Bits. The system of representing pulse levels by the symbols '0' and '1' corresponds to a system of representing numbers called the **binary number system.** The binary number system also uses only the two symbols '0' and '1'. Further details will be given in the next chapter. For the time being remember that **B**inary dig**ITS** are called **BITS** and note that the pulses in fig. 2.3 are represented by the ten bits which are labelled Bit 0 to Bit 9 inclusive.

7. Character Codes. The particular combination of 0's and 1's used for bits 1 to 7 inclusive in fig. 2.3 has been chosen to represent the character "T". Thus we have a *"7 bit code"* representing the character "T".

8. ASCII. The 7 bit code just described conforms to a standard called ASCII. ASCII stands for American Standard Code for Information Interchange. ASCII codes are widely used throughout the computer industry. The ASCII character set is shown in Fig. 2.4.

Binary Code	Decimal Value	Char-acter	Binary Code	Decimal Value	Char-acter	Binary Code	Decimal Value	Char-acter	Binary Code	Decimal Value	Char-acter
010 0000	32	<sp>	011 1000	56	8	101 0000	80	P	110 1000	104	h
010 0001	33	!	011 1001	57	9	101 0001	81	Q	110 1001	105	i
010 0010	34	"	011 1010	58	:	101 0010	82	R	110 1010	106	j
010 0011	35	#	011 1011	59	;	101 0011	83	S	110 1011	107	k
010 0100	36	$	011 1100	60	<	101 0100	84	T	110 1100	108	l
010 0101	37	%	011 1101	61	=	101 0101	85	U	110 1101	109	m
010 0110	38	&	011 1110	62	>	101 0110	86	V	110 1110	110	n
010 0111	39	'	011 1111	63	?	101 0111	87	W	110 1111	111	o
010 1000	40	(	100 0000	64	@	101 1000	88	X	111 0000	112	p
010 1001	41	)	100 0001	65	A	101 1001	89	Y	111 0001	113	q
010 1010	42	*	100 0010	66	B	101 1010	90	Z	111 0010	114	r
010 1011	43	+	100 0011	67	C	101 1011	91	[	111 0011	115	s
010 1100	44	,	100 0100	68	D	101 1100	92		111 0100	116	t
010 1101	45	–	100 0101	69	E	101 1101	93	]	111 0101	117	u
010 1110	46	.	100 0110	70	F	101 1110	94	^	111 0110	118	v
010 1111	47	/	100 0111	71	G	101 1111	95	_	111 0111	119	w
011 0000	48	0	100 1000	72	H	110 0000	96	`	111 1000	120	x
011 0001	49	1	100 1001	73	I	100 0001	97	a	111 1001	121	y
011 0010	50	2	100 1010	74	J	110 0010	98	b	111 1010	122	z
011 0011	51	3	100 1011	75	K	110 0011	99	c	111 1011	123	{
011 0100	52	4	100 1100	76	L	110 0100	100	d	111 1100	124	
011 0101	53	5	100 1101	77	M	110 0101	101	e	111 1101	125	}
011 0110	54	6	100 1110	78	N	110 0110	102	f	111 1110	126	~
011 0111	55	7	100 1111	79	O	110 0111	103	g	111 1111	127	<del>

NB. The binary codes corresponding to the decimal value from 0 to 31 are used as "control characters" ie. they are used to control the transmitting devices rather than to represent data. (details later)

Fig. 2.4. The ASCII character set

9. **Start Bits and Stop Bits.** Bit 0 in fig. 2.2 is called a "start bit". It is the first bit in the pulse train to be transmitted. Its purpose is to signify the start of a character transmission to the receiver (the computer in this case). Bit 9, the "stop bit", signifies the end of the transmission. The start bit and stop bit are always of opposite polarity (ie. if one is 1 the other is 0) so that a change of pulse level takes place when a start bit is transmitted. On some systems two stop bits are used.

10. **Protocols.** A convention used to control the transmission of data is called a protocol. The use of start bits and stop bits is an example of a very simple protocol.

11. **Asynchronous transmission.** The transmission of the characters in fig. 2.2 is asynchronous. That is, the characters pulse trains are *transmitted singly* as they occur at *irregular intervals in time.* However, within pulse trains all bit transmissions occur at a fixed rate.

12. **Synchronous transmissions** occur at fixed intervals and at fixed rates. For example a prepared set of characters may be transmitted synchronously as a single block of character which will be more efficient than transmitting them singly by asynchronous means.

13. The purpose of the parity bit shown in figure 2.3 will be discussed later.

DATA REPRESENTATION ON MAGNETIC MEDIA.

14A. Data in the form of character codes may also be represented on magnetic media. Invisible "spots" of magnetism are created in the magnetic surface of the medium. These spots, which can be magnetised in one of the two directions, correspond to binary 0 or 1 according to the direction of magnetisation. Fig. 2.5 shows an example of how data may be stored on magnetic tape which is a common type of magnetic storage medium.

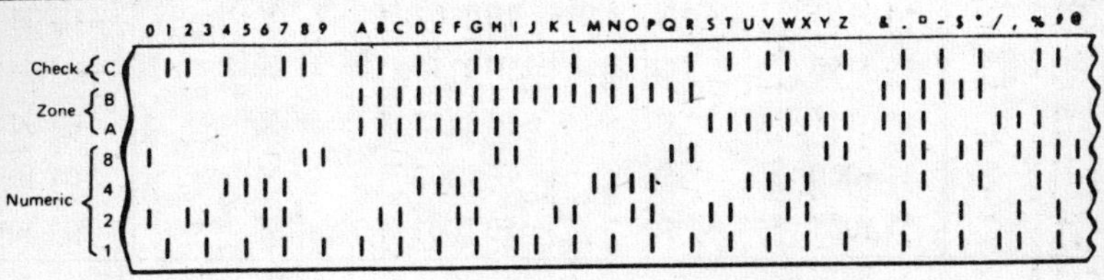

NB. There are 7 "channels" on this tape labelled 1,2,4,8,A,B and C.

Fig. 2.5. How data is recorded on Magnetic Tape

BINARY CODED DECIMAL (BCD)

14B. BCD is a 4 bit code used for coding numeric values only, as follows:–

DECIMAL DIGIT	0	1	2	3	4	5	6	7	8	9
BCD CODE	0000	0001	0010	0011	0100	0101	0110	0111	1000	1001

Example. The number 109_{10} would be coded thus:–

DECIMAL NUMBER	1	0	9
BCD CODE	0001	0000	1001

Note that each decimal digit is coded separately.

15. Standard BCD 6-bit code. This code is formed by extending the BCD 4-bit code by a further two bits in order to allow non-numeric characters to be coded. It is the code used on the magnetic tape shown in fig. 2.5. The 'check' bit is not part of the code. Note that zero is coded as 001010 on some machines rather than 000000. (See Fig. 2.5).

ALPHA CHARACTER	BINARY CODE	ALPHA CHARACTER	BINARY CODE	ALPHA CHARACTER	BINARY CODE
A	11 0001	J	10 0001	–	–
B	11 0010	K	10 0010	S	01 0010
C	11 0011	L	10 0011	T	01 0011
D	11 0100	M	10 0100	U	01 0100
E	11 0101	N	10 0101	V	01 0101
F	11 0110	O	10 0110	W	01 0110
G	11 0111	P	10 0111	X	01 0111
H	11 1000	Q	10 1000	Y	01 1000
I	11 1001	R	10 1001	Z	01 1001

Fig. 2.6. Representation of alphabetic characters in BCD 6-bit code

16. Extended Binary Coded Decimal Interchange Code (EBCDIC). EBCDIC code (usually pronouned "Eb–see–Dick") is sometimes called "8-bit ASCII" and is a newer code than 6-bit BCD. There are 256 characters in EBCDIC character set but only 64 characters in the Standard BCD 6-bit code. (See fig. 2.7).

ALPHA CHARACTER	BINARY CODE	ALPHA CHARACTER	BINARY CODE	ALPHA CHARACTER	BINARY CODE
A	1100 0001	J	1101 0001	–	–
B	1100 0010	K	1101 0010	S	1110 0010
C	1100 0011	L	1101 0011	T	1110 0011
D	1100 0100	M	1101 0100	U	1110 0100
E	1100 0101	N	1101 0101	V	1110 0101
F	1100 0110	O	1101 0110	W	1110 0110
G	1100 0111	P	1101 0111	X	1110 0111
H	1100 1000	Q	1101 1000	Y	1110 1000
I	1100 1001	R	1101 1001	Z	1110 1001

Fig. 2.7. Representation of alphabetic characters in EBCDIC

PARITY

17. We now examine the purpose of the "parity bit" shown in fig 2.3 and the "check bit" of fig. 2.5 which has the same purpose. These extra bits are added to codes in order to allow the detection of errors in data transmission or data recording. Such errors are usually the result of using poor or faulty equipment. The principle is explained here with reference to magnetic tape (fig. 2.5).

18. Even parity. If you examine the magnetic tape codes of fig. 2.5 you will discover that the parity bit has been added (vertical mark) to some codes on the tape so that the 7-bit code *including* parity always has an *even* number of bits. This is an even parity system. As each character code is read from the tape the number of bits including the parity bit is checked. Should an odd number of bits be discovered in an even parity system then an error must have occurred.

19. Odd parity. In an odd parity system the number of bits in the tape for each character code is made odd by the appropriate use of the parity bit.

20. Longitudinal parity checks. Parity bits may also be added to the end of blocks of characters so as to make the total number of holes along each channel even numbered. Longitudinal checks are most commonly used on magnetic media. (See fig. 2.8). Longitudinal checks can be used in synchronous data transmissions.

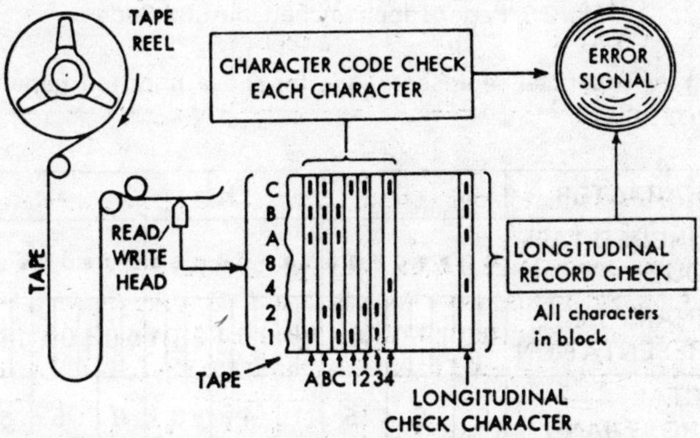

Information read from tape is checked two ways. A character code check (vertical check) is made on each column of information to ensure that an even number of bits exists for each character read. If an odd number of bits is detected for any character or column of bits, an error is indicated, unless the computer operates in odd parity. A longitudinal record check is made by developing an odd or even indication of the number of bits read in each of the seven bit tracks of the record, including the bits of the check character. If any bit track of the record block indicates an odd number of bits after it is read, an error is indicated, unless odd parity is required by system design.

Fig. 2.8. Longitudinal parity checks

TRADITIONAL MEDIA

21. Two traditional media, which were of major importance until the early '70s, are punched paper tape and punched cards. *These media are obsolete* for most modern applications.

22. Paper Tape Codes. Individual characters are converted to a "machine sensible form" by representing them in a code consisting of a combination of holes and spaces in the eight hole positions across the tape.

Fig. 2.9. Paper Tape Punched in ASCII Code

23. The binary and octal representations for these punched paper codes are shown in fig. 2.10.

CHARACTER	5	K	–
PUNCHED TAPE CODE	o o ● ● o ● o ●	o ● o o ● o ● ●	o o ● o ● ● o ●
BINARY RE-PRESENTATION	0 0 1 1 0 1 0 1	0 1 0 0 1 0 1 1	0 0 1 0 1 1 0 1
OCTAL 'SHORTHAND'	0 6 5	1 1 3	0 5 5

Fig. 2.10. Examples of punched codes on Tapes

24. Punched Cards. Here each character is represented by holes punched in a column of the card. Note that:–

a. Numeric 'digits' have *one* hole punched.

b. Alphabetic characters have *two* holes punched. (One 'zone' plus one other.)

c. Special characters may have one, two or more holes punched.

d. The characters printed across the top of the card make the card 'human-sensible' and punched holes also make the card 'machine-sensible'.

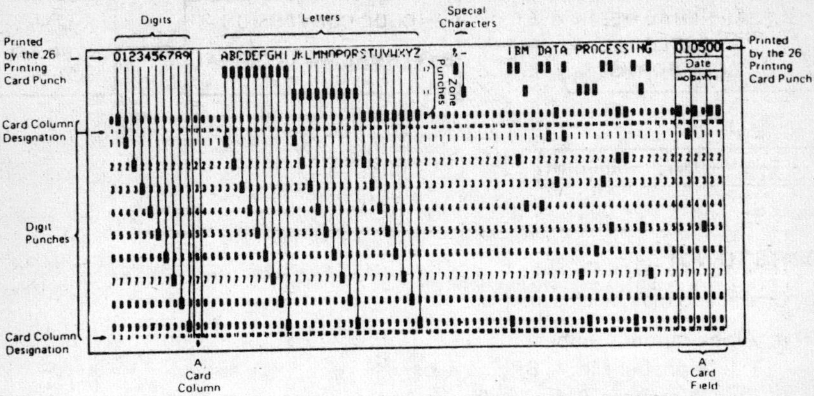

Fig. 2.10. A Punched Card

INTERNAL AND EXTERNAL CHARACTER CODES.

25. Data may be presented to the input devices in a variety of binary codes according to the media used, but it is common practice to use one particular binary code for all data within the CPU. This code is called the **internal code** and the choice of internal code differs from one manufacturer to another eg. IBM uses EBCDIC. The codes used on the various peripherals are called **external codes** eg. punched card code is always an external code.

26. Code conversion from external to internal forms may take place:

a. within a peripheral device,

b. within a device called an **interface** as data enters the CPU,

c. within the CPU itself.

SUMMARY.

27. a. Character codes for the various input media can all be represented in binary form.

b. Parity bits are added to the character codes so that parity checks performed at each code transfer can be used to detect errors in data preparation or transmission.

c. Data may be transmitted synchronously or asynchronously in the form of pulse-trains.

d. Each computer uses its own internal code.

e. Data forms and movement is summarised by this block diagram.

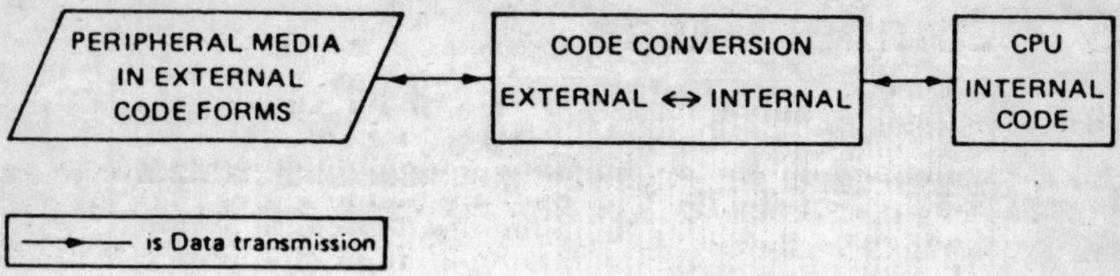

POINTS TO NOTE.

28. Characters may be classified as

a. Alpha-numeric, either
   i. Alphabetic ie. A, B, ... Z, or
   ii. Numeric ie. 0, 1, ... 9.

b. Special Characters eg. . , – / +.

OR

c. Control Characters which are used to control devices.

By convention alphanumeric also refers to b.

29. Codes are defined excluding parity bits so we regard ASCII as a 7 bit code which with parity gives an 8 bit code on tape.

30. The number of bits in a code limits the number of characters which can be coded. An n bit code can provide 2^n different character codes, eg. with ASCII n = 7, so the size of the character set = 2^7 = 128.

STUDENT SELF TESTING QUESTIONS (answers begin page 679)

1. Refer to in Fig. 2.5.

a. Is an odd or even parity system being used?

b. Make a table of numeric and alphabetic character codes in Binary (exclude the check digit).

2. Why are start and stop bits required for each character in asynchronous transmission but not in synchronous transmission?

3. Assuming an even parity system add parity bits to the following binary codes:

a. 1011100

b. 0111101

QUESTIONS WITHOUT ANSWERS.

4. What is meant by the term 'character set'? Identify the character set on the computer keyboard you will be using on your course.

5. Look up the ASCII codes for the letters and spaces in the phrase "A Pulse Train" and draw a diagram like that in fig. 2.2.

3 Number Bases

INTRODUCTION.

1. This chapter introduces numbers in base two, called binary numbers, which are used by digital computers when they store and process data. We will see that several other number bases also have uses in computing, and so the general idea of number bases, together with the methods we will need for converting from one base to another, are developed in this chapter.

2. Decimal Numbers are the numbers in everyday use, and are also known as **Denary** numbers, or numbers to **base 10,** because ten is the *basis* of the number system. To write a number in decimal we make use of the ten **digit** symbols 0, 1, 2, 3, 4, 5, 6, 7, 8 and 9 and also use the method of **place value** (ie the position of a digit affects its meaning).

Example. The number '235' in decimals is made up thus:–

PLACE VALUE	10^3 (1000)	10^2 (100)	10^1 (10)	10^0 (1)		10^2 (100)	10^1 (10)	10^0 (1)
Digit '5' in position 10^0				5	$= 5 \times 10^0$	0	0	5
Digit '3' in position 10^1			3		$= 3 \times 10^1$	0	3	0
Digit '2' in position 10^2		2			$= 2 \times 10^2$	2	0	0
					TOTAL	2	3	5

BINARY NUMBERS.

3. Binary Numbers are numbers to base 2. The binary number system uses just *two* symbols, 0 and 1, and place values increasing in powers of *two.*

Examples. (You should memorise these first 8 values for future use).

BINARY NUMBERS				$2^3=8$ $2^2=4$ $2^1=2$ $2^0=1$		DECIMAL EQUIVALENTS
0	0	0	1	$= (0 \times 2^3) + (0 \times 2^2) + (0 \times 2^1) + (1 \times 2^0)$	=	1
0	0	1	0	$= (0 \times 2^3) + (0 \times 2^2) + (1 \times 2^1) + (0 \times 2^0)$	=	2
0	0	1	1	$= (0 \times 2^3) + (0 \times 2^2) + (1 \times 2^1) + (1 \times 2^0)$	=	3
0	1	0	0	$= (0 \times 2^3) + (1 \times 2^2) + (0 \times 2^1) + (0 \times 2^0)$	=	4
0	1	0	1	$= (0 \times 2^3) + (1 \times 2^2) + (0 \times 2^1) + (1 \times 2^0)$	=	5
0	1	1	0	$= (0 \times 2^3) + (1 \times 2^2) + (1 \times 2^1) + (0 \times 2^0)$	=	6
0	1	1	1	$= (0 \times 2^3) + (1 \times 2^2) + (1 \times 2^1) + (1 \times 2^0)$	=	7
1	0	0	0	$= (1 \times 2^3) + (0 \times 2^2) + (0 \times 2^1) + (0 \times 2^0)$	=	8

4. Subscripts are used to indicate the base of a number in its written form. For example when we see 101_2 the subscript 2 tells us we are looking at a binary number, which from our table we identify as being equivalent to 5 in decimal.

Without the subscript we would probably read 101 as meaning one hundred and one in decimal. So *at all times use subscripts* to indicate the base used if there is any risk of confusion without them. The subscript itself is always in decimal.

5. Conversion from Binary to Decimal.

Example Convert 1101101_2 to Decimal.

PLACE VALUES	2^6 (64)	2^5 (32)	2^4 (16)	2^3 (8)	2^2 (4)	2^1 (2)	2^0 (1)	DECIMAL VALUE
BINARY NUMBERS	1	1	0	1	1	0	1	
CONVERSION	(1 x 64) + (1 x 32) + (0 x 16) + (1 x 8) + (1 x 4) + (0 x 2) + (1 x 1)							= 109

6. Conversion from Decimal to Binary. We use repeated *division* by 2.

Example. Convert 109 Decimal to Binary. *Arrows* are used here to emphasise the direction in which the Binary Number should be read.

USUAL LAYOUT OF WORKING		DETAILS
109	1 ↑	109 ÷ 2 = 54 Remainder 1
54	0	54 ÷ 2 = 27 Remainder 0
27	1	27 ÷ 2 = 13 Remainder 1
13	1	13 ÷ 2 = 6 Remainder 1
6	0	6 ÷ 2 = 3 Remainder 0
3	1	3 ÷ 2 = 1 Remainder 1
1	1	1 ÷ 2 = 0 Remainder 1 → 1 1 0 1 1 0 1

We have thus checked our previous result, $109_{10} = 1101101_2$

OCTAL NUMBERS

7. Octal numbers are numbers to **base 8.** There are eight symbols used in the octal system (0, 1, 2, 3, 4, 5, 6 and 7) and place values increase in powers of 8. Octal numbers are used as a shorthand for binary.

8. Conversion between Octal and Decimal.

Example. Convert 109_{10} to octal and convert back to decimal as a check.

a. Conversion to Octal is done by repeated division by 8. In other respects the method is the same as conversion from Decimal to Binary.

WORKING		DETAILS
109	5 ↑	109 ÷ 8 = 13 Remainder 5
13	5	13 ÷ 8 = 1 Remainder 5
1	1	1 ÷ 8 = 0 Remainder 1

Thus:–
$109_{10} = 155_8$

b. Conversion *to* Decimal *from* Octal.

PLACE VALUES	8^2 (64)	8^1 (8)	8^0 (1)	DECIMAL VALUE
OCTAL NUMBER	1	5	5	
CONVERSION	(1×64) +	(5×8) +	(5×1)	= 109

Thus:–
$155_8 = 109_{10}$

9. Conversion between Octal and Binary. A simple relationship exists between octal and binary, because eight is the cube of two. To do conversions it is merely necessary to remember binary equivalents for the eight octal symbols. Octal is often used as a 'shorthand' for binary because of this easy conversion.

Conversion Table

OCTAL NUMBERS	0	1	2	3	4	5	6	7
BINARY EQUIVALENTS	0 0 0	0 0 1	0 1 0	0 1 1	1 0 0	1 0 1	1 1 0	1 1 1

Example a. Convert 155_8 to Binary

OCTAL NUMBER	1	5	5
BINARY EQUIVALENTS FROM THE CONVERSION TABLE	0 0 1	1 0 1	1 0 1

Thus:–
$155_8 = 001\ 101\ 101_2$

Example b. Convert 1110111000010_2 to octal. In order to use the conversion table we group the binary digits into threes working from right to left, adding extra zeros at the left end if necessary.

GROUPED BINARY DIGITS	0 0 1	1 1 0	1 1 1	0 0 0	0 1 0
OCTAL EQUIVALENT FROM THE CONVERSION TABLE	1	6	7	0	2

Thus:–
001110111000010_2
$= 16702_8$

Note: Conversions between Decimal and Binary are often quicker via Octal, ie using Binary to Octal to Decimal, or Decimal to Octal to Binary.

HEXADECIMAL NUMBERS.

10. Hexadecimal numbers, usually abbreviated to **'Hex'**, are numbers to **base 16.** The sixteen symbols used in the Hex system are 0, 1, 2, 3, 4, 5, 6, 7, 8, 9, A, B, C, D, E and F, and place values increase in powers of sixteen. We need to remember that A, B, C, D, E and F are equivalent to 10, 11, 12, 13, 14, and 15 DECIMAL. Hex numbers are used as a shorthand for binary.

11. Conversions between Hexadecimal and Decimal follow the same pattern used for Binary and Octal.

Example. Convert 109_{10} to Hex and back again.

a.

WORKING		DETAILS
109 6	$13 = D_{16}$ ↑ $6 = 6_{16}$	109 ÷ 16 = 6 Remainder 13 6 ÷ 16 = 0 Remainder 6

Thus:–
$109_{10} = 6D_{16}$

b. Conversion *to* Decimal from Hex

PLACE VALUES	16^2 (256)	16^1 (16)	16^0 (1)	DECIMAL VALUE
HEX NUMBER	0	6	D	
CONVER-SION	(0x256)+(6x16) + (13 x 1)			= 109

Thus:–
$6D_{16} = 109_{10}$

12. Conversion between Hex and other bases. Conversion between Hex, Octal and Binary is done in much the same way as the Octal/Binary conversions in paragraph 9. A conversion table is given below.

Conversion Table.

DECIMAL	0	1	2	3	4	5	6	7
HEX	0	1	2	3	4	5	6	7
BINARY	0000	0001	0010	0011	0100	0101	0110	0111
OCTAL	0	1	2	3	4	5	6	7

DECIMAL	8	9	10	11	12	13	14	15
HEX	8	9	A	B	C	D	E	F
BINARY	1000	1001	1010	1011	1100	1101	1110	1111
OCTAL	10	11	12	13	14	15	16	17

Example a. Convert $6D_{16}$ to Binary and Octal. A conversion between Hex and Octal is most easily made via Binary.

Stage 1 (Hex to Binary)

HEX NUMBER	6	D
BINARY EQUIVALENT FROM THE TABLE	0 1 1 0	1 1 0 1

Stage 2 (Binary to Octal)

BINARY	0 0 1	1 0 1	1 0 1
OCTAL	1	5	5

Example b. Convert 1110111000010_2 to Hex. We group binary digits into fours from the right, then use the conversion table.

GROUPED BINARY DIGITS	0 0 0 1	1 1 0 1	1 1 0 0	0 0 1 0
HEX EQUIVALENT FROM THE CONVERSION TABLE	1	D	C	2

13. SUMMARY

a. A Numbering system is characterised by the base and symbolised. The table summarises those considered.

NUMBER SYSTEM	BASE	SYMBOLS USED
Binary	2	0, 1.
Octal	8	0, 1, 2, 3, 4, 5, 6, 7.
Decimal or Denary	10	0, 1, 2, 3, 4, 5, 6, 7, 8, 9.
Hexadecimal or Hex	16	0, 1, 2, 3, 4, 5, 6, 7, 8, 9, A, B, C, D, E, F.

b. The base of a number is indicated by a subscript.

14. POINTS TO NOTE

a. Another name sometimes used instead of 'base' is **'radix'**.

b. Octal and Hex numbers can be used as 'shorthands' for binary.

c. You will need to use the methods described in this chapter, so practice on the questions given here.

d. The simplest sequences to adopt when converting between bases are shown here:–

i. Decimal ⇌ Octal ⇌ Binary.

ii. Hexadecimal ⇌ Binary ⇌ Octal.

STUDENT SELF TESTING QUESTIONS (answers begin page 680)

1. *Convert these decimal numbers to (a) Octal (b) Binary (c) Hex.*
   - *i. 22*
   - *ii. 26*
   - *iii. 31*
   - *iv. 38*
   - *v. 44*
   - *vi. 53*
   - *vii. 58*
   - *viii. 93*
   - *ix. 751*
   - *x. 1453.*

2. *Convert these Octal numbers to (a) Decimal (b) Hexadecimal (c) Binary.*
   - *i. 73*
   - *ii. 347*
   - *iii. 1521*
   - *iv. 2354*
   - *v. 3733.*

3. *Convert these Hexadecimal numbers to decimal.*
   - *i. 6A*
   - *ii. EF*
   - *iii. 2C8*
   - *iv. 347*
   - *v. 6DA.*

4. *Express this binary number in Octal and Hex. 11011101010110101011.*

Hardware

1. Hardware is the name given to all the physical devices found in a computer system. In the computer room, the devices look like large, inert, metal cabinets and there is little visible evidence of the phenomenal speeds at which data is being processed within. The converse is 'Software' which is the term given to the programs which are required to put life into the Hardware.

2. Chapter 4 gives an overview of this Part by introducing hardware and its uses.

3. Input devices are described in chapter 5. They are used to transfer data into the Central Processing Unit. These devices either accept data at a keyboard and then convert the data into machine-sensible form or they accept data which has already been created in machine sensible form (eg. a machine readable document).

4. Output devices are described in chapter 6. They are used to receive data from the Central Processing Unit and produce the data in a humanly sensible form (or in a machine sensible form for later re-input).

5. Main Storage is described in chapter 7. Main Storage is part of the CPU and holds data and programs currently in use.

6. Auxiliary Storage devices are described in chapter 8. They are used to provide mass storage of data/records.

7. Computer System Architecture is described in chapter 9. The chapter starts by describing how the CPU processes data and then goes on to describe hardware features of systems with more than one processor.

4 An Overview of Hardware

INTRODUCTION.

1. The purpose of this chapter is to provide an overview of hardware, in order to prepare you for the subsequent chapters which go into more detail.

2. Common types of hardware are introduced by the use of suitable examples.

3. The six main headings under which hardware is discussed in this chapter are:-

a. Semi-conductor processors and memories.

b. Data Storage.

c. Backing Storage.

d. Data entry.

e. Data transmission and networks.

f. Output.

4. Although the basic uses of hardware are mentioned in this chapter, a full discussion of its uses is deliberately excluded, because a full knowledge of hardware capabilities and limitations must precede any evaluation of which hardware is best suited to a particular application.

SEMI-CONDUCTOR PROCESSORS AND MEMORIES

5. Although the CPU carries out a number of different functions (fig. 1.1), from a hardware viewpoint the basic components of a modern CPU are all very similar. This similarity arises from common manufacturing processes.

6. Complex circuits such those found in the ALU, Control Unit or main storage are manufactured on single minutely sliced wafers of silicon crystal. Such devices are called **"silicon chips"** or **"semi-conductor devices"** (see fig. 4.1).

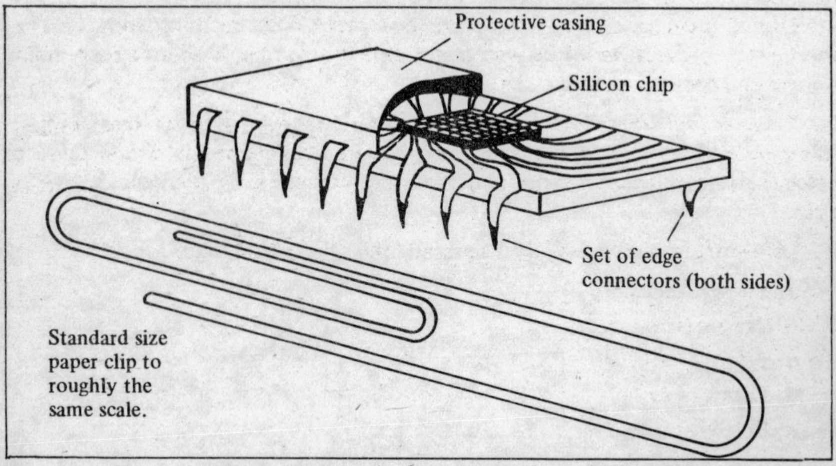

Fig. 4.1. A Computer Component Containing a Silicon Chip.

7. **Micro-processors.** A micro-processor is an entire small computer processor (usually excluding main memory) manufactured on a single chip. Computers built around such devices are called **"micro-computers"**, or more correctly **"micro-computer based systems"**.

8. The first micro-processor was produced in 1972 by the Intel corporation.

9. Most micro-processors do not contain main storage which is normally produced on separate silicon chips.

10. **Semi-conductor memory** is the name given to main storage manufactured on silicon chips. Semi-conductor memory rapidly replaced a former main storage medium, called *"core store"*, during the mid seventies.

11. The most common types of semi-conductor memory are **"volatile"** which means that all data is lost if the power supply is removed.

12. **Main features.** The semi-conductor devices within the CPU have the following features:-

a. Their operation is wholly electronic, and consequently they are very fast and reliable.

b. Despite the complexity of these devices, modern manufacturing methods have enabled them to be produced at costs which represent only minor portions of the total costs of whole computer systems. eg. In a micro-computer costing £1000, the micro-processor may only constitute £10 of the total cost or even less.

c. These devices are highly miniaturised. This feature may be exploited in order to provide computer hardware which can be accommodated comfortably in the office, home, petrol pump, washing machine, car etc.

DATA STORAGE.

13. Some specific aspects of data storage have just been discussed under the heading of semi-conductor processors and memories, but now we turn our attention to *general hardware aspects of data storage* applicable to both main storage and backing storage.

14. There are several different common types of hardware used for data storage. This variety stems from the fact that there are a number of physical characteristics which must be considered in deciding the appropriateness of a particular device in a given situation.

15. Data storage devices will be discussed under these headings:-

a. Storage capacity.

b. Access facilities.

c. Size.

d. Robustness.

e. Relative costs.

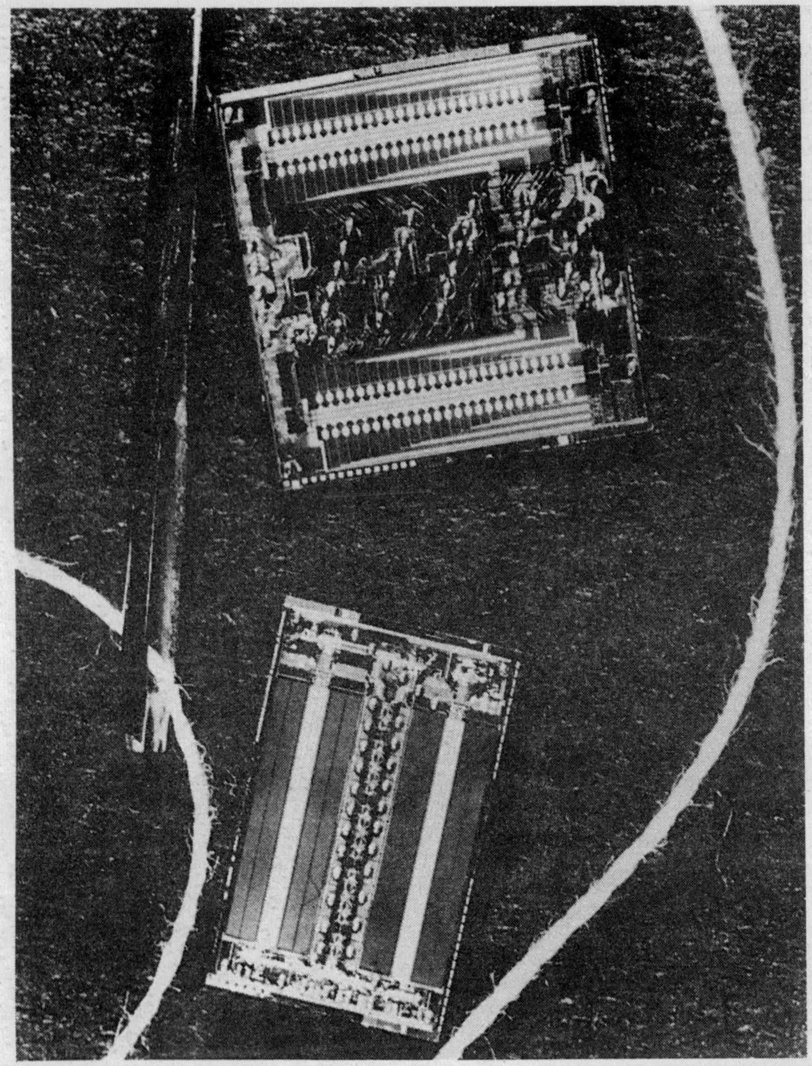

An IBM 64,000 Bit Dynamic Ram Chip, older model and new model (40% smaller) compared with a needle and thread. Picture courtesy of IBM.

STORAGE CAPACITY.

16. Storage capacities may be expressed and compared in terms of the number of **'characters'** stored (2.2).

For example, *main storage* of a small computer may be expressed in terms of tens of thousands of characters whereas *backing storage* of a larger computer may be expressed in terms of tens of millions of characters.

ACCESS FACILITIES.

17. Broadly speaking, the two main factors are:-

a. Mode of access.

b. Speed of access.

18. For the time being an everyday example will provide a basic distinction between mode of access and speed of access. You may 'access' data (ie. get facts) from this book in two modes:-

a. *Serially,* by reading through from the first page to the last,

or b. *directly* by using the index to go straight to the data you need.

19. The first alternative is more efficient if you require most or all of the facts, but the latter is faster if you only want a few facts. If you require to have the *immediate* recall of facts, then you may need to use your own memory, instead of the book, as your 'data storage medium'.

20. These ideas will be related to particular items of hardware later.

SIZE.

21. Despite major strides in miniaturisation, (the components within modern chips are more densely packed than the cells of the human brain although they do not have the same intelligence as brains), some backing storage devices and media remain undesirably bulky. Most backing storage devices have some electro-mechanical parts which contribute to their bulk. When data is to be stored for long periods with minimal access the most compact backing storage media are favoured because of the value of saving space.

22. Compared with normal paper based data storage, as in the form of rows of filing cabinets, computer storage methods are all incredibly more compact.

ROBUSTNESS.

23. Compared with paper based storage, computer data storage may appear to be less robust. Such a view is based upon the fact that most computer storage media may only be used in carefully controlled environments. In practical terms this is seldom a serious problem for commerical applications, since the "office environment" is one which is suitable for most computer hardware. In industrial environments, such as on the factory floor, environmental problems are less easy to solve.

RELATIVE COSTS.

24. There are sharp differences in costs between the various types of computer storage. Awareness of the various alternatives allows the most economical alternative to be selected in a given situation. Conversely, if the storage requirements have not been properly specified, an unduly expensive alternative may be selected unnecessarily.

BACKING STORAGE.

25. The main backing storage media in use today are:

a. Magnetic Disk (hard or floppy).

b. Magnetic Tape.

These media will be described in detail in later chapters. Magnetic Disks are flat rotating circular plates coated with magnetic material. Some magnetic disks are rigid and called **hard disks,** others are *flexible* and are called **floppy disks** or **diskettes.** Hard disks are more expensive but are faster more reliable and bigger.

26. Disks provide direct data access (4.18).

27. **Magnetic tapes** are similar in principle to the tapes used domestically for audio or video recording. Tape is a serial medium (4.18) and is mainly used as a "backup" or archiving medium. Tape is also used as an input medium because data on other media may be converted onto magnetic tape prior to input in order to give faster input.

28. **Magnetic Media Problems.** The common forms of backing storage media in use today are similar in principle to the medium of the domestic tape of cassette recorders. Consequently they are susceptible to stray magnetic fields and to dust.

29. There are some advantages associated with these features of magnetic media. For example, whereas confidential data on paper may prove difficult to dispose of, magnetic media are not directly readable by humans and may be wiped clear magnetically.

DATA ENTRY.

30. There are problems associated with entering data into computers because humans communicate less quickly than computers and in a different way ie. by speech, writing etc. A computer's internal communication is based upon codes formed from high frequency electronic pulses (2.3).

31. The basic problems are overcome by using devices which can encode our data into a form which is usable by the computer.

Modern methods fall into three board categories:-

a. Keyboard entry.

b. Document reading.

c. Data capture.

32. Keyboard entry. One typical keyboard input device is the **VDU** (Visual Display Unit). See fig. 4.2.

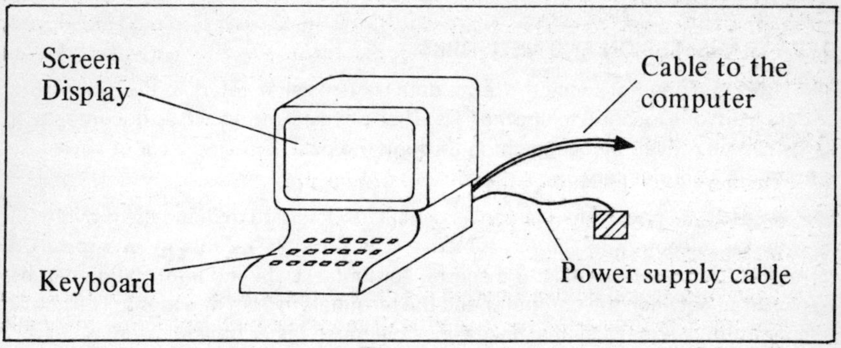

Fig. 4.2. A VDU.

33. The VDU is really two devices in one; one for input, one for output. Data is fed in via a keyboard, which is like a typewriter keyboard, and is both passed into the computer and displayed on the screen. The VDU can also receive and display messages from the computer.

34. There are many different types of VDU (details later) but the two main ways of using VDUs are:

a. To connect the VDU directly to the computer. This is known as **on-line** data entry. Any devices used for on-line data entry in this manner is called a **terminal.**

b. To use the VDU in conjunction with some other data entry system in order to prepare data on a fast and reliable input medium. A popular modern example of this is the **key-to-floppy-disk** or **key-to-diskette** system. These are microcomputer based systems which take in data from the VDU and store it on floppy disks. At some later stage the floppy disks are used for input to the main computer.

35. In both the cases just given the data can be *checked and corrected as it is being input* and no non-reusable medium is being wasted.

36. Document Reading. The idea behind document reading is to get a machine to read source documents (ie. the documents on which the data is originally recorded). This avoids the problems associated with transcription and verification of data when using keyboard devices. The data is recorded on the documents using special marks or characters, and is read by optical or magnetic reading techniques. Details will be given later.

37. Data Capture. This heading covers a wide variety of methods all of which try to combine data creation with data entry ie. the data is 'captured' at source in a machine sensible form. For example pre-recorded, or pre-printed, data on some suitable medium attached to goods, may be read or collected as the goods are sold. This application is known as **PoS** (Point of Sale) data capture. Further details of this and other data capture methods will be given later.

DATA TRANSMISSION AND NETWORKS.

38. Used in a general sense the term 'data transmission' refers to the movement of data from one location to another. Data in a physical form such as documents or cards can be moved by despatching through the post, by using a car or van or by employing a courier service.

39. Nowadays, 'data transmission' is usually understood to mean the movement of data by telecommunications systems. It is possible by this means to link a number of remote terminals to a central computer. Data and information can be transmitted between the computer and the terminals in both directions. The use of telecommunications facilities makes possible much faster transmission.

40. The basic components of a data transmission system are:

a. a central computer

b. terminal devices

c. a telecommunications link between a and b.

41. When they were first introduced the basic data transmission systems, like the one just described, were regarded as another part of the data entry system. It took no time at all to recognise and exploit the possibilities of *two way* point-to-point transmission.

42. Many organisations set up their own *local private systems.* British Telecom (BT) (Formerly part of the Post Office) set up *public services* in the UK with the trade name DATEL.

43. Newer developments. In recent years the whole concept of data transmission has been extended in two ways:

a. Many systems now have computers at *both ends* of the telecommunications link, and several computers may be interlinked in a similar manner to form a complete **computer network.**

b. The networks are able to do more than pass data from point-to-point. **Messages** can be despatched from one point in the network and passed by the network to one or more destinations specified when the messages are sent. This is a form of **"electronic mail."**

44. There are local, national and international networks in current use, and most major networks are interconnected.

45. Data transmission equipment has also been exploited as part of local or national **information retrieval systems.** For example in the UK, BT offer a computer based service connected to users by telephone links. Its trade name is "PRESTEL" and is one example of a **'Viewdata'** system. More details will be covered in later chapters.

A R800/70 System. An integrated system which supports 8 viewdata intelligent colour TV parts and 8 "Writeaway" handprint terminals. Picture courtesy of Rediffusion Computers Ltd.

OUTPUT.

46. At the present time most information produced by computers is output in the form of printed paper documents, reports etc. Over the last few years an increase in the number of computer systems being used for "on-line" information retrieval has meant that considerable volumes of data are displayed on VDU screens instead of being produced in printed form.

47. In both these cases the information is expressed in terms of characters, (2.2) but in the long term more information may be provided in the form of **images** (ie. pictures or diagrams).

48. Quite apart from a number of valuable innovations over many years, the development of output devices has been largely concerned with trying to find ways of improving the speeds, costs and reliability of printers. Print quality and quietness have been additional aims for some printer applications.

49. The two main types of printer currently in use are:

a. character printers
b. line printers.

50. Character Printers are low speed printers which mimic the action of typewriters by printing *one character at a time*. Most of the printers which produce high quality print are character printers.

51. Line Printers. The majority of high speed printers *print whole lines at a time* (or appear to) and are consequently called *line printers*. Line printers usually have a considerable work load on mini or mainframe computers used for DP (Data Processing), ie. Business applications.

SUMMARY.

52. a. The chapter has provided an overview of computer hardware under these main headings.

i. Semi-conductor processors and memories.
ii. Data storage.
iii. Backing storage.
iv. Data entry.
v. Data transmission and networks.
vi. Output.

b. General characteristics have been introduced, with examples, so that when you encounter details of particular hardware in later chapters, you will have some basic criteria by which to evaluate them.

POINTS TO NOTE.

53. Note the difference between "on-line" ie. connected to the CPU and under its control, and "off-line" ie. away from the computer.

54. The hardware examples given in this chapter represent the most widely used types and have a commercial bias: Approximately 80% of all money spent upon computer systems is spent on systems for commercial purposes. However, there are many important types of hardware used in industrial applications such as manufacturing and examples of these will be given in later chapters. In terms of numbers of processors in use the majority of computer use is now industrial, with processors found in everything from watches to weigh-bridges.

STUDENT SELF TESTING QUESTIONS (answers begin page 681)

1. *Define the term 'volatile' in the context of computer memory.*
2. *Name two common backing storage media.*
3. *Name three categories of data entry methods.*
4. *What is 'data transmission'?*

QUESTIONS WITHOUT ANSWERS.

5. *What is the size of main storage and backing storage on the computer system which you use?*

5 Input Devices and Media

INTRODUCTION.

1. The following devices and the media associated with them will be described:-

a. Keyboard devices
   i. VDUs
   ii. Terminal typewriters
   iii. Consoles

b. Document readers – documents with characters/marks in special formats.
   i. Optical readers
   ii. Magnetic ink readers

c. Data Capture devices
   i. Direct input devices
   ii. Data loggers/recorders

d. Magnetic media and storage devices
   i. Magnetic tape unit – magnetic tape
   ii. Floppy disk unit – floppy disk (diskette)

e. Others
   i. Card reader – Punched card
   ii. Paper tape reader – Punched paper tape.

Some of these devices can be used for *both* input and output. In this chapter they will be regarded purely in their input role, except where the input and output operations are inextricably linked, as in the case of the VDU.

KEYBOARD DEVICES.

2. Visual Display Unit (VDU). (as introduced in 4.32) There are many different types of VDU in use today. Only the more common features and variants will be described.

3. *Features*

a. It is a dual purpose device with a keyboard for data input and a cathode ray tube display for output. The latter is similar to a TV screen.

b. The keyboard resembles the QWERTY typewriter keyboard, but usually has several additional keys which are used to control and edit the display.

c. Characters (2.2) are displayed on the screen in a manner which resembles printed text. A typical full screen display is 24 rows by 80 columns (ie. 1920 characters).

d. The display can normally be generated in two different modes:-
   i. **Scrolling mode** in which lines appear at the bottom and move up the screen rather like credits on a movie screen.
   ii. **Paging mode** in which one complete screen full is replaced by another rather like a slide projector display.

An IBM 3277 model 2 Information Display Station and Light Pen. Picture courtesy of IBM.

e. Most VDUs, have features which allow particular parts of the display to be highlighted or contrasted eg.

i. Inverse (Reverse) video ie. black on white instead of white on black.
ii. Blinking displays.
iii. Two levels of brightness.
iv. Colour – on the more expensive models.

f. Cursor controls. A cursor is a small character-sized symbol displayed on the screen, which can be moved about the screen both vertically and horizontally by means of special keys on the keyboard. During data input, the display may resemble a blank form. In this case data may be entered by first moving the cursor to a space on the 'form' and then typing in the data. Further keys may allow the data to be edited or corrected.

g. Inbuilt microprocessors. The numerous internal functions of almost all modern VDUs are controlled by inbuilt microprocessors. The more expensive models are often called **Work Stations** or **Intelligent terminals.** These devices are sometimes capable of limited amounts of processing, and with further enhancements these devices can often be turned into small microcomputer systems in their own right.

4. Variations on the VDU.

a. **Graphics Versions.** Some VDUs have high quality displays which can be used for line drawings, draftsmens' drawings etc.

b. **Light Pens.** A special pen used in conjunction with a graphics VDU. The VDU can detect the location of light shining on the screen by means of special hardware and software. This is a design aid which simplifies input of details of positions on the screen.

c. **Touch Terminals.** An alternative to the light-pen. The VDU can detect when a point on the screen is touched.

d. **Voice Data Entry (VDE).** Additional circuitry plus a microphone is added to the VDU. The unit can be switched to "learn" a number of words, typically less than 200, which it achieves by recording a "sound pattern" for each word typed in. When the unit is switched to input it displays and inputs any word which it recognises. These units are particularly suitable for people wishing to use a few words again in situations where their hands are not free to use a keyboard eg. people in laboratories, invalids etc.

5. Terminal Typewriters. A Terminal typewriter is also a dual-purpose device. It has a keyboard for data input and a small printer for output. It closely resembles a modern electric typewriter, hence its name. One manufacturer of these devices is the Teletype corporation and these devices are often called teletypewriters for that reason.

6. *Features.*

a. The keyboard resembles the QWERTY typewriter keyboard, but usually has several additional keys which are used for device control.

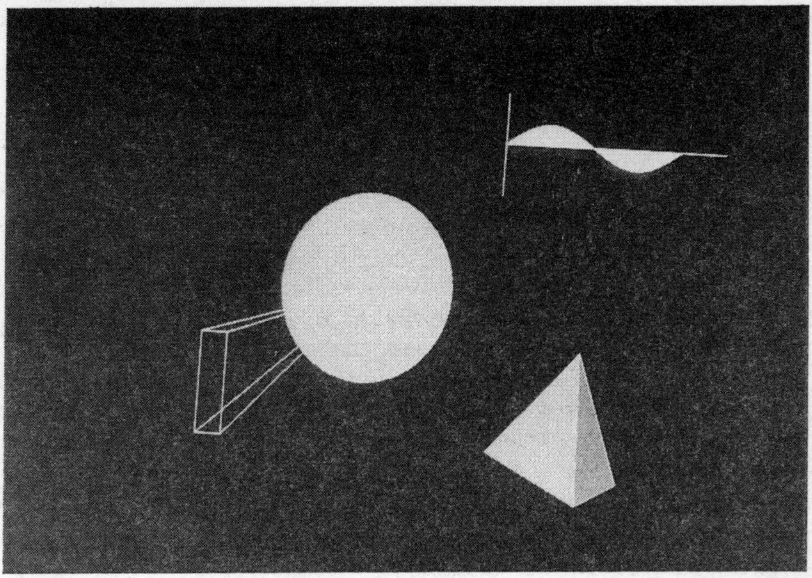

Simple VDU graphics output.

A terminal typewriter.

b. The printer is usually a character printer (4.50). Details will be covered in the next chapter.

7. As is the case of VDUs, terminal typewriters may be used either as terminals or as part of some other data entry system (see 4.34).

8. Consoles. A console is a device which is being used for communication between the *operator* (ie. the person responsible for operating the computer) and the program which is controlling the computer. (This special program is often called the **monitor.**) Terminal typewriters and VDUs can both be used as consoles, although the use of a terminal typewriter is usually prefered because of the permanent printed record which they produce.

9. Control messages are keyed in by the operator (eg. the next task required) and acted upon by the program. Messages can also be typed by the monitor for action by the operator (eg. indicating that a 'run' has finished). All messages are printed by the typewriter. Note that the input in this case consists of *operating messages* for controlling the system.

10. Note that when a terminal is used it is sometimes necessary to be able to communicate control messages as well as data and information. The terminal may therefore be able to perform *console* functions.

DOCUMENT READERS.

11. Optical Readers and Documents. There are two basic methods of Optical Document Reading:

a. **Optical Character Recognition (OCR).**

b. **Optical Mark Recognition (OMR).**

These two methods are often used in conjunction with one another, and have much in common. Their common and distinguishing features are covered in the next few paragraphs.

12. Features of an Optical Reader.

a. It has a document feed hopper and several stackers including a stacker for "rejected" documents.

b. Reading of documents prepared in optical characters or marks is accomplished as follows:

i. **Characters.** A scanning device recognises each character by the amount of reflected light (ie. OCR) (see fig. 5.1). The method of recognition, although essentially an electronic one, is similar in principle to matching photographic pictures with their negatives by holding the negative in front of the picture. The best match lets through the least light.

ii. **Marks.** A mark in a particular position on the document will trigger off a response. It is the *position* of the mark that is converted to a value by the Reader. (ie. OMR) (see fig. 5.2). The method involves directing thin beams of light onto the paper surface which are reflected into a light detector,

unless the beam is absorbed by a dark pencil mark, ie. a mark is recognised by the reduction in reflected light.
[**NB.** An older method of mark reading called **mark sensing** involved pencil marks conducting electricity between two contacts and completing a circuit.]

c. Documents may be read at up to 10,000 A4 documents per hour.

Fig. 5.1. Specimen characters from two common OCR character sets.
[Upper Set : OCR-A Lower Set : OCR-B]

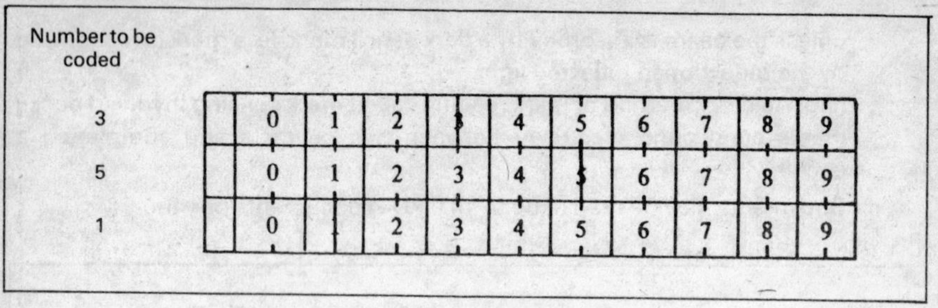

Fig. 5.2. A marked document ready for OMR.

13. Features of a document.

a. Documents are printed in a stylised form (by printers etc fitted with a special type-face) which can be recognised by a machine. The stylised print is also recognisable to the human eye. Printing must be on specified areas on the document.

b. Some documents incorporate optical marks. Pre-determined positions on the document are given values. A mark made in a position using a pencil is read by the reader.

c. Good quality printing and paper are vital.

d. Documents require to be undamaged for accurate reading.

e. Sizes of documents, and scanning area, may be limited.

14. Magnetic Ink Reader and Documents. The method of reading these documents is known as **Magnetic Ink Character Recognition (MICR).**

15. *Features of Magnetic Ink Readers.*

a. Documents are passed through a strong magnetic field causing the iron oxide in the ink encoded characters, to become magnetised. Documents are then passed under a read head when a current flows, at a strength according to the size of the magnetized area (ie. characters are recognised by a magnetic pattern).

b. Documents can be read at up to 2,400 per minute.

16. *Features of documents.*

a. The quality of printing needs to be very high.

b. The characters are printed in a highly distinctive type style using ink containing particles of iron oxide which gives the required magnetic property. (see Fig. 5.3). Examine a bank cheque for a further example.

DATA CAPTURE DEVICES

17. These devices are mostly special purpose devices intended for use in particular applications. Common, special and typical examples are described in the next few paragraphs.

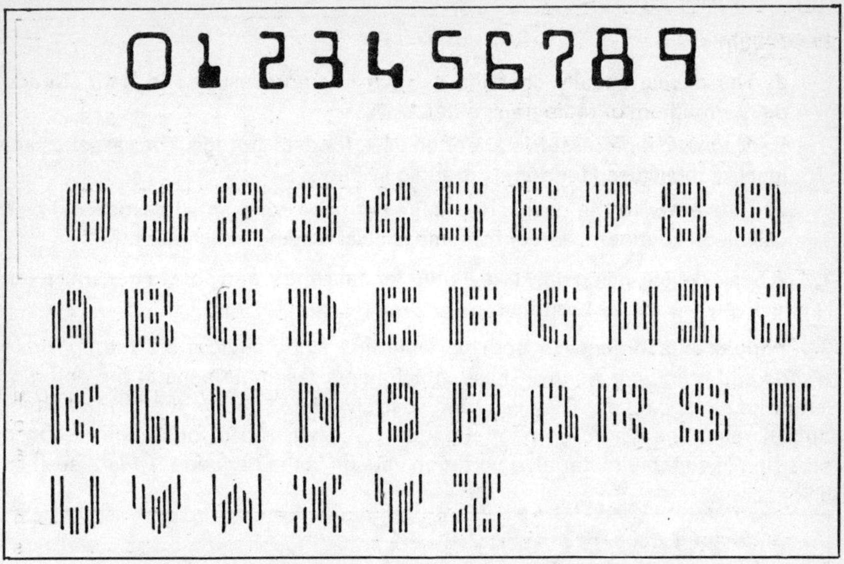

Fig. 5.3. Specimen characters from two common MICR character sets.
[Upper Set : E13B Lower Set : CMC7]

18. Direct Input Devices.

a. Special sensing devices may be able to detect events as they happen and pass the appropriate data directly to the computer. For example:

i. On an automated production line, products or components can be 'counted' as they pass specific points.

ii. At a supermarket checkout a *laser scanner* may read coded marks on food packets as the packets pass by on the conveyor.

This data is used by the computerised till to generate a till receipt and maintain records of stock levels.

iii. In a computer controlled chemical works, food factory or brewery industrial instruments connected to the computer can read temperatures and presssures in vats.

b. **Voice Data Entry Devices.** (5.4d) Data can be spoken into these devices. Currently they are limited to a few applications in which a small vocabulary is involved.

19. *Features.*

The specific features of these devices tend to depend upon the application for which they are used. However, the data captured by the device must ultimately be represented in some binary form in order to be processed by the *digital* computer. For some devices the input may merely be a single bit representation which corresponds to some instrument, such as a pressure switch, being on or off.

20. Data Loggers/Recorders. These devices record and store data at source. The data is input to the computer at some later stage.

21. *Features.*

a. The device usually contains its own microprocessor and data storage device/medium or radio transmitter.

b. *Magnetic tape cassettes* are often used for data storage. The cassettes are just like those used for domestic audio systems.

c. Data entry to the device is usually by means of a small keyboard, like a calculator keyboard, and/or by some special reading attachment.

22. A basic device, using only a keyboard for data entry, and able to transmit data, is effectively a portable terminal.

23. Popular attachments to both portable and static devices are the *light-pen wands* and *magnetic wands.* These attachments resemble pens at the end of a length of electrical flex. They can read specially coded data in the form of either optical marks/characters, or magnetic codes, which have previously been recoded on strips of suitable material. A common version is the *bar-code reader.* (see Fig. 5.4).

10 0116971 0

Fig. 5.4. A bar-coded strip readable by a light-pen wand.

MAGNETIC MEDIA STORAGE DEVICES.

24. Under this heading we will consider:-

a. Magnetic tape unit – magnetic tape.

b. Floppy disk unit – floppy disk (diskette).

These devices and media may also be used for data storage or output.

25. It should be noted that magnetic tapes and floppy disks normally come to have input data on them for one of three reasons:-

a. The data has been entered at some other device (eg. VDU) and encoded on the tape or diskette by some suitable hardware.

b. The data has been converted from a slow medium to enable faster input.

c. The data has previously been output by a computer. eg. in order to transfer data from one computer to another.

26. Magnetic Tape Unit and Magnetic Tape. The main magnetic tape medium is half inch reel-to-reel tape. Two lesser alternatives are magnetic tape cassette and magnetic-tape cartridge. The following description deals mainly with ½" reel-to-reel versions.

27. *Features of the Tape Unit.*

a. It holds the magnetic tape reel and also a second reel for 'taking up' the tape (similar in concept to a tape recorder). (See Fig. 5.5).

b. It has a 'read head' for 'reading' the information stored on the tape, ie. for transferring data from the tape into main storage.

c. The tape moves past the read head at up to 200 inches per second. (ips) Typical speeds are 30, 45, 75 and 125 ips when the tapes are travelling at these speeds data can be read from them at rates between 100,000 and 200,000 characters per second or even higher!

d. The tape can be accelerated to maximum speed or decelerated from maximum speed to a halt in approximately 5-15 ms while the tape travels about 1/4 to 3/8 of one inch.

28. *Features of the Magnetic Tape.*

a. It is 1/2" wide and 300, 600, 1200, 2400 or 3600 feet long.

b. It has a plastic base, coated with magnetisable material on *one* side.

c. Data is stored in tracks. There are 7 or 9 tracks (depending upon the tape unit) which run the length of the tape. The data is coded so that one CHARACTER is recorded across the 7 or 9 tracks. (See Fig. 5.6 which illustrates 7 track tape).

d. An aluminium strip, called a 'load point marker', marks the physical beginning of the tape for recording purposes; (the first 20 ft. or so is not used, apart from threading into the unit). Similarly the physical end of the tape is marked by an 'end of reel marker' (the *last* 20 ft. or so is not used for recording).

e. The *density* of recording can *vary* between 200–6,250 characters to the inch. Common forms are 800 bpi NRZI and the newer 1600 bpi PE. "bpi" stands for bits per inch but is effectively characters per inch. "NRZI" stands for Non-Return Zero Inverting and "PE" stands for Phase Encoding. Both are more sophisticated than the simple coding conventions for 0's and 1's explained in 2.14.

f. The tape is re-usable ie. can be overwritten (as can tape used with tape recorders) – 20,000 – 50,000 passes are possible.

g. It has a practical storage capacity of 40 million characters (approx) per reel.

29. Unlike a tape recorder, the tape on a magnetic tape unit stops and starts between blocks of recorded data. (Details later).

Reading takes place when the tape is moving at a high, *constant* speed past the read head. Reading automatically ceases when the inter block gap is sensed by the read head. The tape decelerates to a stop on termination of one "read" and accelerates up to its reading speed at the commencement of the next "read".

30. The speed with which the tape can be moved past the read head, and the density of characters, combine to give the data transfer speed, ie. the number of characters per second which are transferred into the Central Processing Unit. A *rate* of up to 1,250,000 characters per second can be achieved on the latest models.

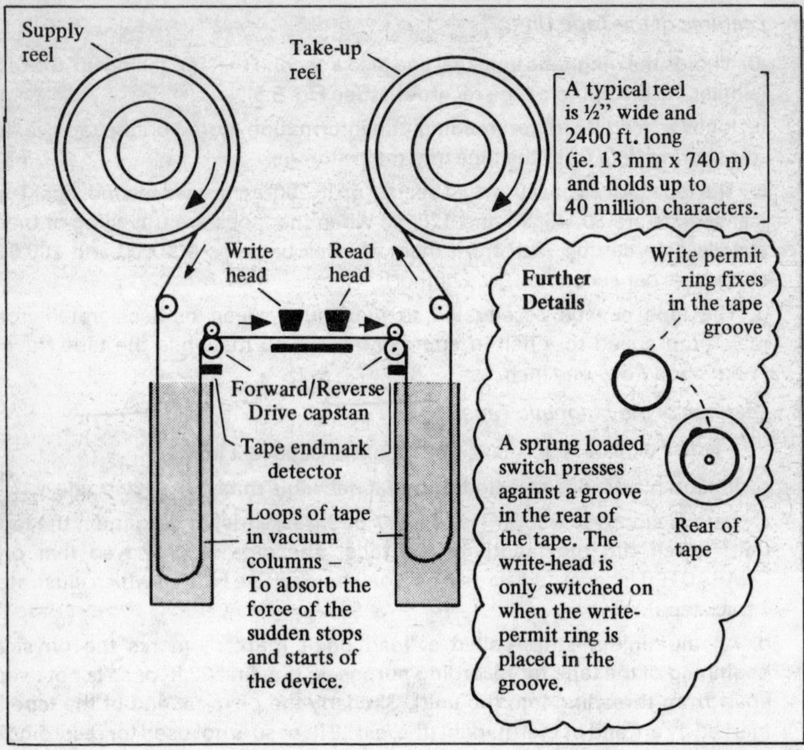

Fig. 5.5. Main features of a Magnetic Tape Unit.

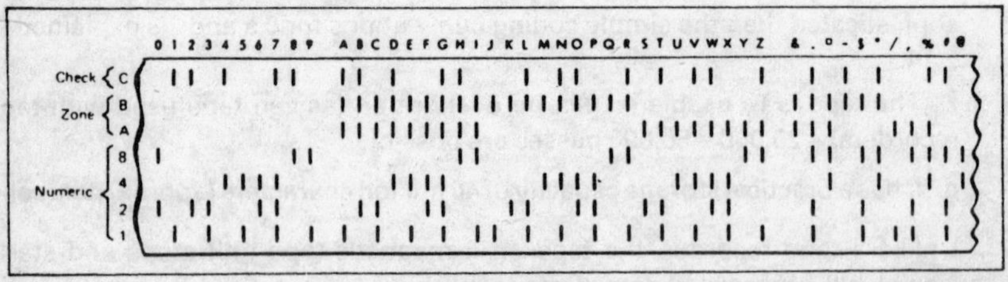

Fig. 5.6. Magnetic Tape Coding.

31. The theoretical storage capacity (ie. length x maximum density) is reduced considerably because of the Inter-Block Gaps which are required, each taking up about .75 inches. Thus the practical capacity can be as little as 20 million characters.

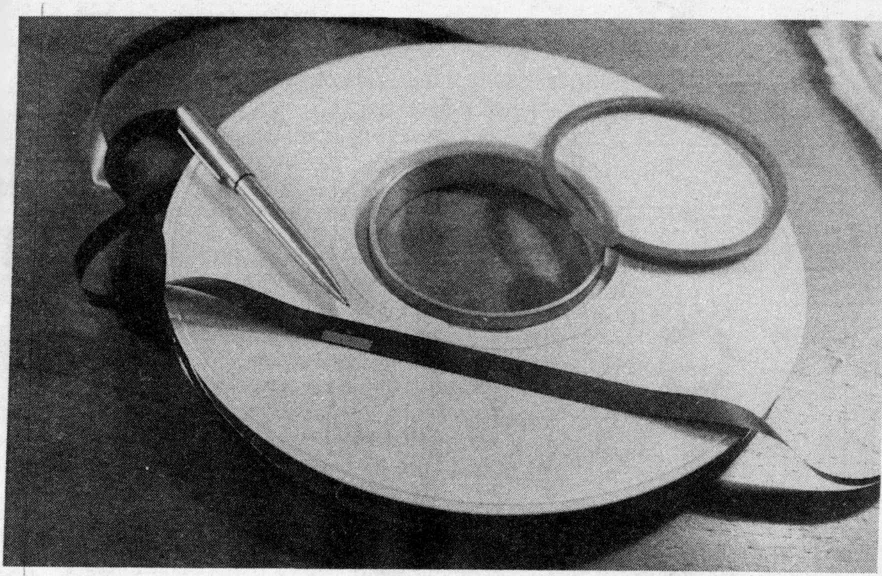

A magnetic tape (reverse side) with a write permit ring visible and removed from the back of the tape.

The pen tip is pointing to the 'Load point marker' at the start of the tape.

32. *Cassettes and Cartridges* operate on the same principles as ½" tape but have smaller capacities and are slower. eg. a cassette may store up to 340,000 characters at 800 characters to the inch on a 280 foot tape. Cassettes are commonly ⅛" two track and cartridges are commonly ¼" 4 track.

Label

■ Represents exposed disk surface

Index hole. Used to locate start of data recording on each track.

Security tag holes which can be covered by tape. Used when needed to stop recorded data being accidentally lost. This serves the same function as a magnetic tape write permit ring. (On some disks adding the tape protects the disk – a less sound practice).

Spindle hole surrounded by surface gripped by spindle clamp in order to rotate the disk.

The read/write head presses against this slot supported by a pressure pad below and moves across the slot from track to track rather like the arm on a record player.

A Floppy Disk in its protective envelope. Typical sizes 5¼" square or 8" square.

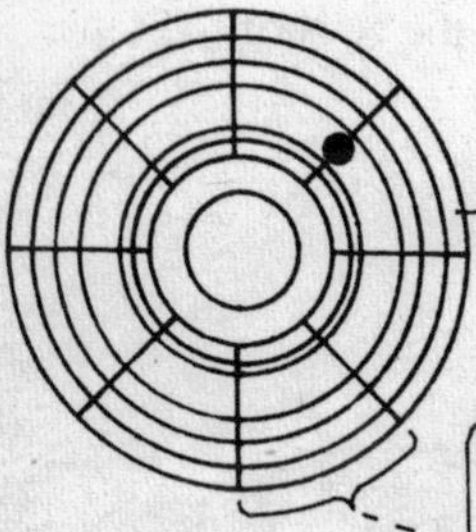

Concentric tracks (invisible). Typically 77 per side on 8" disks and 40 per side on 5¼" disks but there are many common variations.

1 sector
Typically 10, 16 or 32 sectors per track

NB
The data from each sector can be read into main storage without having to first read data from inner or outer tracks ie. **direct access** not **serial access.**

A Floppy Disk

Storage capacity.

"Single sided" disks only use one surface for data recording.

"Double sided" disks use both recording surfaces.

Techniques can be exploited to double the data storage capacity of each track ie. the choice is between "single density" or "double density".

The typical capacity of a single sided single density floppy disk is 125 thousand characters (5¼") or 250 thousand characters (8"). Figures for double sided double density floppy disks are four times those for single sided single density.

Fig. 5.7. Floppy Disk (Diskette) Details.

8″ floppy disk with part of its cover removed, with a 5¼″ floppy disk by its side.

33. Floppy Disk Unit and Floppy Disk (Diskette).

Features of the Floppy Disk Unit.

a. Most floppy disk units are *dual drive* units, ie. able to hold two separate floppy disks at a time.

b. Each disk is inserted into a narrow slot in the front of the disk drive. The slot has a small flap over it, which must be clipped shut once the disk is inserted.

c. The action of closing the flap engages a turntable which rotates the disk and also brings a "read/write head" into contact with the disk. The read/write head is moved to and fro across the disk in order to either record data on the disk surface (a "write"), or 'read' back data which has previously been recorded.

d. Floppy disks rotate at 360 rpm.

e. Floppy Disk Units are sometimes incorporated physically into the VDU associated with the system.

34. *Features of the floppy disk.*

a. A pliable disc permanently sealed within a rigid, smoothly lined, protective plastic envelope. (see Fig. 5.7).

b. Data is stored on tracks.

c. The two most common size are 8" and 5¼".

d. Storage capacities range from 60 thousand characters to 1¼ million characters.

35. "Microfloppy". A more recent variation on the floppy disk is the 3½" "microfloppy". A typical single sided microfloppy stores about 315,000 characters.

OTHER MEDIA.

36. At one time the two main input media were *punched cards* and *paper tape.* They are still to be found in use on some computer systems and so are described here. The reader should note that punched cards and paper tape are cumbersome, slow, costly and laborious to use compared with many newer alternatives.

37. Card Reader and Punched Cards.

Features of the Card Reader.

a. It has a feed hopper and a stacker and a photo electric reader for sensing holes in a card.

b. The whole deck of cards is placed in the feed hopper and under control of the CPU each card passes through the photo electric reader which senses the hole patterns (by light passing through the holes) and transmits the data to the CPU. Cards are then automatically fed out of the machine into the stacker.

c. Cards can be read at speeds of up to 2000 cards per minute.

38. *Features of the Punched Card.*

a. Cards are the same type as those used on the earlier electro-mechanical

Punch Card Systems, and date back to their invention by Dr. Hermann Hollerith in the USA in the mid 1880's.

b. See fig. 2.11.

39. The cards are read completely ie. there is no *absolute character transfer rate* as it depends upon the *number of characters* punched per card.

40. The highest possible transfer rate would be 30 (cards) × 80 (characters) = 2400 characters per second *if all columns* in the card were punched. Because it is not usual for every column to be punched, the average character transfer rate would be between 1,000-2,000 characters per second.

41. Paper Tape Reader and Punched Paper Tape.

Features of the Paper Tape Reader.

a. Paper tape is sprocket fed past a photo electric cell reader (as with punched cards).

b. The tape is usually moved at a speed of 100 inches per second.

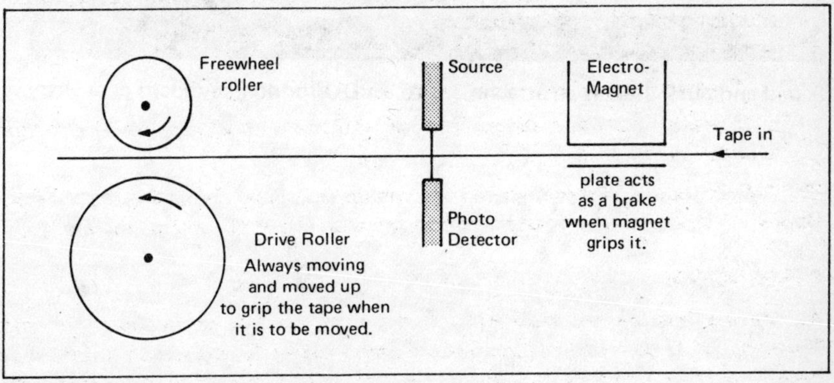

Fig. 5.8. Paper Tape Reader.

42. *Features of Punched Paper Tape.*

a. The width of paper tape varies between ¾ – 1 inch (depending upon code); it is 300–1,000 ft. in length and is stored in reels.

b. Data is coded in the form of punched holes.

c. Data is stored in TRACKS (in the same manner as magnetic tape) with 10 columns per inch. See Fig. 2.9).

43. The usual transfer rate is 1,000 characters per second.

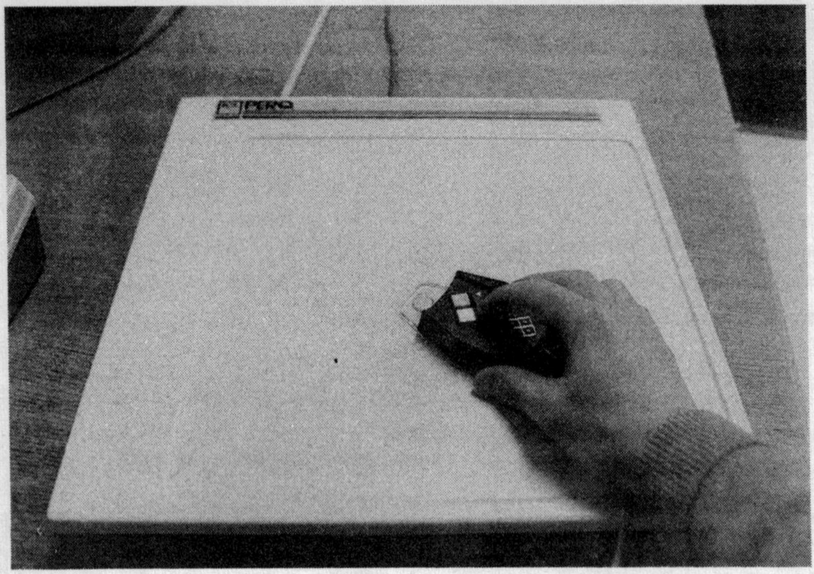

A pad and puck used as an attachment to a VDU for non-keyboard data entry.

SUMMARY.

44. The features of the *main* hardware units and media, for transfering data into the computer, have been covered. They are:-

a. Visual Display Unit (VDU).
b. Terminal Typewriter.
c. Optical reader – Documents.
d. Magnetic ink reader – Documents.
e. Direct input devices.
f. Data loggers/recorders.
g. Magnetic tape unit – Magnetic tape.
h. Floppy disk unit – Floppy disk (Diskette).
i. Card reader – Punched card.
j. Paper tape reader – Paper tape.

POINTS TO NOTE.

45. a. Only the units in 44a-44d handle data in forms which are both machine *and* human sensible.

b. The actions of the input devices are under the control of the computer's processor because the devices are "on-line" to the computer when being used for input purposes. Note however that these devices may also be used "off-line" in some cases ie. away from the computer.

c. Some VDUs now have hand held devices for moving the cursor about the screen. eg. "joysticks" and "mice".

d. Note the use of magnetic tape cassettes and cartridges in conjunction with devices such as data loggers/recorders. The cassette and cartridge use a short length of magnetic tape in a rigid plastic case. The cassette is identical to that used in audio systems. The cartridge is similar but more suited for computer input.

The advantage of these devices is that they are highly portable and inexpensive.

e. Many manufacturers have introduced novel methods of providing backing storage on small computers in recent years. One notable example is the "microdrive" produced by Sinclair Computers.

STUDENT SELF TESTING QUESTIONS (answers begin page 682)

1. What is the difference between "scrolling" and "paging" on a VDU?

2. Explain the presence of a gap between adjacent blocks of data on a magnetic tape.

QUESTIONS WITHOUT ANSWERS.

3. Find out exactly what features are present on the VDU which you use.

4. Explain the term "double density, double sided, one megabyte floppy disk".

6 Output Devices and Media

INTRODUCTION.

1. The following devices and media will be described:-

   a. Printers – Single sheet or continuous stationery.

   b. Terminals – VDU or Terminal typewriter.

   c. Microform recorder – Microfilm or Microfiche.

   d. Magnetic tape unit – Magnetic tape.

   e. Floppy-disk-unit – Floppy disk (diskette).

   f. Graph Plotters – Single sheet or continuous stationery.

   g. Actuators.

   h. Others.

PRINTERS.

2. A basic classification of printers is:

   a. **Character Printers** which print one character at a time.

   b. **Line Printers** which print whole lines at a time.

   c. **Page Printers** (also called **Image Printers**) which print whole pages at a time.

3. **Print Speeds** tend to be expressed in terms of cps (characters per second) or lpm (lines per minute). Printers may be classified as

   a. **Low speed** (10 cps to approx 300 lpm) – usually character printers.

   b. **High speed** (Typically 300 lpm – 3000 lpm) – usually line printers or page printers.

4. **Basic Methods of producing print.**

   a. **Impact or Non-Impact printing.** Impact printers *hit* inked ribbons against paper whereas non-impact printers use other methods of printing eg. Thermal or electrostatic. Most impact printers are noisy.

   b. **Shaped or Dot-Matrix printing.** The difference is explained in Fig. 6.1. A dot matrix can also be used to produce a whole **picture** or **image,** (6.2c) similar in principle, but superior in quality, to the minute pattern of dots in a newspaper picture.

LOW SPEED PRINTERS.

5. **Dot matrix impact character printers.** These are the most popular and widely used low speed printers. They are often loosely referred to as **"dot matrix printers"**.

An IBM 3284 Printer. Picture courtesy of IBM.

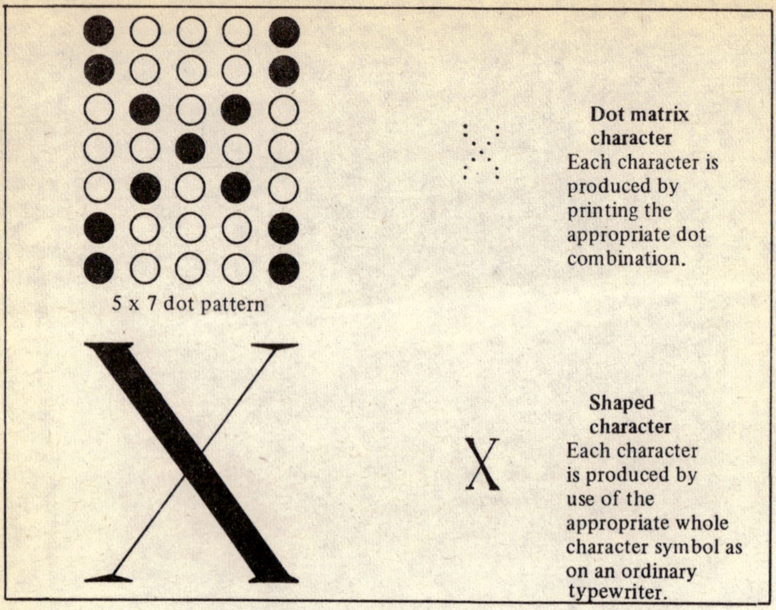

Fig. 6.1. Shaped and Dot Matrix Character.

6. *Features.*

a. As with all character printers the device mimics the action of a typewriter by printing single characters at a time in lines across the stationery. The print is produced by a small 'print head' which moves to and fro across the page, stopping momentarily in each character position to strike a print ribbon against the stationery with an array of wires.

b. According to the number of wires in the print head, the character matrix may be 7 × 5, 7 × 7, 9 × 7, 9 × 9. The more dots the better the image.

c. Line widths are typically 80, 120, 132 or 160 characters across.

d. Speeds are typically from 30 cps to 200 cps.

e. Multiple print copies may be produced by the use of carboned paper (eg. 4-6 copies using NCR paper).

f. Some higher quality versions have:-

i. Inbuilt alternative character sets.

ii. Very good print quality.

iii. Features for producing graphs, pictures, and even colour by means of multiple print ribbons.

7. Daisywheel Printers. Another popular type of low speed printer which is favoured when high print quality is demanded.

8. *Features.*

a. An impact shaped character printer.

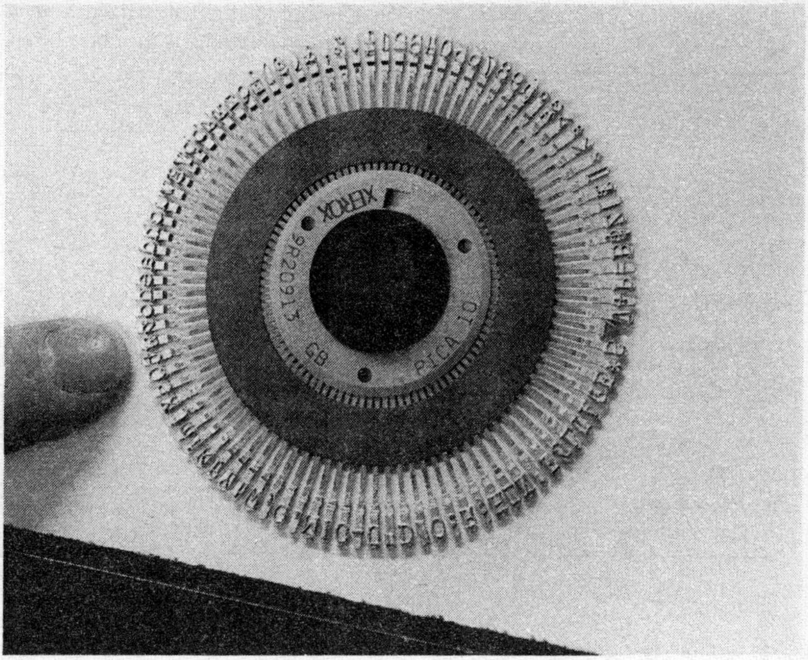

A daisy wheel.

b. These printers are fitted with *exchangeable* print heads called **daisywheels.** (See Fig. 6.2). To print each character the wheel is rotated and the appropriate spoke is struck against an inked ribbon.

c. Speed typically 45 cps.

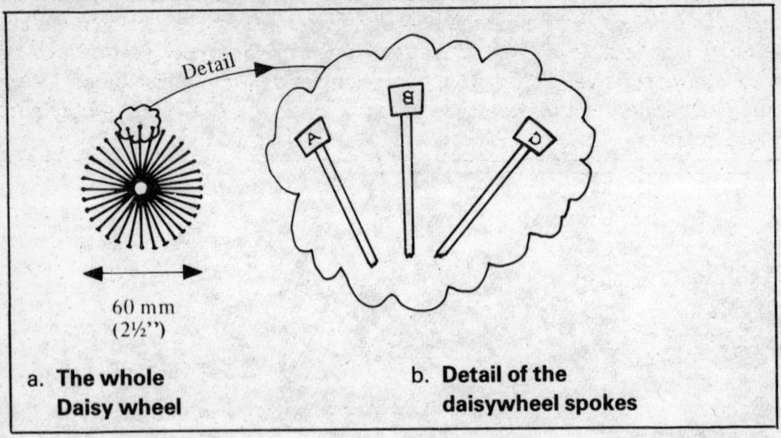

Fig. 6.2.

d. Similar to dot matrix printers in terms of page size and multiple copy printing.

9. **Other low speed printers.** There are many other low speed printers too numerous to mention. Two others worth a mention are:–

a. **Thermal Printers.** These are non-impact character matrix printers which print onto special paper using a heated print head. They are very quiet and this gives them a big advantage for some applications.

b. **Inkjet Printers.** These are non impact character matrix printers which fire ink droplets onto the paper by using an "electrostatic field". They too are very quiet but are not so widely used at present.

HIGH SPEED PRINTERS.

10. There are two basic types of high speed printers:-

a. Line Printers.

b. Page Printers.

Both types operate with continuous stationery.

11. Line printers. These are impact shaped-character printers which, as their names suggest, print whole lines at a time. There are three main types:

a. Drum printers. Fig. 6.3a.

b. Chain printers. } Fig. 6.3b.

c. Band printers. }

12. It will suffice to indicate how *b* and *c* work. A principle of operation typical of the faster models, is that of a moving chain, with the links being engraved character printing slugs, moving at a high constant speed past printing positions. The band printer has an embossed steel loop instead of a chain. Magnetically controlled hammers force *the paper* against the appropriate print slugs. Typically, there are 120 printing positions to a 'line'. Speeds of up to 50 lines per second *can* be achieved although, as yet, 20 (approx) per second is a more typical speed. Using continuous stationery with interleaved carbons, up to 7 copies can be obtained. (See Fig. 6.3b).

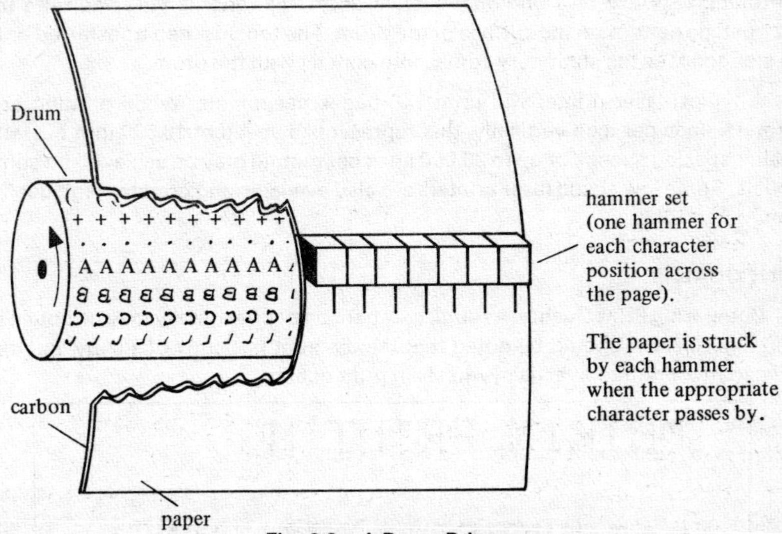

Fig. 6.3a. A Drum Printer

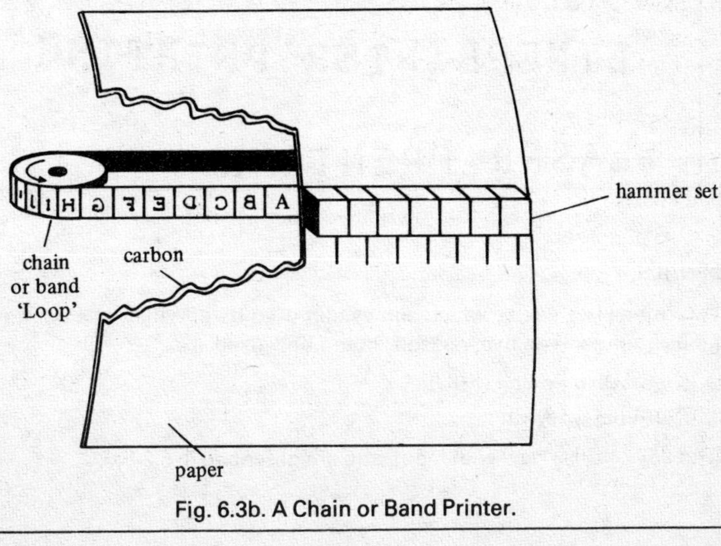

Fig. 6.3b. A Chain or Band Printer.

The bands in a band printer may be exchanged quite readily to provide a variety of character sets.

13. Page Printers. The printers print an *"image"* of a whole page at a time. The image may consist of conventional print, diagrams, pictures, or a combination of these thus making pre-printed stationery unnecessary.

14. According to technical features given emphasis in particular designs, these printers are also known as **Optical printers, Laser printers** or **Xerographic printers.**

15. An electronically controlled laser beam marks out an electrostatic image on the rotating surface of a photoconductive drum. Ink toner is attracted onto the electrostatic pattern on the surface of the drum. The toner is then transferred onto the stationery as the stationery comes into contact with the drum.

16. A typical laser printer will print 146 pages per minute. When printing at a normal 6 lines per inch vertically, this represents a speed of 10,500 lpm but with smaller spacing speeds of up to 30,000 lines per minute may be achieved on some models. Some low speed laser printers are also available and produce high quality print.

PRINT QUALITY.

17. Comparing Print Quality. A *rough* comparison of print quality may be obtained from Figure 6.4. It should be noted that the diagram is a copy of a copy and that *some* matrix printers rival daisywheels in print quality.

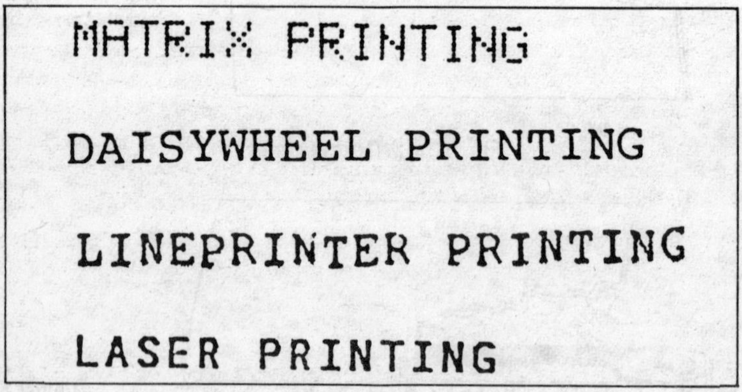

Fig. 6.4. Alternative types of print.

TERMINALS.

18. A terminal is a device which allows output to be provided at a point remote from the computer. The two methods commonly used are:

a. Visual Display Unit (VDU).

b. Terminal typewriter.

The devices also deal with input, and are described in 5.2-5.6.

19. Visual Displays. In 5.2-5.4 the emphasis was placed upon the use of VDUs for input. However, there are applications in which visual displays like those of the VDU are used by themselves. The most common examples occur in industrial applications where the display may be used to provide an animated representation of a measuring instrument's data in order to allow visual monitoring of some process.

20. Types of Display Technology. There are three basic types of display technology:

a. **Vector scan refresh display.**

b. **Direct view storage tubes.**

c. **Raster scan display.**

21. Vector scan refresh display. This is the oldest type of display technology. Details of the image are held in a "display file" in storage. The display file is repeatedly scanned and the appropriate image is displayed on the phosphor screen. The method is relatively expensive, prone to flicker in the case of large complex images, but responds quickly to changing images.

22. Direct view refresh storage tubes. This method was pioneered by Tecktronics. A grid behind the screen has the image displayed upon it and is able to retain the image and allow its transfer to the screen. This prevents flicker but can give a slower response because the image is changed by clearing the grid completely and then redisplaying the image.

23. Raster Scan Display. This method involves the used of a stored image of the display within the device, in a binary form known as a "bit map". The screen is treated as a set of dots in rows and columns with each dot being represented by a single bit (1 for bright, 0 for dark). The bit map is repeatedly scanned within the device and the corresponding image is displayed on the screen. The method produces clear flicker-free images but until recently has lacked adequate resolution for some applications. At the current time the number of dots on the screen (called pixels) is not normally more than 1500 × 1000.

24. Terminal Typewriters. These were discussed in 5.5-5.6. Most terminal typewriters incorporate matrix or daisy-wheel impact printers.

MICROFORM RECORDERS AND MICROFORMS.

25. Microforms are photographically reduced documents on films. There are two types:

a. **Microfilm** – 16 mm roll film.

b. **Microfiche** – sheet film 105mm × 148mm.

Both types are produced in the same manner.

26. Output is written onto magnetic tape, which is then fed into a machine called a microform recorder which reads the magnetic tape and copies the data onto microforms. The information can subsequently be inspected by using a viewer which projects onto a screen. Full-size copies can be printed if required. This technique is useful when large volumes of information are used internally, since economies can be made in stationery costs and storage space. It is usually referred to as COM (Computer Output on Microfilm/Microfiche).

27. Storage Capacities.

a. A typical 16mm roll will hold the equivalent of 3,000 A4 pages.

b. *One* typical microfiche will hold the equivalent of about 98 A4 pages.

MAGNETIC TAPE UNIT AND MAGNETIC TAPE.

28. Features of the Tape Unit. The *same* device is used for both input *and* output, therefore the features are those already described except that a *"write"*-head is used to encode information onto the tape.

29. Features of Magnetic Tape. The same media are used for both input and output. For security purposes a special device called a "write-permit" ring must be attached to a tape reel when writing onto the tape is required.

30. Manner of recording. Data is recorded (written) in blocks as the tape moves past the "write" head at a *constant* rate. After a block has been written, the tape slows down and stops. On being instructed to write again, the tape accelerates up to the speed required for writing and another block is written onto the tape. No writing takes place during the acceleration and deceleration time and this therefore leaves a gap between each block of data on the tape. This INTER BLOCK GAP measures some ¾".

FLOPPY DISK UNIT AND FLOPPY DISK (DISKETTE).

31. The *same* devices and media are used for both input *and* output. Details were given in 5.33.

32. It should be noted that the most common reason for producing output on magnetic tape or floppy disk is to enable subsequent re-input to the same computer, or to some other computer.

GRAPH PLOTTERS

33. These devices provide a completely different form of output and have a variety of applications. Two basic types are:–

a. **Flat bed type.** The pen moves up, down, across or side to side.

b. **Drum type.** The pen moves up, down and across. The paper provides sideways movement.

NB. The up/down movements allow the pen to move from point to point with or without making a line.

a. A desk top, A3 size flatbed 8-pen plotter from CalComp designed for plotting business and scientific graphs and charts on paper or on clear acetate for projection. Photograph with caption by courtesy of CalComp Ltd.

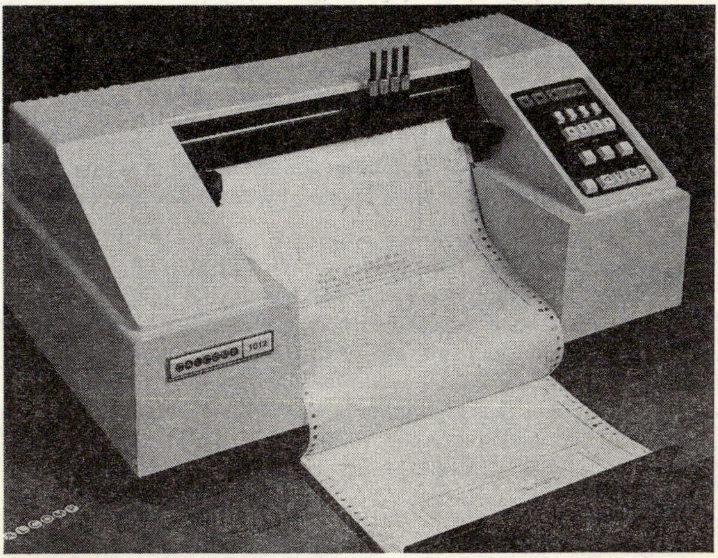

b. A high-speed desk top drum plotter from CalComp which uses A4 size continuous fan folded paper or clear film. Photograph with caption by courtesy of CalComp Ltd.

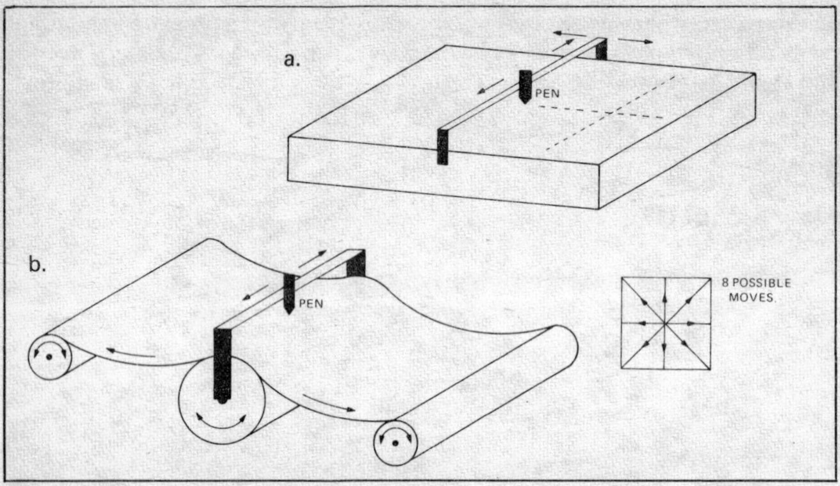

Fig. 6.5. Flat bed plotter (above) and Drum plotter.

34. Digital Plotters and Incremental Plotters. The difference between these two types of plotter is in the way they are given instructions to move:–

a. **Digital Plotters** receive digital input which specifies the position to which the pen should move ie. like a map reference.

b. **Incremental Plotter** receive input which specifies changes in position eg. move 2 mm left.

35. Colour. Many plotters have multiple pens of different colour which may be changed under machine control.

36. Some plotters use "electrostatic" printing rather than pen and ink.

37. Applications. Graph plotters are used for scientific and engineering purposes. One special application is CAD (Computer Aided Design) in which for example machine or architectural designs are created by computer and then output on graph plotters.

ACTUATORS.

38. Computers are frequently used to control the operation of all manner of devices, appliances, mechanisms and processes. Any computer output device which is used to communicate some required action to a machine may be called an **Actuator**. For example a microcomputer operating a washing machine would use actuators to operate the motors and pumps. In a chemical plant controlled by computer actuators would operate valves, pumps etc.

OTHER DEVICES.

39. Most other output devices are limited to use in specific applications. One notable exception is speech output.

40. **Speech Output.** In principle, spoken output should be an extremely useful medium. Unfortunately the devices currently available produce unnatural sounds and are limited to a few specialist applications. The situation is likely to improve over the next few years.

SUMMARY.

41. The *features* of the *main* hardware units and media for the output of data from the CPU have been covered. They are:-

a. Printers – Single sheet or continuous stationery.

b. Terminals – VDU or terminal typewriter.

c. Microform recorder – Microfilm or Microfiche.

d. Magnetic tape unit – Magnetic tape.

e. Floppy disk unit – Floppy disk (diskette).

f. Actuators.

g. Others.

POINTS TO NOTE.

42. a. Line printers can print in *Optical Character Recognition* form, ie. allowing later re-input without further transcription.

b. Some matrix printers can be used to produce bar-coded strips eg. for use as stock labels.

7 Main Storage

INTRODUCTION.

1. We were introduced to Main Storage in chapter one, where it was seen to be an important element in the Central Processing Unit (CPU). The general features of Main Storage are described in this chapter. Another very appropriate name for Main Storage is **Main Memory,** because like the human memory it is able to retain or store information which may later be recalled or accessed.

2. Features of Main Storage.

a. Its operation is wholly electronic, and consequently very fast and reliable. In the most modern computers the electronic memory circuits are also highly miniaturised.

b. Data is almost instantly accessible from main memory because of its electronic operation and close proximity to the rest of the CPU. For example, an item of data may be retrieved from main storage in less than one millionth of one second. For this reason main storage has yet another name, **immediate access storage.**

c. Data *must* be transferred to main storage before it can be processed by the CPU. High access speeds then contribute to fast processing.

3. Uses of Main Storage. Ideally, Main Storage would be used to store all data requiring processing, in order to achieve maximum processing speeds. However, there are practical limitations on the size of main storage that processors can easily be made to operate with. Main storage is also relatively expensive, although modern RAM is much less expensive than core store which was used in the past. So, the practical solution is to limit the size of main storage and supplement it with less expensive auxiliary storage (1.15). Thus limited capacity, coupled with the need to hold data in main storage for processing, results in main storage being *used* as a short term memory.

It stores

a. Instructions awaiting to be obeyed,

b. Instructions currently being obeyed,

c. Data awaiting processing,

d. Data currently being processed,

e. Data awaiting output.

4. An area of main storage being used for data currently being processed is called a **working storage** area and an area being used for data awaiting processing or output is called a **buffer area.**

THE OPERATIONAL FEATURES OF MAIN STORAGE.

5. To understand the principles of how data is placed into main storage we will imagine it to be arranged like a set of boxes, and deal with the physical details of main storage later. The boxes are numbered from zero upwards so that each box can be identified and located. What is usually called a **'Location in main storage'**

corresponds to one of our boxes, and the **'location address'** corresponds to the number of the box.

eg	0	1	2	3	4	5	etc.

Once data is stored in a location in main storage it remains there until it is replaced by other data. Data placed into the same location will destroy what was there previously (rather like the latest recording you make on a tape recorder will destroy the previous one). Accessing and fetching data from main storage is really a copying action which does not result in the data being deleted from main storage (just as playing a tape recorder does not erase the tape).

6. Random Access. It is possible to fetch data from the locations in main storage in any order, and the time taken does not depend on the position of the locations. We summarise this by saying we have **random access** to data in main storage. This is also known as **direct access.**

7. Volatility. Depending on its physical characteristics, main storage may be either **volatile,** in which case data is lost once the power is turned off, or **non-volatile,** where no such data loss occurs.

8. Details of a single location. Each location in main storage consists of a set of tiny devices each of which can be in one of two states at any one time (eg On or Off). The two states of each device are used to represent binary 0 (Off) and 1 (On), and hence the complete set of **two-state devices** in each location provides a method of coding data, rather like that used with input media such as magnetic tape. We may thus talk of a location in main storage as being so many bits long. For a given computer the number of bits in each location will be the same fixed number for all locations eg *each* location could contain 16 bits, and *each* location would be addressable.

BYTES AND WORDS.

9. Each location in main storage is usually said to hold a unit of data called a **word.** Words can often be subdivided into smaller units called **bytes.** The real situation is much more complicated than this because of the many different approaches to computer design. The next few paragraphs discuss common design approaches.

10. Fixed Word length Computers (Word Machines). In a fixed word length computer **1 word = 1 location in main storage** ie data is transferred into main storage one location at a time. The number of bits in each location (word), known as the *word length* will depend on the make and model of computer. Typical word lengths are, 8, 12, 16, 24, 32 and 48 bits. Several characters might be placed or *'packed'* into one word, eg two 6-bit BCD characters could be packed into a 12 bit word as shown in the following example.

11. Example of data storage in a word machine. In this example the characters 'ABC' are stored in a 12 bit word length machine using these codes: A is coded

110001, B is coded 110010, and C is coded 110011. (Fig. 2.6).

LOCATION NO.	201		202	
CONTENTS	1 1 0 0 0 1	1 1 0 0 1 0	0 0 0 0 0 0	1 1 0 0 1 1
COMMENT	Code for 'A'	Code for 'B'	Unused	Code for 'C'

12. Example of instruction storage in a word machine. In word machines, instructions are of *fixed length,* usually one (possibly 2 or 3) instructions per location. For the time being you should regard an instruction as a single binary code. The following example shows the storage of two instructions.

LOCATION NO.	201	202
CONTENTS	1 1 0 1 1 0 1 0 1 1 0 1	1 0 1 1 0 1 1 0 1 1 1 0
COMMENT	Binary Code for the first instruction	Binary Code for the second instruction

13. In general, storage space tends to be wasted by using fixed length units of storage for variable length data eg having to use a 12 bit word to store one 6 bit character as for 'C' in paragraph 11. As this problem occurs in most situations where data is to be transferred or stored, some designers have produced variable word length computers.

14. Variable Word Length Computers. In these computers a word is one or more whole locations in length, and is set to the required length at each data transfer. There are two types of variable word length machines:–

a. **Character Machines** in which each location is 6 bits long.

b. **Byte Machines** in which each location is 8 bits long.

15. Character Machines. The location length of 6 bits allows an internal code (Fig. 2.6) with a character set of $2^6 = 64$ characters. Examples of storage are now given.

a. **Data Storage.** eg The storage of 'ABC' using the codes from paragraph 11.

LOCATION NO.	201	202	203
CONTENTS	1 1 0 0 0 1	1 1 0 0 1 0	1 1 0 0 1 1
COMMENT	Code for A	Code for B	Code for C

The characters 'A', 'B' and 'C' could be stored one at a time by setting the word length to one, or stored all three at once by setting the word length to three.

b. **Instruction Storage.** Instructions may be of *fixed length* (eg all 3 characters long) but usually they are of *variable length* as shown below.

LOCATION NO.	201	202	203	204	205
CONTENTS	1 0 1 1 1 0	1 0 1 1 0 1	1 1 0 1 0 1	0 1 1 0 0 0	1 1 0 1 1 1
COMMENT	Binary Code for the first instruction which is 2 ch. long.		Binary Code for the second instruction which is 3 ch. long.		

16. Byte Machines. The location length of 8 bits allows an internal code character set of $2^8 = 256$ characters. An added advantage is that two 4 bit BCD numeric characters will pack into one byte as shown below.

a. **Data Storage** eg "A" using ASCII (Fig. 2.4) and 12 using 4 bit BCD code.

LOCATION NO.	201	202	
CONTENTS	0 1 0 0 0 0 0 1	0 0 0 1	0 0 1 0
COMMENT	Code for 'A'	Code for 1	Code for 2

A is coded 01000001.

1 is coded 0001.

2 is coded 0010.

b. **Instruction Storage.** The points made for character machines apply except that each location is 8 bits long. A separate diagram is not merited.

17. In both fixed and variable length machines, locations may be used to store instructions or data, and the stored codes are indistinguishable. In principle there is nothing to prevent a stored instruction from being used as data or vice versa! In practice storage must be used carefully to avoid such errors.

18. Variation with machine size. The smaller computers tend to be fixed word length machines. The smaller microcomputers have word lengths of 8 bits. They are **not** variable word length byte machines, however, because the number of bytes transferred between the processor and main storage is always of the same fixed size for every transfer. The larger micro computers and small mini computers tend to have word lengths of 16 bits. Larger mini computers and some mainframes have word lengths of 32 bits, and so on.

19. Parity check. We have been referring to storage as consisting of eg. 6, 8 or 32 bit groups. In fact each one of these groups will have a parity bit added to it in the same way that transmitted codes do. (See Fig. 2.3). The parity bit aids the detection of errors caused through bits being "lost" in the process of storing or transmitting the data.

Note: Small computers do not always incorporate parity checking systems and this can bring their reliability into question in some situations.

PHYSICAL FEATURES OF MAIN STORAGE.

20. To have a sound understanding of main storage we need to be aware of some features of its construction and technology. These features are illustrated here by reference to the most common type of main storage called **semiconductor memory**. Until the mid 1970s main storage was normally constructed of **"core storage"** which is now obsolete (see Appendix 2.1).

21. Semi-conductor memory. The common type, the **RAM** (Random Access Memory) is described here.

a. Each bit in semiconductor memory is represented by a single cell which may be regarded as a microscopic electronic circuit with two distinguishable states used to represent '0' and '1' Cells arranged into rows and columns are built onto a single 'chip' of silicon some 3 mm x 3 mm, in what is clearly a most advanced manufacturing process, since 2048 cells may be formed on a single chip and thousands times more on the larger chips!

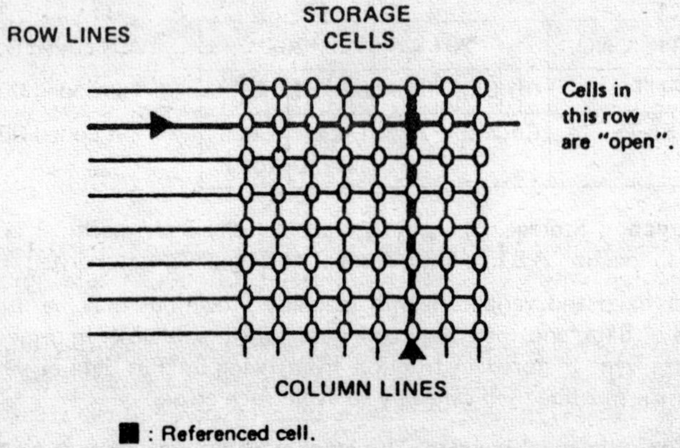

b. Each cell can be *electrically charged* **or** *not electrically charged* representing '1' and '0' respectively. If a row line is made electrically active it causes all cells in that row to switch open so that they can be charged or discharged through a column line. A column line for one cell in the row may then be switched on, **either** to pass charge into the cell (State '1') **or** to allow the cell to discharge (State '0'). Since charge can only flow from a charged cell, an observable discharge reveals the state of a cell and provides the means of reading from memory. A cell discharged by reading from it must be recharged to preserve its state.

c. Charge slowly leaks from the cells and has to be topped up constantly. This is called "refreshing". Strictly speaking this is a feature of one type of RAM called **dynamic RAM.** Refreshing is not required in the other type of RAM which is called **Static RAM.** In static RAM the "cells" stay "latched" in a '1' state or '0' state by the provision of a constant power supply. This dependence on a constant power supply by both static and dynamic RAM means RAM memory is *volatile.* (ie. data is lost if the power supply is removed).

d. Semiconductor memory replaced the older core store because it is faster to access, more compact and much less expensive than core store.

22. **ROMS.** A non-volatile semiconductor alternative to the RAM is the ROM (Read Only Memory) in which all cell states are set permanently during manufacture. A set of instructions stored in this way is said to be a **'hard wired',** and is often called **firmware.** This technique is often used to extend the instruction set of the computer by storing special purpose subroutines, these are called **microprograms.** ROM is also frequently used to store data or instructions which the computer needs all the time from the moment it is switched on.

23. Other types of ROM.

Apart from the basis types of ROM, just described, there are several newer variations which are briefly described here:

a. **PROM** (Programmable Read Only Memory). In contrast to normal ROM, in which the pattern of stored data is permanently incorporated into the chip using a 'Mask' during the last stage of manufacture, the PROM can be programmed by the user of PROM. However, the data is held permanently once the PROM has been programmed.

b. **EPROM** (Erasable Programmable Read Only memory). This is like PROM in that it maybe programmed by the user but has the advantage that it may be erased and reprogrammed. The EPROM must be removed from the computer in order to be erased. Special devices called "EPROM erasers" and "EPROM programmers" are used for these tasks.

c. **EAROM** (Electrically Alterable Read Only Memory). These memories can be read, erased and re-written without removing them from the computer. However, the erasing and re-writing process is very slow compared with reading which limits their use. For this reason they are sometimes called **RMMs** (Read Mostly Memories).

d. **EEROM** (Electrically Erasable Read Only Memory). Essentially the same as EAROM.

SEMI-CONDUCTOR FABRICATION TECHNOLOGIES.

24. The chips used for main storage and the chips used for processors are normally made from one of two basis types of manufacturing process. The two basic fabrication processes are:–

a. BIPOLAR Technology.

b. MOS Technology.

25. There are several variations on these basic technologies eg. Schottky bipolar and I^2L (Integrated Injection Logic) are variations on bipolar technology and PMOS, NMOS, CMOS, SOS, VMOS and HMOS are all variations on MOS technology. Do not attempt to remember all these variations they are mentioned here merely to show the wide variety of technologies that exist.

26. These types of fabrication technology have a direct bearing on the operational features of the semi-conductor devices. Factors affected include

a. Cost.

b. Power consumption.

c. Speed of access.

d. Reliability.

27. Very broadly, speaking MOS technology is more widely used on micro-computers and BIPOLAR technology is mostly used on minicomputers and mainframe computers which should indicate some general differences between the two technologies.

SUMMARY.

a. Main storage is a fast, wholly electronic, random access memory which is used as a short term memory for data awaiting processing or output, or which is being processed.

b. Data stored in main memory is identified and located by the memory location address.

c. Computers are described a 'Character', 'Byte' or 'Word' machines according to the units of data transfer to and from main storage.

d. The two main types of main storage are:–

i. Core Storage. (Now outdated).

ii. Semiconductor memory.

POINTS TO NOTE.

a. Main storage has several names e.g. Main Memory, Immediate access memory, internal storage, primary storage, core storage etc.

b. For simplicity most examples in this chapter have referred to data storage, but the methods described apply equally well to the storage of instructions.

c. You may see main storage size described in terms of K. ($K = 2^{10} = 1024$). eg. 32K words = 32×1024 words = 32768 words. 1000K is normally written M (for Mega). eg. 20 M bytes means 20,000K bytes.

d. Most microcomputers are fixed word length computers with word lengths of either 8 bits or 16 bits hence the common terminology "8 bit micro" and "16 bit micro".

e. Generally speaking computers with longer word lengths operate faster than computer with shorter word lengths because data and instructions can be moved in and out of main storage in bigger units.

STUDENT SELF TESTING QUESTIONS (answers begin page 682)

1. Draw a diagram showing how the word "RAM" could be stored using the ASCII code in:

a. An 8-bit microcomputer's memory.

b. A 16-bit microcomputer's memory.

8 Auxiliary or Backing Storage

INTRODUCTION.

1. Ideally, all data for processing should be stored in main storage so that all internal operations can be carried out at maximum speed. As it is, main storage is relatively expensive and is therefore only used for storing the necessary instructions and the data currently being operated on. Auxiliary storage is provided for the mass storage of programs and files, ie. those programs and files not currently being operated on but which will be transferred to the main storage when required.

2. Although data in the form of files held on auxiliary storage is not immediately accessible, as it would be if held in main storage, it is nevertheless within the computer system. It can therefore serve an important purpose as part of a pool of maintained and accessible data.

3. There are many media for auxiliary storage. The *main* media, which will be described here, are in magnetic form:–

a. Magnetic tape unit – magnetic tape.
b. Magnetic drum unit – magnetic drum.
c. Magnetic disk unit – magnetic disk.
d. Magnetic diskette unit – magnetic diskette (floppy disk).
e. Optical disk unit – optical disk.
f. Solid state storage devices.
g. Mass storage devices and media.

MAGNETIC TAPE UNIT AND MAGNETIC TAPE.

4. In addition to its role as an input/output medium, magnetic tape is also used as an auxiliary storage medium. The devices and media have already been explained.

NB. Tape cassettes and tape cartridges are smaller versions which work on broadly similar principles, but the tapes are narrower and are held in small plastic cases.

MAGNETIC DRUM UNIT AND MAGNETIC DRUM.

5. Features of the Drum Unit.

a. It holds the magnetic drum and has a motor which rotates the drum at a high constant rate (several thousand revolutions per minute, depending on the size of the drum).

b. It has read/write heads situated a fraction of an inch away from the surface of the drum for reading/writing information from/to the drum. There is *normally* one read/write head per track.

6. Features of the Drum. See Fig. 8.1.

a. The drum is a cylinder, varying in length (but, typically, 3 ft) having an outer surface of magnetisable material.

b. It has an outer surface divided into a number of parallel tracks on which data is stored.

c. Typically the drum stores between 100,000 and 8,000,000 characters.

d. It is *not removable* from the drum unit, in the way that tape reels are removable from their tape units.

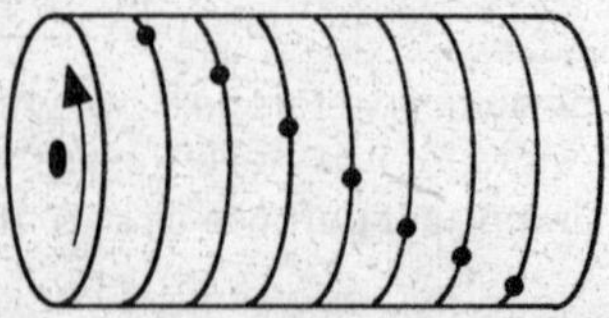

Fig. 8.1. A magnetic drum.

7. It should be noted that the use of drums is limited to large systems and special applications.

EXCHANGEABLE MAGNETIC DISK UNIT AND MAGNETIC DISK PACK.

8. a. **Features of an Exchangeable Disk Unit.**

i. The disk unit is the device in which the disk pack is placed. The disk *pack* is placed into the *unit* and connects with the drive mechanism.

ii. Once the pack is loaded into the unit the read/write mechanism, located inside the unit, positions itself over the first track of each surface. The mechanism consists of a number of arms at the ends of which there is a read/write head for each surface. All arms are fixed together and all move together as one when accessing a surface on the disk pack. See Fig. 8.2.

iii. The disk when loaded is driven at a high number of revolutions (several thousand) per minute and access can only be made to its surfaces when the disk revolves.

b. **Features of an Exchangeable Disk Pack.**

i. Disks are of a size and shape similar to a long playing record.

ii. The surfaces of each disk are of a magnetisable material (except the outer-most surfaces of a pack which are purely protective). Thus there are 10 recording surfaces in a 6 disk pack and 20 in an 11 disk pack.

iii. Each surface is divided into a number of *concentric tracks* (typically 200).

An exchangeable disk pack removed from its protective cover.

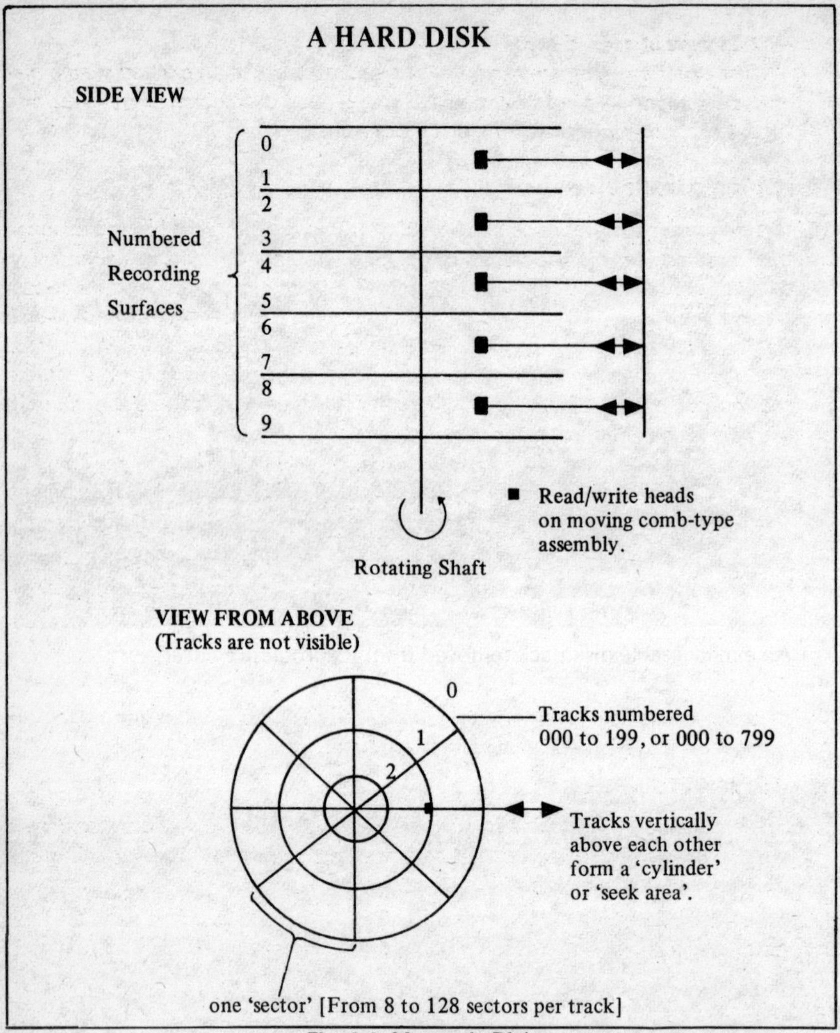

Fig. 8.2. Magnetic Disk.

iv. The disks within a *pack* are inseparable ie. the pack, of either 6 or 11 disks, is *always* used as a single unit.

v. The latest models of disk pack can store 200 million characters. Disks with a capacity of 30 to 60 million characters are now common.

FIXED MAGNETIC DISK UNIT AND MAGNETIC DISK.

9. a. **Features of a Fixed Disk Unit.**

i. The unit houses a number of non-removeable disks.

ii. It has read/write heads, either located on the end of 'arms' (as with exchangeable disks) or serving each track (as with the magnetic drum).

iii. It has a motor that rotates the drive at a high constant rate but because of its size, the speed will be slower than that of exchangeable disk units.

b. **Features of a Fixed Disk.**

The older systems are generally *larger* than disks in an exchangeable disk pack. Some modern computers use a single fixed disk which is the same size as the exchangeable disk, for storing programs.

WINCHESTER DISKS.

10. "Winchester" technology disks were developed by IBM just a few years ago in order to overcome some problems associated with established disk technology. Winchester disks are fixed disks in hermetically sealed disk units and have robust mechanical features. They have toughened surfaces, and read/write heads which move even closer to the disk surface. The heads actually 'land' on the disks surface when the disk finally stops! They can operate in adverse environments which are dusty or humid, have greater reliability and also have greater storage capacities in comparison with the earlier technology disks of the same size.

MAGNETIC DISKETTE UNIT AND MAGNETIC DISKETTE (FLOPPY DISK).

11. In addition to their role as input/output media, magnetic diskettes are also used as auxiliary storage media. However, their use for this purpose is usually limited to small microcomputer based systems. The devices and media have already been explained. (5.33–5.35).

OPTICAL DISK UNIT AND OPTICAL DISK.

12. These devices have been under development for many years but have only recently become available as marketable products.

13. Features of the Disk Unit.

a. The device is similar in appearance to a fixed magnetic disk unit but data is written onto the disk by burning a permanent pattern into the surface of the disk by means of a high precision laser beam.

b. Data is read back by using the laser at lower intensity and detecting the pattern of light reflected from its beam by the surface of the disk.

Features of the Disk.

a. A typical disk has a surface of 40,000 tracks each divided into 25 sectors and a total capacity of a staggering one gigabyte (ie. 1000 million characters).

14. The disks are less prone to data loss than magnetic disks but are non reusable at present.

SOLID STATE STORAGE DEVICES.

15. New forms of storage have been developed which are called **solid-state.** (ie. no moving parts). The (comparative) slowness of current devices is caused by the physical movement of the recording surface and (with disks) of the heads. There is no such physical movement in solid-state devices. These devices are another category of semiconductor memory but give somewhat slower access speeds to the data than RAM and ROM and are therefore not suitable for main storage.

16. The two common types of solid state storage devices used for backing storage are:–

a. **Magnetic bubble memory.**

b. **CCDs (Charge Coupled Devices).**

17. Magnetic Bubble Memory. In **'bubble memories'** data is stored as tiny magnetic domains (the bubbles) which continually circulate past read/write heads.

18. CCDs (Charge Coupled Devices). These are produced by a form of MOS technology. They are relatively fast compared with bubble memory but are volatile whereas bubble memory is not.

19. In the current state of development, solid-state storage is halfway between established memory systems and backing storage. It provides access to data which is faster than conventional backing storage devices but slower than memory. On the other hand, it has a capacity higher than memory but lower than backing storage.

20. Solid state backing storage has for some time looked poised to supersede disk storage, but so far it has not been able to compete in terms of cost.

MASS STORAGE DEVICES AND MEDIA.

21. Some large corporations and government agencies have a need for vast data storage capacities. This need can be met by mass storage devices. These devices are "automated libraries" of disk and tape cartridges. The total capacity of such a system may be as much as 500 billion bytes! Further detail is not merited.

SUMMARY.

22. a. Auxiliary storage is used, as its name suggests, to supplement main storage.

b. The Physical features *only* have been discussed.

c. The main auxiliary storage media is a *magnetic* form.

d. The main hardware devices and media for Auxiliary Storage are:-

i. Magnetic tape unit – Magnetic tape.

ii. Magnetic drum unit – Magnetic drum.

iii. Magnetic disk unit – Magnetic disk.

iv. Magnetic diskette unit – Magnetic diskette (floppy disk).

v. Solid state storage media.

vi. Mass storage devices and media.

vii. The comparative performance of backing storage media/devices is shown in the following table:-

Devices and Medium	Typical Access Time	Typical Storage Capacities	Typical Transfer Rates	Types of Storage SAS (Serial Access Storage) DAS (Direct Access Storage)	Where Used as a Backing Storage Medium (see earlier notes on input/output)
1. Magnetic tape Cassette or tape Cartridge.	A search is required – several minutes).	Up to 145,000 ch (cartridge 256,000 ch).	10–3,000 cps (cartridge 3,000 cps).	SAS	Used on small microcomputer based systems. Cartridge used on small minicomputers sometimes.
2. Floppy-disk (Diskette)	260 ms	180 k bytes to 1.25 M bytes.	24,000 cps.	DAS	Used on microcomputer based systems.
3. Magnetic Tape.	A search is required – several minutes.	40 M bytes.	160,000 cps.	SAS	Used on minicomputer and mainframe computer systems.
4. Magnetic Disk (Hard Disk) (Exchangeable)	60 ms	60 M bytes.	312,000 cps.	DAS	Used on minicomputer and mainframe computer systems.
5. Magnetic Drum. *(Medium not removable).*	6 ms	2 M bytes.	325,000 cps.	DAS	Used on mainframe computers mostly for programs and data which constantly need transfering into main memory.
6. Optical Disk.	100 ms	1 G bytes.	600,000 cps.	DAS	Used on minicomputer and mainframes.

POINTS TO NOTE.

23. a. Note the terms "on-line" and "off-line". "On-line" means being accessible to and under the control of, the CPU. Conversely, "off-line" means *not* accessible to, or under the control of, the CPU. Thus, magnetic drums and *fixed* magnetic disks are *permanently* "on-line"; a magnetic tape reel or an exchangeable magnetic disk pack is "on-line" when placed in its respective units, but "off-line" when stored away from the computer, terminals, *wherever* their physical location, are said to be "on-line" when directly linked to the CPU.

b. On exchangeable disks, the read/write heads serving each *surface* will be positioned over the *same relative track* on *each surface* because the arms on which they are fixed move simultaneously.

c. In any answer involving magnetic disks, you should concentrate on the *exchangeable* disk as this is the most commonly used.

d. The devices and media have been separated for ease of explanation. It should be noted however that in the case of drum and *fixed* disk, the media are permanently fixed to the device, and therefore they are not talked of as being separate.

e. Auxiliary storage is also referred to as *backing storage.*

f. Input, output and storage devices are referred to collectively as peripheral devices.

g. A description of the magnetic drum has been included, but it must be mentioned that in many situations where drums were once used, modern types of fixed disk are used instead. These fixed disks are of standard 14" size, and much smaller than their large predecessors.

h. Some disk packs are produced in side loading version containing just one or two platters. They are normally called **disk cartridges.** Some removable Winchester disks are available in cartridge form.

i. Punched cards and paper tape are still occasionally used as off-line storage media.

j. Simplified versions of magnetic tape or cartridge units known as **"streamers"** may be used to create "backup copies" from Winchester disks.

9 Computer System Architecture

INTRODUCTION.

1. The style of construction and organisation of the many parts of a computer system are its "architecture". Although the basic elements of the computer are essentially the same for almost all digital computers, there are variations in construction which reflect the differing ways in which computers are used. In this chapter we first consider the basic architectural features common to all systems. Then we consider variations in architecture which arise through differences in system use and size.

LEVELS WITHIN COMPUTER ARCHITECTURE.

2. There are a number of levels at which we must study the construction and organisation of computer systems. The simplest distinction between levels is that between hardware and software (1.6). We may view hardware as the lowest and most basic level of the computer onto which a "layer" of software is added. The software sits above the hardware, using it and controlling it. The hardware supports the software by providing the operations the software requires.

3. The idea is easily extended by viewing the whole computer system as a "many layered machine" consisting of several layers of software on top of several layers of hardware. In this chapter we are primarily interested in the various levels of hardware and the lowest levels of software. A discussion of the various levels of software is postponed until later chapters.

LEVELS OF HARDWARE.

4. We may identify four levels of hardware. From lowest to highest they are:

a. Electrical and Electronic component level.

b. Digital logic level.

c. Micro-programmed level.

d. Machine level.

5. The **electrical and electronic component level** is very important but is largely outside the subject of Computer Science and more in the province of Computer Technology. We do need to be aware that even the most sophisticated modern computer devices are built from simple electronic components such as transistors, capacitors and resistors and that these components rely on suitable power supplies and operating environments.

6. We need to know little more than that, however, except that the transistor can act as an electronic switch which is either ON (binary '1') or OFF (binary '0').

7. At some time in the future computers may be based upon some different technology such as optics or biochemisty. There is little chance of such a revolutionary change in the immediate future, however.

8. The **digital logic level** is of considerable importance in Computer Science. All the most basic operations of the machine are provided at this level. The basic elements at this level can store, manipulate and transmit data in the form of simple binary representations.

9. These digital logic elements are called **gates.** A gate is normally constructed from a small number of transistors and other electronic components. However, many gates may be combined onto a single chip, as has already been outlined in 4.5 – 4.12.

10. Digital logic will be discussed more fully in chapter 26. For the time being it is sufficient for you to realise that standard digital logic devices are combined together to form computer processors or computer memories.

11. The **micro-programmed level** is not present in all computers. In order to understand its role more clearly we will consider the machine level first.

12. In the early generations of computers, and in the small micro-processors of today, the processor was constructed from a combination of digital logic components. This was the **machine level** at which the basic elements of the computer (fig. 1.1) were all present.

13. In most modern computers the situation is slightly more complicated than that because there is a level of architecture between the level of digital logic and the machine level, namely, the micro-programmed level. Only the basic ideas will be introduced at this stage so don't expect to gain a full understanding just yet. That will come with later chapters.

14. Hidden within what appears to be the processor is another CPU! This inner processor has its own control unit, ALU and main memory but it operates under the control of special program instructions stored permanently in ROM. These program instructions are called **micro-code.** They are one example of **firmware** (ie. software in ROM).

15. The details of this micro-programmed level of the architecture are not always disclosed by the manufacturers in order to protect trade secrets. For example, Motorola have not disclosed all details of the micro-programmed level of their MC68000 16-bit microprocessors. The details of the micro-programmed levels of larger computers, such as minis or mainframes, are sometimes published by the manufacturers.

16. Over the next few paragraphs the basic features of a CPU will be described, including the functions and operations of its elements. Bear in mind that what is being described is the **machine level** of the architecture and that there are several levels of hardware beneath it.

BASIC FEATURES OF THE CPU.

17. The diagram of the elements of a computer system (Fig. 1.1) shows the CPU as consisting of three parts and all three are wholly electronic. They are:

a. The main storage.

b. The control unit.

c. The arithmetic and logic unit.

18. As was indicated in Fig. 1.1, there is a strong trend towards regarding main memory as external to the CPU. This newer choice of terms reflects modern methods of computer construction and aids classification of systems. In order to overcome this difficulty and to avoid ambiguity *we will use the term "CPU" as in paragraph 2 but use the single word "Processor" to mean the CPU without main memory.*

19. The functions of the CPU are:

a. to store data *and* instructions (7.3)

b. to control the sequence of operations,

c. to give commands to all part of the computer system,

d. to carry out processing.

20. The CPU receives data into main storage, processes it, and then sends the results to output units of various types. At all stages data transmission is electronic. (2.3–2.13).

21. Fig. 9.1 gives an overall view of the CPU and the movement of data, instructions and command signals within. It will be explained in the following sections.

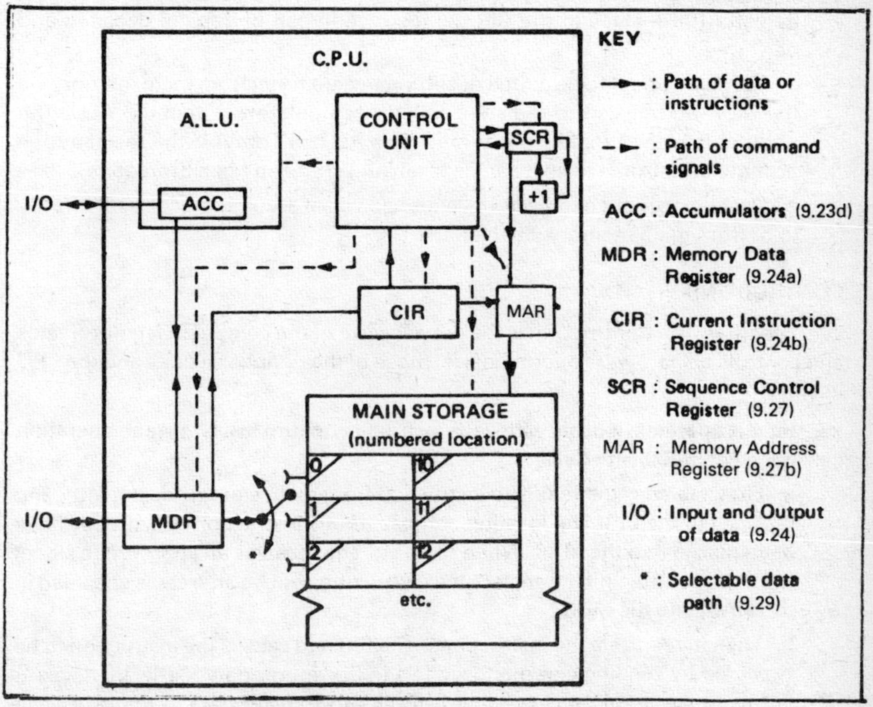

Fig. 9.1. [See Appendix 2.2] for a full diagram

REGISTERS.

22. Registers are special purpose temporary storage locations within the processor or other devices which are quite separate from the locations in main storage although they can be similar in structure. The role of registers in the movement of data and instructions within the CPU is shown in Fig. 9.1. Try to gain an overall view of the paths of data and instructions through the registers.

23. Features and Uses. Registers are constructed so that their contents can be accessed and altered much faster than the contents of locations of main storage. They have several uses, for example:–

a. All data and instructions pass in and out from main storage through a register called the **Memory Data Register (MDR). NB.**There may be two registers for the data to pass through; one in the processor and one in main storage.

b. Prior to each transfer between the MDR and main storage the exact source or destination of the data in main storage must be specified. This is done by loading the appropriate location address (7.5) into the **Memory Address Register MAR.**

c. An instruction which is about to be obeyed will first be taken from main storage via the MDR and placed in a register called the **Current Instruction Register (CIR).** Once in the CIR the instruction can be rapidly decoded and performed.

d. Numbers about to be added or subtracted are taken from main memory via the MDR and placed in registers called **Accumulators** within the ALU. The arithmetic is then rapidly performed. The ALU will provide the result in one accumulator, from which it can be taken and stored in Main Storage.

e. Data being input or output will either go via an accumulator or pass directly to or from main memory via the MDR.

CONTROL UNIT.

24. Function. The Control Unit is the nerve centre of the computer. It co-ordinates and controls all *hardware* operations, ie, those of the peripheral units and the CPU itself.

25. How it operates. It deals with each instruction in turn in a two stage operation called the **Fetch-Execute Cycle:–**

a. First it *fetches* the requisite instruction from main storage via the MDR and places it in the CIR. The location address of this instruction will already have been placed into the MAR. When main storage receives an appropriate signal from the control unit it transfers the instruction, whose address is specified in the MAR, into the MDR.

b. Then it *interprets* the instruction in the CIR and causes the instruction to be *executed* by sending command signals to the appropriate hardware devices. For example, it might cause main storage to transfer data to the MDR or it might cause the ALU to perform some operation on data in the accumulators.

26. Control of the sequence of instructions. The control unit automatically deals with instructions in the order in which they occur in main storage. It does this by using a register called the **Sequence Control Register (SCR)** which holds the location address of the *next* instruction to be performed. Prior to each instruction fetch the contents of the SCR are copied into the MAR. Each time the control unit fetches an instruction, it immediately increases the contents of the SCR by one, so that it is ready to be referred to when the next fetch takes place. Therefore, for most of the time the SCR contains the location address of the *next instruction* to be fetched.

ARITHMETIC AND LOGIC UNIT (ALU).

27. Functions. The ALU has two main functions:–

a. It carries out the arithmetic, eg. add, subtract, multiply and divide.

b. It performs certain 'logical' operations eg. testing whether two data items match.

28. How it operates.

a. Data items about to be processed are taken from main storage, as directed by the control unit, and pass via the MDR into the accumulators in the ALU where they are stored. This step is referred to as *'Loading'* data into an accumulator from main storage. We should also note at this point that the location addresses of these data items will have been contained in instructions in the CIR, from where they will have been transferred to the MAR prior to loading the data.

b. The ALU then performs the required operation(s) on the data (eg. adding) as directed by the control unit. The ALU leaves the result in an accumulator.

c. Results are placed in main storage, again under the direction of the control unit. This step is referred to as *'Storing'* data.

29. Decision Making. Some logical operations of the ALU give the computer its decision making ability. They do this by allowing the result of an operation determine which instruction the control unit fetches next, eg. if two data items matched, then the SCR could be altered to some new value contained within an instruction in the SCR. If the data items did not match it could be left unaltered.

PHYSICAL ORGANISATION OF THE CPU.

30. We now turn to some aspects of the physical organisation of the CPU which were deliberately omitted from figure 9.1 in order to avoid introducing too many ideas all at once.

31. Designing and building a new computer from scratch is an expensive process. Also, the unit costs of individual components are high unless the components are mass produced. These factors cause most computer manufacturers to construct their computers from varied combinations of standard components. For example, many *different micro-computers* contain the *same microprocessors.*

32. This principle of **modular construction** applies to different levels of design. At one level it might be a matter of "plugging in" one peripheral device instead of another. At a lower level it might be a matter of using one type of memory chip instead of another.

33. Standard components are much easier to interconnect if the means of interconnection is standardised. One important method for doing this is using **"buses"** (Also spelt "busses").

34. A **bus** is a collection of parallel electrical conductors called 'lines' onto which a number of components may be connected. Connections are made at points along the length of the bus by means of connectors with multiple electrical contacts.

There are two basic types of bus

a. **Internal buses,** used within the processor and an integral part of its construction.

b. **External buses,** used to connect separate hardware elements together eg. connecting the processor to main memory.

35. Buses may be used to convey:

a. data signals,

b. data address signals,

c. control signals,

d. power.

See Fig. 9.2 for a simple example based upon Fig. 9.1.

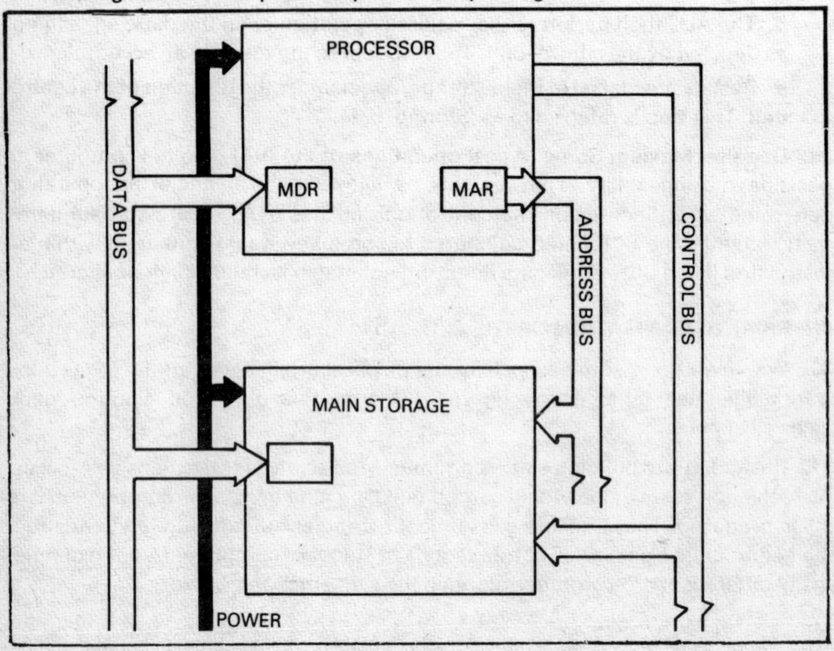

Fig. 9.2. Simplified example of the use of buses.

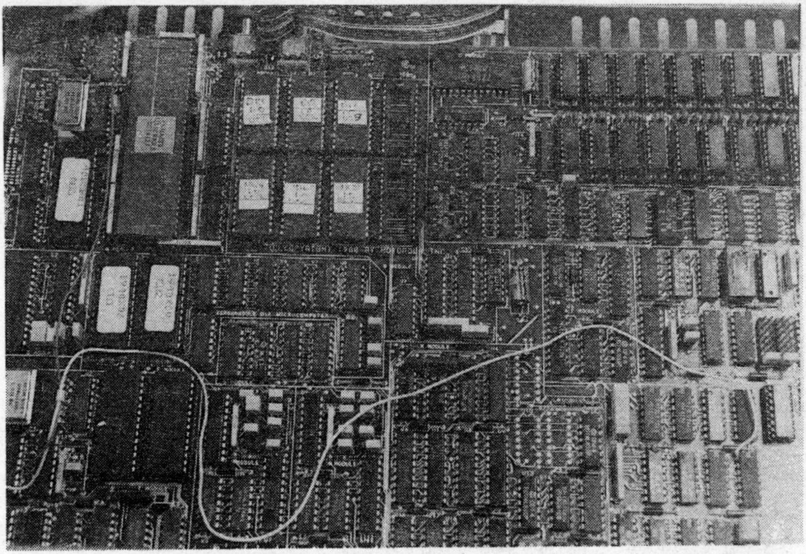

A computer on a single board. The larger chip (top left) is a 16-bit microprocessor. To its right is a block of 6 ROM chips. Further to the right is a block of 18 RAM chips. The remaining chips are for various Input/Output ports etc.

36. **The influence of size on construction** deserves some discussion before we move on to look at the architecture of complete systems. Three distinctly different forms of construction are, from smallest to largest:

a. Single chip computers.

b. Single board computers.

c. Multiple board, bus based computers.

37. **Single chip computers** are those found in such devices as watches, cameras etc. The processors are specialised, they are programmed to do a specific task and, apart from the remarkable operations some of these devices can do, they are not immediately recognisable as computers.

38. **Single Board Computers.** These computers are usually much bigger than single chip computers but are still relatively small. They are constructed on thin flat sheets of electrical insulator onto which the components can be fixed and interconnected. **Printed Circuit Boards (PCBs)** are often used for volume production.

39. The single board computers fall into two broad categories:

a. Small general purpose micro-computers such as the small computers used by hobbyists or for personal business use.

b. Small special purpose computers which are often used for applications involving the control of physical processes. Typical examples would be systems controlling a small scale chemical distillation plant or controlling the operation of complex milling machines.

In both cases buses are used but as integral parts of the board's circuitry.

40. **Multiple Board, Bus Based Computers** are usually general purpose computers. They are normally too large to fit onto a single board. Instead, each board has a particular function and all boards are interconnected by plugging them into individual slots on a general purpose bus. One board may contain the processor, another board may contain main storage, and so on.

41. Having considered some specific issues of size and use relating to the physical organisation of the CPU it is now time to move on and examine the same issues in the broader context of system architecture.

ARCHITECTURE OF SMALL COMPUTER SYSTEMS.

42. The architecture of a typical configuration for a microcomputer based system is shown in Fig. 9.3. Provided that sufficient slots are present in the bus, other units may be plugged in. A Winchester disk might be added, for example.

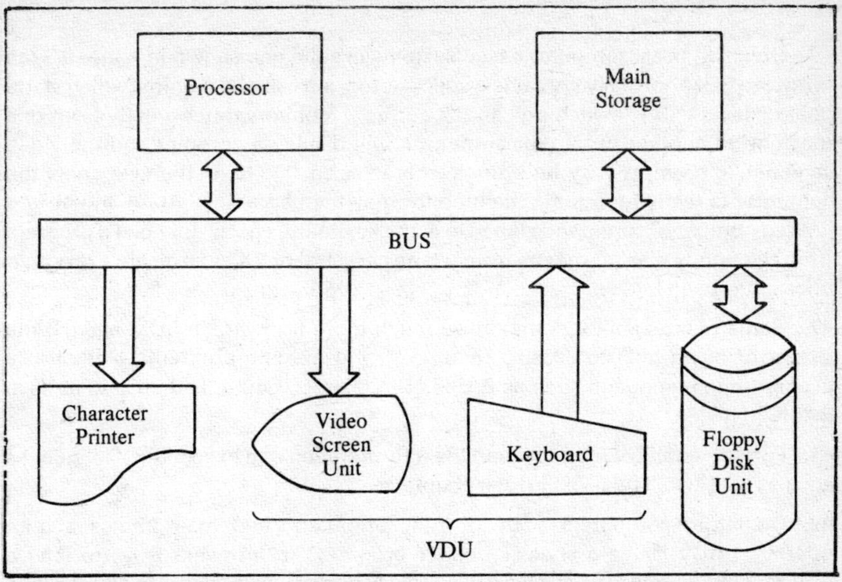

Fig. 9.3. Simplified typical architecture of a small micro computer based system.

43. Memory Organisation. In a small system like that shown in Fig. 9.3 the main storage may be organised as shown in Fig. 9.4.

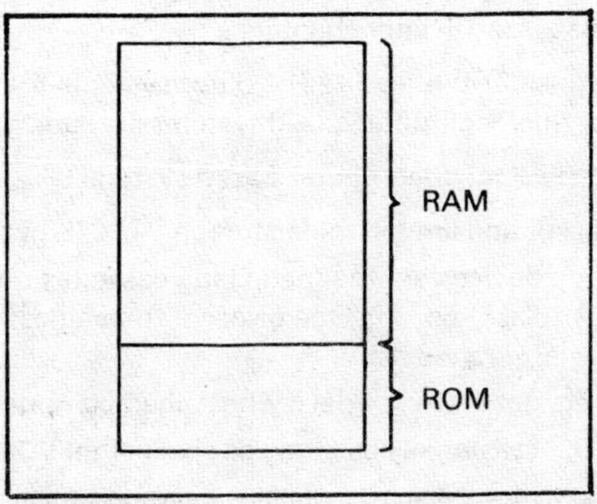

Fig. 9.4. Organisation of main storage in a typical micro computer.

44. Firmware. Programs held in ROM are called **firmware.** They are stored permanently in the ROM and are ready for use when the computer is switched on. (Also see 9.14)

45. When a microcomputer is switched on it is normally made to start executing the instructions held in ROM. This either takes place automatically as part of switching on, or sometimes a "boot" button has to be pressed too. This is known as a "booting up the system".

46. On small microcomputer based systems like the one shown in figure 9.3 the firmware ROM normally contains a special program called a **monitor** which starts being executed on "switch-on" and "boot-up". Monitors differ greatly from one machine to another but a typical monitor will display a "prompt" on the video screen. (A "prompt" may be a single character eg. "*" to let the user know the computer is ready for input). The monitor may then accept, interpret and obey a limited number of commands typed in at the keyboard. eg. "L" for Load a program from the floppy disk (or maybe from a tape cassette) or "X" to execute a program once it has been loaded.

47. Some microcomputers may have much more firmware in ROM even to the extent of being able to accept, "interpret" and execute programs written in a programming language such as BASIC. The microcomputer is then said to have BASIC in ROM.

48. Further details of monitors and the interpretation and execution of languages such as BASIC will be given in later chapters.

49. On larger computers such as mini-computers, and main-frames a boot operation may cause a special "loader program" in firmware ROM to load a program into memory from a hard disk. This first program loaded into memory will also be a monitor, but rather different in character from the one found on a microcomputer based system. What both monitors will have in common is a function in controlling the use of hardware, but on the larger machines the monitor will be just part of a large set of software called the **operating system.** Monitors and operating systems will be discussed in later chapters.

50. Before moving on to consider the features of other systems the basic characteristics of the hardware of microcomputer based systems are summarised here.

51. Hardware features of typical microcomputer based systems:-

a. A single microprocessor and limited main storage (eg. 64K bytes).

b. Small backing storage devices eg. magnetic tape cassettes on very small machines, dual floppy disks on the majority of machines, and small Winchester disks on the larger models.

c. Low speed printers eg. dot matrix or daisywheel character printers.

d. *Usually* a single VDU, occasionally as many as six or eight VDU's.

NB. In some machines several items may be built into a single cabinet eg. the VDU may also house the processor and disk drives.

THE ARCHITECTURE OF MINI AND MAIN FRAME COMPUTER SYSTEMS.

52. The smaller mini-computer systems can be indistinguishable from the larger micro-computer based systems. However, a typical minicomputer has noticably different features from a microcomputer and is essentially a scaled down version of its 'big brother' the main frame computer.

53. Hardware features of a typical minicomputer systems:-

a. Medium size processor and main storage. ie. sufficient to handle the data processing needs of a number of terminals (eg. 1 Megabyte of main storage).

b. Hard disk storage, and magnetic tape storage in some cases.

c. Line printer. eg. 300 lpm versions.

d. Multiple terminals. eg. 20 VDUs or more.

54. It is also difficult to draw a line of demarcation between the larger mini-computers and small main frame computers. The hardware in a main frame may be similar to the hardware in a mini-computer, but there is usually much more of it eg.

a. Very large processors with massive amounts of main storage eg. hundreds of megabytes.

b. Large number of magnetic disk and tape units.

c. High speed line printers eg. 200 lpm.

d. The ability to support large numbers of terminals eg. 100 or more VDUs.

55. Front End Processors (FEPs). Many main frame computers incorporate minicomputers which are used to handle input and output from various terminals, thus relieving the main computer of some tasks associated with input and output. The minicomputer being used for this purpose is called a Front End Processor (FEP).

56. The front end processor may not only deal with terminals close to main computer it may also deal with *remote* terminals which are situated at the end of data transmission lines.

MULTI-PROCESSOR SYSTEMS.

57. Traditionally, multi-processor systems have been very large computers with two or more main processors and large main storage which has been wholly or partially shared. This arrangement not only serves to handle a large processing load but also provides backup in the case of breakdown. (ie. if one processor fails the system can continue to operate). Such systems are called **multi-processing systems** (see Fig. 9.5).

58. In recent years, other ways of exploiting a multiple number of processors within a single system have been devised. Even some microcomputer based systems use forms of multi-processing.

59. The two common approaches towards interconnecting separate computers *into one system* are:

a. **Distributed Systems.**

b. **Computer Networks.**

NB. A computer which is *not* connected to other computers is a **"stand alone system"**. eg. many micro computers operate as stand alone computers.

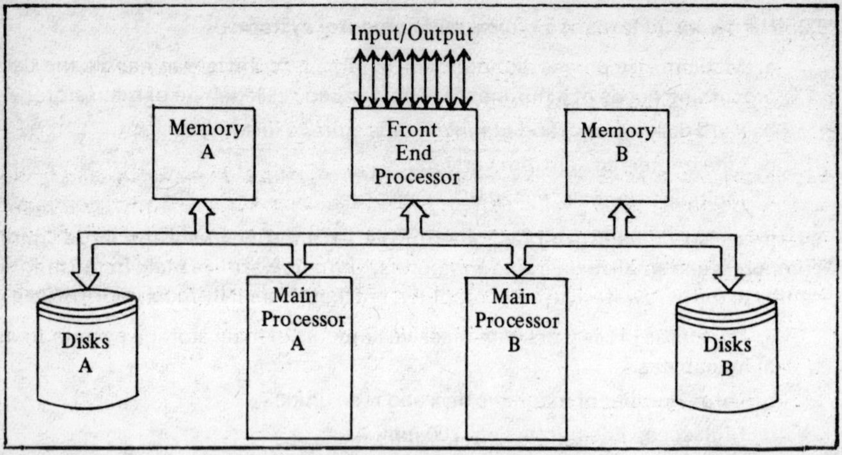

Fig. 9.5. A multiprocessing system with front end processor and duplicated disk storage and memory.

60. Distributed Systems. Over recent years there has been a steady trend towards using computer systems which have several interconnected processors placed in separate locations. Each processor tends to have its own "local" peripherals (disks, printers, terminals) in addition to any peripherals attached to some central processor. See Fig. 9.6.

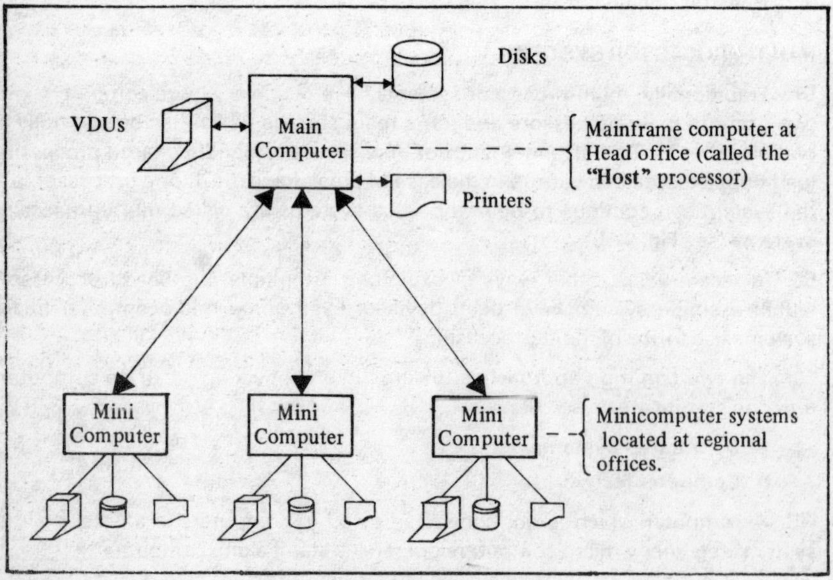

Fig. 9.6. A distributed system.

61. The advantages of distributing the processing include:-

a. Reduction in costs and delays in transmitting and processing data.

b. Reduced load on the "host".

c. Better local control and service.

62. Local networks. Even on one site there may still be an advantage in using distributed processing. For example, suppose a number of microcomputer systems are to be used in various offices in the same building. There are considerable advantages to be gained from linking them all together into one system called a **local area network (or LAN).** This will provide these advantages:-

a. The sharing of resources such as disks and printers.

b. The sharing of data files,

c. Sending messages (Electronic Mail).

NB. Larger computers may be used in LAN's too.

63. Two strategies for providing such a network are:

a. The linear network eg. on a bus, }

b. The ring. } See Figure 9.7

64. Any discussion of networks and distributed systems is incomplete without some details of modern data transmission systems. However, the topic merits its own chapter and so further details have been left till chapter 22.

NEWER ARCHITECTURAL FEATURES.

65. Cache Memories. These are high speed RAMs which work at speeds which match the processor. They are used to hold data which has recently been accessed from disk in anticipation of its use in the near future. Subsequent accesses if they occur will be fast because the disk will not require accessing again. The least accessed data in cache memory is replaced by newly accessed data.

66. Content Addressable Storage (CAS). This storage works in a different way from normal storage. Suppose that each word in memory can hold 4 characters and that location 200 contains "FRED". In normal storage the address, 200 would be used to load "FRED". In content addressable memory "FRED" would be passed along a data bus and the memory would pass 200 back indicating the location of "FRED". Thus a paragraph of stored text could be retrieved by supplying a word contained in the paragraph. CAS is very useful for rapid data selection or retrieval but is expensive at present.

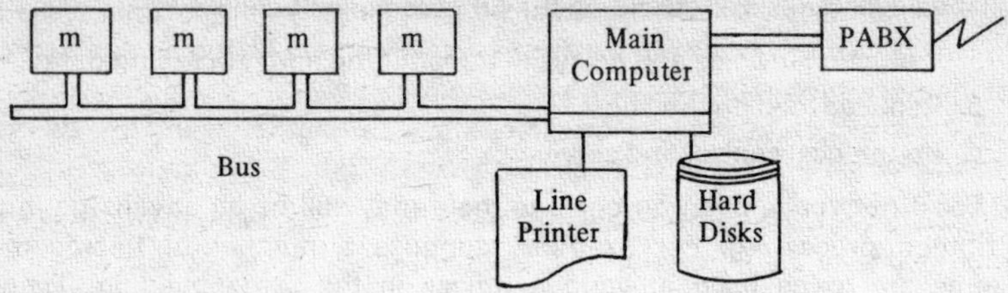

a. **Linear network.**

Key

m: A microcomputer based system with character printer, floppy disks etc.

PABX: PRIVATE AUTOMATIC BRANCH EXCHANGE (An automatic telephone exchange).

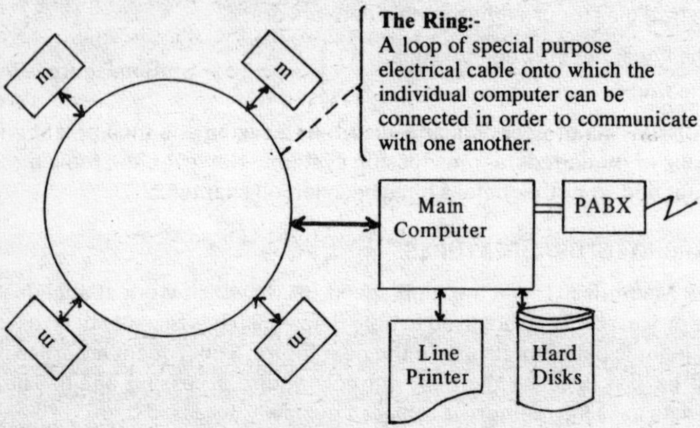

b. **Ring network.**

Fig. 9.7. Local area networks.

ALTERNATIVE ARCHITECTURES.

67. All the examples in this chapter which have been considered so far have been concerned with single or multiple processors all of which conformed to the basic model first presented in Fig. 1.1. However, in recent years these have been moves to create computers to radically new designs.

68. Many of these computers have been designed with the object of gaining greater computational speed. Two approaches which have had some measure of success are:

a. **Pipeline machines.**

b. **Array Processors.**

69. In the **pipeline machine** architecture each stage in the fetch-execute cycle (9.25) is handled by a separate hardware unit. The first unit fetches an instruction from memory, passes it to a unit which decodes it and immediately starts fetching the next instruction. At any one time there may be four or five instructions within the processor each at different stages of execution in different units.

70. In the **array processor** there is one control unit but multiple ALUs which are able to work in parallel with one another. They are particularly suited to applications in which sets of values require the same operation to be performed on each value eg. converting every value in a table to a percentage of the total.

SUMMARY.

71. a. The various levels of architecture were introduced.

b. The CPU has no mechanically moving parts. Electronic pulses moving at nearly the speed of light are used in data representation.

c. Main Storage, Control Unit and the Arithmetic and Logic Unit are the constituent parts of the CPU. The "processor" is the CPU excluding memory.

d. Modern computer "architecture" is characterised by *modular components* which are linked together in a building block fashion, often by means of *buses*.

e. Hardware features of typical micro-computers, mini-computers and main frames were described.

f. *Networks* and *distributed systems* were discussed.

g. Newer and alternative architectural features were introduced.

POINTS TO NOTE.

72. a. The fact that some larger micro-computers perform as well as some smaller mini-computers and some larger mini-computers perform as well as smaller main frames is just one indication that some applications can be computerised in a number of different ways. It also shows the limited value of using rigid classifications of computers.

b. In some situations the same service to the user may be provided by systems of greatly differing design. For example *one* moderately sized processor may support a number of user terminals *or* alternatively a number of single user computers might be connected into a network. The former is called **"shared logic"**, the latter is called **"distributed logic"**.

c. The term **'Distributed Processing'** is now widely used in relation to micro and mini-computers. It implies of course, that a processing facility is made available at a number of sites instead of at a single computer centre. The term can imply:-

i. A number of micros and minis at different sites, not linked to each other.

ii. A network of micros and minis linked to a central main frame computer.

iii. A network of micros and minis linked to each other without a central main frame.

d. Note that the 'floppy disk' is widely used with 'micros' and 'minis' both for input and storage of data.

e. A clear technical difference between a micro-computer and a mini-computer is that in a micro-computer the processor is contained on a single micro-processor chip but in mini-computers the processor is larger and comprises of a number of chips. This technical difference has minor practical significance to the user. Indeed, a larger multi-board micro-computer based system is probably better classified as a mini-computer as far as the user is concerned.

f. A greater understanding of the CPU will come after studying Programming and the chapters on Machine Operation and Language.

g. Most registers are also known by other names. Be prepared for this by noting these alternatives.

i. SCR; also known as Program Counter, Instruction Counter, Instruction Address Register.
ii. CIR; also known as the Instruction Register (IR).
iii. MDR; also known as the Memory Buffer Register.

h. Computer systems developed for special purposes in which the computer is largely hidden within the application, like those mentioned in 9.38 and 9.39b, are often referred to as **"embedded systems"**.

STUDENT SELF TESTING QUESTIONS

(Answers page 683)

1. *a. Distinguish between the terms 'CPU' and 'Processor' as used in this text.*
   b. Described the functions of the CPU.
2. *Describe and distinguish between the following.*
   a. Current Instruction Register.
   b. Program Counter.
   c. Memory Address Register.
   d. Memory Data Register.
3. *Define and distinguish between the terms:*
   a. hardware
   b. firmware
   c. software
   d. ROM
   e. RAM
   f. EPROM.

4. Define the terms.

a. Front End Processor.

b. Distributed System.

c. Computer Network.

5. The number 973 is to be stored in main storage using a 4-bit BCD code. Show how it might be stored in:–

a. A word with 16 bits.

b. A character machine.

c. A byte machine.

Assume storage is to start at location 301.

6. Show how fixed length instructions 32 bits long might be stored in:–

a. A word machine with a 32 bit word.

b. A byte machine (Remember 1 byte = 8 bits).

Assume storage is to start at location 401, and show the storage of two instructions.

7. a. Account for the growth in popularity of the visual display unit (VDU) as an interactive computer terminal. Mention at least one practical disadvantage in having VDUs as the sole input/output device. (10 marks)

b. Explain how a character generated by striking a VDU key might be transferred to the computer main store. (5 marks)

c. A simple VDU can be converted to an intelligent terminal by the provision of extra facilities. Describe some of these extra facilities available on intelligent VDUs. (5 marks)

***AEB** (1980)*

8. a. What is the difference between the main store and the backing store of a computer? [3]

b. Explain the terms speed of access, cost per bit, and capacity for backing stores, and give an account of the ways in which they are related. [3, 3, 3, 4]

c. Explain why most backing stores are at present based on magnetic devices which need to be in motion. What advantages might be gained if they could be replaced by devices without moving parts, and why is this not done? [5, 4]

Oxford

*9. A disc pack has some 20 recording **surfaces, 400 tracks** and 12 **sectors** per track. In operation, the pack spins at constant speed. Data is accessed by moving the read/write assembly (comprising 20 read/write heads) to the required **cylinder,** then reading the sector concerned into main store.*

*a. With the aid of diagrams, explain the terms in **italics.** (10 marks)*

b. When reading data, a read/write head must be positioned over the desired track and must be able to identify the required sector as it spins under the head. To provide positioning information, one surface is formatted so that its read head can pass data on radial and angular position to the control unit. Since all the read/write heads are synchronized, the positioning data is common to all surfaces. Suggest what information might be recorded on this surface:

i. to indicate the track number currently under each read/write head,

(4 marks)

ii. to indicate the sector number which is currently under each read/write head.

(6 marks)

***AEB** (1983)*

QUESTIONS WITHOUT ANSWERS.

10. Describe the notion of a 'bus' in computer architecture and identify an advantage of using buses over alternatives.

11. Identify the computer you use on your course as either a mainframe, mini-computer or micro-computer and justify your choice of category.

Programming

1. A set of instructions which describe the steps to be followed in order to carry out an activity is called an **algorithm** or **procedure.** If the algorithm is written in the computer's language then the set of instructions is called a **program.** The task of producing a computer program involves going through several stages, not all of which involve writing in the computer's own language. The complete task is called programming, but, as you will see, programming involves more than just *writing* programs.

2. Programs consist of sequences of instructions specifying controlled and ordered operations on data which are to be performed by a computer. This Part gradually builds up a complete picture of programs and programming by dealing with different aspects of the subject in turn.

3. Chapter 10 deals with **operations on data.** It considers various types of data, the ways we represent them and the ways we represent operations upon them. Since, ultimately, all operations upon data must be performed by the computer's hardware the representations of the data within the computer are considered too.

4. Chapter 11 deals with **program structures.** In other words it deals with the various component parts of programs and how they are organised. As with chapter 10 the material is also related to what goes on within the computer.

5. One important aspect of chapter 11 is a discussion of the basic features of a programming language. The chapter makes extensive use of a **pseudo-code.** A pseudo-code is a simple language with a few basic grammatical constructions which avoids the ambiguities and complexities of English but which can easily be converted into a programming language. *It is strongly recommended to the reader that, as an exercise, all examples given in pseudocode be converted into whatever programming language the reader is using for practical programming.*

6. Chapter 12 explains what **data structures** are. It gives examples of the more common and important data structures and explains the uses of data structures in programming.

7. Chapter 13 is concerned with **program design.** It examines the aims of programming and how the stages in programming must be followed systematically in order to achieve these aims. It makes use of methods and ideas introduced in chapter 9, 10 and 11.

8. Chapter 14, the last chapter in this part, discusses **program specification.** It examines a number of methods and notations which are used to specify what programs are required to do and how they are required to do them.

9. Some other aspects of programming are not included within this Part because they fit more naturally into the subject matter of later chapters.

10 Operations On Data

INTRODUCTION.

1. This chapter introduces some basic concepts which the reader needs to be familiar with before attempting to understand programming. It describes simple data types and their representation, and explains the operations which may be performed upon data of these simple types.

DATA TYPES.

2. A **data type** consists of:

a. a set of data values

b. a set of operations which may be applied to the values.

3. Having defined data types we can classify individual data items. Some data items may be used singly whilst others may be combined together and arranged to form other data items. The former are classified as **simple data types** whereas the latter are classified as **data structures** or **data aggregates**. Data structures will be discussed in later chapters.

4. **Data type classification.** Several classifications are possible. The following classification is appropriate for study at this level. The simple data types are:-

a. Numeric Integer.

b. Numeric Real.

c. Character.

d. Boolean (logical).

5. These data types will now be considered in two stages. First, the sets of values and methods of representing them will be considered for each type in turn. Then the types will be considered in turn again in order to investigate the operations which may be performed upon them.

TYPE VALUES AND THEIR REPRESENTATION.

6. **Integers** are the positive and negative whole numbers, and zero (0, ±1, ±2, ±3, ±4, ...).

7. The positive integers (+1, +2, +3, +4, ...) are called the **Natural Numbers,** or **Cardinal Values,** and are often written without the "+" sign. In practical work you will probably come across the terms **"unsigned integer"** (1, 2, 3, 4, ...) and **"signed integer"** (+1, +2, +3, ...). Of course, negative integers *must* be signed to distinguish them from positive integers.

8. The integers may be represented on a numerical scale. (See Fig. 10.1)

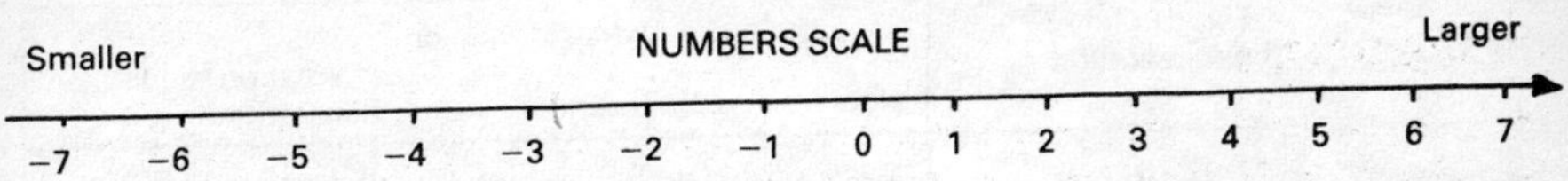

Integers to the right hand side are larger than those to the left hand side. Therefore +3 **is larger than** −**6** but +**3 is has a smaller numerical value than** −**6.** Great care must therefore be taken when using the words "larger" and "smaller".

NB. The lefthand end digit of an integer is called the **most significant digit** and the righthand end digit of an integer is called the **least significant digit.**

Example:–

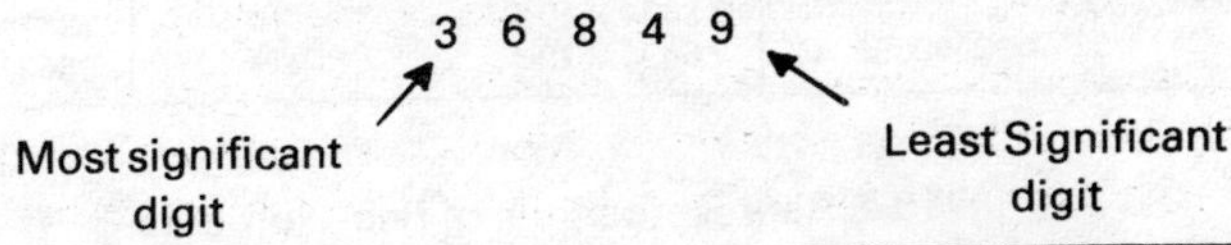

Fig. 10.1. Representations of Integers.

9. Real Numbers. These are **all** the numbers on the number scale shown in Fig. 10.1 (ie. including those between the integers). Real numbers include *all* the integers and *all* the fractions. These are all real numbers: 0, −0.5, 9, $-1^1/_7$, 39.864, $^7/_8$. Positive real numbers may be represented in signed or unsigned forms.

10. The **Numerical Value** (or magnitude) of any real number, and hence any integer, is its value disregarding its sign. Thus +3.2 and −3.2 have the *same* numerical value. Another term for numerical value is **absolute value.**

11. Fixed Point Representation of Real Numbers. The usual way of representing real numbers is to write the number with the decimal point **fixed** in its correct position between the two appropriate digits eg. 13.75 or 3862.4. This is **fixed point representation** and it proves very useful in data processing for example where sums of money are to be processed or printed. However this representation becomes laborious and cumbersome when dealing with several very large or very small numbers eg. 1375000000, 386240000, 0.000001375, 0.00000038624. The answer is to use floating point representation.

12. Floating Point Representation of Real Numbers. This concept is best introduced by some simple examples. See Fig. 10.2.

Fixed Point Representation	Floating Point Representation: Notation used in Science	Notation used in Computing
13.75	1.375×10^1 (Note $10^1 = 10$)	$.1375 \times 10^2$
137.5	1.375×10^2 (Note $10^2 = 100$)	$.1375 \times 10^3$
1375.	1.375×10^3 (Note $10^3 = 1000$)	$.1375 \times 10^4$
1375000000.	1.375×10^9	$.1375 \times 10^{10}$
1.375	1.375×10^0 (Note $10^0 = 1$ by definition)	$.1375 \times 10^1$
0.1375	1.375×10^{-1} (Note $10^{-1} = 1/10$ by definition)	$.1375 \times 10^0$
0.01375	1.375×10^{-2} (Note $10^{-2} = 1/100$)	$.1375 \times 10^{-1}$
0.001375	1.375×10^{-3}	$.1375 \times 10^{-2}$
3862.4	3.8624×10^3	$.38624 \times 10^4$
386240000.	3.8624×10^8	$.38624 \times 10^9$
.00000038624	3.8624×10^{-7}	$.38624 \times 10^{-6}$

Fig. 10.2. Representations of Real Numbers.

13. In each of the floating point representations just given in the table the decimal points have been moved or *floated* along the digits to position it between the first and second non zero most significant digits. (Note that Science and Computer Science differ in notation here) There are three components to a floating point representation:–

a. the **mantissa** sometimes called the **argument,**

b. the **radix** or **base,**

c. the **exponent** sometimes called the **characteristic.**

14. The components of a floating point representation are shown here:–

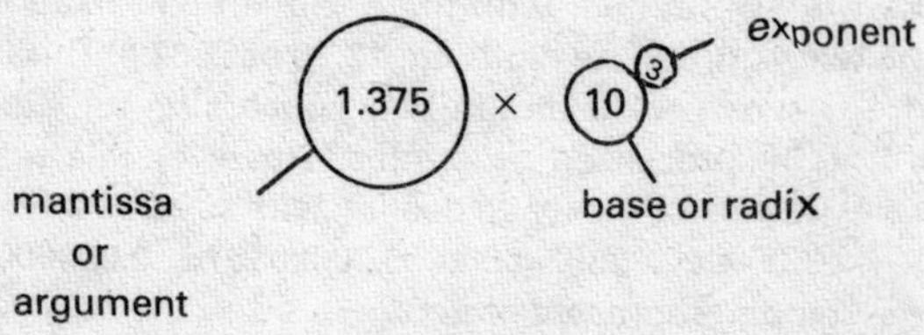

Note i. The exponent takes integer values.

ii. 13.75×10^2, 0.01375×10^5 and 1.375×10^3 are *all* floating point representation of the fixed point number 1375 but the last of the three like those in the table is in a **standard form** with the point between the first and second non zero most significant digits. (Note that there are two "standard forms; one for Science one for Computer Science).

iii. In some applications computer input and output of floating point numbers is printed on one line as shown here:–

Handwritten floating Point representation	Computerised version
1.375×10^3	+1.375E + 3
3.8624×10^{-7}	+3.8624E − 7

The "E" separates the exponent from the mantissa and base 10 is assumed.

15. Characters. Characters have already been introduced (2.2). For practical purposes it is most useful to define the type character by reference to some standard character set eg. ASCII or EBCDIC. One consequence of such definitions is that each character has an associated ordinal value corresponding to its position in the character set (eg. ASCII 'A' has ordinal value 65, see Fig. 2.4).

16. There are many situations when writing programs in which there is a need for simple data items consisting of sequences of characters, for example, when representing names like "Alex" or "James". Such sequences of characters treated as single data items are called **character strings.** We cease to think of strings as simple data types the moment we cease to treat them as single indivisible units and start to manipulate their individual character components. We then consider strings to be **data structures.**

17. Boolean (Logical) Data Types. In one respect booleans are the simplest data types of all because boolean type data items can only take one of two possible values at any one time. The two values are **"True"** and **"False"**. The name "Boolean" comes from the name of a logician called George Boole who did much pioneering work in the algebra of logic.

REPRESENTATION OF DATA TYPES WITHIN THE COMPUTER.

18. The basic ideas of data representation within the computer were introduced in chapter 2 and were expanded upon in some later chapters. Here, we relate these ideas to the data types under discussion in this chapter; some more detailed discussion will be provided in later chapters where appropriate.

19. Further classifications of numeric data types arise from the alternative ways in which numerical data types are coded for storage purposes. The basic types of representation are:

a. **BCD** representation in which each decimal digit in the number is coded separately as in 2.19 (eg. 39 decimal is represented as 0011, 1001).

b. **Pure Binary** representation in which the whole number is converted to binary. (eg. 39 decimal is represented as 100111).

20. Single and Double Precision. This concept is best explained by a simple example. Suppose we wish to represent positive integers in pure binary in an 8-bit microcomputer. We might choose to use one memory location to store each number. The number 39 would be stored using 8 bits as 00100111. With this arrangement the largest positive integer we could store would be 11111111_2 which corresponds to 255 decimal. Clearly, this is rather small and so we might wish to use two 8-bit words instead. The largest positive integer we could store would then be 65536. The two alternatives here are between **single precision,** using 8-bits and **double-precision** using, 16-bits. A more practical example might involve using 16-bits for single precision and 32-bits for double precision.

21. Further details of numeric representations will be given in later chapters. We now turn to the representation of other data types.

22. Character representations within the computer have already been discussed in sufficient detail in chapter 2.

23. Boolean data items are easy to represent in binary. There is a simple choice between '1' for 'True' and '0' for 'False' or '0' for 'True' and '1' for 'False'. In this book we will use the former when such a representation is required.

24. From the preceding paragraph it should be apparent that at machine level the binary representations of all these different data types are indistinguishable. That fact creates a potential source of error when data is processed and something to guard against when programming.

25. We now consider the other aspect of data types; the operations which may be applied to them.

OPERATIONS, OPERATORS AND OPERANDS.

26. An **operation** is a defined action upon data. For example the addition 3 + 5 is an **arithmetic operation** on two integers. The **result** of the operation 3 + 5 is 8. The **operator** used to signify this operation is the symbol '+'. The **operands** are the data items operated upon, in this example the operands are 3 and 5.

27. It is very important to recognise that particular operations can only be defined in terms of what happens to values of the data type to which they are applied.

28. Dyadic operations and Unary operations, operations which act upon *two* operands are called **dyadic operations** and operations which act upon single operands are called **unary operations.** The "+" and "−" signs are used both for dyadic operations and for unary operations.

29. Examples:

a. **Dyadic operations** 3 + 5 and 5 − 3.

b. **Unary operations** +3 and −5.

30. Dyadic operations are also called **'binary operations'** for fairly obvious reasons but ambiguities can arise from that choice of terms, so beware! Unary operations are also called **"monadic operations"**.

ARITHMETIC OPERATIONS.

31. The arithmetic operations of addition, subtraction, multiplication and division are normally indicated by the use of the operaters +, −, × and ÷. However, in computer programming languages other symbols are commonly used instead because of limitations in character sets.

32. There are variations in symbols used between programming languages. Also, there are variations in symbols used which take account of difference between integers and reals.

33. Fig. 10.3 shows the more commonly used symbols.

Normal Representation	Symbols Used In Programming Languages
+	+
−	−
×	*
÷	/ or div
3^2	3 ↑ 2 or 3 ** 2

Fig. 10.3. Symbols for Arithmetic Operators.

OPERATIONS ON INTEGERS.

34. All five operations in Fig. 10.3 may be applied to integers but in the case of division there are some special considerations. Dividing one integer by another does not necessarily give rise to an integer result. For example, 11/4 is 2.75 which is of type real. However, in some situations we might want to obtain the result of division in the forms of an integer quotient and integer remainder. For example, in asking the question how many lots of four items can be made from eleven items and how many will be left over. The remedy is to use **div** and **mod.**

35. Div and Mod. These two operations apply to integers and produce integer results. **Div** produces an integer quotient and **mod** produces an integer remainder.

36. Examples:

a. 11 **div** 4 has the result 2.

b. 11 **mod** 4 has the result 3.

OPERATIONS ON REALS.

37. All five operation in Fig. 10.3 may be applied to reals, and division does not present the same problems encountered with integers. However, there is one more point to note regarding division which applies to integers and reals; the case of attempting to divide by zero. Division by zero leads **either** to an *infinite result or,* in the case of dividing zero by zero, to an *undefined result.* When writing programs which involve divisions the programmer should *always* consider these two special cases and allow for them.

OPERATIONS ON CHARACTERS.

38. A few operations may be applied to individual characters and far more operations may be applied to character strings. It is more instructive to postpone the discussion of the operations for the time being and to give just one example here to illustrate the general idea.

39. **Concatenation** is an operation which adds one string onto the end of another string. The operator symbols commonly used for concatenation are either '+' or '&'. Although the '+' sign is the same symbol as that used in arithmetic *it has a completely different meaning* when used as a string operator. To avoid any confusion "&" will be used in this text.

40. Example.

"ALEX" & "JAMES" has the result "ALEXJAMES"

LOGIC RELATIONAL OPERATORS.

41. Before considering boolean operators which apply to boolean values to give boolean results we will consider **relational operators** which give boolean values when applied to data types such as integers, reals and characters.

42. The relational logic operators are set out in the following table.

OPERATOR	MEANING
=	equal to
≠ or < >	not equal to
<	less than
>	greater than
≤ or < =	less than or equal to
≥ or > =	greater than or equal to

43. Examples.

a. $3 = 4$ is **false**

b $3 \neq 4$ is **true**

c. $3 < 4$ is **true**

d. $3 > 4$ is **false**

e. $3 \leq 4$ is **true**

f. $3 \geq 4$ is **false**

44. The relational logic operators can only be applied to characters if the characters have a defined order. For example, the ASCII characters have a defined order (see Fig. 2.4). In fact, the order of the ASCII characters has been chosen very carefully so as to be consistent with the numerical order of the digits 0 to 9 and the alphabetic sequence A to Z. Note, however, that in ASCII "A" < "B" but "a" > "B"! (See Fig. 2.4)

45. Propositions. A proposition is a statement which can be either **true** or **false**. For example, the statement "You are reading this book" is true but the statement "3= 4" is false.

NB. Questions and exclamations are **not** propositions. Propositions have boolean values and boolean operations may be applied to them.

OPERATIONS ON BOOLEANS.

46. The three basic boolean operations are:-

a. NOT.

b. OR.

c. AND.

47. The 'NOT' operation. Application of the NOT operation to a boolean value is called **negation.** Negating a true value gives a false result and negating a false value gives a true result. The two possible cases are set out in the following table.

P	NOT p	
true	false	When proposition 'p' is true NOT p is false.
false	true	When proposition 'p' is false NOT p is true.

48. Truth tables. Tables like the one just given are called truth tables. They define logic operations by tabulating all possible operation cases and results.

49. The 'OR' Operation. First consider this example of the OR operation.

OPERATION	RESULT
(3 > 5) OR (8 < 4)	false
(3 > 5) OR (8 > 4)	true
(3 < 5) OR (8 < 4)	true
(3 < 5) OR (8 > 4)	true

50. The truth table for the OR operation is given here:

p	q	p OR q
false	false	false
false	true	true
true	false	true
true	true	true

51. Inclusive and Exclusive ORs.

a. In everyday usage the word OR has two possible meanings:–
   i. OR can mean one or the other or both. (the **inclusive** OR)
   ii. OR can mean one or the other but **not** both. (the **exclusive** OR).

b. **Examples.**
   i. **Inclusive** OR. To qualify for a competition you might have to subscribe to a magazine OR belong to a club. (You might do both).
   ii. **Exclusive** OR. You are rich OR you are poor. (You can't be both).

You can see from the truth table that this OR operation is in fact an inclusive OR operation.

52. The 'AND' operation is defined by the following truth table.

p	q	p OR q
false	false	false
false	true	false
true	false	false
true	true	true

Note that *both* p and q must be true for p AND q to be true.

REPRESENTING OPERATIONS BY DIAGRAMS.

53. Diagrammatic representations of operations can often aid understanding.

54. Simple examples:

a. 3 + 5 can be represented by:

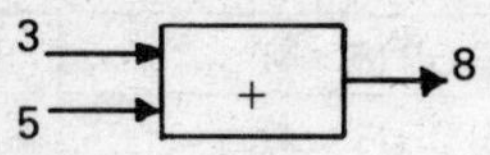

b. True OR False can be represent by:

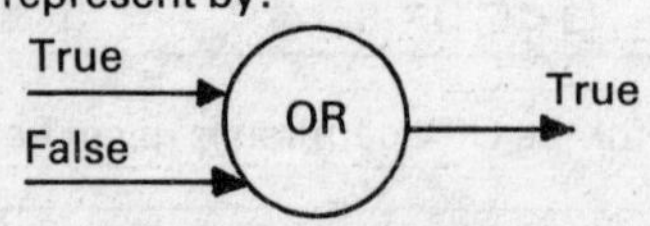

55. We will find a number of uses for these diagrams before we reach the end of this text. We will use them first in our discussion of *expressions.*

EXPRESSIONS.

56. Expressions are formulae containing operations or combinations of operations. It is necessary to have rules which govern the order in which the operations are carried out. Such rules are called **rules of precedence.** Without rules of precedence many expressions would be ambiguous. For example, 3 + 4 * 5 could mean *either* add 3 to 4 and multiply the result by 5 *or* multiply 4 by 5 and add the result to 3. The former evaluation gives the final result 35 whereas the latter evaluation gives the final result 23.

57. Here is are examples which show how the potential ambiguities are overcome.

a. The expression

3 + 4 * 5

could mean

either

i. add 3 to 4 and then multiply that result (ie. 7) to 5 to give the final result (ie. 35).

or

ii. multiply 4 by 5 and then add that result (ie. 20) to 3 to give the final result (ie. 23).

b. Case a ii is consistent with normal practice because, although it is natural to evaluate expressions by working from left to right, the rules of precedence require multiplication to be performed before addition.

c. parentheses may be used to override the order of operator precedence. So the expression (3 + 4) * 5 would be evaluated as in a i because expressions within parentheses are evaluated first.

The following rules of precedence should be easier to follow if you relate them to the example just given.

58. Precedence rules for arithmetic expressions are:

a. Operators of higher precedence are evaluated *before* operators of lower precedence.

b. Operators of equal precedence are evaluated in the order they appear when scanning the expression from left to right.

c. The inclusion of parentheses in the expression requires that the expression within parentheses be evaluated first by applying rules a, b and c.

The order of precedence is given in the following table.

ORDER OF PRECEDENCE	OPERATOR
4	– (unary)
3	↑
2	* / **mod div**
1	+ –(dyadic)

Fig. 10.4. Order of Precedence for Arithmetic Operators.

59. Example. The precedence rules just given are applied to the following expression and are illustrated by means of Fig. 10.5.

Expression – ((3 + 5) * 2 ↑ 3) / (10 – 6)

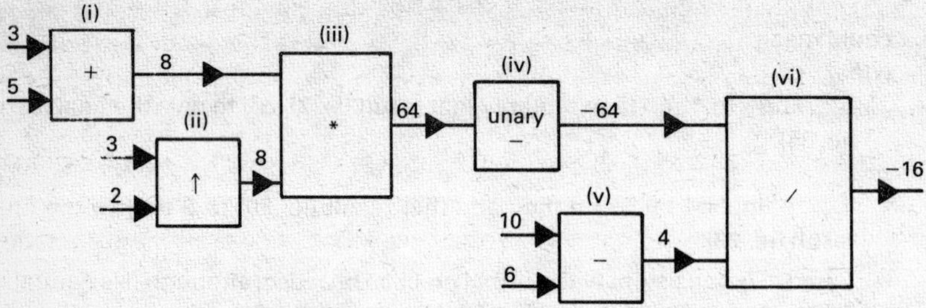

Evaluation of the expression under the precedence rules given in pargraph 58.

NB. Roman numerals indicate the order of evaluation.

Fig. 10.5. Expression Evaluation.

60. For boolean expressions the order of precedence is, from highest to lowest, NOT, AND, OR.

61. Mixed-Mode Expressions. It is possible for expressions to contain data of different types. Such expressions are called **mixed-mode** expressions. In most programming languages there are rules which restrict the use of mixed mode expressions. For example, mixed mode arithmetic which involves mixing integers and reals, is governed by very strict rules in the programming language Pascal.

62. Mixed mode expressions are always governed by carefully devised precedence rules. The precedence rules of 10.57 may be applied to mixed mode expressions if used in conjunction with the orders of precedence specified in Fig. 10.6.

NB. Careful use of parentheses is needed for these expressions.

ORDER OF PRECEDENCE	OPERATOR
8	– (unary)
7	↑
6	* / **div mod**
5	+ – (dyadic)
4	= ≠ < ≤ > ≥
3	**NOT**
2	**AND**
1	**OR**

Fig. 10.6. Order of Precedence for general expressions.

FUNCTIONS.

63. Representing operations by means of operands and operator symbols proves to be unsatisfactory when devising new operations on a regular basis. In such case the *functional notation,* borrowed from Mathematics, is used.

At this point the reader familiar with mathematics should note that the things called "functions" in the subject Computer Science are defined differently from function in Mathematics, although they have many similar properties. Only Computer Science "functions" are discussed here.

64. Functional Notation. The operation "3 + 5" could be written in functional notation as "Add (3, 5)". Note the following points about this notation:

a. Instead of using an operator symbol the action to be performed upon the data is identified by the function name, "Add" in this case.

b. Function names help to convey the meaning of the function.

c. What would be called operands in operation notation are called **arguments** (sometimes also called **parameters**) in functional notation.

d. The function notation is easy to extend so as to allow for multiple arguments eg. Add (3, 5, 2) could represent a function which performed 3 + 5 + 2.

65. Examples of functions.

a. Functions which perform mathematical computations, such as sine or absolute value. These functions use numeric arguments and evaluate to numeric results.

b. Functions which *convert* from one numeric type to another such as an 'Int' function which has a real argument and evaluates to the largest integer not greater than the real eg. Int (3.6) evaluates to 3.

c. Functions which apply to characters to give their successor or predecessor in their character set.

d. Functions which *convert* from characters to their integer ordinal value or vice versa. eg. a function with argument 'A' which evaluates to 65 (See Fig. 2.4).

66. Note how the result of a function always has a type so we may think of the function as being of that type.

SUMMARY.

67. a. Data types were defined, including simple types and data structures.

b. Simple data types were classified as:

i. Numeric integer.

ii. Numeric real.

iii. Character.

iv. Boolean (Logical).

c. Representations of data items of various types were discussed.

d. Operations, operators and operands for various data types were introduced.

e. Expressions and their precedence rules were introduced.

f. Functions and functional notations were discussed.

POINTS TO NOTE.

68. a. A data type is only fully defined if *both* its set of values *and* its related operations are specified.

b. Ensure that operators and operands used together are of consistent type when programming. That will guard against nonsensical operations being carried out at machine level, at which all data is in binary form. The rules of some languages enforce data type consistency.

STUDENT SELF TESTING QUESTIONS

(Answers page 685)

1. *Show how the value 79_{10} may be represented in a 16-bit word as*

   a. *two BCD numeric digits*

   b. *two BCD 6-bit codes*

   c. *two ASCII characters, where an 8th bit is present in each code as an even parity bit.*

   d. *a pure binary natural number.*

2. *What two things must be specified in order to define a data type?*

3. *Distinguish between the terms "operation", "operator", "operand" and "function".*

4. *Suggest a probable fault with the way these expression are written and a suitable correction.*

   a. *15 < "26"*

   b. *5 < 10* ***OR*** *19.*

5. *Evaluate these expressions:*

   a. *((15 − 7) / 2) * (−3 * 2 ↑ 5)*

   b. *(3 < 9)* ***OR*** *(7 < 2)*

   c. *((2 ↑ 10 − 24) = 1000)* ***AND*** *((2 ↑ 3 = 16)* ***OR*** *(24/2 ≤ 3 * 4))*

6. *Suppose that a function called "ORD" takes an ASCII character as its argument and evaluates to the ordinal value of the character as defined in Fig. 2.4. For example ORD ("A") is 65. Also suppose that a function called "CHR" takes an*

integer argument and evaluates to the ASCII character as defined in Fig. 2.4. For example, CHR(65) = "A".

Evaluate these expressions:

a. *ORD ("1") + ORD ("3")*

b. *CHR(67) & CHR(65) & CHR(84)*

c. *CHR (ORD("7") + 1)*

QUESTIONS WITHOUT ANSWERS.

7. *What value does the binary code 01110101 represent each of the following case:*

a. *A two digit BCD numeric code.*

b. *A pure binary integer.*

c. *A single ASCII character.*

State any assumptions which you make.

8. *Evaluate these expressions.*

a. *((17* ***div*** *5) + (17* ***mod*** *5)) ≥ (4 * (−2))*

b. ***NOT*** *((5 < 2) OR (16 = 2 ↑ 4))*

c. *(2 ↑ 7 = 128)* ***AND*** *(2 ↑ 9 − 512 = 0)* ***OR*** *(12/4 ≤ 5)*

11 Program Structures

INTRODUCTION.

1. This chapter introduces program structures which are what we may call the forms in which program components are constructed, organised and interrelated.

2. In order to aid a clear understanding of the material covered in the chapter we start by providing the necessary background knowledge of programming languages and the forms in which programs are written.

3. When considering features of programs it pays to recognise how these features relate to the operational features of the computers for which the programs are written. Therefore, the chapter is organised in a way which highlights these relationships.

4. Particular aspects covered in the chapter are:

a. Language, its syntax and semantics.

b. Data declarations.

c. Basic operations on data.

d. Control structures.

e. Subprograms.

PROGRAMMING LANGUAGES.

5. The subject of programming languages forms a complete Part of this text (Ch.28-30). So, as was mentioned in the introduction, only background information needed for this chapter will be discussed here.

6. When learning a programming language we need to learn about two important aspects of the language:

a. its **syntax**.
and b. its **semantics.**

7. The **syntax** of a language are the grammatical rules which govern the ways in which words symbols, expressions and statements may be formed and combined.

8. The **semantics** of a language are the rules which govern its *meaning.* In the case of computer language, meaning is defined in terms of what happens when the program is executed.

9. **Natural Language and Formal Languages.** Languages used for everyday human communication, such as English, French and Chinese, are called **Natural Languages.**

10. **Natural languages** have complexities which make them unsuitable as computer programming languages. Instructions written in such languages often suffer from ambiguities. For example, this simple English question has several interpretations: "Calculate 4 and 6 divided by 2".

It could mean add 4 to 6 and then divide that answer by 2, or divide 6 by 2 and then add that result to 4, or it could mean divide 4 by 2 to get one result and then divide 6 by 2 to get another result, and so on. Another example is "I want ham or eggs and chips".

11. Formal Languages differ from natural languages in that they have precise semantics. Properly defined programming languages are formal. Every instruction written in such languages has just one meaning.

12. In practical terms what all this boils down to is that when we learn a programming language, as we learn each new instruction, we must learn both its syntax (how to write it down correctly) and its semantics (what will happen when it is executed) so that we use it sensibly.

13. When we considered computer architecture in chapter 9, we saw that hardware could be viewed at different levels. The same is true of software. Some computer languages are at higher levels than others.

14. At machine level (9.12) the operations performed on data are very simple. Just to add together two numbers may take three of these simple operations. For each of these operations there will be one corresponding program instruction in what is called **machine language.** In the early days of computers all programs were written in machine language.

15. These days, programs are seldom written in machine language. Instead, programs are most frequently written in what are called **"High Level Languages"**.

16. The program instructions in high level languages are much closer to sentences in English or expressions in Mathematics. This makes them easier to use than machine languages.

17. The price paid for using these easier and more powerful languages is that each high level language program must first be translated into machine language because the computer can only operate using instructions in machine language. This translation is normally carried out by the computer.

18. Further details of programming languages at various levels, and of the translation processes involved, will be given in later chapters. In this chapter the examples will be given in forms akin to high level languages. This should have the advantage of preventing the details of the hardware from obscuring programming concepts. This language form is a kind of **pseudocode** (See the Part introduction).

NB. Instructions written in high level languages or pseudocode are normally called *statements.*

THE PROGRAM LEVEL VIEW OF THE COMPUTER.

19. When writing programs we need some concept of what the computer is doing when the program is used. This *program level view of the computer* is a much simpler one than the "true" picture but is ideal for its purpose. This situation is comparable to a car driver's view of the car's controls. The driver merely thinks that when the accelerator is pressed harder the engine goes faster, without giving any thought to what actually happens under the car bonnet.

20. The main features of the computer are still visible in features of the language.

a. Storage.

b. Input and output.

c. Operating on data.

d. Control.

We will consider each of these in turn.

STORAGE.

21. In all but the lowest level programming languages data items are identified by name rather than by their location addresses in main storage. The names which we associate with stored data values are called **identifiers** because an identifier is the name by which the data value may be identified.

22. Constants and Variables. An identifier is a **'constant'** if it is always associated with the same data value and it is a **'variable'** if its associated data value is allowed to vary or change. Changing a variable's value implies changing what is stored.

23. Literals. When referring to letters or names in programs we must be careful to specify whether we mean them to be taken *literally* or to be treated as identifiers. When names or letters are used literally we call them **literals,** and we enable them to be distinguished from identifiers by placing them within quotation marks. So the instruction PRINT "N" means print the letter N, and the instruction PRINT N means print the value associated with N. Note that PRINT 2 + 4 means print the value 6 but PRINT "2 + 2" mean print the character "2" followed by the character "+" followed by the character "2".

DATA DECLARATIONS.

24. The data types of constants and variables must be defined within a program so that the appropriate operations may be performed upon the data values. Such information should be given at the start of each program.

25. Some programming languages have special statements which must be used for this purpose. They are called **"declarative statements"** because they state properties of the data and are not executed. They differ in that respect from most of the statements to be discussed in the remainder of this chapter, which are executed, and are called *"procedural statements"*.

26. A typical data declaration is given in Fig. 11.1. Most of the data items declared in Fig. 11.1 will be used in later examples. Two more have been added to make the example complete; the constant "pi", used in Mathematics, and a boolean value "rate-code-valid".

```
constants
                pi = 3.141592654

variables
                quantity_required,
                number_of_inputs,
                i,
                product                        : integer
                unit_price,
                product_price,
                side_one,
                side_two,
                area,
                rate,
                charge,
                units_used,
                unit_cost                      : real
                rate_code                      : character
                rate_code_valid                : boolean
```

NB. Variables of the same type are presented in a list separated by commas.

Fig. 11.1. An example of a data declaration.

27. Some programming languages declare data types in very different ways. For example, in BASIC the use of a "$" sign at the end of an identifier declares the variable to be a string. The absence of the "$" declares the variable type to be numeric by default. In BASIC variable need not be declared in declarative statements.

28. In the declaration of the real constant pi in fig. 11.1 a value has explicitly been *assigned* to the identifier "pi". All the other identifiers in the example have no values asociated with them at the end of the declaration.

29. A variable name does not have an associated value until it has been assigned one. This may be done either by using an assignment statement (details follow in paragraph 39) or by using them as arguments in input functions (detail follow in paragraph 33). This process of assigning values to variables before using them is called **"initialisation"**.

30. Initialisation must be done in a systematic way. Otherwise, unexpected things may happen during the program's execution if non initialised variables are used as operands. The program may give an error message and stop, or possibly worse still, carry on and give the wrong results or cause something dangerous to happen.

INPUT AND OUTPUT.

31. Programming languages have special functions for dealing with input and output. Common names for these functions are **input, read, get, accept, output, write, print, put** and **display.**

32. It is not appropriate to consider all possible cases at this stage. Rather, we will take one typical example to illustrate the basic ideas.

33. Suppose that data input and output is taking place at a VDU or similar device and that two numbers are to be input. Let us suppose that these two numbers represent the unit price and quantity purchased of some product from which it is intended to calculate the price for all the products. The instructions in the program dealing with the input might appear in a form similar to that shown in Fig. 11.2a. In Fig. 11.2b we see what would appear on the VDU screen when the program was executed.

a. PART OF THE PROGRAM (in pseudocode)	b. OUTPUT DURING PROGRAM EXECUTION (what appears on the VDU screen)
output ("Key in the unit price in pounds") **input** (unit_price) **output** ("Key in the quantity required") **input** (quantity_required)	Key in the unit price in pounds 1.25 Key in the quantity required 20

NB. i. The real number 1.25 and the integer 20 are keyed in by the user and are displayed on the VDU screen as they are keyed in.
ii. Outputs of variables are also possible although not shown here.

Fig. 11.2. Programming Simple Input and Output.

34. Try to rewrite these instructions in the language which you are using as part of your course.

35. When input, the numbers shown in fig. 11.2b will be stored in main storage and referred to by the appropriate identifier. (See Fig. 11.3).

Identifier	Data Type	Associated Stored Data Value
unit_price	real	1.25
quantity_required	integer	20

Fig. 11.3. Data Item Identifiers and Associated Stored Values.

OPERATIONS ON DATA.

36. The operations which may be applied to data items of various types were discussed in some detail in the previous chapter. It remains for us to examine how these operations are incorporated into programs.

37. The ideas are best introduced by a simple example. We will continue with the example given in paragraph 33.

38. The price for all products is calculated by multiplying the unit price by the quantity required. A program instruction for doing this might take the form:

products_price := unit_price * quantity_required

This is an example of an **assignment statement.**

39. The **assignment statement** has three basic components:

a. An **assignment operator** which is represented by some appropriate symbols; (In the example ":=" is used.)

b. A **result,** with an identifier ("products_price"); to the left of the assignment operator;

c. an **expression** to the right of the assignment operator.

40. Performing this instruction involves fetching the values associated with the operands in the expression from main storage, performing the required operations (multiplication in this case) and then storing the result in the location(s) in storage associated with the identifier "products_price". Thus, the outcome will be that the value of the result has been *assigned* to the identifier "products_price".

41. In some cases an identifier may appear on *both* sides of an assignment statement. This often occurs when counting or accumulating totals.

42. Examples. Suppose we wished a program to count how many inputs had been made. To do this we could place this assignment statement at the start of the program to *initialise* the counter to zero:

number_of_inputs := 0

and place this assignment statement after each input instruction to count the inputs;

number_of_inputs := number_of_inputs + 1

NB. The result of evaluating the expression on the right hand side of the assignment statement *replaces* the value associated with the identifier "number_of_inputs" *before* the expression is evaluated.

43. The exact form of the assignment statement varies from language to language. The examples just given take the form used in a number of languages including Pascal, Modula and ADA. Some readers may be using the language BASIC which has an assignment statement of the form

LET P = U * Q

In COBOL the assignment could take the form

MULTIPLY U BY Q GIVING P

CONTROL.

44. The order in which program instructions are performed by the computer must be carefully controlled and programming languages contain features which allow the order of instruction execution to be controlled.

45. All programming problems, no matter how complex, may be reduced to combinations of controlled sequences, selections or repetitions of basic operations on data. This fact was established by two Italian Computer Scientists, C Bohm and G Jacopini in 1966. It is part of the important theory which is behind the concept of **"structured programming"**, a term first used by Professor E Diskstra in the mid 1960s and now widely used and misused!

CONTROL STRUCTURES.

46. Program control structures are used to regulate the order in which program statements are executed. They fall into three categories:

a. **sequences**

b. **selections**

c. **repetitions.**

We will consider these three categories in turn.

SEQUENCES.

47. In the absence of selections or repetitions program statements are executed in the sequence in which they appear in the program:

```
statement_1
statement_2
statement_3
     .
     .
     .
```

48. In the following paragraphs we will use the term **"statement sequence"** to mean a sequence of one or more statements.

SELECTIONS.

49. Selections form part of the decision making facilities within programming languages. They allow alternative actions to be taken according to the conditions which exist at particular stages in program execution.

50. Conditions are normally in the form of expressions which when evaluated give boolean results (**true** or **false**).

51. The if_then_else statement. Versions of this simple selection statement appear in most high level languages. A typical form of syntax for this statement is given here:

```
if
        condition
then
        statement_sequence_1
else
        statement_sequence_2
endif
```

52. The semantics of this statement is as follows. When the statement is executed the condition's expression is evaluated. If the result of the evaluation is **true** then statement_sequence_1 will be executed *otherwise* statement_sequence_2 will be executed. After *either* statement_sequence_1 *or* statement_sequence_2 has been executed the statement following "endif" is executed. (See fig. 11.4).

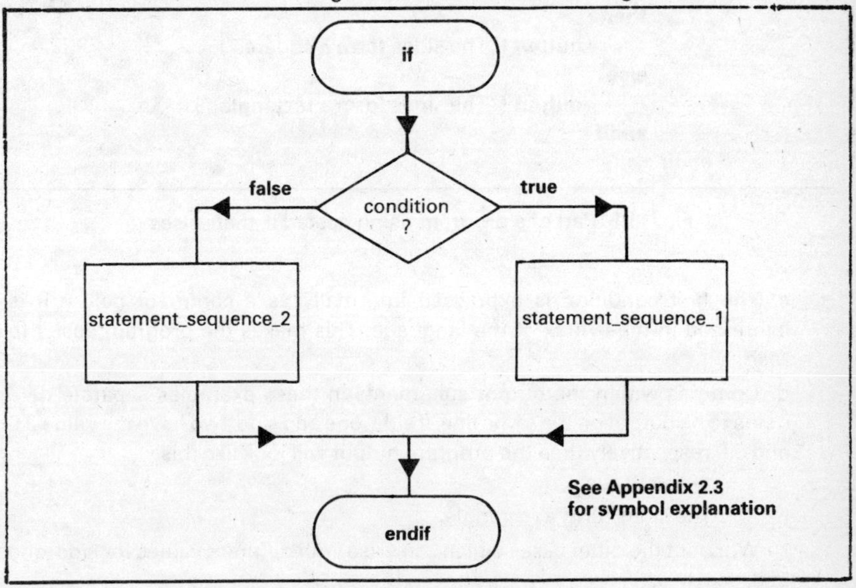

Fig. 11.4. The semantics of the selection if_then_else.

53. Example. In this simple example we consider part of a program in which two real numbers representing the two sides of a rectangle are to be used to determine the area of the rectangle and to indicate whether or not the sides form a square. (See Fig. 11.5).

54. Note the following points about this example.

a. Within the first if_then_else statement there is another if_then_else statement. This is an example of **"nesting"** ie. a structure containing other structures of the same type.

b. The program is made easier to read by indenting statements progressively with each level of nesting.

NB. i. In this and further examples comments within programs will be enclosed between the symbols (* and *).

ii. In this example "side_one", "side_two" and "area" are all real numbers.

```
if
        (* The values of the sides are invalid. *)
        (side_one < = 0) OR (side_two < = 0)
then
        output ("The sides do not form a rectangle.")
else
        area : = side_one * side_two
        output ("The area is ", area)
        if
                side_one = side_two
        then
                output ("The sides form a square.")
        else
                output ("The sides form a rectangle.")
        endif
endif
```

Fig. 11.5. Part of a program using nested if_then_elses

c. The first condition is expressed informally as a comment before it is expressed in the syntax of the language. This makes the program easier to read.

d. Commas within the output statements in these examples separate data items to be output on the same line. If side_one and side_two have the value 2.0 and 3.0 respectively then the program output will look like this:

The area is 6.0
The sides form a rectangle.

Work out the other cases which can arise with different values for side_one and side_two.

55. A more general form of selection is the **CASE** statement. Again, a number of languages have their own versions of case statements. A simple case statement could have syntax like that shown in Fig. 11.6a. Fig. 11.6b explains the semantics.

```
selectcase
                    expression
          case      case_list_1
                    statement_sequence_1
          case      case_list_2
                    statement_sequence_2
            .            .
            .            .
            .            .
          case      case_list_n
                    statement_sequence_n
          case      else
                    statement_sequence_n+1
endselectcase
```

a. **Syntax of a typical case statement.**

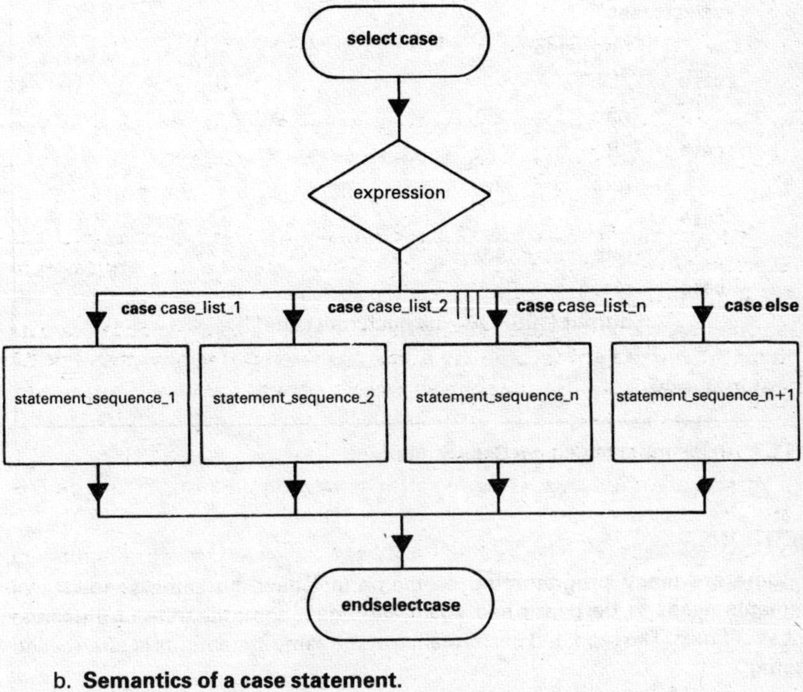

b. **Semantics of a case statement.**

Fig. 11.6. A Case Statement.

56. Example. Suppose for the purpose of this example that the cost of a telephone call is to be calculated from the formula

charge := units_used * unit_cost * rate

where all four items are reals. Also assume that "units_used" and "unit_cost" have already been assigned values but that the "rate" must be determined from the "rate_code" which is a single character. The following table summarises the relationship between "rate_code" and "rate".

rate_code	rate
L (local)	2
A (short distance)	2
B (long distance)	2.5
C (overseas)	4.0

The part of the program which determines the rate is given in Fig. 11.7.

```
NB  Assume that the character "rate_code" has
    already been assigned a value.
    selectcase
            rate_code
    case    "L",   "A"
            rate   : =   2.0
    case    "B"
            rate   : =   2.5
    case    "C"
            rate   : =   4.0
    case    else
            output ("ERROR – no such rate code!")
            rate   : =   0
endselectcase
```

Fig. 11.7. An example of using a **Case** Statement.

*

REPETITIONS.

57. There are many programming problems in which the same sequence of statements needs to be performed again and again some definite or indefinite number of times. The repeated performance of the same statements is often called **"looping"**.

58. Fig. 11.8 shows three common "loop constructs" for performing repetitions. The "while" and "repeat" loops are used for *indefinite* repetitions. That is, they do not define the number of repetitions which will occur when the loop is executed. They merely gives conditions for looping to stop. The "for" loop is used for *definite repetition.* It defines the number of repetitions which will occur during execution.

THE "WHILE" LOOP

while condition
statement_sequence
endwhile

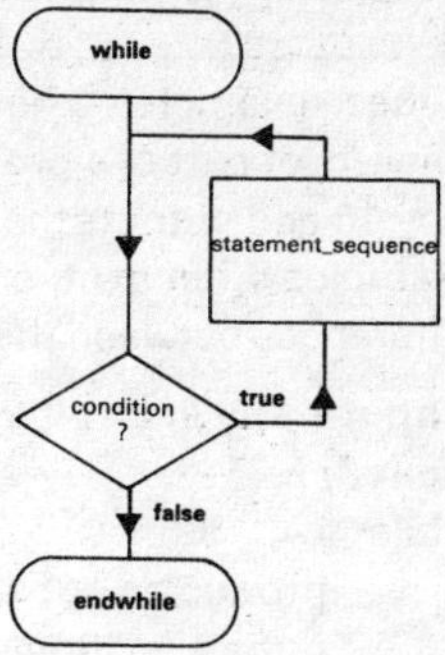

THE "REPEAT" LOOP

repeat
statement_sequence
until condition

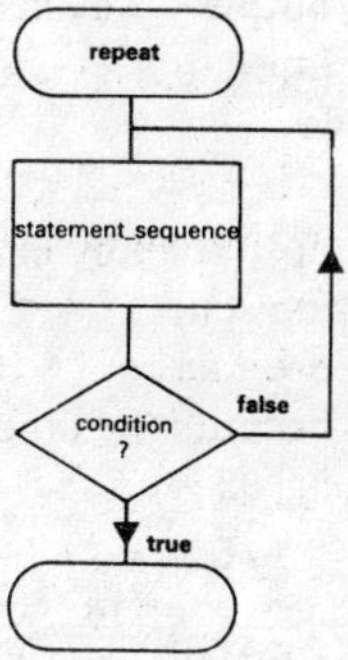

THE "FOR" LOOP

for controll_value : =expression **to** endvalue
statement_sequence
endfor

NB This **for-endfor** statement can replace an assignment followed by a **while** loop. In some languages the **for** loop may replace an assignment followed by a **repeat** loop.

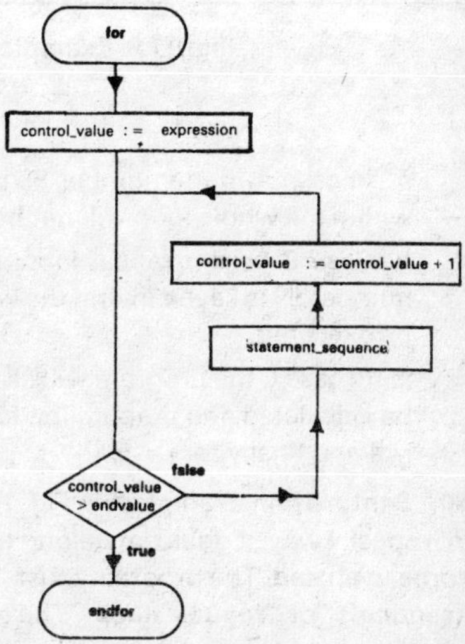

Fig. 11.8. Loop Constructs for Repetitions.

59. Examine Fig. 11.9 which gives examples of using the three loop constructs.

NB In these examples "i" and "product" are integers. Each example consists of part of a program which takes the value of "i", multiplies it by 16 and outputs the result each time the loop is repeated. The examples differ in other respects which help to highlight the differences between the loop constructs.

```
A.  output ("Key in an integer. Key in 99 to stop.")
    input (i)
    while  i <> 99
               product : = i * 16
               output (i, "times", 16, "is", product)
               output ("Key in an integer. Key in 99 to stop.")
               input (i)
    endwhile
B.  repeat
               output ("Key in an integer. Key in 99 to stop.")
               input (i)
               product : = i * 16
               output ("i, "times", 16, "is", product)
    until      i = 99
C.  for i : = 1 to 5
         product : = i * 16
         output (i, "times", 16, "is", product)
    endfor
```

Fig. 11.9. Examples of loop constructs in use.

a. In case A, if the number 99 is keyed in first then the statement sequence within the whole loop will not be executed at all.

b. Case B uses a repeat loop. It looks simpler than case A but even if the number 99 is keyed in first the whole statement sequence within the loop will be executed.

c. In case C the program will always output the same values. The product will be calculated and output, first for i = 1, then for i = 2, then for i = 3, then for i = 4 and finally for i = 5.

60. Sentinels. In example A in Fig. 11.9 it is clear that the number 99 is being used in a special way. It does not belong to the data instead it signifies that the data has come to an end. The program must "keep watch" for such values which are called **"sentinels"** or **"rogue values"**. The term sentinel is probably preferable, although less widely used, because there are situations in which sentinels occur naturally as part of the genuine data.

61. We have now considered all the language features listed in paragraph 20: Storage, Input and Output, Operations on data and Control. However, there is one aspect of program structuring which still requires attention and that is the subject of **subprograms.**

SUBPROGRAMS.

62. The term "subprogram" may be used to describe a component part of a program. Used loosely the term may merely refer to any set of statements forming part of a program used to perform a specific task. However, a properly constructed subprogram should be self-contained, perform well defined operations on well defined data and have an internal structure which is independent of the program in which it is contained. When a subprogram has all these properties it is sometimes called a program **module.**

63. The two basic types of subprograms are:

a. **functions,**
and b. **procedures.**

Note that here the term "procedure" is being used with a far more precise meaning than that used previously (see the Part introduction). Unfortunately, there is some considerable variation in the use of terms such as "function", "procedure", "module" and "subprogram." Within this text every effort has been made to use the most widely adopted terms and to use them consistently, where general and specific meanings exist the context should make it clear which sense is intended.

FUNCTIONS.

64. Many high level programming languages have inbuilt functions such as those mentioned in 11.65. A common example is the square root function "sqrt". The reader may remember that the square root of a number x is that number y with the property $y^2 = x$. Thus the square root of 9 is 3 because $3^2 = 9$. We will assume, for the sake of mathematical simplicity, that the square root function in the following example is only to be used for positive arguments.

65. Fig. 11.10 shows a simple program using an inbuilt square root function.

```
Program Find_root
                    (* This program has the name "Find_root".
                       It inputs a number and outputs the
                       value of the square root of the number.
                    *)
variables
                    number,
                    root      : real
Begin
          output ("Key in the number whose square root you require.")
          input (number)
          if
                    number < 0
          then
                    output ("No root obtainable for negative numbers.")
          else
                    root : = sqrt (number)
                    output ("the square root of ", number, "is", root)
          endif
end
```

Fig. 11.10. A simple program using an inbuilt function.

66. When a required function is not inbuilt it is sometimes possible for the programmer to define it for him or herself. Unfortunately, full facilities to do this are less common features of programming languages despite their usefullness.

67. Suppose we wish to have a function for calculating the area of a rectangle, as we did in Fig. 11.5. It may be argued that this operation is a little too simple to merit defining a special function but it serves as a useful example nevertheless.

68. The program which uses the function will contain a *declaration of the function.* This declaration defines the function. The function will also be used or "called" within the sequence of executable statements. Fig. 11.11 shows the relevant parts of the program.

```
                 Program Rectangle
                 variables
                          side_one,
                          side_two,
                          area      : real
               ┌ function rectangular_area (first_side: real, second_side: real):real
               │          (* This function calculates the area of a rectangle from the
               │             lengths of its two sides. If the value of either side is not
               │             positive it assignes the value zero to the area.
               │          *)
The            │          Begin
function       │                if
declaration   <│                    (first_side <= 0) OR (second_side <= 0)
(definition)   │                then
               │                    rectangular_area := 0
               │                else
               │                    rectangular_area := first_side * second_side
               │                endif
               └          end
         (* Now the procedural part of the program *)
         Begin
               .       .       .       .       .
               .       .       .       .       .
               .       .       .       .       .
The
function  {  area := rectangular_area (side_one, side_two)
call
               .       .       .       .       .
               .       .       .       .       .
         end
```

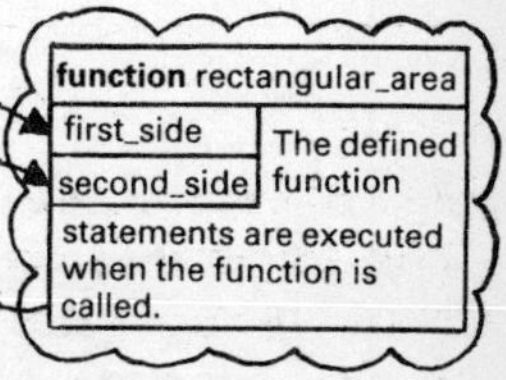

Fig. 11.11. Declaring and using functions.

69. The arguments used in the function declaration ie. "first_side" and "second_side" are called **"formal arguments"**. The arguments used in the function call are called **"actual arguments"**.

PROCEDURES.

70. Any defined way of carrying out some actions may be called a "procedure" but here we are using the term more precisely.

71. Programming procedures are defined operations on defined data and may be used as program components.

72. Procedure definitions are similar to function definitions but procedure calls are statements whereas function calls appear in programs as expressions. These points should be clearer after the following example.

73. A procedure call is a program statement. This point will be easier to understand if we compare a procedure call with a function call. The function call in Fig. 11.11 had the form:

area : = rectangular_area (side_one, side_two)

Had an equivalent procedure been used instead the procedure call could have taken the form:

call rectangular_area (side_one, side_two, area)

74. Parameters. In the procedure example just given "side_one", "side_two" and "area" are the **"actual parameters"** of the procedure. You will no doubt have noticed their similarity with **"actual arguments"** of functions. However, there are some important differences. To see these, first consider Fig. 11.12.

```
procedure rectangular_area (IN first_side,
                                second_side: real
                               OUT area : real)
            (* This procedure takes in the values of first_side and
               second_side.
               If either value is not positive then the procedure returns
               area with value zero. Otherwise, the procedure multiples
               first_side by second_side and returns area with the value of
               the result.
            *)
Begin
    if
        (first_side < = 0) OR (second_side < = 0)
    then
        area : = 0
    else
        area : = first_side * second_side
    endif
end
```

a. **Declaration of the procedure "rectangular_area**

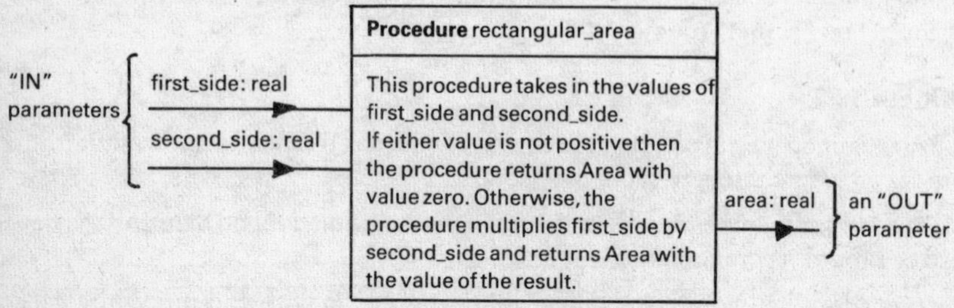

b. **A diagrammatic representation of the procedure.**

Fig. 11.12. Using a procedure.

75. Note that the IN parameters of the procedure correspond to the arguments of a function. The OUT parameter of the procedure serves the same purpose as the value returned by a function.

76. There is a third type of parameter not present in this example, the IN-OUT parameter which is used when data is to be passed into a procedure, manipulated by it in some defined way and then passed out again.

77. There are a number of further features of functions and procedures still to be discussed but they fit more usefully into the remaining chapters in this Part.

SUMMARY.

78. a. The idea of program structures was introduced.

b. The syntax, semantics and other basic properties of programming languages were introduced.

c. Data declarations were explained.

d. Identifiers, constants, variables and literals were defined.

e. Simple input and output functions were explained.

f. The assignment operation was discussed.

g. Control structure were introduced and explained including:
   i. **Statement Sequences**.
   ii. **Selections**: if-then-else, and case
   iii. **Repetitions**: While-loops, Repeat-loops and For-loops.

h. Subprograms were introduced, including the basic features and uses of:
   i. **functions.**
   ii. **procedures.**

POINTS TO NOTE.

79. a. This chapter has placed an emphasis on the "building blocks" from which programs are constructed. The **methods** for designing complete programs from these building blocks *will be explained in the following chapters.*

STUDENT SELF TESTING QUESTIONS

(Answers page 686)

1. *Explain the difference between syntax and semantics.*
2. *Distinguish between constants, variables and literals.*

*3. Using the definition of **input** and **output** given in paragraph 33 show what would be displayed on the VDU screen if the following statements were executed.*

NB. Assume

i. the values input are 6 and 8.

ii. all variables have been declared as integers.

```
output ("Key in an integer.")
input (first_number)
output ("Key in another integer.")
input (second_number)
result := (first_number + second_number) div 2
output ("The result is ", result)
```

4. Write a procedure in pseudocode to calculate the discount that is allowed on purchases according to the following scheme:

If the total value of purchases is over £100 10% discount is given, between £20 and £100 5% is given and below £20 no discount is given. Be careful to define all your variables.

5. Explain the differences in use between actual parameters and formal parameters.

QUESTIONS WITHOUT ANSWERS.

6. Write a program which uses the procedure of question 4 and which deals with several purchase totals in turn terminated by a negative purchase total.

7. Use a case statement to write the following procedure. The IN parameter is a single character. If the character is an octal digit then the corresponding binary value is output as a literal string. For example, if the parameter is "3" the string "011" will be output. Any other character should result in "NOT OCTAL" being output.

12 Data Structures

INTRODUCTION.

1. This chapter explains what **data structures** are. It introduces the more important and common data structures and explains their uses in programming.

2. A **data structure** is an organised grouping of data items treated as a unit. They may be regarded as complex data types (10.3). Data structures are sometimes called **"data aggregates"**.

3. The principal data structures considered in this chapter are:

a. Arrays.

b. Strings.

c. Records.

d. Lists.

e. Trees.

4. The operations associated with these data structures will be explained and the most common programming methods related to these structures will be described with the aid of suitable examples.

5. There are so very many different types of data structure and so many related processing activities. Therefore, the discussion of some topics will be postponed until later chapters.

ARRAYS.

6. In many situations, sets of data items, such as the set of examination marks for a class, may be conveniently arranged into a sequence and referred to by a single identifier eg.

MARK = (56 42 89 65 48).

Such an *arrangement* is a data structure called an ARRAY.

7. **Individual data items in the array** may be referred to separately by stating their position in the array. Thus MARK (1) refers to 56, MARK (2) refers to 42, MARK (3) refers to 89, and so on. The position numbers given in parentheses are called **subscripts.** Variables may be used as subscripts eg. MARK (i) so when i = 2 we are referring to MARK (2), ie. 42, and when i = 4 we are referring to MARK (4), ie. 65.

SIMPLE ARRAY HANDLING.

8. The basic methods used will be explained by means of examples. Suppose that individual exam marks are to be read into an array, and further, suppose that the largest mark, smallest mark, average mark, total mark and number of marks below the average are to be calculated and output.

9. The program to do this task will be easier to understand if taken in steps. First of all we can identify four main stages in the program:

a. Input all the data.

b. Calculate the largest mark, smallest mark, total mark and average mark.

c. Calculate the number of marks below the average.

d. Output the results.

10. These stages suggest four corresponding stages in the program. An outline program is shown in fig. 12.1. Note that the first two stages of the program are in the form of procedures. The two accompanying procedure declarations have been omitted from fig. 12.1 because they are to be discussed separately in the following paragraphs. The third stage is a function which is set as a question at the end of this chapter.

11. First we shall consider the input of the data into the array. Examine fig. 12.2 which shows the details of the procedure declaration.

12. **Note** the following points about the procedure in fig. 12.2:

a. The formal parameters "number_of_marks" and "marks" are both OUT parameters. In this example they have the same identifiers as the actual parameters used but this makes no difference to their meaning.

b. The variable "subscript" is a **local variable** ie. it is used within the procedure and is only defined there. In contrast, variables which are defined throughout the program are called **global** variables. In general terms it is bad practice to *use* variables globally. They should alway be passed into procedures as parameters if they are to be used there. This matter will be discussed more fully in a later chapter.

c. If the user of the program repeatedly fails to key in a valid value for "number_of_marks" the procedure repeatedly outputs an error message and asks the user to try again. A more sophisticated procedure might be designed to abort the procedure after some specific number of errors.

d. In the for-loop in the last part of the procedure the subscript is increased by one each time the loop is repeated. So, for example, if number_of_marks = 3 the loop is equivalent to:–

```
output("key in a mark ")
input(mark(1))
output("key in a mark ")
input(mark(2))
output("key in a mark ")
input(mark(3))
```

```
Program      Marks
        (*   This program inputs a set of not more than 100 marks into an array, determines the
             lowest mark, highest mark, total mark, average mark and number of marks below the
             average. It then outputs each of the values it has determined.
         *)
variables
             number_of_marks,
             number_below_average        : integer
             total_mark,
             smallest_mark,
             largest_mark,
             average_mark                : real
        (*   The next declaration indicates that "mark" is an array able to hold up to 100 real num-
             bers.
         *)
             Mark         : array [1 . . 100] of real
Begin
        (*   Determine how many marks are to be input and input them into the array.
         *)
             call   input_marks(number_of_marks, mark)
             (* Calculate the required values. *)
             call   calculate_results(number_of_marks, mark
                                      total_mark,
                                      smallest_mark,
                                      largest_mark,
                                      average_mark     )
             number_below_average : = below_average(number_of_marks, mark,average_mark)
             (* Output the results *)
             ouput ("Number of marks entered    ",number_of_marks)
             output ("Smallest mark:    ",smallest_mark, "Largest mark:    ",largest_mark)
             output ("Total mark:    ",total_mark, "Average mark:    ", average_mark)
             output ("There were    ",number_below_average," marks below average.")
end
```

Fig. 12.1. Outline program for an array handling problem.

```
procedure   input_marks( OUT number_of_marks:  integer
                              mark            :  array[1 . . 100] of real
                         )
          (* This procedure gets the user to key in the number of marks
             to be entered, which must be an integer between 1 and 100
             inclusive. Then it gets the user to key in the numbers which
             it stores in the array.
          *)
variables
             subscript : integer
Begin
          (* Get the user to key in the number of marks. *)
          output("Key in the number of marks to be entered.")
          output("At least one mark and not more than 100 marks")
          output("may be entered.")
          input(number_of_marks)
          while     (* invalid number entered *)
                    (number_of_marks < 1) OR (number_of_marks > 100)
                    output("ERROR – number must be between 1 and 100")
                    output("Please key in the correct value.")
                    input(number_of_marks)
          endwhile
          (* Get the user to key numbers into the array *)
          for subscript: = 1 to number_of_marks
              output("key in a mark ")
              input(mark(subscript))
          endfor
end
```

Fig. 12.2. A procedure for the input of numbers of an array.

```
procedure     calculate_results(IN number_of_marks: integer
                                   mark           : array[1 . . 100] of real
                               OUT total_so_far,
                                   smallest_so_far,
                                   largest_so_far,
                                   average_mark : real)
              (* This procedure finds the smallest mark, the largest mark, the
                 total of all the marks and the average of all the marks.
              *)
variables
              subscript        : integer
Begin
              (* Initialise the total, smallest and largest values *)
              total_so_far : = 0
              smallest_so_far : = mark(1)
              largest_so_far : = mark(1)
              (* Take each mark in turn adding it to the total and checking it
                 for any change to the smallest or largest value met so far.
              *)
              for     subscript : = 1 to number_of_marks
                      total_so_far : = total_so_far + mark(subscript)
                      if
                            mark(subscript) > largest_so_far
                      then
                            largest_so_far : = mark(subscript)
                      else
                            if
                                  mark(subscript) < smallest_so_far
                            then
                                  smallest_so_far : = mark(subscript)
                            endif
                      endif
              endfor
              average_mark : = total_so_far / number_so_marks
              (* There must be at least one mark so division by zero cannot
                 occur.
              *)
end
```

Fig. 12.3. A procedure for calculating results.

13. Now for the second procedure which is called "calculate_results". (fig. 12.3). Note that this procedure relies upon the fact that there will be at least one mark value in the "mark" array. In this case it is a reasonable assumption because of the way "input_marks" is written. In general, however, it is a good idea to incorporate checks on IN parameters of procedures if their validity cannot be guaranteed.

OTHER FEATURES OF ARRAYS.

8. Array Elements. The individual data items in an array are often called its **elements.** Strictly speaking however, a data item *occupies* an element, ie elements, rather like pigeonholes, are regarded as locations into which data-items may be placed and removed.

15. Main storage as an array. You may have observed a close similarity between arrays and the operational characteristics of main storage. Indeed we may regard main storage as an array in which:–

a. Locations correspond to elements, and

b. Location addresses correspond to subscripts.

One particular use of this fact is that skills learned in handling arrays are transferable to the handling of storage.

16. Matrices are arrays containing only numbers and no alphabetic data. (One matrix, many matrices).

17. Two dimensional arrays have elements arranged into rows and columns and are used for a variety of data tables. For example the examination marks of a class for several subjects could be placed in a two dimensional array thus:–

Pupil or Row Number	English Column 1	Maths Column 2
1	A(1,1) = 56	A(1,2) = 44
2	A(2,1) = 42	A(2,2) = 36
3	A(3,1) = 89	A(3,2) = 73
4	A(4,1) = 65	A(4,2) = 86
5	A(5,1) = 48	A(5,2) = 51

This table can be represented in an array called $A = \begin{bmatrix} 56 & 44 \\ 42 & 36 \\ 89 & 73 \\ 65 & 86 \\ 48 & 51 \end{bmatrix}$

Individual elements can be specified by two subscripts used like map reference, Rows 1st, Columns 2nd. (To remember this order think of Rhubarb and Custard.) eg A(3,1) = 89; A(4,2) = 86. Again subscripts may be variables, as for a one dimensional array, so for A(r,c), if r = 3 and c = 2 we are referring to A(3,2) = 73.

18. 2D Array Handling. In this example the data is entered row by row. The pseudo-code shown in fig. 12.4 shows part of a procedure which reads data into the array. Assume that in the first part of the procedure valid values for the number of rows and columns in the array have been input.

```
{ NB.   "number_of_rows" and "number_of_columns" are          }
{       integer numbers to which valid values have been assigned. }
{       "row_position" and "column_position" are local integers.  }
{       "A" is an array of real numbers.                          }
for     row_position : =1 to number_of_rows
            for column_position : = 1 to number_of_columns
                output("Key in value for row,", row_position,"column", column_position)
                input(A(row_position, column_postion))
            endfor
endfor
```

Fig. 12.4. Part of a procedure to read data into a 2D array.

SORTING AN ARRAY.

19. There are many situations in which the data items within elements of an array need to be rearranged into an ascending or descending sequence. The order of the sequence is often based upon the numerical or alphabetic order of the data. For example, the data in the "mark" array of paragraph 6 could be sorted (ie. re-arranged into order) from

MARK = (56 42 89 65 48)

into *ascending sequence* to be come.

MARK = (42 48 56 65 89).

20. There are many methods of sorting data. The following example is based on a simple method called the **"straight Insertion Sort"**. This method is effective when sorting small arrays but is rather slow when sorting larger arrays. A superior but more complicated method will be described later.

21. A procedure for the straight insertion sort is given in fig. 12.5. Read fig. 12.5 in conjunction with the example in fig. 12.6.

```
procedure    sort_marks(IN      number_of_marks : integer
                        IN-OUT  mark            : array[1. .100] of real
             (* This procedure takes in the array "marks", sorts it into
                ascending numerical order using a straight insertion
                sort and returns it.
             *)
variables
         current_value            ; real
         current_value_position,
         pointer_position         : integer
Begin
         (* Start at element 1 *)
         current_value_position : = 1
         while (* some elements have not yet been reached *)
            current_value_position < number_of_marks
            current_value_position : = current_value_position + 1
            (* get the current value *)
            current_value : = mark(current_value_position)
            (* put it in its correct position relative to the present
               and lower elements *)
               (* set a pointer to the current value position *)
               pointer_position : = current_value_position
               while (* pointer not at insert position *)
                        (pointer_position > 1)
                     AND
                        (current_value < mark(pointer_position – 1))
                     (* copy adjacent value up to pointer position *)
                     mark(pointer_position) : = mark(pointer_position - 1)
                     (* move pointer position down one *)
                     pointer_position : = pointer_position – 1
            endwhile
            (* insert value *)
            mark(pointer_position) : = current_value
         endwhile
end
```

NB. The expression at the start of the inner while loop is assumed to evaluate to **false** when pointer_position = 1 ie. the left most operand will be evaluated first so that mark(0) is not evaluated.

Fig. 12.5. A Straight Insertion Sort Procedure.

Starting with current_value_position = 1

1 2 3 4 5
MARKS = (56 42 89 65 48)

Increase current_value_position by 1 ↑ { Current_value_position = 2
Current_value = 42

Put 42 in position

MARKS = (42 56 89 65 48)

Increase current_value_position by 1 ↑ { Current_value_position = 3
Current_value = 89

Put 89 in position

MARKS = (42 56 89 65 48)

Increase current_value_position by 1 ↑ { Current_value_position = 4
Current_value = 65

Put 65 in position

MARKS = (42 56 65 89 48)

Increase current_value_position by 1 ↑ { Current_value_position = 5
Current_value = 48

Put 48 in position [See fig. 12.6b)

MARKS = (42 48 56 65 89)

a. **Outline example of the straight insertion sort.**

MARKS = (42 56 65 89 48)
↑ pointer_position = 5
(Pointer > 1) AND (48 < 89)
Copy 89 up. Move pointer down.
MARKS = (42 56 65 89 89)
↑ pointer_position = 4
(Pointer > 1) AND (48 < 65)
Copy 65 up. Move pointer down.
MARKS = (42 56 65 65 89)
↑ pointer_position = 3
(Pointer > 1) AND (48 < 56)
Copy 56 up. Move pointer down.
MARKS = (42 56 56 65 89)
↑ pointer_position = 2
(Pointer > 1) BUT (48 > 42)
Place 48 into element pointed to
MARKS = (42 48 56 65 89)

b. **More detailed example of an insertion.**

Fig. 12.6. Examples to illustrate the procedure of Fig. 12.5.

SEARCHING AN ARRAY.

22. If we wish to know whether or not a particular value is present within an array we may find out by conducting a **search**. Searching is a useful and common processing activity and there are many methods which can be used.

23. A simple method, known as the **linear search,** is described in the next few paragraphs. There are more advanced methods of searching but they will be discussed in later chapters.

24. If the data in the array has already been sorted into order then the search can usually be performed faster than if the data had been left unsorted. This highlights another advantage of sorting data. That is, in addition to helping in the presentation of the data, sorting may also make processing faster and possibly simpler too.

25. Suppose that we require a function which searches through an array of examination candidate numbers to see if a particular candidates number is in the array. The function will return the boolean value **true** if the candidates number is found, otherwise it will retain the value **false.**

26. The **linear search** is conducted by examining each array element in turn, from first to last, until the required value is found. Clearly, if the value has not been found by the time the last element has been examined the search has failed. If the array has been sorted into order the failure may be detected even sooner. Figures 12.7 and 12.8 give the details.

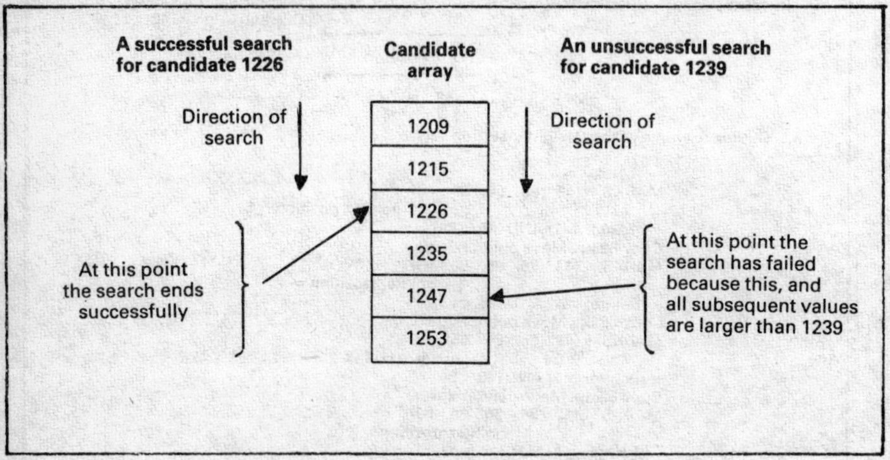

Fig. 12.7. Searching a sorted array.

```
function    found(number_of_elements, search_value: integer,
                  search_array        : array [1 . . 100] of integer): boolean
            (* This function performs a linear search of the search array
               to find the search value. If it finds the search value it
               returns true otherwise it returns false.
            *)
            variables
                      subscript : integer
            Begin
                 (* Initialise values *)
                 subscript : = 0
                 found : = false
                 (* search elements in turn  *)
                 repeat
                      subscript : = subscript + 1
                      if
                        search_array(subscript) = search_value
                      then
                        found : = true
                      endif
                 until  found
                 OR
                   (subscript = number_of_elements)
                 OR
                   (search_array(subscript) > search_value)
end
```

Fig. 12.8. A function for performing a linear search of an array.

STRINGS.

27. We now turn our attention to data structures which are used for text handling and related problems. As you may remember from 10.16, a sequence of characters handled as a single unit of data is called a **string.** For example, "ABC –, 3gh" and "THE CAT SAT ON THE MAT" are **literal strings.**

28. In the programming language BASIC all string identifiers have the "$" sign as a suffix. In most other languages in which strings are used they are present in the form of one dimensional arrays of characters. In paragraphs 29 to 35 assume that the variables A, B, C, V and F have been declared to be strings by a declaration such as

A, B, C, V, F : **string**

29. a. When strings are joined together they are said to be **concatenated** (10.39). So, if A = "ALEX" and B = "JAMES" the assignment

C : = A & B

concatenates A and B to form C where

C = "ALEXJAMES"

b. **Part of a string** is called a **substring** eg. A = "ALEX" and B = "JAMES" are substrings of C = "ALEXJAMES".

30. In the following paragraphs we are primarily concerned with strings as *data structures* comprised of substrings which can be operated upon individually whereas in chapter 10 we merely considered strings as simple indivisible data items.

STRING HANDLING.

31. String handling notation.

a. We number each character position in the string in sequence just like the elements in a one-dimensional array.

b. We refer to each substring by stating its *first* and *last* character position separated by a ":". The following pseudocode and table (fig. 12.9) illustrate the method.

		The appearance of the string after each stop.																						
		Character position																						
Begin		1	2	3	4	5	6	7	8	9	10	11	12	13	14	15	16	17	18	19	20	21	22	23
A	: = "THE CAT SAT ON THE MAT.".	T	H	E		C	A	T		S	A	T		O	N		T	H	E		M	A	T	.
A(6:7)	: = "OW"	T	H	E		C	O	W		S	A	T		O	N		T	H	E		M	A	T	.
A(20:20)	: = "H"	T	H	E		C	O	W		S	A	T		O	N		T	H	E		H	A	T	.
A(9:14)	: = "ATE UP"	T	H	E		C	O	W		A	T	E		U	P		T	H	E		H	A	T	.
end																								

Fig. 12.9. Basic string handling operations

32. Fixed and Variable length strings. We return here to the concept of fixed and variable length storage which was introduced in 7.10 and 7.11.

a. *Fixed length strings* have a fixed number of character places available for data storage.

b. *Variable length strings* provide the data with just the number of spaces it needs.

The significance of these differences is illustrated by the following examples.

NB. These examples are important for two reasons:

i. The manipulation of fixed and variable length data is often needed in programming problems.

ii. They illustrate the ways in which fixed and variable length data is manipulated in main storage. The character positions in strings F and V in these examples may be compared with location addresses in main storage where each location is able to store one character.

33. Example 1.

a. This diagram shows five fixed length strings concatenated into a single string called F. Each string is 5 characters long.

Details of F.

Character Position	1	2	3	4	5	6	7	8	9	10	11	12	13	14	15	16	17	18	19	20	21	22	23	24	25
Contents	J	A	M	E	S	K	A	T	Y		A	N	N			A	L	E	X		J	O			
Comment	1st String					2nd String					3rd String					4th String					5th String				

b. This diagram shows five variable length strings concatenated into a single string called V. The same data is used but the end of each string is indicated by a "*". Note the saving in storage space.

Details of V.

Character Position	1	2	3	4	5	6	7	8	9	10	11	12	13	14	15	16	17	18	19	20	21	22	23	24	25
Contents	J	A	M	E	S	*	K	A	T	Y	*	A	N	N	*	A	L	E	X	*	J	O	*		
Comment	1st String						2nd String					3rd String				4th String					5th String			Saved Storage	

34. Handling fixed length strings. This example shows how the separate sub strings in F can be printed in turn. (See Fig. 12.10).

a.

```
(* This is part of a procedure to output substrings of length 5 from a string
   F. The IN parameter "number_of_substrings" is of type integer, as is the
   local variable "substring_number".
*)
Begin
    for substring_number : = 1 to number_of_substrings
        output(F(5 * substring_number – 4 : 5 * substring_number))
    endfor
end
```

b. Here are the successive values which occur during execution when F is as in 12.33a and "number_of_substrings" has the value 5.

substring_number	5 * substring_number – 4	5 * substring_number	value output
1	1	5	JAMES
2	6	10	KATY
3	11	15	ANN
4	16	20	ALEX
5	21	25	JO
6			

Note : Fixed substring length allows us to claculate the position of each substring.

Fig. 12.10. The output of a fixed length substrings.

35. Handling variable length strings is more difficult than handling fixed length strings but does have the important advantage of saving space. This example shows how the **first** substring in V can be printed and the example in 12.36 will show how to handle all V. Here we assume we have no prior knowledge of the string's length and so we take out each character in turn until we meet the terminator '*'.

```
(* These few lines of pseudocode output the first substring of V. The local
   variable "position" is of type integer.
*)
Begin
      position : = 1
      while V(position : position) <> "*"
            output(   V(position : position) )
            position : = position + 1
      endwhile
end
```

Note i. Further strings may be output in a similar fashion.

ii. An alternative storage strategy would be to have an integer at the start of each substring which indicated its length. eg.

V = "05JAMES04KATY03ANN04ALEX02JO"

Fig. 12.11. Output from a variable length string.

36. A simple example of an access table is an array which holds details of the locations of data values. We will consider such a case now and leave more complicated examples for later discussion. An access table called A is shown in fig. 12.12. It provides a means of accessing the strings held in V of paragraph 12.33b.

Row Number [Corresponds to substring i]	Position of 1st character in string i	Position of Last character in string i
1	A(1, 1) = 1	A(1, 2) = 5
2	A(2, 1) = 7	A(2, 2) = 10
3	A(3, 1) = 12	A(3, 2) = 14
4	A(4, 1) = 16	A(4, 2) = 19
5	A(5, 1) = 21	A(5, 2) = 22

Fig. 12.12. Details of access table A.

```
(* This is part of a procedure to output the substrings of V by using the access
   table "A". The local variable "i" is of type integer: see fig. 12.12. Other
   variables are as defined previously.
*)
   Begin
      for i : = 1 to number_of_substrings
             output(V(A(i,1) : A(i,2)))
      endfor
   end
   NB. For Fig. 12.12 number_of_substrings has value 5.
```

Fig. 12.13. Part of a procedure using an accessible.

RECORDS.

37. Records will be easy to understand if we compare them with arrays. Records are like one dimensional arrays in that they are comprised of a series of related data items. Records differ from arrays in that, whereas all the elements in an array have the same Type, the successive data items in a record may differ in type. The following simple example should clarify these ideas.

38. Example. Suppose we wish to organise the following three items of data, relating to an individual examination candidate, into a single data structure:

candidate_number : **integer**
candidate_name : **string**
average-mark : **real**

39. Although the three data items belong together they cannot be stored in an array because they are of different types. The answer is to store them in a record. A suitable record declaration could take the form:

```
candidate : = record
                  candidate_number : integer
                  candidate_name : string
                  average_mark : real
              endrecord
```

40. In the example just given a record called "candidate" was declared. The three elements of the record each had their own identifiers, unlike array elements which are merely referred to by subscripts. The elements of a record are called **fields.**

41. Reference to the individual fields of a record may be made as shown in the following example.

42. Example. Suppose we wish to create a record for candidate 1209, named Smith who gained an average mark of 55.2. The assignments of these values to the three fields of the record called candidate may be performed in two ways:

a. Using the **"dot"** notation. Consider these lines of pseudocode:

```
Begin
    candidate.candidate_number : = 1209
    candidate.candidate_name : = "Smith"
    candidate.average_mark : = 55.2
end
```

Each record field is identified by the record name followed by a "dot" followed by the field name. Clearly this notation is rather clumsy when referencing several fields from the same record. In such cases the following method is preferable.

b. The **"with"** notation. The following pseudocode is equivalent to that given in 'a'.

```
Begin
    with  candidate
          candidate_number : = 1209
          candidate_name : = "Smith"
          average_mark : = 55.2
    endwith
end
```

43. Not all high level languages provide facilities for creating records. Pascal, COBOL, Modula and Ada do but few versions of BASIC have such facilities.

ARRAYS OF RECORDS (TABLES).

44. Suppose we wish to store the following table of data for a set of examination candidates.

CANDIDATE NUMBER	CANDIDATE NAME	AVERAGE MARK
1209	Smith	55.2
1215	Brown	86.4
1226	Jones	49.2
1235	Robinson	66.0
1247	Finlay	59.8
1253	Johnson	71.3

45. This data could be stored in an array of records declared in the following manner:

```
variables
                    candidate : array [1 . . 6] of record
                                                    number : integer
                                                    name : string
                                                    av_mark : real
                                              endrecord
```

46. Assuming that the data had already been assigned to records in the array, and that "i" had been declared as an integer, the data could be output using the following pseudocode:

```
Begin
    for i : =1 to 6
        with candidate(i)
              output(number, name, av_mark)
        endwith
    endfor
end
```

LISTS.

47. Lists provide a flexible way of handling data items in order. Changes to the order can be achieved with minimal data movement and little loss of storage space.

48. Example. The sentence 'Alex does not like cake' is written below as a list.

We regard each word in our sentence as a data-item or **datum** which is *linked* to the next datum by a **pointer.** Datum plus pointer make one **element** of the list. The last pointer in the list is a terminator. This list may be stored in an array of records as shown in Fig. 12.14. Each row of the array is one element in the list. Two other pointers are useful. A **start pointer** saying where the first datum is and a **free storage pointer** saying where the next datum can go.

START POINTER: 1 → row 1

FREE STORAGE POINTER: 6 → row 6

Row Number	Datum	Pointer to Next Datum	Comment
1	"ALEX"	2	Next datum is in row 2
2	"DOES"	3	Next datum is in row 3
3	"NOT"	4	Next datum is in row 4
4	"LIKE"	5	Next datum is in row 5
5	"CAKE"	–1	Last Datum: –1 is a terminator
6		7	Empty
7		8	Empty

Note: –1 is used as a terminator in this example.

Fig. 12.14. A list stored in an array of records.

49. A data declaration for this list might take the form:

```
variables
        sentence : array [1 . . 7] of record
                                    datum : string
                                    next : integer
                            endrecord
```

50. Assuming that the start pointer ("start") and row value "row" have been declared as integers then the following pseudocode could be used to output the list elements in the correct order.

```
Begin
    (* Get first datum's row *)
    row : = start
    while   (* terminator not found *)
            row <> –1
            (* output next datum *)
            output(sentence(row).datum)
            (* get next row *)
            row : = sentence (row).next
    endwhile
end
```

51. Deletions. When elements are deleted from a list, the freed storage can be reused. In the example given here 'NOT' has been deleted so the list now reads 'ALEX DOES LIKE CAKE'.

START POINTER 1 → row 1

FREE STORAGE POINTER 3 → row 3

Row Number	Datum	Pointer to Next Datum	Comment
1	"ALEX"	2	
2	"DOES"	4	Pointer to deleted item changed to deleted pointer.
3		6	Deleted pointer replaced by free storage pointer
4	"LIKE"	5	
5	"CAKE"	–1	
6		7	
7		8	

The free storage pointer is replaced by the pointer to the deleted item.

52. Insertions. The free storage pointer is used for insertions. In this example the list is changed to 'ALEX DOES LIKE CREAM CAKE' by inserting 'CREAM'.

START POINTER 1 → row 1

FREE STORAGE POINTER 6 → row 6

Row Number	Datum	Pointer to Next Datum	Comment
1	"ALEX"	2	
2	"DOES"	4	
3	"CREAM"	5	Old pointer given to free storage.
4	"LIKE"	3	Old pointer given to new item. New pointer from free storage.
5	"CAKE"	–1	
6		7	
7		8	

53. The pseudocode of paragraph 50 can be used to output the lists of paragraphs 51 and 52. Extreme cases can be dealt with in these ways:–

a. An empty list can be indicated by a terminator (eg –1) in the start pointer.

b. A full list can be indicated by a terminator in the free storage pointer.

54. In the examples just given we have, strictly speaking, only been considering one method of **implementing** lists namely linked lists in the form of arrays of records. A more general notation for lists is one in which the data elements are written in sequence thus:

$< e_1, e_2, e_3, \ldots\ldots, e_n >$

55. As with all data types what characterises a list is not only the set of values it takes but the operations which may be performed upon it. One would normally expect to be able to perform these operations upon a list:

a. Find the position and value of the first element.

b. Insert an element.

c. Delete an element.

d. Find the next element (sometimes the previous element too).

e. Find a specific element.

f. Output the list elements in order.

h. Create an empty list.

TREES.

56. Trees are **hierarchical data structures** rather like the familiar family tree. They are constructed using a rule of precedence for the data items eg using alphabetic or numerical sequence. The **elements** of a tree are called **nodes** and each element consists of a datum and at least two pointers. In the example about to be given the examination marks used in 12.6 are entered into a tree so as to indicate their numerical order. Each element looks like this:–

LEFT POINTER	DATUM	RIGHT POINTER

57. Example. These numbers are placed into a tree: 56, 42, 89, 65 and 48.

a. 56 is the *first* datum placed into the tree its node is therefore called the **parent** or **root node.**

b. We add 42 to the tree next using the rule 'lower numbers to the left, higher numbers to the right'. The tree then looks like this:–

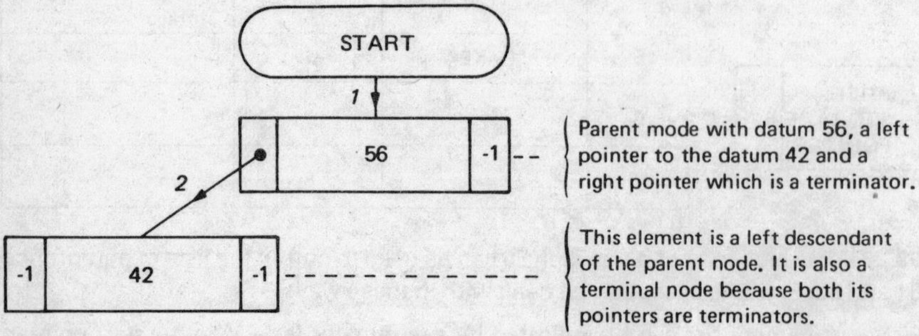

c. 89 is added next. It is larger than 56 so we add it to the right of the parent node thus:–

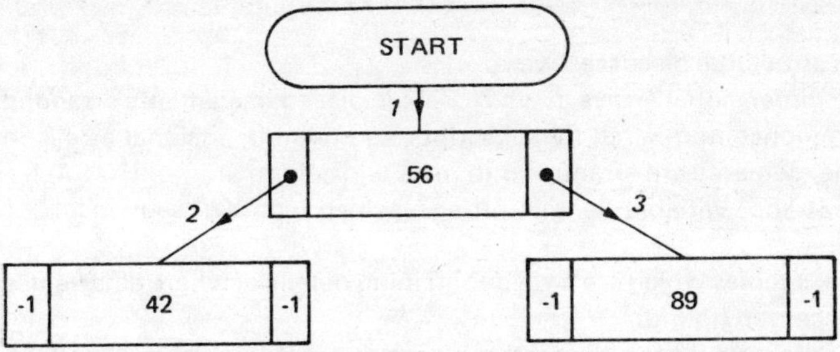

d. 65 is added next. It is larger than 56 so we go right at the parent node but left at 89 because it is smaller.

e. 48 is added next. We go left at 56 because it is smaller and right at 42 because it is larger. Our tree finally looks like this:–

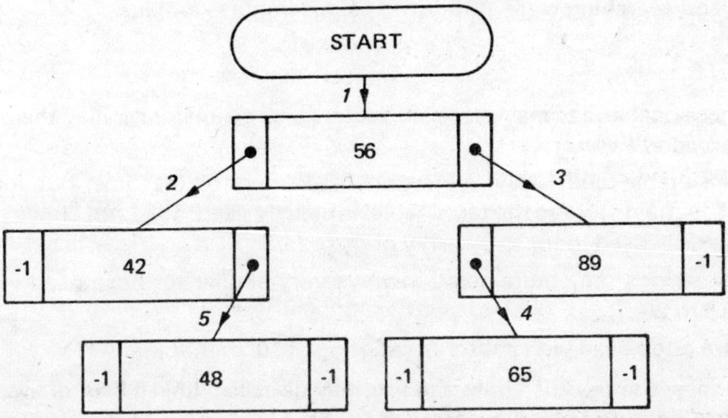

Note. i. The leftmost node contains the smallest number.

ii. The rightmost node contains the highest number.

58. The tree just given in the example could be placed in an array of records as shown below.

Left Pointer	Datum	Right Pointer
2	56	3
–1	42	5
4	89	–1
–1	65	–1
–1	48	–1

59. The procedures for inserting and deleting items from trees together with other methods for trees are left till chapter 31.

SUMMARY.

60. a. The data structures discussed were:

i. One dimensional **arrays** in which data is placed in **elements** arranged into a sequence numbered by **subscripts** and two dimensional arrays in which the elements are arranged into rows and columns.

ii. Fixed and variable length **strings** which contain sequences of characters.

iii. **Access tables** which are arrays containing details of where data values can be accessed (found).

iv. **Records** in which the elements are a series of **fields** which may each be of different type.

v. Arrays of records in which each element of the array is a record.

vi. **Lists** in which individual elements containing data and **pointers** are connected together by the use of the pointers.

vii. **Trees** in which data is organised in a hierarchical manner. Each **element** (node) has left and right pointers.

b. **Sorting** and **searching** were introduced using simple examples.

POINTS TO NOTE.

61. a. One dimensional arrays may be called **vectors** and main storage may therefore be regarded as a vector.

b. The terms 'table' and 'array' are synonymous most of the time, but for applications in main storage the term 'table' is usually used. The term "table" is also commonly used to mean an array of records.

c. Arrays of strings may be handled in ways very similar to those used in paragraphs 8 to 26.

d. Arrays are often used with subscripts starting at "0" rather than "1".

e. Pointers may also be called **links** and lists may be called **'linked lists'** or even **'threaded lists'** because of their appearance.

f. The **trees** introduced in this chapter had nodes with just *two* pointers and are called *binary trees.* More complicated trees will be dealt with later.

g. A data type or structure considered purely in terms of the sets of values which variables of the type can take and the set of operations which may be performed upon those variables *without* considering how it is implemented is called an **abstract data type** (A DT).

STUDENT SELF TESTING QUESTIONS

(Answers on page 687)

1. The array B shown below contains 6 characters. Give the order in which you would select elements in order to spell the word "MATRIX".

T R X
I A M

2. *Enter the letters of "MATRIX" Into a tree one at a time in the order they are spelt. Use the rule "earlier in the alphabet to the left".*

3. *Write the function "below–average" used in Fig. 12.1.*

4. *Write a procedure to reverse the order of elements in*

   a. *an array eg. [3, 6, 2, 5] becomes [5, 2, 6, 3]*

   b. *a string eg. "MATRIX" becomes "XIRTAM".*

5. *Describe a suitable data structure for a details of stock items numbered in the range 1 to 100. Each stock item may be held at each of 20 locations. The numbers of items held at each location needs to be recorded.*

QUESTIONS WITHOUT ANSWERS.

6. *The linked list shown in this chapter allows us to pass through the list in one direction only ie. given the location of an item we do not know its predecessor. Write a record declaration for a list so that from a single element we know both the location of its predecessor and its successor. How does this differ from a tree?*

7. *Write a function which determines the number of words in a string such as that shown in Fig. 12.9. State any assumptions that you make.*

13 Program Design

INTRODUCTION.

1. Today, there are many amateur programmers writing all kinds of programs. Just as the do-it-yourself enthusiast who builds a shed in the garden usually has only a rudimentary knowledge of building design, most amateur programmers have little knowledge of program design.

2. In this chapter we consider program design as it applies to the production of professional software. The chapter is only an introduction to program design because of the scope of this text. However, it must be stressed that although only a basic knowledge of program design is needed to write small programs of reasonable quality, a sound and detailed knowledge of program design is essential for the production of large scale software. Look at it this way. Would you let a do-it-yourself shed builder build a house for you?

THE IMPORTANCE OF GOOD PROGRAMMING METHODS.

3. Today, great reliance is placed upon computers for all kinds of applications, including banking, insurance, public and private administration, national defence, and so on. Computers are only machines and will slavishly follow the program instructions given them.

4. The costs of programming have risen because the shortages of skilled personnel, as required for programming, have pushed up labour costs, whereas the costs of hardware have fallen because of technical innovation and increased automation. It is a false economy to reduce programming standards in order to achieve greater programmer output, because of potentially damaging effects of errors, high correction and maintenance costs and difficulties experienced in transfering sub-standard programs from one computer to another.

5. The need for good quality programming is greater than ever, but there is also a need to reduce programming costs. Experience has shown that it pays to put greater effort into program **design** rather than into trying to get a badly designed program to work. The longer an error goes undetected the more costly it is to correct and so the early stages of program design are **very** important.

PROGRAM DESIGN AIMS.

6. These are summarised as follows:–

a. **Reliability**. ie. the program can be depended upon always to do what it is supposed to do.

b. **Maintainability**. ie. the program will be easy to change or modify when the need arises.

c. **Portability**. ie. the program will be transferable to a different computer with a minimum of modification.

d. **Readability.** ie. the program will be easy for a programmer to read and understand (this can aid a, b and c).

e. **Performance.** ie. the program causes the tasks to be done quickly and efficiently.

f. **Storage saving.** ie. the program is not allowed to be unnecessarily long.

Some of these aims are in conflict with others eg. e and f.

PROGRAM SPECIFICATION AND CORRECTNESS.

7. A programmer is usually given a specification of *what* the proposed program is required to do. The programmer must then design and implement the program so that it meets the specification. A program which meets its specification is said to be **"correct"**.

8. There are some serious complications to this basic picture of design and implementation. First, the specification could be wrong in that it might not specify what was really required. This could lead to a program being "correct" but unsuitable! Secondly, even if the specification is right it may be very difficult to ensure that the program is correct. It is in this respect that good programming methods can be of great value.

9. The issues of how to provide good program specifications will be dealt with in later chapters. In this chapter we concentrate on program design and implementation with the emphasis on the design methods throughout.

10. What the general points made so far boil down to is this. We need to produce **correct** programs from specifications which truly express the requirements. The programs need to be reliable, maintainable, portable, readable and efficient. The programs must also be produced in reasonable time and without undue expense.

METHODS FOR PROGRAM DEVELOPMENT.

11. There are a number of methods for designing and implementing programs. Broadly speaking, the methods are influenced both by the size of the programming problem and by the programming languages available for its solution.

12. We will start by considering the stages in programming which apply to program development for typical programs in most computer languages. Then we will look at how these stages may differ if more advanced methods are used.

STAGES IN PROGRAMMING.

13. In the process of producing the necessary instructions making up a program, the following stages can be recognised:-

a. Understanding the problem.

b. Planning the method of solution.

c. Developing the method using suitable aids eg. pseudocode.

d. Writing the instructions in a programming language.

e. Transcribing the instructions into "machine-sensible" form.

f. Testing the program.

g. Documenting all the work involved in producing the program. This documentation will be developed stage by stage.

14. If during testing the program an error is discovered then *it is important to go back to earlier stages* in order to correct the error. If the error comes from misunderstanding the problem it will probably be better to start again from the beginning. An outline of what happens at each programming stage now follows.

15. Understanding the problem. The programmer needs to know exactly what the program is required to do and normally works from a **program specification**. This program specification is normally part of a **"System Specification"** which defines the whole system, of which the program may be only a small part. For example, the program might be just one of a suite of programs for use in a particular application.

16. Broadly speaking, the program specification will define the inputs, processing and outputs required. A good specification will normally specify *what* processing is needed by giving the exact relationship between outputs and the inputs from which they are derived rather than prescribing *how* the program should be written.

17. Planning the method of solution. Depending upon the extent of the task, the program preparation may be shared amongst many programmers. Such cooperation requires an overall plan. Large programs may require each programmer to write a separate part of the program. These separate parts are often called modules or segments. The modules may be prepared and tested separately, then linked together to be tested as a whole, a process known as **integration.**

18. Developing the method by using suitable aids such as pseudocode. Modern approaches to programming recognise the fact that complicated problems can be solved most easily if they are broken down into simpler more manageable tasks in a step by step fashion. At each step the problem is broken down further and consideration of details is put off as long as possible. This general approach is known as **Top Down Programming by Stepwise Refinement.** (More details later).

19. Writing the instructions in a programming language. This may be regarded as the last step in Stepwise Refinement. The instructions written in pseudocode are written in a programming language. There are different types of programming "languages" and details will be given in later chapters. Programs are first written on special-forms called "Coding Sheets."

20. Transcribing instructions into "machine-sensible" form. In order to input the program to the computer the program instructions on the Coding Sheets must either be copied onto an input medium eg. punched cards or typed directly into the computer eg. via a VDU Keyboard.

21. Testing the program. Once written a program has to be subjected to various tests to check that it has been written out and transcribed correctly, and does what it is supposed to do ie. is correct. These tests invariably reveal errors which have to be corrected. This can be quite a lengthy, and expensive process. Careful and thorough design in the early stages of programming will help to minimise these errors. The later an error is discovered the more expensive and troublesome it will be to eliminate.

22. Documentation. It is very important that the work of the programmer in producing a finished program is fully documented. This documentation will include a statement of the problem (System Specification), pseudocode, coding sheets, test data and results, technical details, details and instruction for the user etc. *Producing these documents should be done as part of each stage in programming and not as an afterthought.* If this is done the documentation will aid the programmer in programming and good documentation will aid the maintenance of a program during its lifetime. Some programs have very long lives. For example, some programs written during the 1960's are still in use today, although they may have been subjected to *regular maintenance* eg. modification or bringing up to date.

COMPUTER STAFF.

23. Is is easier to see programming in context if at this stage we give some consideration to the work of the staff involved. An outline of the work is given in the following paragraphs. Greater detail will be given in a later chapter.

24. Systems Analyst. The main jobs of the analyst are:-

a. To examine the feasibility of potential computer applications.

b. Analysis of existing systems with a view to their computerisation.

c. Design of computer-based systems, their implementation, and review.

25. It is very likely that systems analysts would work in project teams with a senior analyst in charge.

26. Programmers. Following the design process the job of programming begins. The programmer:-

a. Encodes the procedures detailed by the analyst in a language suitable for the specified computer.

b. Will liaise very closely with the analyst and the user to ensure logical correctness of programs.

27. Programmers also frequently work in project teams.

CONCEPTS WHICH LIE BEHIND PROGRAM DESIGN.

28. There are a number of concepts which have a relevance to the general problems of program design which the reader should be aware of. Three particular concepts are:

a. Computability.

b. Complexity.

c. Correctness.

The last was introduced in paragraph 7.

29. Computability. Throughout this text we are concerned with what tasks computers can do and how they do them. Here, we stop briefly to face the fact that there are many problem which computers cannot solve, not just for practical reasons but because the task can be proven to be theoretically impossible. A task may be said to be **computable** if it can in principle be performed by a machine.

30. Strange though it may at first seem most tasks are not computable. It is relatively easy for example, to discover non-computable mathematical functions. There are also some celebrated unsolvable problems in the theory of computability. One rather interesting problem in this category is **"The halting problem"**. Put simply, there is no algorithm which can take an arbitrary program and its input and decide whether the program's execution will stop if the program is given that input. Such an algorithm would have great practical value but cannot exist. Further discussion is beyond the scope of this book.

31. Complexity. Even when a task is computable, and is therefore possible to express as an algorithm, it may still not be amenable to solution because of its complexity. In other words although a task may be computable and therefore theoretically possible it may not be feasible.

32. Complexity is measured in terms of the quantity of resources used. The main resources considered are time and storage.

33. The general idea is easier to understand by considering a simple example. Suppose that we wish to perform a processing operation on a set of "n" numbers. For a simple task, such as finding the total, the complexity in terms of storage requirements will not be affected by n because we need only store the cumulative total. The complexity, in terms of time taken, will be in direct proportion to n. For some other task, sorting say, not only will all the n values require storing but the time taken for methods such as the straight insertion sort is proportional to n^2.

34. Clearly, for many tasks there may be alternative algorithms and for practical reasons a knowledge of their complexity will help us make the best choice. Also, we may be interested in average cases and worst cases.

35. Correctness. As was mentioned in paragraph 7, a program is correct if it meets its specification. Ideally, when we complete the implementation of any program we want to be able to say for certain that the program is correct. Unfortunately this is seldom possible. To **prove** that a program is correct it is necessary to show for certain that for all permissible input to the program the program will produce the required results. Such proofs require methods comparable to those for proving theorems in Mathematics and can become very complicated even for simple programs.

36. In practice, rather than attempt a proof, we **test** the program using a set of carefully selected **"test data"**.

37. Testing may be conducted by executing the program on the computer or by simulating its execution by a manual pencil and paper exercise called a **"dry run"**. There are two basic types of testing:

a. **Functional testing** (also called **black box testing**). This form of testing is based upon typical, extreme and invalid data values which are representative of those covered by the specification.

b. **Logical testing** (also called **white box testing**). This form of testing is based upon examining the internal structure of the program and selecting data which gives rise to the alternative cases of control flow eg. both paths through an If-else.

38. Functional testing is often used at the final stage of programming as a basis for accepting or rejecting the program. Functional testing is not adequate by itself and logical testing by the programmer during program development tends to be far more beneficial.

39. Debugging. A program fault which causes a program to fail during testing, or after it has been commissioned is called a **bug.** The process of finding and getting rid of bugs is called **debugging.**

40. The presence of bugs in a program is often symptomatic of poor workmanship on the part of the persons who produced the specification or who wrote the program. When a bug is discovered it is important that the reasons for its occurence are investigated fully and that the program's design and implementation are reworked where necessary. Quick and easy alterations to the program to remove bug, often called **"fixes"** or **"patches"**, invariably produce "new bugs for old".

PROGRAMMING METHOD.

41. Armed with the additional background knowledge provided by the preceding paragraphs we now return to the ideas introduced in paragraph 18.

42. Many of the terms used to describe programming method have been so badly overused that they have become almost meaningless slogans. Even so, these "popular" terms deserve some explanation and the next few paragraphs will provide such explanations where appropriate.

43. "Top Down" and "Bottom Up" methods. It is clear that many problems which occur in programming, and system design, are too large to be solved all at once. The answer is to try to solve such problems in stages, but where should one begin? If the problem is different from anything met before it may be necessary to set about solving a part of the problem which is understood, and then, as other parts of the problem become clearer, solving them until the whole problem is solved. Such an approach in which the whole solution is built up by joining together the completed parts is called a "bottom up" approach.

44. There is one severe danger inherent in the bottom-up approach: the various parts may not fit together properly and, in some cases, considerable effort may be necessary to overcome this problem. "Top down" methods attempt to avoid such problems by starting with the general concept of what is required, breaking the whole into component parts, and then tackling the component parts in the same manner. The interrelationships between components are decided upon before the components are created so that the final integration of the parts into the whole should be more straightforward. A number of methods in use today may be described as top down.

45. Decomposition is the term used to describe the process of breaking down a program into component parts. (When applied to rotten programs it seems even more appropriate!) Since there is almost invariably a choice over what the components should be, both for top down methods and for bottom up methods, it is possible to examine the completed program and classify it as a good decomposition or a bad one.

46. Most standard methods of decomposition are **control oriented,** that is to say, they concentrate on working out the flow of control within the program. Methods based upon flowcharts and pseudocode are almost invariably control oriented. The alternative to **control-oriented** programming is **object oriented** programming in which attention is directed towards identifying objects such as data structures and the operations performed upon them. A detailed discussion of object oriented programming is beyond the scope of this book.

47. The simplest forms of program decompositions produced by top down design methods are based upon standard control structures. The ideas are illustrated by the following example.

48. Example. A program is required which will enable the user to check whether a particular number is a factor of several other numbers (ie. to check whether the particular number divides an exact number of times into the other numbers). The number to be checked is to be keyed in first. Then a series of numbers are to be keyed in and checked in turn. Zero is to be used as a sentinel.

49. These possible stages in top down development of this program are shown in fig. 13.1. Note the following points:

a. In stage 1 (fig. 13.1a) the data items to be processed have been identified and declared, and the program has been decomposed into a *sequence* of two actions given in the comments between **Begin** and **end.**

```
Program    factor_checker
           (* See paragraph 13.48 for details. *)
variables
           possible_factor,
           number_for checking : integer
Begin
     (* get a value for the possible factor *)
     (* get numbers for checking and check the possible factor on each *)
end
```

a. Stage 1

```
Program     factor_checker
            (* See paragraph 13.49 for details *)
variables
            possible_factor,
            number_for_checking : integer
Begin
    (* get a value for the possible factor *)
       output("Key in the number to be checked as a factor")
       input(possible_factor)
    (* get numbers for checking and check the possible factor on each *)
       output("Key in a number to be checked (Key in 0 to stop)")
       input(number_for_checking)
       while(* number keyed in is not zero *)
           (* check the number and get the next number *)
       endwhile
end
```

b. Stage 2

```
Program     factor_checker
            (* See paragraph 13.49 for details *)
Begin
    (* get a value for the possible factor *)
       output("Key in the number to be checked as a factor")
       input(possible_factor)
    (* get numbers for checking and check the possible factor on each *)
       output("Key in a number to be checked (Key in 0 to stop)")
       input(number_for_checking)
       while(* number keyed in is not zero *)
              number_for_checking <> 0
              if
                   (* possible factor divides exactly into number entered *)
                   number_for_checking mod possible_factor = 0
              then
                   output(possible_factor,"is a factor of", number_for_checking)
              else
                   output(possible_factor,"is not a factor of", number_for_checking)
              endif
              output("Key in number to be checked (Key in 0 to stop) ")
              input(number_for_checking)
       endwhile
end
```

c. Stage 3

Fig. 13.1. Stages in a top-down development of a simple program.

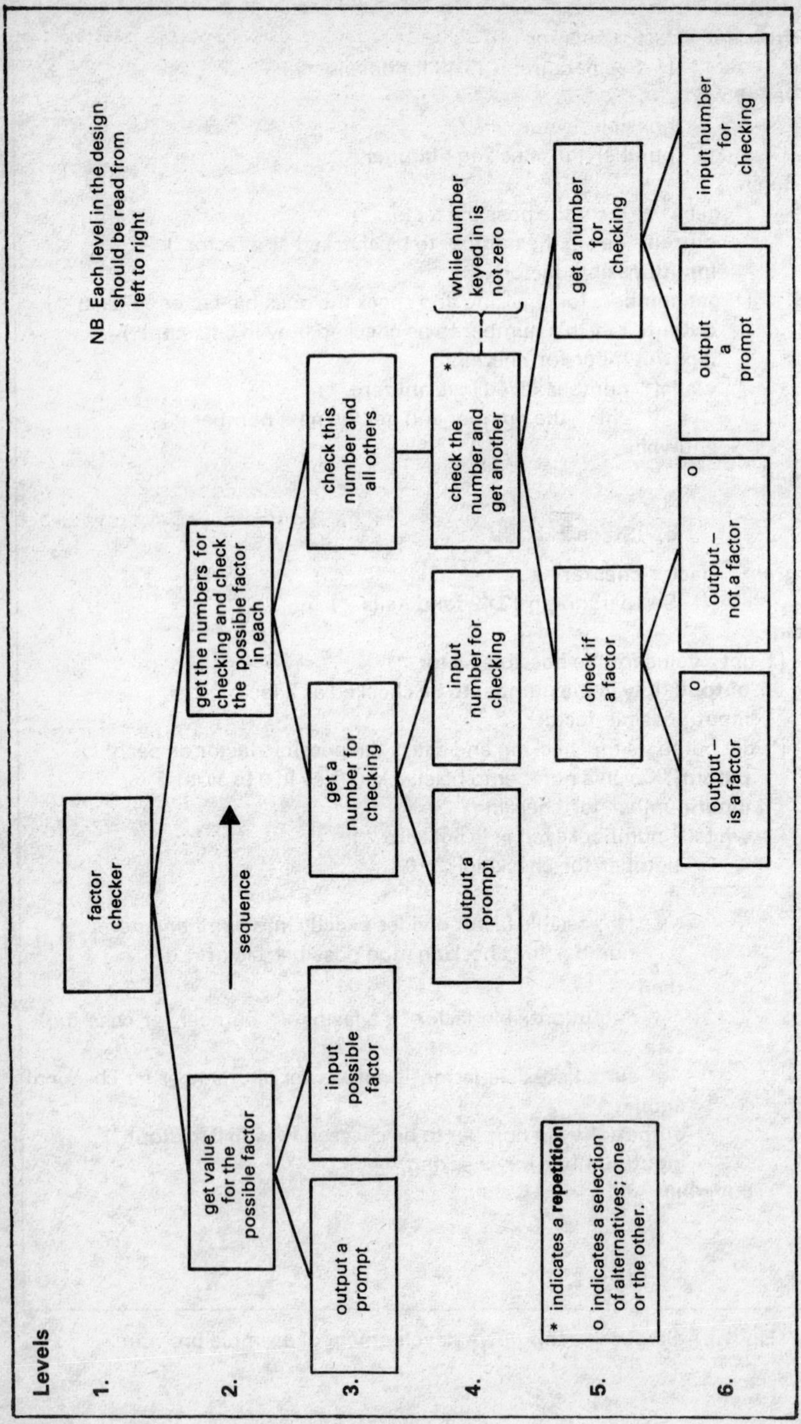

Fig. 13.2. A Structure diagram.

b. In stage 2 (fig. 13.1b) the sequence of actions has been decomposed further by adding details to the first action and splitting the second action into a *sequence* comprised of an input followed by a loop.

c. In stage 3 (fig. 13.1c) the final level of detail has been added.

Notice how this approach allows the whole problem to be solved in a series of manageable steps.

50. The example just given was of a kind of decomposition known as **hierarchical** decomposition. Hierarchical decompositions may be represented by **structure diagrams.**

51. An example of a structure diagram is given in fig. 13.2 which corresponds to the program in fig. 13.1.

52. Stepwise refinement is a top down design method which takes the idea of hierarchical decomposition and extends it. It is often used in order to arrive at a **functional decomposition** of the program. The objective of functional decomposition is a program in which the program components are functions, which themselves may be comprised of other functions, and so on, right down to the lowest level of the design.

53. These "functions" are required to have certain properties. They should:

a. Perform well defined operations on well defined data.

b. Have internal structures which are independent of the program or function which contains them.

When used correctly, the functions and procedures of the types first introduced in 11.63 have these required properties.

54. The method of stepwise refinement takes the design development in steps in which each step is broadly comparable to the *levels* in fig. 13.2. It differs from hierarchical decomposition in that each step involves a complete definitions both of the data and of *what* the functions do at that level.

```
Program     Rectangle
            (* See paragraph 13.57 for details of the specification *)
variables
            side_one,
            side_two,
            area : real
procedure   get_two_valid_sides(OUT first_side,
                                    second_side : real)
            (* This procedure obtains positive values for the two sides from
               the user of the program.
            *)
            Begin
                (* code will be written at next step in refinement *)
            end
procedure   put_sides_into_order( IN-OUT first_side,
                                    second_side: real)
            (* This procedure checks the values of the two sides and swaps
               them around if necessary to ensure that the larger value is
               first. Equal values are not altered.
            *)
            Begin
                (* code will be written at next step in refinement *)
            end
function    rectangular_area(first_side:real,second_side:real):real
            (* See fig. 11.11 *)
            Begin
                (* code will be written at next step in refinement *)
            end
procedure   output_results( IN first_side,
                               second_side,
                               area       : real)
            (* This procedure outputs the results
            *)
            Begin
                (* code will be written at next step in refinement *)
            end
Begin
      call get_two_valid_sides(side_one,side_two)
      call put_sides_into_order(side_one,side_two)
      area := rectangular_area(side_one,side_two)
      call output_results(side_one,side_two,area)
end
```

Fig. 13.3. First step in the refinement of a program.

55. The careful definition of functions at each step allows the program to be tested in steps which makes testing better and simpler.

56. The merits of the method becomes more obvious when writing medium to large sized programs but the following example should give the basic ideas.

57. Example. A program is required which takes in values corresponding to the lengths of two sides of a rectangle. It must put the values into order with the larger value called "the length" and the other "the breadth". It must calculate the area and then output the result. For example if the values input are 3.0 and 5.0 the output should be:

"The length 5.0 multiplied by breadth 3.0 gives an area of 15.0"

NB. Some aspects of this problem have already been considered in fig. 11.11.

58. Step 1 involves specifying the top level functions and procedures in the program and the top level control structures of the program. (See fig. 13.3) In this case the main structure of the program is a simple sequence of procedures and functions. The combination of procedures and functions at the higher levels of the program design using standard control structures is called **"program level structure".** In contrast with this, the combination of basic operations at the lowest level of design using standard control structures is called **"code level structure".**

59. Even at this first step the program can be transcribed into a programming language and tested for correct syntax. Some languages, such as Pascal, can act as their own pseudocode thus making testing even easier.

60. Testing at lower levels is achieved by using "dummy" procedures and functions, sometimes called **"stubs".**

61. Step 2 involves writing and testing the code for each of the functions and procedures defined in step 1. This may require the definition of functions at a lower level, in which case a further step in refinement will be necessary.

62. At this second step we may first write the "output_results" procedure. The procedure can be tested by creating dummy procedures. For example, the values 5.0 and 3.0 may be *assigned* to first_side and second_side respectively in the procedure "put_side_in_order" and the value 15.0 may be *assigned* to "rectangular_area".

63. Having established that the output results procedure is correct we might then write and test the "get_two_valid_sides" procedure.

64. As each procedure or function is written new local variables procedures and functions may be created. For example, within the procedure "put_sides_into_order" we might have the following:

```
variables
            swap_value : real
Begin
    if
            second_side > first_side
    then
            (* swap the values around *)
            swap_value := first_side
            first_side := second_side
            second_side := swap_value
    endif
end
```

NB. "Swap_value" is a variable local to this procedure.

65. Functions and procedures must be used with care when attempting to produce a good functional decomposition. We now turn to some basic principles concerning their use.

USING SUBPROGRAMS.

66. Most programming languages have restrictions upon the ways functions, procedures, their arguments and their parameters may be used. Some restrictions may prevent the programmer from doing what is ideal and may also permit the programmer to indulge in bad practices. Either way, a greater burden of responsibility is placed upon the programmer.

67. Here is an outline guide to the main points to bear in mind:

a. Constants should always be declared in the main heading of the program rather than be hidden within subprograms. Inclusion in subprograms may lead to inconsistencies between different values for the same constant.

b. Variables should only be passed between a calling program and the called subprogram by means of parameters or arguments. Neglect of this principle makes it harder to keep the program components independent of one another which in turn complicates understanding the program, testing it or modifying it.

c. Use IN, OUT and IN-OUT parameters in the appropriate way. In particular do not allow a procedure to change an IN parameter, or a function to change its arguments. Neglect of this principle leads to confusion and errors. For example, we would not want a function which found the square root of "x" to change the value of x. A function which does changes its argument or data external to it is said to have "side effects".

68. Recursive Functions are functions which are defined with reference to themselves. When recursive functions are executed they call themselves. These ideas are best understood by means of an example.

69. Suppose we wish to have a function which generates powers of 2 and that the " ↑ " operator is not available. eg. given the argument 3 we want to obtain 2^3. In this particular case we could implement a solution, without the need for recursion, by calculating $y = 2^n$ in the the following way:
NB. Assume that n is a non-negative integer and that "y" and "i" are declared as integers.

```
Begin
    y := 1
    i := 0
    while     i < n
              y := y * 2
              i := i + 1
    endwhile
end
```

However, this is rather removed from the definition of what the function does.

70. A recursive definition of the function could take this form:

NB. Assume that the function is not used if n is negative.

```
function    two_to_power( n: integer) : integer
            (* finds the value of two to the power n *)
            Begin
                if          n = 0
                then
                            two_to_power := 1
                else
                            two_to_power := 2 * two_to_power(n – 1)
                endif
            end
```

71. Recursive functions and the use of recursive definitions in general, is of considerable importance in Computer Science but further discussion is inappropriate in a text at this level.

PARAMETER PASSING MECHANISMS.

72. There are a number of methods by which parameters may be passed from the calling program to the called subprogram and back again. The principal methods are:

a. **call by value**

b. **call by address** (also known as "call by reference" and "call by location"

c. **call by result**

d. **call by value-result**

e. **call by name.**

73. Call by value is an appropriate way to handle "IN" parameters or function arguments. When the subprogram is called the actual values of the parameter are placed in the memory locations associated with the formal parameters of the called subprogram (see fig. 13.4a.)

74. Call by address is an appropriate way to handle "IN-OUT" parameters. When the procedure is called the address of the memory locations of the actual parameter is passed to the called procedure so that it can access and alter the actual parameter. In call by address both the calling program and the called procedure access the same data whereas in the case of call by value the calling program has no access to the formal parameter data. (See fig. 13.4b).

75. Call by result is an appropriate way to hand "OUT" parameters. When the procedure is called the formal parameter is not initialised. At the end of procedure execution the value is copied back in a similar manner to that used to pass values in by call by value.

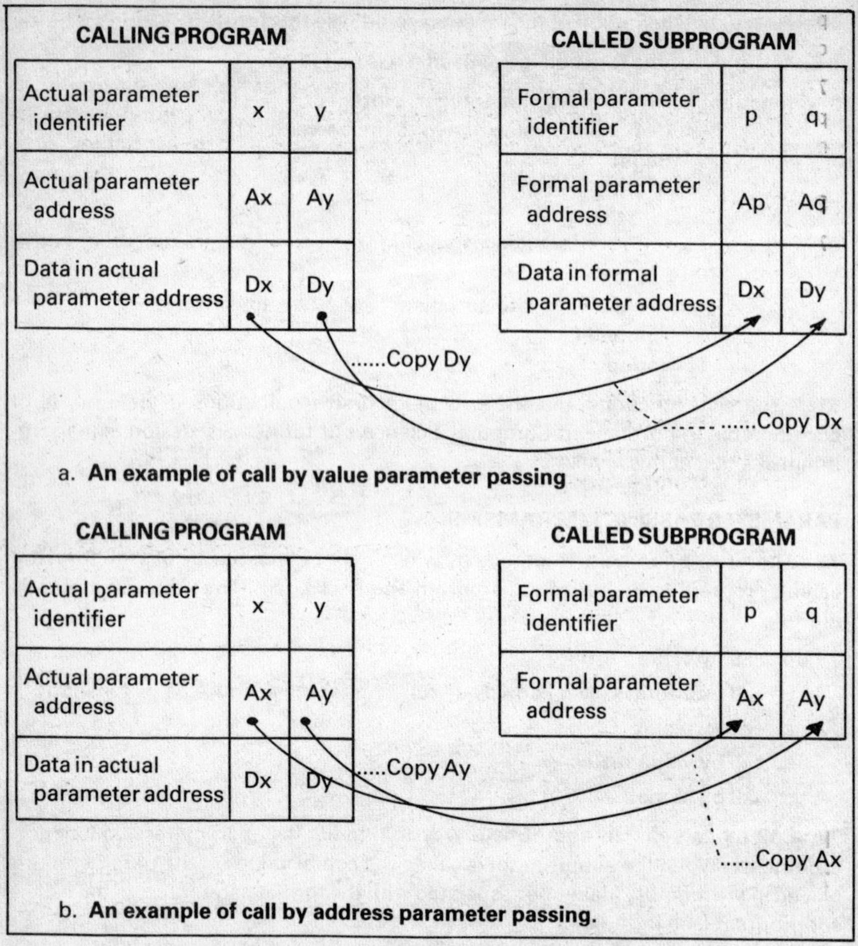

Fig. 13.4. Parameter passing mechanisms.

75. Call by value-result is an alternative way of providing IN-OUT parameter passing. The actual value is passed in as for call by value and is passed back as in call by result. There is a slightly more complicated form of call by value-result in which actual parameters are passed in and out by call by address but the called program uses local values which are copied from the formal parameters after entry and copied back again before return.

76. Call by name is a rare method of parameter passing in which the *effect* of the call is as if the actual parameters textually replace the formal parameter. Thus, for example, if the actual parameter were "z" and an expression such as "x + y", and the corresponding formal parameters were "a" and "b", then the expression a := 2 * b in the called subprogram would effectively be z := 2 * (x + y). The parameter passing mechanism is implemented by a special type of function rather oddly called a **"thunk"**! Further discussion is not merited.

77. These variations in parameter passing mechanisms affect the behaviour of the programs and so the programmer needs to be aware of the parameter passing mechanism being used when using a particular language implementation.

SUMMARY.

78. a. Good program design is essential for the economic production of correct programs.

b. Programming aims include:
   i. Reliability.
   ii. Maintainability.
   iii. Portability.
   iv. Readability.
   v. Performance.
   vi. Storage saving.

c. Programming takes place in stages.

d. Computability, complexity and correctness are concepts which lie behind program design.

e. Modern program design methods were introduced.

f. Functional decomposition and stepwise refinement were discussed.

g. The use of subprograms was discussed further, including parameter passing mechanisms.

h. Recursion was introduced and explained.

i. The work of computer staff was introduced.

POINTS TO NOTE.

79. a. Good programs only come from good program design and good program design only comes from giving sufficient thought and effort in the early stages of programming.

b. The programmer cannot solve a programming problem satisfactorily if the problem has not been properly stated.

c. Subprograms are also sometimes called "subroutines".

d. One subprogram may be called upon several times, in different places within the same program.

e. Functional decomposition as described in this chapter is a form of **modular decomposition**. "Modular decomposition" is a term which also applies to object oriented programming (13.46) and so its use has been avoided here.

f. Further aspects of parameter passing and memory allocation for sub-programs will be covered in later chapters.

g. Inbuilt functions are sometimes called **intrinsic functions**.

h. A function call is sometimes called a **"function reference"**.

i. Formal parameters and arguments are sometimes called **"dummy arguments"**.

j. **"Structured programming"** is a term used to describe programming methods which employ program level structuring and code level structuring (13.58).

STUDENT SELF TESTING QUESTIONS

(Answers on page 689)

1. *State seven aims of program design and give possible reasons for these aims.*

2. *What is meant when we say that a program is "correct"?*

3. *The following program is required to obtain a set of real number values from the user in a "user-friendly" way and to output the total. The numbers are to be terminated by 999.*

   a. *Is the program correct? If not why not?*

   b. *What is wrong with the program design?*

   c. *Re-write the program properly.*

```
program a
variables
t, r : real
Begin
repeat
input (r)
t : = t + r
until r = 999
output (t)
end
```

4. *List the main sections of program documentation and explain the purpose of each section.*

5. *Distinguish betwen the roles of Systems Analysts and programmers.*

6. *Suppose that you may use an output function called* ***"out"*** *which is the same as* ***"output"*** *except that it does not cause a new line to be executed. For example, the statements:*

```
out ("a")
out ("b")
```

give rise to the output "ab" on a single line.

NB. *Assume* ***output*** *by itself cause a new line to be generated.*

Produce a design, in pseudocode, for a program which for a given pair of positive integers outputs a suitably sized rectangle of asterisks. Suppose 5, 4 is input the output will be:

```
* * * *
* * * *
* * * *
* * * *
* * * *
```

QUESTIONS WITHOUT ANSWERS.

7. *Distinguish between "program level structure" and "code level structure".*

8. *Explain the difference between "IN", "OUT" and "IN-OUT" parameters. "IN-OUT" parameters could be used instead of "IN" or "OUT" parameters but why shouldn't they be used in this way?*

9. *Assuming you may use the **"out"** function of question 6 produce a design in pseudocode for a program which takes in a single positive integer and output a triangle of corresponding size. eg. if 3 is input the output will be:*

```
*
* *
* * *
```

14 Program Specification

INTRODUCTION.

1. This chapter examines methods and notations which are used to specify what programs are required to do and how they are required to do them.

2. A **program specification** is usually part of a **system specification** which defines the whole system. In order to avoid needless repetition, the more general aspects of program specification are included in the chapter on system design (ch. 42) and merely introduced in this chapter.

GENERAL REQUIREMENTS.

3. Much of the detail within a program specification is specific to the particular problem to be solved. However, some general design aims (13.6) may be expressed explicitly as part of the program specification irrespective of the particular problem. The following requirements of a program design fall into this general category:

a. Program design style and its presentation.

b. Program reliability.

c. Program efficiency.

d. Program development time.

e. Program development costs.

f. Program documentation.

PROGRAM DESIGN STYLE AND ITS PRESENTATION.

4. An insistence upon **structured programming** can directly contribute to the overall quality of programs and the achievement of many design aims. (13.6) Structured programs are not only more comprehensible they are much easier to test and essential if program proving (13.35) is to be attempted.

5. Program presentation is another important issue. Aids to presentation include:

a. The use of long meaningful identifiers for programs, subprograms, variables and constants.

b. The indenting of code to highlight its structure.

c. The use of appropriate program structures.

d. Restricting the size of subprograms to manageable lengths eg. insisting that no subprogram occupies more than one page.

e. Incorporating comments within the program which explain what is being done and how it is done.

6. The use of more advanced methods based upon object oriented programming may provide even further benefits. In these methods each data structure is contained solely within one program **module.** The idea is to keep all information about the data structure within the one module so that changes to its design and implementation can be localised. Access to the data is provided by a set of functions controlled by the module but visible outside it. For example, a module might be used for an array and provide functions to input data to the array and output values from the array sorted into sequence. Such methods are called **"data encapsulation"** or **"information hiding"** and use the idea of an **abstract data type** (12.61g).

PROGRAM RELIABILITY.

7. It is common for program specification to be accompanied by carefully laid down methods for testing the program. Appropriate methods were discussed in the previous chapter. A program which passes its test may be "certified" and put into use. If the program continues to work for some appreciable time without failure it may be regarded as reasonably reliable. It is useful to quantify reliability in some way. One measure of reliability, borrowed from engineering, is **mean time between failures.** This is the average time which elapses between program failures being detected. A failure could be anything from the output of a wrong result to a non recoverable and unexpected termination of execution called a "crash".

PROGRAM EFFICIENCY.

8. The efficiency of a program may be expressed in terms of its use of resources such as time and storage space. There are some obvious links between efficiency and complexity (13.31). For example, a less complex method of sorting an array will be more efficient than a more complex method. There is often a trade off between time and storage saving.

9. Efficiency is better achieved by adopting a sound design method rather than by using programming "tricks" which result in compact but unreadable programs which will undoubtedly fail to achieve any other requirements of the program's specification. It is better to design a program to work first and make it efficient later.

10. A well written program containing a simple subprogram to sort an array, say, can easily be made to perform faster by merely rewriting that subprogram. The same idea applies on a larger scale. A good design may turn out to be efficient enough by itself. If it is not, it will be much easier to make efficient than a poorly designed program.

11. The use of subprograms may slow down execution speeds slightly because of the time taken for parameter passing but can be turned to advantage in dealing with the efficient use of restricted storage space. This happens where **segmentation** is possible.

12. A **segmented program** is one which when executed allows some parts of the program (segments) to take turns in occupying the same area of main storage. Segments will occupy main storage when they are executed and be held on disk, say, the rest of the time.

13. Overlays. Copying programs or subprograms, into the same area of main storage during execution is known as performing an overlay.

PROGRAM DEVELOPMENT TIME.

14. There is usually some limit set on the amount of time to be used in designing and implementing a program. Such limits may cause the quality of the program to suffer but the quality should not be allowed to suffer unnecessarily. The urgent desire to get a program up and running can tempt the programmer to economise on the design and hurry on to the implementation. This "rushing to the coding sheet" usually makes matters worse. The better strategy is to produce a good design from which a quick and simplified implementation can be produced if necessary.

15. Milestones. Some program specifications state dates by which specific parts of the programming task must be completed. These are called "milestones". To the programmer they may seem more like millstones!

PROGRAM DEVELOPMENT COSTS.

16. Programs must usually be produced within specific budgets. The consequences of such limits are very similar to those for time.

PROGRAM DOCUMENTATION.

17. Here, we build on the basic ideas of program documentation introduced in 13.22. Program documentation varies according to its intended use. Three main areas of use are:

a. For the programmer's own present or future use, as an aid to all stages in programming.

b. For the present or future use of other programmers, including the programmer's supervisor, eg. for maintenance, modification, debugging etc.

c. For the users of the program, which may themselves vary in expertise.

18. The following items may be expected as part of the complete process of documentation.

a. A statement of the problem (System and Program Specification).

b. Documents specifying the formats of inputs and outputs, including checks on the validity of data.

c. Details of the data structures used plus details of how data in files is to be organised, accessed and kept secure. (details later)

d. Details of the algorithms and procedures used to solve the problem. These must be in a suitable form eg. pseudocode.

e. A suitably self documented or annotated program.

f. A carefully devised set of test data with evidence to show that the test data has been used to good effect.

g. Evidence to show that the program not only works but that it has simple, effective, unambiguous and error free methods of input and output for the program's user. (ie. a good **"user interface".)**

h. Detailed instructions to the user (or installer) eg.

i. Limitations of the program.

ii. Requirements in order to run the program (eg. hardware needed).

iii. Details of how to run the program.

iv. Instructions, with examples, on how to use the program. These may take the form of a **user manual** with additional instructions output by the program when it runs.

DETAILED SPECIFICATION.

19. The discussion of documentation concluded the general aspects of program specification and also introduced some specific aspects which need more detailed attention. The three areas of specification important to each particular application are the specification of:

a. inputs.

b. outputs.

c. processing.

INPUT SPECIFICATION.

20. The two main considerations here are the definitions of:

a. The data items to be input, their data types, what values it is valid for them to take, and what actions are to be taken if an attempt is made by a user to enter invalid data.

b. The formats in which input data values are to be entered. For example, the layout of VDU screens may need specifying along with a description of how a dialogue with the user should take place.

21. Screen layouts for data input (or output) may be specified on special forms called **screen layout charts** which consist of boxes set out in a grid in rows and columns which correspond to character positions on the screen. They are similar to print layout charts which will be described shortly.

22. Many modern systems provide special programs which enable screen layouts to be designed directly on the screen. This avoids the need for pencil and paper specifications.

OUTPUT SPECIFICATION.

23. The main considerations here are the definitions of:

a. What data is to be output, how it is to be derived from the input data, when it is to be produced and the form in which it is to be produced.

b. The formats in which the data is to be output.

24. Print layout charts are used to give precise definitions of how the output data is to be printed. One output report may take several print layout charts to define. One chart might provide a specimen layout, another might give a precise definition of the formats of the individual data items. (See fig. 14.1).

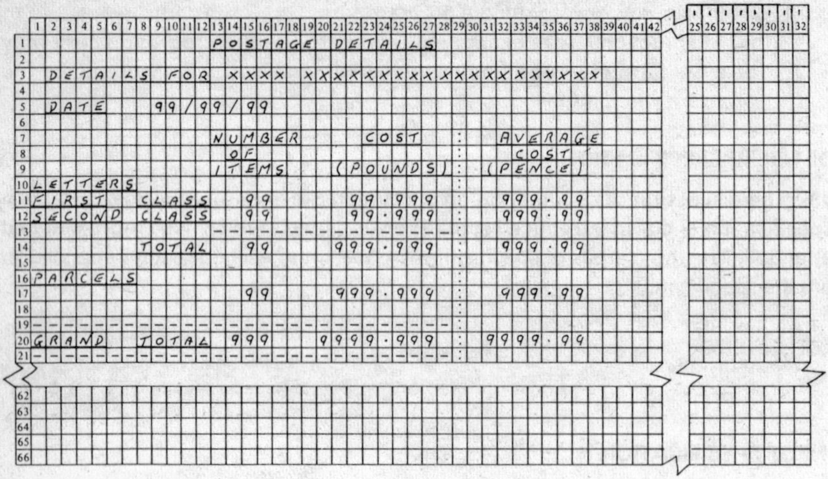

Note.

a. The full size chart is 132 columns wide by 66 lines deep which corresponds to a typical line printer page size.

b. The characters "X" and "9" are used to indicate character positions occupied by alphanumeric and numeric data respectively.

c. The document may be used both for screen layouts and print layouts. The layout shown is for a 40 column screen.

d. It is often necessary to provide several print layout sheets for one form in order to cover all the necessary information.

Fig. 14.1. A Print Layout Chart

PROCESS SPECIFICATION.

25. The specification of how the processing is to take place needs to give a precise definition of *what* processing is needed by giving the relationship between the input data and the output data. At times some details of *how* the processing is to be done are also given but if the definition is too prescriptive of how the processing is to take place the definition has taken over a significant part of the task of programming and may exclude alternatives which merit consideration.

26. Some standard ways of specifying processing will now be considered. They are:

a. English.
b. Pseudocode.
c. Flowcharts.
d. Program structure block diagrams.
e. Warnier diagrams.
f. Decision tables and trees.

ENGLISH.

27. English is often used for an initial expression of processing requirements but, as was discussed in 11.10–11.18, English is a natural language which lacks the precision of meaning and simplicity needed when programming a computer. The chief use of English in producing specifications is as a means of providing informal explanations to formal languages and notations.

PSEUDOCODE.

28. Pseudocode should need no introduction by this stage in the text. Its basic advantages have already been explained (11.18) and the reader can judge for him or herself how useful pseudocode is.

PROGRAM FLOWCHARTS.

29. Flowcharts are a traditional means of showing, in diagrammatic form, the sequence of steps in performing a programming task (see Appendix 2.3).

30. Program flowcharts are generally produced in two stages representing different levels of details:-

a. Outline program flowcharts.
b. Detailed program flowcharts.

31. Outline Program Flowcharts. Outline program flowcharts represent the first stage of turning the systems flowchart into the necessary detail to enable the programmer to write the programs. As implied by the title they present the actual computer operations in outline only. (See Fig. 14.2a.)

32. Detailed Program Flowcharts. These charts are prepared from the outline charts and will contain the *detailed* computer steps necessary to perform the particular task. It is from these charts that the programmer will prepare his or her program coding sheets. Such is the amount of detail involved that these charts are often prepared by individual programmers each taking a segment of the outline charts. (See Fig. 14.2b.)

THE LIMITATIONS OF FLOWCHARTS.

33. Flowcharts were originally introduced as aids to a systematic process of analysing problems and developing suitable computer based solutions. In recent years flowcharts have been heavily criticised as being cumbersome and inefficient tools for the job. Newer alternatives have been introduced and widely adopted.

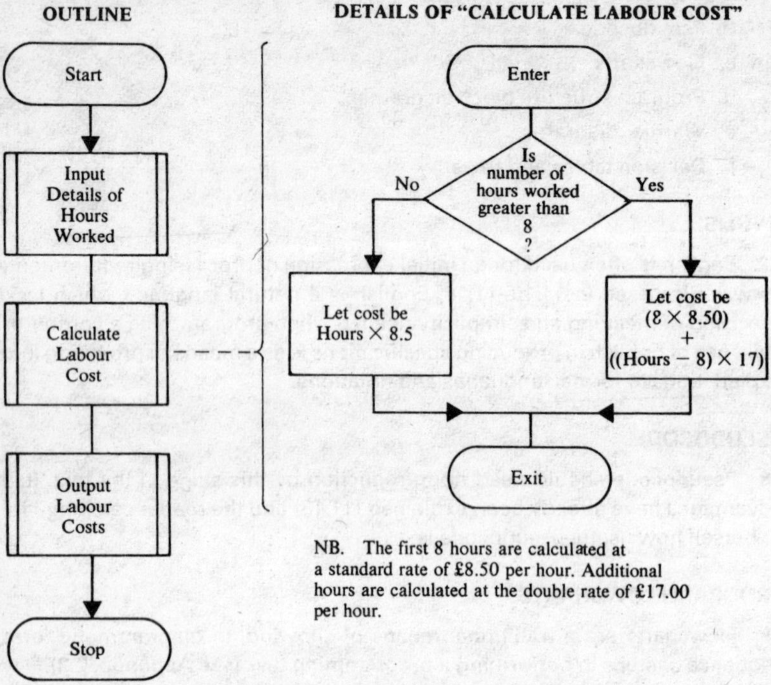

Fig. 14.2a.
Simple Outline Flowchart.

Fig. 14.2b.
Detailed Flowchart.

34. Particular limitations of flowcharts are:-

a. Different levels of detail can easily become confused eg. details of a particular implementation can be inadvertently introduced too early in the design.

b. There are no obvious mechanisms for progressing from one level of design to the next eg. from System flowchart to outline program flowchart.

c. The essentials of *what* is done can too easily be lost in the technical details of *how* it is done.

d. Program flowcharts, although easy to follow, are not such a natural way of expressing procedures as writing in English, nor are they easily translated into programming languages.

PROGRAM STRUCTURE BLOCK DIAGRAMS. (Also see **structure diagrams** Fig. 13.2)

34. There are many varieties of program structure block diagrams. They are all based upon the original idea proposed by **Nassi and Shneiderman** in 1973. Their "Nassi Shneiderman Structured Flowcharts" **NSSF** were intended as a replacement for traditional flowcharts which aided the writing of structured code. NSSFs, and variations upon them have had some measure of success but are often criticised as only being suitable for low level specifications. Typical examples are shown in fig. 14.2.

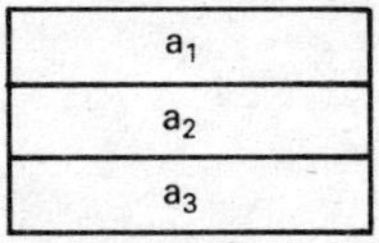

A simple **sequence** of three actions

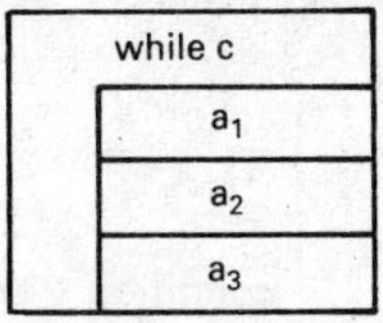

A **while** loop of 3 actions terminated by condition C

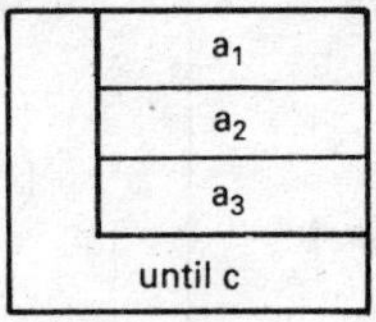

A **repeat** loop of 3 actions

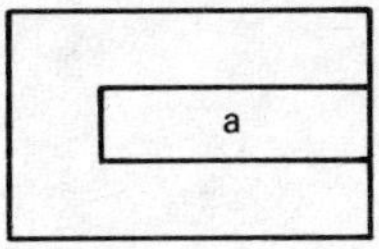

A loop repeating action a indefinitely

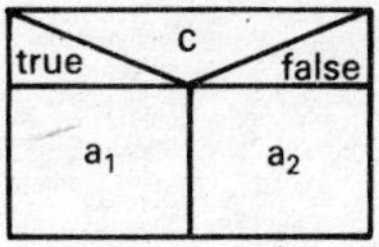

If c **then** a_1, **else** a_2

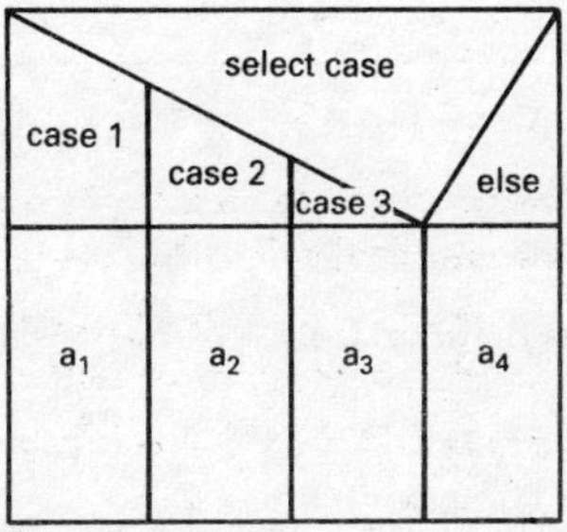

A case structure

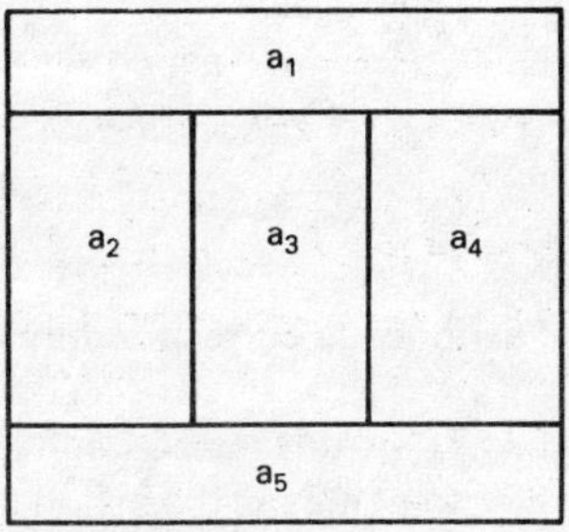

After action a_1, the actions a_2, a_3 and a_4 may take place concurrently followed by action a_5

NB. These diagrams may be combined together into larger units.

Fig. 14.2. Program Structure Block Diagram Examples.

WARNIER DIAGRAMS.

35. Warnier diagrams are a simple way of writing out processing requirements in a structured form. They are mostly used for drafting out simple procedures before attempting to express the procedures in more precise forms such as pseudocode.

36. There are several variations to the way in which they may be written but they are all essentially the same.

37. The basic notation is explained by means of the example in fig. 14.3.

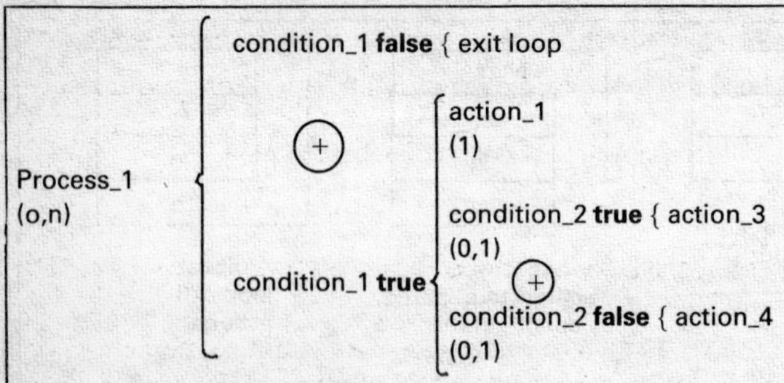

a. **WARNIER DIAGRAM.**

```
Begin
    while     condition_1
              (*Process_1*)
              action_1
              if
                   condition_2
              then
                   action_3
              else
                   action_4
              endif
    endwhile
end
```

b. **Pseudocode corresponding to Warnier diagram (a).**

Note i (1) means the action happens exactly once.

ii. (o,n) means the action happens no times or n times.

iii. ⊕ between two items means they are mutually exclusive ie. either one or the other but not both may happen.

Fig. 14.3. An Example of a Warnier diagram.

DECISION TABLES AND TREES.

38. In considering a particular problem it is sometimes difficult to see all the possible factors involved and how they interact. Decision tables are used to analyse a problem. The conditions applying in the particular problem are set out, and the actions to be taken, as a result of any combination of the conditions arising, are shown. Decision trees are a graphical representations of decision tables. Their purpose is to aid the construction of decision tables.

39. Decision tables and trees are means of expressing process logic. They may therefore be used in conjunction with, or in place of, flowcharts or pseudocode.

40. This chapter begins with a very simple example of a commercial situation involving conditions and actions. The example is then used in the succeeding paragraphs to illustrate the concepts of decision tables and trees.

EXAMPLE 1.

41. A clerk, in assessing the amount of discount allowed on a customer's order is required to comply with the following policy:–

'Any order of £500 or more received from a credit worthy customer attracts discount of 5%, and, similarly, orders of less than £500 attract discount of 3%. Other circumstances must be referred to the supervisor for a decision'.

Now see this policy illustrated in the form of a decision tree at Fig. 14.4, and as a decision table at Fig. 14.5.

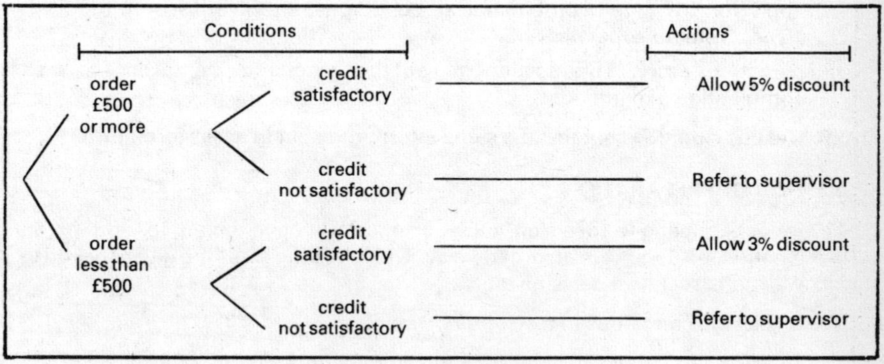

Figure 14.4. A Decision Tree.

CONDITIONS	RULES 1	2	3	4
Is order £500 or more?	Y	Y	N	N
Is credit satisfactory?	Y	N	Y	N
ACTIONS				
Allow discount of 3%			x	
Allow discount of 5%	x			
Refer to Supervisor		x		x

KEY		
	Y	YES
	N	NO

Figure 14.5. A Decision Table.

FORMAT.

42. Decision tables have a standardised format and are comprised of four sections (separated by double lines):-

a. **Condition stub.** This section contains a list of all possible conditions which could apply in a particular problem eg. "order of £500 or more", "satisfactory credit".

b. **Condition entry.** This section contains the different *combinations* of the conditions, each combination being given a number termed a 'Rule'.

c. **Action stub.** This section contains a list of the possible actions which could apply for any given combination of conditions, eg. give discount of "3%", "5%", "refer to supervisor".

d. **Action entry.** This section shows the actions to be taken for each combination of conditions.

NB. The decision tree contains the same information but in a less formal way.

METHOD OF PREPARATION.

43. In constructing a decision table from a narrative given to you in an examination, go about it in an orderly way. The following steps are given for you to follow in constructing a decision table.

a. List the conditions in the *condition* stub.

b. Work out the possible number of combinations of conditions ie. 2^n where n = the number of conditions. This will give you the number of rules and ensures that the table is complete.

In the worked example, there are 2 conditions, thus 2^2 $(2 \times 2) = 4$ possible combinations (rules).

c. Rule up sufficient columns in the condition entry section for the number of combinations, ie. 4.

d. When entering 'Y' or 'N' the combinations must be *unique* (ie. no two columns must be alike). The 'halve' rule is applied to each row of condition rules as follows:-

i. **Row 1.** Y's are inserted for half the number of rules (2 in our case) then N's are inserted for the other half.

ii. **Row 2.** Alternate the Y's and N's, the groups being half the size of those in Row 1. (The group size in our example is 2 therefore the second row size will be 1 ie. Y, N, Y, N).

In an example where there are more than two rows, the halve rule is continued for the other rows.

e. Enter the action stub.

f. Follow down each rule and mark in the appropriate action to be taken.

NB. The decision tree is drawn from left to right. Each question is filled in the same order as the corresponding decision stub entry.

EXAMPLE 2.

44. The unit price of a particular product is £15 if less than 10 are purchased, £14 if between 10 and 49 are purchased, and £13.80 if 50 or more are purchased. If the customer also has preferred customer status then the purchase is subject to a discount of 10%.

This policy is illustrated in the form of a decision table in Fig. 14.6 which is arrived at by setting out all 16 rules and then eliminating impossible cases leaving just the six shown.

CONDITIONS	RULES					
	1	2	3	4	5	6
order < 10	Y	Y	N	N	N	N
10 ≤ order < 50	N	N	Y	Y	N	N
50 ≤ order	N	N	N	N	Y	Y
Preferred Customer	Y	N	N	Y	N	N
ACTIONS						
charge £15 per item		x				
charge £13.5 per item	x					
charge £14 per item				x		
charge £12.6 per item			x			
charge £13.80 per item						x
charge £12.42 per item					x	

Figure 14.6.

45. The form of decision table dealt with is called LIMITED ENTRY because the *conditions* and *actions* are *limited* to the condition/action *stub* respectively. EXTENDED ENTRY tables are ones showing a *part* only of the condition/action in the *stub* with the balance in the *entry* eg. in the action *stub* of Fig. 14.5 the first two actions could be combined as "allow discount" and in the action *entry* "3%" and "5%" shown in place of the crosses.

46. Limited entry format and extended entry format can both be used in a single table for individual conditions or actions. Where a table contains *both* types of format it is called a MIXED ENTRY decision table.

a. When one type of format is used in preference to another depends on particular circumstances. In general terms, extended entry and mixed entry tables use fewer conditions and actions and are thus more compact, but are not so easily checked for completeness as are limited entry tables.

b. It is possible to present processing requirements to the computer in the form of decision tables, instead of programs, provided a special item of software called a "decision table processor" is available. Although some decision table processors have been available for a number of years they have not been widely adopted.

SUMMARY.

47. a. General requirements present in all program specifications were discussed.

b. Detailed specifications of inputs, outputs and processing were described.

POINTS TO NOTE.

48. a. Many of the problems of specifying, designing and implementing individual programs are present on a larger scale when specifying designing and implementing whole systems.

b. The "dash" rule can sometimes be used to simplify the problem when constructing decision tables. For example, if these two column result in the same action.

Y	Y
N	Y

they may be replaced by the single column

Y
–

where the dash "–" means yes or no.

STUDENT SELF TEST QUESTIONS.

(Answers on page 691)

1. *Refer to the algorithm of fig. 13.1 and rewrite using*

   a. *a flowchart.*

   b. *a program structure block diagram.*

   c. *a Warnier diagram.*

2. *Briefly describe eight items to be included in program documentation.*

3. *A programmer's salary scale has three points. Applicants for posts are placed on the scale according to the following criteria: people over 25 years of age with either a degree in computing or three years programming experience are placed on the scale on point two; where applicants over 25 have both of these qualifications they are placed on point three; applicants under 25 with either a degree in computing or three years programming experience are placed on point one while those with both are placed on point two. All other applicants are rejected.*

   Construct a decision table for the placing of candidates on the salary scale. Show that your table covers all possibilities and reduce the table to eliminate redundancy.

4. *Work from the answer to question 3 to produce a program design in pseudocode which takes in the requirerd data and generates suitable results.* ***Before*** *you write your pseudocode design suitable layouts for the inputs and outputs.*

QUESTIONS WITHOUT ANSWERS.

5. *A publisher produces short books on topics in computing. These are published in two page sizes, A4 and A5; they are also available in paperback or hardback. The selling price will depend on these two factors and the expected sale. The A4 size books cost £2 more than the corresponding A5 book. The hardback copy costs £3 more than a paperback copy. The selling price for paperback A5 copies is £15 per copy if the expected sale is greater than 5000 and £18 otherwise.*

   Construct a decision table for this pricing scheme. Show that the table is complete and eliminate any redundancy if possible.

6. *Design a program in pseudocode which can determine the selling price of a book from suitable input using the answer from question 5 as the basis for your design.*

7. *The stamp charge on a letter or postcard is based upon the class (1 or 2) and the weight in grams. Obtain up to date information from your post office and then design a decision table and program based upon the values you have obtained. The user of the program should be asked to key in the class and number of grams and the program should output the stamp required.*

8. *A common programming problem in computer payroll systems is* ***Coin Analysis.*** *Given a sum of money to be paid the appropriate notes and coins*

required for payment must be determined. For example given the sum £57.93 payment could be made as follows.

2 × £20 note	*40.*
1 × £10 note	*10.*
1 × £ 5 note	*5.*
2 × £ 2 note	*2.*
1 × 50p piece	*.50*
2 × 20p piece	*.40*
1 × 2p piece	*.02*
1 × 1p piece	*.01*
	£57.93

Design a program which is able to perform coin analysis on an input sum.

9. a. Define the term, and explain the importance of, subroutines. Explain ***two*** *ways of passing information to and from a subroutine.* **6**

b. A list is held in store which contains the mark that each student gained in a particular examination. A subroutine must be produced to find the maximum mark gained, the minimum mark gained, and the mark which was gained by most students.

i. Using a flowchart, or some other suitable method, describe an algorithm for this subroutine. **6**

ii. Describe how this subroutine may be used by another programmer. **4**

iii. Explain how you would test this subroutine after it had been coded into a suitable high-level language. **4=20**

JMB 1982

Computer Files

1. Files are named collections of stored data. Files tend to be too large to be held in main storage and are therefore held on backing storage devices such as magnetic disks and magnetic tapes. When data in a file is required for processing the file is read into main storage in manageable amounts.

2. Named programs are also often held on backing storage ready for use and may be regarded as "files" too. In this Part of the text we are primarily concerned with file stored for data processing which we may call **"data files"** to distinguish them from files containing programs.

3. Chapter 15 sets out the concepts of magnetic files. Chapter 16 describes the methods of organising a file on magnetic *tape* and how access is made to the records in such a file. Chapter 17 does the same with regard to magnetic *disk*.

4. In the interests of clarity only two magnetic storage devices are used as a basis for discussing computer files. These are:-

a. Magnetic tape – Serial Access Storage (SAS).

b. Magnetic disk (Hard or Floppy) – Direct Access Storage (DAS).

5. The *general* principles discussed with regard to magnetic *tape* or magnetic *disk* can be applied to other media according to whether the media are SAS media or DAS media.

15 Computer File Concepts

INTRODUCTION.

1. The purpose of this chapter is to look at the general concepts which lie behind the subject of computer files before going on to discuss the different methods of organising them. At all times the term 'file' will refer to computer data files.

2. Purpose. A file holds data which is required for providing information. Some files are processed at regular intervals to provide this information (eg payroll file) and others will hold data which is required at irregular intervals (eg a file containing prices of items).

3. There are two common ways of viewing files:-

a. **Logical files.** A "logical file" is a file viewed in terms of *what* data items its records contain and *what* processing operations may be performed upon the file. The user of the file will normally adopt such a view.

b. **Physical files.** A "physical file" is a file viewed in terms of *how* the data is stored on a storage device such as a magnetic disk and *how* the processing operations are made possible.

4. A logical file can usually give rise to a number of alternative physical file implementations. These alternatives are considered in later chapters.

ELEMENTS OF A COMPUTER FILE.

5. A file consists of a number of **records.** Records were defined in 12.37. Here we consider records in a slightly different way because we are concerned with the way they are commonly stored. Each record is made up of a number of **fields** and each field consists of a number of **characters.**

a. **Character.** A character is the smallest element in a file and can be alphabetic, numeric or special. (2.2)

b. **Field.** An item of data within a *record* is called a field – it is made up of a number of *characters,* eg a name, a date, or an amount.

c. **Record.** A record is made up of a number of related fields, eg a customer record, or an employee payroll record. See Fig. 15.1

CLOCK NUMBER	EMPLOYEE'S NAME	DATE OF BIRTH	SEX	GRADE	HOURLY RATE
1201	P J JOHNS	06 12 45	F	4	850

Characters — Field

Notes:
1. Clock number is the Key field. (15.10)
2. Grade is coded.
3. Hourly rate is expressed in pence.

Fig. 15.1. PAYROLL RECORD (Part only)

ALTERNATIVE TERMINOLOGY.

6. The terminology of pargraph 5 (ie. record, field and character) is firmly established as a means of describing the characteristics of files in general situations. However, the use of this terminology can lead to excessive attention being directed towards physical details, such as how many characters there should be in a field. Such issues can divert attention from matters of high priority, such as what fields should be recorded in order to meet the information needs of the user. To overcome this difficulty, two alternative sets of terms have been developed, one set for physical files, and other set for logical files. They are:-

a. **For physical files**
   i. Physical Record.
   ii. Field.
   iii. Character (a physical feature).

b. **For logical files.**
   i. Logical Record – of an "entity".
   ii. Data item – "attributes" of the "entity".

7. Entities are things (eg. objects, people, events etc.) about which there is a need to record data eg. an item of stock, an employee, a financial transaction etc. The individual properties of the entity, about which data is recorded, are its **"attributes"** eg. the attributes of an invoice (entity) will include the "name"; "address"; "customer order number"; "quantity"; "price"; "description".

A logical record is created for each entity occurrence and the logical record contains one **data item** for each **occurrence** of the entity's attributes. eg. the "customers name" would be a data item and there would be **one** only in the logical record. Whereas the attribute "quantity" would have as many data items as there are entries on the invoice.

8. The relationship between the various terms used is summarized in the following table:-

Things about which there is a need to record data	Entities	– each entity has a number of *attributes*
How the data is recorded	Logical records (1 per entity occurrence)	– each logical record contains a number of *data items*
Physical details of how the data is recorded	Physical record (1 or more per logical record)	– each Physical record contains a number of *fields.*

TYPES OF FILES.

9. a. **Master file.** These are files of a fairly permanent nature eg customer ledger, payroll, inventory, etc. A feature to note is the regular *updating* of these files to show a current position. For example customers' orders will be processed increasing the "balance owing" figure on a customer ledger record. It is seen therefore that master records will contain both data of a static nature, eg. a customer name and address, and data which, by its nature will change *each time* a transaction occurs, eg. the "balance" figure already mentioned.

b. **Movement file.** Also called Transaction file. This is made up of the various transactions created from the source documents. In a sales ledger application the file will contain all the orders received at a particular time. This file will be used to update the *master file.* As soon as it has been used for this purpose it is no longer required. It will therefore have a very short life, because it will be replaced by a file containing the *next* batch of orders.

c. **Reference file.** A file with a reasonable amount of permanency. Examples of data used for reference purposes are price lists, tables of rates of pay, names and addresses.

ACCESS TO FILES.

10. Key field. Once having created files of data in magnetic form one must have the means of access to particular records within those files. In *general* terms this is usually done by giving each record a "key" field and the record will be recognised or identified by that particular key. Examples of key fields are:–

a. Customer number in a customer ledger record.

b. Stock code number in a stock record.

c. Employee clock number in a payroll record.

11. Not only does the key field assist in accessing records but the records themselves can, if required, be *sorted* into the sequence indicated by the key.

STORAGE DEVICES.

12. Mention is made here of the two storage devices which will be considered in connection with the storage of files. (ie. Physical Files).

a. **Magnetic tape.** The significant feature with regard to its use as a storage medium is the fact that it is a serial access medium. (4.18).

b. **Magnetic disk.** This device on the other hand is a direct access medium (4.18) and therefore has a distinct advantage over tape in this respect.

NB. This advantage is reflected in the fact that disk is the major medium used for on-line storage.

13. These characteristics will loom large in our considerations about files in the chapters that follow. Note then that they are inherent in the *physical* make up of the devices and will clearly influence the *type* of files stored on each one, and how the files can be *organised* and *accessed.*

PROCESSING ACTIVITIES.

14. We will need to have access to particular records in the files in order to process them. The major processing activities are given below:–

a. **Updating.** When data on the master record is changed to reflect a current position, eg. updating a customer ledger record with new orders. Note that the old data on the record is replaced by the new data.

b. **Referencing.** When access is made to a particular record to ascertain what is contained therein, eg reference is made to a "prices" file during an invoicing run. Note that this does *not* involve any alteration to the record itself.

c. **File maintenance.** New records must be added to a file and records need to be deleted. Prices change, and the file must be altered. Customer's addresses also change and new addresses have to be inserted to bring the file up to date. These particular activities come under the heading of "maintaining" the file. File maintenance can be carried out as a separate run but the insertion and deletion of records is sometimes *combined* with Updating.

d. **File enquiry or interrogation.** This is similar in concept to referencing. It involves the need to ascertain a piece of information from, say, a master record. For example a customer may query a Statement sent to him. A "file enquiry" will get the data in dispute from the record so that the query may be settled.

FIXED/VARIABLE LENGTH RECORDS.

15. The question whether to use records of a fixed or variable length is one which usually does not have to be considered in manual/mechanical methods.

a. **Fixed.** Every record in the file will be of the same fixed number of fields and characters and will never vary in size.

b. **Variable.** This means that not *all* records in the file will be of the same size. This could be for two reasons:—

i. Some records could have more *fields* than others. In an invoicing application for example (assuming a 6 character field to represent "total amount for each invoice") we would add a new field to a customer record for each invoice. So a customer's record would vary in *size* according to the *number* of invoices he had been sent.

ii. Fields *themselves* could vary in size. A simple example is the "name and address" field because it varies widely in size.

16. It should be noted, however, that in the examples at 15b a fixed length record *could* be used. In 15bi. the record could be designed in the first instance to accommodate a fixed number of *possible* invoices. This means the records with less than the fixed number of invoices would contain blank fields. Similarly in 15bii. the field could be made large enough to accommodate the *largest* name and address. Again records with names and addresses of a smaller number of characters would contain blanks.

17. Fixed length records make it easy for the programmer because he or she is dealing with a known quantity of characters each time. On the other hand they result in less efficient utilisation of storage. Variable length records mean difficulties for the programmer but better utilisation of storage.

HIT RATE.

18. This is the term used to describe the rate of processing of master files in terms of active records. For example if 1,000 transactions are processed each day against a master file of 10,000 records, then the hit rate is said to be 10%. Hit rate is a measure of the **"activity"** of the file.

OTHER FILE CHARACTERISTICS.

19. Apart from **activity,** which is measured by hit rate, there are other characteristics of the file which need to be considered. These are:

a. **Volatility.** This is the frequency with which records are added to the file or deleted from it. If the frequency is high the file is said to be *volatile.* A file which is not altered is *"static".* If the frequency is low the file is said to be *"semi-static".*

b. **Size.** This is the amount of data stored in the file. It may be expressed in terms of the number of characters or number of records.

c. **Growth.** Files often grow steadily in size as new records are added. Growth must be allowed for when planning how to store a file.

DATA HIERARCHY.

20. The data structure of a file forms part of a **data hierarchy** as shown below.

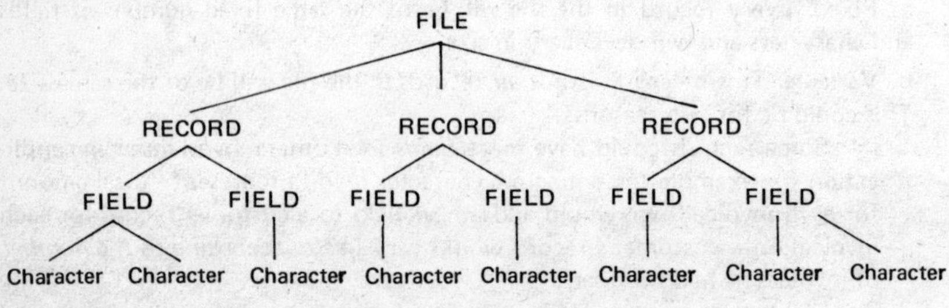

OTHER FILE TYPES.

21. Files may also be referred to in the following ways:

a. **Program file.** A file in which the "data" held in the file is some item of software such as a simple program or collection of program parts.

b. **Data file.** The types of file described so far, as opposed to **program file.**

c. **Input and Output files. Either** files formed from source documents but not sufficiently organised for use as transaction files (eg not sorted) **or** files holding processed data awaiting output.

d. **Text file.** A file containing the words of a document. Each record usually corresponds to a line of printed words. A high level language program may be stored as a text file.

e. **Work file.** A file created during an intermediate stage in processing.

f. **Scratch file.** A file no longer needed which may be overwritten.

SUMMARY.

22. a. A file is a collection of *related* records.

b. A file is made up of **records,** which are made up of **fields,** which are made up of **characters.**

c. It is often advantageous to distinguish between physical files and logical files.

d. Fields within logical records are normally called **"data items"** (or just **"items"**).

e. A record is recognised or identified by the record KEY.

f. Files can be broadly classified as, master files, movement (or transaction) files, and reference files.

g. The physical nature of the storage device will have a direct bearing on the way files are organised on it, and also on the method of access.

h. Four processing activities are: Updating, Referencing, File Maintenance and File Enquiry or Interrogation.

i. Referencing is usually carried out during updating and is incidental to it.

j. Files can consist of records of fixed length or variable length. The decision on which is adopted is a question of programming ease v storage utilisation.

POINTS TO NOTE.

23. a. Magnetic tape is a serial medium, disk is a direct access medium.

b. **Direct access** should be distinguished from **immediate access** which refers to access to main store.

c. **Direct access** is also called **Random access** because it means access in no set order.

d. In terms of levels of storage Direct access is below Immediate access and above Serial access.

e. A file may be described in terms of its **"structure"** and in terms of its **organisation.** Its *structure* is determined by which data items are included in records and how the data items are grouped within records. Its *organisation* is determined by how the records are arranged within the file.

f. Files are not normally held in **primary storage** (ie. main storage). They are normally held on on-line backing storage **(secondary storage)** or on off-line backing storage.

STUDENT SELF TEST QUESTIONS.

(Answers on page 695)

1. An organisation runs a simple savings scheme for its members. Members pay in sums of money to their own accounts and gain interest on the money saved. Data about the accounts is stored in a masterfile.

What would you suggest would be the entities used in this systems. Also suggest what attributes these entities might have.

2. Define the Term "key field". Discuss the suitability of the following data items as key fields.

a. A person's surname in a personnel file.

b. A national insurance number in a payroll file.

c. A candidate number in an examinations file.

3. Define the terms "hit rate" and "volatility" with regard to computer files. Where else have you come across the term "volatility" in Computer Science?

QUESTIONS WITHOUT ANSWERS.

4. Suppose that exam results for all students in your college or school were maintained in a master file. Comment on the probable characteristics of the file in terms of its

a. Volatility,

b. Activity,

c. size,

d. growth.

16 Magnetic Tape

INTRODUCTION.

1. Before tackling this chapter revise 5.24–5.32 which describes the physical attributes of tape itself (in the form of reels) and the "reading" and "writing" devices called the Tape Unit. File organisation is the arrangement of records within a particular file. We start from the point where the individual physical record layout has already been designed ie. the file "structure" has already been decided? How do we organise our many hundreds, or even thousands of such records (eg. customer records) on magnetic tape? When we wish to access one or more of the records how do we do it? This chapter sets out to explain how these things are done.

WRITING ON TAPE.

2. Records are "written" in the first place from main storage onto the tape by the CPU. Each record is written onto tape in response to a "write instruction". This process will be repeated until all the required records are written onto the tape ie. until the file is complete. Fig. 16.1 illustrates what the tape will look like in diagrammatic form.

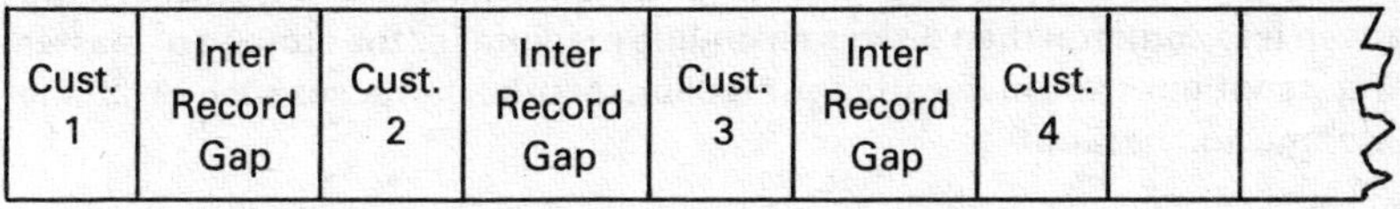

Fig. 16.1. Diagram illustrating records on Magnetic Tape.

Notice the inter-record gap (IRG) which is caused by the tape slowing down at the conclusion of one "write" and accelerating at the beginning of the next.

READING FROM TAPE.

3. Having created (ie. written) a file of records onto tape, we will later need to *process* the file. To do this, we take the reel of tape and mount it on to a tape unit. Records are now "read" *from* the tape into main storage. Each record is read in response to a "read instruction". Notice that when "reading", the tape automatically stops when the IRG is reached. It "knows" when to stop *either* because the length of the record is known in advance *or* because control data recorded on the end of the record marks the end of the record.

FILE ORGANISATION.

4. Organisation of a file on tape is simply a matter of placing the records one after the other onto the tape. There are two possible arrangements of files:-

a. **Serial.** When records are written onto tape *without* there being any relationship between the record keys. *Unsorted* transaction records would form such a file.

b. **Sequential.** When records are written onto tape in *sequence* according to the record keys. Examples of sequential files are:-

i. **Master** files.

ii. **Sorted** transaction files.

ACCESS.

5. a. **Serial files.**The only way to access a serial file on tape is SERIALLY. This simply means to say that each record is read from the tape into main storage one after the other in the order they occur on the tape.

b. **Sequential** files. The method of access used is still SERIAL but of course the file is now in sequence, and for this reason the term SEQUENTIAL is often used in describing serial access of a sequential tape file. It is important to note that to process (eg. update) a sequential master tape file, the transaction file must *also* be in the sequence of the master file. Access is achieved by first reading the transaction file and then reading the master file until the matching record (using the record keys) is found. Note therefore that if the record required is the twentieth record on the file, in order to get it into storage to process it, the computer will first have to read in *all* nineteen preceding records.

NB. These limited methods of organisation and access have lead to tape becoming very much less common than disk as an on-line medium for the storage of master files. Tape continues as a major storage medium for other purposes such as off-line data storage and backup.

UPDATING THE FILES.

6. a. Because of the design of the tape unit it is not possible to write records back to the same position on the tape from which they have been read. The method of updating a tape file therefore is to form a *new* master file on a *new* reel of tape each time the updating process is carried out.

b. Updating a master file held on tape entails the following:-

i. Transaction file and master file must be in the same sequence.

ii. A transaction record is read into main storage.

iii. A master record is read into main storage and written straight out again on a new reel if it does not match the transaction. Successive records from the master file are read (and written) until the record matching the transaction is located.

iv. The master record is then updated in storage and written out in sequence on the new reel.

The four steps are repeated until all the master records for which there is a transaction record have been updated. The result is the creation of a *new* reel of tape containing the records that did not change plus the records that have been updated. The new reel will be used on the next updating run. (See Fig. 16.2).

DAY 1

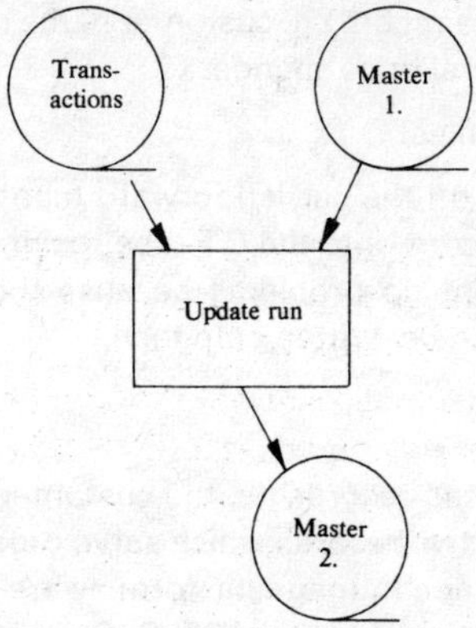

Note:

1. **Master 1** "gives birth" to Son M2.

2. Therefore M1 is said to be the 'Father Tape' and M2 the 'Son Tape'.

DAY 2

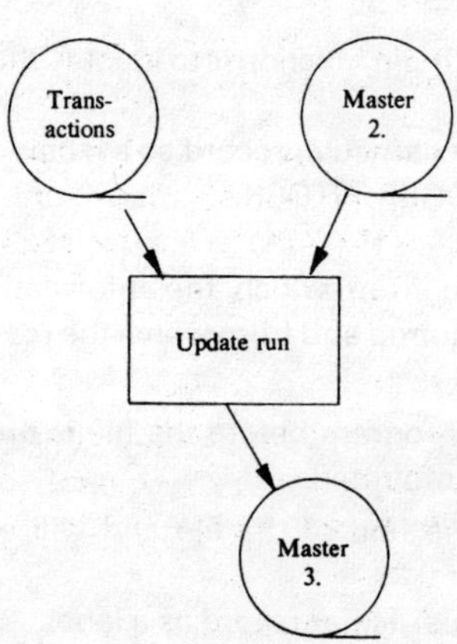

Note:

1. M2 from Day 1 is now the input Master. M2 now gives birth to a Son M3.

2. The position is now:-
M1 is the Grandfather tape.
M2 the Father tape.
M3 the Son tape.

This can be carried on ad infinitum but there will be a definite policy with regards to how *many* generation are kept; Grandfather – Father – Son should be adequate. If an accident should befall M3 on Day 3's Update run then no matter, we can recreate it by doing Day 2's Run again. The keeping of the Master and appropriate Transaction files ensure security of the system's files. Notice as new 'generations' are born the oldest tapes are re-used. The old information they contain is overwritten.

Fig. 16.2. File Security on Tape – the Father-Son Concept.

FILE MAINTENANCE.

7. File maintenance is the term used to describe the following:-

a. Removing or adding records to the magnetic file.

b. Amending static data contained in a record eg. customer name or address, prices of stock items following a general price change.

The term generally applies to master files.

8. Removing a record entails leaving it off the carried forward tape reel, while adding records entails writing the new record onto the C/F tape reel in its correct sequence. Variable length records present no problems because there are no constraints on the size of records which can be written onto tape.

FILE LABELS.

9. In addition to its own particular 'logical' records (ie. the customer or payroll records) each *tape file* will generally have two records which serve organisational requirements. They are written onto the tape in magnetic form as are the logical records. These two records are usually referred to as LABELS. One comes at the beginning of the file and the other at the end.

a. **Header label.** This is the first and its main function is to identify the file. It will contain the following data:-

i. A specified field to identify the particular record as a label.

ii. File name – eg. PAYROLL; LEDGER; STOCK.

iii. Date written.

iv. Purge date – being the date from which the information on the particular tape reel is no longer required and from which the reel can be re-used.

This label will be checked by the Program before the file is processed to ensure the correct tape reel has been mounted.

b. **Trailer label.** This will come at the end of the file and will contain the following data:-

i. A specific field to identify the particular record as a label.

ii. A count of the number of records on the file. This will be checked against the total accumulated by the Program during processing.

iii. Reel number if the file takes up more than one reel of tape.

CONTROL TOTALS.

10. Mention is made here of one further type of record found on tape files – one which will contain control totals, eg. financial totals. Such a record will precede the Trailer Label.

BLOCKING OF RECORDS.

11. The gaps created between each record on tape represent wasted space but more importantly they represent unproductive *time* spent by the tape unit in slowing down and accelerating in between each write and read operation. In order to reduce the number of IRGs and thus speed up the *total* time to process a tape file the technique of blocking records is adopted. Thus a single "read" or "write" instruction will cause a number of records to be read or written. See Fig. 16.3.

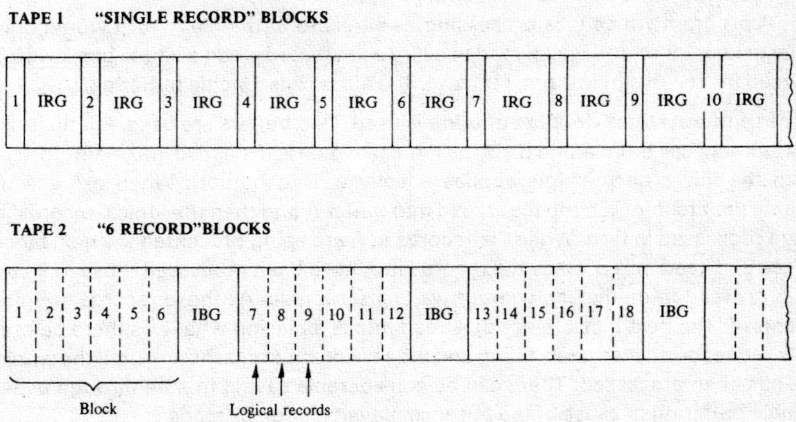

Notes:

1. The saving in the *overall* input/output time. Each IRG (IBG) represents time *wasted.* Tape 2 cuts out 15 IRGs (17 are required in tape 1 for 18 records) representing a *very significant* speed up in the process of transferring records to main storage.

2. The saving in *space* used on tape, although the saving in time is more important.

3. The number of records comprising a block is known as the *blocking factor.*

4. The block is the *physical* unit of transfer between the tape and internal storage and the IRG is now referred to as the IBG.

5. The Block may be called a **physical record**.

6. The individual records making up the block are known as the **logical records.**

7. The size of each block will depend on:-

a. The size of the logical records.

b. The size of internal storage available for input/output purposes.

Fig. 16.3. Blocking Records on Magnetic Tape.

BUFFERS AND BUFFERING.

12. The area of main storage used to hold the individual blocks, when they are read in or written out, is called a **buffer**.

13. In the example shown in fig. 16.3 tape 2, where the blocking factor is 6, the buffer will be at least as long as 6 logical records because records are transferred between the tape unit and main memory one complete block at a time.

14. A program which was processing each record in the file in turn would only have to wait for records to be read in every sixth record when a whole block would be read in. The use of just one buffer for the file is called **single buffering.**

15. In some systems **double buffering** is used. Two buffers are used. For the sake of argument call them A and B and assume that data is to be read into main storage from the file. (The principle applies equally well to output). When processing begins the first block in the file is read into buffer A and then the logical records in A are processed in turn. While the records in A are being processed the next block (block 2) is read into B. Once the records in A have been processed those in B can be processed immediately, *without waiting for a read.* As those records in B are processed the next block (block 3) is read into A replacing what was there before. This sequence of alternately filling and processing blocks carries on until the whole file has been processed. There can be considerable saving in time through using double buffering because of the absence of waits for block reads.

16. Note that single and double buffering are generally carried out by the operating system not by the application program. Further aspects of buffering and double buffering will be covered in later chapters.

FILE CALCULATIONS

17. Two basic types of calculation are often needed when using magnetic tape files:

a. The space occupied by the file.

b. The time taken to read or write the file.

A simple example now follows.

18. Example. (NB. Metric units are still seldom used in practice so they are not used here).

a. Assume that a magnetic tape on which a file is to be stored has these characteristics.

i. 1600 bpi recording density
ii. length 2,400 feet
iii. IBG ½″
iv. Speed 75 ips (inches per second)
v. Stop/Start time 10 ms

} See 5.26–5.28

b. Assume a file of 10,000 records, each 200ch long, is to be stored on magnetic tape four records to a block.

c. Find:

i. The space occupied by the file.

ii. The time taken to read the file if it is single buffered.

d. **Solution.**

i. **Space occupied.**

One block of 4 records is 800 characters long.

Therefore it occupies $\frac{800}{1600}$ inches ie. ½"

Therefore a block plus its IBG will occupy 1"

10,000 records occupy 2,500 blocks.

Therefore the file occupies 2,500 inches or approximately 208 feet.

ii. **Time taken.**

$$\text{Total time taken} = \left[\text{start time} + \left[\begin{matrix}\text{time to read}\\\text{one block}\end{matrix}\right] + \text{Stop time}\right] \times \left[\begin{matrix}\text{Number}\\\text{of blocks}\end{matrix}\right]$$

If the speed of the tape is 75 ips and the recording density is 1600 bpi then data will be transferred at a rate of 75 × 1600 characters per second.

Therefore the time to read one block will be, in ms

$$\frac{800}{75 \times 1600} \times 1000 \text{ ms} = 6\tfrac{2}{3} \text{ ms}$$

So the total time take = $[10 + 6\tfrac{2}{3} + 10] \times 2{,}500$ ms

= 66,666 ms

ie. approximately 1 minute.

OTHER 'SERIAL ACCESS' MEDIA.

19. You have seen that records on magnetic tape are stored serially or sequentially and *accessed* serially.

Other 'Serial Access' media are:-

a. **Punched cards.**

b. **Punched paper tape.**

20. These media are now obsolete for storage purposes because they are bulky, difficult to store and maintain, non reusable, have low storage capacities and have slow data transfer speeds.

SUMMARY.

21. a. An inter block gap is created after each block is *written* on tape.

b. When the tape is being read the IBG terminates the "read" operation (ie. the transfer of the data in that particular block).

c. Tape is a serial medium and can only be accessed serially.

d. Updating is achieved by creating a physically different file each time.

e. File maintenance involves adding and deleting records and the amendment of static data contained in records.

f. Labels are provided for control/organisational purposes.

g. A diagram showing the components of a tape file is shown in Fig. 16.4.

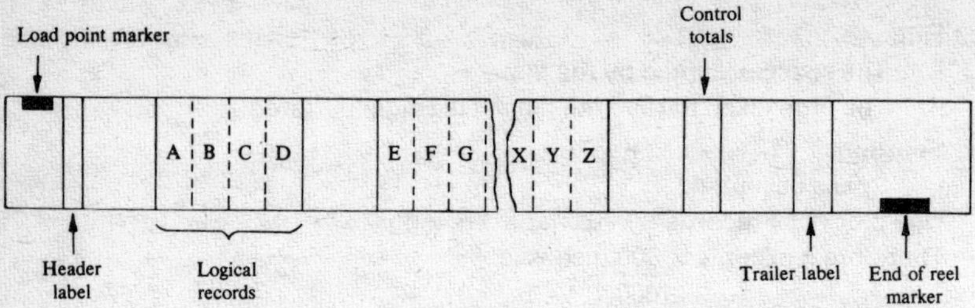

Fig. 16.4. Diagram Illustrating Components of a Tape File.

POINTS TO NOTE.

22. a. Note the amount of data transfer *time* saved by blocking records together on tape. (Fig. 16.3).

b. When we talk of "transferring" or "reading" from tape, this really means *copying* it from tape because the data is still *there* on the tape. This concept holds good *whatever* the medium in computers.

c. Data can also be written onto tape "off-line" ie. by a Magnetic Tape Encoder, (19.11), and by transferring from another medium to tape eg. from punched cards to tape (done by means of a special type of tape unit linked to a card reader). Transaction files are generally associated with these methods of "preparing" tape.

d. The size of blocks is limited by the amount of main storage available for the input/output area.

e. Tape labels are *magnetic* labels for use by the computer program.

f. The expression "reading the master/transaction file" really means in effect "reading *one* block into main storage". A separate "read" instruction is required for each block on tape to be "read" into main storage.

g. The use of the term "generation" in connection with master files (Fig. 16.2).

h. Magnetic tape is *not* normally used as a storage medium for master files undergoing processing, but is frequently used for "backup copies" of all kinds of files.

i. Some tape units may be operated in a mode in which data is transferred between the tape and main storage in a continuous stream for "backup" or "recovery" purposes. This is known as **streaming.**

j. A file is "open" for input once its header label has been read and checked and it is "open" for output once its header label has been written successfully.

STUDENT SELF TESTING QUESTIONS

(Answers on page 695)

1. *Why are gaps required between physical records on a magnetic tape file? What improvements are made by blocking records together?*

2. *Why is the updated master file stored on a new reel during a file update run?*

3. Assume the tape characteristics given in paragraph 18 and secondly assume that a file has 15,000 records each of 250 ch in length.

a. Find the space occupied by the file.

b. Find the time taken to read the file if it is single buffered.

Compare the answers for blocks of 1 record only with those for 5 records per block.

Explain the effect double buffering could have on the read time.

QUESTIONS WITHOUT ANSWERS.

4. What is the Father-Son concept with regard to the updating of magnetic tape files?

5. What data would you expect to find in header and trailer labels and comment on each item. Give an example of a header label and trailer label for a particular application.

17 Magnetic Disk

INTRODUCTION.

1. The exchangeable type disk will be used as a basis for this chapter because it is most often used in practice. Hard disks are the main file processing medium on mini and mainframe computers, and floppy disks are the main file processing medium on microcomputers. The principles covered by this chapter are applicable to both hard and floppy disks. Any relevant differences will be highlighted when appropriate.

2. You should be thoroughly conversant with the relevant hardware described in 5.33–5.34 and 8.8–8.11 before going on with this chapter, which is concerned with the organisation of files on disk and how files are accessed.

WRITING ON DISK.

3. Records are "written" onto a disk as the disk pack revolves at a constant speed within its disk unit. Each record is written in response to a "write" instruction. Data goes from main storage through a read-write head onto a track on the disk surface. Records are recorded one after the other on each track. .

NB. All references to "records" in this chapter should be taken to mean "Physical records" unless otherwise stated.

READING FROM DISK.

4. In order to process files stored on disk the disk pack must first be loaded into a disk unit. Records are read from the disk as it revolves at a constant speed. Each record is read in response to a "read" instruction. Data goes from the disk to the main storage through the read-write head already mentioned. Both reading and writing of data are accomplished at a fixed number (thousands) of characters per second.

5. We will take for our discussion on file organisation, a "6 disk" disk pack, meaning it has ten usable surfaces (the outer two are not used for recording purposes). But before describing how files are organised let us look first at the basic underlying concepts.

CYLINDER CONCEPT.

6. Consult Fig. 8.2 where the disk pack is illustrated and note the following:

i. There are *ten* recording surfaces. Each surface has 200 tracks.

ii. There is a read-write head for *each* surface on the disk pack.

iii. *All* the read-write arms are fixed to *one* mechanism and are like a comb.

iv. When the "access" mechanism moves all ten read-write heads move *in unison* across the disk surfaces.

v. Whenever the access mechanism comes to rest *each* read-write head will be positioned on the *equivalent* track on *each* of the ten surfaces.

vi. For *one* movement of the access mechanism access is possible to *ten* tracks of data.

7. In the case of a floppy disk the situation is essentially the same but simpler. (Fig. 5.7) There is just *one* recording surface on a "single sided" floppy disk and *two* recording surfaces on a "double sided" floppy disk. The other significant differences are in terms of capacity and speed.

8. Use is made of the physical features already described when organising the storage of records on disk. Records are written onto the disk starting with track 1 on surface 1, then track 1 on surface 2, then track 1 on surface 3 and so on to track 1 on surface 10. One can see that conceptually the ten tracks of data can be regarded as forming a CYLINDER.

9. Data is written onto successive cylinders, involving *one* movement only of the access mechanism for each cylinder. When access is made to the stored records it will be advantageous, in terms of keeping access mechanism movement to a minimum, to deal with a cylinder of records at a time.

10. Conceptually the disk can be regarded as consisting of 200 CYLINDERS. Cylinder 1 comprises track 1 on each of 10 surfaces; cylinder 2 comprises track 2 of each of the 10 surfaces and so on to cylinder 200 which comprises track 200 on each of the 10 surfaces. This CYLINDER CONCEPT is fundamental to an understanding of how records are organised on disks. An alternative term for cylinder is SEEK AREA, ie. the amount of data which is available to the read-write heads as a result of one movement or SEEK of the access mechanism.

HARD SECTORED DISKS AND SOFT SECTORED DISKS.

11. The tracks on a disk are sub divided into **sectors** (see Fig. 17.1). There are two alternative design strategies for the division of tracks into sectors. One is called **soft sectoring,** the other is called **hard sectoring.**

In either case *whole* sectors of data are transferred between the disk and main storage.

NB. A disk said to have "no sectors" is effectively a soft sectored disk.

12. A **soft sectored** disk has sectors which may be varied in length, up to some maximum value which is never more than the size of a complete track. Sector size and position is *soft*ware controlled, hence the term "soft sectored".

13. A *hard sectored* disk has sectors of fixed length. There may be anything from 8 to 128 sectors per track. Sector size and position is pre-determined by hardware, hence the term "hard sectored".

14. You may compare a sector with a physical record or block on magnetic tape (Fig. 16.3). In fact it is common to use "sector" and "blocks" as synonyms. However, in the case of hard sectored disks, blocks may be grouped together into larger units called "buckets" or "logical blocks". It is therefore prudent to call a sector a "physical block" so as to avoid any possible ambiguity.

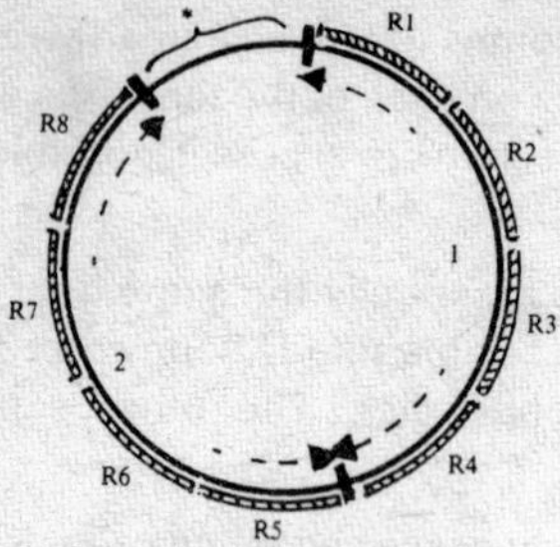

a. **A Soft Sectored Disk.**

The start of each track is marked physically by a notch or hole. The start of each sector is marked by special data recorded there.

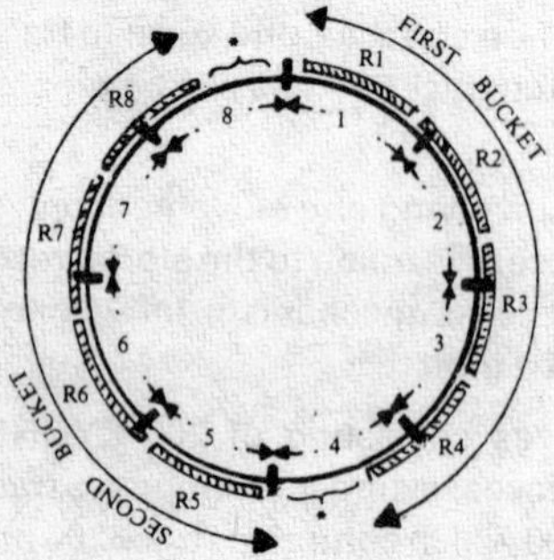

b. **A Hard Sectored Disk.**

The start of each track and sector is marked physically by a notch or hole. There may also be recorded marks as on the soft sectored disk.

Key

SECTORS (ie. BLOCKS) ARE NUMBERED 1, 2, 3 ....

LOGICAL RECORDS: ARE NUMBERED R1, R2, R3, ...

* INDICATES WASTED STORAGE SPACE.

Note

Reading a bucket is treated as a single read operation, although in reality it is a sequence of hard sector reads.

Fig. 17.1. Blocking Records on Magnetic Disk.

BASIC ADDRESS CONCEPTS.

15. As the disk is a direct access device a record can be accessed independently of other records. To enable the disk to locate a record, the record must have some form of ADDRESS. The whole area of each disk can be sub-divided to enable this to be accomplished.

a. **Cylinder.** The major subdivision as we have seen is the cylinder.

b. **Track.** Each cylinder is comprised of a number of tracks (10 in our quoted example).

c. **Block.** The smallest addressable part of a disk is a block (ie. a sector). This forms the **unit** of transfer between the disk and main storage.

d. **Bucket.** When the block size is fixed (ie. when the disk is hard sectored) a number of blocks (ie. sectors) are grouped to form a larger unit of transfer. This unit is called a bucket or **logical block.**

16. The block or the bucket is therefore the unit of input/output on disk. As on magnetic tape, records will be combined together to form one of these units. The optimum size for a block or bucket is determined by:

a. the need to optimise fillage of a track – eg. if a size were chosen for a variable length block which did not divide exactly into the track size, space would be wasted. (See Fig. 17.1).

b. the need to minimise the number of transfers between main storage and disk storage. The larger the block or bucket size, the more records will be brought into main storage at each transfer. (eg. in Fig. 17.1a, four records are transferred at a time).

c. the need to economise in the use of main storage. A large block or bucket may occupy so much main storage that insufficient space is left for other data and programs.

17. In basic hardware terms, the address of a record is given thus:-

a. cylinder number

b. track number

c. block number (which will be the first block in the bucket if this concept applies).

NB. On a single sided floppy disk the address would be simply

a. "track" number } (ie. one of a number of concentric tracks).
b. block number. }

Thus the address 1900403 indicates.

a. cylinder 190

b. track 4

c. block 3.

ACCESS TIME.

18. Access time *on disk* is the time interval between the moment the command is given to transfer data from disk to main storage and the moment this transfer is completed. It is made up of three components:-

a. **Seek time.** This is the time it takes the access mechanism to position itself at the appropriate cylinder.

b. **Rotational delay.** This is the time taken for the bucket to come round and position itself under the read-write head. On average this will be the time taken for half a revolution of the disk pack. This average is called the **'latency'** of the disk.

c. **Data transfer time.** This is the total time taken to *read* the contents of the bucket into main storage.

19. Access time will vary mainly according to the position of the *access mechanism* at the time the command is given. For example if the access mechanism is already positioned at cylinder 1 and the record required happens to be in cylinder 1 no movement of the access mechanism is required. If, however, the record required is in cylinder 200, the access mechanism has to move right across the surface of the disk. Once the bucket has arrived at the read-write head, the transfer of data to storage begins. *Speed of transfer* of data to main storage is very fast and is a constant rate of so many thousand characters per second. A hard disk will operate at speeds roughly 10 times faster than a floppy disk.

FILE ORGANISATION.

20. There are four basic methods of organising files on disk:-

a. **Serial.** Exactly as for tape. Records are placed onto the disk one after the other with no regard for sequence.

b. **Sequential.** Again as for tape; records are written onto the disk but in a defined sequence according to the record keys.

c. **Indexed sequential.** Records are stored in sequence as for 20b but with one important difference – an *index* is provided to enable individual records to be located. Strictly speaking the records may not always be stored in sequence but the index will always enable the sequence to be determined.

d. **Random.** Records are actually placed onto the disk "at random", that is to say there is no *obvious* relationship between the records as with 20b and c. A mathematical formula is derived which when applied to each record key, generates as an answer, a bucket address (as illustrated in para 17). The record is then placed onto the disk at this address. (eg. one possible formula might be: given key = 37099. Divide by 193 giving 192 remainder 43. (Address is taken as cylinder 192, track 4, block 3).

ACCESS.

21. a. **Serial files.** As for tape the only way to access a serially organised file is SERIALLY.

b. **Sequential files.** As for tape also, in fact the comments under 16.5b apply equally to sequentially organised files on disk.

c. **Indexed sequential files.** There are three methods of access:

i. **Sequential.** This is almost the same as in b above; the complete file is read in sequential order using the index. The method is used when the hit rate is high. The method makes minimal use of the index, minimises head movement and processes *all* records in each block in a single read. Therefore, the index is used once per block rather than once per record. Any transaction file must be pre-sorted into the sequence of the master file.

ii. **Selective Sequential.** Again the transaction file must be pre-sorted into the same sequence as the master file. The transaction file is processed against the master file and *only* those master records for which there is a transaction are selected. Notice that the access mechanism is going forward in an ordered progression (never backtracking) because both files are in same sequence. This minimises head movement and saves processing time. This method is suitable when the hit rate is low, as only those records for which there is a transaction are accessed.

iii. **Random.** Transactions are processed in a sequence which is not that of the master file. The transactions may be in another sequence, or may be unsequenced. In contrast to the selective sequential method, the access mechanism will move *not* in an ordered progression but back and forth along the file. Here the index is used once per record rather than once per block as in (c i). This method is used when transactions are processed immediately – ie. there is not time to assemble files and sort them to sequence. It is also used when updating two files simultaneously. For example, a transaction file of orders might be used to update a stock file *and* a customer file during the same run. If the order file was sorted to customer sequence, the customer file would be updated on a *selected sequential* basis and the stock file on a random basis. (Examples will be given in later chapters).

NB. In ci and cii the ordered progression of the heads relies upon an orderly organisation of the data and no other program performing reads from the disk at the same time, which would cause head movement to other parts of the disk. In multi-user systems these things cannot always be relied upon.

d. **Random files.** Generally speaking the method of access to random files is RANDOM. The transaction record keys will be put through the *same* mathematical formula as were the keys of the master records thus creating the appropriate bucket address. The transactions in random order are then processed against the master file, the bucket address providing the address of the record required.

METHODS OF ADDRESSING.

22. For direct access one must be able to "address" (locate) each record whenever one wants to process it. The main methods of obtaining the appropriate address are as follows:-

a. **Index.** The record keys are listed with the appropriate disk address. The incoming transaction record key is used to locate the disk address of the master record in the index. This address is then used to locate the appropriate master record. We referred to this method in para 21c.

b. **Address generation.** This is another method which has been mentioned earlier in para. 21d. The record keys are applied to a mathematical formula which has been designed to generate a disk hardware address. The formula is very difficult to design and you need not worry about it. The master records are placed on the disk at the addresses generated. Access is afterwards obtained by generating the disk address for each transaction.

c. **Record key = disk address.** It would be convenient if we could use the actual disk hardware address as our record key. Our transaction record keys would then also be the appropriate disk addresses and thus no preliminary action such as searching an index or address generation would be required in order to access the appropriate master records. This is not a very practical method, however, and has very limited application.

NB. Files organised as in 22b and 22c are said to be "self indexing".

UPDATING DISK FILES.

23. As individual records on disks are addressable, it is possible to *write back* an up-dated record to the same place from which it was read. The effect is therefore to *overwrite* the original master record with the new or updated master record. This method of updating is called **"Updating in place"** or **"overlay".** Note the sequence of steps involved:-

a. The transaction record is read into main storage.

b. The appropriate master record is located on disk and is read into main storage.

c. The master record is updated in main storage.

d. The master record (now in updated form) is written from main storage to its original location, overwriting the record in its *pre*-updated form.

24. a. The method described can only be used when the *address* of the record is *known;* ie. when a file is organised Indexed Sequentially or Randomly.

b. Files organised on a Serial or Sequential basis are processed in the same way as magnetic tape files ie. a physically different carry forward master file will be created each time the file is processed. Such a new file could be written onto a different disk pack or perhaps on a different area of the same disk pack.

25. The Grandfather-son method of file security cannot be applied to "update in place". A common alternative is shown in an example in Fig. 17.2.

FILE MAINTENANCE – DISK FILES.

26. a. If disk files are organised and processed in the same manner as magnetic tapes then the remarks made in the previous chapter apply.

b. Disk files which are updated using the "overlay" method present certain problems:

i. When new records are to be inserted it may not be possible to put them, there and then, in sequence on the file.

ii. Similarly if during the process of *updating* a variable record it were to be made longer, it may not be possible to write it back to the disk in its original place, unless of course sufficient space had been allowed for such expansion.

c. To cater for such circumstances, an OVERFLOW area is usually included in the disk file and such records as those referred to above are placed in this area temporarily and an indication of their whereabouts placed on the main part of the file (usually called the HOME area).

d. Records which are to be removed from the file have a deletion marker placed on them during a file maintenance run.

FILE REORGANISATION.

27. As a result of the foregoing the number of records in the overflow area will increase. As a consequence the time taken to locate such a record will involve first

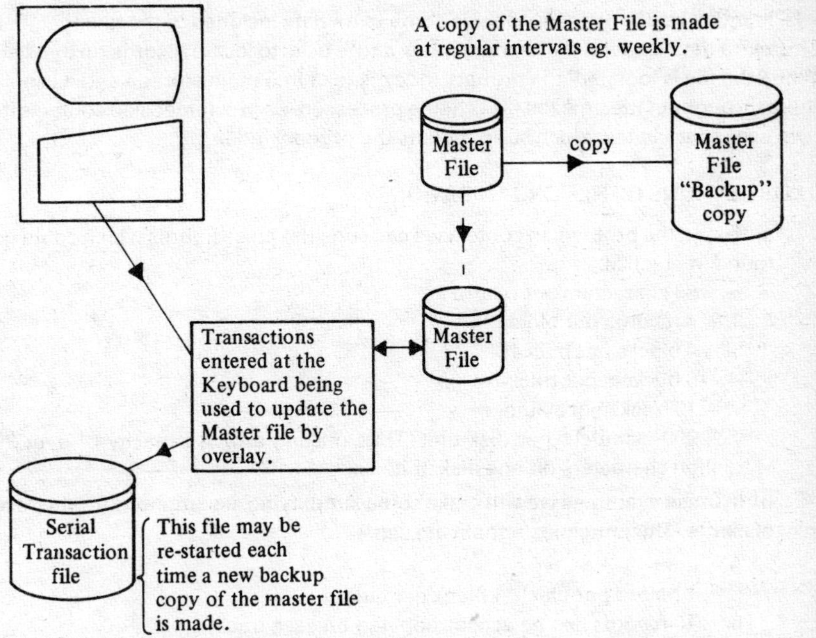

If for any reason the Master file is lost or damaged a new copy can be obtained by bringing the Master file "backup copy" up to date using the transaction file data.

Fig. 17.2. This diagram gives an example of file security for disk files updated by overlay.

seeking the home track and then the overflow track.

Periodically it will be necessary to reorganise the file. This will entail rewriting the file onto a new disk pack:-

i. Putting the records that are in the overflow area in the home area in the proper sequence.
ii. Leaving off the records which have a deletion marker on them.
iii. Rewriting any index which is associated with the file.

LABELS/CONTROL TOTALS.

28. Header and trailer labels and control totals – akin to those on magnetic tape – are used on disk files too.

29. In index sequential files there is some extra data included in the header label. This extra data is called the **primary index** and is used to locate records on the disk. When the file is 'opened' the primary index is read into main storage and it is held there throughout the time the file is being processed. Each cylinder also contains its own **secondary index** which supplements the primary index.

ILLUSTRATIONS OF FILE ORGANISATION.

30. a. To put the problem in context we can consider these figures which could be found in practice.

i. 80 characters per record
ii. 4 records per block
iii. 4 blocks per bucket
iv. 8 buckets per track
v. 10 tracks per cylinder
vi. 200 cylinders per disk unit. Thus making a total capacity of over 20 million characters on one disk unit.

b. In these examples we will make some simplifying assumptions for the sake of clarity. The principles remain the same.

Assume:

i. 1 record per block, 1 block per bucket
ii. 10 records can be accommodated on each track
iii. Records in the file have keys in the range 100 to 299 inclusive
iv. Not all keys are used.

Only the keys will be shown on the diagrams rather than whole records since the records are organised by their key numbers.

31. Sequential file Organisation. Consider a file which is placed on a cylinder corresponding to all the tracks numbered 1. Records would be written on the disk one surface at a time in sequence as shown in this diagram.

LOCATIONS OF RECORDS 101 to 299										
Position on Track	Track 1 Surface 0	Track 1 Surface 1	Track 1 Surface 2	Track 1 Surface 3	Track 1 Surface 4	Track 1 Surface 5	Track 1 Surface 6	Track 1 Surface 7	Track 1 Surface 8	Track 1 Surface 9
1	101	132	158	219	265					
2	104	137	167	224	270					
3	105	138	171	228	275					
4	107	140	177	231	277					
5	111	145	179	237	282					
6	113	146	183	241	287					
7	119	149	188	245	293					
8	123	151	197	252	294					
9	128	154	200	256	299					
10	130	156	206	263						

Note: Working from surface to surface on the same cylinder does not require movement of the read/write heads.

32. Index Sequential Organisation. (The example shown here is explained by the notes which follow).

LOCATIONS OF RECORDS 101 to 299 ON CYLINDER 1												Overflow Tracks	
Position on Track	Track 1 Surface 0 (Secondary Index for Cylinder 1) see b.				Track 1 Surface 1	Track 1 Surface 2	Track 1 Surface 3	Track 1 Surface 4	Track 1 Surface 5	Track 1 Surface 6	Track 1 Surface 7	Track 1 Surface 8	Track 1 Surface 9
1	1	119	119	•	101	123	145	167	200	241	275		
2	2	140	140	•	104	128	146	171	206	245	277		
3	3	158	158	•	105	130	149	177	219	252	282		
4	4	197	197	•	107	132	151	179	224	256	287		
5	5	237	237	•	111	137	154	183	228	263	293		
6	6	270	270	•	113	138	156	188	231	265	294		
7	7	299	299	•	119	140	158	197	237	270	299		
8													
9													
10													

The index sequential file is created from a file which is already in sequential order. The indexes are generated and included as the index sequential file is organised and stored. The indexes are subsequently updated as the file is updated.

a. The **primary index** is created in main storage as the file is organised, and stored on the disk when organisation and storage of the file is completed. It is loaded into main storage again at the start of any subsequent access. The primary index on surface '0' track '0' say would have a record such as this one:–

Cylinder Number	Highest Key number on cylinder
1	299

Cylinder Number '1' is comprised of all tracks numbered '1'.

b. A **secondary index** is also created in main storage while each cylinder is organised and stored. There is one secondary index per cylinder. During the organisation of each cylinder provision is made for **local overflow** ie the provision of spare storage on the *same* cylinder, for tracks which subsequently may become full and therefore unable to accommodate further records. (**Global overflow** ie overflow of the whole file may be catered for in a similar way). The secondary index for cylinder '1' would have records such as this one:–

Surface Number	Highest Key Number on the track	Highest Key Number in overflow from the track	Pointer to First Overflow Key
1	112	119	T1S9B2 ie Track 1 Surface 9 Block 2

If there is no overflow the second and third field will contain the same number and the overflow pointer will be a terminator eg '*'.

c. Space has been left on each surface during the initial organisation so that a few additions can be made before overflow occurs. To find the key numbered 188 on a subsequent access. Reference to the primary index directs us to cylinder 1. The secondary index on cylinder 1 directs us to surface 4.

d. The following diagram shows the same cylinder after a number of records have been added.

LOCATIONS OF RECORDS 101 to 299 ON CYLINDER 1													Overflow Tracks			
Position on Track	Track 1 Surface 0 (Secondary Index for Cylinder 1) see b.				Track 1 Surface 1	Track 1 Surface 2	Track 1 Surface 3	Track 1 Surface 4	Track 1 Surface 5	Track 1 Surface 6	Track 1 Surface 7	Track 1 Surface 8		Track 1 Surface 9	
1	1	112	119	T1 S9 B2	101	123	145	167	200	241	275	119	*	118	T1 S8 B1
2	2	140	140	*	103	128	146	168	206	245	277	197	*	113	T1 S9 B1
3	3	158	158	*	104	130	149	170	219	252	282	188	T1 S8 B2		
4	4	185	197	T1 S8 B3	105	132	151	171	224	253	287				
5	5	237	237	*	106	137	154	177	228	254	293				
6	6	270	270	*	107	138	155	178	231	256	294				
7	7	299	299	*	108	140	156	179	237	263	299				
8					109		158	183		265					
9					111			184		270					
10					112			185							

Again use the index and pointers to find key number 188.

33. Random File Organisation. In this method the keys are used to allocate record positions on the disc. For example a record whose key was 149 could be allocated the position surface 1 track 49. We say that the **disk address** of the record has been *generated* from the key and so the technique is called **address generation.** The generated disk address usually gives just enough detail to specify the block in which the record is to be placed or found; so that when a record is to be accessed the whole block is input, and the record is searched for within the block. We thus have **organisation by address generation** and **access by address generation.** Sometimes an index of generated addresses is produced as the file is created. This index is then stored with the file. It is then possible to access the file by means of this **random index.** We then have **organisation by address generation** and **access by random index.**

34. Hashed Keys. When disk addresses are generated directly from keys, as in the example just given, there tends to be an uneven distribution of records over available tracks. This can be avoided by applying some algorithm to the key first. In this case we say the key is **hashed.** Examples:—

a. Squaring, eg for key number 188

188^2 =	3 5	3	4	4
DISC ADDRESS	Track Number	Surface Number	Bucket Number	Block Number

b. Division method, eg for Key number 188.

188 ÷ 7 = 26 Remainder 6. So we could use track 26 surface 6 say.

Hashing reduces the chances of overflow occurring but when overflow does occur records are normally placed on the next available surface in the same cylinder so as to minimise head movement.

OTHER ORGANISATION AND ACCESS METHODS.

35. The methods of file organisation and access described so far are closely related to the physical features of the disk. It is now common practice for much of this detail to be "hidden" from programmers or users of the system. Instead the operating system (9.49) handles the physical levels of organisation and access, and provides standard *logical file* organisation and access methods.

36. Some examples of logical file organisation.

a. **Sequential files.** A programmer need merely regard the file as a sequence of records, and need have no concern for their physical location. A program instruction to read the next record will result in the appropriate record being transferred into memory ie. the programmers "view" may just be like this:-

R1	R2	R3	R4	R5	R6 etc.

R1 . . . . R6 are logical records.

b. **Direct Files.** These are files which provide fast and efficient direct access. ie. they are normally *random files* with *one* of a number of appropriate addressing methods. A common type of direct file is the **Relative File.** The logical organisation of a relative file is like this:-

R1	R2	R3	R4	R5	R6 etc.
1	2	3	4	5	6 etc.

R1 . . . . R6 are *logical records* with *logical keys* 1 . . . 6.

A relative file may be accessed sequentially or randomly.

c. **Index Sequential Files.** Logical versions of index sequential files are simpler than their physical counterparts, in that logical keys are used instead of disk addresses, and details of overflow are hidden from the programmer. The accessing methods are the same as those given in 21c.

FILE CALCULATIONS.

37. Basic calculations of storage requirements and times are often needed for magnetic disk files, just as they are for files on magnetic tape (16.17).

38. From paragraph 18 we may deduce that:

average access time = seek time + latency + Data transfer time

39. For a random file where N records were read the total read time would simply be N × average access time. Note that a whole sector would have to be read in just to get each individual record.

40. For a sequential file, where the disk was not being used for any other accesses at the same time, there would be a seek for each cylinder and then all sectors in the cylinder would be read. This suggests a formula such as:

$$\text{Total read time} \approx \left[\text{seek time} + \left[\text{latency + data transfer time} \right] \times \left[\text{number of sectors per cylinder} \right] \right] \times \left[\text{number of cylinders per file} \right]$$

OTHER 'DIRECT ACCESS' MEDIA.

41. The ability to access records independently of others within the file, ie. at random or *directly* has resulted in the term *direct access* devices being given to those devices able to offer this facility. The magnetic drum is another direct access device.

MAGNETIC DRUM.

42. The physical nature of drums, ie. having a read-write head per tracks, reduces the elements of access time to rotational delay and transfer time (no seek time being involved as with disk).

As electro-mechanical movement is a major part of access time, the elemination of seek time makes access to drums faster than to disks.

SUMMARY.

43. a. Conceptually the disk is regarded as being composed of so many concentric CYLINDERS.

b. Disk is an addressable medium and therefore specific records can be accessed leaving the rest of the file undisturbed.

c. Organisation on disk is by cylinder, track, and bucket (or block).

d. Access time on disk consists of three components, seek time, rotational delay, and data transfer time.

e. The overlay or "in place" method of updating *can be* used on disk.

f. Methods of file organisation on disk are:
   i. Serial.
   ii. Sequential (with or without an index).
   iii. Random.

g. Methods of access to disk files are:-
   i. Serial (for serial and sequential files).
   ii. Selective sequential (for indexed sequential files).
   iii. Sequential (for sequential and indexed sequential files).
   iv. Random (for random and indexed sequential files).

h. File maintenance on disk raises problems:-
   i. When inserting new records.
   ii. When updating variable length records.

i. Special overflow areas are designated on disk to take new records and over-length records temporarily.

j. A periodic file reorganisation run is required with disk files to place records residing temporarily in overflow areas into their correct sequence in the file and to leave off "deleted" records. Any index also has to be reconstructed during this run.

k. A summary of normally accepted methods of File Organisation on disk and associated methods of access is given in Fig. 17.3.

FILE ORGANISATION METHOD	METHOD OF ACCESS
1. Serial } (Sequential)	Serial } (Sequential)
2. Sequential } (Sequential)	Serial (Sequential) } (Sequential)
3. Indexed Sequential	a. Sequential b. Selective sequential c. Random (Direct)
4. Random (Direct or Relative)	Random (Direct)

Fig. 17.3.

NB. Terms in parentheses are alternative terms normally used at a logical level.

POINTS TO NOTE.

44. a. The expression "the disk" has been used in this chapter. It is probably more correct to use the slightly more verbose expression "the disk pack".

b. "Seek area" or "cylinder" constitutes the amount of data available at any one time to the read-write heads, for only one movement of the access mechanism. Note however that data can only be read or written from *one* read-write head at any one time.

c. Although it is a direct access device, the disk is very often used without making use of the particular characteristic of direct access for reasons which will be stated later.

d. Updating in place (overlay) is generally adopted in conjunction with *fixed* length records.

e. The methods of file organisation and access were dealt with separately in the text for clarity. They are however very much related.

f. If you are asked a question about "File Organisation" the chances are you will be required to talk about the whole subject including, of course, access.

g. Although dealt with separately in the interests of clarity File Maintenance and File Reorganisation are closely related and should both be included in an examination answer on either subject.

h. It is desirable to have a disk overflow area on the *same* cylinder as the home area. If the overflow area is on a different cylinder then the access mechanism has to move *twice* for one access; once to the home area and then to the overflow area. The second movement is not required if the home area and the overflow area are on the same cylinder.

i. Note the implication of an overflow area during the Sequential access of an Indexed Sequential file on DISK. Access is made to every record in their *logical* sequence, which may *not* be the same as the *physical* sequence because some of the records will be residing temporarily in an overflow area.

j. Details of file processing methods will be covered in later chapters.

STUDENT SELF TEST QUESTIONS.

(Answers on page 696)

1. *What factors would govern choice of storage media?*

2. *Outline the methods by which files may be organised and accessed on:*

   a. *magnetic tape,*

   b. *magnetic disk.*

For files on each medium, state the contents of file labels and explain how they are used.

(A.E.B. 1977)

3. *Describe a method of file organisation on a direct-access storage device, which involves a hash algorithm (address generation algorithm).*

A file on a direct-access device occupies 100 blocks, each block containing 1000 characters.

*The records are of variable length, terminated by *; the last record terminator in each block being followed by /. The key of each record is contained in the first 6 characters, and the file is organised with a specified hash algorithm.*

a. Draw a flowchart to show how, given a key, you would obtain the required record, assuming that the record is not in an overflow block.

b. Explain what is meant by overflow, and describe briefly how you obtain a record from an overflow block.

(A.E.B. 1976)

4. *Describe briefly each of the following methods of file organisation, listing the particular merits of each.*

a. Sequential

b. Direct

c. Index Sequential.

(B.C.S. Part 1 1974)

5. *Describe the way sectors are addressed on a disk pack.*

6. *Discuss the problems of file security on disk files.*

7. *Design an access method for a situation where records are stored in a relative file with physical records numbered I . . N but with logical records numbered 2501 to 3500. Design two methods:*

a. using address generation

b. using an index.

State any assumption that you make.

8. *A disk drive and its exchangeable disk pack have the following characteristics:*

i. The disk is hard sectored with 8 sectors of 512 characters per track and 200 tracks on each surface. There are six usable surfaces per pack.

ii. The disk has a seek time of 20 ms when seeking an adjacent track but an average seek time of 40 ms.

iii. The disk rotates once every 24 ms and has a data transfer rate of 256000 ch per second.

A file to be stored on the disk consists of 19200 records each 128 ch in length.

a. How many records can be stored in each sector?

b. What percentage of available disk space will the file occupy?

c. If the file is stored with sequential organisation how long will it take to read the whole file sequentially.

d. If the file is stored with random organisation how long will it take to read the whole file in key sequence?

State any assumptions made and comment on your results.

9. a. Information is stored in the form of records on a sequential file sorted on a particular key and held on a magnetic tape. Explain how records can be inserted into and deleted from such a file. [7]

b. What is meant by an indexed file and how can it be accessed?

An insurance company has records for each of its 700,000 clients, each record contains 300 characters including a 20 character sort key. If the disk block size is 2400 characters, how could an index for the file be organised?

Write down the operations that would have to be performed to find a record with a given key. [13]

Welsh Joint Education Committee (1983)

QUESTIONS WITHOUT ANSWERS

10. Distinguish between the way sectors are located on a hard sectored disk from the way they are located on a soft sectored disk.

Find out the kind of sectoring used on the types of disks you use.

11. Find out the operating characteristics of the types of disk you use eg. seek time, latency. Calculate the time taken to read one record from the disk.

12. The characteristics of a particular disk drive are as follows:

i. the disk has a single recording surface consisting of 200 tracks;
ii. the disk rotates at 3000 revolutions per minute (i.e. 20 milliseconds per revolution);
iii. moving the head from one track to another takes approximately 25 milliseconds plus 10 milliseconds per track moved;
iv. after moving the head it takes on average half a revolution to find the marker which indicates the start of data on the track.

A file occupies tracks 151 to 200 of a disk and is to be moved to occupy tracks 1 to 50 of the same disk. A program exists which copies a file by reading a complete track and then writing a complete track, continuing until all tracks of the file have been copied. Assuming that a complete track is transferred in a single operation and that the processor time involved in initiating read and write operations is negligible compared to the transfer times, calculate approximately the time taken to move the file.

If a second disk drive is available which may be accessed concurrently with the first one, by what method and by approximately how much may this time be reduced?

Explain all your timing calculations.

Cambridge (1981)

13. a. Explain the following terms:

i. file creation,

ii. file reorganisation,

iii. master file. **6**

b. A magnetic disk cartridge has 10 usable disk surfaces. Each surface has 200 tracks, with 10 blocks per track. The timing for the disk is as follows.

Time for one revolution	*25 msecs*
One track seek	*10 msecs*
Average time for a random seek	*40 msecs.*

i. For this disk calculate the file size for 20,000 records packed at 10 records/block.

ii. The above file is to be updated with 200 records. Calculate the time for this update for both a sequential and a random update, stating any assumptions you make. Comment on your answers. **14 = 20**

JMB 1983

14. A fully indexed file which has a large number of records of variable length, and which is subject to very frequent insertions and deletions, is held on a disk. The structure of the file is illustrated and described below.

The file occupies a number of blocks, some of which contain records, some of which contain the index, and the rest of which are free. The records in the file are not stored in any particular order, but each has a key field by which it is referenced. After the last record in each record block there is an end marker.

The index consists of two parts, a primary index which occupies a single block, and a secondary index occupying several blocks. The secondary index contains an entry for each record in the file, consisting of a copy of the record key field and the number of the block in which the record is stored. Each block of the secondary index contains a count of the number of entries in it followed by the entries, and all the entries in the secondary index are held in ascending order of key. The primary index block contains the block number of the first free block (or −1 if there are none), and a count of the number of secondary index blocks, followed by an entry for each block in the secondary index. These entries consist of the highest key referred to in that secondary index block, together with its block number, and they are held in ascending order of key.

Each free block contains a single entry, the block number of the next free block or −1 if there is none, to form a chain starting with the first free block referred to in the primary index.

Describe briefly the actions which may need to be taken when a record with a given key is to be deleted from the file. Your description should include consideration of the special cases that may arise. *[19]*

(Cambridge 1983)

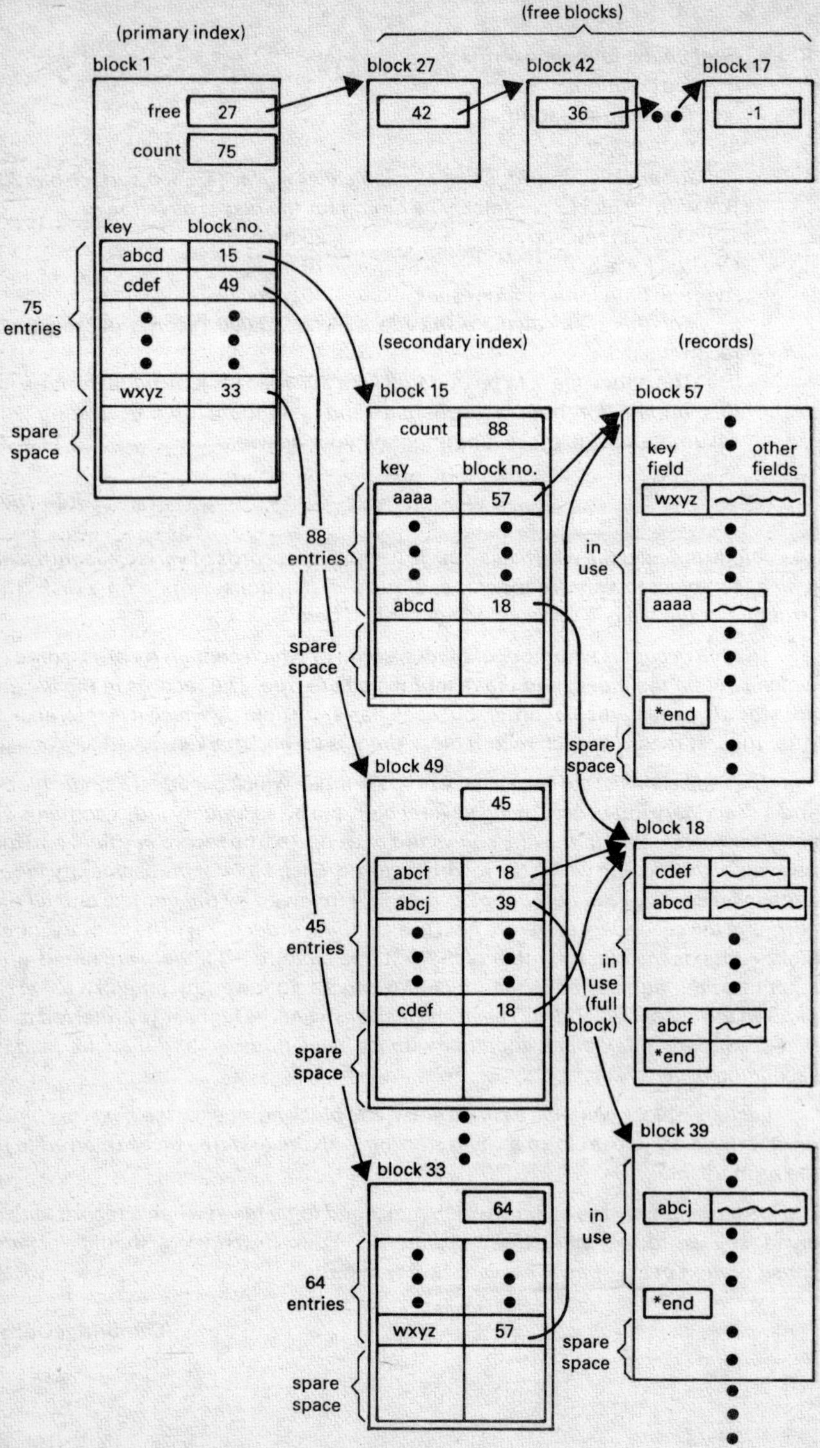
(primary index)
block 1
free
27
count
75
key
block no.
abcd
15
cdef
49
wxyz
33
75 entries
spare space
(free blocks)
block 27
42
block 42
36
block 17
-1
(secondary index)
block 15
count
88
key
block no.
aaaa
57
abcd
18
88 entries
spare space
block 49
45
abcf
18
abcj
39
cdef
18
45 entries
spare space
block 33
64
wxyz
57
64 entries
spare space
(records)
block 57
key field
other fields
wxyz
aaaa
*end
in use
spare space
block 18
cdef
abcd
abcf
*end
in use (full block)
block 39
abcj
*end
in use
spare space

Data Collection and Controls

1. The data which is required to be processed by the computer must be presented to it in a *machine-sensible* form. Therein lies the basic problem since most data *originates* in a form which is *far* from machine sensible. Thus a painful error-prone process of transcription must be undergone before the data is suitable for input to the computer.

2. The process of data collection involves getting the original data to the "processing centre", transcribing it, sometimes converting it from one medium to another, and finally getting it into the computer. This process involves a great many people, machines and much expense.

3. A number of advances have been made in recent years, towards automating the data collection process so as to bypass or reduce the problems. This Part will consider both traditional and modern methods. Emphasis will be placed upon the methods used in data processing because of their widespread use and importance. Specialist methods used for industrial computer applications will be covered in the chapter on analog and hybrid computers.

4. Chapter 18 traces the various stages through which data travels before being used for processing against master files. Chapter 19 describes the various methods/media used for the collection of data. Chapter 20 discusses the factors which influence the choice of a particular method/medium. Chapter 21 examines the subject of system controls both in connection with data collection and computer processing. Chapter 22 looks at Data Transmission and Networks.

18 Data Collection Stages

INTRODUCTION.

1. Data can originate in many forms but the computer can only accept it in a machine-sensible form (ie. the language of the particular input device). The process involved in getting the data from its point of origin to the computer in a form suitable for processing against master files is called Data Collection. This chapter outlines the stages involved in this process.

2. Before dealing with the individual stages of data collection it should be noted that data collection *starts* at the source of the raw data and *ends* when valid data is within the computer in a form ready for processing. (eg. as a valid sorted transaction file).

STAGES IN DATA COLLECTION.

3. a. Data creation. eg. on clerically prepared source documents.

b. Transmission of data.

c. Data preparation. ie. Transcription and verification.

d. Possible conversion from one medium (eg. diskette) to another (eg. magnetic tape).

e. Input of data to the computer for validation.

f. Sorting.

g. Control – all stages must be controlled.

4. Not all data will go through every stage and the sequence could vary in some applications. A high proportion of input data starts its life in the form of a manually scribed or typewritten document and would have to go through all the stages. However, efforts have been made to reduce the number of stages. Progress has been made in preparing the source document itself in a machine-sensible form so that it may be used as input to the computer without the need for transcription. In practice the method/medium adopted will depend on factors such as cost, type of application, etc. This will be discussed further in chapter 20.

STAGES EXPLAINED.

5. a. **Data Creation.** There are two basic alternatives, the first of which is the traditional method:-

i. **Source Documents.** A great deal of data still originates in the form of clerically prepared source documents.

ii. **Data Capture.** Data is produced in a machine sensible form at source and is read directly by a suitable device eg. a bar code reader.

b. **Data transmission.** This can mean different things according to the method/medium of data collection adopted.

i. If the computer is located at a central point, the documents will be physically "transmitted" ie. by the post office or a courier to the central point. (eg. posting batches of source documents).

ii. It is also possible for data to be transmitted by means of telegraph lines to the central computer in which case no source documents would be involved in the transmission process. (eg. transmitting data captured at source).

c. **Data preparation.** This is the term given to the *transcription* of data from the source document to a machine-sensible medium. There are two parts; the original transcription itself and the verification process that follows.

NB. Data Capture eliminates the need for transcription.

d. **Media conversion.** Very often data is prepared in a particular medium and converted to another medium for faster input to the computer, eg. data might be prepared on diskette, or captured onto cassette, and then converted to magnetic tape for input.

e. **Input.** The data, now in magnetic form, is subjected to validity checks by computer program before it is used for processing against the appropriate master file.

f. **Sorting.** This stage is required to re-arrange the data into the sequence required for processing eg. into the sequence of the master file. (This is a practical necessity for efficient batch processing of sequential files).

g. **Control.** This is not a *stage* as such, because control is applied throughout the *whole* data collection.

DATA COLLECTION MEDIA/METHODS IN OUTLINE.

6. a. Source document keyed directly into diskette (key-to-diskette) from some documents.

b. Source data punched into cards or paper tape from a source document.

c. Source data keyed directly onto magnetic tape (Key-to-Tape) from a source document.

d. Source data keyed onto magnetic tape but via a disk (Key-to-Disk) from a source document.

e. Portable encoding devices.

f. The source document itself prepared in machine-sensible form using Character Recognition techniques.

g. Source data captured in 'Tags'.

h. Use of Plastic Badges or Data Carriers.

i. Creation of data for input as a by-product of another operation.

j. On-line transmission of data from source.

SUMMARY.

7. a. Data collection is the process of getting data into a form suitable for processing against master files.

POINTS TO NOTE.

8. a. Many traditional methods require data preparation, eg: Key-to-Disk, key-to-tape etc.

b. Many modern methods collect data in machine sensible form thereby eliminating data preparation eg. Character recognition, source document capture etc.

STUDENT SELF TEST QUESTIONS.

(Answers on page 699)

1. At what stages in data collect is control applied?

2. Distinguish between "human-sensible" and "machine-sensible". Give an example of a form of computer input which is both machine-sensible and human-sensible.

19. Methods and Media

INTRODUCTION.

1. This chapter explains the various media/methods used in the data collection process. We will go through them one by one in the order previously indicated.

2. In earlier chapters we concentrated on devices and media. Now we consider the whole data entry process.

KEY-TO-DISKETTE.

3. We start with key-to-diskette systems because they represent a major modern method of data entry.

4. The simplest key-to-diskette system is a stand alone workstation consisting of a high quality VDU with inbuilt dual diskette units and microprocessor. (Fig. 19.1a.)

5. The workstation operates under the control of its own programs which format the screen like a document, verify and validate input data, and transfer the data onto diskette. Programs for dealing with different source documents may be held on diskette and loaded by the workstation user when required.

6. The workstations are compact, robust, reliable, portable and operate autonomously. They therefore enable distributed data entry (close to the source of the data) together with a simple means of transfering data to a central computer.

7. Larger systems often include local printers to provide hard copy (ie. on paper) of the disk input (eg. for audit trail purposes, and electronic data transmission facilities. (Fig. 19.1b). The largest systems normally form part of a distributed data processing system in which work stations are multi-purpose devices and facilities for data storage and transmission are varied and flexible, eg. a workstation may act as an interactive terminal to the main computer, or large volumes of data on diskette may be converted to magnetic tape for faster bulk input. (Fig. 19.1c).

8. The systems just described represent the new generation in a line of developments intended to lead to the total replacement of punched card systems. Methods which represent earlier attempts are Key-to-tape, and Key-to-disk.

PUNCHED CARD.

9. a. Data from a source document is 'punched' into cards.

b. A verification process follows which is a virtual repeat of 9a.

c. Batches of cards then go as computer input. (Documents are returned to the appropriate clerical department).

d. Because of very slow input speeds cards are invariably converted to magnetic tape for faster input.

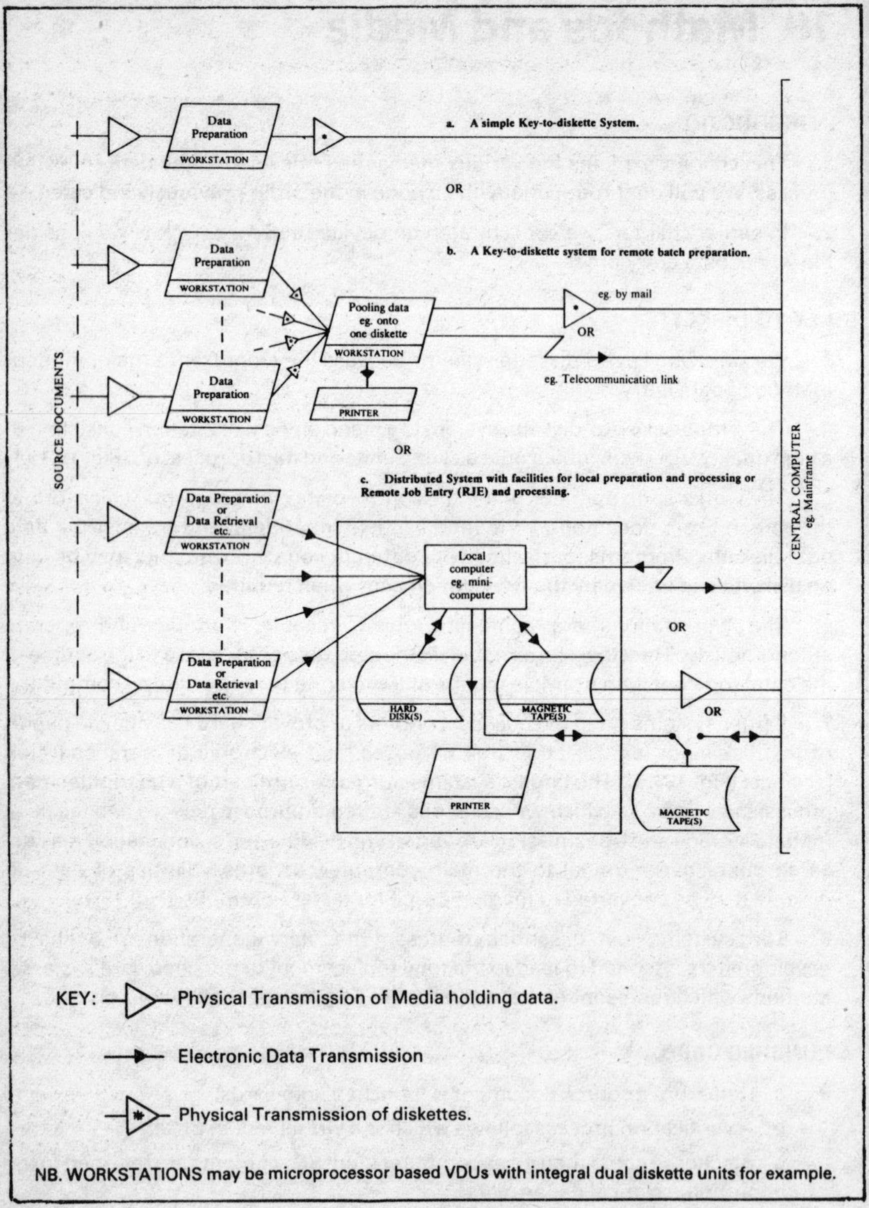

Fig. 19.1. Some Typical Data Entry Systems.

PUNCHED PAPER TAPE.

10. a. Data is punched into rolls/spools of paper tape.

b. A verification process follows. There are two *main* methods of verifying punched paper tape:-

i. **Call-over methods.** A tape-punch machine is linked to a printer which prints a copy of the data which is punched into the tape. The printed copy is visually checked against the source document.

ii. **Two-tape method.** A tape is punched from the source document and then fed into a Tape Verifier. A different operator punches a *fresh* tape and as this is being done, the Verifier compares each character with the corresponding character in the *first* tape. The verifier stops if an error is detected.

c. Spools of punched paper tape then go as computer input.

d. Again a conversion process is likely for faster input.

KEY-TO-TAPE.

11. This involves the use of a machine called a Magnetic Tape Encoder. The machine consists of a keyboard, a small electronic memory, and a reel of magnetic tape which is removable. It can be regarded as a replacement for the punched card method. The steps involved are as follows:-

a. Data from a source document is keyed by an operator on to the tape reel via the encoder's 'memory'. Before passing from memory to the tape, limited validity checks are carried out, eg. if the operator is keying-in a 'name' field the machine will not accept a numeric character.

b. When a *batch* of documents has been encoded onto tape, verification follows.

c. This is done by re-loading the tape and switching the encoder to 'Verify' status. The keying-in process is repeated and the machine carries out a comparison with the data already on the tape. The machine stops if an error is detected. Errors can be corrected there and then by *overwriting* the incorrect data on the tape.

d. A *different* operator usually performs the verification process.

e. Each encoder is equipped with one tape reel, and the reels from a *number* of encoders are pooled (merged onto *one* reel). The "pooled" reel is then used as input to the computer. (See Fig. 19.2).

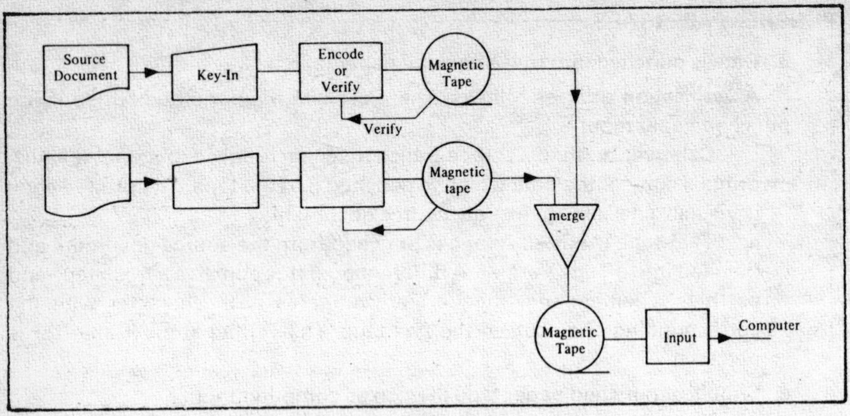

Fig. 19.2. A Key-to-Tape System.

KEY-TO-DISK.

12. These are complete "systems" consisting of a number (between 5-60 depending on model) of Key Stations linked directly to a mini computer (processor). The processor itself consists of a small memory, an arithmetic and logic unit, and a control unit. Directly linked to the processor is a disk unit and a tape unit. All the key stations and the processor will generally be located together in one room. The system operates as follows:-

a. Data from a source document is keyed in at a key station by an operator. Data is automatically formatted and stored on the disk under control of a program in the processor. (The program is changed for each different type of application ie. payroll, invoice etc).

b. Verification is done by a different operator who keys in the same data from the source documents. This is compared with the data already residing on disk and errors can be corrected there and then. Data to be verified is identified by batch numbers.

c. On instructions keyed in by the supervisor via a console typewriter completed batches are written from disk to a magnetic tape reel which is taken to the computer and used as input.

d. A limited amount of sorting and validation is carried out by the system.

e. Each key station be used for both keying and verification.

f. Control totals are automatically assembled by the processor. (See Fig. 19.3).

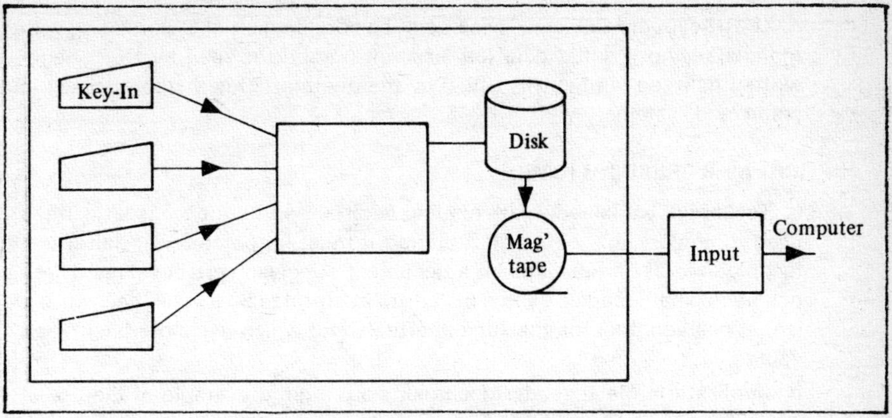

Fig. 19.3. A Key-to-Disk System.

PORTABLE ENCODING DEVICES.

13. Portable encoding devices are now in common use eg. data loggers (5.20). Note that these devices often employ magnetic cassettes or cartridges for storage purposes.

CHARACTER RECOGNITION.

14. The methods described so far have been concerned with turning data *into* a machine-sensible form as a pre-requisite to input. By using Optical Character Recognition (OCR) and Magnetic Ink Character Recognition (MICR) techniques, the source documents *themselves* are prepared in a machine-sensible form and thus *eliminate* the transcription stage. Notice however that such characters can *also* be recognised by the human eye. (See Fig. 5.1 and 5.3).

OPTICAL CHARACTER RECOGNITION (OCR).

15. a. **Technique explained.**

i. Alphabetic and numeric characters are created in a particular type style which can be "read" by special machines (5.12). The characters look so nearly like 'normal' print that they can *also* be read by humans.

ii. Characters are *created* by a variety of machines (eg. line printers, typewriters, cash registers etc.) fitted with the special type-face.

iii. The special optical character reading machines *can* be linked to a computer, in which case the data is read from the document into the CPU.

b. **Applications.**OCR is used extensively in connection with billing, eg. gas and electricity bills and insurance premium renewals. In these applications the bills are prepared in OC by the computer, then sent out to the customers who return them with payment cheques. The documents re-enter the computer system (via. the OC reader) as evidence of payment. This is an example of the "turn-around" technique. Notice that no transcription is required.

c. **OCR/Keyboard Devices.** These permit a combination of OCR reading with manual keying. Printed data (eg. account number) is read by OCR; handwritten data (eg. amount) is keyed by the operator. This method is used in credit card systems.

OPTICAL MARK READING (OMR).

16. a. **Technique explained.** Mark reading is discussed here because it is often used in conjunction with OCR although it must be pointed out that it is a technique in *itself.* Positions on a document are given certain values. These positions when 'marked' with a pencil are interpreted by a machine. Notice it is the 'position' that the machine interprets and which has a predetermined value.

b. **Application.** Meter reader documents are a good example of the use of OMR in conjunction with OCR. The computer prints out the document for each customer (containing name, address, *last* reading etc.) in OC. The meter reader records the current reading in the form of 'marks' on the same document. The document re-enters the computer system (via. a reader which reads OC *and* OM) and is processed (ie. results in a bill being sent to the customer). Note that this is another example of a **"turnaround"** document. (See Fig. 19.4).

MAGNETIC INK CHARACTER RECOGNITION (MICR).

17. a. **Technique explained.** Numeric characters are created in a highly stylised type, by special encoding machines using magnetic ink. Documents encoded thus are 'read' by special machines (5.14).

b. **Application.** One major application is in Banking (look at your own cheque book) although some local authorities use it for payment of rates by instalments. Cheques are encoded at the bottom with account number, branch code, and cheque number *before* being given to the customer (ie. pre-encoded). When the cheques are received *from* the customers the bottom line is completed by encoding the *amount* of the cheque (ie. post-encoded). Thus all the details necessary for processing are now encoded in MIC and the cheque enters the computer system via a magnetic ink character reader to be processed.

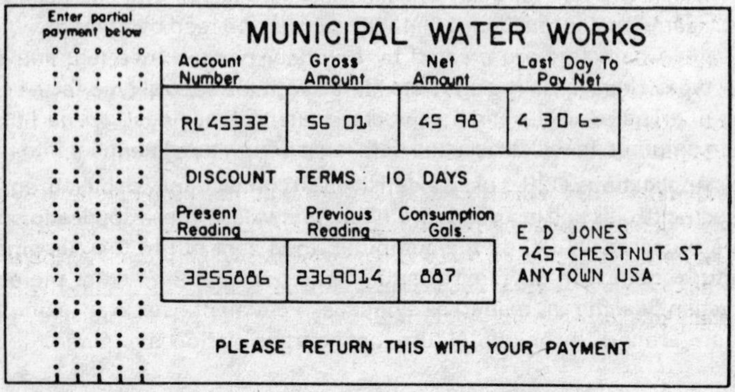

Fig. 19.4. Turnaround Document (OCR/OMR).

PUNCHED TAGS.

18. The use of tags as a data collection technique is usually associated with clothing retailing applications although they are also used to some extent in other applications.

a. Small cardboard tags are used as miniature punched cards.

b. Using a special code, data such as price of garment, type and size, and branch/dept are *punched* into the tag, by a machine. Certain of the data is also *printed* on the tag.

c. Tags are affixed to the garment before sale and are *removed* at the point of sale. At the end of the day's trading each store will send its tags (representing the day's sales) in a container to the Data Processing Centre.

d. At the centre the tags are *converted* to more conventional diskette or magnetic tape for input to the computer system.

e. Note that data is "captured" at the source (point of sale) in a machine-sensible form and thus needs no transcription and can be processed straight-away by the machine. (See Fig. 19.5).

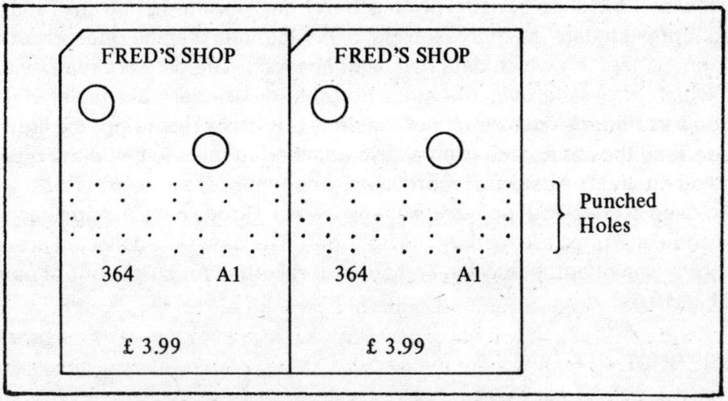

Fig. 19.5. Punched Tags.

EMBOSSED PLASTIC BADGES.

19. The use of plastic 'data carriers' as the plastic badges are sometimes called is similar in concept to the BARCLAYCARD. They are usually incorporated in a data collection system designed for a specific application. They are in use as Shop Floor data collection systems. Three elements make up such a system:-

a. **A plastic card.** This is embossed with both machine and human-sensible data. These cards can carry a variety of data according to the application. There may be a set of two or three cards. The first will contain the identification details of an operative eg. number, machine etc. The second will contain details of a job eg. number of units etc.

b. **A data recorder.** To record a job the operative inserts the cards into the recorder and presses a lever. The data is automatically transcribed into a card (similar to a punched card). Also produced is a flimsy copy for immediate control purposes. Most recorders have facilities for manual insertion of variable data, eg. items of production are recorded by *setting keys* on the machine.

c. **Converter.** This machine accepts the output (the card) from the data recorder and converts it into a medium acceptable as computer input eg. magnetic tape.

Note that the data finally captured at the conversion stage is then processed by a computer to produce the necessary information eg. production figures etc. The system described is an off-line system of data collection but the data recorder can be linked *direct* to a computer to give an on-line system of data collection.

BAR-CODED AND MAGNETIC STRIPS.

20. Data can be recorded on small strips which are read optically or magnetically. Optical reading is done by using printed 'bar codes'; ie. alternating lines and spaces which represent data in binary (see Fig. 5.4). Magnetic reading depends on a strip of magnetic tape on which data has been encoded. The data are read by a 'light-pen' which is passed over the strip. Portable devices are available which also include a key-board. An example of their use is in stock recording; the light-pen is used to read the stock code from a strip attached to the shelf, and the quantity is keyed manually. The data are recorded on a magnetic tape cassette. This technique is also used at check-out points in super-markets. Goods have a strip attached and stock code and price are read by the light-pen. The data thus collected are used to prepare a receipt automatically, and are also recorded for stock control purposes. (See Fig. 19.6).

BY-PRODUCT.

21. All the systems describe up to now have been designed specifically with data collection in mind but data can very often be collected as a by-product of some other operation. Two good examples of this are found with the operation of accounting machines and cash registers:-

a. **Accounting machines.** Paper tape punches are attached to the accounting machine thus collecting immediately in machine-sensible form, sales statistics (invoicing application) stock figures (stock ledger) etc. The data is thus in a form suitable for computer processing.

b. **Cash registers.** These are fitted with paper tape punches, tally roll printers or magnetic tape cassette units. A mass of statistical data is captured at source without any intermediate operation. The rolls of tape etc. are forwarded to the Data Processing Centre for input to a computer.

0 12345 67890

11-Digit Symbol

0 003190

7-Digit Symbol

Courtesy IBM

The type of bar-coding shown here is used on packets of consumable products such as foods. The numbers are coded in bar-coded strips and printed in OCR characters. The code is called a **UPC** (Universal Product Code) in the USA and a **EAN** (European Article Number) in Europe. The lefthand digit, '0' in 'a' above, represents the country of origin eg. '0' is the USA, '5' is the UK. The next four digits are the manufacturers code and the last five are the product number.

Such details would not be asked for in an examination but serve as a good illustration of a specialised coding system.

Fig. 19.6. An example of an application of Bar-coding.

ON-LINE SYSTEMS.

22. The ultimate in data collection is to have the computer linked *directly* to the source of the data. If this is *not* feasible then the next best thing is to 'capture' the data as near as possible to its source and feed it to the computer with little delay.

23. Such methods involve the use of data transmission equipment. The computer is linked to the terminal point (the source of data or near) by a telecommunication line and data is transmitted over the line to the computer system.

24. Data enters the terminal either by keying in via a keyboard or is transmitted using a paper tape attachment or some other medium (data having been transcribed from the source document previously).

25. On-line methods obviate the need for physical transportation of source documents to the processing point. There is also less delay in producing processed information especially if the data link provides for two-way transmission of data (ie. from terminal to computer and computer to terminal).

The IBM 3660 Supermarket System incorporates a high speed optical scanner. As an item is pulled across the scanner's window a laser beam reads the European Article Number (or Universal Product Code in the US) bar code printed on the side of the package and the system automatically decodes and registers the information on the symbol.
The item can be of any shape or size and the bar code can be passed over the window in any direction. Picture and details courtesy of IBM.

26. Such systems can involve large capital outlay on the necessary equipment which is usually justified in terms of speed of access to computer files and quicker feed-back of information.

27. On-line systems are the only practical choice for some applications. One example is the computer which controls a machine or factory process. It must receive input directly from source in order to be able to respond at a moment's notice.

DIRECT DATA ENTRY (DDE).

28. A Direct Data Entry Station consists of a Visual Display Unit with a keyboard. Data is keyed by the operator, checked, displayed on the screen and then entered for processing.

A DDE station can also be used to interrogate the computer files. The technique is particularly common with the smaller computer systems, but may be used in any configuration.

POINT-OF-SALE TERMINALS.

29. The Point-of-Sale Terminal **(PoS)** is essentially an electronic cash register which is linked to a computer, or which records data onto cassette or cartridge (21b.).

In its simplest form, it may simply transmit the details of a transaction to the computer for processing.

The more complex terminals can communicate with the computer for such purposes as checking the credit position of a customer, obtaining prices from file and ascertaining availability of stock.

The terminal usually includes a keyboard for manual entry of data. A bar code reader may also be provided, typically to read stock codes.

SUMMARY.

30. a. Data collection is accomplished in stages from source document through to actual processing against master files.

POINTS TO NOTE.

31. a. **Terminology.**

i. **Data collection.** The process of getting data to the computer in a machine-sensible form for processing.

ii. **Data capture.** Sometimes used as a substitute term for data collection but more specifically refers to data 'captured' in a machine-sensible form at its *source.*

b. **Differences between Key-to-tape and Key-to-disk.**

i. Key-to-tape uses *separate* machines (called encoders) and individual tapes have to be pooled for input.

ii. Key-to-disk. All key stations are *linked* to a processor and have *simultaneous* access to disk for entry of data. Data is transferred by the processor after verification to one tape reel under control of a supervisor.

iii. *No* operator handling of separate tapes is involved in Key-to-disk.

c. Note how smaller key-to-diskette systems are similar to key-to-tape and larger key-to-diskette systems are similar to key-to-disk.

d. **Key-to-tape.** The process of getting data from the source document to tape is referred to as 'ENCODING'.

e. **Punched tags.** A major manufacturer of systems based on punched tags is KIMBALL and thus you may find that they are referred to as KIMBALL TAGS.

f. Note how *on-line systems* speed up response time.

STUDENT SELF TEST QUESTIONS.

(Answers on page 699)

1. Key-to-diskette systems have replaced many input systems based upon punched cards or paper tape. Suggest how the paper-tape verification methods of paragraph 10 might be adapted for use with key-to-diskette systems.

2. What is a "turnaround document"?

3. Give two examples of systems in which on-line data entry would be essential.

4. a. Describe the use of any ***two*** *of the following methods for collecting data at source in machine readable form from*

i. "Point of Sale" terminals.

ii. MICR.

iii. Kimball tags.

For each method described state a suitable application area. ***[12 marks]***

b. Many computer applications require that a master file of data be held on backing store.

For each of the following methods of file organisation state a typical application which uses that method and explain why it is appropriate:

i. serial

ii. indexed sequential

iii. random (direct) ***[8 marks]***

AEB 1982

20. Choice of Method and Media

INTRODUCTION.

1. The selection of the best method of data collection is often the biggest single problem faced by the computer user, because of the high costs involved and the other problems described. This chapter deals with the factors which influence the choice.

FACTORS.

2. The choice of data collection method/medium may be influenced by the following factors:-

a. **Appropriateness.**

i. **Punched Cards.** Despite their obsolete features these are still used for computer input. This is partly because they are well tried and tested; many computer users converted from punched card installations. Cards have the advantage that they can be used as an off-line 'manual' file. The main replacement for punched cards is the diskette (floppy disk).

Cards are bulky and expensive, and cannot be re-used.

ii. **Paper Tape** was used mainly in 'scientific' applications – eg. research institutes and colleges. It is much cheaper than punched cards and less bulky but also less convenient.

Both punched card and paper tape have the disadvantage that their input speeds are slow. Both media are in rapid decline.

iii. **Magnetic Tape** is now an established method of input. It is re-usable, and can be input at much higher speeds than punched cards or paper tape. Moreover, key-to-disk systems provide an advanced method of data collection with facilities for checking and control as the data are keyed, plus reducing the need for verification. Magnetic tape cassettes and cartridges are also growing in importance, being cheap and easily transportable. Input speeds are not as high as with ½" magnetic tape.

iv. **Magnetic diskettes** (floppy disks) are of major importance as input media. Like magnetic tape, they are re-usable and advanced equipment is available for their preparation. They are compact and relatively cheap.

v. **Character Recognition.**

(a) **MICR** is largely confined to banking. It was developed in response to the need to cope with large volumes of documents (in particular, cheques) beyond the scope of conventional methods (eg. diskettes). It is a very reliable but expensive method.

(b) **OCR** is more versatile than MICR and less expensive. It is suited to those applications which use a turnaround system such as billing in gas and electricity where volumes are too high for conventional methods. It is limited to applications in which a 'turn-around' document can be used – eg. a bill printed by the computer, part of which is returned with the payment.

(c) **OMR** is very simple and inexpensive. The forms can however be prepared only by people who have been trained in the method.

All character recognition techniques suffer from the possible disadvantage of requiring a standardised document acceptable to the document reader.

vi. **Direct Data Entry** is a very simple and convenient method, but is not suitable for large amounts of data.

vii. **Terminals** provide a very fast means of data collection. They may also provide a fast means of output direct to the point of use. But costs are increased by the need to provide terminals at a number of different points and the use of data transmission.

viii. **Special Media** such as plastic badges, perforated tags and bar-coded strips reduce costs, but are essentially tailored to particular types of application.

b. **Cost**. This must be an overriding factor. The elements of cost are:-

i. **Operators.** (probably the biggest).

ii. **Machinery.** (capital and running costs).

iii. **Buildings.** Floor space and environmental requirements.

iv. **Recording media.** Cards and paper tape are *not* re-usable, magnetic tape of course is.

c. **Time.** This can be quite fundamental in the choice of method/medium and is very much linked with cost because the quicker the response required the more it generally costs to get that response. Punched card and paper tape systems are slow and cumbersome having to go through all the stages in the collection cycle, a slowness which is accentuated by rejects having to go through the whole process again.

On-line systems will cut down this delay; so will methods like OCR which prepare source documents in a machine-sensible form.

d. **Accuracy.** This is linked with a. and f., and is a big headache in data collection. Input must be 'clean' otherwise it is rejected and delays occur. Error at the preparation stage also are costly. Substitution of the machine for the human is the answer in general terms.

e. **Volume.** Some methods will not be able to cope with high volumes of source data within a reasonable time scale.

f. **Confidence.** It is very important that a system has a record of success. This is probably why punched cards are still used. OCR and key-to-diskette have gained ground, and will grow in importance.

g. **Input medium.** The choice of input medium is very much tied up with data collection. Often it will be an integral part of data collection eg. on-line systems. Key-to-disk methods have the advantage of collecting data on what is a fast input medium. These two examples are enough to demonstrate the way in which input medium is a prime consideration when looking at the collection of data.

SUMMARY.

3. a. Data collection is a costly, time consuming, and, in many cases, cumbersome process. Therefore methods of reducing cost and/or of reducing the time involved must be worthwhile.

b. Remember the factors which influence choice of system:-

i. Appropriateness or suitability.
ii. Cost.
iii. Time.
iv. Accuracy.
v. Volume.
vi. Confidence.

c. Magnetic media have gradually replaced the punched card and key-to-diskette systems are the main punch card replacement.

d. Specialist methods such as kimball tags and plastic badges are in the minority but are important in their particular fields.

POINTS TO NOTE.

4. a. Note that data preparation is a part of the data collection process.

b. Data is often captured/prepared in one machine-sensible medium and converted to another before input to computer.

c. OCR/MICR "readers" can be of the type that are used off-line or on-line to the computer. The off-line readers may be linked to a magnetic tape unit so that the optical character/magnetic ink documents can be converted to tape for much faster input.

STUDENT SELF TEST QUESTIONS.

(Answers in page 700)

1. What do you consider to be the advantages and disadvantages of the various methods/media of data collection?

2. Compare the relatives advantages of a VDU and printer terminals for on-line computing.

3. Explain how the factors in paragraph 3b could influence the choice of printer to be used on a system.

QUESTIONS WITHOUT ANSWERS.

4. There is an advantage to retailers in keeping track of how many of each stock item are sold. Assuming that a computerised system is to be used, suggest a variety of methods and media which could be used to collect the data required for this purpose. State under what circumstances you think each of your suggestions would be most appropriate.

21. System Controls

INTRODUCTION.

1. This chapter is concerned with controls within a DP system. The objects of control are:

a. To ensure that all data are processed.

b. To preserve the integrity of maintained data.

c. To detect, correct and re-process all errors.

d. To prevent and detect fraud.

The different controls are dealt with under the following headings:

a. Manual controls – applied to documents prior to computer processing.

b. Data preparation controls.

c. Validation checks.

d. Batch controls.

e. File controls.

DESIGN CONSIDERATIONS.

2. Controls are a major consideration of the systems designer. They must be designed into the system and thoroughly tested. Failure to build in adequate control has caused many expensive system failures.

3. The need for controls must be clearly defined at the outset to enable the appropriate action to be taken to provide them. User staff and auditors should be fully consulted.

IMPORTANCE OF CONTROL.

4. Control must be instituted as early as possible in the system. The quality of input data is of vital importance to the accuracy of output. Everything possible must be done to ensure that data are complete and accurate before input to the computer.

TYPES OF ERROR.

5. The systems designer must provide for the following types of error:

a. Missing source documents.

b. Source documents on which entries are omitted, illegible or dubious.

c. Transcription errors (eg. errors in copying data from one form to another).

d. Data preparation errors (eg. errors made when punching cards).

e. Program faults.

f. Machine faults.

Note:
Machine faults are far less common in practice than is often supposed. Modern

computers are self-checking to a very considerable extent (eg. parity) and usually signal any internal failure. The machine is very often blamed for what are really faults in systems design or programming.

MANUAL CONTROLS.

6. Even in advanced DP systems, considerable checking of source documents is often necessary. Such checks may be:

a. **Scrutiny** to detect:
   i. missing entries.
   ii. illegible entries.
   iii. illogical or unlikely entries.

b. **Reference** of the document to a file to verify entries.

c. **Re-calculating** to check calculations made on the document.

DATA COLLECTION CONTROLS.

7. The collection of data for processing involves transcribing it into a form suitable for machine processing. There is a very real possibility of error at this stage, and control must be imposed to prevent or detect transcription errors. The type of control depends on the method of data collection used.

a. **Punched Cards, Paper Tape and Magnetic Tape.** The basic control is to repeat the keyboarding operation, the second stage being known as verification. Verification techniques are described in (19.9–19.11).

b. **Character Recognition.** With these techniques, accuracy depends on the character reader detecting any doubtful character or mark. Some readers provide facilities for display of the character and its immediate manual correction by the operator. Otherwise, the document is rejected by the machine.

c. **On-line systems.** These depend on the data being printed (by a type-writer) or displayed (by a VDU) and checked by the operator before being released for processing.

VALIDATION CHECKS.

8. A computer cannot notice errors in the data being processed in the way that a clerk or machine operator does. Validation checks are an attempt to build into the computer program powers of judgement so that incorrect items of data are detected and reported. These checks can be made at two stages:

a. **Input.** When data is first input to the computer, different checks can be applied to prevent errors going forward for processing. For this reason, the first computer run is often referred to as VALIDATION or DATA VET.

b. **Updating.** Further checking is possible when the data input are matched with master files. The consistency of transactions with master file records can be checked by the program. It is possible to perform checks of this type during the Validation Run if the master file is on-line at the time.

9. The following are the main types of validation check which may be used.

a. **Presence.** Data are checked to ensure that all necessary fields are present.

b. **Size.** Fields are checked to ensure that they contain the correct number of characters.

c. **Range.** Numbers or codes are checked to ensure that they are within the permissible range (eg. costs codes within the series allocated).

d. **Character check.** Fields are checked to ensure that they contain only characters of the correct type (eg. that there are no letters in a numeric field).

e. **Format.** Fields are checked to ensure that the format is correct (eg. that a part number contains the correct number of alphabetic and numeric characters in the correct sequence).

f. **Reasonableness.** Quantities are checked to ensure that they are not abnormally high or low (eg. that the amount of a certain type of goods ordered is "reasonable").

g. **Check Digits.** Use of a check digit enables a number to be self-checking. It is calculated using a mathematical formula and then becomes part of the number. (See Appendix 2.4). When the number is input to the computer, the Validation Program performs the same calculation on the number as was performed when the check digit was generated in the first place. This will ensure the number is correct, eg. no digits have been transposed.

The checks described above are usually applied during the first processing run. When input data are matched with master files, further checks may be made. These are:

a. **New records.** If a complete new record is input for insertion into the master file, a check is made to see that a record with the same key number is not already present.

b. **Deleted records.** If input indicates that a record is to be deleted from the file, an error is reported if the record is not present on the file.

c. **Consistency.** Before the master file record is amended, a check may be made to ensure that the new data is consistent with data already stored in the record (eg. before updating a payroll record with overtime payments, the record would be checked to ensure that the employee was not a salaried member of staff not entitled to overtime).

BATCH CONTROLS.

10. Batch controls are fundamental to most computer-based accounting systems. Similar techniques are used with accounting machines. The stages of batch control in a computer-based system are:-

a. **Batching.** At an early stage in processing, documents are arranged in batches by being placed in a wallet or folder, or clipped together. The number of documents in a batch may be standard (eg. 50) or may represent a convenient group (eg. one day's orders from one sales office). A *batch cover note* is attached to the batch.

b. **Numbering.** Each batch is allocated a unique number, which is entered on the batch cover note.

c. **Batch registers.** Each department or section responsible for processing the batch records its receipt and despatch in a register. It is thus possible to check that all batches have been received and dealt with, and to trace any batch which gets lost or delayed.

d. **Batch totals.** Control totals are obtained for each batch, usually using a desk adding or calculating machine. The control totals comprise:

i. the number of documents in the batch,

ii. totals of the fields which it is required to control (eg. total value of invoices; total value of overtime payments; total quantities of orders).

These totals are entered on the *batch cover* note.

e. **Data preparation.** When input is prepared, the batch totals are included. (eg. if key-to-diskette is used, batch totals are typed in first and checked against the entered data).

f. **Reconciliation.** When the input data are read by the validation program, batch totals are reconciled. The input items are accumulated and the total agreed to the input batch control total. If the two totals do not agree, an error is reported. The report shows the two totals, the difference, and may provide a listing of all the items in the batch. The batch does not go forward for processing; it is re-input after the error has been found and corrected.

g. **Hash totals.** Batch totals are usually used to control the number of forms processed and the quantities they contain. It is also possible to apply the technique to numbers such as customer or payroll numbers. When batch totals are obtained the numbers are also added and entered on the batch cover note. The totals are input and reconciled in the way jut described. Since the totals are meaningless and useful only for control, they are called "hash" or "nonsense" totals.

FILE CONTROLS.

11. It is essential to ensure that data are not only input correctly, but also maintained correctly and processed correctly right through the system. It is also necessary to ensure that data in master files are not corrupted by machine or program failures.

The necessary safeguards are provided by *file control totals.* At the end of each file, there is a special block (sometimes blocks) which hold the total value of the items stored in the file. For example, the net total of the balances, and a count of the number of records. When the file is processed, totals are accumulated from each record. At the end of the run, these totals are compared with those in the file control block. Any difference between the two totals indicates some error in processing or some corruption of data in the file.

File control totals are derived from batch totals, and the following paragraphs explain how this is done.

a. **Transaction files.** When batch totals have been reconciled, data are written onto a magnetic file for further processing. By adding all the correct batch totals for the run, a control total for the transaction file is obtained. This total is used to ensure that the transaction file is correctly processed during subsequent runs, and that all transactions are processed when the master file is updated.

b. **Master files.** When the master file is updated from the transaction file, the processing of the transaction file is controlled as described above. The control totals in the master file are then adjusted by the amount of the transactions which have been inserted into it. Subsequent runs of the master file are reconciled to the control total.

c. **Clerical control.** It is possible to maintain an independent control on computer processing. Records are kept of the batch totals and are added to provide a run total, ie. the total value of transactions passed to the DP department for processing. When the computer outputs are received the control totals printed by the machine can be reconciled to the original batch figures. Adjustments have to be made, of course, for individual items rejected by the computer because they fail validity checks.

EXAMPLE – PURCHASE INVOICE PROCESSING SYSTEM.

12. The operation of these controls is illustrated by the example which follows (Fig. 21.1) of a Purchase Invoice Processing System. Note that the system has been simplified for the sake of clarity. On the left, a system flowchart shows the main processing stages. On the right, the controls imposed at each stage are explained.

COST OF CONTROL.

13. The cost of control should be measured against the cost of *not* having it. It is possible to have too much control as well as too little. The inability of the computer to detect by itself faults in programs or data should always be kept in mind. Controls should be designed in relation to the consequences of an error going undetected, and after investigations into the types of error likely to occur. Controls should be inserted into the system at the point where they give maximum benefit. It is often necessary to adjust controls (particularly validity checks) in the light of practical experience.

SUMMARY.

14. a. Controls need to be designed into a system carefully.

b. Controls are considered under the following headings:

- i. Manual
- ii. Data preparation
- iii. Validation checks
- iv. Batch controls
- v. File controls

c. Control is costly. Consideration should be given to what *should* be controlled rather than what *can* be controlled.

POINTS TO NOTE.

15. a. Note the importance of detecting an error as quickly as possible so that it may be put right and the data re-enter the system quickly.

SYSTEM FLOWCHART

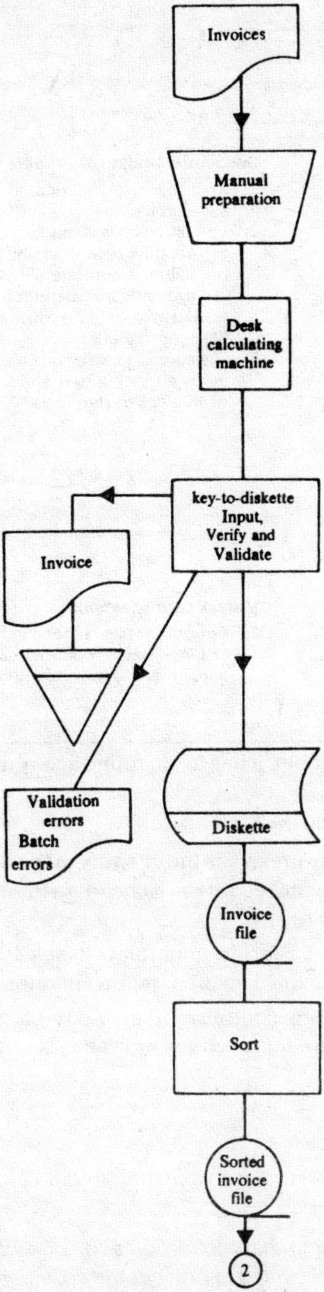

PROCESSING AND CONTROL STAGES

Receipts
Invoices received from suppliers

Manual preparation
1. Supplier number verified by reference to supplier file.
2. Invoice checked against purchase order and goods received note.
3. Invoice scrutinised for legibility.
4. Invoices arranged in batches.
5. Batch Cover note attached and numbered.

Desk calculating machine
1. Invoice calculations checked (quantity x price, discount)
2. Batch totals obtained for
   a. number of invoices.
   b. value of invoices.

Input and verification
1. Key in
   a. invoice details
   b. batch totals
2. Data verified.
3. Errors corrected.

Validation
1. Validation checks (eg)
   a. all fields keyed in correctly.
   b. supplier number (check digit)
   c. invoice value (reasonable)
2. Batch control totals reconciled.
3. Valid data copied to magnetic tape (Invoice File).
4. Invalid data reported (subsequent re-processing and re-input not shown).
5. Batch control totals accumulated to provide file control total.

Sort
1. Invoice details sorted to supplier sequence (sorted invoice file).
2. File control total copied onto new file.

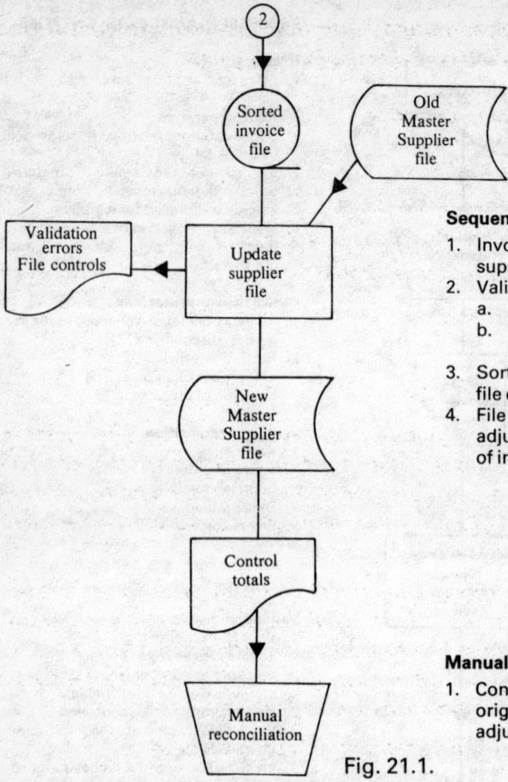

Sequential Update of supplier file.

1. Invoice details posted to supplier file.
2. Validation checks (eg.)
   a. supplier record on file?
   b. value consistent with previous transactions?
3. Sorted invoice file reconciled to file control totals.
4. File control total for supplier file adjusted by number and value of invoices posted.

Manual reconciliation.

1. Control totals reconciled to original batch controls, after adjustment for rejected items.

Fig. 21.1.

b. Long delays are caused by rejected input. It has to 'go round again' and this can cause days of delay.

c. The unit of control for input is usually the batch.

d. Note the use of the check digit. Its use preserves the integrity of the number field and when used in conjunction with the record key it ensures a transaction is processed against the correct master record.

e. Note that good source document design is important. It helps legible entries to be made and eases the task of the data preparation operator.

f. This chapter deals only with system controls. Other types of control, designed to ensure that the DP department functions efficiently and that its files are secure, are dealt with later.

STUDENT SELF TESTING QUESTIONS

(Answers on page 706)

1. *What is the difference between verification and validation in the context of data collection?*

2. *Name six types of error which can occur in data collection and, for each type, give an example of one measure which can be used to prevent the error.*

3. Details of payments to, and withdrawals from, a savings account are recorded on small paper slips. Each slip contains the following data.

- *i. Date*
- *ii. Account holders name(s)*
- *iii. Account number*
- *iv. Amount (in pounds)*
- *v. Account holders signature.*

a. Suggest ways in which this data might be validated.

b. Suggest a suitable layout for a simple batch control slip (batch cover note).

c. Suggest possible record formats if this data is to be stored in a transaction file.

QUESTIONS WITHOUT ANSWERS.

4. It is required to test a program written to the following specification: valid input data is a date in the form DD/MM/YY where D, M and Y represent digits. The program validates the data, calculates the date a week later and outputs it in a full form; eg. if the input is 17/02/85 then the output should be: 24 February 1985, invalid input will be rejected with a message.

Describe the validation checks that can be carried out and construct a set of test data that if presented to the program would establish that the program works according to the specification. Your test data should be chosen to show that invalid input is rejected and that the program can successfully calculate the date a week later in all possible cases (including leap years).

***NB.** You may like to design and implement this program too!*

22 Data Transmission and Networks

INTRODUCTION.

1. This chapter explains the traditional and modern methods of data transmission. It also looks at the broader subject of Computer Networks. Computer networks have been rapidly developed in recent years and support a growing number of important applications. Examples of these developments and applications will be covered within the chapter.

2. You are advised to re-read the following passages before you continue: 2.3–2.13, 4.38–4.45, 9.57–9.64.

BASIC IDEAS IN DATA TRANSMISSION.

6. Consider the simple signals shown in fig. 22.1 and then note the points which follow.

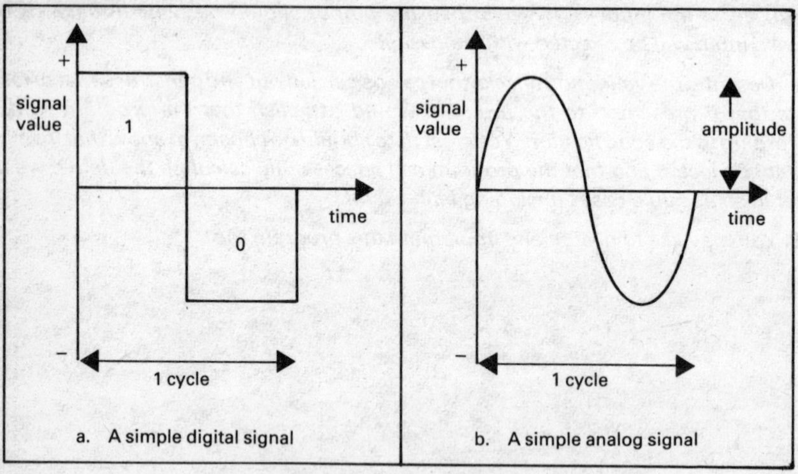

Fig. 22.1. Simple Signals.

7. Data transmission speeds are related to signal **frequencies**. The frequency of a signal is the number of cycles per second and is often expressed in units called **hertz** (Hz for short). 1 Hz is 1 cycle per second.

8. Various physical factors limit the maximum and minimum frequencies that a given medium can carry. A transmission link is called a **channel.** The range of frequencies over which a transmission may take place over a channel is called the **bandwidth** of the channel. **Broadband** channels (ie. those with broad bandwidth) have the ability to carry more data. Broadband channels are also called **wideband channels.**

9. The data carrying capacity of a channel is of prime interest to us and can be related to the channel frequency as follows. You may see from fig. 22.1a that there are two pulses per cycle (a '0' and a '1'). The number of pulses per second is a unit called a **baud.** In simple situations like the one in fig. 22.1a the baud rate is twice the frequency. We have already seen (fig. 2.3) that data can be encoded and transmitted in terms of pulses with the binary values '0' and '1'. However, not all the bits carry data, as is the case for the stop and start bits in fig. 2.3. The rate of data flow called the **data transfer rate** is therefore less than the baud rate. Data transfer rates are often expressed in terms of the number of data bits transmitted per second. The actual units may be Kbits/s (thousands of bits per second) or Mbits/s (millions of bits per second).

10. This is an appropriate point to give some practical examples **A coaxial cable** (see your TV aerial lead) may have a data transfer rate of 140 Mbits/s, enough to carry, at any one time, the information for two TV channels **or** nearly 300 music channels **or** about 2000 telephone channels. Optical fibres have even greater data transfer rates of 500 Mbits/s or more!

11. Transmitted signals become degraded during transmission because of:

a. **Noise** ie. random unwanted signals picked up by the channel. The quality of the channel may be expressed in terms of its **signal-to-noise ratio** which is measured in decibels db. The lower the value the better.

b. **Distortion** ie. changes to the shape of the signal caused by such things as absorbtion of the signal **(attenuation)** and delays by the medium. (See fig. 22.2).

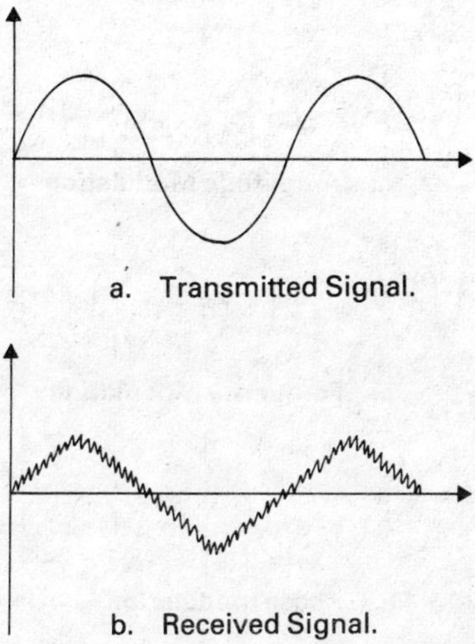

a. Transmitted Signal.

b. Received Signal.

Note how in b

i. Attenuation has reduced the amplitude of the signal.
ii. The signal has been distorted into a more angular form.
iii. The signal has lost its smooth line because of noise.

Fig. 22.2. Signal Degradation.

12. It is relatively easy to restore a digital signal to its original amplitude and free it of noise by means of a unit called a **digital repeater.** However, **analog repeaters** are only able to restore amplitude and, worse still, they amplify noise. Therefore digit signals are preferable to analog signals.

13. Baseband transmission involves directly encoding the signal onto the channel medium eg. using +5v for '1' and −5v for '0'. Baseband transmission is satisfactory over relatively short distances ie. less than 1km. For longer transmissions. **"Carrier waves"** must be used in order to overcome the degradation which occurs to baseband signals.

14. Modulated Carrier Waves are best explained with the aid of an example (fig. 22.3). The basic form of the carrier wave is a simple signal which has the form of a smooth rounded waveform. The characteristics of the carrier's waveform are regulated in accordance with changes in the signal to be carried (the baseband signal). This process is known as **modulation.** Various types of modulation may be used. (See fig. 22.3)

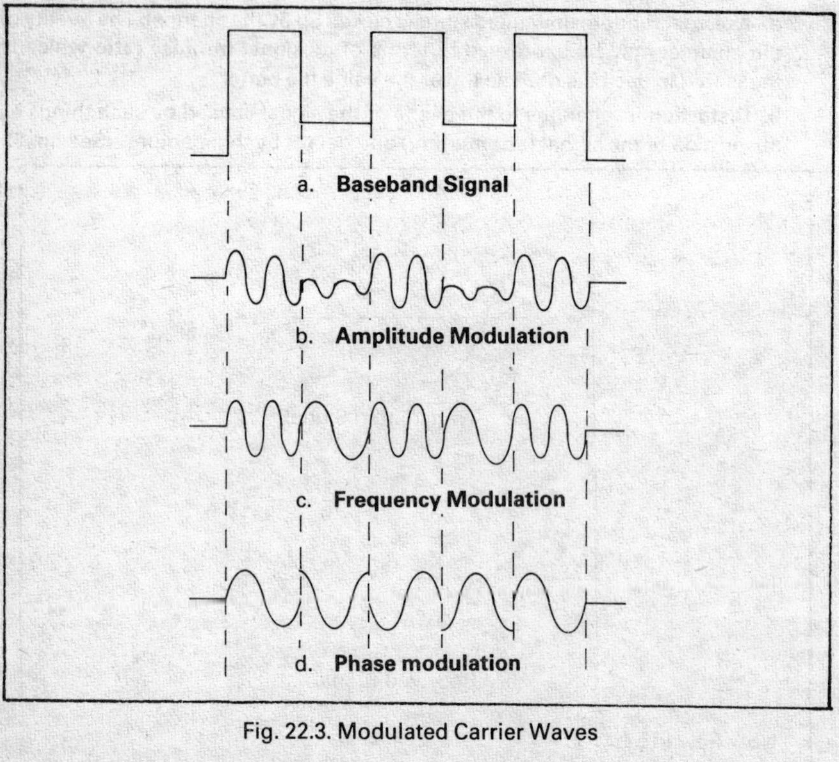

Fig. 22.3. Modulated Carrier Waves

NB. If the carrier wave is thought of as a sound signal then amplitude modulation corresponds to defined changes in volume (amplitude), frequency modulation corresponds to defined changes in pitch (frequency) and phase modulation corresponds to defined displacements in a continuous tone.

15. Multiplexing is the term used in data transmission for using one data link to carry a number of separate data signal's at the same time. There are two basic methods of multiplexing:

a. **Time Division Multiplexing (TDM)** in which the signals take frequent turns at using the carrier wave one after another.

b. **Frequency Division Multiplexing (FDM)** in which different ranges of the bandwidth are used for each signal.

When the signal is received it must be **demultiplexed** back into its constituent signals. Devices able to perform these functions are called **multiplexors** and **demultiplexors.**

NB. multiplexing may be used for both baseband and non baseband signals.

TRADITIONAL TELECOMMUNICATIONS METHODS.

16. The next eight paragraphs outline the traditional methods used for data transmission.

BRITISH TELECOM (BT).

17. In the UK, the BT is a monopoly carrier, and its services *must* be used to transmit data between different locations. Some relaxations of this monopoly have occured in recent years. If it is required to set up a network within a single site (eg. a factory/office complex), non-BT facilities may be used. In practice, most data in the UK is transmitted over the ordinary telegraph and telephone circuits, which are capable of carrying data as well as speech.

DATEL SERVICES.

18. British Telecom offers a number of services under the name of DATEL. These are identified by numbers – DATEL 100, 200, 400, 600, 2400. The numbers indicate (roughly) the baud rate. The most common transmitting speed is 600 – 1,200 baud (bits per second). Much higher speeds can be achieved, up to 48,000 baud by using 'wide-band' circuits.

PUBLIC AND PRIVATE LINES.

19. Data can be transmitted over the ordinary *public* telephone circuits. The connection is made using a normal telephone handset and dialling the number of the computer from the terminal. The link is disconnected when the transmission has finished. Charges are based on the type of service and the amount of time used.

It is also possible to hire a *private* line. The public telephone network is used, but a line is reserved for the exclusive use of the hirer. A fixed charge is made regardless of the actual amount of traffic. The line can also be used for ordinary speech calls.

LINE SYSTEMS.

20. Transmission is possible in three modes:-

a. **Simplex.** Transmission is possible in only *one direction.*

b. **Half Duplex.** Transmission is possible in *both* directions, but not simultaneously.

c. **Duplex.** Transmission is possible in both directions simultaneously.

TRANSMISSION EQUIPMENT.

21. a. Where *telegraph* circuits are used, transmission is direct between the terminal devices, eg. paper tape reader/punch.

b. Where public *telephone* circuits are used, a MODEM must be provided at each end of the line. **'MODEM'** is short for **mod**ulator-**dem**odulator. Its function is to modulate the signals into frequences suitable for transmission and to demodulate them at the receiving end. (See Fig. 22.4).

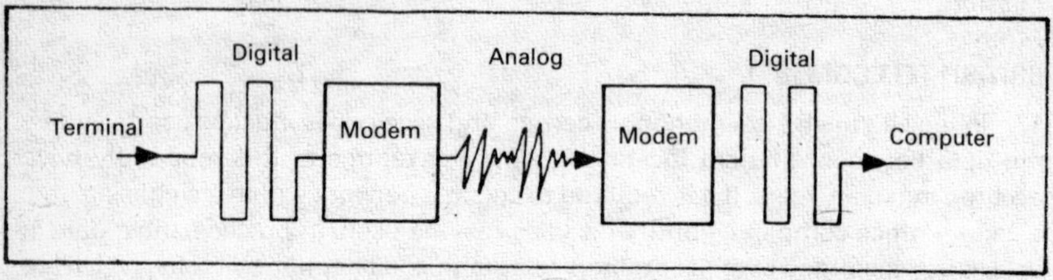

Fig. 22.4.Data Transmission and the use of Modems.

c. A cheaper alternative to the modem is the *acoustic coupler,* which makes it possible to use an ordinary telephone handset for transmission. This is suitable only for low speed transmission.

d. When a number of terminals are linked to a central computer, a *multiplexor* has to be provided as part of the computer hardware. This deals with the routine work of handling incoming and outgoing messages, which would otherwise occupy an excess amount of CPU time.

e. To reduce transmission costs, a *dataplex* or *concentrator* may be used. This connects a number of terminals which are close to each other but not to the central computer. The messages are transmitted in a single stream using multiplexing techniques. Trunk charges thus have to be paid for only one 'stream' of data instead of for each terminal. Concentrators may also be used when the computer is on the same site.

Concentrators usually use a method called asynchronous time division multiplexing in which the signals from each terminal are transmitted at irregular intervals and must therefore be identified by a number transmitted with each data item. This method is also called **statistical multiplexing.**

TERMINAL DEVICES.

22. There is a very wide variety of terminal devices in use, ranging from a teletypewriter to sophisticated devices which permit automatic sending and receiving of data. Any *peripheral device* can if required be used as a terminal ie. a transmitting or receiving device at the end of a transmission line connected to a computer.

ON-LINE/OFF-LINE TRANSMISSION.

23. If the terminal is linked directly to the computer, data is transmitted via the data link directly into the CPU. Such a data transmission system, as you might expect, is called an ON-LINE system.

The terminal can be linked to say, a key-to-diskette or even magnetic tape unit which is *not* itself linked to the computer. Data is transmitted via the data link to the device at the other end. Such data is fed to the computer eventually. Such a data transmission system is called an OFF-LINE system.

APPLICATIONS.

24. a. The use of data transmission is increasing rapidly. Many systems are now designed with a communications network as their basis (details shortly). Other systems which operate on an 'in-house' basis (ie. all data preparation and processing are carried out in one computer centre) are being re-designed to use data transmission.

b. The basic advantages are:

i. **Data collection** is much faster.

ii. **Information** in the files of the central computer is readily available at different locations.

iii. **Hardware** costs can be reduced by use of one large machine instead of a number of small ones at different sites.

iv. **Computing** facilities can be made available to staff (eg. designers requiring complex calculations).

c. Some systems depend on immediate collection of data as soon as it originates. These are known as 'on-line' and 'real-time' systems and are dealt with later.

d. Off-line systems are simpler and less expensive, because the terminals are not connected to a computer. Such systems benefit from the speed with which data are transmitted, even though processing is not as fast.

e. Considerations in the choice of system will be:-

i. Cost

ii. Distance between computer and terminals

iii. Volume of traffic

iv. Type of system

v. Speed required.

NETWORKS DEFINED.

25. An interconnected set of two or more computers may be called a **"computer network"**. However, if the computers in the network operate together as a single unit which to the user appears as a single computer, albeit physically dispersed, then the complete system is more accurately described as a **distributed system.** Therefore, although *any* interconnected set of computers is often conveniently referred to as a "computer network" the use of the term often implies an interconnected set of *independent* computers and not a distributed system. However, it may be useful to recognise distributed systems which are based upon particular types of network.

26. Networks used to interconnect computers in a single room, rooms within a building or buildings on one site are normally of a type called **Local Area Networks** (LANs).

27. The networks which interconnect computers on separate sites, or in separate cities or countries are called **Long-Haul Networks** (LHNs) or **Wide Area Networks** (WANs).

28. In many countries LHNs are provided by specially authorised agencies. In the UK the principal agency for this is BT (British Telecom). The telecommunications facilities provided by BT for the transmission of data vary in sophistication from simple traditional methods of transmitting data to a computer using telephone lines (see paragraphs 17–23) to large LHNs.

29. LANs tend to be privately owned and to use baseband methods.

BASIC ADVANTAGES OF USING NETWORKS.

30. There are many possible advantages in using networks. The basic ones are:

a. The sharing of resources (eg. computers & staff) and information.
b. The provision of local facilities without the loss of central control.
c. The even distribution of work, processing loads etc.
d. Shared risk and mutual support.
e. Improved communication facilities.

NETWORK ARCHITECTURE.

31. Communication between interconnected systems is a complex activity which takes place at a number of different levels. At the lowest level there is the physical transmission of signals and at the highest level there may be communication of messages in natural languages.

32. By deliberately organising a network into a set of distinct **levels** or **layers** it becomes much easier to understand and develop. The communications at each level have their own **protocols** (2.10). The layers plus their protocols constitute what is called the **architecture of the network.**

33. Since one purpose of networks is to interconnect dissimilar computer systems there is an important need to standardise network architectures. Traditional data transmission has been subject to a number of standards for many years. The influential standards body has been the CCITT (Consultative Committee for International Telephone and Telegraphy). The CCITT have produced a series of standards numbered X1 to X29 and V1 to V57. For example, X25 is the standard for packet switching systems (see later) and V24 is the standard which applies to terminals connected to modems.

34. In an attempt to form a basis for standardising all layers in network architecture the International Standards Organisation **(ISO)** has devised a model of network architecture. This model is known as the Reference Model of Open System Interconnection **(OSI).**

35. The OSI model has seven layers. From lowest to highest they are as follows.

a. **The Physical Control Layer** is the level of electrical connections, signal transmission and data in raw binary form.

b. **The data link layer** is the level at which data is transmitted in small units using suitable protocols to contol and check correct transmission. The units of data are **"frames"** ie. asynchronously transmitted characters or synchronously transmitted blocks of characters. (2.11–2.12)

c. **The network layer** is the level which provides the control between adjacent sending and receiving points in the network. The sending and receiving points which are able to *switch* transmissions are "nodes" in the network called **IMPs** (Interface Message Processors). IMPs are special purpose computers. **"Packets"** of information are transmitted at this level. A packet is a unit of data with two main components:

i. Header data which specifies its destination address. (Possibly its source address too)

ii. Data to be transmitted.

d. **The transport layer** is the level which provides an **end-to-end** service between host computers. It deals with addressing, error controls and regulates data transfers.

e. **The Session layer** is the level which handles the establishment of connections between hosts and the management of the dialogue messages created at this level are addressed by the transport layer and split into packets at the network layer.

f. **The Presentation layer** is the level which handles the standard forms for presenting data eg. the layouts used for VDU displays.

g. **The Application layer** is the level which the user has control over in determining what data is to be transmitted and how it is to be sent or received.

NETWORK STRUCTURES.

36. A number of standard network structures are shown in fig. 22.5.

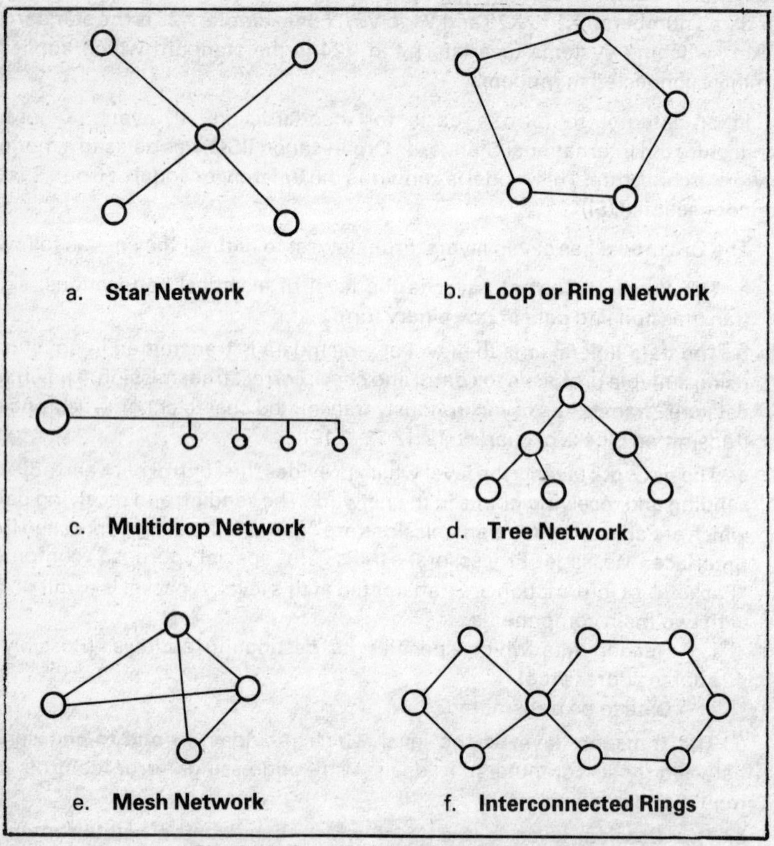

Fig. 22.5. Standard Network Structures.

37. The small circles in fig. 22.5 represent IMPs which would be present in LHNs. Most computers or terminals would be connected to these IMPs. IMPs may communicate directly with one another if connected by cables or indirectly via other IMPs. An IMP may receive, store and forward messages received from one IMP and intended for another. For distances over approximately 400 km it is more economic to use satelite transmissions between IMPs rather than use cable. The IMPs are said to perform a **"message switching"** function.

38. In the case of LANs the arrangements are different from those just described. For example, the circles in fig. 22.5b might represent digital repeaters or access boxes on a ring. A device connected to an access box on a ring might be able to deposit data and addresses into empty packets cirulating continuously on the ring. Another access box to which the message was addressed would be able to pick up the message, clear the packet and transmit an acknowledgement in a similar fashion.

NETWORKS CURRENTLY IN USE.

39. There are numerous networks in use today. Many of them are proprietary. One of the earliest LHNs was **ARPANET** (a mesh network), the network of the **A**dvanced **R**esearch **P**roject **A**gency in the USA and part of the US defense department. ARPANET was set up partly for research purposes and many universities and private corporations have been allowed to use it, both in the USA and elsewhere. There are also networks in Britain and Europe which are connected together and to ARPANET.

40. One popular LAN is **Ethernet** (a ring) pioneered by XEROX, but now used by a variety of manufacturers. Ethernet uses coaxial cable somewhat larger than those used for domestic TV aerials. A popular British LAN is the **Cambridge Ring.**

APPLICATIONS AND RECENT DEVELOPMENTS.

41. British Telecom have developed a digital telephone exchange system known as **System X.** Installation has already begun and is due for completion in 1992. When it is completed MODEMS will be obsolete! The system will be compatible with the bottom three layers of the OSI model, which, incidentially, are compatible with X25.

42. A new version of the old **telex** service has been developed over the last few years. It will be able to send pictures as well as text and is called **teletex.** The intention is to link teletex devices into computer systems and to handle pictures as well as text. These developments will eventually lead to systems compatible with FAX (See below).

Facsimile devices (FAX for short) have been in use for some time to transmit pictures from one place to another using telephone/telex like link.

43. **Viewdata.** This is a service which has the international name **videotex** and the BT (British Telecom) trade name 'PRESTEL'. Essentially it is a computer based service which provides information, via telephone links, to a TV set connected to the user's telephone receiver point. It should not be confused with **teletext** (BBC's *Ceefax* or ITV's *Oracle*) which provides information by using "unused lines" on TV picture transmission.

NB. Note the *two* services **teletex** and **teletext.**

44. Many private organisations use their own automatic telephone exchanges as part of internal transmission. Such exchanges are known as PABX's (Private Automatic Branch Exchanges) as opposed to the older PMBX's (Private Manual Branch Exchanges). Some PABX's now have computers built into them and are able to be programmed to handle a variety of data transmission tasks. These PABX's are sometimes called SPC's (Stored Program Controlled exchanges). Incoming and outgoing transmissions are also handled by the PABX's (See Fig. 9.7).

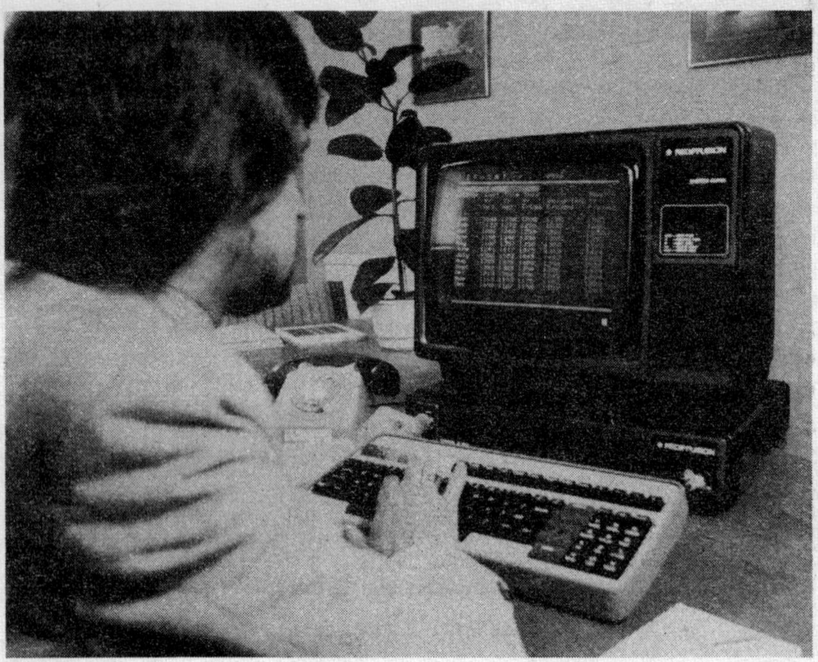

A "System Alpha Model 1 Teleputer" Terminal for use with private Videotex and British Telecom's Prestel. Picture by courtesy of Rediffusion Computers Ltd.

45. Electronic Mail. As its name suggests Electronic mail has features more familiar to the postal service than the telephone service. The main features are given here in outline:-

a. Each main user has a 'mailbox' which is accessed via a computer terminal within the system by entering a password. Messages are drawn to the user's attention when they enter the system. When messages are sent they must consist of two parts a 'header' giving the 'address' of the sender and the body of the text.

b. The mailing system provides computerised ways of preparing, entering and editing text.

c. The mailing system provides means of filing and retrieving messages.

46. The user of an electronic mail system may have the choice of sending messages within their own organisation, via a LAN, or possibly over a public LHN.

47. Packet Switching Systems (PSS). In Britain BT (British Telecom) operate a 'packet switching system' PSS which operates in and between major cities as an alternative to the telephone and telex services mentioned earlier. This is a LHN service. PSSs can be used to provide an Electronic Mail service. A packet consists of details of the sender, the intended destination 'address', a message, and other data for control purposes. The 'packet switched network' is more than just an electronic mail service. It is important as an automated means of transmitting volumes of data between computers which are geographically separated.

SUMMARY.

48. The basic ideas of data transmission were introduced including the concepts of **signal frequency, channels, band width, baud rates, data transfer rates, carrier waves, modulation** and **multiplexing.**

49. Traditional Telecommunications methods were described including the use of BT lines for data transmission.

50. Transmission equipment was described including **modems, acoustic couplers, dataplexes** and **concentrators.**

51. Networks were defined and a distinction was made between **Local Area Networks (LANs)** and **Long Haul Networks (LHNs).**

52. The advantages of networks were outlined.

53. Network architecture and the OSI reference model were introduced.

54. Networks structures were described and current types of network were discussed briefly.

55. Recent developments and applications were considered including:

i. System X
ii. Teletex
iii. FAX
iv. Videotex

v. PABXs
vi. Electronic Mail
vii. Packet Switching Systems.

POINTS TO NOTE.

56. a. Wide-band circuits make possible high speed bulk data transmission.

b. Some "terminals" are in fact micro-computers. They are called 'intelligent terminals' because they have a small CPU and can carry out 'local' processing as well as transmitting data. Banks use them as part of their system for linking branches with their computer centre.

c. It is also possible to use data transmission to link two large computers. One which is busy can then transfer work to the other. This is called 'load-shedding'.

STUDENT SELF TESTING QUESTIONS

(Answers on page 708)

1. *Explain the meaning of these terms:*
   a. *Bandwidth*
   b. *LAN*
   c. *Baseband*
   d. *Multiplexing*
   e. *Carrier wave*
   f. *PSS*
   g. *OSI model*
   h. *Electronic mail.*
2. *Why are carrier waves needed for data transmission in LHNs?*
3. *What is the purpose of a MODEM and where would a MODEM be used?*
   Name one alternative to a MODEM if a portable terminal is to be used.
4. *Explain the terms "Distributed System" and "Computer Network".*
5. *Why was the OSI model created?*

QUESTIONS WITHOUT ANSWERS.

6. *Explain why a transmitted signal using 4 signal levels, instead of two as shown in Fig. 22.1, can have a baud rate of 200 baud but a data signalling rate of 400 baud.*

7. *Explain this statement: "The company uses a LAN in order to provide a distributed computer system on site·"*

Computer Arithmetic

1. In the next three chapters we deal with computer arithmetic in more depth and make use of the ideas on number bases introduced in chapter 3.

2. Chapter 23 deals with arithmetical procedures. Chapter 24 introduces and develops fixed and floating point arithmetic, and lastly chapter 25 explores the problems of errors and accuracy associated with all computer calculations.

23 Arithmetical Procedures

INTRODUCTION.

1. This chapter deals with methods of addition, subtraction, multiplication and division which apply to computer arithmetic. It also introduces methods involving binary fractions, sign bits and number complements.

BINARY ADDITION.

2. Binary addition is performed in a similar way to decimal addition. We apply these rules:–

a.	b.	c.	d.
0	0	1	1
+ 0	+ 1	+ 0	+ 1
0	1	1	10

3. **Example.** $00110_2 + 01101_2$ (Equivalent to $6_{10} + 13_{10} = 19_{10}$)

First Number	0	0	1	1	0	6_{10}
Second Number	0	1	1	0	1	13_{10}
Sum	1	0	0	1	1	19_{10}
Carries	1	1				
Addition rules	a then b	b then d	d	c	b	

4. **Further Examples** set out in the usual way. (The carry is shown where it occurs)

a	b	c
1 0 1 1 0 0	1 1 0	1 0 1
+ 1 0 0 1 0	+ 1 0 1	0 1 1
1 1 1 1 1 0	1 0 1 1	1 0 0 0
	1	1 1 1

These are respectively equivalent to the decimal sums 44 + 18, 6 + 5 and 5 + 3.

5. To add more than two numbers we can apply the same method by adding the first two numbers, and then adding the next number to the subtotal. We repeat additions to the subtotal until all numbers are added. The subtotal is called a **partial sum.**

OCTAL ADDITION.

6. Two methods may be readily employed:–

a. i. Convert to Binary
   ii. Add
   iii. Convert back to Octal.

b. Use the Octal addition table shown here:–

OCTAL ADDITION TABLE								
+	0	1	2	3	4	5	6	7
0	0	1	2	3	4	5	6	7
1	1	2	3	4	5	6	7	10
2	2	3	4	5	6	7	10	11
3	3	4	5	6	7	10	11	12
4	4	5	6	7	10	11	12	13
5	5	6	7	10	[11]	12	13	14
6	6	7	10	11	12	13	14	15
7	7	10	11	12	13	14	15	16

The square [11] in the table illustrates the addition $5_8 + 4_8 = 11_8$

Once familiar, both methods should be achieved without the need to refer to tables.

7. **Examples** of the addition $327_8 + 245_8 = 574_8$

Method (a)

OCTAL NUMBERS	CONVERSION (See 3.9)	BINARY REPRESENTATION		
3 2 7	⟶	011	010	111
+2 4 5	⟶	010	100	101
5 7 4	⟵	101	111	100

Method (b)

OCTAL NUMBERS	COMMENTS (Working Right to Left)
3 2 7	$7_8 + 5_3 = 14_8$ (From table) i e 4 carry 1
+2 4 5	$2_8 + 4_8 = 6_8$ (From table) $6 + 1 = 7_8$ (ie Add carry)
5 7 4	$3_8 + 2_8 = 5_8$ (From table)

Further example $654_8 + 176_8 = 1052_8$

	6	5	4
+	1	7	6
1	0	5	2

	110	101	100
+	001	111	110
001	000	101	010

1052_8 is obtained either way.

HEXADECIMAL ADDITION.

8. Conversion to binary or the use of an addition table are acceptable methods. It is left to the reader to construct a table if he so wishes. An example using conversion to binary is given here (see 3.12 for HEX-BINARY conversion).

Example of $CA3_{16} + 5FB_{16} = 129E_{16}$

HEX NUMBER	CONVERSION	BINARY REPRESENTATION			
C A 3	→		1 1 0 0	1 0 1 0	0 0 1 1
+ 5 F B	→	+	0 1 0 1	1 1 1 1	1 0 1 1
1 2 9 E	←	0 0 0 1	0 0 1 0	1 0 0 1	1 1 1 0

BCD ADDITION.

The procedure here is longer but straightforward. We will take it in two stages.

9. Single Digit Addition. (See 2.14 for the ten BCD codes).
There are two cases to consider:–

a. **Example.**

DECIMAL NUMBERS	BCD NUMBERS
2	0 0 1 0
+ 3	+ 0 0 1 1
5	0 1 0 1

Binary addition of the two BCD Codes gives the correct BCD result 0101 directly. No further work is needed.

b. **Example** (This corresponds to a 'decimal carry'.)

DECIMAL NUMBERS	BCD NUMBERS	COMMENTS
8 + 5	1 0 0 0 + 0 1 0 1	Binary addition results in 1101_2 which is not a BCD code (3.8). To correct for this 0110_2 is added.
13	1 1 0 1	
	+ 0 1 1 0	Correction added to result
13	0 0 0 1 0 0 1 1	BCD codes for 1_{10} and 3_{10} (ie BCD 13)

10. Multi-digit addition. To do this the methods of single digit addition are applied as follows starting with the the right hand column.

a. Add the two BCD digits.

b. Add any carry digits to this sum.

c. Add 0110 if the sum is not an acceptable BCD code.

d. Move to the next column and return to step a.

11. Example. The sum 159 + 473 = 632 in BCD.

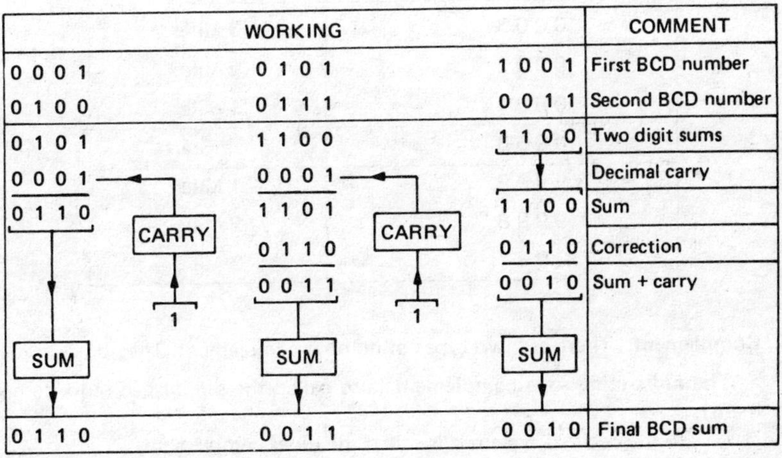

12. You can see from these examples that BCD addition is longer than Pure Binary addition. The time taken to convert to Pure Binary and to convert the Pure Binary result to BCD is avoided however. In general number representation and arithmetic Pure Binary is preferred because the representation is compact and provides computational ease and speed. BCD arithmetic, and other forms of 'string arithmetic' performed on numeric codes can be found in some commercial applications, eg in many versions of COBOL and in BUSINESS BASIC. The conversions between character code and BCD codes are relatively simple as can be seen from inspecting the character codes (see fig. 2.4). Also, some computers have hardware able to perform BCD arithmetic directly.

REPRESENTATIONS OF NEGATIVE NUMBERS.

13. The familiar method of placing a '–' sign before a number to show that it is negative is not the only way to represent a negative number. We will now look at an alternative method and see how it provides certain advantages when using computers. A car milometer can be used to illustrate this alternative method. If the milometer is run backwards we see that eg 9997 represents –3 miles not +9997 miles. This is one example of the **numbers complement** method of representing negative numbers. It provides an **implicit sign** but to avoid ambiguities we must sacrifice the representation of large numbers like +9997. We will now see how to convert to this method of representation.

FOUR DIGIT MILOMETER READING	DISTANCE GONE
0003	3 Miles
0002	2 Miles
0001	1 Mile
0000	Start
9999	– 1 Mile
9998	– 2 Miles
9997	– 3 Miles

14. Complements. There are two types of number complement. They are:–

a. **The radix-minus-one complement** (also called the diminished radix complement).

   i. In the decimal system it is called the **nines complement.**

   ii. In the binary system it is called the **ones complement.**

b. **The radix complement** (also called the *true* or noughts complement)

   i. In the decimal system it is called the **tens complement.**

   ii. In the binary system it is called the **twos complement.**

15. Rules for finding complements of numbers.

a. To obtain the radix-minus-one complement of a number, subtract each digit of the number from one less than the radix (base), eg for decimal (base 10) subtract each digit from 9.

b. To obtain the radix complement add one to the radix-minus-one complement.

16. Examples for 30962 decimal and 10110 binary.

DECIMAL EXAMPLE	COMMENTS		BINARY EXAMPLE	
	One less than the radix			
9 9 9 9 9 9	i e 9	i e 1	1 1 1 1 1 1	
0 3 0 9 6 2	Subtract Number to be complemented		0 1 0 1 1 0	Also see note (i) below.
9 6 9 0 3 7	Result		1 0 1 0 0 1	
	Nines complement	Ones complement		
1	Add 1		1	
9 6 9 0 3 8	Tens Complement	Twos Complement	1 0 1 0 1 0	

Note: For binary numbers the rules simplify to:–

i. change ones to zeros and zeros to ones to obtain the ones complement
ii. add one to this result for the twos complement.

17. Reverse process. The reverse of complementation can be accomplished by using **exactly the same rules** as those used to obtain the complement, hence the complement of a number has the number as its complement – one reason for the choice of the term 'complement'.

18. Using Complements.

a. Complements are mainly used for:–
   i. Representing negative numbers
   ii. subtraction.
b. Reasons for their use are:–
   i. Convenience: Complementation is easy with two-state devices.
   ii. Efficiency: Only one procedure, **addition,** is needed because to subtract a number one can add its complement.
   iii. No provision is needed for separate *explicit* sign representation. The sign is *implicit.*

19. Examples of Use. Assume for simplicity that we are using a representation with just two decimal digits. We can use the numbers 00 to 99. However, if we use tens complement representation for negative numbers we must 'borrow' some positive number forms. An arbitrary, but convenient choice would be to use 00–49 to represent positive numbers and 50–99 to represent negative numbers, eg:–

DECIMAL NUMBER	TENS COMPLEMENT REPRESENTATION
27	27
16	16
– 16	84
– 27	73
49	49 (Most positive number)
– 1	99
– 50	50 (Most negative Number)

To *subtract* a number *add* its complement.

CALCULATION OF 27 + 16		COMMENT	CALCULATION OF 27 – 16		COMMENT
2	7	Normal methods apply	2	7	To subtract 16 its complement, 84, is added. The last carry is lost in the absence of a third column
1	6		8	4	
4	3		1	1	
CALCULATION OF 16 - 27		**COMMENT**	**CALCULATION OF 27 + 27**		**COMMENT**
1	6	The complement of 27 (i e 73) is added. The result 89 is the tens complement representing -11.	2	7	The result is too large to be represented since 54 is the representation for -46!
7	3		2	7	
8	9		5	4	

Binary examples are given in the paragraph 20 and 21.

BINARY REPRESENTATIONS OF NEGATIVE NUMBERS.

20. The different methods of representation can be compared by using the simple 3 bit examples given here. In each example the most significant (ie leftmost) bit indicates the number's sign, (0 for '+' and 1 for '–'), and is called the **sign bit.**

a. Explicit sign method i.e. sign bit plus positive representation.				b. Ones Complement Method (The sign is implicit)				c. Twos Complement Method (The sign is implicit)			
Decimal Integer	Binary Representation: Sign			Decimal Integer	Binary Representation: Sign			Decimal Integer	Binary Representation: Sign		
+3	0	1	1	+3	0	1	1	+3	0	1	1
+2	0	1	0	+2	0	1	0	+2	0	1	0
+1	0	0	1	+1	0	0	1	+1	0	0	1
0	0	0	0	0	0	0	0	0	0	0	0
(Redundant) -0	1	0	0	(Redundant) -0	1	1	1	-1	1	1	1
-1	1	0	1	-1	1	1	0	-2	1	1	0
-2	1	1	0	-2	1	0	1	-3	1	0	1
-3	1	1	1	-3	1	0	0	-4	1	0	0
Range: +3 to -3				Range: +3 to -3				Range: +3 to -4			

21. The use of twos complement representation is preferred for these reasons:–

a. There is no redundant representation of zero. (The twos complement of 000 is 000).

b. The range of representation is extended by one unit as a consequence of a.

Representations using a greater number of bits can be constructed in the same manner. Here we show the 12 bit representation of 107_{10} and -107_{10} in twos complement with the leftmost bit as sign bit.

Decimal Interger	Twos Complement Binary Representation Sign											
+107	0	0	0	0	0	1	1	0	1	0	1	1
–107	1	1	1	1	1	0	0	1	0	1	0	1

c. Twos complement arithmetic is more straight-forward than ones complement arithmetic eg when adding two negative numbers:–

USING TWOS COMPLEMENTS			USING ONES COMPLEMENTS		
111_2	–1	ADD	110_2	–1	ADD
111_2	–1		110_2	–1	
1110_2	–2		1100_2	–3	Wrong Answer!
→ ignore			→ 1		Add Carry (An 'End Around Carry')
			101_2	–2	Correct Answer

OTHER METHODS.

22. Complements in BCD. The method for finding the nines and tens complement is shown in this example. Note that the codes 1010 and 1111 are used to represent the signs '+' and '–' respectively.

LAYOUT (To Complement 275_{10})				COMMENTS
+	2	7	5	Decimal Number
1010	0010	0111	0101	BCD Representation with sign.
0101	1101	1000	1010	Produce ones complement of each BCD digit.
1010	1010	1010	1010	Add 1010 to each BCD digit
1111	10111	10010	10100	Result of adding 1010
1111	0111	0010	0100	To obtain the nines complement:– Bring down the first 4 bits of each sum
0000	0000	0000	0001	Add one to obtain the tens complement
1111	0111	0010	0101	Tens complement
–	7	2	5	Decimal form of tens complement

23. Excess –3 (XS3) Code. This is an alternative code to 8421 weighted BCD code which has the advantage of having a simpler procedure for complementation. Each decimal digit has a code *3 higher* than its 8421 BCD equivalent as can be seen in this table:–

DECIMAL DIGIT	EXCESS–3 CODE	DECIMAL DIGIT	EXCESS–3 CODE
0	0011	5	1000
1	0100	6	1001
2	0101	7	1010
3	0110	8	1011
4	0111	9	1100

Note:–
Other advantages include:

- i. No code is null (all zeros)
- ii. Some arithmetic is simpler and quicker
- iii. Each digit is self complementing.

24. Example. Finding the nines and tens complements of 275 in XS3. 0000 is used for '+' and 1111 for '–' if required.

LAYOUT (To complement 275_{10})				COMMENTS (A zero in the right hand column must be corrected (See 11))
+	2	7	5	Decimal Number
0000	0101	1010	1000	XS3 representation
1111	1010	0101	0111	The ones complement gives the nines complement
0000	0000	0000	0001	Add one to get the tens complement
1111	1010	0101	1000	XS3 form of tens complement.
–	7	2	5	Tens complement in decimal

STUDENT SELF TEST QUESTIONS.

(Answers on page 708)

25. Do these questions before you continue.

1. *Find* a. $1101_2 + 1001_2$
   b. $110110_2 + 100111_2$
   c. $10101_2 + 11011_2$
   d. $11110_2 + 10101_2$

2. *Do these* octal *additions.*
   a. *27 + 53*
   b. *46 + 675*

3. *Do these* Hex *additions*
   a. *D5F + 4AC*
   b. *BCA + E23*

4. *Do these decimal sums using BCD. Check your answer.*
   a. *7 + 4*
   b. *294 + 328*

5. *Give the 8 digit binary ones and twos complement representation of*
   a. -21_{10}
   b. -39_{10}

6. *Use 4 bit representation and twos complements to do this decimal subtraction in binary: 7 – 4 = 3*

BINARY FRACTIONS.

• **26.** Examples of binary fractions are given in this table. (See also 3.3)

BINARY FRACTION	$2^{-1} = \frac{1}{2}$ $2^{-2} = \frac{1}{4}$ $2^{-3} = \frac{1}{8}$ $2^{-4} = \frac{1}{16}$	DECIMAL EQUIVALENT
· 1 0 0 0	= (1 x ½) + (0 x ¼) + (0 x ⅛) + (0 x 1/16)	= ½ = 0.5
· 0 1 0 0	= (0 x ½) + (1 x ¼) + (0 x ⅛) + (0 x 1/16)	= ¼ = 0.25
· 0 0 1 0	= (0 x ½) + (0 x ¼) + (1 x ⅛) + (0 x 1/16)	= ⅛ = 0.125
· 0 0 0 1	= (0 x ½) x (0 x ¼) x (0 x ⅛) x (1 x 1/16)	1/16 = 0.0625

27. Conversion from Binary to Decimal.

Example. Convert 11.101_2 to a decimal value.

PLACE VALUE	2^1 (2)	2^0 (1)	·	2^{-1} (½)	2^{-2} (¼)	2^{-3} (⅛)	DECIMAL VALUE
BINARY NUMBER	1	1	·	1	0	1	
CONVERSION	(1 x 2) + (1 x 1) + (1 x ½) + (0 x ¼) + (1 x ⅛)						3⅝ = 3.625

28. Decimal to Binary Conversion. (The whole number part is converted as in 3.6)

Example 1. Convert 0.625_{10} to binary

WORKING	COMMENT
.625 x 2 1.25 .25 x 2 0.5 .5 x 2 1.0 .0 x 2 .1 0 1	Multiply by 2 and write result beneath. Remove digit before the point to form the binary fraction. Repeat process until a zero fraction value occurs, or the required accuracy is reached.

29. Example 2. Convert — ⅓ to binary using 5 bits for your representation and twos complement form. Note: We convert +⅓ and then find its complement.

WORKING
⅓ x 2 0 + ⅔ ⅔ x 2 1 + ⅓ .0 1 ⅓ x 2 [Repeats]

FURTHER WORKING TO 5 BITS	
0 . 0 1 0 1	⅓ to 5 bits including sign
1 . 1 0 1 0	Ones complement
1 . 1 0 1 1	Twos complement

Note: When fractions are stored in words or registers the position of the point is not shown but recorded separately eg 1.1011 could be stored as:

1	1	0	1	1

SHIFTS.

30. If the bits in a word or register are moved leftwards or rightwards then a **shift** is said to have taken place. A shift one place left corresponds to multiplication by 2 and a shift one place right corresponds to division by 2, provided certain conditions are satisfied.

These conditions are:–

a. The sign of the number must be preserved.

b. Arithmetic meaning must be preserved.

Shifts which satisfy these conditions are called **arithmetic shifts.**

31. Examples. (further examples will be given in 28.12–28.13).

AFTER ONE SHIFT LEFT						STARTING WITH				AFTER ONE SHIFT RIGHT					
Bit lost in shift	Sign Bit	Value + 4			Bit inserted	Sign Bit	Value + 2			Bit inserted	Sign Bit	Value + 1			Bit Lost
0 ←	0	1	0	0	← 0	0	0	1	0	0 →	0	0	0	1	→ 0
Bit Lost	Sign bit	Value - 4			Bit inserted	Sign Bit	Value - 2			Bit inserted	Sign Bit	Value - 1			Bit Lost
1 ←	1	1	0	0	← 0	1	1	1	0	1 →	1	1	1	1	→ 0

MULTIPLICATION AND DIVISION.

32. In General.

a. Binary multiplication is achieved by a combination of shifts and additions.

b. Binary division is achieved by a combination of shifts and subtractions.

The details of these procedures are difficult to grasp, so the reader may wish to leave this for a later reading, and the less mathematical reader may prefer to leave this section completely.

33. Binary Multiplication (A Computer Based Procedure).

The two numbers being multiplied together are called **multiplicand** and **multiplier.** The result obtained at each stage of the calculation is called the **partial product sum.** Its final value is that of the product of the two numbers.

Steps. (These should be read in conjunction with the example.)

a. Negative multiplicands or multipliers should be converted to positive representations and the result complemented back to a negative representation at the end if necessary.

b. Set the partial product sum to zero.

c. Start with the leftmost bit of the multiplier and take multiplier bits in turn until all have been considered. Perform these steps for each multiplier bit:–

- i. Shift the partial product sum left by one bit position.
- ii. If the multiplier bit is a *one* add the multiplicand to the partial product sum.

34. Example. To perform $-13_{10} \times 6_{10} = -78_{10}$ in binary. ($13_{10} = 1101_2$, $6_2 = 0110_2$).

Partial Product Sum Successive Values (Last Value is the Product)	Multiplier Bits labelled A, B, C, D to aid explanation	Comments
		The partial product sum is the combined length of multiplier and multiplicand
(First set to zero)	A B C D	
0 0 0 0 0 0 0 0	0 1 1 0	
0 0 0 0 0 0 0 0	Left shift (Step c.i.) Multiplier bit (A) is zero(c.iii.)	
0 0 0 0 0 0 0 0	Left shift (Step c.i.)	
0 0 0 0 1 1 0 1	Multiplier bit (B) is *one* so add multiplicand (c.ii.)	
0 0 0 0 1 1 0 1	Result of sum.	
0 0 0 1 1 0 1 0	Left shift (Step c.i.)	
0 0 0 0 1 1 0 1	Multiplier bit (C) is *one* so add multiplicand (c.ii.)	
0 0 1 0 0 1 1 1	Result of sum.	
0 1 0 0 1 1 1 0	Left shift (Step c.i.). Multiplier bit (C) is *zero* (c.ii.)	
0 1 0 0 1 1 1 0	This product, 78_{10} must be complemented (Step a.)	
1 0 1 1 0 0 1 0	Twos complement representing -78_{10}	

35. Binary Division. (Computer Based procedures called the **restoring method**).

In the decimal division $-19 \div 6 = -3$ remainder 1, -19 is the **dividend, 6** is the **divisor** and 3 is the **quotient.**

Steps. (These should be read in conjunction with the example).

a. The division should be performed on positive values and the sign corrected at the end.

b. Shift the divisor left until the most significant bits align with the dividend (beneath the lefthand end of the dividend). Record the number of shifts made.

c. Subtract the divisor from the dividend (by adding the twos complement).

d. Shift the quotient one place left.

e. i. If the result of Step c. is negative, *restore* the dividend to its previous value by adding back the divisor.

ii. If the result of Step c. is positive, add one to the quotient.

f. Shift the remainder one place left.

g. With the remainder as the new dividend return to Step c.

h. Repeat these steps as many times as the divisor was shifted in Step b.

36. Example. To evaluate $-19 \div 6$. ($19_{10} = 10011_2$, $+6_{10} = 0110_2$, $-6_{10} = 1010_2$)

WORKING ON DIVIDENDS & REMAINDERS						COMMENTS Three lines of preliminary work followed by main steps.							
Sign Bit													
0	1	0	0	1	1	Dividend							
0	1	1	0	0	0	Step b. The divisor '6' has been shifted 2 places left.							
1	0	1	0	0	0	Twos complement of the divisor		QUOTIENT					
0	1	0	0	1	1	Dividend	Start with zero quotient	0	0	0	0	0	0
1	0	1	0	0	0	Subtract divisor (Step c.)	No change	0	0	0	0	0	0
1	1	1	0	1	1	Result of sub-traction	(Step d.) Shift left	0	0	0	0	0	0
0	1	1	0	0	0	Restore dividend (Step e.i.)	No change	0	0	0	0	0	0
0	1	0	0	1	1	Remainder ie restored dividend	No change	0	0	0	0	0	0
1	0	0	1	1	0	Shift left (Step f.)	No change	0	0	0	0	0	0
1	0	1	0	0	0	Subtract divisor (Step c.)	No change	0	0	0	0	0	0
0	0	1	1	1	0	Result of sub-traction	(Step d.) Shift left	0	0	0	0	0	0
0	1	1	1	0	0	Shift remainder left (Step f.)	(Step e.ii.) one added	0	0	0	0	0	1
1	0	1	0	0	0	Subtract divisor (Step c.)	No change	0	0	0	0	0	1
0	0	0	1	0	0	Result of sub-traction	(Step d.) Shift left	0	0	0	0	1	0
0	0	0	1	0	0	Remainder = 1. The 2 shifts (Step b.) tells us the point is 2 places in from the right	(Step e.ii.) One added	0	0	0	0	1	1
0	0	0	1	0	0		Twos complement	1	1	1	1	0	1

At this stage we have the result −19 divided by 6 is −3 remainder 1. The procedure can be continued to obtain a quotient to greater accuracy.

GRAY'S (OR CYCLIC) CODE.

37. This is also a BCD code but **not** 8421 weighted. The weighting is twice the binary power less one, zeros may be ignored but in calculating decimal values one works from the **leftmost** 1 to the **rightmost,** alternately adding and subtracting weighted values. The table below should make this clearer.

Decimal	Weightings n / 2n – 1	Gray's Code 8 4 2 1 / 15 7 3 1	Comment
0		0 0 0 0	
1		0 0 0 1	
2		0 0 1 1	3 less 1
3		0 0 1 0	3
4		0 1 1 0	7 less 3
5		0 1 1 1	7 less 3 plus 1
6		0 1 0 1	7 less 1
7		0 1 0 0	7
8		1 1 0 0	15 less 7
9		1 1 0 1	15 less 7 plus 1

Note. i. This bizarre code has the feature that the addition of one to any number results in only one bit being altered.

ii. The feature mentioned in i. makes it suitable for use in mechanical, optical or electronic counting mechanisms, because the load or signal changes evenly and aids accurate readings (see iii.)

iii. Gray's code is sometimes used for disc and drum drives for the purpose of reading rotational positions.

iv. The code is *not* useful for arithmetic purposes.

SUMMARY.

38. a. Complements are used for representing negative numbers and for subtraction because they are convenient and efficient.

b. Two types of complement are used.

c. Binary multiplication uses shift and add. Binary division uses shift and subtract.

d. The range of numbers stored in a given word or register depends on the word size, position of the point, and choice of complementation method.

POINTS TO NOTE.

39. A computer which uses BCD arithmetic or some other form of string arithmetic is called a 'decimal computer'.

40. BCD arithmetic is favoured for some commercial purposes because of the saving in conversion time but pure binary arithmetic is usually preferable.

41. The methods illustrated in this chapter are computer based methods as required in examinations. Quicker, manual methods, are inappropriate.

42. When BCD is referred to we should strictly speaking call it 8421 weighted BCD code because there are alternative BCD codes. XS3 is one example of an alternative BCD code. Another example is Gray's Code.

FURTHER STUDENT SELF TEST QUESTIONS.

(Answers on page 709)

7. *Convert these binary numbers to decimal*
   - *i.* 0.11
   - *ii.* 0.1101
   - *iii.* 0.0111
   - *iv.* 10.101
   - *v.* 101.011

8. *Convert from decimal to binary*
   - *i.* 0.3125
   - *ii.* 0.9375
   - *iii.* 6.1875
   - *iv.* 0.53125
   - *v.* 0.2

9. *a. Given that you can convert octal fractions to binary by writing down the binary equivalent of each octal digit convert these octal fractions to binary (eg $0.3_8 = 0.011_2$).*
   - *i.* 0.36
   - *ii.* 0.65
   - *iii.* 0.742

   b. Using a similar rule for hexadecimal fractions (eg $0.3_{16} = 0.0011_2$) convert these Hex fractions to binary.
   - *i.* 0.2B
   - *ii.* 0.3CF
   - *iii.* 0.5B9

10. *Evaluate 11 x 3 and 11 ÷ 3 decimal using binary multiplications and division.*

QUESTIONS WITHOUT ANSWERS.

11. *Convert $1101\ 1101\ 1011\ .\ 1110\ 0011_2$ to decimal, octal and hex.*

12. *Convert $C4F.B_{16}$ and $EB4.5_{16}$to binary Subtract the larger value from the smaller one using two complements and then express your answer in base 10.*

24 Fixed and Floating Point Arithmetic

INTRODUCTION.

1. This chapter introduces the two basic methods of number representation used in computers. A method of representation is judged in terms of the range, scale and accuracy which it provides, so these features are also explained. The basic ideas of number representation were introduced in chapter 10 as part of the description of numerical data types. In that chapter emphasis was placed on considering number types from the point of view of a programmer using a high level language. Here, the emphasis is upon the details of the binary representation of stored numbers and any reference to programming is in the context of low level languages where details of storage are more visible to the programmer than they are in high level languages.

FIXED POINT NUMBER REPRESENTATION.

2. For fixed point number representation the programmer requires:

a. A computer storage location or register of sufficient size to store all the digits of the number.

b. The ability to keep track of where the point lies himself. Convention dictates a **fixed** position for the point at the righthand side of the units column.

3. **Example.** • indicates the position of the point.

a. **Decimal example** for a 5 digit representation.

i. If the programmer assumes the point position to be:–

then	0	1	3	7	5	represents 13.75
and	3	8	6	2	4	represents 386.24

ii. If the programmer assumes the point position to be:–

then	1	3	7	5	0	represents 13.75
and	3	8	6	2	4	represents 38.624

b. **Binary example** for an 8 digit representation.

i. If the programmer assumes the point position to be:–

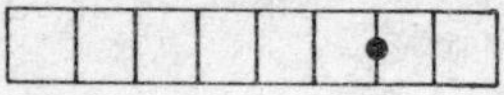

then	0	0	1	1	0	1	1	1	represents 13.75
and	0	0	0	1	0	0	1	0	represents 4.5

ii. If the programmer assumes the point position to be:–

then	0	1	1	0	1	1	1	0	represents 13.75
and	0	0	0	1	0	0	1	0	represents 2.25

4. Usage.

a. Only by knowing the assumed position of the point is it possible to determine the value of a stored number eg compare the storage of the numbers 4.5 and 2.25 in 3b.

b. When using fixed point representation it is the *responsibility of the programmer* to keep track of the point position. This task is simplified by

i. maintaining the same assumed point position throughout all calculations or,

ii. restricting the type of number representation. This leads to three basic classifications of fixed point representation:

A. **Mid-point representation** in which there are digits both before and after the point.

B. **Integer representations** in which there are no digits after the decimal point.

C. **Fraction representations** in which there are no digit before the decimal point.

5. The decimal examples given in paragraph 3, and those given later, could be represented in BCD. However, the same principles apply to BCD representations and so the details have been omitted in the interests of clarity.

FLOATING POINT NUMBER REPRESENTATIONS.

6. For floating point number representations the programmer requires:

a. A computer storage location or register of sufficient size to store all the significant digits of the number. (This part is called the **mantissa**)

b. Additional storage space to store the position of the point. This additional space may be within the same or a separate location. (This part is called the **exponent**).

7. Examples.

a. **Decimal examples** with a 5 digit mantissa and a 3 digit exponent.

MANTISSA ie 5 digits of the number					EXPONENT ie Position of point from the left.			Number represented. **Note** The position of the point 'floats' between the digits
1	3	7	5	0	0	0	2	$.13750 \times 10^2 = 13.75$
1	3	7	5	0	0	0	1	$.13750 \times 10^1 = 1.375$
3	8	6	2	4	0	0	3	$.38624 \times 10^3 = 386.24$
3	8	6	2	4	0	0	0	$.38624 \times 10^0 = .38624$

b. **Binary examples** using a total of 12 bits and twos complement for negative values.

MANTISSA Sign Bit	Fraction							EX-PONENT				Number represented
0	1	1	0	1	1	1	0	0	1	0	0	$.110111_2 \times 2^4 = 1101.11_2 = 13.75_{10}$
0	1	0	0	1	0	0	0	0	0	1	1	$.1001_2 \times 2^3 = 100.1_2 = 4.5_{10}$
0	1	0	0	1	0	0	0	0	0	1	0	$.1001_2 \times 2^2 = 10.01_2 = 2.25_{10}$
0	1	0	0	0	0	0	0	1	1	1	1	$.1_2 \times 2^{-1} = 0.01_2 = 0.25_{10}$
1	0	0	1	0	0	1	0	0	1	0	0	$-.110111_2 \times 2^4 = -1101.11_2 = -13.75_{10}$

c. These examples suggest the **general form** which is $n = f.r^e$ where

i. 'n' is the number,

ii. 'f' is the **mantissa** which is a *fraction* sometimes called the **argument,**

iii. 'r' is the **radix** or base, and

iv. 'e' is the **exponent** which is an *integer* sometimes called the **characteristic.**

8. Take care over the following unfortunate features of this terminology.

a. In **fixed point** computer representations of numbers the points position *between* two bits *need not remain* in a *fixed position* in a storage location since the programmer may move it.

b. In **floating point** computer representations of numbers the point *remains fixed* at the left hand end of the mantissa.

COMPARING FIXED POINT AND FLOATING POINT.

9. Speed. Computers can perform fixed point arithmetic faster than floating point arithmetic because extra work is involved in calculations with floating point numbers. Hardware may be used to do floating point arithmetic but this is usually an option costing extra. Floating point saves the programmer work but is still not as fast as fixed point arithmetic.

10. Range Scale and Accuracy.

a. Fixed point representation limits the range and scale of the numbers being represented.

b. Floating point representation gives greater flexibility in range and scale usually at the cost of accuracy.

11. Examples. We take a simple case to clarify ideas. Suppose just 3 decimal digits may be used to represent positive numbers. We can now see how they may be utilised.

a. **Fixed point case.** *Three figure accuracy* is possible.
The point position determines range and scale.

i. With the point to the extreme left fractional representations •|0|0|0| through •|9|9|9| are possible. The **range** (difference between largest and smallest) is 0.999. The **scale** is such that the right most digit represents units of .001.

ii. With the point to the extreme right, integers from |0|0|0|• through |9|9|9|• are possible. The **range** is 999 and the **scale** unit is 1.

b. **Floating point case.** No more than *two figure accuracy* is possible. We will consider that case ie assume a 2 digit mantissa and single digit exponent.

i. **Range.** The smallest number possible is •|0|0| $\times 10^{\boxed{0}} = 0$ and the largest number is •|9|9| $\times 10^{\boxed{9}}$ = 990 000 000. Hence the range is 990 000 000.

ii. **Scale.** When the exponent is 0 the mantissa is in units of .01 and when the exponent is 9 the mantissa is in units of 10 000 000.

iii. **Accuracy.** Reducing the accuracy to single digit values could allow a 2 digit exponent with even greater range and scale change.

Note: Floating point scale is adjusted automatically for each number represented.

FIXED POINT ARITHMETIC.

12. The procedures introduced in chapter 23 apply directly to fixed point arithmetic. It remains for us to examine the range and accuracy of binary representations in details.

13. Examples of binary representations.

An 8 bit register holds numbers in twos complement form with the leftmost bit as sign bit. Maximum and Minimum positive and negative numbers are represented. Seven bit accuracy is available.

a. Example of integer representation.

REPRESENTATION (In binary) Sign bit		VALUE (in decimal)		COMMENT
0	1 1 1 1 1 1 1	$= 2^7-1$	$= 127$	Maximum positive
0	0 0 0 0 0 0 1	$= 2^0$	$= 1$	Minimum positive
1	1 1 1 1 1 1 1	$= -2^0$	$= -1$	Least negative
1	0 0 0 0 0 0 0	$= -2^7$	$= -128$	Most negative

b. The example is repeated here with a fractional representation

REPRESENTATION Sign Bit	Point Position						VALUE (in decimal)	COMMENT
0	1	1	1	1	1	1	1 $= 1 - \frac{1}{2^7}$	Maximum positive
0	0	0	0	0	0	0	1 $= \frac{1}{2^7}$	Minimum positive
1	1	1	1	1	1	1	1 $= -\frac{1}{2^7}$	Least negative
1	0	0	0	0	0	0	0 $= -1$	Most negative
1	0	0	0	0	0	0	1 $= -(1 - \frac{1}{2^7})$	Most negative fraction

If arithmetic produces results beyond the range of representation they must be handled in some way. We now see how this problem is overcome.

14. Overflow and Underflow.

a. **Overflow** occurs when the result of an arithmetic operation is too large to be stored in the location allocated to it.

b. **Underflow** occurs when the result is too small to be stored in the location allocated to it.

All overflow and underflow should be detected and corrected if possible.

15. Examples given a 5 bit word with 4 bit accuracy and leftmost bit as sign bit. All numbers are integers.

a. Sign Bit	BINARY SUM (ADDITION)				DECIMAL VALUES
0	1	1	0	0	12
0	0	1	1	0	6
1	0	0	1	0	18

	b. Sign Bit	BINARY SUM (ADDITION)				DECIMAL VALUES
	1	0	1	0	0	−12
	1	1	0	1	0	− 6
1	0	1	1	1	0	−18

a and b are examples of overflow, the results are too large, this is easily detected since the sign bit of the sum is different to the sign bits of the two numbers being added together.

c. If 6 were divided by 12 in this representation the result $.1_2$ would be too small to represent ie underflow would occur.

16. Detecting overflow. (Detected values will be lost unless they are stored elsewhere immediately they occur).

a. Using an extra bit which is added to the left of the sign bit. Procedure:–

i. The extra bit is set to the same value as the sign bit before addition or subtraction.

ii. The modified numbers are added or subtracted.

iii. If the extra bit and sign bit differ after the operation then overflow has occurred.

Example.

a. Extra bit	Sign bit	BINARY SUM (ADDITION)				DECIMAL VALUES
0	0	1	1	0	0	12
0	0	0	0	1	1	3
0	0	1	1	1	1	15
0 =	0	Bits the same: no overflow				

Extra bit	Sign bit	BINARY SUM (ADDITION)				DECIMAL VALUES
0	0	1	1	0	0	12
0	0	0	1	1	0	6
0	1	0	0	1	0	18
0 ≠	1	Bits differ: overflow				

b. An alternative method not requiring an extra bit can be used but it is more complicated:–

i. With ADD, if signs differ and with SUBTRACT, if signs are the same overflow cannot occur.

ii. In other cases the sign can be predicted ie:–

For A + B   if sign (A) = sign (B) then result should be sign (A)
For A – B   if sign (A) ≠ sign (B) then result should be sign (A)

A wrong sign will indicate overflow.

17. Double Precision. One way to reduce overflow is to increase the storage length allocated to each number representation. If one location in memory is not long enough then two adjacent locations can be used. A number stored in this way is called a **double-precision number** or **double length number.** Double precision is used:–

a. When the use of a single location will not give sufficient accuracy or range as is often the case with small computers with word lengths less than 24 bits.

b. For multiplication where products will be double the length of the multiplicands.

18. Double-Precision Arithmetic is arithmetic using double precision numbers. It is slower but machines with longer words tend to be more expensive so the method is often employed. The details go beyond the scope of this book but the ideas involved are indicated by this example in which for simplicity we assume each location is 4 bits long.

DOUBLE PRECISION NUMBERS								COMMENT
First Location				Second Location				Example of
Sign bit	More significant bits			Carries 'C'	Less significant bits			$25_{10} + 15_{10}$ ie $11001_2 + 1111_2$
0	0	1	1	0	0	0	1	$25_{10} = 11001_2$
0	0	0	1	0	1	1	1	$15_{10} = 1111_2$
0	0	0	1	1	0	0	0	Pseudocode Step 1
0	0	0	1	1	0	0	0	Pseudocode Step 3
0	0	1	0	0	0	0	0	and Step 4
0	0	1	1	0	0	0	0	Pseudocode Step 5
0	1	0	1	0	0	0	0	Result $101000_2 = 40_{10}$

```
Begin
    Add less significant halves                    (* Step 1)
    if
        carry = 1                                  (* Step 2*)
    then
        Add 1 to the more significant half of the number (* Step 3 *)
        carry : = 0 (* Step 4 *)
    endif
    Add more significant halves                    (Step 5 *)
end
```

FLOATING POINT ARITHMETIC.

19. Standard Form. You will see that 0.125×10^2 and 0.0125×10^3 are alternative floating point representations of the same number. It proves useful in practice to use only those representations which have mantissa values within some specified range. Such representations are said to be in **Standard form.**

20. Example. In decimal we can specify the mantissa 'm' by

$$+0.1 \leqslant m < +1 \text{ and } -1 < m \leqslant -0.1$$

So for example 0.125×10^2 *is* in standard form but 0.0125×10^3 *is not.* The representation of zero is a special case which will be dealt with later.

21. Standard form for binary floating point numbers.

The range for the mantissa 'f' is $\frac{1}{2} \leqslant f < 1$ and $-1 \leqslant f < -\frac{1}{2}$. This choice of mantissa range enables the detection and correction of **temporary overflow** of the mantissa during floating point arithmetic. A 7 bit floating point number is used to illustrate the important points in the following examples. Note carefully that the exponents are powers of 2.

22. Examples with this representation:–

<table>
<tr><td colspan="4">MANTISSA
(fraction)</td><td colspan="3">EXPONENT
(Integer)</td></tr>
<tr><td>sign bit</td><td>●</td><td></td><td></td><td>sign bit</td><td></td><td></td></tr>
</table>

<table>
<tr><td colspan="10">STANDARD FORM MANTISSAS</td></tr>
<tr><td colspan="4">Positive Mantissas
½ ≤ f < 1</td><td>Mantissa Values</td><td colspan="4">Negative Mantissas
−1 ≤ f < −½</td><td>Mantissa Values</td></tr>
<tr><td>0</td><td>1</td><td>0</td><td>0</td><td>½</td><td>1</td><td>0</td><td>0</td><td>0</td><td>−1</td></tr>
<tr><td>0</td><td>1</td><td>0</td><td>1</td><td>⅝</td><td>1</td><td>0</td><td>0</td><td>1</td><td>−⅞</td></tr>
<tr><td>0</td><td>1</td><td>1</td><td>0</td><td>¾</td><td>1</td><td>0</td><td>1</td><td>0</td><td>−¾</td></tr>
<tr><td>0</td><td>1</td><td>1</td><td>1</td><td>⅞</td><td>1</td><td>0</td><td>1</td><td>1</td><td>−⅝</td></tr>
</table>

Assume an exponent value of zero, in which case the mantissa value is the value represented.

Note: The sign bit and adjacent bit differ in *all* cases. *Any* representation in which the sign bit and adjacent bit are *equal* will be *detected* as an illegal (overflow) representation. (ie representation is out of range).

23. Normalisation (Standardisation). The mantissa 0.001 for ⅛ is not in standard form. To convert its representation into standard form ie to **normalize** it we can apply this general procedure for **normalisation:–**

a. Shift the mantissa n bits left or right as necessary
b. If shifted left subtract n from the exponent.
If shifted right add n to the exponent.

Examples

a. Subtracting ½ from ⅝ could give rise to this unconventional representation of ⅛ which must be corrected.

MANTISSA				EXPONENT			COMMENT
0	0	0	1	0	0	0	⅛ **not** in standard form.
0	1	0	0	1	1	0	Mantissa shifted two places left so 2 subtracted from exponent ie ½ x 2^{-2}

b. Adding ⅝ to ⅞ could give rise to this unconventional representation of 1½ which must be corrected.

MANTISSA				EXPONENT			COMMENT
1	1	0	0	0	0	0	1½ **not** in standard form. (could be confused with –½)
0	1	1	0	0	0	1	Mantissa shifted 1 place right so 1 added to exponent ie ¾ x 2^1

24. During addition or subtraction temporary overflow often occurs but normalisation is easy, as can be seen from these further examples.

	REPRESENTATIONS		COMMENTS	
	MANTISSA	EXPONENT	DECIMAL WORKING	
a.	1 0 0 0 0 1 0 0	0 0 0 0 0 0	-1×2^0 $+\frac{1}{2} \times 2^0$ ADD	Signs differ so a left shift will be required.
	1 1 0 0	0 0 0	$-\frac{1}{2} \times 2^0$	Correct result but not in standard form.
	1 0 0 0	1 1 1	-1×2^{-1}	Mantissa shifted left 1 bit NORMALISED RESULT
b.	0 1 1 1 1 0 1 1	0 0 0 0 0 0	$+\frac{7}{8} \times 2^0$ $-\frac{5}{8} \times 2^0$ ADD	Signs differ so a left shift will be required.
	0 0 1 0	0 0 0	$+\frac{1}{4} \times 2^0$	Correct result but not in standard form.
	0 1 0 0	1 1 1	$\frac{1}{2} \times 2^{-1}$	Mantissa shifted left 1 bit
c.	0 1 0 0 0 1 1 0	0 0 0 0 0 0	$+\frac{1}{2} \times 2^0$ $+\frac{3}{4} \times 2^0$ ADD	Signs same so a right shift will be required.
	1 0 1 0	0 0 0	$+\frac{5}{4} \times 2^0$	Correct result but not in standard form.
	0 1 0 1	0 0 1	$+\frac{5}{8} \times 2^1$	Mantissa shifted right 1 bit Least significant bit is lost.
d.	1 0 0 0 1 0 1 0	0 0 0 0 0 0	-1×2^0 $-\frac{3}{4} \times 2^0$ ADD	Signs same so a right shift will be required.
	0 0 1 0	0 0 0	$-\frac{7}{4} \times 2^0$	Correct result but not in standard form.
	1 0 0 1	0 0 1	$-\frac{7}{8} \times 2^1$	Mantissa shifted right. Sign bit replaced. Least significant bit is lost.
e.	0 1 0 0 0 1 0 1	0 0 0 0 0 0	$+\frac{1}{2} \times 2^0$ $+\frac{5}{8} \times 2^0$ ADD	Sign same so a right shift will be required.
	1 0 0 1	0 0 0	$+1\frac{1}{8}$ (Taken for $-\frac{7}{8}$ if left!)	Correct result but sign indicates overflow.
	0 1 0 0	0 0 1	$+\frac{1}{2} \times 2^1$	Mantissa shifted right 1 bit. Least significant bit is lost so value becomes 1 not $1\frac{1}{8}$.

25. Range of standard form floating point representations.

a. In floating point representations:—

i. The most positive number occurs with the largest positive mantissa and largest positive exponent.

ii. The least positive number occurs with the smallest positive mantissa and largest negative exponent. **This number is often used as the standard form representation of zero since a zero mantissa is out of range.** Alternatively, zero must be handled as a special case.

iii. The least negative number occurs with the least negative mantissa and largest negative exponent.

iv. The most negative number occurs with the most negative mantissa and most positive exponent.

Note:

i. **Floating point overflow** occurs if the *exponent* overflows.
ii. Some machines automatically set underflow values to zero.

b. **Examples.**

Zero representations shown here are not typical. Typical values would be $\pm 10^{-30}$ or smaller.

MANTISSA	EXPONENT	COMMENT
0 1 1 1	0 1 1	Most positive number
$+(1-\frac{1}{2^3})$	+3	$(1-\frac{1}{2^3}) \times 2^3 = \frac{7}{8} \times 8 = +7$
0 1 0 0	1 0 0	Least positive number (Represents zero)
$+\frac{1}{2}$	−4	$(\frac{1}{2}) \times 2^{-4} = +\frac{1}{32} = +0.03125$
1 0 1 1	1 0 0	Least negative number (Alternative representation of zero).
$-(\frac{1}{2}-\frac{1}{2^3})$	−4	$-(\frac{1}{2}-\frac{1}{2^3}) \times 2^{-4} = -\frac{1}{2^5}+\frac{1}{2^7} = -0.0234375$
1 0 0 0	0 1 1	Most negative number
−1	+3	$-1 \times 2^3 = -8$

26. General Method for Addition and Subtraction.

a. Line up points by making the exponents equal. (Right hand shifts should be used so as to lose least significant digits instead of most significant digits).

b. Add or subtract mantissas.

c. Normalise result.

27. Examples. The method is demonstrated in decimal for simplicity.

a.	$(0.28 \times 10^3) + (0.12 \times 10^2)$					
0 •	2	8	0	x	10^3	
0 •	0	1	2	x	10^3	Shifted right to align points
0 •	2	9	2			Mantissa added, result in standard form
b.	$(0.2 \times 10^3) - (0.24 \times 10^3)$					
0 •	2	8	0	x	10^3	
0 •	2	4	0	x	10^3	Points already aligned
0 •	0	4	0	x	10^3	Result needs normalisation
0 •	4	0	0	x	10^2	Result in standard form

28. Multiplication and Division of floating point numbers

a. Multiplication rule:–
   i. Multiply the mantissas
   ii. add the exponents
   iii. normalise.

b. Division rule:–
   i. divide the mantissas
   ii. subtract the exponents
   iii. normalise.

ie

If the numbers are $n_1 = f_1 \cdot r^{e_1}$ and $n_2 = f_2 \cdot r^{e_2}$

Then $n_1 \times n_2 = (f_1 \times f_2) \times r^{e_1 + e_2}$

$n_1 / n_2 = (f_1 / f_2) \times r^{e_1 - e_2}$

29. Examples.

a.	$(0.12 \times 10^2) \times (0.253 \times 10^3)$	
0•1 2 0	$\times\ 10^2$	Assume 3 digit accuracy in mantissa fraction.
0•2 5 3	$\times\ 10^3$	
0•0 3 0	$\times\ 10^{2+3}$	Mantissa multiplied. Result is .03036; partial underflow. Exponents added
0•3 0 0	$\times\ 10^4$	Result in standard form
b.	$(0.156 \times 10^3) \div (0.12 \times 10^2)$	
0•1 5 6	$\times\ 10^3$	
0•1 2 0	$\times\ 10^2$	
1•3 0 0	$\times\ 10^{3-2}$	Mantissas divided. Exponents subtracted
0•1 3 0	$\times\ 10^2$	Result in standard form

30. Guard bits. If in example 29a we had provided a temporary extra digit for the result, then our result in its final standard form would have been 0.303×10^4, and a more accurate value. An even more serious problem is the temporary underflow of an exponent, which can be handled by placing an extra bit at the right hand end of the accumulator. This extra bit is called a **guard bit** and preserves floating point accuracy.

31. Exponents of floating point numbers are often represented by **excess 64 code.** This exponent is a 7 bit code in the range –64 to +63 and each value is coded as a positive value in binary by adding 64 eg 5 is coded as (64 + 5) = 69 and –12 is coded as (64 – 12) = 52.

SUMMARY.

32. a. The two basic methods of binary number representation used in computers are fixed point representation and floating point representation.

b. The two methods may be contrasted in terms of range, scale, accuracy, and convenience, speed and cost in doing arithmetic.

c. Floating point numbers are stored in **normal** or **standard** form with limits to the range of representation of the mantissa to allow overflow checks.

d. Double precision may be used to provide greater accuracy.

e. The use of extra bits at the end of the accumulators can aid overflow checking and guard bits can protect accuracy during temporary overflow.

POINTS TO NOTE.

33. a. The physical features of the computer notably word length has a direct bearing on the magnitude of number representable in single precision.

b. It is the responsibility of the programmer to see that his program keeps track of the point when using fixed point arithmetic.

c. Fixed point arithmetic is preferred for most commercial computing because of its speed, and commercial computers usually have an adequate word length to deal with all numbers in single precision. Commercial computers using the language COBOL often store numerical values in fixed point BCD form. This saves the time needed to convert the numbers into fixed point pure binary but arithmetic in BCD is slower. On balance, the saving in conversiontime pays off because of the small amount of arithmetic performed compared with the number of data items which would be converted.

d. Floating point arithmetic is often required for scientific computing in order to handle the variety of number ranges and scales. To cater for the accuracy sometimes required double precision floating point facilities are often available on scientific machines.

e. Extending precision as in double precision fixed point arithmetic is just one example of **extended precision,** eg a microcomputer with 8 bit words may use 7 words to represent a floating point number.

f. To estimate the number of bits required to store a decimal number as a fixed point binary number you may assume that it requires *roughly* 3⅓ bits per decimal digit.

STUDENT SELF TEST QUESTIONS.

(Answers on page 710)

1. A 12 bit register is to be used to hold fixed point numbers. State the largest and smallest positive and negative numbers which can be represented in arrangements a and b below. Use twos complement representation.

a.

b.

2. *Place these decimal numbers into this standard form:* $n = f \times r^e$ *where n is the number, f is a mantissa (fixed point part),* $r = 10_{10}$ *is the radix and e is the exponent.*

Take $0.1 \leqslant f < 1$ *or* $-1 < f \leqslant -0.1$

eg $25 = 0.25 \times 10^2$

i. 36
ii. 159
iii. −276
iv. −56724
v. 376.92
vi. 36.5×10^2
vii. -0.0498×10^3
viii. 9.824×10^{-3}
ix. -15.62×10^{-5}
x. -0.026×10^{-6}

3. **a.** ***Show how each of these decimal numbers would be represented in a binary register using the floating point representation indicated below.***

i. 5
ii. −5
iii. 0.5
iv. −0.5
v. 35
vi. −35
vii. 3.5_{10}
viii. −3.5
ix. 0.125
x. −0.125

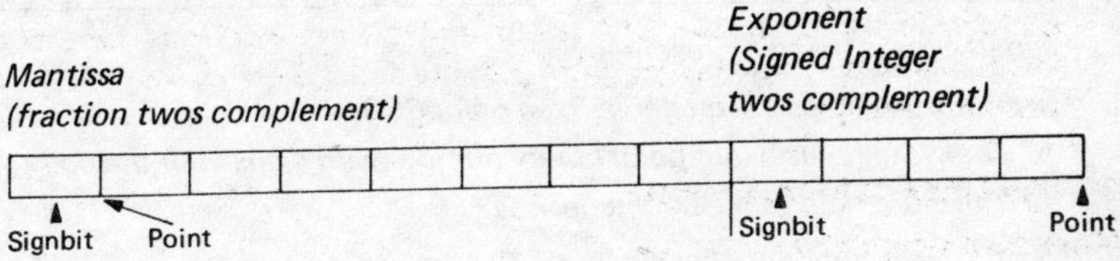

range of mantissa 'm' $-1 \leqslant m < -\tfrac{1}{2}$ $\tfrac{1}{2} \leqslant m < 1$

b. *State in decimal for this representation*

i. *the most positive number*
ii. *the least positive number*
iii. *the most negative number*
iv. *the least negative number*

4. *Give the relative advantages and disadvantages of fixed and floating point representation of numbers in computers.*

5. a. How are signed binary integers represented in digital computers and what are the advantages and disadvantages of each representation?

b. Express each of the following numbers, given in the scale named, in each of the other three named.

- i. Binary +0.101
- ii. Decimal −91
- iii. Octal +237
- iv. Hexadecimal +E8

(B.C.S. Part 1 1976)

6. a. What is the numerically largest negative integer that can be represented by 8 bits, using 2's complement fixed point storage? Give your answers in binary and denary.

b. The floating point representations of numbers are usually normalised. Why?

(London 1977)

QUESTIONS WITHOUT ANSWERS.

7. A 16 bit word is to be used to store floating point numbers with 6 bits allocated to the exponent and 10 bit allocated to the fraction.

a. Suggest how the format of the word could be organised.

b. What is the largest positive number which can be represented?

c. How many decimal digits accuracy can be guaranteed?

8. Consider the contents of the following 16 bit word:

1	0	0	1	0	1	1	1	0	0	1	0	0	1	0	1

What value is being represented if:

a. The word holds an integer in fixed point BCD 8421 weighted code?

b. The word holds a mid-point binary number with 4 bits after the point?

c. The word holds a binary integer?

State any assumption that you make.

25 Errors and Accuracy

INTRODUCTION.

1. This chapter deals with types of errors, sources of error, ways of dealing with errors in computer arithmetic and methods of preserving accuracy or avoiding errors.

2. Errors (Numerical Errors). An **error** occurs when the value used to represent some quantity is not the true value of that quantity, eg errors occur if we use approximate values such as 2.5 instead of 2.53627. **Note that**

a. A value may be *intentionally* used despite the fact that it may incur an error. The reasons for this may be those of:–

i. simplicity,
ii. convenience,
iii. cost,
iv. necessity.

b. An error may be caused by a **mistake,** which is said to occur if the value used is other than the one intended, eg writing 5.2 when meaning to write 2.5.

3. Other Errors. The term "error" may also be used to describe situations which occur when a program **either** is not executed in the manner intended **or** produces results which are not correct. Causes for such errors include

a. Faulty data.

b. Faulty software.

c. Faulty hardware.

(The last is by far the least common).

4. Absolute and Relative Errors. (These definitions are general; computer orientated examples come later).

These are the two main types of error. They have both theoretical and practical importance.

Definitions:–

a. **Absolute error.** This is the difference between the true value of quantity and the number used to represent it.

ie Absolute error = Value used – True value.

eg True value = 2.5, Value used = 3
Absolute error = 3.0 – 2.5 = 0.5

b. **Relative error** $= \dfrac{\text{Absolute error}}{\text{True Value}}$

eg using the figures just given

Relative error $= \dfrac{0.5}{2.5} = 0.2$

We may express the result algebraically as $E = \frac{U - T}{T}$

where E is the relative error, U is the used value and T is the true value. This formula can be rearranged into a useful form which is

$$U = T\ [1 + E]$$

Note:

i. Alternative definitions of the absolute error ignore its sign ie they define it in terms of **numerical values** or **absolute values.**

ii. Since the true value may not always be known, the relative error may be approximated by using

$$\text{Relative error} = \frac{\text{Absolute error estimate}}{\text{Used value}}$$

For small absolute errors this gives a reasonably accurate value.

SOURCES OF ERROR.

5. These may include:–

a. Data errors.
b. Transcription errors.
c. Conversion errors.
d. Rounding errors.
e. Computational errors.
f. Truncation errors.
g. Algorithmic errors.

We will now define and discuss these various sources of error.

6. Data errors. The data input to the computer may be subject to error because of limitations on the method of data collection. These limitations may include:–

a. the accuracy to which it was possible to make measurements,
b. the skill of the observer, or
c. the resources available to obtain the data. (See 21.5)

7. Transcription errors. These are errors (mistakes) in copying from one form to another.

a. **Examples.**
   i. Transposition, eg typing 369 for 396
   ii. 'Mixed doubles' eg typing 3226 for 3326
b. These errors may be reduced or avoided by using
   i. Direct encoding (eg OCR/OMR)
   ii. Validation checks (See 21.8)

8. Conversion. When converting data from its input form, BCD say, to its stored form, Pure Binary say, some errors may be unavoidably incurred because of practical limits to accuracy. On output similar errors may occur. Further discussion will follow later.

9. Rounding errors frequently occur when doing manual decimal arithmetic. They occur with even greater frequency in computer arithmetic.

a. **Examples.**
   i. Writing 2.53627 as 2.54
   ii. Writing ⅓ as 0.3333

b. A rounding error occurs when **not all the significant digits** (figures) are given, eg when writing 2.54 we omit the *less significant digits* 6, 2 and 7.

10. Types of Rounding.

a. **Rounding down,** sometimes called truncating, involves leaving off some of the less significant digits thus producing a *lower* or *smaller* number, eg writing 2.53 for 2.53627.

b. **Rounding up** involves leaving off some of the less significant digits, but the remaining least significant digit is increased by 1, thus making a *larger* number, eg writing 2.54 for 2.53627.

c. **Rounding off** involves rounding up or down according to which of these makes the least change in the stated value, eg 2.536 would be rounded up to 2.54 but 2.533 would be rounded down to 2.53. What to do in the case of 2.535 can be decided by an arbitrary rule such as 'If the next significant digit is odd round up, if even round down.' So using this rule 2.535 would round to 2.54 because '3' is odd.

11. Significant Digits (figures) and Decimal Places. These are the two methods of describing rounded off results. They are defined as follows.

a. **Decimal Places.** A number is given to n decimal places (or nD) if there are n digits to the right of the decimal point.

Examples. 2.53627 is 2.54 to 2 decimal places
ie 2.53627 = 2.54 (2D)
2.53627 = 2.536 (3D)
4.203 = 4.20 (2D)
0.00351 = 0.0035 (4D)

b. **Significant Figures.** A number is given to n significant figures (or nS) if there are n digits used to express the number but excluding
   i. all leading zeros and
   ii. trailing zeros to the *left* of the decimal point.

Examples. 2.53627 = 2.54 (3S)
57640 = 58000 (2S)
0.00351 = 0.0035 (2S)
4.203 = 4.20 (3S)

12. Computational Errors occur as a result of performing arithmetic operations and are usually caused by overflow or rounding of intermediate results.

13. Truncation Errors. We first need to define some terms. When numbers are placed in some specified order they form a **sequence,** eg 1, 3, 5, 7, 9 . . . or ½, ¼, ⅛, 1/16 . . . . . When a sequence is added it is called a **series** eg 1 + 3 + 5 + 7 + 9 + . . .

or ½ + ¼ + ⅛ + $\frac{1}{16}$ + ... Some series have many practical uses. For example the quantity π, used extensively in Mathematics, can be evaluated to *any* required accuracy by using the formula:–

$$\pi = 4 \times (1 - \frac{1}{3} + \frac{1}{5} - \frac{1}{7} + \frac{1}{9} - \frac{1}{11} + \frac{1}{13} \quad \ldots\ldots)$$

The series is an **infinite** series since it goes on as far as we care to take it. In practice we might only use the first few terms to get an approximate value. We **truncate** a series, if when we calculate its sum, we leave off all terms past a given one, eg

$$1 - \frac{1}{3} + \frac{1}{5} - \frac{1}{7}$$

is a truncated series. A **truncation** error is an error resulting from the truncation of a series.

Note: *Rounding down* is also sometimes called *truncation.*

14. Algorithmic Errors. An **algorithm** is a set of procedural steps used in the solution of a given problem and can be represented by pseudocode. Errors incurred by the execution of an algorithm are called **algorithmic errors.** A computer program is one type of algorithm. If two programs are available to perform a specified task, the one which produces the result with the greatest accuracy will have the smaller algorithmic error. Since each step in an algorithm may involve a **computational error,** the algorithm which achieves the result in fewer steps *may* have a smaller algorithmic error.

ERRORS IN COMPUTER ARITHMETIC.

15. In manual arithmetic calculations we may wish to estimate the accuracy of the result given the accuracy of the data used in the calculation. The same problem exists with computer calculations but we have to focus our attention on the errors introduced when the computer stores and handles data.

16. Rounding Errors in Stored Data.
Since all computers have a **finite word length** there is always a limit to the accuracy of the stored data, and many values will be **rounded** each time they are stored. The following factors are relevant.

a. For **fixed point integer representation** there is good control over accuracy within the allowed range since there is no fractional part to be rounded.

b. In **other fixed point representations,** where part or all of the number is fractional, rounding will occur often, but the precision provided may still allow reasonable control over accuracy during addition and subtraction.

c. In **floating point representations** almost all number storage and calculations can lead to rounding errors.

d. Rounding should be **unbiased** if possible, ie numbers should be rounded **off** rather than **up** or **down** when stored.

17. Unbiased Rounding in Binary.

Example. Consider a very simple case where only the first two binary fraction places are available, as shown here. Consider values between ¼ and ½. Unbiased rounding is indicated by this diagram. (N is the number to be rounded).

PLACE VALUES			NUMBER REPRESENTATION
1	½	¼	
0	0	0	= 0
0	0	1	= ¼
0	1	0	= ½
0	1	1	= ¾
1	0	0	= 1

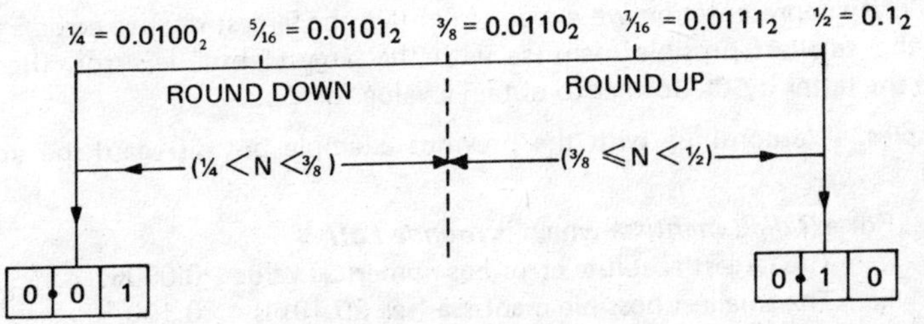

Note that numbers with the *third* binary fraction place zero are rounded down whilst those with the same place a one are rounded up. This suggests a general rule which is:– To round off a binary fraction to n places:

If the $(n + 1)^{th}$ bit is zero, round down
If the $(n + 1)^{th}$ bit is one, round up.

18. Conversion Errors. In converting fractions from decimal to binary for storage, rounding errors are often introduced.

Example. ⅘ is easily represented as the decimal fraction 0.8. However, if we convert 0.8 to binary we discover that it can only be represented as a recurring fraction ie 0.110011001100 . . . . Suppose we are able to store only 6 bits of this fraction ie 0.110011. If we convert this stored value back to decimal we will get the value 0.796875 **not** 0.8! *Conversion errors like this are very common.*

19. Computational Errors.

a. In general every arithmetic operation performed by a computer may produce a rounding error. The cause of this error will be one of :–
   - i. The limited number of bits available to store the result ie finite word length.
   - ii. Overflow or underflow (also a consequence of a.).
   - iii. Rounding in order to normalize a result.

b. The size of the error will depend on these two main factors:–
   - i. The size of the word length.
   - ii. The method of rounding, up, down, or off.

Control over these errors depends on factors listed in paragraph 16.

20. Relative Errors in Floating Point Representation depend on the word length and method of rounding as will now be demonstrated. For simplicity we will consider a decimal example. The results apply equally well to binary representations.

Supppose we have a representation which provides **3 digit accuracy** in the mantissa and adequate representation of the exponent and sign. So the 4 digit number 2594 will be *rounded* when stored as + .259 x 10^{+4}. The relative error in this case is clearly

$$= \frac{-0.0004 \times 10^4}{0.2594 \times 10^4} \triangleq -0.0015$$

You should notice that since the exponents cancel we need only consider mantissas. This we will do in the general case which follows.

21. Maximum Relative Error (denoted by $\in$)
For a given representation we expect to obtain the largest relative error $\in$ when we have the smallest possible mantissa with the largest absolute error. (Because we divide the latter by the former to obtain a value for $\in$).

Examples. (We continue with the previous example but disregard the sign of the error).

a. For a *3 digit mantissa* which is *rounded off.*
   i. The largest absolute error has numerical value 0.0005.
   ii. The smallest possible mantissa (see 20.19) is 0.100.
   iii. The maximum relative error $\in = \frac{0.0005}{0.100} = 0.005$

b. For a *4 digit mantissa* which is *rounded off.*
   i. The largest absolute error has numerical value 0.00005.
   ii. The smallest possible mantissa again is 0.100.
   iii. The maximum relative error $\in = \frac{0.00005}{0.100} = 0.0005$

c. For a *3 digit mantissa* which is *rounded down.*
   i. The largest absolute error has numerical value 0.001
   ii. The smallest possible mantissa again is 0.100.
   iii. The maximum relative error $\in = \frac{0.001}{0.100} = 0.01$

These examples demonstrate that **the word length and method of rounding affect the maximum size of the relative error $\in$.**

22. Errors in Stored Results. All results stored in mantissas of the same length will be subject to the *same* maximum relative error $\in$. This will be the case for *any* floating point arithmetic operation; add, subtract, multiply or divide.

23. The Floating Point Error Formula. This formula is used to find the maximum error in the result of a floating point arithmetic operation. The general method is summarised by the formula:–

$$R(x \circ y) = (x \circ y)(1 \pm \in) \qquad \text{(See paragraph 4)}$$

where 'o' represents one of the operations, +, –, x or ÷.

$\in$ is the <u>maximum relative error</u> for the given method of representation and R(x o y) represents the worst **Result** of the operation x o y.

24. Examples. (We continue with 3 digit decimal representations with $\in = 0.005$ as in 21 a.)

a. Consider the sum 195 + 23.4 = 218.4
We take 'o' as +, x = 195, y = 23.4 and $\in$ = 0.005
substituting in the formula gives

$$R(195 + 23.4) = (195 + 23.4)(1 \pm 0.005)$$

(We use the calculated value on the Right hand side)

$$= 218\,(1 \pm 0.005)$$
$$= 218 \pm 1.09$$

This tells us our *3 figure result* will have a maximum error $\triangleq \pm 1.09$. The actual error is only 0.4 since the correct *result to 4 figures* is 218.4

b. Consider 195 x 23.4 = 4563 = 4560 (3S)
We take 'o' as x, x = 195, y = 23.4 and $\in$ = 0.005
substituting in the formula gives

$$R(195 \times 23.4) = (195 \times 23.4)(1 \pm 0.005)$$

(We use the calculated value on the Right hand side)

$$= 4560\,(1 \pm 0.005)$$
$$= 4560 \pm 22.8$$

This tells us our *3 figure result* will have a maximum error $\triangleq \pm 22.8$.

25. The main use of the floating point error formula is in algebraic rather than numerical problems like those just demonstrated. Before working through an algebraic example we will deal with a problem to which the formula can be applied.

26. Equivalent algebraic formula may not give results to the same accuracy because of the effects of rounding errors.

Example. Consider the well known relation $a^2 - b^2 = (a - b)(a + b)$

If 'a' is close to 'b' then the right hand side may give a more accurate value than the left.

Take a = 3.17 and b = 2.95 and assume that *all intermediate results are rounded off to three figures.* This rounding corresponds to restoring the floating point result at each stage of computer arithmetic. You may check the true result 1.3464 by performing the calculation to full accuracy but we will use 3 figure accuracy.

Using $a^2 - b^2$ we have:–

$$3.17^2 - 2.95^2 = 10.0 - 8.70 = 1.3 \qquad (2S)$$

Using (a – b) (a + b) we have:–

$$(3.17 - 2.95)(3.17 + 2.95) = 0.22 \times 6.12 = 1.35 \qquad (3S)$$

We see that the second method is superior and in this case it gives the true rounded value.

Note: The advantage of using (a – b) (a + b) only occurs when $a \triangleq b$ (try it with a = 31.7) and particularly if a – b is of the **same order of magnitude as** $\in$ ie when $(a - b) \triangleq \in$.

27. A Proof using the floating point error formula. We assume that the floating point arithmetic in a particular computer is such that the result of each individual arithmetic operation has a relative error $\leqslant \in$ in magnitude. It is reasonable to also assume that errors of the order of $\in^2$ may be neglected. We can show that when 'a' is approximately equal to 'b' then (a – b) (a + b) is preferable to $a^2 - b^2$.

Proof using $R(x \circ y) = (x \circ y)\,(1 \pm \epsilon)$

a. Consider $a^2 - b^2$

First Stage.
$$R(a^2) = a^2\,(1 \pm \epsilon) = a^2 \pm a^2\epsilon$$
$$R(b^2) = b^2\,(1 \pm \epsilon) = b^2 \pm b^2\epsilon$$

Second Stage.
$$R[(a^2 \pm a^2\epsilon) - (b^2 \pm b^2\epsilon)] = [(a^2 \pm a^2\epsilon) - (b^2 \pm b^2\epsilon)]\,[1 \pm \epsilon]$$
$$= a^2 - b^2 + 2\,(\pm a^2 \pm b^2)\epsilon + (\pm a^2 \pm b^2)\epsilon^2$$
$$\simeq a^2 - b^2 + 2(\pm a^2 \pm b^2)\epsilon \qquad \text{(i)}$$
(ϵ^2 terms ignored)

b. Consider $(a - b)\,(a + b)$

First Stage.
$$R(a - b) = (a - b)\,(1 \pm \epsilon) = a - b \pm (a - b)\epsilon$$
$$R(a + b) = (a + b)\,(1 + \epsilon) = a + b \pm (a + b)\epsilon$$

Second Stage.
$$R\,([(a - b)\,(1 \pm \epsilon)]\,.\,[(a + b)\,(1 \pm \epsilon)]) = (a - b)\,(a + b)\,(1 \pm \epsilon)^3$$
$$\simeq (a^2 - b^2) \pm 3(a^2 - b^2)\epsilon \qquad \text{(ii)}$$
(ignoring terms in ϵ^2 and ϵ^3)

The magnitudes of the maximum errors in (i) and (ii) are $|\,2(a^2 + b^2)\epsilon\,|$ and $|\,3(a^2 - b^2)\epsilon\,|$ respectively. The second of these errors will be the smaller one if $a \simeq b$.

NB. The floating point error formula is not intended for use in numerical computations. It is for use in establishing *error limits* for given algebraic expressions which are to be evaluated on a floating point machine. For many numerical calculations the formulae may give maximum errors higher than those attainable in practice.

STUDENT SELF TEST QUESTIONS.

(Answers on page 713)

1. *a. Define the terms "Numerical Error", "Absolute Error", "Relative Error".*
   b. State five sources of error.
2. *Give the maximum value of*
   i. the absolute error and
   ii. the relative error

for each of the following numbers. Assume they are rounded off to the number of digits specified.

a. 80 (2S)
b. 0.125 (3S)
c. 350 (2S)
d. 6.25 (2D)

3. *a. State three causes of error in computer arithmetic.*

   b. State the two main factors which affect the size of errors produced in computer arithmetic.

   c. State the floating point error formula.

4. *Assume that arithmetic is being done in 4 digit decimal floating point arithmetic and that rounding off occurs where necessary.*

   a. What is the magnitude of the maximum relative error?

   b. Do this calculation and use the floating point error formula to calculate the error in the result.

   5968 – 43.67

5. *Show that the formula* $\nu(v - w)$ *is preferable to* $\nu v - \nu w$ *if v and w are numbers of similar magnitude.*

FURTHER ERRORS IN COMPUTER ARITHMETIC.

28. Order of operations. It is better to add "floating point" numbers in order of magnitude if possible.

Example. To calculate 0.273000 + 0.001480 + 0.000862.
The true value is 0.275342. We will do this sum two numbers at a time and round intermediate results just as a computer would do it. We have a choice of working (scanning) from right to left or from left to right. Assume the computer truncates intermediate results when it stores them with mantissas only 3 digits long.

a. WORKING LEFT TO RIGHT IN DESCENDING ORDER OF MAGNITUDE	COMMENTS	b. WORKING RIGHT TO LEFT IN ASCENDING ORDER OF MAGNITUDE
0.273000	Add	0.000862
0.001480		0.001480
0.274480	Results	0.002342
0.274000	Truncated to 3 Fig.	0.002340
0.000862	Add next Number	0.273000
0.274862	Results	0.275340
0.274000	Rounded to 3 Fig.	0.275000

The third figure is wrong in a. but correct in b. As a general rule therefore do additions in order of magnitude of the numbers from smaller to larger.

29. Algorithmic Errors. The errors produced when using an algorithm will frequently depend on

a. the order of the operations performed

b. the number of operations performed.

If the errors from one stage of the algorithm are carried over to successive stages then the size of the error may "grow". These **accumulated errors,** as they are called, may ultimately make the result obtained very unreliable.

30. Example. To keep the example simple we will consider an artificial situation, but with modifications it becomes a common practical problem. Suppose the solution of a problem requires the same calculation to be performed on successive values of X from $\frac{1}{3}$ to 6 in steps of $\frac{1}{3}$ ie X takes values $\frac{1}{3}$, $\frac{2}{3}$, 1, etc. Assume the problem is performed in decimal using *3 digit accuracy* at each stage. Two possible algorithms are shown here:–

ALGORITHM A		ALGORITHM B	
	SUCCESSIVE X VALUES	SUCCESSIVE X VALUES	

variables
x : **real**
Begin
x : = 0
repeat
x : = x + .333
(*Perform Calculation*)
until x > 6
end
	0.333
	0.666
	0.999
	1.33
	1.66
	1.99
	2.32
	2.65
	etc.
		0.333
		0.667
		1.00
		1.33
		1.67
		2.00
		2.33
		2.67
		etc.
			variables
			n : **integer**
			x : **real**
			
			Begin
			n : = 0
			repeat
			n : = n + 1
			x : = n / 3
			(*Perform Calculation*)
			until n > 18
			end

Both sets of X values suffer from rounding but algorithm A accumulates errors so that successive values become too low. Many simple decimal fractions became recurring fractions when converted to binary (see paragraph 18). An algorithm requiring steps of 0.1_{10} would need to deal with this problem for example.

METHODS WHICH REDUCE ERRORS AND MAINTAIN ACCURACY.

31. Nesting. This reduces the number of operations thereby reducing error accumulation.

Example. To evaluate $3x^3 + 2x^2 + 5x + 1$ for a given x value use $((3x + 2)x + 5)x + 1$, starting with the innermost bracket and working outwards.

32. Batch Adding. This is an extension of the method in paragraph 28. A set of numbers to be added is grouped into several batches containing numbers of similar magnitude. Each batch total is found, then the batch totals are added.

33. Finding a "small" root of a quadratic equation.
When solving $ax^2 + bx + c = 0$ using the well known formula

$$x = \frac{-b \pm \sqrt{b^2 - 4ac}}{2a}$$

difficulties arise if one root is close to zero. Suppose the roots are α and β then
$(x - \alpha)(x - \beta) = 0$
ie $x^2 - (\alpha + \beta)x + \alpha\beta = 0$
By comparison with $ax^2 + bx + c = 0$ we see that $\alpha\beta = {}^c/_a$ or $\beta = {}^c/_{\alpha a}$. So given one root we can find the other.

Example. To solve $100x^2 + 2502x + 50 = 0$
$a = 100, b = 2502, c = 50$
Working to 3 figure accuracy

$$x = \frac{-b \pm \sqrt{b^2 - 4ac}}{2a}$$

gives $x = -25$ or 0
but taking $\alpha = -25$

$$\beta = \frac{c}{\alpha A} = \frac{50}{-25 \times 100} = -0.02,$$ the correct value for the other root.

ILL CONDITIONING.

34. A **problem** is **ill conditioned** if small errors in the data used for its solution lead to large errors in the answer. **Equations** are **ill conditioned** if small changes in coefficients lead to large changes in the solution.

35. Example 1. Suppose we are asked to solve the equations.

$y = 0.5x + 2$ (i)

$y = mx + 2.2$ (ii) where $m = 0.4 \pm 0.05$

using the value $m = 0.4$ we get the solution $x = 2, y = 3$
using the value $m = 0.45$ we get the solution $x = 4, y = 4$
using the value $m = 0.35$ we get the solution $x = 1\frac{1}{3}, y = 2\frac{2}{3}$
The error in 'm' is 12½% but we have obtained results with errors as much as 100%!

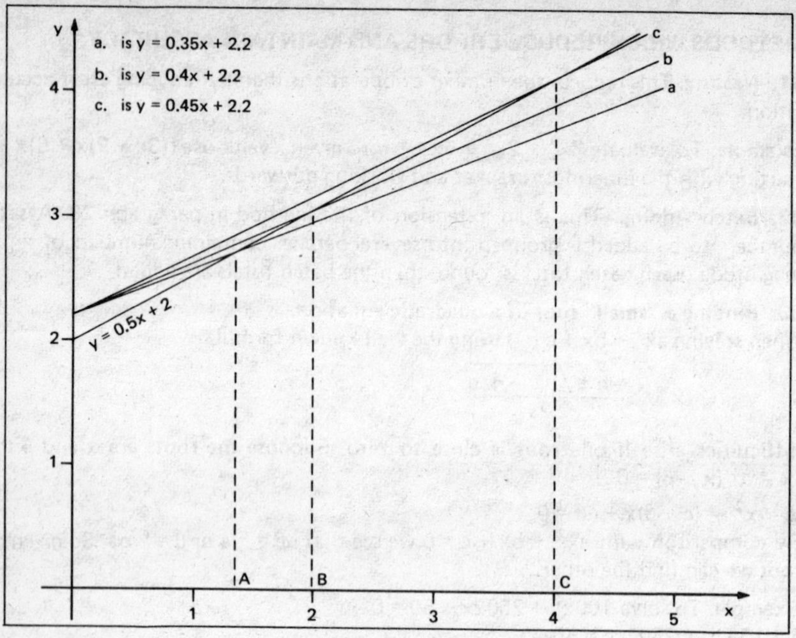

Fig. 25.1.

Fig. 25.1 shows that the three very different values for the root (marked A, B & C) arise because the angle between the lines is very small.

36. Example 2. To solve $50x^2 - 215x + C = 0$ where C = 231 (3S).

Using C = 231 in the formula $x = \dfrac{-b \pm \sqrt{b^2 - 4ac}}{2a}$

we get x = 2.1 or x = 2.2. But C = 231 ± 0.5 and if we use C = 231.5 in the formula we get no real solution!

SUMMARY.

37. a. The two types of numerical error are the absolute error and relative error.

b. Sources of numerical errors are:

i. Data errors
ii. Transcription errors
iii. Conversion errors
iv. Rounding errors
v. Computational errors
vi. Truncation errors
vii. Algorithmic errors.

c. Most values produced in floating point arithmetic are subject to rounding errors.

d. The size of the relative error in computer floating point arithmetic is affected by the word length and method of rounding.

e. In computer arithmetic care should be taken over:–
  i. The order of operations performed
  ii. Accumulated errors
  iii. Choice of alternative formulae
  iv. Ill conditioned problems.

POINTS TO NOTE.

38. a. It is important to relate these topics to computer arithmetic. So in examination questions look for phrases suggesting this such as "working to three figures" which would suggest the rounding of intermediate stored results.

b. Make use of these methods in your own programs particularly your examination project. It will save you time and trouble and improve the quality of your work.

STUDENT SELF TEST QUESTIONS (continued)

(Answers on page 714)

6. a. i. Convert the hexadecimal representation 3F2 into its binary coded decimal form. (Note: F represents the decimal number 15.)

ii. The letters abc represent a number in binary coded decimal form where each letter stands for a group of four bits in an 8421 weighted code. State a simple arithmetic procedure which can be used to convert the number directly into its pure binary form. Where is such a procedure normally used? Use the procedure to convert the BCD number 011101100101 into its pure binary form.

b. Write down an expression for each of the following numbers which can be held in an (n + 1)-bit register where the first bit is a sign bit and twos complementation is used, stating any assumptions made regarding the binary point.

i. The maximum and minimum positive fractions, *and*

ii. the most negative and the least negative fractions.

State the maximum number of bits which can occur in the product of two fractions.

If n = 23 what is the maximum loss of accuracy which can occur when the least significant bits of a product are truncated? State the answer as a decimal fraction.

c. Perform the following integer division in binary arithmetic using the restoring method:

$$35 \div 5$$

Use the twos complement convention. Annotate the working as necessary.

(AEB 1977)

7. a. For the quadratic equation,

$$x^2 - 100.1x + 0.05 = 0$$

use the standard formulae $x = (-b \pm \sqrt{(b^2 - 4ac)})/2a$, working to 5 significant figures, to obtain the two roots.

Explain how the error in the smaller root occurred.

Derive an alternative formula for the smaller root and use it to obtain a more accurate answer.

b. Give the meaning of ill-conditioning.

In the simultaneous equations

$$100x + 100y = 200$$
$$kx + 101y = 201,$$

k is an observed measurement – its nominal value is 100, but the measurement could be in error.

Find the ranges of x and y, if the variation from the nominal value of k could be:

i. ± 0.75%

ii. ± 2%

(AEB 1976)

QUESTIONS WITHOUT ANSWERS.

8. a. Suggest a suitable procedure for evaluating $y = 2x^3 - 9x^2 + 12x - b$ for values of x between 0 and 3 so that accurate graphs based upon 30 points may be drawn for various values of b.

b. Explain how the solution of the equation becomes ill-conditioned when $b \doteqdot 4$.

Boolean Algebra and Machine Logic

1. Chapter 26 is an introduction to Boolean Algebra, which is the algebra of logic. The chapter includes a discussion of the features of logic operations and truth tables along with methods of representing and simplifying logic expressions.

2. Chapter 27 shows how Boolean Algebra applies to the operation of computer devices. In particular it deals with the logic operations of the ALU and the encoding and decoding circuits.

26 Boolean Algebra

INTRODUCTION.

1. Boolean Algebra, named after its pioneer George Boole, is the algebra of logic. The binary nature of logical propositions (true or false) means this subject has applications in computing. Indeed, we have already seen boolean algebra, as applied to programming, in chapter 10. In this chapter we revise the basic ideas and take them a stage further.

PROPOSITIONS AND PREDICATES.

2. Propositions. A proposition is a statement which can either be **true** or **false.** Propositions can be represented by letters.

Examples.

a. 'p' stands for the proposition "You are reading this book" (TRUE)

b. 'q' stands for the proposition $3_{10} + 4_{10} = 10_{10}$ (FALSE)

Questions and exclamations are **not** propositions.

Examples.

a. "Who are you?" (NOT A PROPOSITION)

b. "Oh what a hot day!" (NOT A PROPOSITION)

3. Negation. The **negation** of a proposition 'p' is the proposition which is false when p is true, and true when p is false. The negation of 'p' may be written as $\bar{p}$ $-$p or $\sim$ p. (and pronounced NOT p)

Example.

'p' is the proposition "You are reading this book"
'$\bar{p}$' is the proposition "You are *not* reading this book"

4. Truth Tables. The table shown below is a **truth table.** It shows the possible values of p and $\bar{p}$ It also serves as a concise definition of $\bar{p}$ in terms of p.

p	$\bar{p}$
T	F
F	T

T stands for True. F stands for False.

When p is true $\bar{p}$ is false

When p is false $\bar{p}$ is true

Frequently the digits '0' and '1' are used instead of 'T' and 'F'. *We will use '1' for True and '0' for False.* The truth table then appears as:–

p	$\bar{p}$
1	0
0	1

This binary representation should give you a clue as to how computers handle logic.

5. **Predicates** are like propositions in that they can either be **true** or **false** but differ from propositions in that they contain variables which, until specified, prevent the true or false value from being determined.

Examples.

a. $x > 5$ is a predicate. We need to know the value of x before we can determine whether or not it is true or false. Once a value is assigned to x (8 say) the predicate becomes the proposition $8 > 5$ which is true.

b. "It is red" is a predicate. We need to know what "it" is before we can determine whether or not the predicate is true or false.

6. Conditions in selections and repetitions in programming languages are examples of predicates.

7. Since the substitution of values into the variables in a predicate turns the predicate into a proposition, predicates are sometimes loosely called propositions. Try to avoid this practice if you wish to pursue this subject further.

LOGIC OPERATIONS (BOOLEAN OPERATIONS).

8. **Operations, Operands,** and **Operators** were defined in 10.26. Propositions and predicates may be combined together using logic operators. The propositions and predicates then become **operands** in **logical operations.**

9. **Logic Operations** Propositions may be combined together. The propositions then become **operands** in **logic operations.**

Examples.

a. 'p' stands for "You are reading this book". 'q' stands for "You are drinking coffee". p AND q is a **logic operation** with 'p' and 'q' operands and AND as operator. p AND q stands for "You are reading this book *and* you are drinking coffee".

b. P(x) is a predicate which stands for

$$x > 5$$

Q(y) is a predicate which stands for

$$y = 9$$

P(x) AND Q(y) is a **logic operation** with P(x) and Q(y) as operands and AND as operator. P(x) AND Q(y) stands for "$x > 5$ *and* $y = 9$"

10. Logic Operations may be defined by truth tables. **Negation** is a logic operation and it was defined by truth table in paragraph 4.

11. The AND Operation is defined in the truth table given below. The symbols ∩ ∧ and . are commonly used for AND. So p∧q is pronounced "p AND q"

p	q	p∧q
0	0	0
0	1	0
1	0	0
1	1	1

Note: a. All possible combinations of p and q are given. Only one combination gives p ∧ q true.

b. The AND operation may also be called the **logical product, intersection** or **conjunction.**

12. The OR operation is defined in the following truth table. The symbols U, V and + are commonly used for OR. The OR operation may also be called the logical sum, **inclusive OR, disjunction** or **union.**

p	q	pVq
0	0	0
0	1	1
1	0	1
1	1	1

13. Inclusive and Exclusive ORs.

a. In everyday usage the word OR has two possible meanings:—

i. OR can mean one or the other or both. (the **inclusive** OR)

ii. OR can mean one or the other but **not** both. (the **exclusive** OR).

b. **Examples.**

i. **Inclusive OR.** To qualify for a competition you might have to subscribe to a magazine OR belong to a club. (You might do both).

ii. **Exclusive OR.** You are rich OR you are poor. (You can't be both).

You can see from the truth table that the OR operation, as defined here is in fact an inclusive OR operation.

14. Non-equivalent operation (Exclusive OR Operation). The Exclusive OR symbol $\not\equiv$, is defined in the following truth table.

p	q	$p \not\equiv q$
0	0	0
0	1	1
1	0	1
1	1	0

Compare this with the inclusive OR.

NB $p \not\equiv q$ is a shorter way of writing $\bar{p}.q + p.\bar{q}$

15. The Equivalence Operation (Match), symbol $\equiv$ is defined in the truth table. Note that $p = q$ is true when p and q are the same ie match. An alternative symbol for $\equiv$ is $\Longleftrightarrow$.

p	q	$p \equiv q$
0	0	1
0	1	0
1	0	0
1	1	1

Compare this with non-equivalence where $p \not\equiv q$ *is* true if p and q do *not* match.

NB $p \equiv q$ is a shorter way of writing $\bar{p}.\bar{q} + p.q$

16. Equivalence. Two operations are equivalent if they have the same truth table, and the equivalence operation is used to test equivalence. For convenience we use the = sign for cases where the equivalence operation is true eg $p = q$ means $p \equiv q$ is true.

17. Examples.

a. To show $\overline{p \vee q} = \bar{p} \wedge \bar{q}$ using truth tables.

Truth Table.

p	q	$\bar{p}$	$\bar{q}$	$\bar{p} \wedge \bar{q}$	$p \vee q$	$\overline{p \vee q}$
0	0	1	1	1	0	1
0	1	1	0	0	1	0
1	0	0	1	0	1	0
1	1	0	0	0	1	0

Method.

i. $\bar{p}$ and $\bar{q}$ are filled in using the negation table.
ii. $\bar{p} \wedge \bar{q}$ is filled in using the AND table with $\bar{p}$ and $\bar{q}$.
iii. $p \vee q$ is filled in using the OR table.
iv. $\overline{p \vee q}$ is filled in using negation of $p \vee q$.

The truth table values for $\overline{p \vee q}$ and $\bar{p} \wedge \bar{q}$ match so $\overline{p \vee q} = \bar{p} \wedge \bar{q}$ ie $\overline{p \vee q} \equiv \bar{p} \wedge \bar{q}$ is '1' for *all* values of the expressions.

b. This example uses the alternative notation with . for AND and + for OR so that the reader becomes familiar with both sets of symbols.

To show $A + \bar{A} . B = A + B$

A	B	A + B	$\bar{A}$	$\bar{A} . B$	$A + \bar{A} . B$
0	0	0	1	0	0
0	1	1	1	1	1
1	0	1	0	0	1
1	1	1	0	0	1

The columns are filled in left to right using the appropriate operations to build up the expressions.

c. To show A + 1 = 1 and A . 1 = A

A	1	A + 1	A . 1
1	1	1	1
0	1	1	0

VENN DIAGRAMS.

18. Diagrams in which AREAS represent OPERATIONS or PROPOSITIONS are called **Venn diagrams.**

19. Examples. The area within the rectangle represents all the possible propositions and the shaded area represents the proposition under consideration. **NB. A letter within a circle refers to the WHOLE circle in all these examples.**

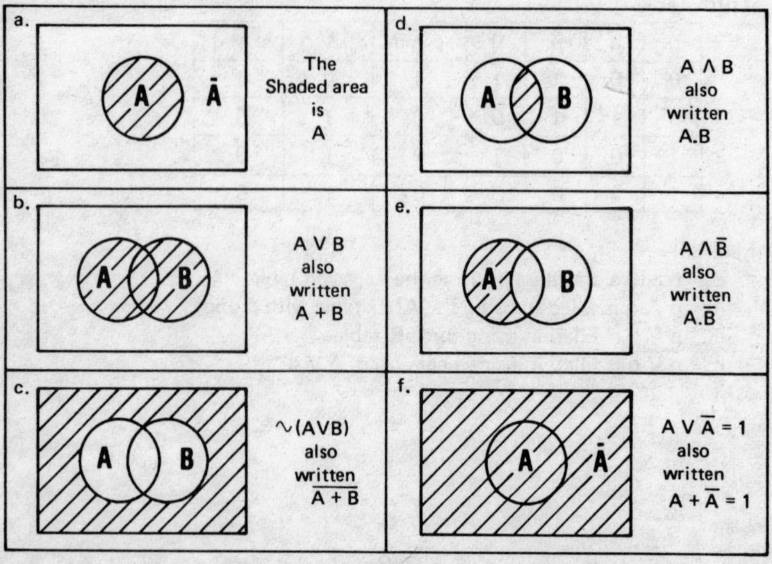

20. Using Venn Diagrams. If two operations have the same Venn diagram they are equivalent. We use this fact to show equivalence.

Examples. Repeating the problems in paragraph 15.

a (i)

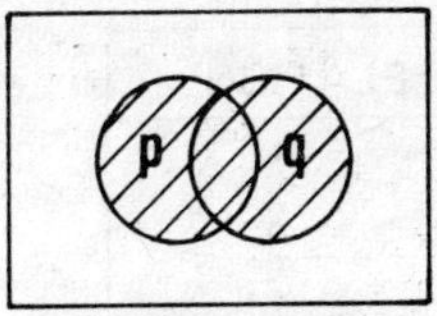

'p' refers to the **whole** of the lefthand circle and 'q' refers to the **whole** of the righthand circle in a(i) and a(ii).
The shaded area represents $p \vee q$, so the unshaded area represents $\overline{p \vee q}$.

(ii)

/// represents $\bar{p}$. \\\ represents $\bar{q}$ so the double shaded area represents $\bar{p} \wedge \bar{q}$ and is the same as the unshaded area in a(i).
So $\overline{p \vee q} = \bar{p} \wedge \bar{q}$

b (i)

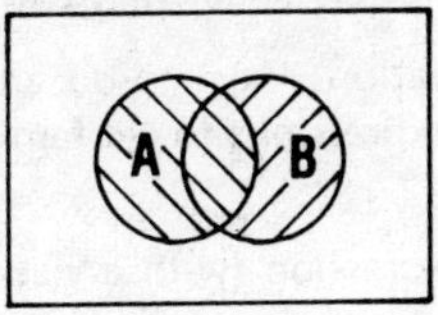

'A' refers to the **whole** of the lefthand circle and 'B' refers to the **whole** of the righthand circle in b(i) and b(ii).
\\\ represents A . /// represents $\bar{A}.B$
So the total shaded area represents $A + \bar{A}.B$

(ii)

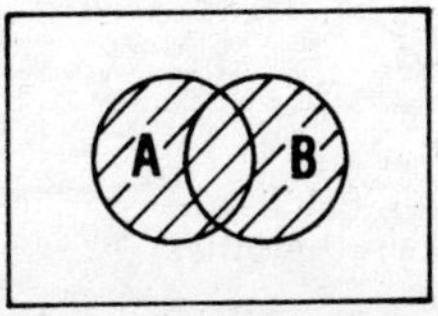

/// represents A + B and is the same as the total shaded area in b(i).
So $A + \bar{A}B = A + B$

c (i)

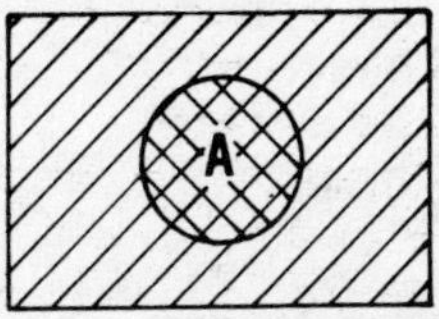

/// represents 1.\\\ represents A
but /// also represents A+1 so A+1 = 1
The double shaded area is A.1 and is the same as \\\ . So A.1 = A

SIMPLIFICATION OF EXPRESSIONS.

21. Broadly speaking simplification involves producing equivalent expressions which contain fewer operators.

Methods. The two methods covered by this book are:—

a. Algebraic Simplification using standard relations.

b. Diagrammatic techniques.

22. Algebraic Simplification. The following relations may be used to reduce expressions to their simplest forms. You are advised

a. to draw a truth table and Venn diagram for each expression to satisfy yourself that they are true.

b. to commit each relation to memory.

23. Duals. One aid in dealing with these and later expressions is the concept of **duality.** If you take a true relation and convert all ones to noughts, all noughts to ones, all ANDs to ORs and all ORs to AND you will obtain the dual of the relation. The dual will also be true which is the reason why duals are so useful.

RELATIONS	DUAL RELATION
$A \cdot 0 = 0$	$A + 1 = 1$
$A \cdot A = A$	$A + A = A$
$A \cdot \bar{A} = 0$	$A + \bar{A} = 1$
$A \cdot 1 = A$	$A + 0 = A$
$A \cdot (A + B) = A$	$A + A \cdot B = A$
$A \cdot (\bar{A} + B) = A \cdot B$	$A + \bar{A} \cdot B = A + B$

Note. The . may be omitted if implied eg A . B may be written AB.

24. De Morgan's Rule. These rules aid simplification. Again you are advised to draw truth tables and Venn diagrams for several expressions to get familiar with the results.

a. To apply De Morgan's Rules to simple expression (with a view to simplification) do the following

i. **change** ANDs to ORs and ORs to ANDs.
ii. **negate** all variables.
iii. **negate** the expression so formed.

Examples. Apply the rule to either side to obtain the other.

$$\left.\begin{array}{l} \overline{A + B} = \bar{A} \cdot \bar{B} \\ \overline{A \cdot B} = \bar{A} + \bar{B} \end{array}\right\} \text{Duals}$$

$$\left.\begin{array}{l} \overline{A + B + C} = \bar{A} \cdot \bar{B} \cdot \bar{C} \\ \overline{A \cdot B \cdot C \cdot D} = \bar{A} + \bar{B} + \bar{C} + \bar{D} \end{array}\right\} \text{Duals}$$

We use these expressions to simplify more complicated ones.

Note. The rules only apply to sum and product expressions.

b. For more elaborate expressions the rule is applied in stages.

Example

Consider	$(\overline{p+q}) \cdot \bar{r}$		
1st Stage	$(\overline{p+q}) \cdot \bar{r}$	$= \bar{p} \cdot \bar{q} \cdot \bar{r}$	[Apply De M' to $(\overline{p+q})$]
2nd Stage	$\bar{p} \cdot \bar{q} \cdot \bar{r}$	$= \overline{p+q+r}$	[Apply De M' to whole expression]

25. Other Rules.

a. **Commutative Law.** (ordering of variables can be changed)

Examples.

i. $A . B = B . A$

ii. $A + B = B + A$

b. **Associative Law** (brackets can be moved)

Examples.

i. $A . (B . C) = (A . B) . C = A . B . C$

ii. $A + (B + C) = (A + B) + C = A + B + C$

iii. $(A + B) + (C + D) = A + B + C + D$

c. **Distributive Law** (Similar rule to multiplying brackets in algebra)

Examples.

i. $A . (B + C) = A . B + A . C$

ii. $(A + B)\ (A + C) = A . A + A . B + A . C + BC = A + BC$

26. Examples of Simplification.

a. To simplify $A + B\ (A + B) + A(\bar{A} + B)$

Solution

$$
\begin{aligned}
& A + B(A + B) + A(\bar{A} + B) & \\
= \; & A + B + A(\bar{A} + B) & \text{(See paragraph 23)} \\
= \; & A + B + A . B & \text{(See paragraph 23)} \\
= \; & A + AB + B & \text{(Commutative law)} \\
= \; & A + B & \text{(See paragraph 23)}
\end{aligned}
$$

b. To simplify $\overline{\bar{A} + (\overline{B . C}) + \bar{C} . B}$

Solution

$$
\begin{aligned}
& \overline{\bar{A} + (\overline{B . C}) + \bar{C}.B} & \\
= \; & \bar{\bar{A}} . \overline{(\overline{B . C})} \; . \; \overline{\bar{C}.B} & \text{(De M' applied as for } \overline{x + y + z} = \bar{x} . \bar{y} . \bar{z}) \\
= \; & A . B . C . (\overline{\bar{C} . B}) & \text{(since eg } \bar{\bar{A}} = A) \\
= \; & A . B . C . (\bar{\bar{C}} + \bar{B}) & \text{(De M' applied to } (\overline{\bar{C} . B})) \\
= \; & A . B . C . (C + \bar{B}) & \\
= \; & A . B . C . C + A . B . C . \bar{B} & \text{(Distributive Law)} \\
= \; & A\,B\,C & \text{(C . C = C and B . } \bar{B} = 0 \text{ and see paragraph 23)}
\end{aligned}
$$

c. To Simplify $A + \overline{(\bar{B} . \bar{C}) + (\bar{B} . \bar{D})} + \bar{A}D$

Solution

$$
\begin{aligned}
& A + \overline{(\bar{B} . \bar{C}) + (\bar{B} . \bar{D})} + \bar{A}D & \\
= \; & A + \bar{A}D + \overline{(\bar{B} . \bar{C} + \bar{B} . \bar{D})} & \text{(Commutative law)}
\end{aligned}
$$

=	$A + D + \overline{(\overline{B} . \overline{C} + \overline{B} . \overline{D})}$	(See paragraph 23)
=	$A + D + (\overline{\overline{B} . \overline{C}}) . (\overline{\overline{B} . \overline{D}})$	(De Morgan)
=	$A + D + (B + C) . (B + D)$	(De Morgan)
=	$A + D + B + CD$	(Distributive law see paragraph 25cii)
=	$A + B + D + C . D$	(Commutative law)
=	$A + B + D$	(See paragraph 23)

STUDENT SELF TEST QUESTIONS.

(Answers on page 718)

1. *Use truth tables to find which of the following relations are true.*
   - i. $A(A + B) = A + A . B$
   - ii. $A . (\overline{A} + \overline{B}) = A . \overline{B}$
   - iii. $A + \overline{A} . B = A . B$
   - iv. $B . (A + 1) = B . (B + \overline{B})$
   - v. $A . 0 + C = C . \overline{C} + C . 1$

2. *Complete this truth table.*

A	B	C	D	(A.B) + (C.D)	(B + D) . C	$(\overline{A} . \overline{D}) + B$	$\overline{B} . \overline{C}$
0	0	0	0				
0	0	0	1				
0	0	1	0				
0	0	1	1				
0	1	0	0				
0	1	0	1				
0	1	1	0				
0	1	1	1				
1	0	0	0				
1	0	0	1				
1	0	1	0				
1	0	1	1				
1	1	0	0				
1	1	0	1				
1	1	1	0				
1	1	1	1				

3. *Simplify these expressions. (26.21).*

   i. $A.\overline{B}+\overline{A}.\overline{B}$

   ii. $A.B+\overline{A}B+\overline{A}.\overline{B}$

   iii. $\overline{\overline{A}.(B+C).\overline{D}}$

   iv. $(x+\overline{x}.y)+v(\overline{v}+w)$

   v. $\overline{\overline{x.(x+y)}+\overline{(y+yz)}}$

   vi. $\overline{\overline{(\overline{u}+0)}.\overline{(\overline{v}+0)}.\overline{(\overline{v}.0)}.\overline{(\overline{\overline{w}}+\overline{\overline{w}})}.\overline{(\overline{\overline{x}}.\overline{\overline{x}})}}$

KARNAUGH MAPS. (A stylized form of Venn diagrams).

27. There are different forms according to the number of variables in the expression to be simplified. We will consider expressions with up to 4 variables. Appropriate diagrams are shown below.

a. Two variable case. The variables A,B and their negations can be combined in 4 ways and by cross reference of row and column labels (as with a map) each can be described.

	A	$\overline{A}$
B	represents A.B	represents $\overline{A}$.B
$\overline{B}$	represents A.$\overline{B}$	represents $\overline{A}.\overline{B}$

To represent an expression a '1' is placed in each square for which a term is present. eg A = A.B + A.$\overline{B}$ is represented below

	A	$\overline{A}$
B	1	
$\overline{B}$	1	

b. **Three variable case.**

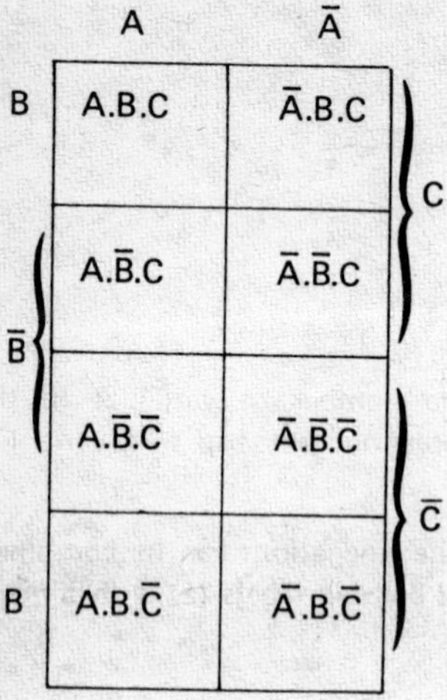

The term represented is shown here in each square.

eg $A.\bar{B}.C + \bar{A}.\bar{B}.\bar{C}.$ is shown below

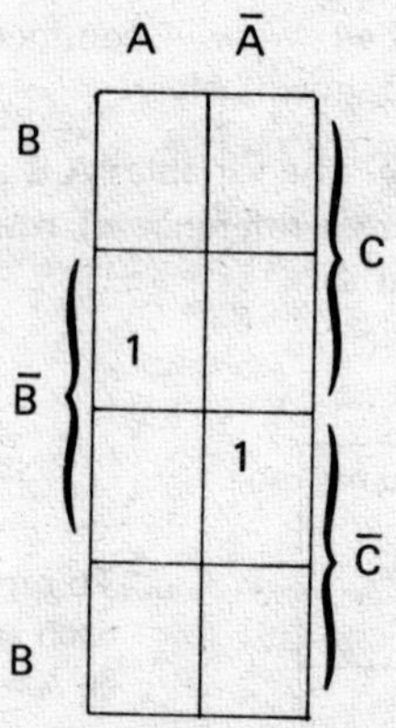

c. **Four variable case.** The diagram is shown below and terms are written in.

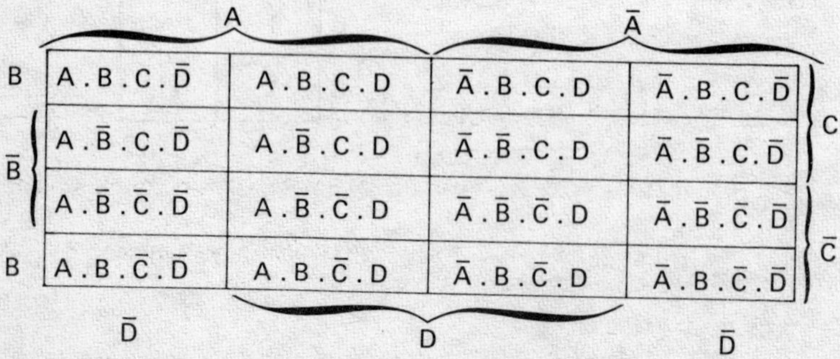

The expression A . B + C . D is shown below.

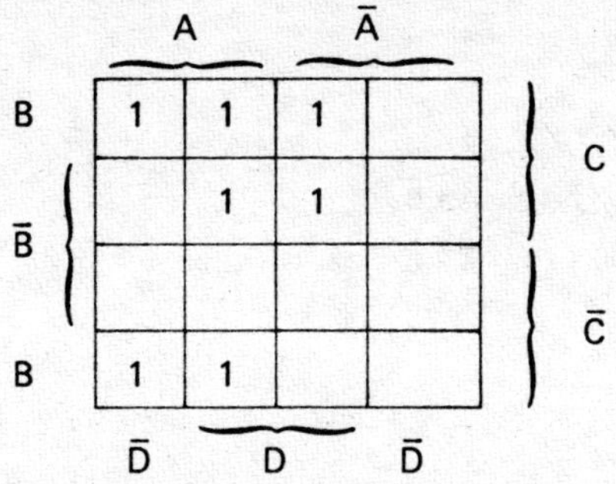

Simplifications using Karnaugh Maps.

28. This is a very useful diagrammatic technique particularly when simplifying expressions which have several terms connected by ORs.

The procedure is as follows

a. Do preliminary sketches to identify terms if you find it helpful.

b. On a new sketch fill in 1's for any term which is present in the expression. Use your preliminary sketches as a guide.

c. Draw loops around groups of 1, 2, 4 or 8 1's which correspond to simple expressions. The simplified expression will be a combination of these simpler expressions.

A little skill is needed to group the 1's correctly but it soon comes with practice.

29. Examples.

a. To simplify $A\bar{B} + \bar{A} . \bar{B} + \bar{A}B$

Solution.

A preliminary sketch serves no useful purpose here

i. Each term in the expression is represented by a 1.

ii. A loop is drawn around the 1's representing $\bar{A}$ and the 1's representing $\bar{B}$.

iii. The two loops include all terms so the simplified expression is $\bar{A} + \bar{B}$ ie $A\bar{B} + \bar{A}\bar{B} + \bar{A}B = \bar{A} + \bar{B}$

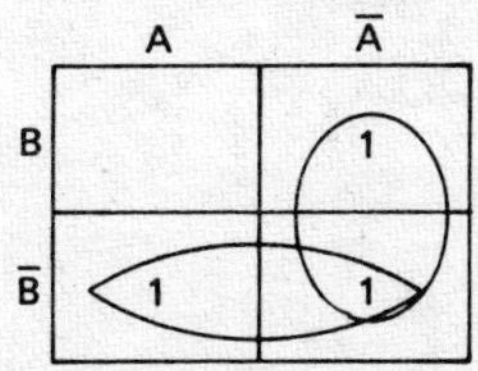

b. To simplify $A + B(A + B) + A(\bar{A} + B)$

Preliminary sketch 1

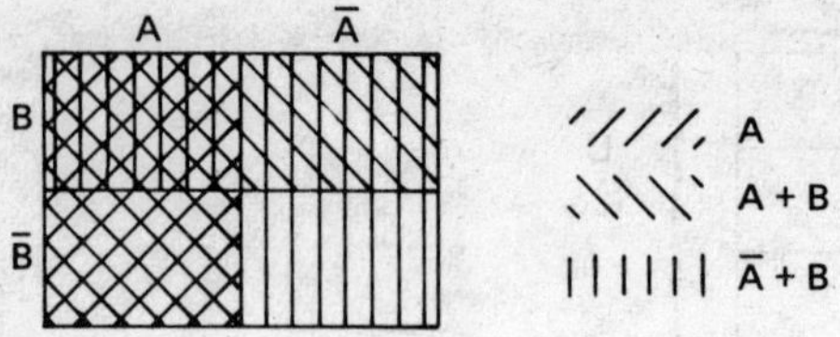

Preliminary sketch 2

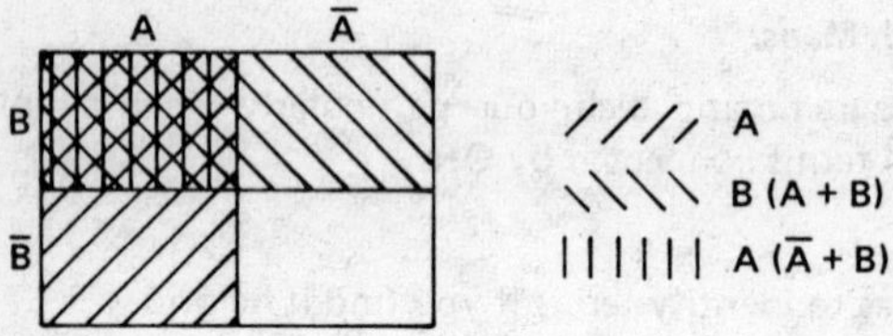

1's diagram with loops

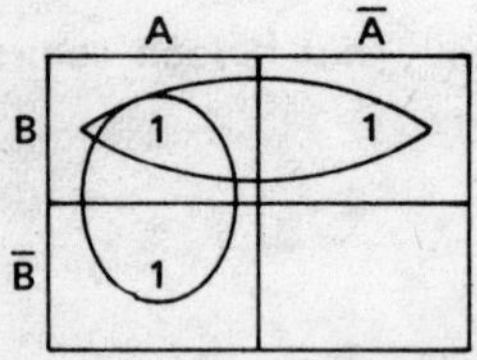

A Loop has been placed about A and B

The simplified expression is $A + B$

c. To simplify $ABC + A\bar{B}\bar{C} + \bar{A}B\bar{C} + \bar{A}BC + AB\bar{C} + \bar{A}\bar{B}\bar{C}$
  i. Each term in the expression is represented by a 1.
  ii. A loop is drawn around the terms representing $\bar{C}$.
  iii. Another 'broken loop' can be placed around the terms representing B.
The simplified expression is $B + \bar{C}$.

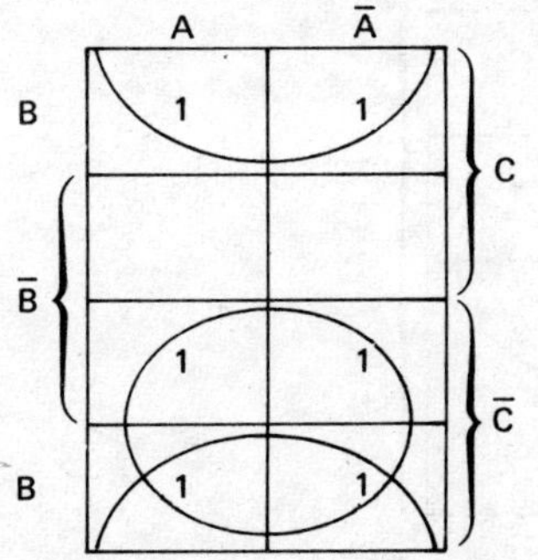

d. To simplify $\bar{A}C + B\bar{C} + \overline{B + C}$
Preliminary manipulation may help ie $\bar{A}C + B\bar{C} + \overline{B + C} = \bar{A}C + B\bar{C} + \bar{B} . \bar{C}$ (De M')

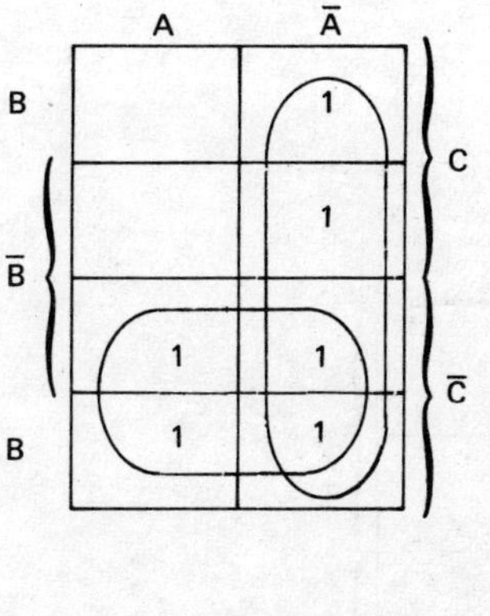

  i. $\bar{A}C$, $B\bar{C}$ and $\bar{B}\bar{C}$ are each represented by two 1's.
  ii. A loop can be drawn around $\bar{A}$ and $\bar{C}$.
  iii. $\bar{A} + \bar{C}$ is a simplified expression but by applying De Morgan's rule we get a further simplification to $\overline{A.C.}$
(See if you can spot the result $\overline{A.C.}$ just by inspecting the Karnaugh map).

e. To simplify $\bar{A}\bar{B}CD + \bar{A}\bar{B}C\bar{D} + A\bar{B}\bar{C}D + \bar{A}\bar{B}\bar{C}D + \bar{A}\bar{B}\bar{C}\bar{D} + AB\bar{C}D + \bar{A}B\bar{C}D$

i. Each term is represented by a 1.

ii. A loop can be drawn around $\bar{A} . \bar{B}$ and $\bar{C}D$.

The simplified expression is $\bar{A}\bar{B} + \bar{C}D$

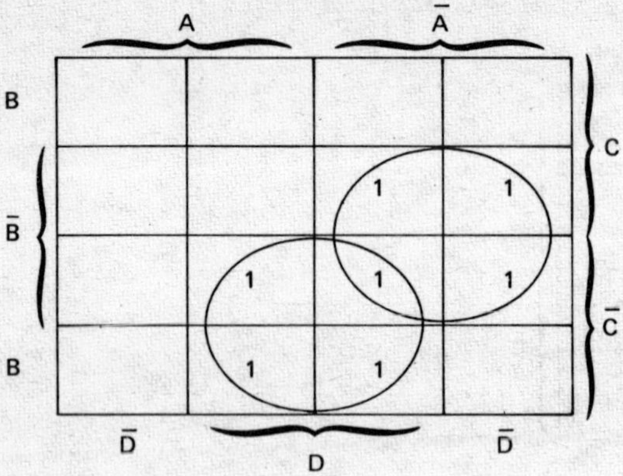

f. To simplify $ABD + \bar{B}CD + \bar{C}D + A\bar{B}C\bar{D} + \bar{A}BCD$

i. 1's are entered in the usual way

ii. Loops can be drawn for D and $A\bar{B}C$.

The simplified expression is $D + A\bar{B}C$.

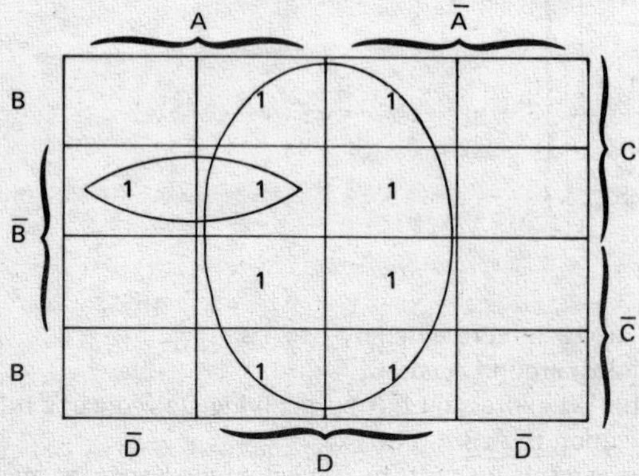

SUMMARY.

30. a. The terms operation, operand and operator were defined.

b. The operations introduced in this chapter were:–

OPERATION	OPERATOR SYMBOL
NOT	– or ~
AND	. or $\wedge$ or $\cap$
OR	+ or V or U
EQUIVALENCE	$\equiv$ or $\Longleftrightarrow$
NON-EQUIVALENCE	$\not\equiv$ or $\oplus$

c. Truth tables may be used to define operations:–

p	q	$\bar{p}$	p . q	p + q	$p \equiv q$	$p \not\equiv q$
0	0	1	0	0	1	0
0	1	1	0	1	0	1
1	0	0	0	1	0	1
1	1	0	1	1	1	0

d. Venn diagrams help in illustrating operations and simplifying expressions.

e. Boolean expressions may be simplified by:–

i. Algebraic methods using standard relations and rules such as De Morgan's rule.

ii. Diagrammatic techniques eg Karnaugh maps.

POINTS TO NOTE.

31. a. It is essential that you commit to memory all the notation terminology and operations because they are used frequently.

b. You should be completely competent in at least one of the methods of simplification preferably both.

c. It is important to distinguish between the equivalence operation $\equiv$ which is performed on operands and the = sign which is used to state that the equivalence of two expressions is true.

d. An alternative approach to this subject makes use of the theory of SETS. There is no need for you to study set theory but if you are already familiar with it you should be able to draw on some common skills already acquired.

e. You may find the non-equivalence operation referred to as just "NEQ" or "XOR" and the equivalence operation referred to as "EQ".

STUDENT SELF TESTING QUESTIONS (Continued).

(Answers on page 719)

4. *Simplify these expressions using Karnaugh maps.*
   - i. $A\bar{B} + \bar{A} \,.\, \bar{B}$
   - ii. $A \,.\, B + \bar{A} \,.\, B + \bar{A} \,.\, \bar{B}$
   - iii. $(X + \bar{X} \,.\, Y) + V(\bar{V} + W)$
   - iv. $\bar{A}\bar{B}CD + \bar{A}\bar{B}\bar{C}\bar{D} + AB\bar{C}\bar{D} + \bar{A}\bar{B}C\bar{D} + AB\bar{C}D + \bar{A}\bar{B}\bar{C}$
5. *Simplify these expressions.*
   - i. $(\bar{A}BC + \bar{A}\bar{B}C) + (A\bar{B}\bar{C} + AB\bar{C}) + (\bar{A}\bar{B}\bar{C} + \bar{A}B\bar{C})$
   - ii. $ABC\bar{D} + (\bar{A}B\bar{C}\bar{D} + AB\bar{C}\bar{D}) + \overline{(A + \bar{B} + \bar{C} + D)}$
   - iii. $\overline{\overline{X(X + Y)} + (\overline{Y + Y\bar{Z}})}$
6. *Simplify the dual of* $(A + B + C) \,.\, (A + B + \bar{C}) \,.\, (A + \bar{B} + C) \,.\, (\bar{A} + B + \bar{C})$. *The dual of the simplified dual, is the simplest form of the original expression. Try checking it.*

QUESTIONS WITHOUT ANSWERS.

7. *A logical operation called "implies" with symbol "⇒" has the following truth table.*

p	q	$p \Rightarrow q$
0	0	1
0	1	1
1	0	0
1	1	1

Find an alternative expression for this operation given that you may only use the symbols for AND, OR and NOT.

8. *Simplify these expressions:*
   - a. $A.\bar{B} + \bar{B}.\bar{C}. + A.\bar{C}. + \bar{A}.\bar{B}.\bar{C}. + \bar{A}.B.\bar{C}.$
   - b. $A.B.\bar{C}.\bar{D}. + \bar{B}.\bar{C}.D + A.C.\bar{D} + \bar{A}.B.\bar{C}.D + \bar{A}.\bar{C}.\bar{D} + A.\bar{B}.C + A.\bar{B}.\bar{D}$

27 Machine Logic

INTRODUCTION.

1. In chapters two and seven we saw how data and instructions are coded and stored in binary form. This chapter shows how the computer handles binary data and instructions at what may be called the **digital logic level** of the machine (9.8).

2. Data and instructions are transmitted between the various parts of the CPU or between the CPU and peripherals by means of **pulse trains** (2.3). Various tasks are performed by passing pulse trains through "electronic switches" called **gates.** Each **gate** is an electronic circuit which may have provision for receiving or sending several pulses at once. Each gate may be regarded as a "black box" which controls the flow of pulses in a particular way.

3. Each gate normally performs some simple function (operation) eg AND, OR, NOT, and for this reason gates are often called **logic elements.** It is the logic operations of gates which will concern us in this chapter, and we will *not* consider how they perform electronically, nor will we consider how they are made. The following background information should suffice.

BACKGROUND INFORMATION.

4. Most of the background information needed for this chapter was given earlier. The key points are summarised here with references to earlier details.

a. In modern computers a large number of components are made from small pieces of semiconductor material called **silicon chips** (4.4). A single chip will contain several components (eg. all the components for one gate) and because of this electronic property may be referred to as an **integrated circuit. (IC).** IC memory, also called **semiconductor memory,** was introduced in 4.10.

b. Chips may be classified according to size as follows:

i. **Small Scale Integration (SSI)** – containing at most 10 gates.

ii. **Medium Scale Integration (MSI)** – containing between 10 and 100 gates.

iii. **Large Scale Integration (LSI)** – containing between 100 and 100 000 gates.

iv. **Very Large Scale Integration (VLSI)** – containing more than 100 000 gates.

NB. This classification is not too strictly adhered to. For example, a circuit with 12 simple gates might be classified as SSI.

c. To gain an idea of what these sizes mean we may note that typical microprocessor-units (MPUs), and memory chips used with them, are examples of LSIs. Many of the devices described in this chapter, adders, decoders, multiplexers etc., may be made using MSI, or from a combination of SSI components.

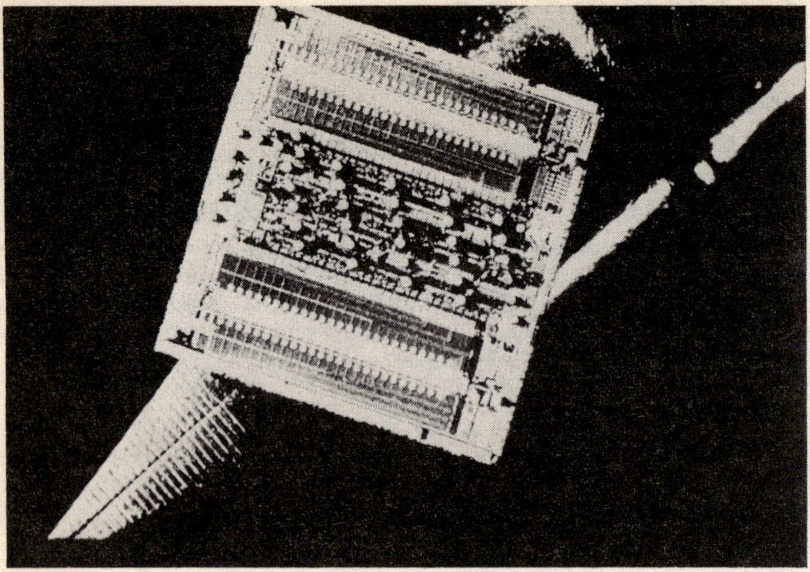

IBM 64K bit chip on a pen nib. Picture courtesy of IBM.

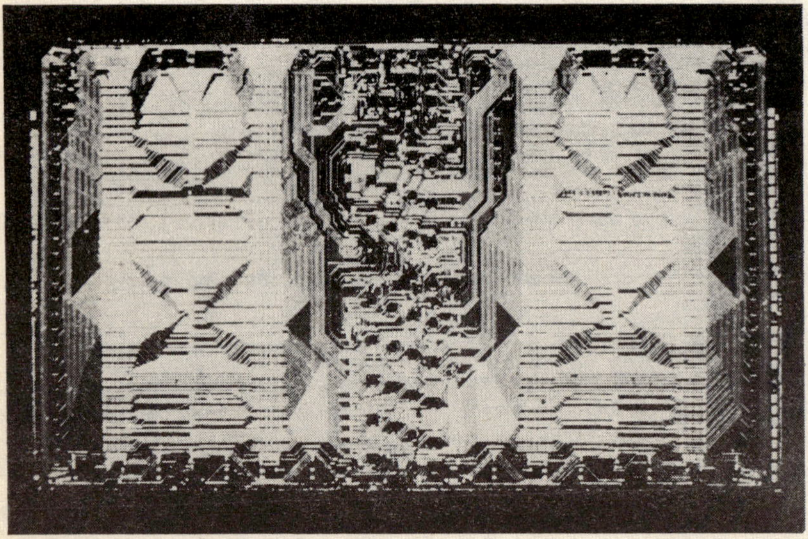

IBM 288K bit chip. Picture courtesy of IBM.

d. LSI design and manufacture is most economic if large numbers of chips are to be used. Therefore, special purpose devices which could be manufactured using LSI may be constructed from common MSI components instead if the numbers required do not make LSI manufacture economic. General purpose LSIs may also be used in such cases. One type, the **PLA (Programmed Logic Array),** may be specially tailored to a particular purpose in a one-off operation broadly comparable to the programming of a PROM.

e. To function properly, all chips require an adequate power supply. The operation of many chips requires precise timing and when this is the case electronic clocks are used to provide pulses to the chip. The operations which a chip performs on the inputs it receives may either depend upon the level of the input signal (0 or 1) or upon transitions in level (0 to 1 or 1 to 0). Where appropriate, these ideas will be discussed later.

LOGIC DIAGRAMS.

5. In logic diagrams *gates* are represented by *symbols* and *inputs* and *outputs* are represented by *arrowed lines* labelled by letters.

Example. In this diagram an AND gate (AND element) has two input signals, X and Y and gives one output signal corresponding to X . Y.

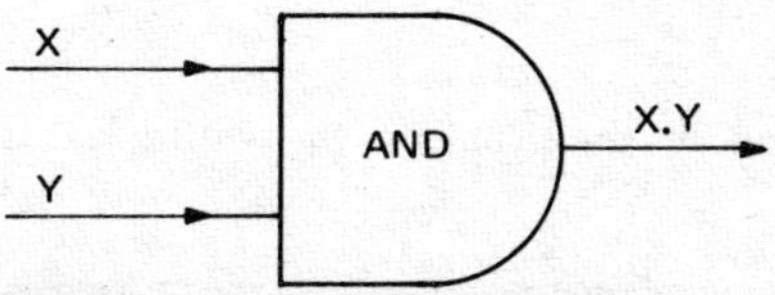

There is no need to write AND inside this AND symbol once it has been learned.

Simplified symbols may be used in which the name of the gate is written inside a circle as shown here.

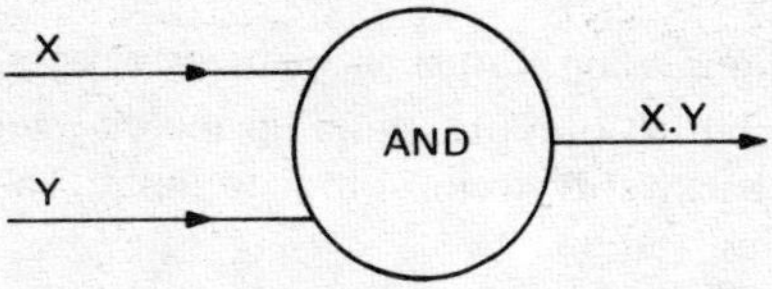

6. The function of a gate corresponds to logic operations and so they may be defined by a truth table.

Example.

X	Y	X . Y
0	0	0
0	1	0
1	0	0
1	1	1

'1' means a 'high' signal. '0' means a 'low' signal. The AND gate will only output a 'high' signal if it receives both X and Y 'high' signals at the same time.

NB. The convention '1' for "high", '0' for low is called **positive logic. Negative logic** may also be used ie. '0' for high '1' for low. All examples in this text use positive logic.

7. Table of Logic Symbols.

OPERATOR	OPERATION	SYMBOL
AND	X . Y	
OR	X + Y	
NOT	$\bar{X}$	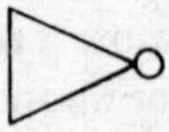

All other operations can be performed by a combinations of these gates. Other useful gates will be introduced later.

SOLVING PROBLEMS IN LOGIC DESIGN.

8. In designing a logic circuit we aim to reduce the number of gates used, thereby reducing cost. The method is outlined here and then illustrated with a simple problem.

Steps in the solution.

a. Start with a well defined description of the problem, eg Identify exact inputs and outputs.

b. Select symbols to represent the input and output variables.

c. Form a truth table in terms of these symbols referring to the problem definition throughout.

d. Form logic expressions from the truth table giving output variables in terms of input variables.

e. Try to simplify the output expressions using Karnaugh maps or algebra.

f. Produce a logic diagram for the simplified outputs. Build up the diagram using ANDs, ORs, or NOTs and work 'backwards' from output to input. The latter is not essential but the method helps later on.

9. Example.

a. **Definition of problem.** Design a 'parity detector' which produces a warning signal if it receives a 2 bit signal which does not have even parity (2.17). (This problem is not typical in all ways but is given because of importance later.)

b. **Symbols.**

i. Let A and B be the two *inputs* forming the 2 bit signal.

ii. Let P be the parity warning signal *output.*

c. **Truth table.**

A	B	P
0	0	0
0	1	1
1	0	1
1	1	0

d. **Form Expression.**

$P = \overline{A} . B + A . \overline{B}$ (Note also that $P = A \not\equiv B$)

This requires *5 gates:–* 2 NOTs, 2 ANDs and 1 OR.

e. **Simplification.**

i. Karnaugh Map.

	A	$\overline{A}$
B	0	1
$\overline{B}$	1	0

ii. From the Karnaugh map we see that

$$P = \overline{A . B + \overline{A} . \overline{B}}$$
$$= \overline{A . B} . \overline{\overline{A} . \overline{B}} \quad \text{(De Morgan)}$$
$$= \overline{A . B} . (\overline{\overline{A}} + \overline{\overline{B}}) \quad \text{(De Morgan)}$$
$$= \overline{A . B} . (A + B)$$

This expression uses only *4 gates:–*
1 NOT, 2 ANDs and 1 OR.

In our example the Karnaugh map does not lead to simplification in the usual way! A more typical simplification of $Q = \overline{A} . \overline{B} + \overline{A} . B + AB$ say is shown here.

i. Karnaugh Map

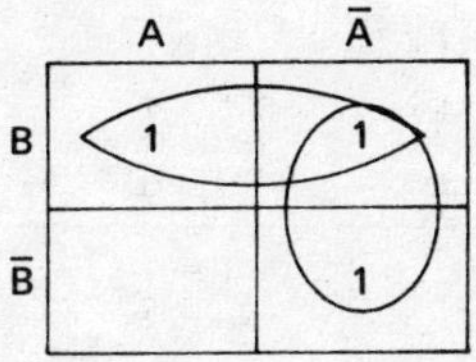

A	B	Q
0	0	1
0	1	1
1	0	0
1	1	1

ii. **or** by Algebra

$$Q = \overline{A} . \overline{B} + \overline{A} . B + A . B = \overline{A} . \overline{B} + \overline{A} . B + \overline{A} . B + A . B$$
$$= \overline{A}(\overline{B} + B) + B(\overline{A} + A)$$
$$= \overline{A} + B$$

f. **Logic diagram** for $P = \overline{A . B} . (A + B)$
The diagram is drawn from the expression working *Right* to *Left.*

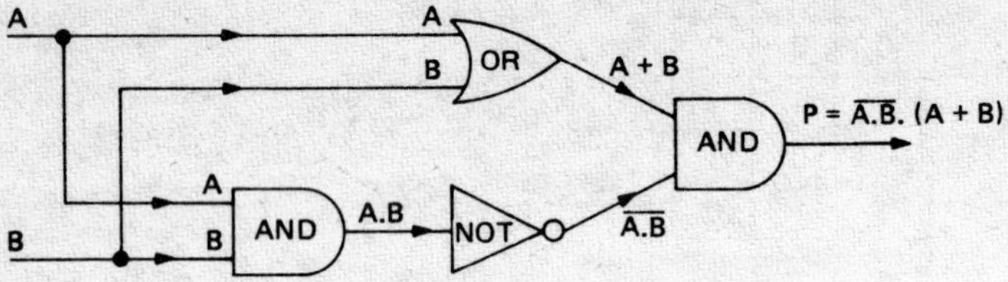

GATES FOR ARITHMETICAL PURPOSES.

10. Addition of two bits. The four possible additions (19.2) are represented in this truth table. The two inputs are X and Y and the outputs are S for SUM and C for CARRY.

X	Y	SUM 'S'	CARRY 'C'
0	0	0	0
0	1	1	0
1	0	1	0
1	1	0	1

From our table we see that

$C = X . Y$

and $S = \bar{X} . Y + X . \bar{Y} = X \not\equiv Y$

S can be represented by $S = \overline{X . Y}\ (X + Y)$, as was demonstrated in paragraph 9. This is illustrated here by truth table.

X	Y	C = X . Y	$\overline{X . Y}$	X + Y	$S = \overline{XY} . (X + Y)$
0	0	0	1	0	0
0	1	0	1	1	1
1	0	0	1	1	1
1	1	1	0	1	0

11. A Half Adder. Gates can be combined to produce a device which gives both **sum** and **carry** outputs. The device is called a **half adder** and is shown here.

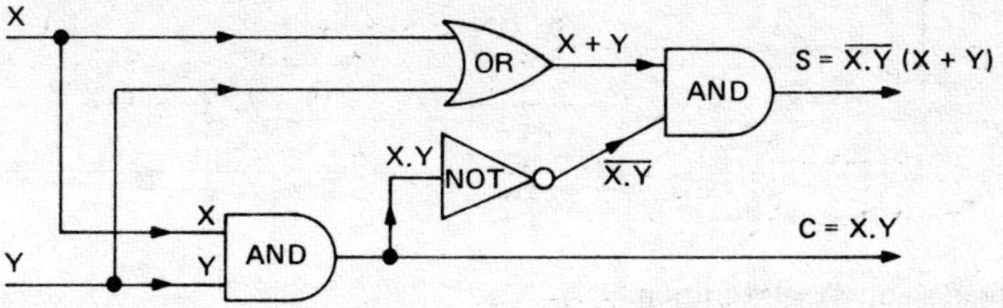

12. The Adder (Full Adder) can deal with a carry from a previous 2 bit sum and has 3 inputs.

INPUTS			OUTPUTS	
P	X	Y	S	C
0	0	0	0	0
0	0	1	1	0
0	1	0	1	0
0	1	1	0	1
1	0	0	1	0
1	0	1	0	1
1	1	0	0	1
1	1	1	1	1

In this truth table, which defines the operation of the adder, the inputs are X, Y and carry from previous sum P. The outputs are S for Sum and C for Carry.

$$S = \overline{P}\,\overline{X}Y + \overline{P}X\overline{Y} + P\overline{X}\,\overline{Y} + PXY$$

$$C = \overline{P}XY + P\overline{X}Y + PX\overline{Y} + PXY$$

From these expressions we may get

$$S = \overline{P}(\overline{X}Y + X\overline{Y}) + P(\overline{X}\,\overline{Y} + XY)$$

$$= \overline{P}(\overline{X}Y + X\overline{Y}) + P(\overline{\overline{X}Y + X\overline{Y}})$$

and $C = XY(\overline{P} + P) + P(\overline{X}Y + X\overline{Y})$

$$= XY + P(\overline{X}Y + X\overline{Y})$$

See 26.12 and 26.13
Also please note $X \equiv Y$
$= \overline{\overline{X \equiv Y}}$
$= \overline{X \not\equiv Y}$

From paragraph 10 we know that $\bar{X}Y + X\bar{Y}$ is the sum output from a half adder. A close look at the terms for S and C should provide the basis of the adder design shown here.

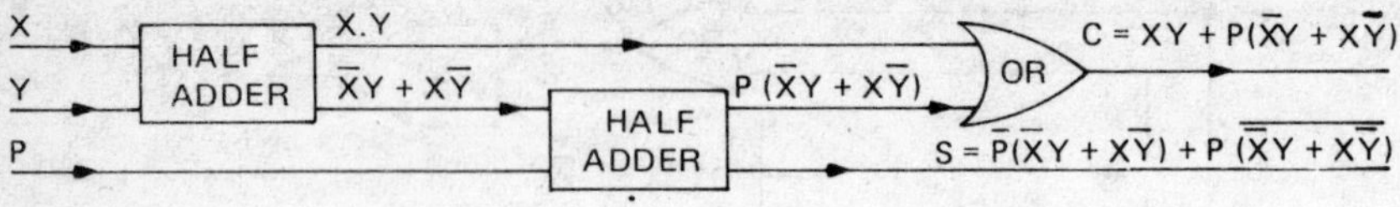

13. Parallel and Serial Addition.

There are two basic methods of adding numbers which are several digits long.

a. Parallel addition in which the columns are added side by side at the same time.

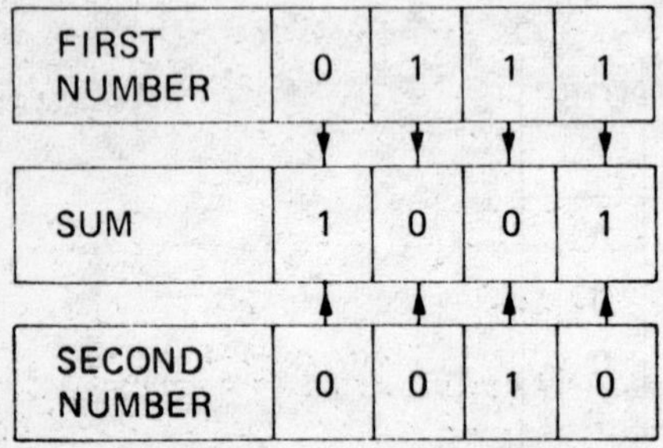

b. Serial addition in which columns are added one at a time, the carry being held over and used in the next column addition.

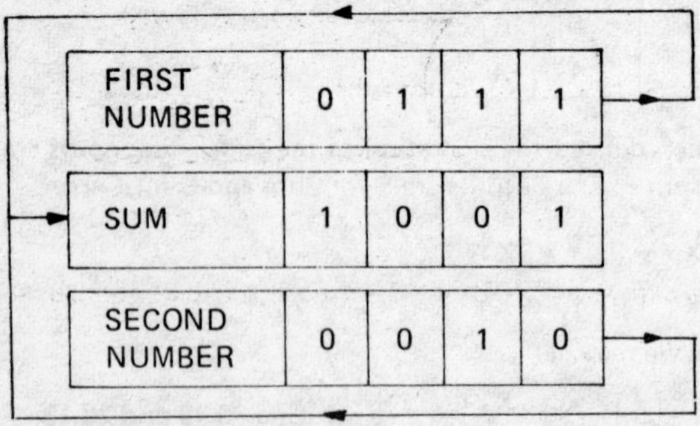

NB. A bit for the sum enters from the left as each column is added, working right to left. As this happens the successive values of the sum in this example are: 0000, 1000, 0100 0010, 1001.

14. Relative merits. Parallel addition is faster than serial addition but requires more **gates** (hardware). The advantage of greater speed usually outweighs cost making **parallel** addition more popular.

15. Registers. Data input to an adder must be held in an appropriate register.

a. In **parallel registers** all bits from the register are applied to the parallel adder simultaneously.

b. In **serial registers** all bits from the register are applied to the serial adder one at a time. The remaining bits in the registers are shifted along towards the end each time until output.

16. Example of a Parallel Adder.
The addition $111_2 + 010_2 = 1001_2$ is shown.

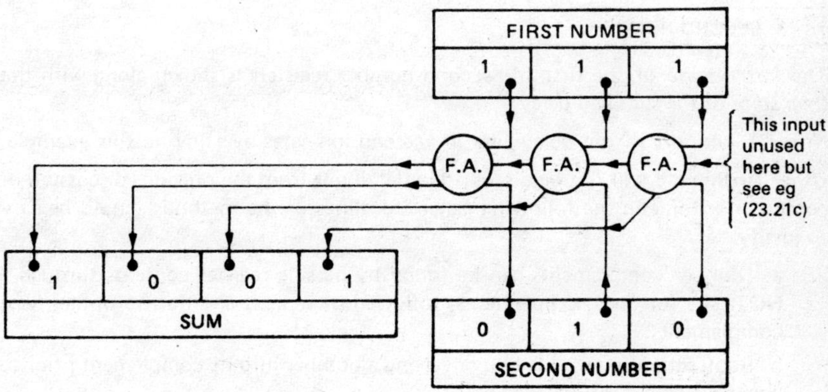

Details of Full Adders (F.A.)

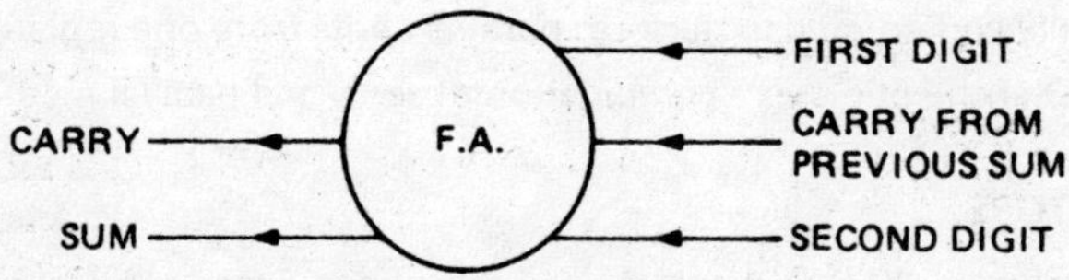

Note. In this example provision is made for a 4 digit sum of 3 digit number. Alternatively the *last carry* can be used to signal overflow.

17. Example of a Serial Adder.
It consists of:

a. **One full adder** which receives pairs of X, Y bits from two serial registers starting with the least significant bits.

b. A **delay store** which consists of a binary store which holds the carry bit until it is needed for the next addition. The store is set to zero prior to the first addition.

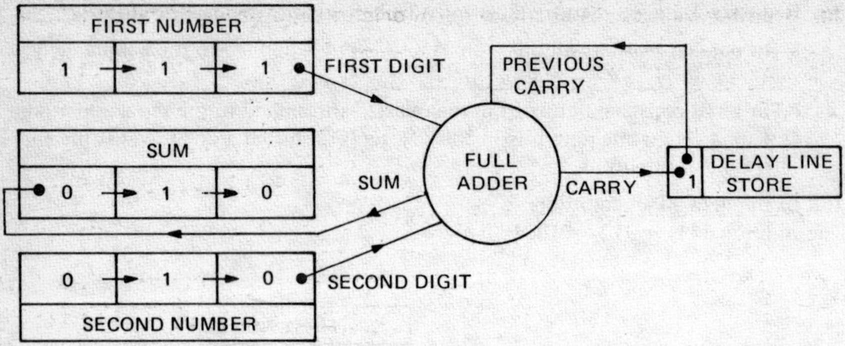

The *initial state* of the first and second number registers is shown along with the *final state* of the sum and delay.

Note. A one left in the delay line at the end indicates overflow in this example.

Other Arithmetic will not be discussed in detail but from the previous discussion of computer arithmetic the following general outlines of the methods should be easy to justify.

a. Number complements can be found by passing register contents through a NOT gate for ones complements, followed by a 1 bit addition to obtain twos complements.

b. Subtraction is possible by converting a number into its complement prior to passing it through an ADDER.

c. Multiplication and division can be accomplished by a combination of shifts, additions and subtractions of numbers held in appropriate registers. The devices which perform the shift operations are called **shifters** and are normally constructed to perform parallel shifts from one register to another.

d. BCD arithmetic uses a combination of serial and parallel methods.

COMPARATORS.

19. The exclusive OR (XOR), which we have already seen used in parity checking and arithmetic, is an example of a simple **comparator.** Its truth table and logic symbol are given here:

X	Y	X≢Y
0	0	0
0	1	1
1	0	1
1	1	0

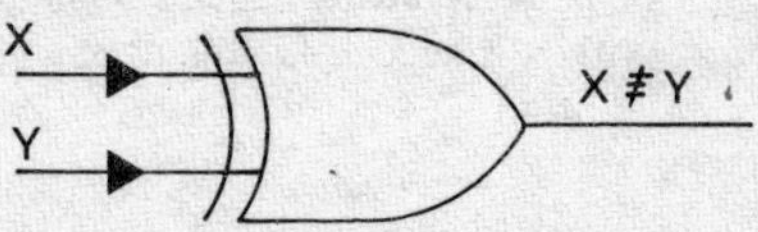

20. A further example of a simple comparator is the equivalence operation (23.13):

X	Y	X≡Y
0	0	1
0	1	0
1	0	0
1	1	1

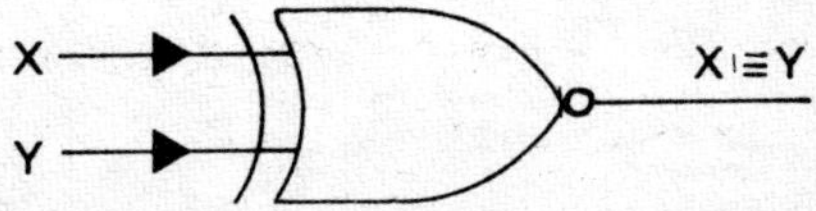

21. In general **comparators** are used to compare two registers, A and B say, to test for the conditions A = B, A = B, A < B and A > B. Here is a simple example of testing A = B for two 3-bit registers.

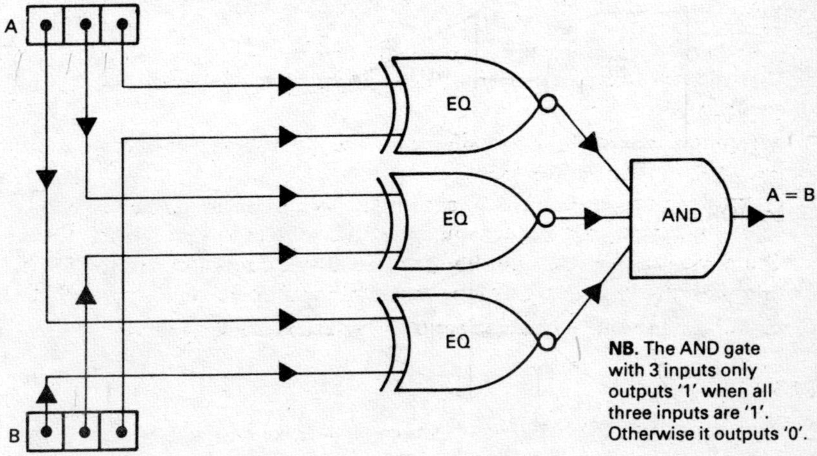

A comparator

NAND and NOR METHODS.

22. Although AND, OR and NOT gate combinations are always sufficient for the construction of any logic operation, alternative methods using NAND and NOR gates are more economical and therefore more widely used. The NAND and NOR operations will be described in this section. *All* logic operations can be performed with combinations of just NANDs or just NORs but a combination of NORs with NANDs is usually preferable to one provided just by NANDs.

23.

OPERATOR	OPERATION	SYMBOL	TRUTH TABLE		
			X	Y	$\overline{X . Y}$
NAND	$\overline{X . Y}$	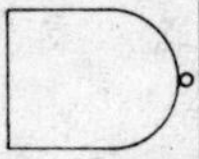	0 0 1 1	0 1 0 1	1 1 1 0
			X	Y	$\overline{X + Y}$
NOR	$\overline{X + Y}$	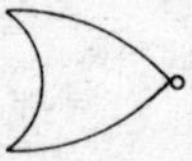	0 0 1 1	0 1 0 1	1 0 0 0

24. The AND-OR-NOT representation of NAND and NOR is shown here.

a. **NAND.**

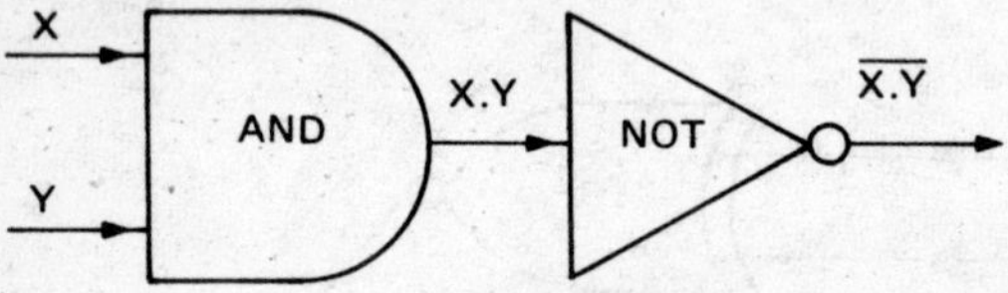

b. **NOR.**

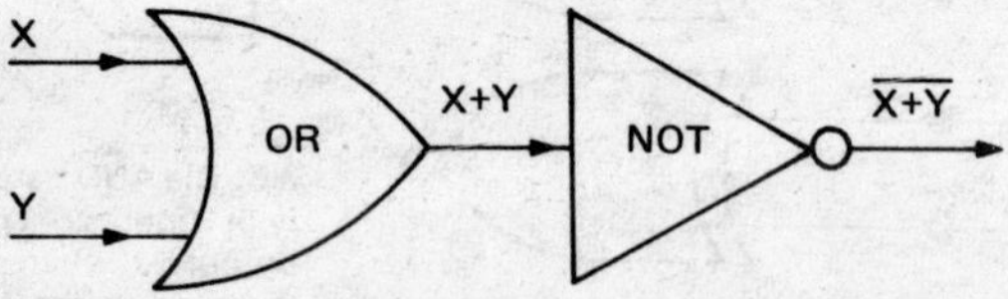

25. Converting from AND-OR-NOT forms to NAND or NOR forms.

a. The AND-OR-NOT expression must be manipulated into a suitable form for conversion:–

i. if NANDs are needed a suitable form is brackets containing ANDs connected by ORs eg $(A . B . C) + (\overline{A}BC) + (A\overline{B}\overline{C})$

ii. If NORs are needed a suitable form is brackets containing ORs connected by ANDs eg $(A + B + C) . (\overline{A} + B + C) . (A + \overline{B} + \overline{C})$

b. De Morgan's rule is then used repeatedly until the desired result is reached.

c. The logic diagram is drawn 'backwards' as with AND-OR-NOT ie starting with outputs and working towards inputs.

26. Standard NAND and NOR representations are shown here.

a. **NOT**

i.

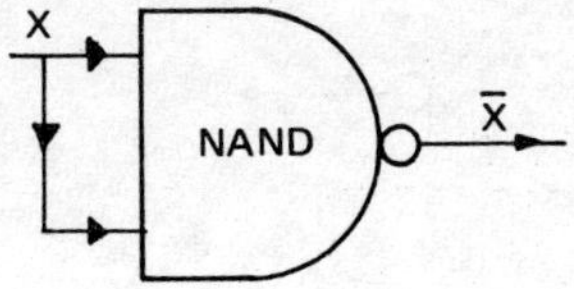

ii.

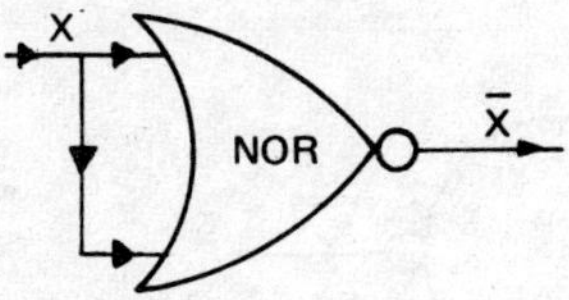

b. **AND**

i. Using NAND

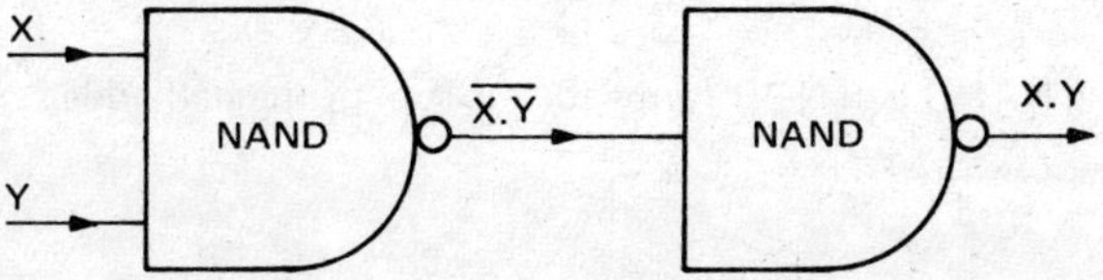

ii. Using NOR. $X \,.\, Y = \overline{\overline{X} + \overline{Y}}$. (De Morgan).

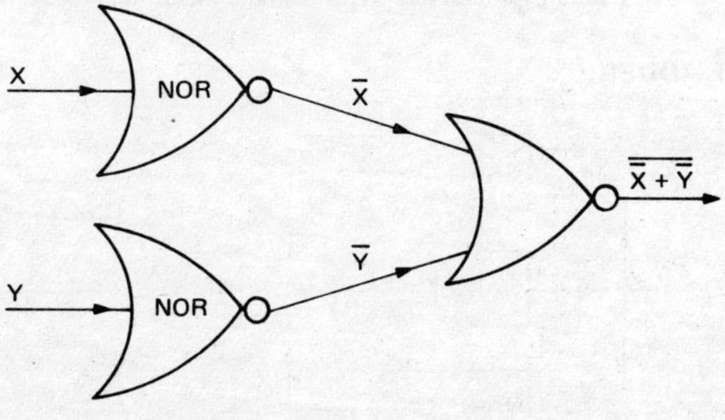

c. **OR**

i. Using NOR.

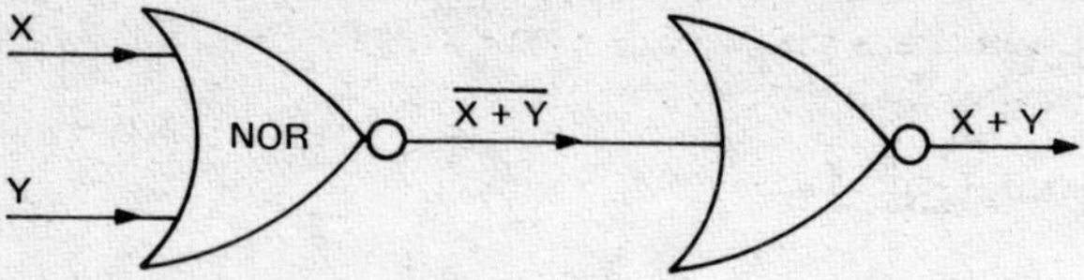

ii. Using NAND $X + Y = \overline{\overline{X} . \overline{Y}}$. (De Morgan)

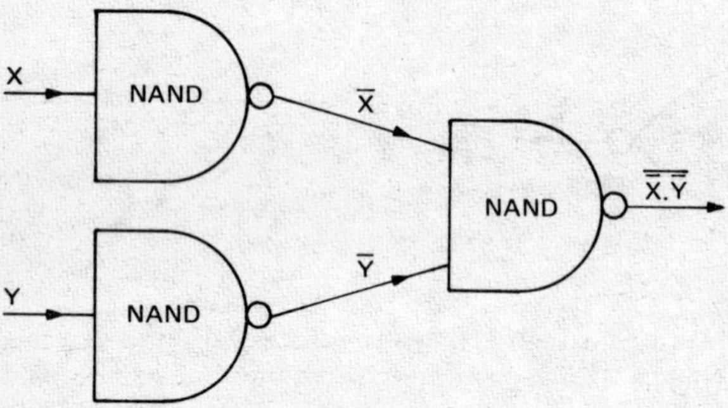

27. Example. Finding NAND and NOR forms for the sum of the half adder

$S \;=\; \overline{X . Y}\,(X + Y)$

a. **NAND Form.**

i. Manipulation into a suitable form. $S = \overline{XY}\,(X + Y) = \overline{XY} . X + \overline{XY} . Y$

ii. Apply De Morgans Rule $S = \overline{\overline{(\overline{XY} . X)} . \overline{(\overline{XY} . Y)}}$

iii. The logic diagram is shown here. An extra NAND has been added to produce a CARRY. (Note that **a NAND with a single input acts like a NOT).**

NAND HALF ADDER.

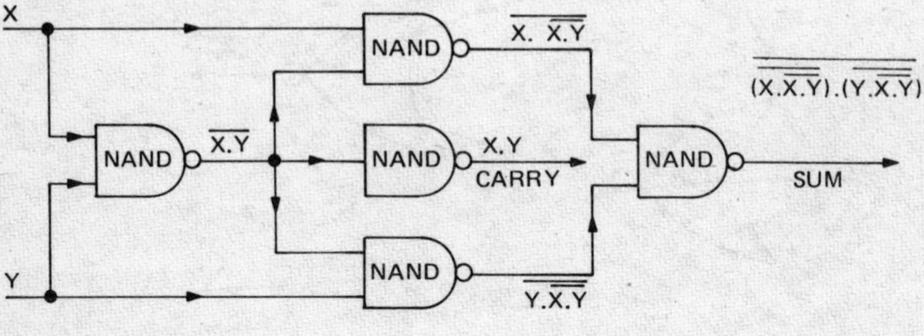

b. **NOR Form.**

i. Manipulation into a suitable form $S = \overline{XY}(X + Y) = (\overline{X} + \overline{Y}) . (X + Y)$ (De Morgan)

ii. Apply De Morgan's Rule again $S = \overline{\overline{(\overline{X} + \overline{Y})} + \overline{(X + Y)}}$

iii. The logic diagram is shown here.

NOR HALF ADDER.

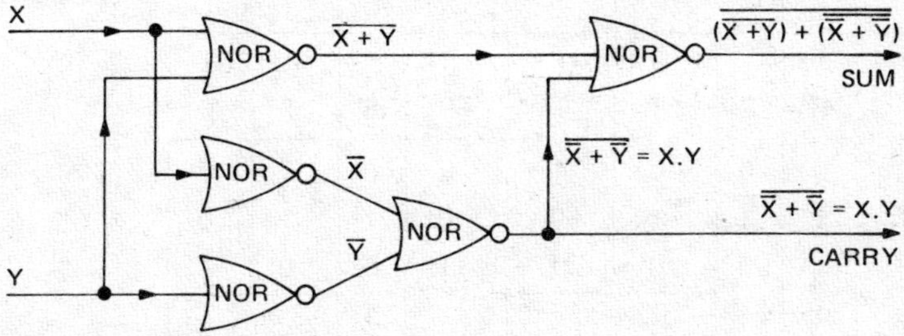

FLIP-FLOPS AND LATCHES.

28. Flip flops are two state devices ie they have two stable operating states corresponding to binary '0' and '1'. They can be switched from one state to another and can be used in multiples to form registers, 'cascaded' in series to form binary counters or used singly as status registers (eg 1 = Device ON 0 = Device OFF). There are two basic types of flip flop. One type has output states which depend upon the signal levels of the inputs (0 or 1) the other type has output states which depend upon transitions in levels (0 to 1 or 1 to 0). The former are often called **Latches,** rather than flip flops, and the latter are sometimes called **edge triggered flip flops** as opposed to **level triggered flip flops** which is the the other name for the former. Flip flops are also called **bistable multivibrators** or just **bistables.** Unfortunately, the terminology in use is far from universal and is sometimes contradictory!

29. A common type of flip flop is the Set-Reset flip flop which has two inputs, one to make the output '1' (the set) the other to make the output '0' (the reset).

25. The Set/Reset Flip Flop. (This can be used as a one-bit memory).

Truth Table.

Note.

i. The combination S = 1 and R = 1 is not possible.

ii. The double *output* $T/\overline{T}$ is held and used as part of the next *input.*

STARTING WITH T = 0 $\overline{T}$ = 1				STARTING WITH T = 1 $\overline{T}$ = 0			
INPUT		OUTPUT		INPUT		OUTPUT	
R	S	T	$\overline{T}$	R	S	T	$\overline{T}$
0	0	0	1	0	0	1	0
0	1	1	0	0	1	1	0
1	0	0	1	1	0	0	1
1	1			1	1	–	

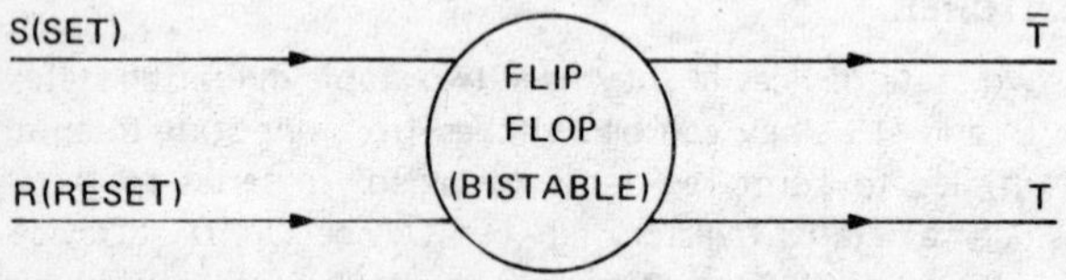

Practical NOR implementation

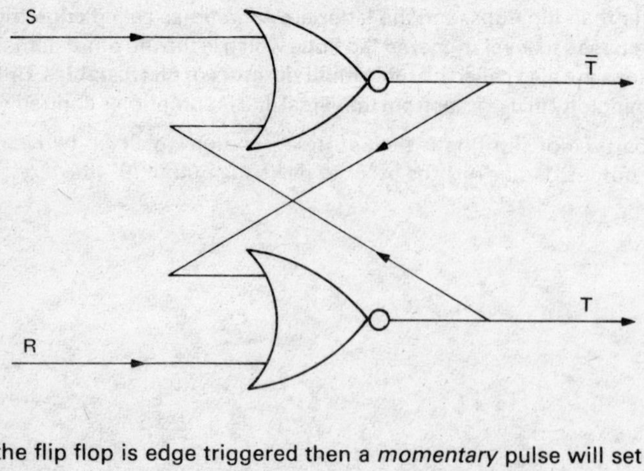

If the flip flop is edge triggered then a *momentary* pulse will set this one bit store to a detectable state held *indefinitely.*

ALU and CONTROL.

30. So far we have seen how gates can be combined to perform particular tasks such as addition. the ALU is comprised of a large number of such gate combinations, but is usually designed as a whole so as to work most efficiently. The selection of the appropriate operation (set of gates) can be handled by passing signals from the CONTROL UNIT through gates.

Example. This example is illustrative rather than practical and also uses ones complement. The inclusion of the half adder in the adder below allows the circuit to **either** add **or** subtract according to the CONTROL UNIT signal 'S'.

If S = 1 subtract Y from X. If S = 0 add Y to X.

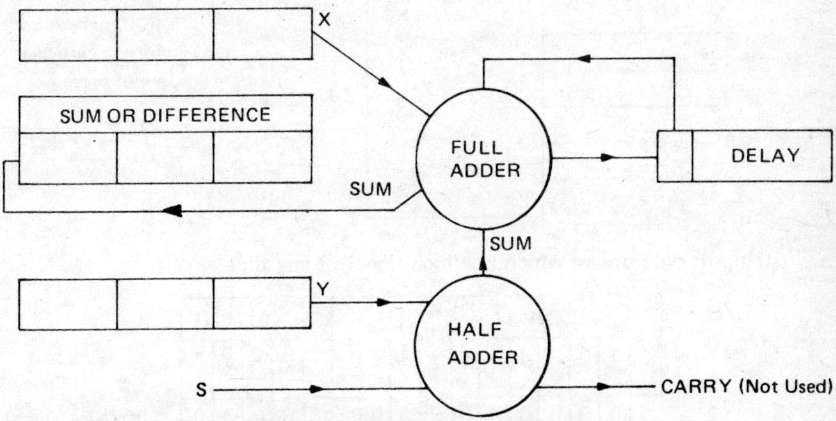

31. A typical diagrammatic representation for a complete ALU is shown here:

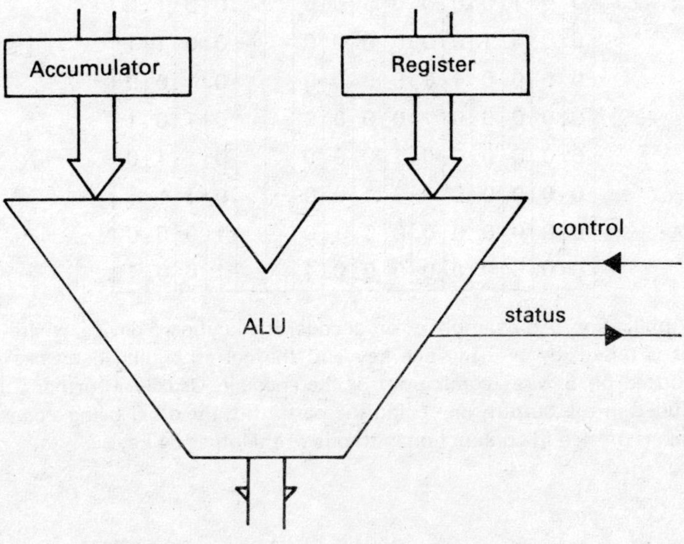

ENCODING AND DECODING.

32. Encoding involves the conversion of **one** signal from one set into a **group** of signals of another set. A device performing this task is called an **encoder.**

a. **Example.**

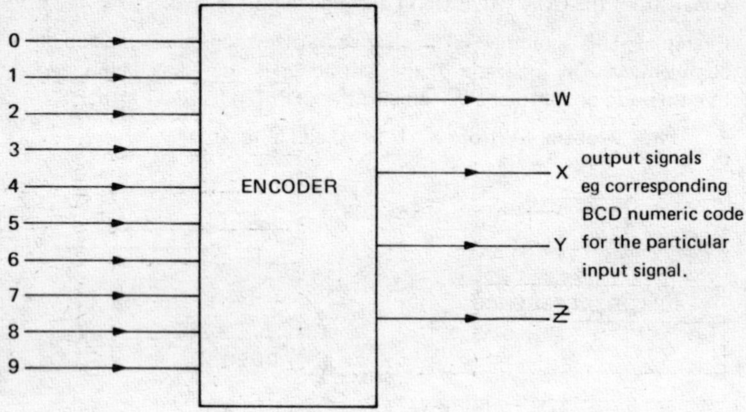

10 inputs **only one of which** is a 'high signal' at any time.

INPUT											OUTPUT			
0	1	2	3	4	5	6	7	8	9		W	X	Y	Z
1	0	0	0	0	0	0	0	0	0		0	0	0	0
0	1	0	0	0	0	0	0	0	0		0	0	0	1
0	0	1	0	0	0	0	0	0	0		0	0	1	0
0	0	0	1	0	0	0	0	0	0		0	0	1	1
0	0	0	0	1	0	0	0	0	0		0	1	0	0
0	0	0	0	0	1	0	0	0	0		0	1	0	1
0	0	0	0	0	0	1	0	0	0		0	1	1	0
0	0	0	0	0	0	0	1	0	0		0	1	1	1
0	0	0	0	0	0	0	0	1	0		1	0	0	0
0	0	0	0	0	0	0	0	0	1		1	0	0	1

1 = high signal.
0 = low signal.

b. **Application.** An example of an **encoder** is a keyboard device, where 1 of 64 lines is raised, by pressing one key and the corresponding 6 bit character is produced on 6 wires coming out of the encoder. Usually a further 2 bits are included in the output, one being the parity bit, the other being a control key which is pressed in conjunction with one of the other 64 keys.

33. a. **Decoding.** This is the opposite operation to **encoding** and the device performing the task is called a **decoder.** If 'n' wires are connected in there will normally be 2^n wires out only one of which will be a logic '1' at an instant.

b. **Example.**

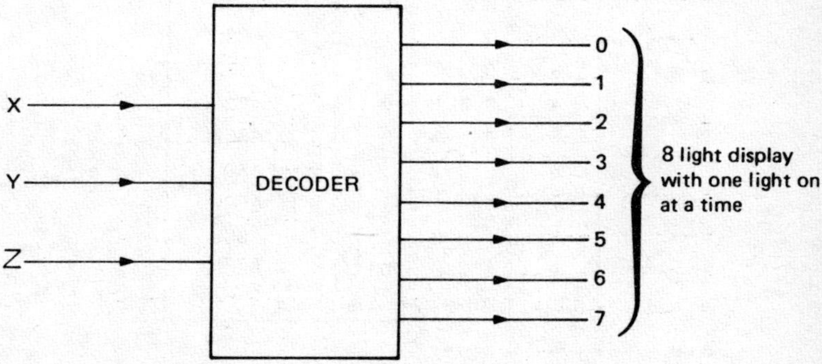

3 bit binary code in.

INPUT			OUTPUT							
X	Y	Z	0	1	2	3	4	5	6	7
0	0	0	1	0	0	0	0	0	0	0
0	0	1	0	1	0	0	0	0	0	0
0	1	0	0	0	1	0	0	0	0	0
0	1	1	0	0	0	1	0	0	0	0
1	0	0	0	0	0	0	1	0	0	0
1	0	1	0	0	0	0	0	1	0	0
1	1	0	0	0	0	0	0	0	1	0
1	1	1	0	0	0	0	0	0	0	1

34. Uses. Encoders and decoders are used for such things as:

a. Translations of **internal** binary codes to or from **external** signals for peripheral input or output actions such as printing characters, reading cards, moving pens in plotters or monitoring device status.

b. The control of hardware, eg selecting output channels from device codes, translating control signals for disc head movements or translating function codes.

35. An example of Decoder design. A decoder for converting a 4 bit 8421 weighted BCD codes into individual decimal equivalents.

BCD DIGIT	CODE BITS A	B	C	D	LOGIC EXPRESSION
0	0	0	0	0	$\bar{A}\bar{B}\bar{C}\bar{D}$
1	0	0	0	1	$\bar{A}\bar{B}\bar{C}D$
2	0	0	1	0	$\bar{A}\bar{B}C\bar{D}$
3	0	0	1	1	$\bar{A}\bar{B}CD$
4	0	1	0	0	$\bar{A}B\bar{C}\bar{D}$
5	0	1	0	1	$\bar{A}B\bar{C}D$
6	0	1	1	0	$\bar{A}BC\bar{D}$
7	0	1	1	1	$\bar{A}BCD$
8	1	0	0	0	$A\bar{B}\bar{C}\bar{D}$
9	1	0	0	1	$A\bar{B}\bar{C}D$
10-15	Arbitrary because unused				

Karnaugh Map. (Arbitrary unused terms called "Don't care terms" are marked with a U).

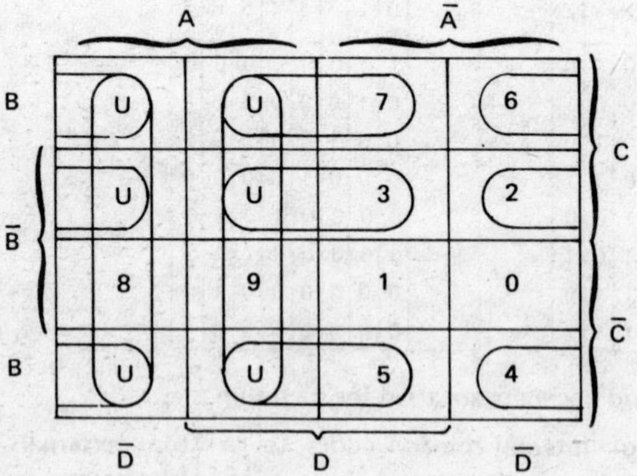

a. We saw earlier that the larger the loop drawn within the map the fewer variables are needed to specify it. We make use of this by combining arbitrary values to make larger loops. Note that each loop represents **one** of the ten outputs required, so on the map we are simplifying 10 boolean equations at once. The corresponding expressions are shown in this Table.

DECIMAL DIGIT	LOGIC EXPRESSION	ALTERNATIVE EXPRESSION
0	$\overline{A}.\overline{B}.\overline{C}.\overline{D}$	$\overline{A+B+C+D}$
1	$\overline{A}.\overline{B}.\overline{C}.D$	$\overline{A+B+C+\overline{D}}$
2	$\overline{B}.C.\overline{D}$	$\overline{B+\overline{C}+D}$
3	$\overline{B}.C.D$	$\overline{B+\overline{C}+\overline{D}}$
4	$B.\overline{C}.\overline{D}$	$\overline{\overline{B}+C+D}$
5	$B.\overline{C}.D$	$\overline{\overline{B}+C+\overline{D}}$
6	$B.C.\overline{D}$	$\overline{\overline{B}+\overline{C}+D}$
7	$B.C.D$	$\overline{\overline{B}+\overline{C}+\overline{D}}$
8	$A.\overline{D}$	$\overline{\overline{A}+D}$
9	$A.D$	$\overline{\overline{A}+\overline{D}}$

b. **An implementation using NOR gates.**

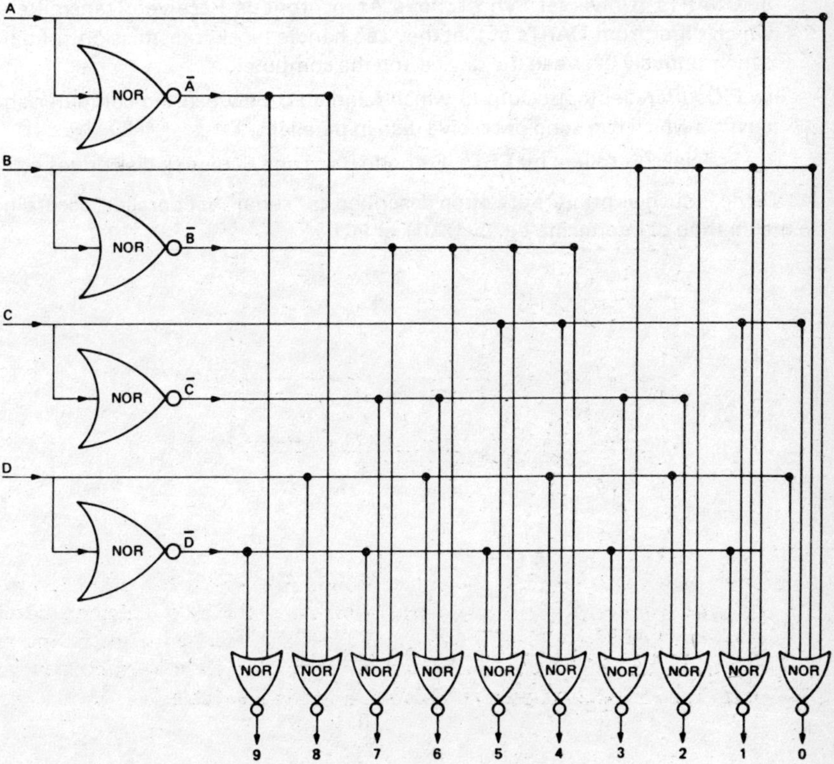

INTERFACING.

36. Interface. A **standard interface** is a **specification** of the logic signals, electrical connections and logic rules of the processors **interface** parts. An **interface** is a piece of **hardware** which converts the electrical signals and logic rules of the peripheral device connected to one side of it, into those of the standard interface, for the CPU which is connected to the other side of the interface. Conversions may take place both ways. Interfaces take over part of the job of controlling the devices to which they are connected. Interfacing provides flexibility and increases efficiency. Encoders and decoders form part of most interface circuits for the translation of control and data signals at the **interface.**

37. On most microcomputer based systems special chips are used to provide input and output with suitable interfacing. Common chips used for this purpose are:

a. **UARTs** (Universal Asynchronous Receiver Transmitters) which handle two way communication between the computer and a *serial device.* On the computer side of the UART, data, such as individual characters, will be transmitted in parallel. On the serial device side data will be transmitted **serially** as a sequence of pulses in a pulse train.

b. **USARTs** (Universal Synchronous Asynchronous Receiver Transmitters) which differ from UARTs in that they can handle block transmissions of data synchronously between the device and the computer.

c. **PIOs** (Parallel Input/Output) which handle I/O between the computer and devices which can send or receive data in parallel.

d. Special controllers for CRTs [Cathode Ray Tube Screens], disk drives etc.

NB. Devices such as printers are often described as "serial" or "parallel" according to the method of interfacing eg. by UART or PIO.

MULTIPLEXERS (MULTIPLEXORS) (MUX for short).

38. Multiplexers are selection mechanisms. They have long had importance in handling multiple numbers of Input and Output devices. They have even more importance today in the way they handle the selection of data and instruction flow within modern CPU's. You may compare them with the points and signal box at a railway junction. Here is a simple example:–

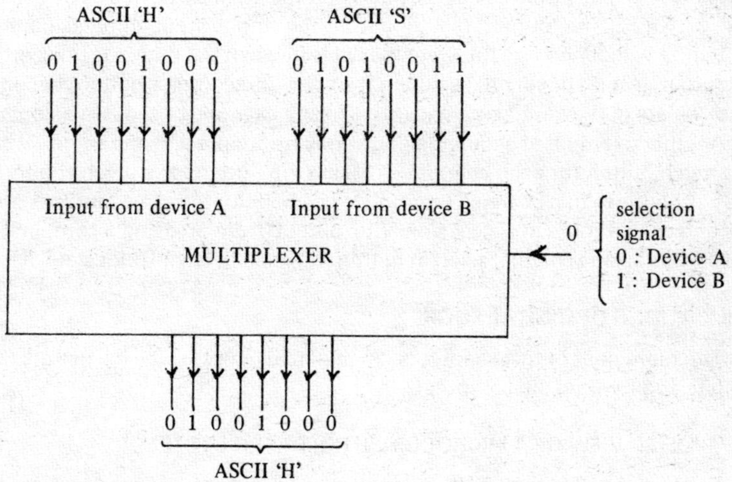

In a demultiplexer the reverse process takes place ie. a single input is switched to an appropriate output path.

39. Highways. You may notice in the example just given that signals are being transmitted in parallel eg. the 8 bits of the ASCII character code for 'H' are being sent along the 8 lines side by side at the same time. Such a 'bundle' of lines is called a **"highway"** or bus. It is now common practice to illustrate such highways by open arrows thus:–

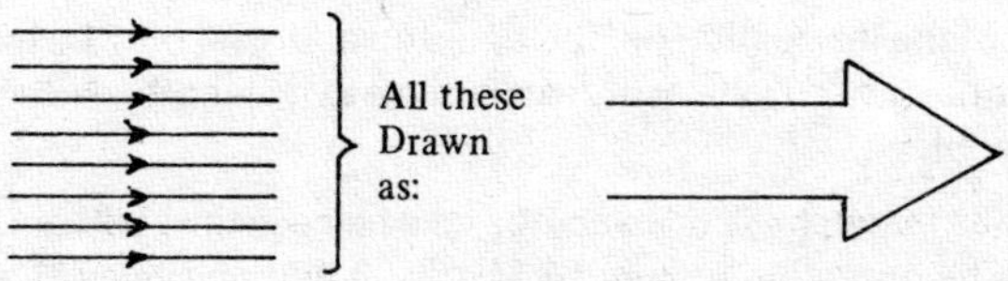

NB. The highway may contain any number of lines, not necessarily 8.

COMBINATIONAL AND SEQUENTIAL LOGIC.

40. A **combinational logic** gate has outputs which are completely defined by the combination of inputs. A **sequential logic** gate differs from combinational logic in that the outputs depend not only on the combination of inputs but on the sequence in which they occur. AND, OR and NOT gates provide examples of combinational logic and a flip-flop provides an example of sequential logic. The idea of sequential logic will be familiar to you although the terminology may not be. For example, a TV set may have a single ON/OFF button and the set may be in one of two *states* "ON" or "OFF". The 'output' resulting from the single 'input' of pressing the ON/OFF button will depend on the state the set is in when the button is pressed. Thus the 'output' (set on or set off) resulting from the 'input' (press button) depends on where we are in the on/off *sequence*. This is one example of sequential logic.

41. Another example of sequential logic may be supplied by the same TV set if it has a push button for each channel. Pressing the button for a given channel may cause a change to that channel, or produce no change if the same button is pressed a second or third time in succession. The 'output' from pressing a combination of ON/OFF button and channel selector button will depend on the prior state of the set.

APPLICATIONS OF DIGITAL LOGIC.

42. The remainder of this chapter is devoted to examples which illustrate the use of digital logic within the computer.

A SIMPLIFIED VIEW OF A MICROCOMPUTER BASED SYSTEM.

43. Examine fig. 27.1 which shows a simplified view of a Microcomputer Based System. Compare fig. 27.1 with fig. 9.1 and note the following points about fig. 27.1.

a. All registers except the MAR and SCR are 8 bits long.

b. The SCR may incorporate sequential logic for increasing it by 1 as part of the fetch-execute cycle.

c. A 16 bit instruction will be spread over two successive 8-bit locations in memory and will therefore require two fetch cycles. 24 bit instructions will require 3 fetch cycles. This is an important factor causing 8-bit micros to be slower than 16 bit machines.

d. The first 8 bits of an instruction may contain opcodes plus address mode details and will be fetched into the opcode register as 8 parallel bits. The remainder of the instruction (ie. the operand address) may be fetched into the MAR on a one or two cycle action according to its length. (NB. An opcode is a function code).

e. The cycles for fetches and executes take place in time with an external clock which may be operating at about 3 MHz ie. 3 million cycles (6 million pulses) per second. (One cycle has two pulses: $\sim$)

f. The use of an index register (IX reg) will be discussed in the next chapter.

g. Note the use of a multiplexer and a decoder.

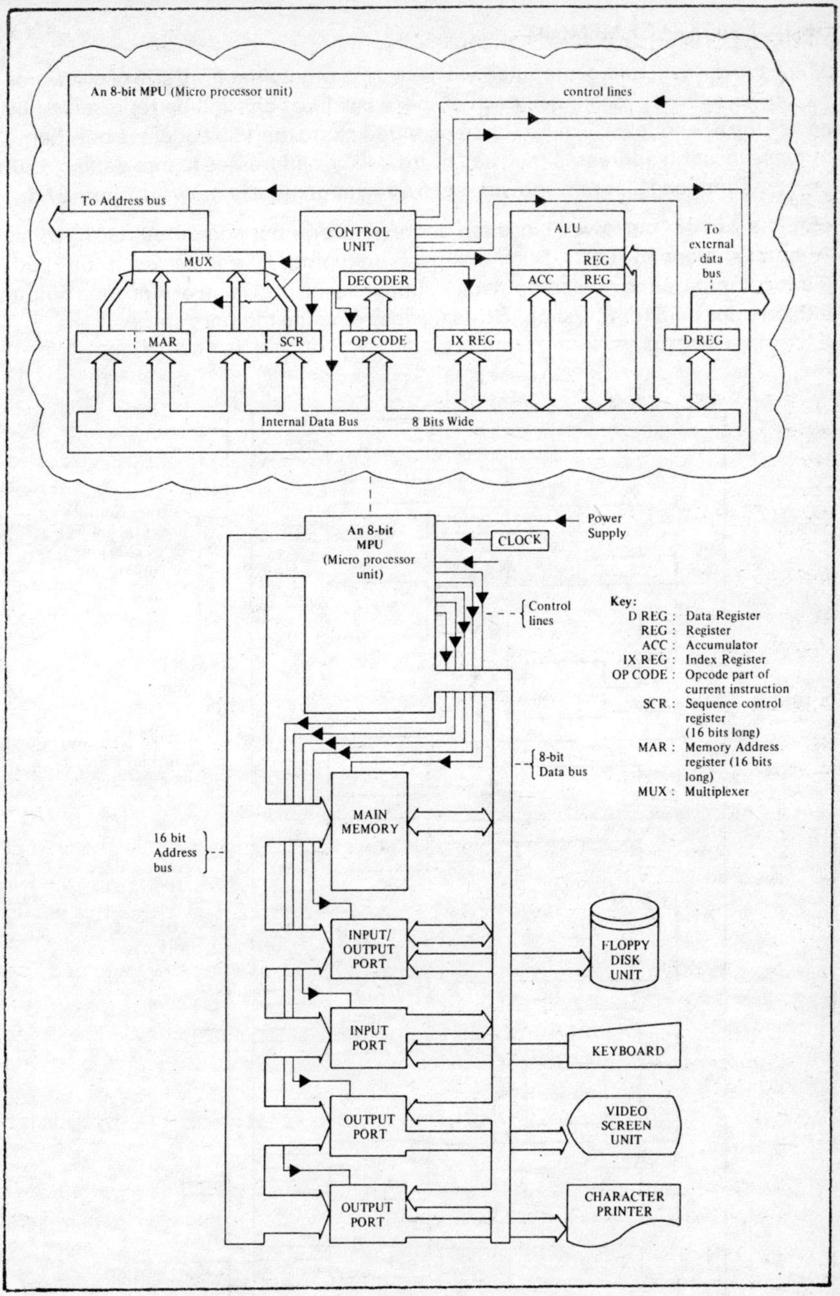

Figure 27.1. A simplified view of a Microcomputer Based System.

ORGANISATION OF MEMORY.

44. A typical 8 bit microcomputer will have a maximum memory size of 64k words (ie. 65535 memory locations). Each of these 64k locations will be represented by one of the 64k codes which can be transmitted along the 16 bit address bus. Some of these location addresses may be "borrowed" as addresses to input and output ports. A simplified diagram showing such an arrangement is shown in figure 27.2.

45. The use of "borrowed" location addresses for input and output is known as **"memory mapped I/O"**. Such memory mapping is widely used on both microcomputers and minicomputers. It simplifies the provision of input and output but the price paid for this simplicity is the loss of some memory space.

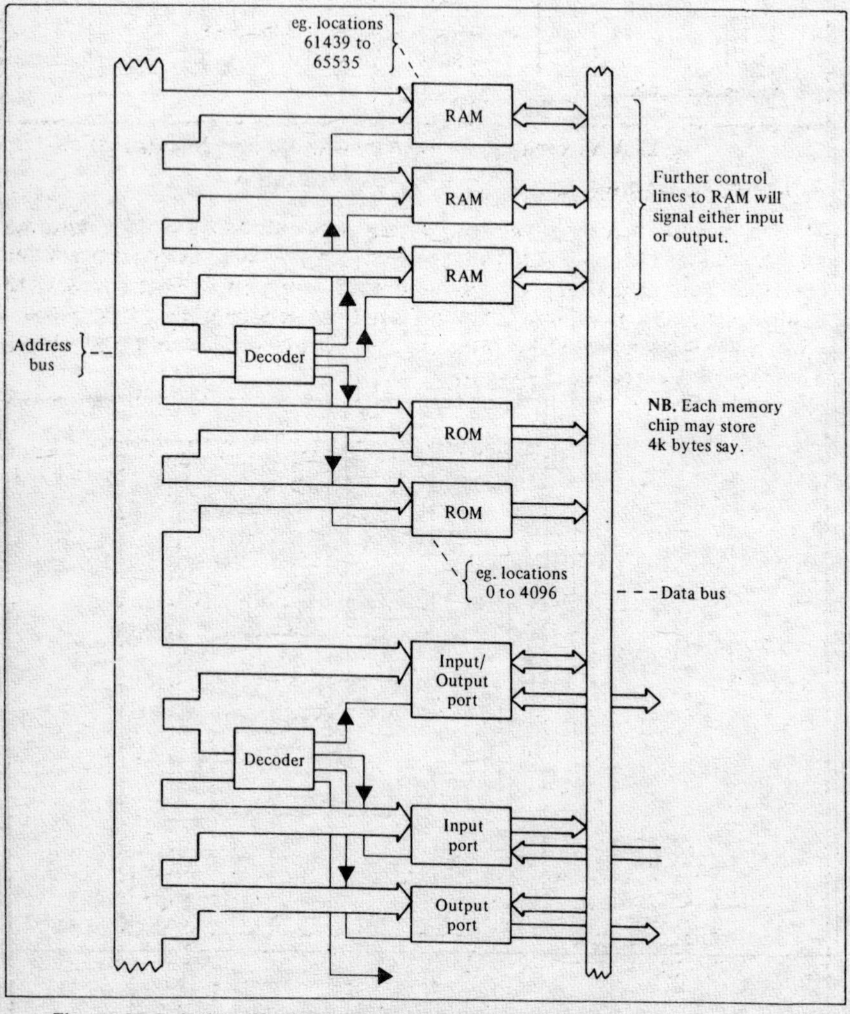

Figure 27.2. A simplified diagram of microcomputer memory organisation and allocation of memory addresses.

46. A typical allocation of 8 bit microcomputer memory addresses for various uses is illustrated in figure 27.3.

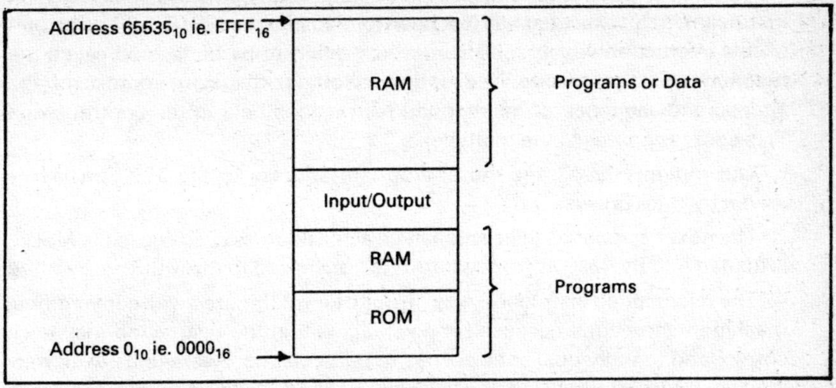

Fig. 27.3. Microcomputer memory with Memory Mapped I/O

MICROCODED MACHINES.

47. The idea of microprogrammed machines was introduced in 9.11. Here, we consider the idea in more detail with the aid of a simplified example (fig. 27.4). Within the control unit of a microprogrammed computer is what appears like another processor. There now follows a simplified version of how this machine works which is intended to convey the principle but which, because it is simplified, is not technically accurate in all respects.

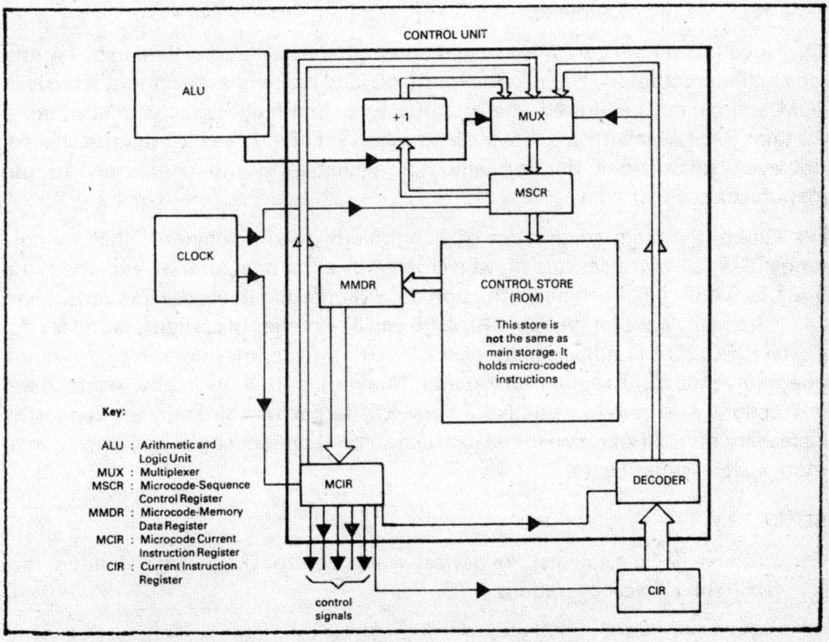

Fig. 27.4. A Simplified View of the Microprogrammed level of the Computer.

48. The microprogrammed machine works as follows:

a. Start at the point when, at the conventional level of the machine, the next instruction to be executed has just been loaded into the CIR (Fig. 9.1). The part of this instruction which specifies the operation to be performed called the **function code** or **opcode** is decoded to obtain the start address of the appropriate sequence of microcoded instructions held in the control store. This address passes to the multiplexer.

b. The multiplexer passes the appropriate address to the MSCR which is driven by clock pulses.

c. The next microcoded instruction, held at the address specified in the MSCR, is loaded into the MMDR, from where it is transferred to the MCIR.

d. The microcoded instruction may be quite long compared with conventional machine instructions because bit positions within the instruction may each correspond to individual control lines to particular hardware units. A '1' may indicate a control signal is to be transmitted and a '0' that it is not. Thus, each micro-coded instruction holds a particular combination of control signals. When the MCIR receives a pulse from the clock these signals are transmitted.

e. Also within the MCIR will be an address for the next micro-coded instruction. This address is used when the sequence of control is to be altered because of conditions signalled to the multiplexer by the ALU. For example, the ALU may signal that it has tested for, and found, a zero result.

f. Normally, the microcoded instructions will be executed in sequence by the contents of the MSCR being incremented by 1 and being reloaded into the MSCR via the multiplexer.

49. Not all computers are microcoded although the exceptions tend to be among the smaller microprocessors. In most microcoded machines the control store is in ROM and cannot be altered after manufacture. In a few cases the control store contains RAM which means that the instruction set of the machine may be altered. However, microcoding is normally not available to the user, only to the manufacturer.

50. One of the main advantages of using microcoded machines is that a whole range of different processors may be created by a manufacturer all with the same basic conventional machine instruction set but differing in processing power and cost. This is the case for the IBM 370, 4300 and 3300 series of computers and for the digital (DEC) PDP 11 minicomputer series. In the smaller machines in such a range one conventional machine instruction may give rise to many microcoded instructions and may be relatively slow. On larger machines in the range the necessary number of microcoded instructions will be reduced by the provision of more specialist hardware.

SUMMARY.

51. a. Gates (logic elements) are devices which control the passage of pulses, thus facilitating logical operations.

b. We discussed the logical operation of gates not their electronic operations.

c. In logic diagrams gates are represented by symbols.

d. A combination of AND, OR and NOT gates may be replaced by just NAND or just NOR gates.

e. A **half adder** adds together two binary digits but does not have provision to deal with the carry from a previous addition as does a **full adder.**

f. Two basic types of addition are:–
   i. Parallel addition (usually faster)
   ii. Serial addition.
   Data must be held in parallel and serial registers respectively.

g. Gates can be used for:–
   i. Arithmetical and logical purposes.
   ii. For control purposes such as selecting operations or devices eg. by multiplexing.
   iii. Encoding and Decoding.

h. Interfacing is used for the electronic and logical communication between the CPU and its peripherals and interfaces themselves have some control tasks.

i. The two basic types of logic are
   i. Combinational logic.
   ii. Sequential logic.

j. Applications of digital logic were provided at the end of the chapter:
   i. A simplified view of a microcomputer based system.
   ii. The organisation of memory.
   iii. Microcoded machines.

POINTS TO NOTE.

52. a. Constructing logic diagrams requires the skills developed in the previous chapter.

b. You will need some practice at constructing logic diagrams before you can produce them in the time allowed in the examination.

c. Constructing a truth table is often a good way of understanding a question or problem and may suggest the correct approach to the solution.

STUDENT SELF TESTING QUESTIONS.

(Answers on page 719).

1. *By using truth tables prove the results:–*

$$X + (\bar{X} . Y) = X + Y$$

$$(X . Y) + (X . \bar{Y}) = X$$

Three binary signals are represented by A, B andC and the output D is related to these signals in the following way:–

AB is a two-digit binary number and C is a control signal;

when AB is non-zero and C = 1 then D = 1;
when AB is odd and C = 0 then D = 1. (In other cases D = 0).

Draw up a truth table for D and hence, or otherwise, find a Boolean expression for D in its simplest form.

Draw a logic diagram for D using NOR elements only.

Note: *In your answer use the following symbols for Boolean operators:—*

OPERATOR	SYMBOL
OR	+
AND	.
NOT	—

(A.E.B. 1976)

2. a. *State* not ((not A) or (not B)) *as simply as possible in terms of A and B. By drawing a Venn diagram, or otherwise show how the two logical statements are connected. Generalise the relationship to more than two variables.*

   b. *The decimal digits 0 to 9 can be represented by a set of binary digits a, b, c, d of values 8, 4, 2 and 1 respectively. Devise a logical function of a, b, c and d which is true if they represent a decimal digit and false otherwise. Explain your derivation.*

(Oxford 1976)

3. *Relate the differing scales of integration of electronic components to the differing generations of computer.*

4. *Distinguish between serial and parallel adders and draw a logic diagram for each. Why are parallel adders preferred to serial adders in most cases?*

5. *Explain the difference between an edge triggered flip flop and a level triggered flip flop.*

6. *Define:* a. *UART*
   b. *USART*
   c. *PIO*

7. *Distinguish between combinational logic and sequential logic and identify the category to which the following gates belong.*

   a. *adder*
   b. *comparator*
   c. *flip flop*
   d. *decoder.*

8. *Here is a simplified multiplexer:*

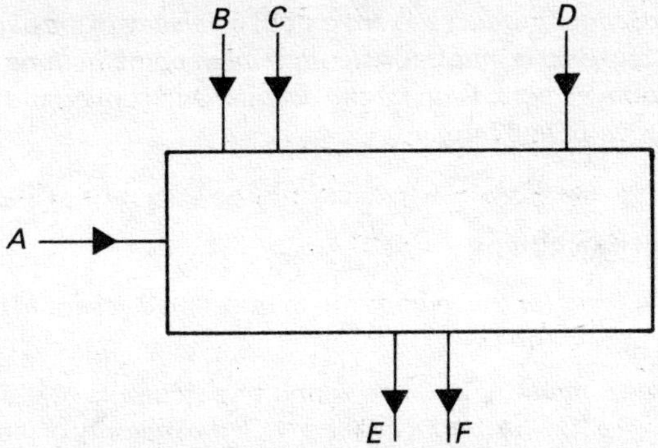

When the signal at A is '0' the output at F is the same as the input signal at D and the output at E is '0' regardless of the signals at B and C. When the signal at A is '1' the output at E is the same as the input signal at B and the output at F is the same as the input signal at C regardless of the signal at D.

a. *Summarise these details in a truth table.*

b. *Construct expressions for the outputs E and F in terms of A, B, C and D.*

c. *Simplify your expressions.*

d. *Create a logic circuit for the multiplexer.*

e. *Justify your choice of gates in d.*

9. *Two 2-bit registers, X and Y are both used to hold 2 digit positive integers where 00_2, 01_2, 10_2, and 11_2 represent 0,1,2 and 3 respectively.*

A comparator has four inputs, two from register X and 2 from register Y, and outputs a '1' when the contents of X are greater than Y, otherwise it outputs '0'.

a. *Represent this comparator diagrammatically.*

b. *Construct a truth table for the comparator.*

c. *Produce a simplified expression for the output of the comparator.*

d. *Derive a logic diagram for the comparator.*

10. a. *What practical advantage is there in employing NAND or NOR components in electronic circuits?* *(2 marks)*

b. *By using a truth (logic) table, or otherwise, show that the Boolean expressions below are all different:*

$$\overline{\overline{A + B} + C}$$

$$\overline{A + \overline{B + C}}$$

$$\overline{B + \overline{C + A}}$$

$$\overline{A + B + C}$$

(5 marks)

c. Using the result in (b), express $(\bar{A}.\bar{B}.\bar{C}) + (A.B.C)$ in NOR logic. (3 marks)

d. A four-input decoder produces a zero output when any of the patterns 0000, 0001, 0010, 0100 or 1000 is input; for all other input combinations, the output is '1'. Derive a Boolean expression for the decoder and convert the expression to NOR logic in a simplified form. (10 marks)

(AEB 1982)

QUESTIONS WITHOUT ANSWERS.

11. Design a demultiplexer for the multiplexer in question 8. It should have inputs A, E and F and outputs B, C and D.

12. A decoder has four inputs A, B, C and D and three outputs X, Y and Z. If the majority of the inputs are '1's the output at X is a '1'. If the majority of inputs are '0's then the output at Y is a '1'. If the number of '0's and '1's are equal then the output at Z is a '1'.

a. Construct a truth table for the decoder.

b. Derive expression for the outputs from the decoder in terms of the inputs.

c. Simplify your expressions as far as possible.

d. Derive a logic diagram for the decoder.

Computer Language and Operation

1. The next three chapters demonstrate and contrast the features of computer languages. Chapter 28 concentrates on machine language and consequently covers several aspects of machine operation.

2. Chapter 29 considers the use of low level programming languages and uses programming examples for that purpose. After reading chapter 29 you may benefit from re-reading chapter 28.

3. Chapter 30 considers the use of high level programming languages and compares them with low level languages.

28 Machine Language

INTRODUCTION.

1. The purpose of this chapter is to demonstrate the various features of machine language. The chapter also explains how a computer can carry out instructions presented to it in machine language. It is assumed that you have by now acquired some programming skill, (eg from chapters 10-14 and practical course work) and are ready to supplement that skill by taking a closer look at machine language facilities. If you feel you still need more programming practice leave the detailed points from this chapter for a second reading.

2. A **machine language** is a (programming) language in which the instructions are in a form which allows the computer to perform them immediately, without any further translation being required.

3. Instructions in **machine language** are in the form of a **binary code,** also called **machine code,** and are called **machine instructions.**

4. Machine instructions are stored in the same way as data (chapter 7), and each instruction corresponds directly to a hardware facility on the machine for which it is written. The handling of instructions in the CPU (chapter 9) will be discussed further in this chapter, and machine logic (chapter 27) is the instrument used.

5. The set of machine instructions which a computer can perform is called its **instruction set.** Any operation not provided by the hardware, and therefore not in the instruction set, can only be provided by using more than one instruction.
NB. This principle applies both at the microprogrammed level and at the machine level. In this chapter we are concerned with the machine level not with micro-programming.

6. The size of the instruction set will affect all of the following items.

a. The cost of the machine:more hardware costs more money.

b. Speed and efficiency: If a large number of different instructions exist, then it is likely that a given task may be performed in fewer instructions than on a machine with a small instruction set.

c. Choice of word size and instruction format: A large instruction set implies that the function field of each instruction must have a larger number of bits. If the machine has a large word size it may be possible to fit each instruction into a single word but in the case of most micro-computers and mini-computers instructions may each occupy several words. For example, in the case of the 8-bit Z80 micro-processor instructions may be 1, 2, 3 or 4 words long. In such cases an instruction fetch is a multiple fetch, one per word, and carries with it an obvious time penalty.

7. Instruction Format. A machine instruction has several components. The **instruction format** is the size and arrangement of these components. Two major components are the **function code (opcode)** which specifies the function or operation performed, and the **operand addresses,** which specifies the locations of the **operands** used. As was indicated in paragraph 6c, on a given machine there may be several instruction lengths and there may be an even greater variation in instruction formats. For example, on an IBM 370 there are 5 basic instruction formats, on the PDP 11 there are 13 and on the Z80 there are 26.

8. **Address Format.** This is the part of the instruction format which deals with specifying the address of operands. Several quite different methods may be used, their general features are given here and details of addressing will be given later. The main methods are:–

a. **The three-address format.**
Each instruction specifies the address of two operands and gives a further address for the result of the operation, eg addresses of two numbers and address for their sum. This method demands a long instruction in order to give the three addresses, and is therefore little used.

Example.

FUNCTION	ADDRESS	ADDRESS	ADDRESS

b. **The two-address format.**
Each instruction specifies the address of two operands. The result of an add operation would **replace** one of the two operands. It is an improvement over the **three address format.**

Example.

FUNCTION	ADDRESS	ADDRESS

c. **The one and a half address format** (or one address format).
One operand is held in a special register or accumulator having first been fetched and placed there. The instruction specifies the address of the other operand, and the number of the accumulator, if there is more than one. The result is placed in the specified accumulator. This gives a further shortening of the instruction since fewer bits are needed to specify accumulators than are needed to specify an operand address.

Examples.

FUNCTION	ADDRESS

Single accumulator machine.

or

FUNCTION	AC	ADDRESS

AC = Accumulator number.

d. **Between accumulator operations.**
A one and a half address format may be used to **fetch** or **load** operands into the accumulators from main store but thereafter the instruction may just specify the two or three accumulators which are to be used for operands and results.

Example.

FUNCTION	AC	AC

AC = Accumulator number.

NB. On small computers these instructions may be spread over several words. For example, a two-address format like the one shown in paragraph 8b would occupy three 16-bit words in a PDP-11.

TYPES OF INSTRUCTION.

9. There are many ways of grouping or classifying the members of an instruction set and the choice of method will depend on the machine being described. The following headings often prove useful.

a. Arithmetic and Logic Operations (Instructions).

b. Transfer of control or branch instruction.

c. Load (fetch) and store instructions.

d. Input/Output instructions.

e. Memory Reference instructions.

f. Processor Reference instructons.

10. Arithmetic and Logic Operations (Instructions). These are instructions which use operations of the ALU. Typical examples are given here:–

11. Arithmetic Operations.

a. Addition, subtraction, multiplication and division. The method will depend on the **address format**. Different operations will be required for fixed and floating point numbers. (Details of arithmetic in chapters 23 and 24).

b. **Incre**ment and **decre**ment operations ie increasing or decreasing the contents of an address or accumulator by 1.

c. Negation and complementing ie producing ones or twos complements. (See logical operations).

d. **Arithmetic shifts** ie moving bits in registers either left or right in order to multiply or divide. Examples are given here in detail because of their practical importance.

12. Examples of Arithmetic shifts.

a. **Arithmetic shift one place left** (Arithmetical meaning is preserved, twos complement convention).

	BEFORE		AFTER		
i.	0 0 0 1	+1	← 0 0 1 0	← zero inserted	+2
ii.	1 1 1 1	–1	← 1 1 1 0	← zero inserted	–2
iii.	0 1 0 0	+4	← 1 0 0 0	← zero inserted	–8

↑ (Has changed) An overflow signal would be set. The result is –8 instead of +8!

Note. In multiple shifts, a further shift after an overflow would cause an arithmetic error signal to occur.

b. **Arithmetic shift one place right** (Arithmetical meanings preserved, twos complement convention).

	BEFORE		AFTER	
i.	0 0 1 0	+2	0 0 0 1	+1
ii.	1 1 1 0	–2	1 1 1 1	–1

The sign is preserved. One shifted in.

(This is called **"sign propagation"**)

13. Logical operations.

a. Various Boolean operations eg AND, OR. They are usually performed between registers as in this example where the AND operation is used to 'mask out' one character in a register.

	ASCII 'A'								ASCII 'B'							
FIRST 'X' REGISTER CONTAINING 2 CHARACTERS	0	1	0	0	0	0	0	1	0	1	0	0	0	0	1	0
SECOND 'Y' REGISTER CONTAINING A 'MASK'	0	0	0	0	0	0	0	0	1	1	1	1	1	1	1	1
RESULTS REGISTER CONTAINING X.Y (Performed on each bit pair)	0	0	0	0	0	0	0	0	0	1	0	0	0	0	1	0

b. Negation, the Boolean NOT also performs ones complementation.

c. **Rotation,** also called logical shift, ie moving bits left or right but replacing each bit at the opposite end of the register. (This terminology is *not* universal).

Examples.

i. **Logical shift (with a rotation) one place left.** (A logical shift need not include a rotation)

BEFORE	AFTER
1 0 1 1	0 1 1 1

'1' removed on left replaced on the right in the case of rotation.

ii. **Logical shift (with a rotation) one place right.**

BEFORE	AFTER
1 0 1 1	1 1 0 1

'1' removed on right replaced on left in the case of rotation.

iii. **Logical shift (without a rotation) one place left.**

BEFORE

1	0	1	1

AFTER

0	1	1	0

← zero inserted

iv. **Logical shift (without a rotation) one place right**

BEFORE

1	0	1	1

AFTER

zero inserted →

0	1	0	1

d. **Swaps** ie changing the lefthand and righthand half of a word.

Example. Swap halves.

BEFORE THE SWAP															
ASCII 'A'								ASCII 'B'							
0	1	0	0	0	0	0	1	0	1	0	0	0	0	1	0

AFTER THE SWAP															
ASCII 'B'								ASCII 'A'							
0	1	0	0	0	0	1	0	0	1	0	0	0	0	0	1

14. Transfer of Control or Branch Instructions.
These are instructions which change the sequence in which instructions are obeyed. Their execution causes a 'jump' to an instruction given elsewhere. The details follow shortly. First we list the two main types of these 'jump' instructions.

a. **Unconditional transfer of control.** The jump always occurs eg
   i. Jump to a specified address
   ii. Skip the next instruction or skip a specified distance.

b. **Conditional transfer of control.** The jump will only occur if the result of an operation has a particular value.

Examples.
   i. Jump to a specified address if the accumulator contains zero.
   ii. Jump to a specified address if the accumulator contains a negative value.
   iii. Skip the next instruction if the accumulator contains zero.
   iv. Increment or decrement specified address, and skip next instruction if result is zero.

(Details of how these jumps are achieved follow in paragraph 18).

15. Load (fetch) and Store Instructions. These instructions cause the transfer of data between accumulators and memory, eg load contents of specified address into a specified accumulator.

16. Input/Output (I/O) Instructions. These instructions implement the transfer of data between peripherals and memory, or between peripherals and accumulators.

Examples.

i. Checking to see if a terminal typewriter has data ready for transfer.
ii. Moving a character from a terminal typewriter into an accumulator.

(Input and Output is dealt with later in chapter 34).

17. a. **Memory Reference Instructions.** These are operations which require access to memory during their execution, hence they include **load and store instructions** and may also include some arithmetic, logic and control transfer instructions.

b. **Processor Reference Instructions.** These are instructions which do not require memory and do not involve input or output eg HALT processor.

HOW INSTRUCTIONS ARE OBEYED.

18. We must continue with the ideas introduced in (9.22 to 9.29) which you may wish to re-read before you continue. This explanation uses details from the CPU diagram in appendix 2.2.

19.

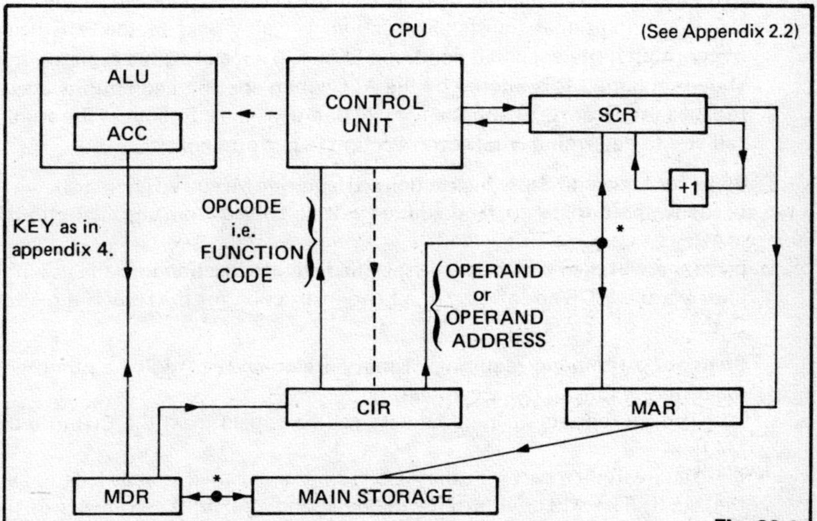

Fig. 28.1

This diagram is simplified in order to highlight the basic features. A more practical example was given in fig. 27.1.

20. Remind yourself of the purpose of each of the registers (9.22) before you read on.

21. Further Details of the Fetch-Execute Cycle. (Follow these steps on this diagram).

a. **Fetching** the required instruction.

i. The MAR is loaded with the address of the instruction to be performed. This address is copied from the SCR.

ii. The controls of the SCR are then increased by 1 so it is ready to be referenced for the next fetch.

iii. The fetch is completed by loading the instruction into the CIR via the MDR.

b. *Executing* the instruction.

i. The **opcode** or function part of the instruction is decoded by the control unit. What happens next depends on the type of instruction.

Examples:–

Steps for instructions NOT requiring memory reference.

ii. The control unit sends command signals to the appropriate devices in the desired sequence until execution is completed.

Steps for transfer of control instructions.

ii. An unconditional transfer instruction causes the address held in the SCR to be overwritten by the address held in the righthand half of the CIR, thereby ensuring that the desired instruction is obtained in the next fetch. A conditional transfer instruction will only lead to the SCR being overwritten if the specified condition is met. A special **status register,** not shown in fig. 28.1, is altered by the ALU when specified conditions occur (eg. accumulator zero) and the control unit uses the contents of the status register to determine what control action to perform next.

Steps for Load and Store instructions. (Requiring Memory Reference).

ii. The appropriate operand address will be copied from the CIR into the MAR.

iii. Data will then pass from the specified storage location into the accumulator via the MDR in the case of a Load instruction (or the reverse direction in the case of a store).

Steps for Arithmetic requiring Memory Reference eg Adding a number in main store to one in the accumulator.

ii. The appropriate operand address will be copied from the CIR into the MAR.

iii. Data will then pass into the ALU from the specified storage location via the MDR. The ALU will receive the data, adding it to the contents of the accumulator which may then be replaced by the result.

AN IMAGINARY MACHINE LANGUAGE.

22. We are now going to consider the machine language for an imaginary computer.

There is great variation between computer manufacturers in their design of machine codes. In order to give a balanced picture we will consider alternative examples in many cases. Familiarity with a real machine language should be obtained in your practical work if possible. It is very important that the reader realise that the imaginary computer described is much simpler than a real computer. To create a balanced view some more practical examples will be provided later in this chapter.

23. Aids to the programmer.

Remembering the binary codes for each instruction, or just each function, is troublesome so the following aids are often used by programmers.

a. Symbolic and MNEMONIC codes.

Groups of letters (symbols) are used by the programmer when writing his program. These codes are usually MNEMONIC which means that their sound suggests their meaning eg LDA might stand for the function **L**oa**D** **A**ccumulator. It is usual to describe the function code as mnemonic and addresses or labels as symbolic.

Example. "LDA N" means "Load Accumulator with contents of address N" LDA is a mnemonic opcode (function code) and N is a symbolic address.

b. Binary codes may be converted to octal or hex to make them more manageable.

c. A special program called an **Assembler** may be provided which will convert a program in symbolic and mnemonic form into machine code. The mnemonic and symbolic program is called the **source program** for the Assembler and the machine code produced by the assembler is called the **object program.**

24. The number of bits in an instruction which are allowed for the function code will determine the number of possible codes. (The same principle applies when considering the number of bits required to represent a given number of characters). If two bits were allowed then 4 function codes would be possible ie, 00, 01, 10, 11. In general n bits allow 2^n function codes. However, the situation is more complicated than this in practice because of the variations which occur in instruction format within the same machine. For each format the same principle applies though.

25. For our imaginary computer we will take an example where in a fixed (word) length instruction 4 bits are used to represent a possible 16 function codes. The codes, their functions and associated mnemonics are given below.

MACHINE CODE (BINARY CODE)	OCTAL EQUIVALENT	FUNCTION (OPERATION)	MNEMONIC
0000	00	**L**oad **A**ccumulator with contents of specified address	LDA
0001	01	**ST**ore contents of **A**ccumulator in specified address	STA
0010	02	**L**oa**D** specified **N**umber into accumulator	LDN
0011	03	**ADD** contents of specified address to accumulator contents	ADD
0100	04	**SUB**tract contents of specified address from accumulator contents	SUB
0101	05	**AD**d specified **N**umber to contents of accumulator	ADN
0110	06	**SU**btract specified **N**umber from contents of accumulator	SUN
0111	07	Perform a Boolean AND on specified address and accumulator contents	AND
1000	10	Perform a Boolean OR on specified address and accumulator contents	OR
1001	11	**J**ump to specified address if **A**ccumulator contents **Z**ero	JAZ
1010	12	**J**um**P** **U**nconditionally to specified address	JPU
1011	13	**J**ump to specified address if **A**ccumulator contents **G**reater than zero	JAG
1100	14	**J**ump to specified address if **A**ccumulator contents **L**ess than zero	JAL
1101	15	**J**ump to specified address if **A**ccumulator contents **N**ot zero	JAN
1110	16	Perform specified **I**nput/**O**utput operation	IO
1111	17	**STOP** the program ie HALT the processor	STOP

Note.

a. In instructions where there is no memory reference, eg. I/O operations, the operand address bits may be used to extend the function options.

b. It is in this respect of having just one instruction format that this imaginary computer is particularly simple compared with most real computers.

26. Suppose that our imaginary computer has a fixed word length of 16 bits. The function code requires 4 bits so 12 bits remain for the operand addresses. If the machine had two accumulators we would require one bit, set to 0 or 1 to specify the accumulator. We will assume there is just one accumulator and hence it will not require **explicit** addressing. We will thus have the following arrangement:–

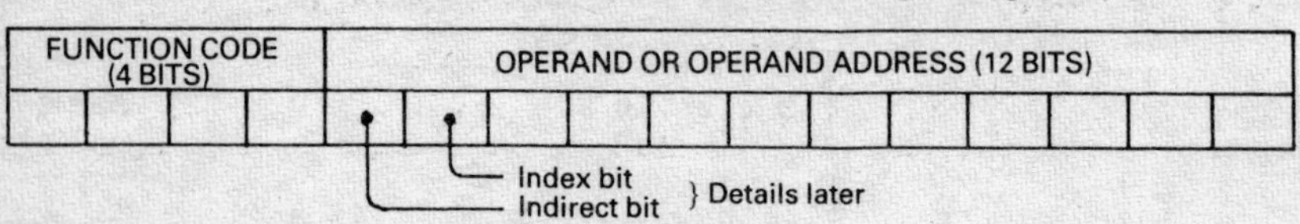

METHODS OF ADDRESSING.

27. The location address ultimately determined by hardware is called the **absolute address.** Within the instruction various methods may be used. The main methods of addressing are:—

a. Direct addressing.

b. Indirect Addressing (also called deferred address).

c. Indexed Addressing.

d. Modified Addressing.

e. Relative Addressing.

f. Page Addressing.

g. Immediate Addressing.

h. Symbolic Addressing. (Not possible in machine language).

Hardware determines the address type by decoding the operand part of the instruction in the SCR. It then produces the correct absolute address. The data path from CIR to MAR in Fig. 28.1 therefore gave a simplified view of what happens.

28. Direct Addressing is being used if the number given in the operand part of an instruction is the actual address of the operand (data) to be used.

Example.

FUNCTION CODE: LDA				ADDRESS $111_2 = 7_8$											
0	0	0	0	0	0	0	0	0	0	0	0	0	1	1	1

In this example the instruction would be to load the contents of Location 7 into the accumulator.

29. Direct addressing is simple, fast and effective but the number of locations addressable is limited. In the above example the 12 bits available allow just $2^{12} = 4096_{10}$ locations to be specified. This problem may be overcome by

a. Using longer words.

b. Using more than one word for the address by using the next location. (called an **extended address**). This is common in micro computers.

c. Using alternative methods. Since a. and b. are frequently impractical on the one hand because longer words prove wasteful and expensive and on the other because the method is slow and complicates the fetch execute cycle.

30. Indirect Addressing. When **indirect addressing** is used the address given in the address part of the instruction is NOT the address of the required operand. Instead the address part is the address of the location which contains the required address. An address is **either** direct **or** indirect.

Example.

FUNCTION CODE :LDA				ADDRESS OF LOCATION CONTAINING OPERAND ADDRESS											
0	0	0	0	*1	0	0	0	0	0	0	0	0	1	1	1

*This bit (the indirect bit) is set to '1' to signify indirect addressing or '0' for direct addressing.

CONTENTS OF LOCATION 7															
* 0	0	0	0	0	0	0	0	0	0	0	0	1	0	0	1

a. **Note.**

i. The data to be loaded is in location 9. It is **not obtained directly** because its address must **first** be found in location 7. Hence the term **indirect address.** (Two memory accesses will be necessary).

ii. Almost **all** of location 7 may be used to specify the data address so $2^{15} = 32768_{10}$ locations may be accessed, a considerable improvement.

b. Practical difficulties with this example arise because it is not possible to access locations greater than $2^{11} = 2048_{10}$ directly. One unavoidable drawback of indirect addressing is the need for two memory accesses instead of one.

c. Indirect addressing is sometimes called **deferred addressing** and if the second address is yet a further indirect address then the address is called a **multi-level address.** (Note the * in location 7 shown in the diagram).

31. Indexed Addressing.

In this method the required address is obtained by **adding** the contents of the address part of the instruction to a number stored in a special register called the **index register** or **modifier register.**

Example.

FUNCTION CODE: LDA	INDIRECT BIT	INDEX BIT	REMAINDER OF OPERAND ADDRESS
0 0 0 0	0	1	0 0 0 0 0 0 0 1 1 1

THE CONTENTS OF THE INDEX REGISTER IS 9_{10}															
0	0	0	0	0	0	0	0	0	0	0	0	1	0	0	1

Index bit set to '1' to signify the use of the index register. DATA ADDRESS = 9 + 7 = 16.

Note.

a. The need to do an addition makes this method slower than direct addressing but once the address is calculated it can be accessed in one step ie directly.

b. A further bit has been used in our example to indicate whether or not the index register is to be used. This further limits the range of the address given in the instruction.

c. The index address and indirect bits could both be set to one thus allowing an **indirect indexed address** where the address given by address part + index register contents would be an indirect address.

d. No index register is shown in fig. 28.1 which highlights the limitations of this imaginary computer. In some later examples we will take memory location zero to be the index register which is not so unrealistic as it may first appear because it is not unknown for the first few locations in memory to be constructed and used as registers.

32. You can see from the previous examples that bits may be taken from the address part of the instruction in order to specify such things as the accumulators to be used or the type of addressing to be used. For a given machine the instruction format must be designed to allow for these different **modes of addressing** to be added in some way.

33. Other methods of addressing will now be described. It would be uncommon for all these methods to be used on any one machine, although all are used, on different machines, but on a given machine the mode of address would be specified by a suitable part of the instruction format.

34. Modified Addressing.
If an instruction is altered or modified so that the same function is performed again but on an operand in a different address then a **modified address** has been used. Two basic methods are:–

a. Using indexed addressing and changing the contents of the index register before the instruction is repeated.

NB. A common use is to successively add one to the index register so as to access successive locations in memory.

b. Changing the address part of the instruction. This can be done by treating the instruction as an operand (data) and either adding or subtracting some number from it.

NB. The use of this method is almost invariably a bad practice because it is a threat to program readability and reliability. In any case, it limits the ways in which the code can be reused.

35. Relative Addressing.

a. The address part of the instruction is used to give a **displacement** from some **stated** address. In one sense an index address is a relative address since the address part of the instruction gives the location of the operand as so many places **past** the location **stated** in the index register.

b. A further example occurs when the address part of the instruction specifies an address relative to the instruction currently being performed. The address field requires one bit to specify this type of address, the remainder of the address field may be a positive or negative. When the instruction is performed the hardware uses the value in the Sequence Control Register + the displacement to generate the absolute address.

Example. JPU (SCR)–2 ie Jump back two instructions.

36. Base Address.
The address to which the relative address is referred is frequently called the **base address.** Thus the **displacement** is added to the **base address.**

37. Page Addressing. (Used where word length limits the size of the address field) This is a special form of **relative addressing.** The main storage area is divided into units of equal size (512 locations say) and the units, called pages, are numbered 0, 1, 2, 3 etc. A register can be set to the value of a given page number and then until it is altered all addresses given in the address part of the instruction are added to the zeroth address for that page.

Usually the size of the address field in the instruction is such that it can only specify N different locations, where N is the size of the pages.

38. Immediate Addressing.
If instead of giving the location of the data in the address part of the instruction the address part itself is used as data then immediate addressing is being used., ie the address part is used as the operand. In paragraph 25 we saw functions LDN, ADN and SUN which would be using immediate addressing. (The operand is an **immediate operand**).

39. Symbolic Addressing.
Symbolic addressing is NOT possible in **machine code** but it is used by the programmer when he or she uses an Alpha-numeric symbol to specify an address. The symbolic address must at some stage be translated into a **machine address.**

Example. (Program section adding two numbers and storing the result).

labels	A:	3	Contents of these locations
	B:	5	
	C:	Ø	
Instructions using symbolic addressing	LDA	A	Load accumulator with contents of address labelled by A.
	ADD	B	Add to accumulator the contents of the address labelled by B.
	STA	C	Store the sum in the address labelled by C.

FURTHER FEATURES OF THE MACHINE.

40. The imaginary machine described earlier in this chapter, and used as a basis for simple examples, is too simple to serve as a basis for all the points requiring discussion here. The simplified machine shown in fig. 28.2 will be used from now on.

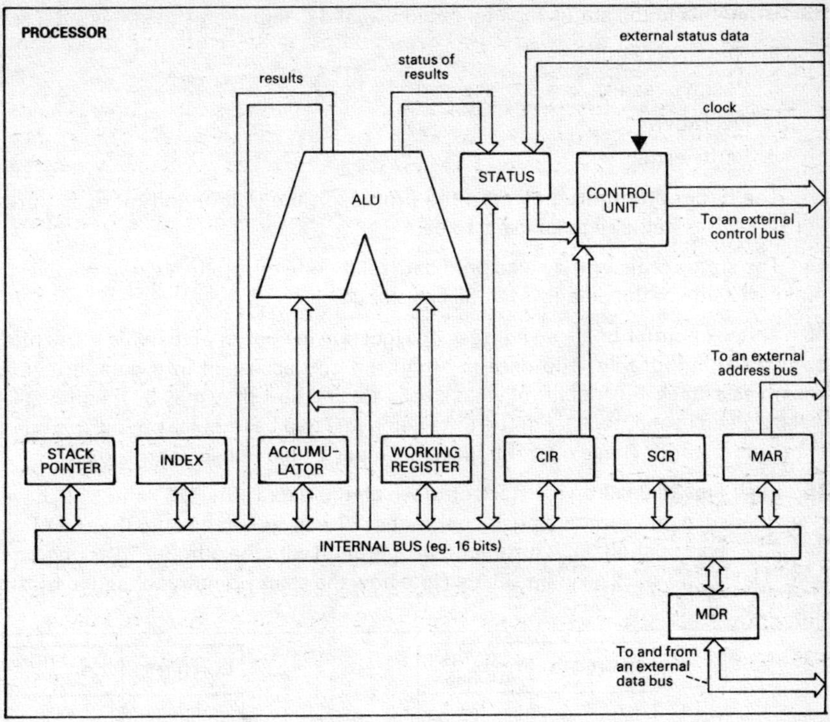

Figure 28.2. A Simplified View of a Typical Processor

41. Examine fig. 28.2 and note the following points.

a. Many of the registers are the same as in fig. 28.1.

b. Data is transferred in parallel and many transfers use the internal data bus.

c. The index register (28.31) is represented in the diagram. The ALU could be used to perform the arithmetic needed for indexed addressing.

d. Two registers met for the first time in fig. 28.2.

i. A **Status Register.**

ii. A **Stack Pointer.**

42. A Status Register such as the one shown in fig. 28.2 has its contents set by hardware devices such as the ALU and is used by the control unit. For example, one bit in the status register might be used to signify whether or not the last ALU result was zero. The control unit would examine this bit when it controlled a conditional branch instruction such as JAZ or JAN.

43. Other bits in the status register could be used to signify result states such as:

a. Negative result.

b. Positive result.

c. Overflow.

d. Parity error.

The larger and more powerful the processor, the longer and more comprehensive is the status register likely to be.

44. The status register may also hold data relating to the state of external devices but discussion of the details is left till chapter 34.

45. A **stack pointer** holds an address of a location in memory into which data may be placed temporarily. The data is organised and accessed in a data structure known as a **stack.** Full details of what stacks are and how they may be manipulated will be given in chapter 31. For the time being just two basic stack operations need to be understood. These operations are normally called **"push"** and **"pop"**.

46. Push Fig. 28.3a shows a stack onto which the data value "15" and "12" have been placed in two separate push operations. 15 was "pushed" onto the stack first then "12" was pushed on. A further push operation with the number 23 as operand would leave the stack as in fig. 28.3b. Note how the stack pointer is changed by the push operation.

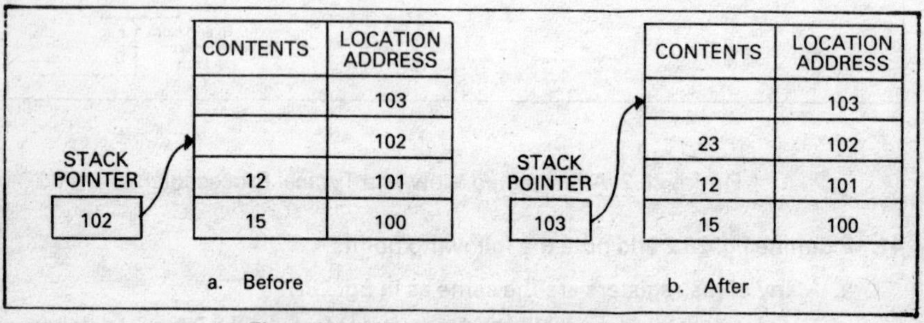

Figure 28.3. Pushing '23' onto a stack.

47. A **pop** operation is the reverse of a push operation ie. the item is removed from the stack and the stack pointer is altered. Thus fig. 28.3b shows the stack before a pop which removes "23" and fig. 28.3a shows the stack after the pop operation.

48. Push and pop operations are often provided as machine instruction. Even some 8-bit microprocessors have this facility eg. the Z80.

49. In some machines special registers are provided within the processor to form a stack and may be used instead of memory.

50. The three main uses of stacks at machine level are:

a. Use in simple computations to hold intermediate results.

b. Use in handling subprogram calls.

c. Use in handling interrupts.

The last two of these three will be discussed in later chapters. An example of (a) would be a simple swap operation when two variables (a = 9 and b = 12 say) were to exchange values. A possible method would be:

i. push a's value onto the stack.
ii. copy b's value to a.
iii. pop the value off the stack into b.

The code for this could be something like this:

```
PUSH A
LDA B
STA A
POP B
```

LOADING AND STORING PROGRAMS IN MACHINE CODE.

51. Nearly all modern computers have programs available which are called **loaders** or **loading routines.** A loader will take a program written in machine code and in some suitable input form such as disk, and input the instructions from the disk into their specified storage locations. The loader is often permanently in main memory. You may ask "How is the loader loaded?" We shall now answer this question.

52. Manual Communication. Information about the CPU is displayed on a special panel called the **console** which may often be used in conjunction with a typewriter called the **console typewriter.** The console panel will have lights to display the contents of various registers or addresses and switches by which those contents may be altered. On a 16 bit word machine there would probably be 2 rows of 16 lights to represent in one row the binary addresses, and in the other the contents of that address in binary. Underneath these lights there might be 16 switches used for selecting addresses or changing their contents.

53. By the manual use of these switches one could enter a whole program in machine code by setting the binary code for each instruction on the switches one at a time. On the early computers this was the only way! Today one would use this method in two main situations which are

a. to "key in" a very simple loader by hand in order to load all other programs. This might be done when for some reason the loader was not in memory.
b. to make very minor alterations to programs already loaded.

54. Bootstraps. Bootstraps or Bootstrap loaders are very simple loaders which are **either** placed in memory manually by use of the console **or** placed in memory by a special piece of **hardware** which will place instructions into the first few locations in core for input of instructions from some specified device. These 'hardware' instructions would be provided by a ROM.

55. Absolute and Relocatable Programs. (The need for relocatable programs will be discussed in chapter 39). An **absolute address** is an address as determined by hardware. An **absolute program** is one which is always loaded into the same fixed locations in main store for which the **absolute addresses** are known. A **relocatable program** is one which may be loaded into different locations in mainstore each time it is run. When writing a **relocatable program** it is common to assume that it starts at location zero ie all addresses are relative to an assumed base address at zero.

SUMMARY.

56. a. Instructions in **machine language** can be performed without further translation.

b. The address format can be classified by the number of addresses specified eg one address format.

c. Types of instructions can be classified under the headings:—

- i. Arithmetic and logic
- ii. Transfer of control
- iii. Load and Store
- iv. Input/Output
- v. Memory Reference

or more concisely

- i. Memory Reference
- ii. Processor Reference
- iii. Input/Output.

d. Symbolic, mnemonic codes aid programming in machine code.

e. Methods of addressing possible are:—

- i. Direct
- ii. Indirect (deferred) and multilevel
- iii. Indexed addressing
- iv. Address Modification
- v. Relative
- vi. Page Addressing
- vii. Immediate
- viii. Symbolic (Not possible in machine language)

f. The absolute address is the address determined by hardware.

g. Status registers and stacks were introduced.

h. A program must be placed in main store before it is performed. This may be done by

- i. A loader program
- ii. Manual setting of switches
- iii. A hardware load.

i. A loaded program may be either absolute or relocatable.

POINTS TO NOTE.

57. a. Once the instruction format is fixed there are limits set on the number of different instructions which can be coded and the number of locations directly addressable in a single instruction.

b. Indexed addressing and indirect addressing overcome the limitation to the range of addresses accessible by a single instruction at the cost of either extra arithmetic or further access.

c. The relative speeds of indirect addressing and index addressing depend entirely on the hardware of the particular machine on which they are used. Usually Index addressing offers a greater flexibility.

d. Exam questions are often set on imaginary machine instruction set so be prepared to get familiar with an instruction set in a hurry.

e. When working through a machine language program it often helps to tabulate successive contents of relevant locations.

f. Relocatability mentioned in this chapter is 'static'. Some machines can relocate programs while they are being executed ie they provide 'dynamic relocatability'. (Further discussion will occur in chapter 39).

g. Specimen programs are given in the next chapter.

h. The reader is advised to get a working knowledge of at least one real machine having first become familiar with the contents of this chapter and the next one.

STUDENT SELF TEST QUESTIONS.

(Answers on page 726)

1. *A small one-address computer has storage for 4096 eighteen-bit words. Each machine instruction is one complete word and must be able to address directly any cell in the store. How many different machine instruction operation codes can there be?*

2. a. Briefly explain two *methods of inserting instructions in machine code into the store without using peripheral transfers. What part does this type of input play in setting up a machine to read in and process its first user program?*

b. Discuss the role within a control unit of

i. the Sequence Control Register, and

ii. the Current Instruction Register.

Sketch a flow-diagram to show the basic operations of a control unit during the 'fetch-execute' cycle, showing particularly a route through the diagram for the following instructions:—

add operand to contents of accumulator,

subtract operand from contents of accumulator,

store contents of accumulator,

conditional jump and unconditional jump.

(AEB 1976)

3. What is meant by an instruction format? Describe the following forms of addressing.

a. Direct.

b. Immediate.

c. Indexed.

d. Symbolic.

4. Distinguish between a logical shift instruction and an arithmetic shift instruction. Show what happens to the following bytes after

a. a 2 bit arithmetic shift right.

b. a 2 bit logical shift right.

i. 00110110

ii. 11010111

QUESTIONS WITHOUT ANSWERS.

5. Repeat question 4 for 2 bit left shifts.

6. Investigate the word length and instruction formats of the computer you use.

29 Low Level Languages

INTRODUCTION.

1. This chapter is primarily concerned with low level languages and how programs are written in low level languages. Low level language programming requires some knowledge of machine language and so some aspects of machine language programming have been included in this chapter, rather than the previous chapter, in order to make the subject matter more coherent.

MACHINE LANGUAGE PROGRAMMING.

2. We will now consider three machine language programs in order to illustrate programming features. These examples are based on the imaginary computer introduced in 28.22. We will use the instruction format 28.31, signed integer arithmetic using twos complement and the instruction set specified in 28.25.

3. In writing specimen programs the following notation will be used.

a. Machine instructions will be shown in octal as well as binary to show how octal coding aids the programmer.

eg the instruction "Store contents of accumulator in Location 7" is

COMMENTS	FUNCTION CODE:LDA	INDIRECT BIT	INDEX BIT	REMAINDER OF OPERAND ADDRESS
BINARY	0 0 0 0	0	0	0 0 0 0 0 0 1 1 1
OCTAL	0 0		0	0 0 7

b. In writing MNEMONICS the address notation will be as shown in the following instruction examples.

- i. STA 7 — Store accumulator contents in location 7. (Direct address)
- ii. STA @ 7 — The @ indicates an indirect address. In this case store accumulator contents at the location specified in location 7.
- iii. STA 5, X — The ",X" indicates that the inde**X** register is to be used. In this case store accumulator in location given by (Contents of index register) + 5.

c. Numerical values will be in OCTAL.

4. Example 1. A program to add two numbers stored in locations 5 and 6, and to place the result in location 7. (Look at the MNEMONICS **FIRST**).

LOCATION OF INSTRUCTION (OCTAL)	MACHINE INSTRUCTION (OR DATA) (BINARY) Function Code	Operand or Operand Address	MACHINE INSTRUCTION (OR DATA) (Octal Coded)	MNEMONIC EQUIVALENT (Numerics octal)
0	0000	000000000101	000005	LDA 5
1	0011	000000000110	030006	ADD 6
2	0001	000000000111	010007	STA 7
3	1111	000000000000	170000	STOP
4	0000	000000000000	000000	0
5	0000	000000000110	000006	6
6	0000	000000001010	000012	12
7	0000	000000000000	000000	0

Note. i. Simple direct addressing is being used here.

ii. Data and instructions are stored in **exactly the same way** so data can be treated as an instruction or an instruction as data, eg had the STOP instruction been omitted the data value 0 held in location 4 would be treated as the instruction LDA 0 and the CPU would continue to obey each word of store as an instruction until a STOP code was met.

5. Example 2. The same task is performed as in example 1 but different methods of addressing are used for illustration although they are unnecessary.

LOCATION OF INSTRUCTION (OCTAL)	MACHINE INSTRUCTION (OR DATA) (BINARY) Function Code	Operand or Operand Address	MACHINE INSTRUCTION (OR DATA) (Octal Coded)	MNEMONIC EQUIVALENT (Numerics octal)
INDEX REGISTER	0000	000000000100	000004	4
1	0010	000000000110	020006	LDN 6
2	0011	100000000101	034005	ADD @ 5
3	0001	010000000011	010003	STA 3, X
4	1111	000000000000	170000	STOP
5	0000	000000000110	000006	6
6	0000	000000001010	000012	12
7	0000	000000000000	000000	0

Note. i. LDN 6 results in the number 6 being loaded with the accumulator.

ii. ADD @ 5 results in the address of the data being found in location 5.

That address 6 leads to the data 12_8. This results in the data 12_8 being added to the accumulator.

iii. STA 3, X results in the sum, 18, being stored in location 3 + Contents of index register ie location 3 + 4 = 7.

6. Example 3. Extending the previous program.

a. The STOP instruction in location 4 could be replaced by an unconditional jump to the next instruction in location 10 (OCTAL) say. The appropriate instruction would be JPU 10. The binary and octal forms are:–

BINARY																OCTAL				
1	0	1	0	0	0	0	0	0	0	0	0	1	0	0	0	1	2	0	0	1 0

To terminate the program, eg if the sum is 20, the following group of instructions would suffice. (Binary and Octal codes are omitted for clarity).

LOCATION	INSTRUCTION MNEMONIC	COMMENT
10	SUN 20	Test for 20 by subtracting 20 and
11	JAN 13	skipping the STOP if the result is non zero
12	STOP	Performs this STOP if sum 20
13	etc.	This instruction is obeyed if the sum is not 20

7. Final points on machine language programming.

a. All the machine's operation codes (function codes) have to be memorised.

b. All memory addresses have to be assigned and a track kept of them (ie we must give each variable an address and record our action).

c. Instructions have to be written in the sequence in which they are to be executed. Thus insertions or deletions entail the **movement** of all succeeding instructions. (eg to insert code between location 6 & 7).

d. Subsequent revision of a completed program would be so impractical as to almost require a complete **rewrite.**

e. The whole process is very time consuming and inefficient in terms of human effort.

LOW LEVEL LANGUAGES.

8. We saw the advantages of using MNEMONICS to describe machine language instructions. It seems logical to write the program in this SYMBOLIC form and to get the machine to do the translation to machine language and this is what is done with **low level languages.**

9. Definition. Low level languages are **machine orientated languages** in which each instruction corresponds to or resembles a machine instruction.

10. Common Features of Low Level Languages.

a. **MNEMONIC** codes are used in place of machine codes eg using LDA 5 in place of 0000000000000101.

b. **Symbolic addresses** are frequently used instead of actual machine addresses eg using LDA N where N stands for the address which can be assigned a numerical value at a more convenient time.

11. The (symbolic) low level language must be translated into machine language before use, because although easier for the programmer to work with it is not usable by the machine in symbolic/mnemonic form.

The translation is actually done by the computer by means of a special translating program.

12. Assembly language.

a. Each computer manufacturer normally devises a low level language which corresponds closely to the particular machine language used by that manufacturer. This language is called an ASSEMBLY LANGUAGE. The manufacturer provides a program called an ASSEMBLER or ASSEMBLER PROGRAM which translates the ASSEMBLY LANGUAGE into MACHINE CODE.

b. A program written in ASSEMBLY LANGUAGE is called the SOURCE PROGRAM. The translated program in MACHINE CODE is called the OBJECT PROGRAM.

(The features of ASSEMBLERS will be left until chapter 32).

13. Pseudo Assembly Languages. Assembly languages differ, since the features of each assembly language depends on the particular computer on which it is used. This makes computer courses and examinations difficult to standardise. To answer this problem several low level assembly-like languages which are **machine independent** have been devised for educational purposes. They are **pseudo assembly languages** since they do not fulfil the usual task of an assembly language, but are useful educationally.

Examples are:

a. CESIL Computer Education in Schools Instruction Language

b. City and Guilds 319 Mnemonic coded.

The mnemonic code used for examples in the previous chapter may also be regarded as a pseudo-assembly language.

ILLUSTRATIVE PROBEMS IN ASSEMBLY LANGUAGE.

14. The assembly language instruction format used here is based on the instruction format used in the earlier examples. Here are the details.

Instruction Format

LABEL : FUNCTION CODE OPERAND OR OPERAND ADDRESS

eg A : LDA 5

Note.

a. The LABEL is **optional** and may be used either
   i. to give an instruction a symbolic address, or
   ii. to give a numerical value a symbolic address.

b. The operand address can take these forms:
   i. a direct address or operand eg 5
   ii. a direct index address eg 5, X
   The address will be 5 + contents of index register.
   iii. indirect, indicated by an @ eg @ 5 or @ 5, X.
   iv. up to three letters used as a symbolic address eg. N.

c. Examples.
   i. LDA 5 — Load accumulator with contents of address 5.
   ii. LDA N — Load the contents of (symbolic) address N into the accumulator. Further down the contents of N are specified next to the label.
   N : 5
   iii. LDA @ N — The symbolic address N holds the address of the data to be loaded into the accumulator.
   iv. LDA 5, X — Load the contents of location 5 + (X) where (X) means *contents* of index register.

15. Specimen Problem 1. To add a set of numbers stored in successive locations starting at location 30_8 and terminated by a location containing zero. The program will be placed in location 10_8 to 25_8 inclusive and the data is organised as shown here:

LOCATION ADDRESS (OCTAL)	CONTENTS	
26	pointer value (initialised to 30)	A **pointer** to the address of the next number to be added.
27	total value	value of the **total.**
30	15	Specimen data with sentinel value zero
31	18	
32	14	
33	0	

16. The method is given in pseudocode in the following table. **All** numbers are in octal. The pointer contains the address of the next number to be added. Indirect addressing is used in the assembly program and this is indicated in pseudocode by the use of parentheses. Thus, for example, "(pointer)" means the data whose address is currently assigned to pointer.

PSEUDOCODE	ASSEMBLY LANGUAGE	COMMENTS
(* Take all variables to be non-negative integers. *)		
Begin	.START 10	A **directive** to the assembler to start the program storage at location 10
total : = 0	LDN 0 STA 27	Setting the contents of location 27 to zero ie. **total** : = 0
pointer : = 30	LDN 30 STA 26	Loading the number 30 into location 26 where it is to be used as an indirect address
number : = (pointer)	LDA @ 26	Loading the number whose address is in location 26
While number < > 0	A: JAZ B	Checking for zero terminator (label used later)
total : = total + 1	ADD 27 STA 27	Adding number to total then store the new total
pointer : = pointer + 1	LDN 1 ADD 26 STA 26	Increasing the address stored in location 26 by 1 so that next time it is used it refers to the next number to be added.
number : = (pointer)	LDA @ 26	Same as before
	JPU A	Jump to load next number.
endwhile		
end	B: STOP	STOP
	.END	A **directive** to the assembler to end the translation.

17. Note the following points about this assembly language program.

a. A **while loop** has been constructed using a combination of conditional and non-conditional jump instructions.

b. The way the data is stored in memory from location 30 onwards is comparable to the way data is stored in an array and the pointer is comparable with the subscript of an array.

c. The use of a "directive".

18. Directives. .START and .END are *not* ASSEMBLY LANGUAGE instructions. They are DIRECTIVES ie. instructions to the ASSEMBLER requiring immediate execution and *not* requiring translation as part of the program.

19. Specimen Problem 2. The main purpose of this problem is to show how **if-then-else** may be implemented using an assembly language. Location 3 and 4 hold integer values corresponding to the costs, in pence, of purchased goods. If the sum of these two values is no more than 100p then the additional postage and packing cost is 30p. If the sum is more than 100p then the additional postage and packing cost is 50p. The program is to calculate the total cost and store it in location 5.

20. The method is given in pseudocode in the following table. **All** numbers are in octal. Note the way in which the jump instructions are used to select the appropriate actions.

PSEUDOCODE	ASSEMBLY LANGUAGE
Begin	.START 10
total_cost : = first_cost + second_cost	LDA 3 ADD 4 STA 5
if total_cost < = 100	LDN 100 SUB 5 JAN G
then total_cost : = total_cost + 30	LDN 30 ADD 5 STA 5 JPU E
else total_cost : = total_cost + 50	G: LDN 50 ADD 5 STA 5
endif **end**	E: STOP .END

SUBROUTINES (SUBPROGRAMS)

21. A subprogram (11.62) written in a low level language is usually called a subroutine. Subroutines were invented as an aid to efficiency but have become even more important in high level programming as a program structuring feature. In the following paragraphs the low level language feature which support subprograms will be discussed.

22. A subroutine is a set of program instructions forming **part** of a program and used to perform a specific task. Used wisely the **same** subroutine may be used to do the same task at different stages in the main program without the need for rewriting it each time.

Figure 29.1 illustrates the basic principles.

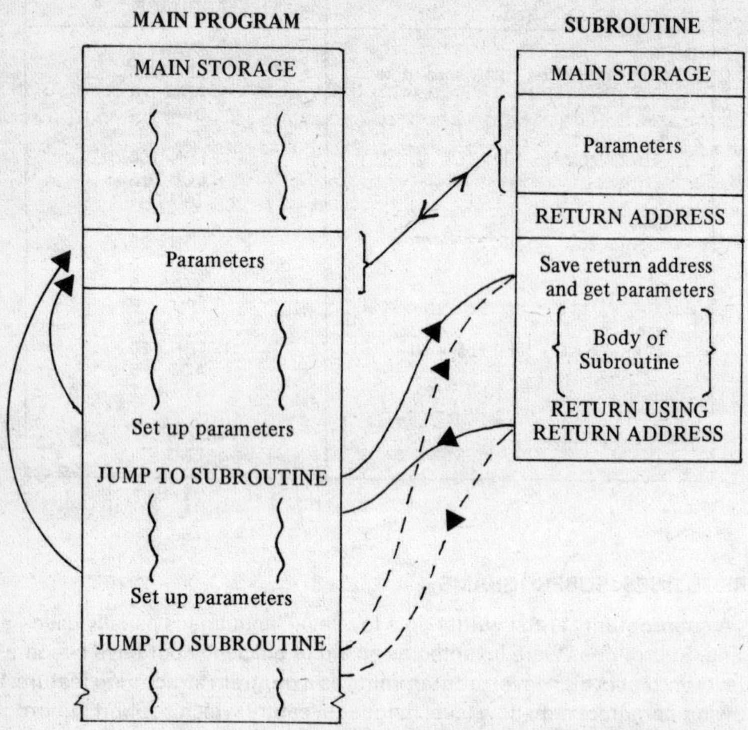

NB. There are many ways of dealing with subroutines depending upon the facilities available in the machine language. Some computers automatically handle the return address as part of their hardware operation. This diagram merely illustrates the basic principles.

Figure 29.1. Handling Subroutines.

23. In the simplest cases there will be no parameter passing and no hardware to handle the subroutine calls and returns. The former is often the case when a high level language does not support full subprogram facilities. The latter is rare these days. Nevertheless it is convenient to start with the simplest case in order to introduce the ideas in easy stages.

24. Subroutine Example 1.

At different places in a program a character must be input by a terminal typewriter and its code placed in the accumulator. Suppose that a subroutine is available for doing the task and that the subroutine starts at location 400. Show how the **same** subroutine may be used each time that it is needed.

Comments:–

a. The last instruction in the subroutine will be an unconditional jump back to the appropriate location in the main program. This return address must be stored (saved) for use by the subroutine, prior to entering the subroutine.

b. There are two common ways of returning from subroutines when there is no explicit hardware facility provided. These are by using **either** Indirect addressing **or** Address modification.

25. Instructions for entering the subroutine.

LOCATION	MNEMONIC EQUIVALENT OF INSTRUCTION STORED IN LOCATION	COMMENTS
16	LDN 21	Load return address
17	STA 0	Store return address in location 0
20	JPU 400	Unconditional jump to subroutine.
21		1st instruction on return from subroutine.

(See Fig. 29.1)

To return from the subroutine if the return address is stored in location 0.

Last instruction in subroutine could use:

a. **Indirect addressing** eg JPU @ 0

b. **Address modification** eg JPU 0,X (Assume location zero is used as the index register).

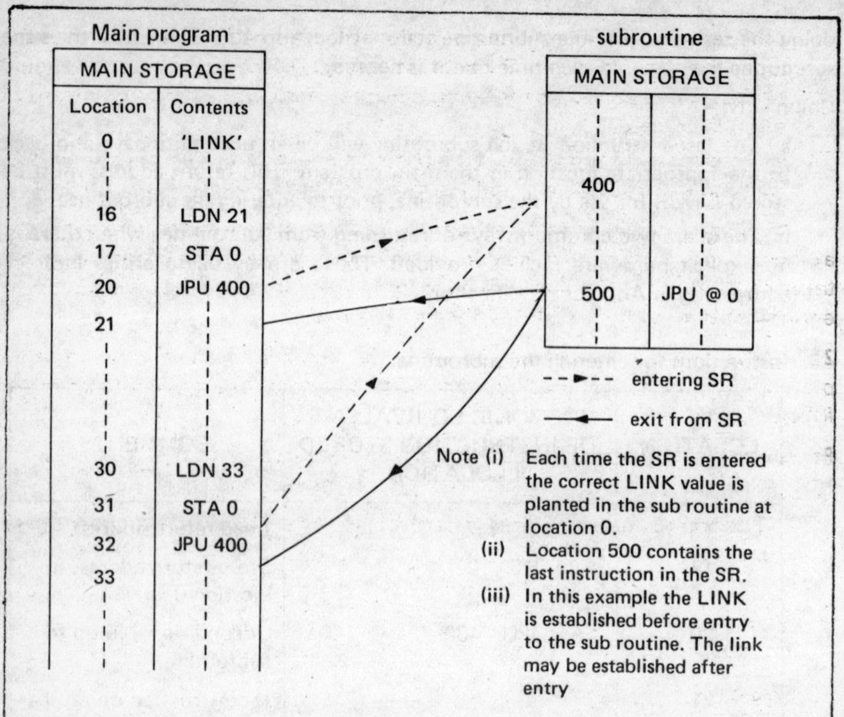

Fig. 29.2.

26. Subroutine Example 2. In this example we consider a case where hardware is provided for handling the subroutine calls and returns and we also deal with parameter passing.

27. For the purpose of this example we will assume a machine architecture like that shown in fig. 28.2, in which a stack pointer is present. We will further assume the following extensions to our assembly language. These instructions are included in the language:

a. The **PUSH** and **POP** operations described in 28.46–28.47.

b. A **MOVE** instruction which takes the form MOVE A B where A is register whose contents are moved to register B and where the accumulator, index register, stack pointer and sequence control register have the symbolic addresses ACC, INDEX, STACK and SCR respectively.

For example, MOVE INDEX STACK moves the contents of the index register into the stack pointer.

c. A Jump To Subroutine instruction with mnemonic **JSR** where, for example, the instruction JSR B will cause the contents of the SCR to be pushed onto the stack, thereby saving the return address, and a jump equivalent to JPU B will be performed.

d. A Return From Subroutine instruction with mnemonic **RTN** which pops the top of the stack into the SCR where the contents of the top of the stack should be the return address for the subroutine previously placed there by means of a JSR instruction.

e. An instruction to increment the contents of a register with mnemonic **INC.** For example, INC ACC will add 1 to the contents of the accumulator.

In addition to these features we will assume that all labels and symbolic addresses may be up to 5 characters long. In other respects the language will be taken to be the same as that defined in 29.14. So, for example LDA 5, INDEX is equivalent in meaning to LDA 5, X shown in 29.14iv.

28. In this example a procedure called "order_and_add" is to take two integers place them in ascending order, and calculate their total. The procedure takes the following form.

```
Procedure order_and_add (IN-OUT first, secon : integer
                          OUT total          integer)

  (* This procedure places first and secon in ascending order and calculates their
     total.
  *)
  Variables
      temp : integer
  Begin
      if
          first > secon
      then
          (* swap first and secon *)
          temp : = first
          first : = secon
          secon : = temp
      endif
      (* calculate total *)
      total : = first + secon
  end
```

29. The part of the main program which deals with calling the procedure and returning from it is shown in the following table.

PART OF THE MAIN ASSEMBLY PROGRAM		COMMENTS
⋮	⋮	
MOVE	STACK INDEX	Save the current base address of the stack in the index register.
PUSH	FIRST	Place the first parameter on the stack (ie first number).
PUSH	SECON	Place the second parameter on the stack (ie. second number).
INC	STACK	Make space on the stack for the third parameter (ie. total).
JSR	OAA	Jump to the subroutine which orders and adds.
POP	TOTAL	Remove the OUT parameter (total) from the stack.
POP	SECON	Remove the IN-OUT parameter (SECON) from the stack.
POP	FIRST	Remove the IN-OUT parameter (FIRST) from the stack.
⋮	⋮	

30. The contents of the stack at critical stages in the execution of the program part just described are given in fig. 29.3.

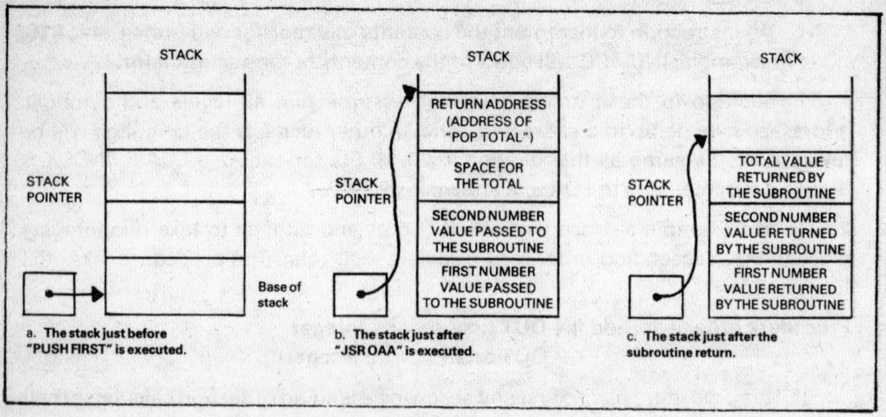

Figure 29.3. Stack contents for subroutine calls and returns.

31. The subroutine is given in the following table.

ASSEMBLY SUBROUTINE			COMMENTS
	PUSH	INDEX	Save the contents of these
	PUSH	ACC	registers on the stack.
	LDA	1,INDEX	Check whether first number is
	SUB	0,INDEX	greater than second.
	JAN	N	Dont swap if numbers are already in order.
	PUSH	0,INDEX	Swap numbers if they
	LDA	1,INDEX	are not in order.
	STA	0,INDEX	See 28.50.
	POP	1,INDEX	
N:	LDA	0,INDEX	Add the two numbers
	ADD	1,INDEX	and store the
	STA	2,INDEX	total.
	POP	ACC	Restore the register
	POP	INDEX	values.
	RTN		Return to the main program.

32. Note the following points about this example:

a. A local variable, corresponding to "TEMP" in the pseudocode, is created on the stack during subroutine execution.

b. The use of the stack base address, held in the index register, which makes it easier to locate variables even though the stack pointer changes.

c. The way the stack base address is used means that this subroutine could be called from within another subroutine, which had already placed items on the stack, and would work in exactly the same way as shown in this example.

33. OPEN and CLOSED Subroutines. These are the two types of subroutine.

a. **OPEN** subroutines are part of the main program and inserted into the program where required.

b. **CLOSED** subroutines are not part of the main program. They are **linked** to the main program by the entry and return procedures outlined in the last four paragraphs. The term **Link** is often used to refer to either the return address or the return instruction from the subroutine.

The example just given was a closed subroutine; an open subroutine is shown here in Fig. 29.4.

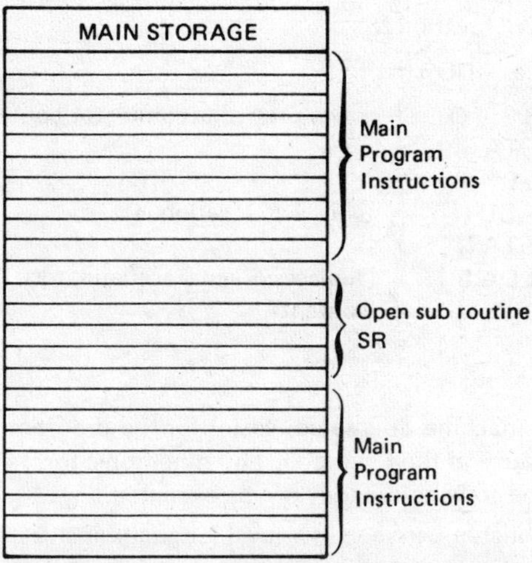

Note The open sub routine really becomes part of the main program.

Fig. 29.4.

34. It should be noted that:–

a. The subroutine has to be in main storage in order to be entered. It must either be loaded along with the main program (if not already in main store) or the main program will be halted while the subroutine is loaded. In the latter case the loading is done automatically by software provided for the purpose. Most frequently the subroutines would be available on disc in such cases.

b. The subroutines may even be written in a different language from the main program.

c. Closed subroutines save main storage space.

MACRO Instructions.

35. Notice that low level languages made program writing easier, but the programmer had still to write out **every** single instruction in source language. A macro instruction is a **single** instruction written as part of the source program language which when assembled will generate **many** machine code instructions. These 'Macros' (some written by the manufacturer, some by the user) are used as a library of open subroutines to perform common tasks such as input/output operations. The Assembler does the job of inserting the instruction for the MACROS into the object program.

Example.

A macro to add 1 to the contents of location N

MACRO INSTRUCTION written as ADD 1(N)

```
ADD 1(N)   generates  { S : Ø    } saves present accumulator contents
                      { STA S    }
                      { LDN 1    }
                      { ADD N    } adds 1 to location N
                      { STA N    }
                      { LDA S    } replaces original accumulator
                                   contents.
```

SUMMARY.

36. a. Low level languages are machine orientated, easier for the programmer than machine language because of their symbolic and mnemonic forms but require translation to machine code before they can be executed.

b. There is a one-one relationship between low level language instructions and machine language instructions, with the exception of macros.

c. It is possible to build the high level program constructs such as control structures and data structures from low level language instructions. One high level instruction may take several low level instructions to implement.

d. When a subroutine is called, parameters have to be set up prior to the call, the return address and contents of registers need to be saved for the return and within the subroutine local variables may be created. The exact mechanisms vary considerably from machine to machine.

e. The two types of subroutine are:

i. Open subroutines: essentially part of the program.

ii. Closed subroutines: linked to the program at various stages in its execution.

POINTS TO NOTE.

37. a. The reader is strongly recommended to gain practical experience of a real assembly language having once gained familiarity with the contents of this chapter.

b. Assembly language instructions may be referred to as "external symbolic machine instructions".

STUDENT SELF TEST QUESTIONS.

(Answers on page 728)

1. Described the action of the following instruction.
   a. SUN 7
   b. ADD @ 7
   c. ADD 7
   d. SUB 7,X
2. Distinguish between low level languages and machine language.
3. Define the terms
   a. assembler program
   b. assembly language
   c. assembly process
4. Given that the ASCII value of "*" is 52_8 and that
   a. LDN 52
      IO 2
   will cause the output of a "*"
   b. LDA CR
      IO 2
      LDA LF
      IO 2
   will terminate the current line of output and prepare the printer for the next line.

   Write a program in assembly language to output a triangle of asterisks thus:

   ```
   *
   **
   ***
   ****
   ```
5. a. Using the mnemonic code given below, write sections of code to add together the contents of 50 locations, starting at location 100, storing the sum in location 99, using:
      i. indirect addressing,
      ii. address modification.

   b. A subroutine is stored from location 500 onwards; location 499 is reserved for the return address. Give:
      i. instructions to enter the routine from location 200,

ii. two alternative instructions for exit from the routine, one using address modification, the other using indirect addressing.

Mnemonic code

A single address sequential machine with one accumulator interprets instructions as follows:

LA	*n/m*	*Copy contents of location n + (m) into cleared accumulator*
LN	*n/m*	*Load integer N + (m) into cleared accumulator*
ST	*n/m*	*Store contents of accumulator in location n + (m)*
AD	*n/m*	*Add contents of location n + (m) to contents of accumulator.*
AN	*n/m*	*Add integer n + (m) to contents of accumulator*
SB	*n/m*	*Subtract contents of location n + (m) from contents of accumulator*
SN	*n/m*	*Subtract integer n + (m) from contents of accumulator*
JG	*n/m*	*Jump to location n + (m) if contents of accumulator are greater than zero*
JZ	*n/m*	*Jump to location n + (m) if contents of accumulator are equal to zero.*
JM	*n/m*	*Jump to location n + (m) unconditionally.*
ILA	*n/m*	
IST	*n/m*	
IAD	*n/m*	
ISB	*n/m*	*As above, but with address n taken to be indirect*
IJG	*n/m*	
IJZ	*n/m*	
IJM	*n/m*	

Notes: *(m) = contents of m. Where address modification is not required /m is omitted from the format.*

(AEB 1976)

QUESTIONS WITHOUT ANSWERS.

6. Rewrite your answer to question 4 as a subroutine where the vertical height is passed as a parameter.

7. Write a subroutine which takes three IN parameter values, arranges them into ascending numerical sequence and returns them together with their total.

30 High Level Languages

INTRODUCTION.

1. This chapter explains why high level languages have been developed. It describes both the general features of high level languages and the particular features of a cross section of high level languages in use today.

THE DEVELOPMENT OF HIGH LEVEL LANGUAGES.

2. The development of high level languages was intended to overcome the main limitations of low level languages which are:—

a. Program writing is a relatively time consuming business for the programmer because the assembly process produces machine instructions on a ONE for ONE basis.

b. Low level languages are **machine orientated,** each conforming to the instruction set of the machine on which they are used and therefore restricted to use on that machine.

3. High level languages are intended to be machine independent and are problem orientated languages (POLS) ie they reflect the type of problem solved rather than the features of the machine. Source programs are written in statements akin to English, a great advance over mnemonics.

4. The first high level language to be released was FORTRAN (FORmula TRANslation) in 1957. Over the next few years many other high level languages appeared and established themselves. In fact, new high level languages have been coming into existence ever since. Most, but not all, have disappeared into obscurity.

5. The machine independence of high level languages means that in principle it should be possible to make the same high level language run on different machines and then write programs in that language which are portable. Such portability has a number of advantages:

a. A user of a program can change to a newer or bigger computer without the need to rewrite programs.

b. Users of different computers may be able to share or exchange programs and thereby reduce costs.

c. An organisation producing software for sale can sell the same program to users of different computers without the need to rewrite the program for each type of computer. Again, this reduces costs.

6. In practice, there are a number of obstacles to such portability. Perhaps the most serious obstacles are those resulting from variations which occur between different versions of each language. Each different *dialect* is usually the deliberate creation of a computer manufacture who will try to attract new customers with a "better" product and who will then keep existing customers because their programs will no longer be portable to the computers of other manufacturers.

7. Despite these seemingly unavoidable variations which have proliferated over time, the development of high level languages has been accompanied by many successful moves to standardise high level languages and the ways they are defined.

8. Standardisation is organised on an international basis. The international body is the **ISO** (International Standards Organisation). Member countries have their own representative bodies on the ISO committees. For example, in Britain the representative body is the **BSI** (British Standards Institution) and in the USA it is **ANSI** (American National Standards Institution). The standardisation of high level languages has often been carried out in the USA. Subsequently the ANSI standard has become the ISO standard. Britain has produced some standards too, notably the standard for the language **Pascal.**

9. Every few years new versions of high level languages appear in the form of new standards. For example, COBOL '68, COBOL '71 and COBOL '8x are versions of COBOL based on ANSI standards for those years.

GENERAL FEATURES OF HIGH LEVEL LANGUAGES.

10. a. They have an extensive vocabulary of words, symbols and sentences.

b. Programs are written in the language and whole statements are translated into **many** (sometimes hundreds) of machine instructions. This translation is often done by a special program called a **compiler** which is described in chapter 32.

c. Libraries of macros and subroutines can be incorporated.

d. As they are **problem orientated** the programmer is able to work at least to some extent independently of the machine.

e. A set of rules must be obeyed when writing the source program (akin to rules of grammar in writing English if you like).

f. Instructions in high level languages are usually called **statements.**

TYPES OF HIGH LEVEL LANGUAGES.

11. Types of High Level language.
Five main types are:–

a. Commercial languages.

b. Scientific languages.

c. Special purpose languages.

d. Command languages for operating systems.

e. Multipurpose languages.

COMMERCIAL LANGUAGES.

12. The most well known commercial language is COBOL (Common Business Oriented Language). It is the most widely used Commercial and Business language and the fact that something like 80% of all computer usage is of this type reflects its importance.

13. COBOL was devised by an independent committee called **CODASYL** (Committee on Data Systems Languages) in 1959. CODASYL intended that any program written in COBOL would be compiled and within reason, run on any computer. This has not worked out in practice, however, for reasons discussed earlier in paragraphs 5 to 9.

14. There are many other high level languages used for commercial computing, full **BASIC** and **UCSD-Pascal** are often used on small computers for example, but COBOL will be discussed further here because it is still the major commercial language.

FEATURES OF COBOL.

15. The main features of COBOL and other Business languages are:–

a. Extensive file handling facilities such as the naming, movement and processing of files, records, fields, etc.

b. Close resemblance to English in terms of incorporating common English terms in sentence-like forms and avoiding mathematical notation.

c. Suited to structuring and handling layouts of tabulated outputs, reports, special forms etc.

16. Each COBOL program is written in what appears to be a stylised but mostly readable form of English. Every COBOL program consists of *four divisions.*

a. **Identification division.** This contains the title of the program for identification purposes. It may also contain the date on which the program was written and the name of the author.

b. **Environment division.** Specifies the particular configuration (hardware) on which the object program will be compiled and executed eg. Model of machine (IBM 4341), internal storage size needed for running the object program, peripheral units etc.

c. **Data division.** All items of data to be used in writing the program are listed and identified. Names or labels are given for each *file* and any *records* or *fields* which are referred to later. Record/field *sizes* and *contents* (eg. whether alpha or numeric) are also specified. Working storage areas are defined.

d. **Procedure division.** Contains the program instructions necessary to solve the particular problem indicated in pseudocode. These are to be in the form of statements written in a type of English and which conform to the rules of the language. (Cobol language). The statements written must use the data labels as defined in divisions 2 and 3. The compiler will report any inconsistencies. Also used are RESERVED WORDS which can only be used in a specific context because they convey a special meaning to the compiler. (Misuse of these words is reported by the compiler).

17. COBOL examples are given here:

a. **Illustration of reserved words.**
"ADD TAX TO GRADPENS".
ADD . . . . . . TO are reserved words indicating to the compiler that two items of data must be added together.

"TAX" and "GRADPENS" are labels (identifiers) of two items of data defined in the Data Division.

b. **Examples of COBOL Statements.**

(The statements are in block capitals; explanatory notes in small letters).

i. **Peripheral Instructions.**

OPEN INPUT-PAY-FILE. (prepares a file for processing)

READ PAY-FILE AT END MOVE "EOF" TO FILE-STATE (Reads a record from a file into memory).

WRITE PAY-LINE AFTER ADVANCING ONE LINE. (print after throwing paper up by oneline.)

ii. **Arithmetic Instructions.**

MULTIPLY HOURS BY RATE GIVING BASICPAY.

ADD BONUS TO BASIC PAY GIVING GROSSPAY.

SUBTRACT INCTAX FROM GROSSPAY GIVING NETPAY.

iii. **Branch Instructions.**

GO TO PENSION-RTN. (unconditional branch)

IF GROSS-PAY GREATER THAN 100 GO TO EXCEPTION-RTN. (conditional branch).

iv. **Control Structures** (other than the unstructured forms just given).

```
IF GROSS-PAY GREATER THAN 100
   PERFORM HIGH-PAY
ELSE
   PERFORM LOW-PAY
```

(A **selection** between two paragraphs to be performed)

PERFORM READ-FILE UNTIL END-OF-FILE.

(A simple loop structure)

v. **Data Handling Instruction.**

MOVE DEDUCTIONS TO DATAC. (transfers a field to working store).

SCIENTIFIC LANGUAGES.

18. The first scientific language was **FORTRAN** (paragraph 4). The first standard for FORTRAN was established in 1966 but that standard has since been replaced by the 1977 standard. FORTRAN is still widely used for engineering applications and scientific use.

19. An early competitor with FORTRAN was **ALGOL** (**ALG**orithmic **O**riented **L**anguage). ALGOL was devised by a working group of **IFIP** (International Federation for Information Processing) in 1960 and the language definition was published in a report that year. The report was particularly significant in that for the first time the syntax of a language was defined formally, using a notation called BNF. BNF will be discussed in chapter 33.

20. Later forms of ALGOL, notably **ALGOL 68,** were so much more extensive that they are probably better regarded as different languages.

21. A third language which deserves an explicit mention here is BASIC (**B**eginners **A**llpurpose **S**ymbolic **I**nstruction **C**ode). BASIC was created in 1964 by J. G. Kemeny and T. E. Kurtz at Dartmouth College USA. The language was originally designed as a simplified version of FORTRAN for use in teaching programming.

22. Early versions of BASIC, and sadly many versions in use on small computers today, deserve strong criticism for features which encourage bad programming methods. However, some newer versions such as the product "True BASIC", devised by T. E. Kurtz and based upon the latest ANSI standard, are very significantly better.

23. It is expected that the reader will use a language such as **BASIC** or **Pascal** as part of the practical coursework and will thereby gain experience of the features found in a scientific language. **Pascal** will be discussed later, under a separate heading, but has many similarities with ALGOL.

24. General Features of Scientific languages are:

a. Extensive arithmetic computational ability.

b. Large library of inbuilt mathematical function.

c. Ability to handle mathematical expressions and procedures.

d. Array handling facilities.

SPECIAL PURPOSE LANGUAGES.

25. These are languages intended to be 'tailor made' for a particular type of problem, eg. Machine Control, Wages, Simulation, Control of Experiments. Examples are:

a. **C.S.L.** which is a Simulation language.

b. **Coral-66** which is used for real-time applications such as process control, ie. the direct control of physical processes, eg. experiments.

c. **RTL/2** also used for real-time application.

d. **Ada** a relatively new language used for real-time and possibly general purpose application. Ada will probably replace Coral-66.

e. **Modula** and **Modula-2**. This is a compact language, almost an extended form of **Pascal** (see later). It allows object oriented programming methods (as does Ada) and is suitable for real-time applications.

f. **QUEL** (**QUE**ry **L**anguage) and **QBE** (**Q**uery **B**y **E**xample) are examples of database query languages. Further discussion will be given in chapter 37.

g. Some languages are special purpose in that they adopt radically different approaches to programming. Examples will be discussed later in the chapter. Such languages include **LISP** (a list processing language), **SNOBOL** (a string processing language) and **PROLOG** (**Pro**grammed **Log**ic).

COMMAND LANGUAGES FOR OPERATING SYSTEMS.

26. These are languages used to control the operation of the computer. The required facilities will be apparent after you have read chapter 39.

MULTIPURPOSE LANGUAGES.

27. Example: International Business Machines (IBM) introduced the language PL/1 which it claimed can cope with business **and** scientific use. "Pascal" is a somewhat different example. It was originally intended as a language for teaching programming. It is now widely used for a variety of applications, particularly on small computers.

LANGUAGE FEATURES.

28. Common features upon which comparisons between languages may be made are:

a. **Control Structures.** Pascal and PL/1 are languages rich in control structures eg. Pascal has WHILE, REPEAT . . UNTIL and FOR loops. IF . . THEN . . ELSE and CASE statements and allows the nesting of control structures. Minimal BASICs have very limited control structures. Full ANSI BASIC competes favourably with Pascal and PL/1 in terms of control structures.

b. **Data Structures and Files.** Pascal and PL/1 provide a variety of data types and structures. Pascal allows more complex types of structures to be built from simpler ones. COBOL has a variety of basic data types, provides a wide variety of file types and also has facilities for dealing with databases. Again BASIC varies greatly according to the level of implementation.

c. **Computations.** FORTRAN, ALGOL, Pascal and BASIC provide facilities for mathematical expressions and functions. Computations in COBOL may be expressed in mathematical form but are more usually expressed in an English like form (see para. 17bii).

d. **Procedures and Subprograms.** Pascal, FORTRAN and ALGOL have facilities for handling procedures and subprograms. Comparable features in minimal or small implementations of BASIC are almost **non existent.** COBOL has facilities which give a flexible combination of procedure calls and control structures.

29. There are many other features which could be discussed eg. facilities to deal with controlling the format of data being input or output but the reader should by now have some feel for the ways in which features may be compared.

OTHER FORMS OF HIGH LEVEL LANGUAGE.

30. The high level languages so far described in this chapter may be described as **procedural languages** in that they provide facilities for the programmer to express procedures or algorithms. Procedural languages necessarily require a style of programming in which the programmer must express **how** computations are to be carried out, ie. what to do and in which order. This is known as an **imperative style** of programming and these languages are also known as **imperative languages.**

31. There are alternatives to imperative languages which employ an **assertional method** of programming in which the programmer expresses (asserts) **what** is required in a calculation rather than how it is done.

32. The ideas of assertional programming are much simpler than they first sound. For example, if you require the square root of the number 'x' **what** you require is 'y' such that $y^2 = x$ and this is easy to express compared with how to find y.

33. Clearly, sooner or later the "what" must be translated into a "how" and so we may regard assertional languages as being at a higher level than imperative high level languages.

34. There are two basic approaches to assertional programming

a. **Logic Programming** for which one popular language is **Prolog.**

b. **Functional Programming** for which one popular language is **LISP.**

35. The current state of Computer Science is such that, although the properties of assertional languages are seen to be of possibly great importance in the future, the current forms of assertional languages are too restricted and inefficient to deal with many practical problems currently handled by procedural languages.

PROLOG

36. PROLOG deals with "objects" and "relationships" between them. The three main ways in which it does so are: declaring facts, asking questions and defining rules. Facts about what people will eat may be expressed in PROLOG thus

```
eats (fred, chips).
eats (john, fish).
eats (bruce, caviar).
. . . . etc . . . .
```

Having keyed in these statements we may pose the question "will fred eat chips?" by keying in

```
? – eats (fred, chips).
```

PROLOG will respond with the answer "yes".

LISP

37. LISP was devised around 1960 at Massachusetts Institute of Technology by J. McCarthy. This was some 10 years before the arrival of PROLOG. It also shows how long it is taking for functional languages to get established for general applications.

38. There are many versions of LISP. A typical LISP program operates upon items of data in *symbolic* form referred to as S-expressions (S for symbolic). The program is expressed in terms of procedures which operate upon S-expressions and which are called M-expressions (M for Metalanguage).

39. Further discussion is not merited in a book at this level.

SUMMARY.

40. a. The development of high level languages was discussed starting with the release of FORTRAN in 1957.

b. High level languages are problem oriented, rather than machine oriented, and are intended to be largely machine independent.

c. Types of high level languages are:

i. Commercial languages, eg. COBOL.

ii. Scientific languages, eg. FORTRAN.

iii. Special Purpose languages, eg. CSL, Ada, QUEL,

iv. Command languages for operating systems.

v. Multipurpose languages, eg. PL/1, full ANSI BASIC.

POINTS TO NOTE.

41. a. The choice of programming language in a particular situation may be severely restricted both by the availability of languages for the particular machine which is to be used and by the expertise of the staff whose responsibility it will be to write the programs.

b. High level languages are altered as time goes by in order to respond to changes in technology or new knowledge about the subject.

STUDENT SELF TEST QUESTIONS.

(Answers on page 732)

1. What are the advantages and disadvantages of high level languages?

2. What advantages can be obtained from high level language program portability? What are the practical obstacles to such portability?

3. Two friends have each purchased home microcomputers. The computers are of different makes but are both claimed to provide the BASIC language.

The friends find that they are unable to use one anothers programs despite the fact that all programs are written in BASIC. Explain this state of affairs and suggest what could be done to help this particular problem and what measures can be taken in general to prevent such situations arising.

QUESTIONS WITHOUT ANSWERS.

4. Critically describe the language(s) which you use as part of your practical coursework.

5. a. Name one general purpose high level language, and discuss its suitability for each of the following:

i. scientific programming,

ii. commercial programming. *(10 marks)*

b. Give a typical sequence of assembly language instructions which would execute a loop. *(5 marks)*

c. State, with reasons, one application where an assembly language would be more suitable than a high level language. *(5 marks)*

(AEB 1980)

Further Data Structures

1. This Part continues with the topics introduced in chapter 12 but also uses the methods described in the programming Part. You may find it useful to re-read chapter 12 before you continue.

31 Queues, Stacks, Further Trees and Tables

INTRODUCTION.

1. This chapter introduces data structure called STACKS and QUEUES and also shows further methods of using TREES. The problems associated with trying to find data elements quickly and easily are examined. That leads into a broadening of the discussion on ACCESS TABLES (12.36).

QUEUES.

2. Consider this example. It is a common occurrence for a computer to create data for output at a speed which cannot be matched by the output device for which the data is intended. When this happens the data may be placed in a "buffer area" (7.4) of main storage, where it takes its place in a **queue,** and waits its turn to be output. **Queues** have many uses but remember this example as we now define a queue more precisely. The technical meaning of 'queue' is not quite its everyday meaning.

3. Features of a queue. Data is added to the 'end' of a queue but is removed from the 'front'. The term "FIFO" is used to describe queues because the First datum In is the First datum Out. Data in what we call a **queue** is *not* moved along like people in a cinema queue. Instead, each datum stays in its storage location until its turn comes, thereby reducing time spent in data movement. The use of pointers makes this possible.

4. Example.

NEXT REMOVAL POINTER	101

NEXT ENTRY POINTER	106

LOCATION ADDRESS	101	102	103	104	105	106	107	108	109	110
CONTENTS	20	4	19	12	16					
ORDER OF ARRIVAL AND REMOVAL	1	2	3	4	5					

5. Overflow and Underflow.

a. **Overflow** occurs when an attempt is made to add data to a queue when all available locations are occupied.

b. **Underflow** occurs when an attempt is made to remove data from an empty queue.

6. Example of queue handling. Assume locations 101 to 110 are available to store a queue with each location storing just one number. Assume that two procedures called "place" and "fetch" are available as follows:

procedure place (**IN** pointer, number : **integer**)
    (* This procedure places number in the memory location whose address value is pointer.
    *)

procedure fetch (**IN** pointer : **integer**
        OUT number : **integer**)
    (* This procedure fetches number from the memory location whose address value is pointer.
    *)

The methods for entering and removing numbers from the queue are outlined in the pseudocode in Figure 31.1. You should note that the boolean variable called overflow is set to true if overflow is attempted. Assume that initially entry-pointer = 101 and removal-pointer = 100. In this example locations at the front of the queue are not reused once they become empty. Instead, the process is restarted once the whole queue is empty.

```
(* Entering a number *)
(* outline method *)
variables
    entry-pointer,
    removal-pointer,
    number              : integer
    overflow            : boolean
Begin
  (* assume previous initialisation *)
  if
    entry_pointer = 111
  then
    overflow : = true
  else
    (* place number in location given
      by entry_pointer *)
    call place (entry-pointer, number)
    (* update pointers *)
    entry-pointer : = entry_pointer + 1
    if
      removal_pointer = 100
    then
      removal-pointer : = 101
    endif
  endif
end

a.
```

```
(* Removing a number *)
(* outline method *)
variables
    entry-pointer,
    removal-pointer,
    number              : integer
    underflow :         : boolean
Begin
  (* assume previous initialisation *)
  if
    removal_pointer = 100
  then
    underflow : = true
  else
    (* fetch number from location given
      by removal_pointer *)
    call fetch (removal-pointer, number)
      if
        (* queue is now empty *)
        removal_pointer = 110
        OR
        entry_pointer = removal_pointer + 1
      then
        (* reset the queue for reuse *)
        removal-pointer : = 100
        entry_pointer : = 101
      else
        (* update removal_pointer *)
        removal_pointer : = removal_pointer + 1
      endif
    endif
end

b.
```

Figure 31.1. Queue Handling Example.

NB. Use this pseudocode to create and then remove the data given in paragraph 4.

7. The reader should be able to see ways in which to adapt the methods of Fig. 31.1 into two procedures called "enter" and "remove" say. Let us pursue the idea a stage further and see what other functions or procedures should be considered:

a. There is a need for a function which initialises the queue to an empty state. The same function could possibly also be used subsequently to reset the queue so let us call the function "clear".

b. The methods described in Fig. 31.1 deal with attempts to either enter data to a full queue or to remove data from an empty queue. Provision of boolean function called "q-is-full" and "q-is-empty" would help to avoid such a mistake.

8. Some programming languages allow sets of functions and procedures associated with a data structure such as a queue to be grouped together into a single programming unit called a **module** or **package.**

9. The user of a queue module might have the following simple functions and procedures provided by the module:

a. **Procedure** clear.
A parameterless procedure which sets the state of the queue to empty.

b. **function** q-is-empty: **boolean**
A parameterless function which returns **true** when the queue is empty and returns **false** otherwise.

c. **function** q-is-full: **boolean**
A parameterless function which returns **true** when the queue is full and returns **false** otherwise.

d. **Procedure** enter (**IN** number)
This procedure places a number on the end of the queue. If the queue is full the procedure has no effect.

d. **Procedure** remove (**OUT** number)
This procedure removes a number from the head of the queue and returns it. If the queue is empty an undefined value is returned.

10. When entering and removing data these functions need to be used in conjunction with one another, eg.

a. To add a number

```
if
  q-is-full
then
  output ("Queue is full")
else
  enter (number)
endif
```

b. **if**
  q-is-empty
then
  output ("No data in queue")
else
  remove (number)
  output ("next value is", number)
endif

11. Note the following points which arise from these examples

a. A data structure describe in terms of the operations performed upon it, as the queue was in paragraph 9, may be called an **abstract data type.**

b. The functions in paragraph 9 do not pass either the stored form of the queue or its pointers because they are already contained within the module and are **global** to all functions and procedures within the package. They are **local** to the module, however, which is why this method of representing and handling data structures is sometimes called **information hiding.**

NB. In functional decomposition these data items would be passed as parameters.

12. The use of abstract data types (information hiding) is important in advanced programming but further discussion of such methods are beyond the scope of this text.

13. Queue organisation in Lists. Queues may be stored in the form of Lists (12.47) A list used to store a queue is called a **Push Up List.**

Example.

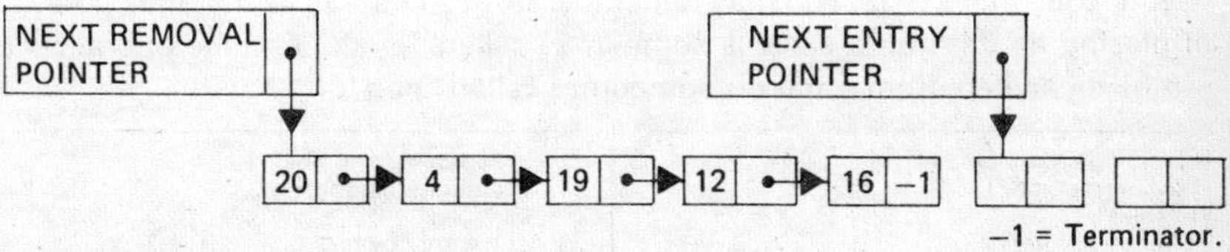

STACKS.

14. Stacks are frequently used for temporary storage but in a different way from queues. A **stack** differs from a queue in the method of data addition and removal. Data is added to the 'top' of a stack and is also removed from the 'top'. The **L**ast datum **I**n is the **F**irst datum **O**ut (LIFO). Compare this with a pack of cards on a table for which cards are either added or removed from the top.

NB. Examples of stacks at machine level were given in 28.45 and 29.30.

15. a. **Example.**

NEXT REMOVAL POINTER			NEXT ENTRY POINTER	Or use Removal Pointer + 1
	105	106		

LOCATION ADDRESS	101	102	103	104	105	106	107	108	109	110
CONTENTS	20	4	19	12	16					
ORDER OF ARRIVAL	1	2	3	4	5					
ORDER OF REMOVAL	5	4	3	2	1					

Note. The stack provides the facility to *retrace* the steps of data insertion.

b. **Example of Use.** One common application of stacks is for storing return addresses (link values) for closed subroutines (29.30). When entering a subroutine, the return address is placed on top of the stack. Should a second subroutine be entered from the first, then the return address will again be placed on the stack. When the time comes to return from the second subroutine to the first, the correct return address will be on top of the stack. The return address will be removed revealing the return address to the main program. The same method can be applied when many subroutines are 'nested' in this manner and proves useful in other applications discussed later.

16. Example of stack handling. (We make the same assumptions made in paragraph 6 except that locations will be reused if they become vacant). The methods for entering and removing numbers from the stack are outlined in pseudocode in fig. 31.2. You may remember from 28.46 – 28.47 that the operation of placing an item on a stack is sometimes called **"push"** and the operation of removing an item from a stack is sometimes called **"pop"**.

```
(* Entering a number *)
(* outline method *)
variables
    entry-pointer,
    removal-pointer,
    number              : integer
    overflow            : boolean
Begin
  (* assume previous initialisation *)
  if
    entry_pointer = 111
  then
    overflow : = true
  else
    (* place number in location given
       by entry_pointer *)
    call place (entry-pointer, number)
    (* update pointers *)
    removal-pointer : = entry_pointer
    entry_pointer : = entry_pointer + 1
  endif
end
a.
```

```
(* Removing a number *)
(* outline method *)
variables
    entry-pointer,
    removal-pointer,
    number              : integer
    underflow           : boolean
Begin
  (* assume previous initialisation *)
  if
    removal_pointer = 101
  then
    underflow : = true
  else
    (* fetch number from location given
       by removal_pointer *)
    call fetch (removal-pointer, number)
    (* update pointers *)
    entry-pointer : = removal_pointer
    removal_pointer : = removal _pointer – 1
  endif
end
b.
```

Figure 31.2. Stack Handling Example.

NB. Use this pseudocode to create and then remove the data given in paragraph 15.

17. As for the queue, the stack may also be described in terms of the operations which may be performed upon it. There are numerous ways in which this may be done. Typical functions are:

a. A **clear** procedure analagous to that described for the queue.

b. Functions called "stack-is-empty" and "stack-is-full", also analagous to those for the queue.

c. A **push** procedure eg. **procedure** push (**IN** number), to insert numbers on to the top of a non-full stack.

d. A **pop** procedure. The pop procedure, which involve removing the top items from the stack, is sometimes split into two operations:

i. **pop** which merely deletes the top item from the stack,

and ii. **top** which returns the top item from the stack without deleting it.

18. Stack organisation in Lists. Lists used to store stacks are called **Push Down Lists.**

Example. (Note the use of 'backward' pointers rather than 'forward' pointers).

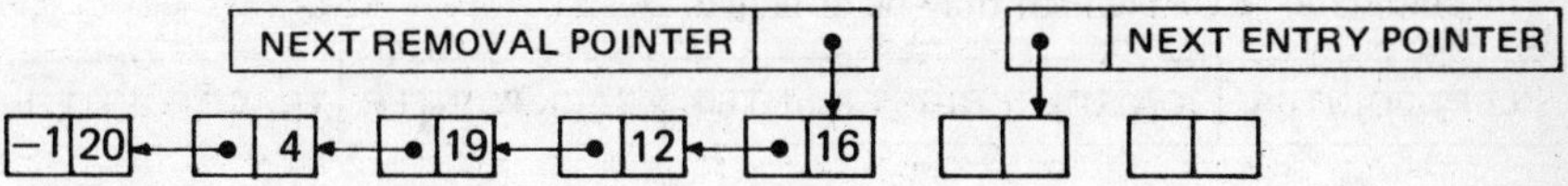

–1 = Terminator.

TREES CONTINUED.

19. You may first wish to re-read (12.56 – 12.59) in which TREES were introduced and constructed.

20. Deletions from a TREE. We will use this TREE as an example.

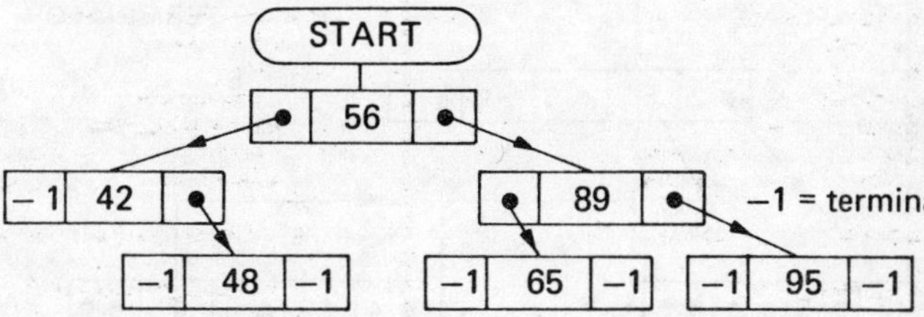

a. **Method**

Case (i) **Deletion of a terminal node** eg 48. Replace the pointer to the node by a terminator.

Case (ii) **Deletions within the TREE** eg 89. Change the *rightmost node* of the *lefthand subtree* below the node to be deleted. (If there is no lefthand subtree change the first righthand node below the node to be deleted).

b. **Example.** (48 has been deleted as in case (i) and 89 has been deleted as in case (ii).

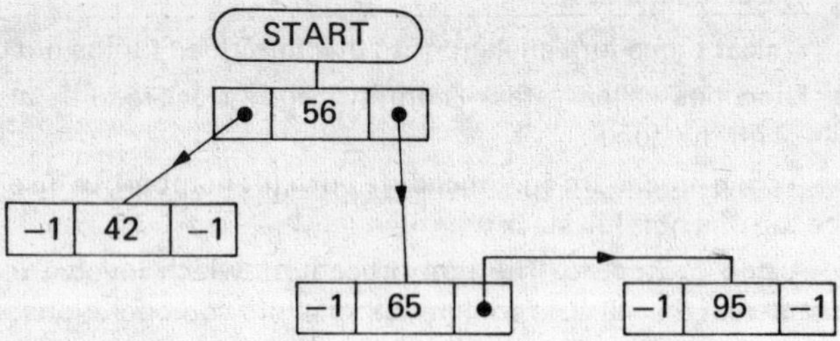

21. Other TREE Pointers.

These pointers are often used as part of the TREE elements:–

a. **Back pointers,** which give the position of the parent of each node.

b. **Trace pointers,** which point to the next node in numerical order for each node. This allows data to be read in sequence.

The complete TREE element may be arranged thus:–

LEFT POINTER	DATUM	RIGHT POINTER	BACK POINTER	TRACE POINTER

Each extra pointer uses more storage space so they should only be included when they are needed.

22. Example. (Pointers are arranged as just indicated).

a. **Flowchart.**

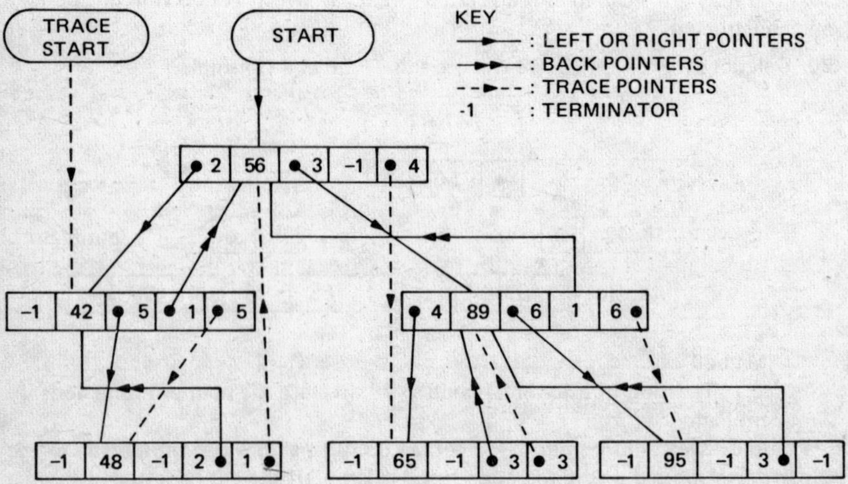

b. Possible Array Representation

START POINTER	1

START TRACE POINTER	2

ORDER OF ENTRY INTO THE TREE	LEFT POINTER	DATUM	RIGHT POINTER	BACK POINTER	TRACE POINTER
1	A(1, 1) = 2	A(1, 2) = 56	A(1, 3) = 3	A(1, 4) = –1	A(1, 5) = 4
2	A(2, 1) = –1	A(2, 2) = 42	A(2, 3) = 5	A(2, 4) = 1	A(2, 5) = 5
3	A(3, 1) = 4	A(3, 2) = 89	A(3, 3) = 6	A(3, 4) = 1	A(3, 5) = 6
4	A(4, 1) = –1	A(4, 2) = 65	A(4, 3) = –1	A(4, 4) = 3	A(4, 5) = 3
5	A(5, 1) = –1	A(5, 2) = 48	A(5, 3) = –1	A(5, 4) = 2	A(5, 5) = 1
6	A(6, 1) = –1	A(6, 2) = 95	A(6, 3) = –1	A(6, 4) = 3	A(6, 5) = –1

NB. If elements were of different data types an array of records would be used.

23. Using stacks instead of trace pointers. This method can be used if trace pointers have not been provided. If traces are only occasionally needed this may be the best way of providing trace facilities. In this example we use the TREE given in paragraph 22.

Procedure.

a. Find the **leftmost node** placing old pointers on the stack as you go. When we reach '42' the stack looks like this:–

1					

(The first number '42' is read).

b. If there is a **righthand pointer** to the node then enter the righthand subtree and repeat step a. in the subtree. When we reach '48' the stack looks like this:–

1	2				

(The second number '48' is read).

c. If you reach a terminal node, remove the top pointer on the stack and use it. Continue with step b. Stack:–

1	4				

(the fourth number '65' is read).

When the stack is empty **and** there are no more righthand subtrees the trace is completed. Try to use the method to complete the trace.

SEARCH AND ACCESS.

24. Search Time and Search Length. (When accessing data).
An important characteristic of a data structure is its search time. The **search time** is the **average time** taken to find a datum in the structure. It is often expressed in terms of the **search length** which is the average number of elements examined in order to find a datum.

In situations where data items are required individually the data structure with the shortest **search length** will be prefereable, since it will save CPU time and thereby increase efficiency.

25. The Linear Search. (The simplest and most common type of search).
To perform a **linear search** the data is examined one element at a time in physical order until the required datum is found. (See 12.26 for the method).

Example.

a. Suppose we had a table with 5 entries. The 5 possible search lengths are 1, 2, 3, 4, 5 eg to find the third entry takes 3 examinations. The average search length will be

$$\frac{1+2+3+4+5}{5} = 3$$

b. For a table with N entries the average search length would be:

$$\frac{1+2+3+4+\ldots\ldots\ldots+(N-1)+N}{N}$$

This sum can be simplified if we notice that writing the series backwards we can add it twice easily:–

Add columns	1	+ 2	+ 3	+ 4	+ .. + (N–1)	+ N
	N	+ (N–1)	+ (N–2)	+ (N–3) + .. +	2	+ 1
	(N+1)	+ (N+1)	† (N+1)	+ (N+1) + ..	+ (N+1)	+ (N+1)

There are N terms.

So **twice** the sum 1 + 2 + 3 . . . . .+ N is N(N + 1)

$$\text{so average search length} = \frac{N(N+1)}{2N} = \frac{(N+1)}{2}$$

A linear search can be performed on all the data structures described so far. (Structures like TREES are constructed so as to reduce search length).

26. Search length for a binary TREE. For a well balanced tree the search length is approximately $\log_2$ N, where N is the number of elements in the tree. (eg If N = 32 the search length is 5, because $2^5 = 32$ or $\log_2 32 = 5$.)

To justify the use of this formula we can see that:–

If we had two (2^1) nodes we would find the datum after one examination. If we had four (2^2) nodes we would find the datum after 2 examinations. If we had eight (2^3) nodes we would find the datum after 3 examinations, etc.

27. Binary Search. A sorted array can be searched in a way analagous to the method used for searching a binary tree called a binary search. In a binary search the value in the middle of the array is examined to see if it is equal to the value being searched for. If the searched for value is not equal to the middle value then the process is repeated with either the first half of the array or the second half of the array according to whether the middle value is larger or smaller than the searched for value. (If the middle value is too small, for example, there is clearly no point in searching the first half of the array when those values are even smaller than the middle value). The process is repeated with smaller and smaller subdivisions of the array until either the value is found or there are no more subdivisions to make. A procedure for performing a binary search is given in fig. 31.3. The method should be compared with that given for the linear search in Fig. 12.8. Note that the function called int(x) returns the largest integer less than or equal to x.

NB. The binary search has a search length of $\log_2$ N.

```
Procedure search_array ( IN  number_of_elements, search_value : integer
                             search_array : array [1 . . 100] of integer
                         OUT subscript : integer
                             found : boolean )
  (* This procedure performs a binary search through the search_array for the
     search_value. If it finds the search_value it returns found = true and the
     subscript of the found value. Otherwise, it returns found = false and the
     subscript value last checked.
  *)
  variables
     high,                     (* high and low designate the *)
     low : integer             (* range of subscripts still *)
                               (* to be searched. *)
     search_failed : boolean
```

```
Begin
  (* initialise variables *)
  found : = false
  search_failed : = false
  high : = number_of_elements
  low : = 1
  repeat
    (* get a subscript mid way between low and high *)
    subscript : = int ( (high + low) /2)
    if
      search_value = search_array (subscript)
    then
      found : = true
    else
      if
        (* at last stage in search *)
        subscript = low
      then
        if
          search_value = search_array (high)
        then
          found : = true
        else
          search_failed : = true
        endif
      else (* still searching *)
        (* reduce range of search *)
        if
          search_value > search_array(low)
        then
          low : = subscript
        else
          high : = subscript
        endif
      endif
    endif
  until found OR search_failed
end
```

Figure 31.3. A Procedure for Performing a Binary Search.

28. Many attempts to reduce search times are based upon the use of tables such as the ACCESS TABLE (12.36). Various types of table used to improve the access by reducing search time are described in the following paragraphs.

TABLES AND THEIR USES.

29. Keys. Accessing most tables described in this section involves using **Keys.** A Key is a data item which is associated with the data and which can be used to locate or identify other data. It may form part of the data to be located, or it may be quite separate. A subscript of an array may be thought of as a Key of this second type.

30. To illustrate the various types of table we will take as an example some data which is the telephone numbers of various people. You may think of the telephone number as the data item to be accessed and the persons name as a key to that number.

NAME (KEY)	TELEPHONE NUMBER (DATUM)
ALEX	3012
CHARLOTTE	7641
EMMA	5962
JAMES	4243
KATY	2126
LUCY	3562

31. LOOK-UP Tables. (Types of access table used independently or in conjunction with other data structures).

a. Suppose that each location in main memory can store *4 characters.* The telephone numbers can be stored like this for example.

LOCATION ADDRESS	101	102	103	104	105	106
CONTENTS	3012	7641	5962	4243	2126	3562

b. Given a name "CHARLOTTE" say we may want to find the corresponding telephone number. The Key "CHARLOTTE" is too long to fit into one location in this case, but using just the first four letters may do just as well, and that is what we use in this example. (eg here we use CHAR).

c. This is the LOOK-UP TABLE:

KEY	ADDRESS OF CORRESPONDING DATA
ALEX	0101
CHAR	0102
EMMA	0103
JAME	0104
KATY	0105
LUCY	0106

N.B. In this simplified example the 4 character data could occupy the space given to its 4 character address thus removing the need for the LOOK-UP TABLE! *In general the data may occupy several successive locations, the first of which is specified in the LOOK-UP TABLE.*

d. This is how the LOOK-UP TABLE could be stored:–

LOCATION ADDRESS	81	82	83	84	85	86	87	88	89	90	91	92
CONTENTS	ALEX	0101	CHAR	0102	EMMA	0103	JAME	0104	KATY	0105	LUCY	0106

e. To find the required datum we perform a **linear search** in the Look-Up table for the datum's key and thereby find the address of the datum.

32. DIRECT ACCESS Tables. Any datum in a DIRECT ACCESS TABLE can be accessed directly ie *without a search.* This is achieved by using a *mapping function* ie a formula or procedure which is applied to each key to produce the location address of the corresponding datum.

33. Example.

a. **Mapping function.** Consider a simple example in which the first letter of each key is given a value corresponding to its position in the alphabet ie A = 1, B = 2, C = 3 etc. A possible mapping function is

LOCATION ADDRESS = 100 + KEY VALUE

eg For "CHARLOTTE" the key value is '3' and the location address of the datum will be 100 + 3 = 103.

b. The data is stored and accessed as shown in this table. *Only the data is stored.*

KEY	FIRST LETTER OF KEY	KEY VALUE	LOCATION ADDRESS (= 100 + KEY VALUE)	CONTENTS
ALEX	A	1	101	3012
	B	2	102	
CHARlotte	C	3	103	7642
	D	4	104	
EMMA	E	5	105	5962
	F	6	106	
	G	7	107	
	H	8	108	
	I	9	109	
JAMEs	J	10	110	4243
KATY	K	11	111	2126
LUCY	L	12	112	3562
	M	13	113	

c. **Note**

i. There is a waste of storage space; the price of direct access.

ii. This simple mapping function would not be suitable if two Keys started with the same letter, so it is hardly practicable.

34. HASH tables. (These use methods very similar to those described in (17.34) on Random Files). The Hash table is a compromise between the direct access table technique, and the need to reduce unused storage space. Hash table mapping functions are allowed to be ambiguous ie generate the same location address for two different keys. When this happens, and data is allocated to storage space which is already occupied, a procedure is used to find it alternative storage space within the table.

35. Example: The 'open' HASH table.

a. In this example

i. The datum's key is also stored with the datum, so that the datum may be identified when accessed.

ii. The mapping function is:

DATUM LOCATION ADDRESS = 100 + (2 x KEY VALUE)

KEY LOCATION ADDRESS = DATUM LOCATION ADDRESS –1

eg CHARLOTTE's datum will have the location address 100 + (2 x 3) = 106 and the Key CHAR will have location address 106 – 1 = 105.

iii. If a datum is assigned a location which is already occupied the datum will be placed in the next empty location instead. (This is the 'open' hash method).

b. The HASH table looks like this after seven entries:—

KEY	FIRST LETTER OF KEY	KEY VALUE	DATUM LOCATION ADDRESS [100 + 2 x (KEY VALUE)]	DATUM CONTENTS	KEY LOCATION ADDRESS [DATUM ADDRESS –1]	KEY CONTENTS
ALEX	A	1	102	3012	101	ALEX
BERNard	B	2	104	4251	103	BERN
CHARlotte	C	3	106	7641	105	CHAR
	D	4				
EMMA	E	5	110	5962	109	EMMA
	F	6				
	G	7				
	H	8				
	I	9				
JAMEs	J	10	120	4243	119	JAME
KATY	K	11	122	2126	121	KATY
LUCY	L	12	124	3562	123	LUCY
	M	13	126			

c. If we now try to add a datum '5482' with the Key 'ANN', it will be allocated location 102 which is occupied. The next available space is that normally used by 'D' and so the datum '5482' will be placed in location 108 and its key 'ANN' will be placed in location 107.

d. The table is **'circular'** if values not accommodated at its end are referred to the start of the table. (eg refer 'Z' to 'A').

36. Other features of HASH tables in brief. (A detailed understanding is not called for).

a. Hash tables work most efficiently when the data is evenly spread out rather than clustered together. If clustering does occur then either the method of choosing the next available location must be changed, or a complete **rehash** must be made (ie the table must be remade using a different mapping function.

b. An alternative to the **open hash** is the **closed hash** in which instead of using adjacent locations in the table for surplus data a **pointer** is placed in the table indicating where the **'overflow'** data may be found.

c. The search length for a hash table is approximate

$$\frac{2L - N}{2(L - N)}$$

where L is the length of the table and N is the number of entries. The proof of this formula is beyond the scope of this book.

37. The Binary Search in Tables. When direct access tables or hash tables *have not been used* it is often possible to improve over a **linear search** by means of a **binary search** provided the table is in some logical order.

SUMMARY.

38. a. The data structures discussed in this chapter were:—

i. **Queues** in which the first item added is the first item removed (FIFO).

ii. **Stacks** in which the last item added is the first item removed (LIFO).

iii. **Look-Up tables** in which the address of a datum is found by a linear search for its key.

iv. **Direct Access tables** in which mapping functions are used on the Key of a datum to give its location directly.

v. **Hash tables** in which mapping functions are also used but for which the location generated is not unique.

b. The **search length** for various structures was discussed:—

i. The **linear search** is a basic method which may be used in any data structure. Search length = (N + 1)/2.

ii. The **binary search** which can be used on tables in logical order usually proves quicker than a linear search. Search length = $\log_2$ N.

iii. The **binary tree** structure produces the same search length as a binary search.

iv. A direct access table provides access to the data without a search ie search length = 1.

v. A hash table is almost as fast as a direct access table when it only has a few entries but otherwise still gives fast access.

Search length $\triangleq$ (2 L – N)/(2L – 2N)

POINTS TO NOTE.

39. a. If you are asked to compare data structures then consider these points:

i. Method of access/storage.

ii. Use and wastage of storage space.

iii. Application. (Nature and use of data).

iv. Flexibility in handling variable data, overflow etc.

b. Try to gain practical experience in setting up and handling various data structures.

c. **Double Buffering** is an alternative to Buffering. One **queue** is filled while the other is emptied.

STUDENT SELF TEST QUESTIONS.

(Answers on page 732)

1. *What advantages can a list have over simple strings or tables. Make reference to data storage within main store to illustrate your answer.*

2. *Name three types of table and compare their features.*

3. a. i. *Explain what is meant by a* tree *and a* binary tree

ii. *Describe how you would represent a* binary tree *in main store.*

b. A knock out tournament has sixteen competitors; matches are played between two competitors and the winner goes on to the next round, where again players are paired. Eventually, a single winner emerges. Show how this may be represented by a binary tree, and draw a flowchart to extract and print the competitors who played against the eventual winner of the tournament.

(A.E.B. 1977)

4. *Assume that an array called "S" with 20 elements is to be used to hold the contents of a stack and write pseudocode for the functions outlined in paragraph 17.*

QUESTIONS WITHOUT ANSWERS.

5. *What is generally understood by*

a. A LIFO (last in first out) stack

b. a FIFO (first in first out) queue?

Describe with the aid of diagrams how a one-dimensional array may be used efficiently for the storage of such structures.

Explain what is meant by overflow and underflow in relation to stacks and queues.

Give sets of instructions for

i. the insertion of an item in, and

ii. the deletion of an item from a queue, taking account of extreme situations.

(London Specimen Paper)

6. The diagram shows a representation of an English sentence stored in a computer. Part of the store is given in the diagram (with addresses 100 to 120) together with its contents. Some of the cells shown contain pointers to the beginning of words and some contain codes for letters themselves so that A is coded as 1, B as 2 and C as 3 etc. Zeros are used as terminators.

i. What sentence is stored here?

ii. What is the purpose of the zero in cell 109?

iii. What is the purpose of the zero in cell 104?

iv. How is the ordering of the words achieved?

v. Describe, using a flowchart or a set of written instructions, an algorithm which, when supplied with two of the word-pointers, may interchange them so that an alphabetic ordering of the words is achieved.

100	105
101	115
102	119
103	110
104	0
105	13
106	1
107	18
108	25
109	0
110	12
111	11
112	13
113	2
114	0
115	8
116	1
117	4
118	0
119	1
120	Ø

(London Specimen Paper)

7. a. A list of N records is maintained in immediate access memory in sequential order of key field.

i. Explain the sequential search method to find a record in the list and state what the average number of accesses will be 4

ii. Explain the binary search method to find a record in the list and state what the maximum number of accesses will be. 4

b. Describe an efficient hashing algorithm to store a record in a randomly ordered list held in immediate access memory, assuming that collisions can occur and that the record keys are randomly distributed. State why the algorithm is efficient. 8 = 16

(JMB 1983)

8. Show, by means of diagrams or otherwise, what constitutes the type of data structure called a stack.

Explain how it is used and describe the operations which make use of it. [6]

(CAMBRIDGE 1981)

9. A warehouse for tinned foodstuffs keeps records of the stock in a fully indexed direct access file. A record is held containing data about each type and size of tinned foodstuff and the record key is a code consisting of five letters. The index is arranged as a hash table, with chains (linked lists) for index entries held in a table. A hashing algorithm applied to the record key identifies a hash table entry which points to the first item in a chain. The items in the chain consist of the record key, the number of the disk block which contains the record, and the chain link. The free space in the chain table is itself held as a chain. This structure is illustrated in the following diagram, which includes some example entries.

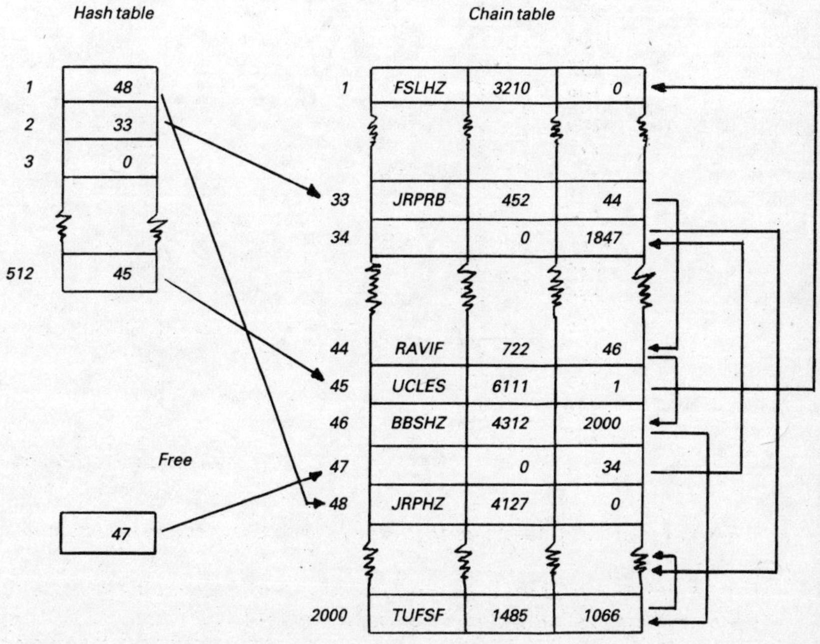

The example data shows only a single tinned foodstuff (record key JRPHZ) with a hash value of 1, many with a hash value of 2, none with a hash value of 3, and two with a hash value of 512.

Describe algorithms for the following operations:

a. accessing the record corresponding to a given record key;

b. inserting a new record and record key corresponding to a new variety of tinned foodstuff;

c. deleting a record and record key corresponding to a discontinued variety of tinned foodstuff.

In each case assume that the record key gives a hash value denoted by H. Your algorithms need not give details of any reorganisation of the records in the file made necessary or desirable by (b) or (c).

(CAMBRIDGE 1982)

10. *In the queue example in this chapter the queue was allocated addresses 101–110. When the next entry pointer became 111 the queue was declared to be full. However, there may have been space at the front end. eg. if the removal pointer was 105 then 101 to 104 were available to be used for new items. This leads to the idea of a circular buffer where after address 110 we would use 101. Write pseudocode for the functions and precedures identified in paragraph 9 for the manipulation of a queue stored in this way in a "circular buffer".*

Translation

The next two chapters consider the problems of converting one computer language into another, which is part of the broader problem of communication with machines. In chapter 32 we concentrate on special programs which do the translation called **translators** and in chapter 33 we examine the techniques used in these programs.

32 Translators

INTRODUCTION.

1. This chapter deals with **translators,** how they are used, and how they work. A **translator** is a program which converts statements written in one language to statements in another language, eg converting assembly language to machine code. The assembly language program would be called the **source program** and the machine code program would be called the **object program.**

2. There are three types of translator:–

a. Assemblers

b. Compilers

c. Interpreters

3. The meaning of the terminology is not completely universal but generally accepted definitions are:–

a. **Assembler.** A program which translates assembly language into machine code. One machine instruction is generated for each source instruction. The resulting program can only be executed when the assembly process is completed. (See fig. 32.1)

b. **Compiler.** A program which translates a high level language into a machine orientated language, often the machine code. **Many** machine instructions are generated for each source statement. The resulting program can only be executed when compilation is completed. (See fig. 32.1)

c. **Interpreter.** A program which translates and executes each source statement in logical sequence as the program is executed.

4. The assembler:–

a. Translates mnemonic operation codes into machine code, and symbolic addresses into machine addresses.

b. Includes the necessary linkages for closed subroutines and inserts appropriate machine code for macros.

c. Allocates areas of storage.

d. Detects and indicates invalid source language instructions.

e. Produces the object program on cards, tape or disc as required.

f. Produces a printed **listing** of the source and object program with comments.

(Rather like the table in 29.4). The listing may also include error codes if appropriate.

5. To illustrate the methods used we will make use of the imaginary assembly language introduced in the (29.14 – 29.20). We must first look at the **directives** (25.18) in more detail.

6. A Directive is used to control the Assembly process, it is not assembled, but is obeyed by the Assembler when it is encountered eg ".END" indicates to the Assembler that no more source code follows. The function code of a directive

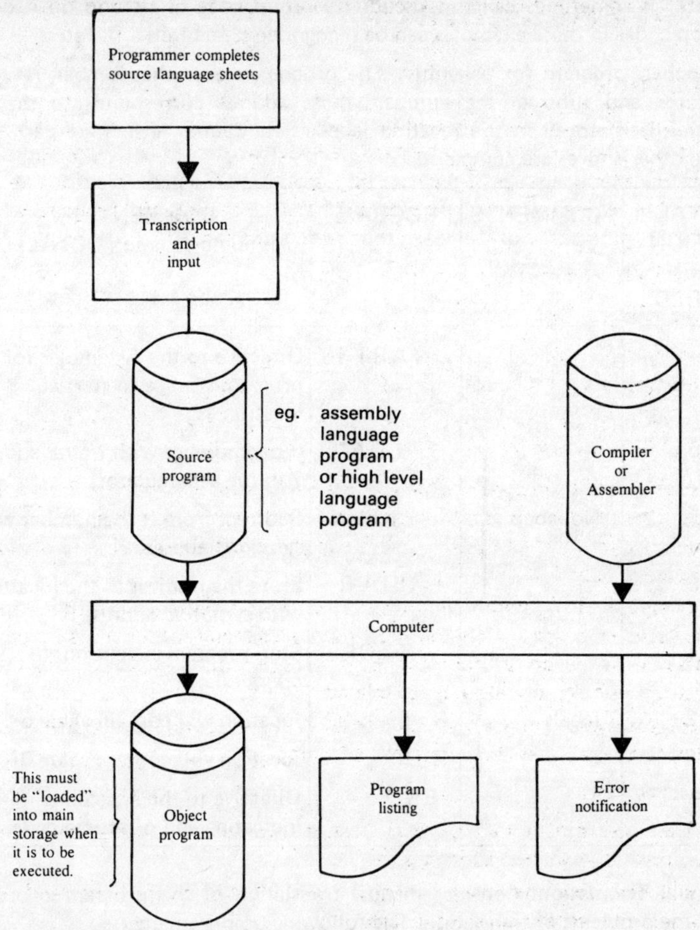

Note:

1. The errors notified are compilation errors (including errors of *syntax*).
2. The object program will later be subjected to testing for *logical* correctness.
3. You must be careful to differentiate between *compilation* errors and errors of logic which are only brought to light when the program is run against test data.

Figure 32.1. Using Assemblers or Compilers to produce object programs.

eg ".END" is sometimes called a **pseudo-operation code** or **pseudo op code.** All pseudo op codes in these examples can be recognised by an initial full stop.

7. **Specimen program for assembly.** The program places the number 7_8 in the accumulator and subtract the number whose address corresponds to the label N. The result is stored in the location labelled R. Capital letters are part of the program, other entries are comments.

OCTAL LOCATION WHEN STORED	COMMENTS	PROGRAM	COMMENTS (All numbers are in OCTAL)
–		. START 16	Directive to the Assembler for program storage to start at location 16.
16	No labels	LDA 7	Load number with *literal* address 7 in the accumulator.
17		SUB N	Subtract from it the number with *symbolic* address N
20		STA R	Store the result into the location with *symbolic* address R
21		STOP	Stop program execution. (*no operand*).
22	labels	N : 5	location will contain value 5
23		R : 0	location will contain value 0
–		. END	Directive to the Assembler indicating end of source code.

8. **Manual Translation.** Consider manual translation of this program in order to identify the problems of translation. The following points emerge:–

a. It is necessary to keep track of the location of each instruction.

b. Instructions must be checked for legality.

c. A conversion table of mnemonic/machine equivalents must be available (28.25).

d. If we try to translate the instructions one at a time, when we reach "SUB N" we will find that it is not possible to proceed because we have not yet determined the location corresponding to the symbolic address N. By looking ahead we can see that N is at location 22_8 but this information is not yet reached when we are processing "SUB N".

9. **Two pass assembler.** The problems of forward reference described in 8d. is overcome by the use of a two pass assembler in which the source program is scanned twice as follows:–

a. On the first pass or scan

i. **symbol tables** are constructed in which each symbolic operand or label is entered together with its corresponding address.

ii. **pseudo-operation tables** are constructed in which the addresses are the entry points for the appropriate directives if they are to be interpreted on the second pass.

b. On the second pass the tables are available, thus the directives may be executed and the object programs and listings are output to appropriate devices.

Note. Only on very simple systems is the source program input twice. It is normally either held in main memory for the second pass or placed on backing store and read from there for the second pass.

10. The two-pass assembly process may be summarised by these diagrams of one example.

a. **PASS 1**

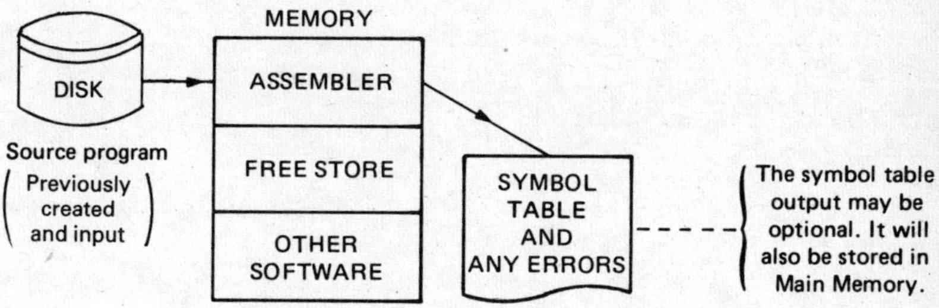

b. **PASS 2**

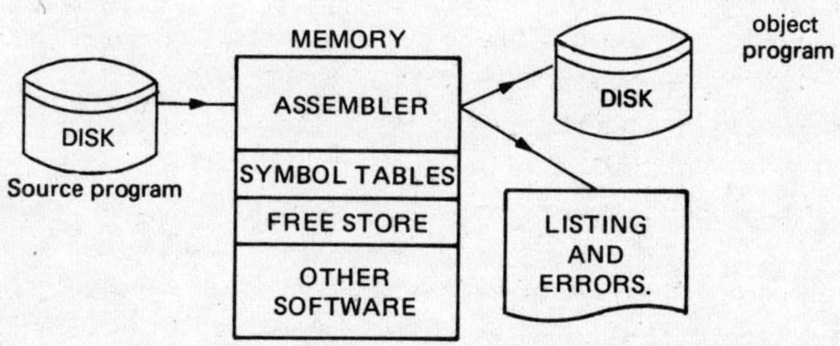

11. How the first pass works.

a. A variable called the *load pointer* is used to keep track of the location of the instruction currently being examined and is incremented when necessary.

b. opcodes are checked for legality and type.

c. Labels are entered in the symbol tables and addresses in the pseudo-op table.

d. Errors are entered in the error table.

Note. Labels and symbolic address operands may either be matched up as the first pass proceeds and checked at the end or they may be entered each time they are encountered and linked at the end of the first pass. The first method is used in the example which follows.

12. The main features of the first pass are outlined in the following pseudocode.

MAIN FEATURES OF THE FIRST PASS

```
Begin
    load_pointer : = 0
    while more source instructions need processing
        read next source instruction
        check legality and identify instruction type
        if
            instruction is a pseudo-op
        then
            translate
            enter start address of directive in the table
            execute pseudo-op if it is relevant to the 1st pass
        else
            if
                label present in instruction
            then
                seek in symbol table
                if
                    label present in symbol table
                then
                        if
                            address present
                        then
                            the address is ambiguous so
                            enter error in error table
                        else
                            enter load_pointer in symbol table
                        endif
                else
                        enter label in symbol table
                        enter load_pointer in symbol table
                endif
            endif
            if
                operand present
            then
                if
                        operand is symbolic
                then
                        seek in symbol table
                        if
                                absent from table
                        then
                                insert symbol in symbol table
                        endif
                endif
            endif
            load_pointer : = load_pointer + 1
        endif
    endwhile
end
```

13. Comments on the pseudocode with reference to the program in paragraph 7.

a. The ".START" directive with pseudo op START will be translated *and executed* thus setting 'L' to the value 16_8.

b. The instruction "LDA 7" has no label and a literal operand so the only action is the incrementing of 'L' to 17.

c. i. "SUB N" has no label but does have the symbolic operand 'N' so the 'N' will be inserted in the symbol table as follows.

SYMBOL TABLE	
SYMBOL	(OCTAL) ADDRESS
N	

The address is not yet defined.

ii. 'L' will be set to 20_8.

d. "STA R" will be treated in the same way as "SUB N" and 'L' will be set to 21_8.

e. STOP has no label and no operand so the only action is to increment 'L' by one to 22_8.

f. Label 'N' will be found in the symbol table and the current location counter value $L = 22_8$ added. The same will happen with R to give this symbol table.

SYMBOL TABLE	
SYMBOL	(OCTAL) ADDRESS
N	22
R	23

g. The directive ".END" will be translated *and executed* resulting in the output of a symbol table, error messages (none in this case). If no errors occur in pass 1 the ".END" directive starts pass 2.

h. If N : 5 had occurred before "SUB N" then both the symbol 'N' and its address would have been entered at the same time.

i. Other pseudo-ops beside .START and .END might include macros to
   i. change the location counter 'L'
   ii. reserve blocks of storage
   iii. evaluate expressions
   iv. make alterations to the symbol table.

j. **Conclusion.** The output for pass 1 is the table in f. and a corresponding table in memory.

14. Here are the main features of the second pass, again in pseudocode.

MAIN FEATURES OF SECOND PASS

```
Begin
  location_counter : _ 0
  while there are more instructions
      (* NB The directive ".END" terminates the pass *)
    read next source instruction
    while instruction is a pseudo-op
        if
            relevant to second pass
        then
            obtain start address from table and execute macro
        endif
        read next source instruction
    endwhile
    if
        function code
    then
        find binary value of function code (from table)
    else (* must be a constant *)
        find binary value of constant by calculation
    endif
    (* NB This is the first step in building a complete *)
    (*    binary machine instruction.                    *)

    obtain (binary) machine address from symbol table
    add to machine function code
    (* NB The remainder of the instruction is added. *)
    (*    Immediate operands will be converted to binary form *)

    output object instruction in required forms
    (* NB i.  The binary machine instruction will be output as an *)
    (*    object program. *)
    (*    ii. The machine instruction will be output on a listing *)
    (*    octal or hex form beside its octal or hex address and *)
    (*    mnemonic form. Error notes may be included *)

    location_counter : = location _counter + 1
  endwhile
end
```

15. The Listed output from pass two for the program in (32.7) would look like this:–

OCTAL LOCATION ADDRESS	OCTAL CONTENTS INSTRUCTION OR DATA	SOURCE PROGRAM
		.START 16
000016	000007	LDA 7
000017	040022	SUB N
000020	010023	STA R
000021	170000	STOP
000022	000005	N : 5
000023	000000	R : 0
		.END

16. Absolute or Relocatable. In the examples given here we are dealing with **absolute programs** (28.55) in which the absolute address of each instruction is determined, ie given ".START 16" we can work out the machine address of each instruction. A **relocatable program** (28.55) in which instructions may occupy different instructions each time they are loaded, can be assembled assuming ".START 0". If it is to be loaded into memory starting at location 16 then all addresses will be increased by 16 when the program is loaded.

17. The assembler may add extra binary data to the front of the object program to tell the loader program where program storage starts. (Compare with .START 16) Further data may be added to specify the **run time start address** ie which instruction in the program should be executed first.

COMPILERS.

18. The compiler:–

a. Translates the source program statements into machine code.

b. Includes linkage for closed subroutines.

c. Allocates areas of main storage.

d. Generates the object program on cards, tape or disc as required.

e. Produces a printed listing of the source and object programs when required.

f. Tabulates a list of errors found during compilation eg the use of 'words' or statements not included in the language vocabulary; or violating the rules of syntax.

19. Although in outline a compiler appears to do much the same job as an assembler in fact it does far more, particularly in the translation of source statements and the linkage of subroutines.

20. Form of the object program. It is sometimes not practical for the compiler to complete the translation process because of the large amount of storage required. Instead the object program is stored as a table of macros with appropriate linkage entries, and the program is put together **("consolidated")** when the program is loaded into main storage for execution. The program which performs these tasks is often called a **linker loader.**

STAGES OF COMPILATION.

21. The compilation process may be broken down into stages just like the passes of an assembler. The compiler may have to translate instructions which are combined into simple sentences and each sentence will require analysis as a whole, in terms of its words grammar and logic but not its semantics (meaning). The three major parts of compilation process are

a. Lexical analysis.

b. Syntactical analysis.

c. Code generation.

22. Lexical Analysis. This stage often includes such things as:

a. Checking for valid 'words' eg valid data names or operator symbols, or detecting double decimal points in a single number.

b. Placing all input forms into the same form, eg disk and tape may have different forms.

c. Coding 'reserved words' (ie words which have a special meaning to the compiler and which may not be used as data names) eg in a printing instruction containing a reserved word "PRINT" the word print may be replaced by a single non alphanumeric character code. Codes representing words and operators are called **tokens.**

d. Standardising formats and removing spaces so that a standardised format is presented to the next stage. As part of this standardised format the tokens may be replaced by pointers to **symbol tables.** A symbol table for programmer defined identifiers would be created during lexical analysis and would contain details of attributes such as data types.

Pre-defined symbol names such as arithmetic operands would be held in permanent symbol tables within the compiler.

23. Syntactical Analysis. This stage often includes such things as:

a. Checking statements for correct grammatical form. (Their **meaning** is **not** determined at this stage). This process may go beyond grammatical analysis of individual statements however, eg there may be checks to see that every **"if"** has a matching **"endif"**. (This may be considered as a separate semantics stage).

b. Complex forms may be broken down into simpler equivalent and more manageable forms.

NB. The part of the compiler which performs this lexical analysis is called a **parser.** Further details of *parsing* will be covered in the next chapter.

24. Code Generation. This stage often includes such things as:

a. Translating each statement into its equivalent form. This involves
   i. The use of tables as in the assembly process,
   ii. the setting up of various linkages
   iii. fetch subroutines from the systems library.

Since many instructions are of a similar form use is often made of **Skeleton** subroutine linkages which are modified to suit the particular case.

b. Optimisations where possible.

25. The code generation phrase is often sub-divided into three distinct stages:

a. **Intermediate code generation.** This intermediate code is obtained fairly directly from the parser. It has a simple form which is easy to optimise.

b. **Optimisation.** The intermediate code is transformed so as to make the program execute faster and need less storage space.

c. **Code generation.** The optimised code is finally used to produce the object code. The object code is usually in machine language but could be in higher level forms such as assembly language, or an "ideal" machine code which is then interpreted.

26. The efficiency of the compiler will depend primarily on the way in which the various tables are constructed and accessed. Efficient use of storage although relevant is still largely in the hands of the programmer since it is he who should make economies in his choice of variables, storage requirements, etc.

INTERPRETERS.

27. Interpreters are more easily understood by comparing them with compilers.

28. Both compilers and interpreters are commonly used for the translation of high level language programs but they perform the translation in two completely different ways.

29. The **compiler** translates the *whole* of the high level language source program into a machine code object program prior to the object program being loaded into main memory and executed. Contrast this with the **interpreter** which deals with the source program *one instruction at a time,* completely translating *and* executing each instruction before it goes onto the next. Interpreters seldom produce object code but call upon inbuilt routines instead. Some intermediate code is usually produced temporarily, however.

30. If a **compiler** is used, the same program need only be translated once. Thereafter, the object program can be loaded directly into main storage and executed.

31. If an **interpreter** is used, the source program will be translated every time the program is executed. Executions carried out in this way may be ten times slower than the execution of the equivalent object programs!

32. Despite their apparent inefficiency interpreters are widely used, particularly for the programming language BASIC on small computers, because they are easier to use than compilers.

33. Uses. Interpreters are used for such things as:

a. Handling user commands in an interactive system.

b. Debugging programs as they run (ie removing program faults).

c. Handling software produced for or by a different computer. In this case the interpreter may be essential if:

i. Two dissimilar machines are to be connected together for operation, or

ii. If software produced on an old model and not yet converted had to be run on a new one.

NB. Interpretive routines have many uses, eg. handling individual commands or directives.

34. Simulation and Emulation.

a. The procedure described in 33c. ii. is often referred to as simulation since the interpreter allows the new computer to simulate the behaviour of the old. Interpreters can also be used to simulate a new machine not yet provided but for which software is already written.

b. As was discussed in 27.45, sometimes it is possible to encode the microsteps that describe each instruction cycle in a special memory in the CPU called a control store. In this way, the instruction set can be readily altered, and the technique is termed microprogramming. Microprogrammable computers can therefore be set up to obey the instruction set of any other computer, and this process is called emulation.

OTHER TRANSLATOR VARIATIONS.

35. Generators.

These are programs which create programs to a given specification. For example the generator might be able to produce programs which print out the contents of files on a choice of devices. The generator would be given data which specified such things as output device, type of file, name of file, format of output. The generator would then create the desired program.

36. Compiler-Compilers.

Compiler-Compilers are generators which produce a compiler for a given language from a definition of the language. They are intended to save man-hours in compiler writing and speed up the production of compilers.

37. Cross Compilers and Cross Assemblers. Cross Compilers and Cross Assemblers are translators which are used on one computer in order to produce object programs for use on a second computer. Usually the computer used for the translation is a mini-computer or main frame and the object program is used on a microcomputer.

SUMMARY.

38. a. The 3 types of translators are

i. Assemblers
ii. Compilers
iii. Intepreters.

b. Assemblers can use two passes to translate assembly language into machine code. The first pass creates a symbol table and the second to do the translation. On large machines the two passes can be handled in one in which case the loader may handle forward references in the table.

c. Compilers translate high level language programs to machine orientated language in stages, the main ones being

i. Lexical analysis
ii. Syntax analysis
iii. Code generators.

d. Interpreters are not efficient alternatives to assemblers and compilers but have uses in debugging simulation and, because they are easy to use, in small systems.

e. The relationship between level of language and type of translation needed is shown in this table:

LANGUAGE	TRANSLATOR	INSTRUCTIONS GENERATED	ORIENTATION
Machine	None	N/A	N/A
Low level (symbolic)	Assembler	1 for 1 (+ macros)	Machine
High level	Compiler	Many for 1 statement	Problem

POINTS TO NOTE.

39. a. Translation to machine code is only the first step towards using a program. Before it is performed it must be **loaded into main storage** and only then can the **execution phase** be started.

STUDENT SELF TEST QUESTIONS.

(Answers on page 736)

1. *Name three types of translator and distinguish between them.*

2. *Use the methods described in 32.10 – 32.15 to assemble this program and produce a listing.*

```
        START 200
D:      LDA X
        JAZ E
        SUB 100
        JAL E
        STA X
        LDA Q
        ADN 1
        STA Q
        JPU D
E:      STOP
Q:      0
X:      60
.END
```

What does this program do?

3. a. *Explain the difference between internal machine instructions and external symbolic machine instructions.*

   b. *Describe what takes place during:–*

      i. *the* assembly *phase, and*

      ii. *the* execution *phase,*

   for an instruction such as ADD COST, 3 when COST refers to a fixed length binary store location and the third operand (ie 3 in this case) refers to a modifier register.

(AEB 1976)

4. a. *In the context of the compilation of a source program into executable machine code, state what you understand by*

      i. *lexical analysis,*

      ii. *parsing,*

      iii. *code generation.*

(6 marks)

b. In a particular high-level programming language, only the first two characters of a variable identifier are significant. Thus, TIME and TITLE will be treated identically. What are the advantages and disadvantages of this feature of the language?

(2 marks)

c. A particular high-level language allows assembly code to be inserted at any point between high-level statements. What are the advantages of this feature of the language.

(4 marks)

d. A programmer uses an iterative loop executed 1000 times, but containing no executable instructions other than those controlling the loop, in order to provide a pause while a particular complex diagram is held on the VDU screen. Explain why this technique may give satisfactory results when the program is interpreted, but may not when it has been compiled.

(3 marks)

(London 1983)

QUESTIONS WITHOUT ANSWERS.

5. *Compare the use of compilers and interpreters for the translation of high level languages.*

6. *a. Explain the relationship between an assembly language and the corresponding machine code, and describe the major features of an assembly language which make it easier to use than machine code.* *[6]*

   b. Describe in broad outline how an assembler works. *[11]*

(Cambridge 1982)

33 Techniques needed in Translation

INTRODUCTION.

1. Two main topics will be discussed in this chapter, both are applicable to translation and compiler writing. They are:–

a. Language definition and description.

b. Reverse Polish notation for handling expressions.

LANGUAGE DEFINITION AND DESCRIPTION.

2. Uses of Language Definition. Language definitions are of use in:–

a. Producing all legal sentences or expressions in a language.

b. Checking the legality of a sentence or expression. In computer applications this leads to the production of unambiguous code.

(b. is of more interest to us).

3. Syntax, Lexicons and Semantics.

a. The **syntax** of a sentence is the structure of the sentence and the grammatical rules governing the structure.

b. A **lexicon** is a dictionary of valid words in a language, ie a list of valid words.

c. **Semantics** is concerned with the meaning of words and sentences.

The following paragraphs are concerned **mainly** with a., **partly** with b. but **not** with c.

4. Language definition. A language may be defined by

a. a **generative** scheme ie a procedure for generating all legal sentences in the language, or

b. **recognition** in which a procedure is defined for deciding the legality of any sentence.

The **generative** method is more common in the context of definition of programming languages but **recognition** is closer to the implicit language definition provided by most compilers.

5. Most schemes of language definition run into trouble when applied to natural languages like English, because of the inherent ambiguities, and metaphors and imprecise meanings, but these schematic methods work well on computer languages.

BNF GENERATIVE CLASSIFICATION.

6. The B.N.F. (Backus-Naur Form) is a notational method of presenting language generation. B.N.F. may itself be regarded as a special language and languages of this type are called **meta-languages.**

7. Notation, Terminology and Method.

a. → means "is defined by" (sometimes ∷ = is used instead of →)
| means "or"
< > are used to enclose **syntactic variables** as shown in these examples:–

b. **Example 1.** A language rule which defines operands used in the language. < operand > → A | B | C | D means the **syntactic variable** (an operand) is defined by the **terminal** symbols A or B or C or D, ie In the given language an operand is one of the characters A, B, C or D.

c. **Example 2.** A language rule which defines operators used in the language. < operator > → + | – | / | *. In examples 1 and 2 A, B, C, D, +, –, /, and * are all examples of **syntactic elements,** and **terminal symbols.**

8. Producing legal sentences or legal expressions.

a. **Example.** To define a legal expression. The following rules could be given.
i. <expression>→<operand><operator><operand>
ii. <operand>→ A | B | C | D
iii. <operator>→ + | – | / | *

Such rules or definitions are called **productions.**

b. To **generate** or **produce** a legal expression **recursion** may be used, ie the **lefthand sides** of **productions** are substituted into the **righthand sides** again and again. Intermediate expressions containing both syntactic elements and syntactic variables are called **sentential forms**
(eg. i. < expression > → A < operator > < operand > is a sentential form).
Once all syntactic variables have been replaced by syntactic elements we have produced a sentential form which is a **legal expression** or **legal sentence** in the language, as shown in C.

c. Apply rules a.i., a.ii. and a.iii. to get a **legal expression.**

a.i.	<expression>→<operand>	<operator>	<operand>	} sentential forms
Use a.ii.	A	<operator>	<operand>	
Use a.iii.	A	+	<operand>	
Use a.ii.	A	+	B	} legal expression

9. Example of forming a legal sentence.

a. Given the following production
i. <sentence>→<subject phrase><verb><object phrase>
ii. <subject phrase>→<article><adjective><noun>
iii. <object phrase>→<article><adjective><noun>
iv. <verb>→ ate | has | saw
v. <article>→ a | the
vi. <adjective>→ bad | big | nice | small
vii. <noun>→ boy | bird | chocolate.

Note: The **lexicon** is defined by iv., v., vi and vii, and each word in the lexicon is a **terminal symbol.**

b. Constructing a legal sentence.

< sentence >

Using production i. < subject phrase >< verb >< object phrase >

Using production ii. < article >< adjective >< noun >< verb >
< object phrase >

Using production iii. < article >< adjective >< noun >< verb >< article >
< adjective >< noun >

Using production iv. < article > < adjective > < noun > ate < article >
< adjective >< noun > etc.

Until we arrive at legal sentences such as:–

"the bad chocolate ate the small bird"

"the nice boy saw the big chocolate"

Note. The semantics may be incorrect, but syntactically these examples are legal.

10. Defining a statement in high level languages.

Example. A simplified version of the PRINT statement in BASIC could be defined as follows:–

< PRINT Statement > → PRINT | PRINT < expression >
< expression > → < variable > | < variable >, | < variable >;
< variable > → < letter > | < letter >< digit >
< letter > → A | B | C | D | E | F | G | H | I | J | K | L | M | N | O | P | Q | R | S | T | U | V | W | X | Y | Z
< digit > → 0 | 1 | 2 | 3 | 4 | 5 | 6 | 7 | 8 | 9

So statements such as the following would be legal.

i. PRINT
ii. PRINT A
iii. PRINT A,
iv. PRINT B;
v. PRINT C9
vi. PRINT Z2,

11. Syntax Diagrams are sometimes used as an alternative to BNF.

Examples

a. < operand > → A/B/C/D could be written in syntax diagram form as

operand

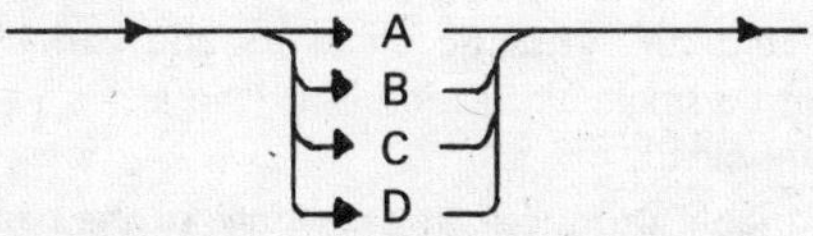

b. < assignment > → < variable > : = < expression >

assignment

→| *variable* → : = → *expression* →

PARSING. (Used in syntax analysis stage of compilation).

12. Parsing is the breaking down of sentences into their components. We will **parse** in order to check the legality of sentences. More precisely, parsing is defined as the process of defining the productions which when applied by recursion result in giving legal sentences or expressions.

13. Example of parsing.

a. Given these language definition productions
(1) <expression>→<operand><operator><operand>
(2) <operand>→W | X | Y | Z
(3) <operand>→+ | – | * | /

b. Parsing the expression W – X

Using (2) <operand> – X
Using (3) <operand><operator> X
Using (2) <operand><operator><operand>
Using (1) <expression>

The parse is described by the sequence of production ie (2, 3, 2, 1).

c. The parsing of an expression can be represented by a TREE called a **syntax tree** or a **parse tree**. The syntax tree for the parse in b. is shown here:–

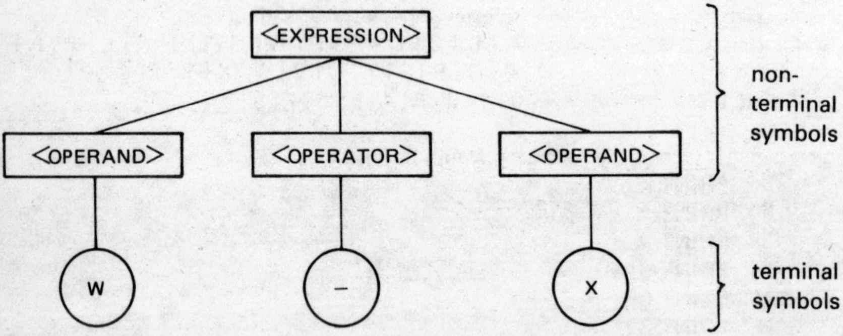

14. The Canonical parse is a procedure which ensures well defined parsing as follows

a. i. Find a production which when applied would have produced the **left most** syntactic elements and replace these elements by the syntactic variable from which they came.

ii. The process is repeated on syntactic elements and variables (always working from the left) until a single expression is arrived at.
(The parse in 13b. was canonical).

b. The lefthand syntactic variable produced at each stage of the parse is called the **handle.**

15. A sentence (or expression) is **unambiguous** if only *one* canonical parse exists for that sentence. **Computer languages** must be defined so that *all* sentences in the language are unambiguous, in which case the language is said to be **unambiguous.** When a *canonical* parsing procedure is not adhered to, a sentence can only be unambiguous if just **one** parse exists for the sentence regardless of parsing procedure. The following example shows how a language definition can be unsatisfactory with non canonical parsing producing ambiguous expressions.

16. Example. Ambiguous language definition.

(1) < expression > → < operand > | < expression > < operator > < expression >

(2) < operand > → W | X | Y | Z

(3) < operator > → + | – | * | /

a. **Canonical parse** of W – X * Z

Using (2) < operand > – X * Z
Using (1) < expression > – X * Z
Using (3) < expression > < operator > X * Z
Using (2) < expression > < operator > < operand > * Z
Using (1) < expression > < operator > < expression > * Z
Using (1) < expression > * Z
Using (3) < expression > < operator > Z
Using (2) < expression > < operator > < operand >
Using (1) < expression > < operator > < expression >
Using (1) < expression >

The canonical parse is (2, 1, 3, 2, 1, 1, 3, 2, 1, 1)

b. **Syntax tree of the canonical parse.**

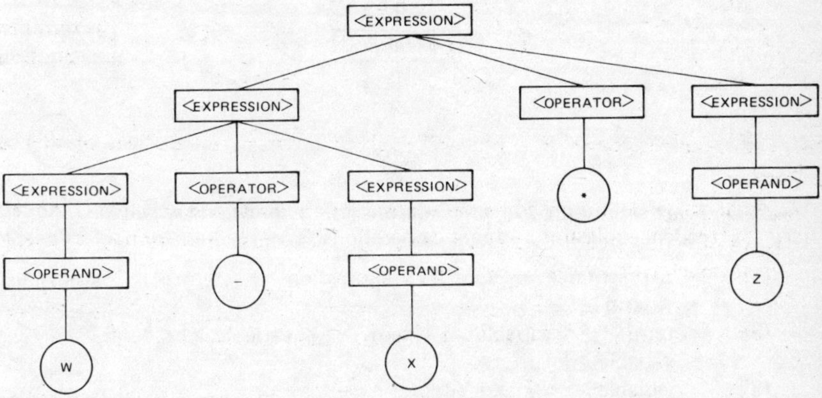

c. **Note.** A further deficiency of this language definition is apparent from this parse, namely that the order of operations is contrary to normal practice. We would normally expect to perform the * before the –. A good language definition for arithmetic expressions will provide the necessary **precedence rules.**

d. **Alternate non-canonical parse** of W – X * Z

2 < operand > – X * Z
3 < operand >< operator > X * Z
2 < operand >< operator >< operand > * Z
3 < operand >< operator >< operand >< operator > Z
2 < operand >< operator >< operand >< operator >< operand >
1 < expression >< operator >< operand >< operator >< operand >
1 < expression >< operator >< expression >< operator >< operand >
1 < expression >< operator >< expression >< operator >
< expression >
1 < expression >< operator >< expression >
1 < expression >

The parse is (2, 3, 2, 3, 2, 1, 1, 1, 1, 1)

e. **Syntax tree of this parse.**

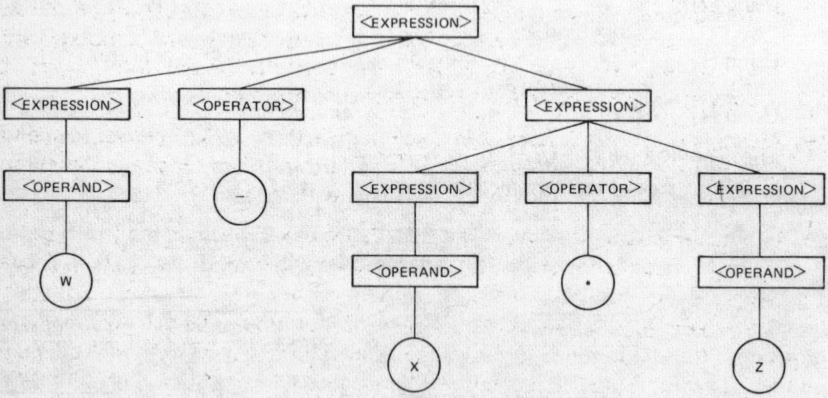

17. A language definition for simple arithmetic expressions which provides the normal precedence rules for arithmetic operations.

(1) < expression > → < term > | < expression > + < term > | < expression > – < term > |

(2) < term > → < variable > | < term > * < variable > | < term > / < variable > |

(3) < variable > → W | X | Y | Z

a. A canonical parse of W – X * Z is performed here. Notice the need to **backtrack** when the parse fails to complete.

i. Using (3) <variable> – X * Z ⎤ **NB.** No rule for <variable> followed
ii. Using (2) <term> – X * Z ⎦ by operator so try another rule.
iii. Using (1) <expression> – X * Z
iv. Using (3) <expression> – <variable> * Z
v. Using (2) <expression> – <term> * Z
vi. Using (1) <expression> * Z
vii. Using (3) <expression> * <variable>
viii. Using (2) <expression> * <term>

The parse fails here so we **backtrack** to step v.

vi. Using (3) <expression> – <term> * <variable>
vii. Using (2) <expression> – <term>
viii. Using (1) <expression>

The canonical parse is (3, 2, 1, 3, 2, 3, 2, 1)

Note. Backtracking can also be used to search for ambiguous expressions.

18. From these parsing examples we may draw some useful conclusions:

a. Computer language definitions should be unambiguous and cater for precedence rules where appropriate.

b. A satisfactory computer language definition will allow the parsing procedure
i. to detect illegal expression (when the parse fails despite all backtracks)
ii. to find the legal parse. It is the correctly parsed form which is converted into code within a translator such as a compiler.

19. Awareness of what features of language definitions lead to efficient parsing methods has led to the development of standard forms of language definition together with parsing methods which work well with them.

20. In outline, the methods work like this. Expressions are scanned left to right. Parsing procedures associated with each non-terminal symbol are applied. These procedures either parse left to right or right to left. The language definition (grammar) will have been constructed to favour one of these two parsing directions. In order to parse the expression the parser may have to look ahead a number of symbols (K say). Parsers, and their associated grammars, are classified according to the methods used. Thus an **LL (1)** parser, based on an LL (1) grammar, scans left to right (the first 'L') parses left to right (the second 'L') and is very simple because it only needs to look ahead 1 symbol. The basic alternatives are LL(K) parsers and LR(K) parsers. Further details are beyond the scope of this book.

REVERSE POLISH.

21. Reverse Polish is useful for handling expression for which evaluation is governed by precedence rules. These expressions often constitute an unsophisticated language and in such cases the application of Reverse Polish methods quickly yield usable legal parsed forms without the need for backtracking canonical parses.

22. Infix notation. The conventional way of writing formulae, and the way used in many high level languages, is called **infix notation.** The operators (+, −, etc) are within the expression between the appropriate operands

eg in (A + B) * (C − D) (* means 'multiply')

23. The problem of infix notation is that the order in which the expression is written down is **not** the same as the order in which the operands are required, or the operations are performed. This is even more apparent if we consider the order in which a computer might do the calculation, eg

1 Fetch A
2 Fetch B
3 Add A and B (then store intermediate result (A + B))
4 Fetch C
5 Fetch D
6 Subtract D from C
7 Multiply by intermediate result (A + B)

The order in which the terms of the expression were used is indicated here:

1	3	2	7	4	6	5
(A	+	B)	*	(C	−	D)

24. Reverse Polish notation. (First devised by a Polish logician J. Łukasiewicz). In **Reverse Polish** notation each operator is written *after* the appropriate operands eg the infix expression (A + B) * (C − D) would be written as AB + CD − * which as you can see is the *useful* order shown in the previous paragraph. Reverse Polish notation is sometimes called **postfix notation.**

AIDS TO TRANSLATION.

25. The unary minus. The + and − signs of normal arithmetic are used in two ways.

a. **For binary operations** ie those requiring **two** operands such as 3 + 5 or 7 − 4.

b. **For unary operations** ie to designate sign value where only **one** operand is present such as + 4 or − 9.

In case b the − is called the **unary minus** sign and in conversion to Reverse Polish we may ignore the unary + but must treat the unary minus differently than the normal 'binary ' minus.

26. Restricting the use of the unary minus. The use of the unary minus is often restricted in a high level language and may only be used after an : = or a (sign.

eg X : = A * − B is not allowed but X : = A * (− B) is.

A further general restriction is that operands must always be explicit

eg A * B may **not** be written as AB.

27. Operators. The following notation will be adopted to comply with the more usual notation of BASIC and FORTRAN. Note the use of "=" rather than ": =" for assignment in these examples.

Assigning values	=	eg LET X = 3 (ie. X : = 3)
Parentheses	(or)	
Add	+	
Subtract	–	
Unary minus	∿	(for identification only)
Multiply	*	
Divide	/	
Exponentiate	↑	eg 3^2 written 3 ↑ 2

28. Precedence Rules. In order to carry out the translation it is advantageous to give the operators a rule of precedence (ie a rule to decide which to do when all else is equal). The following convention is adopted throughout this book, there are variations used elsewhere.

OPERATOR	PRECEDENCE
=	0
(	1
+ –)	2
* / ∿	3
↑	4

TRANSLATION TO REVERSE POLISH FROM INFIX.

29. Preliminary comments. The method will be described with the aid of pseudocode, but the following points should be noted first:–

a. The infix expression will be regarded as a (one dimensional) string called infix-string and scanned left to right one symbol at a time.

b. The Reverse Polish expression will be regarded as a (one dimensional) string called reverse-polish-expression filled left to right.

c. Use will be made of L.I.F.O. stack of the type described in the chapter on data structures. The top entry in the stack will be called top-of-stack.

d. The symbol in the infix string currently being examined will be called current symbol.

e. The method used here is called Dijkstra's method.

f. Operands may be
   i. **Constants** eg 5, 19, etc, or
   ii. **Literals** eg A, B, C, etc.

g. You are advised to use the pseudocode to work through the table which follows it.

30. Pseudocode for converting well formed infix strings to reverse polish. (Some error checks are included). This pseudocode merely gives an outline of the method. In many places comments are given instead of the actual code.

```
variables
        current_symbol,
        top_of_stack                        : character
        infix_string,
        reverse_polish expression           : string
        end_of_infix_string,
        error_found,
        stack_empty,
        process_needed                      : boolean
Begin
    error_found : = false
    while (* more characters in infix_string *)
        AND NOT error_found
        if
            end_of_infix_string
        then
            (* empty stack into reverse_polish_expression *)
            (* but omit "(" or ")". *)
        else
            (* assign next infix-string symbol to the *)
            (* current_symbol *)
            if
                (* current_symbol is an operand *)
            then
                if
                    (* the previous current_symbol was an operand *)
                then
                    error_found : = true
                else
                    (* add current_symbol to the *)
                    (* reverse_polish_expression *)
                endif
            else    (* current_symbol is an operator
                       a "(" or a ")" *)
                if
                    stack_empty
                then
                    (* add current_symbol to stack *)
                else
                    if
                        current_symbol = "("
                    then
                        (* add current_symbol to stack *)
                    else
                        (* adjust stack
                           NB. Details shown separately *)
                    endif
                endif
            endif
        endif
    endwhile
end
```

```
(* Details of "adjust stack" *)
        process_needed : = true
        repeat
            if
                (precedence of current_symbol)
                >
                (precedence of top_of_stack)
            then
                if
                    current_symbol = ")"
                    AND
                    top_of_stack = "("
                then
                    (* remove "(" from the stack *)
                else
                    (* add current_symbol to the stack *)
                endif
                process_needed : = false
            else
                if
                    top_of_stack = "("
                    OR
                    top_of_stack = ")"
                then
                    error_found : = true
                else
                    (* transfer top_of_stack *)
                    (* to reverse_polish_expression *)
                    if
                        stack_empty
                    then
                        (* add current_symbol to stack *)
                        process-needed : = false
                    endif
                endif
            endif
        until (NOT process_needed) OR error_found
```

31. Examples using the Pseudocode.

Example 1. Convert (A + B) * C – D) to Reverse Polish.
Use the pseudocode and refer to the table given below. The table is filled by working through the pseudocode so tick entries in pencil as you do them.

Current_ symbol	Precedence (if an operator)	Stack top_of_stack to the right	Precedence of top_of_stack	Reverse_Polish_ String
(	1	(	1	
A				A
+	2	(+	2	
B				AB
)	2	(	1	AB +
*	3	*	3	
(		* (	1	
C				AB + C
–	2	* (–	2	
D				AB + CD
)	2	* (	1	AB + CD –
		*		
End of infix_string Stack empty				AB + CD – *

(A + B) * (C – D) is AB + CD – * in Reverse Polish.

32. Example 2. Convert X = (– W + A * (5 * Y – Z ↑ 3))/2 into Reverse Polish (postfix) notation.

Note. We identify that the unary minus occurs after the (and rewrite the expression

X = (∼ W + A * (5 * Y – Z ↑ 3))/2

33. Table illustrating the conversion of X = (∼ W + A * (5 * Y – Z ↑ 3))/2 to Reverse Polish notation.

Symbol currently scanned	Precedence (if an operator)	Stack (Top value to the right)	Precedence of top value	Reverse Polish String P
X				X
=	0	=	0	
(	1	= (	1	
∼	3	= (∼	3	
W				XW
+	2	= (	1	XW ∼
		= (+	2	
A				XW ∼ A
*	3	= (+ *	3	
(	1	= (+ * (	1	
5				XW ∼ A5
*	3	= (+ * (*	3	
Y				XW ∼ A5Y
–	2	= (+ * (	1	XW ∼ A5Y *
		= (+ * (–	2	
Z				XW ∼ A5Y * Z
↑	4	= (+ * (– ↑	4	
3				XW ∼ A5Y * Z3
)	2	= (+ * (–	2	XW ∼ A5Y * Z3 ↑
		= (+ * (	1	XW ∼ A5Y * Z3 ↑ –
		= (+ *	3	
)	2	= (+	2	XW ∼ A5Y * Z3 ↑ – *
		= (	1	XW ∼ A5Y * Z3 ↑ – * +
		=	0	
/	3	= /		
2				XW ∼ A5Y * Z3 ↑ – * + 2
empty stack				XW ∼ A5Y * Z3 ↑ – * + 2 / =

X = (∼ W + A * (5 * Y – Z ↑ 3))/2 is XW ∼ A5Y * Z3 ↑ – * + 2 / = in Reverse Polish.

Note.

i. The *operands* are in the *same* order as the operands in the infix string.
ii. The *operators* are now in 'operational' order.

34. Well Formed Formulae (WFF) in Reverse Polish. Before generating code form, or evaluating expressions in Reverse Polish, the Reverse Polish expression should be checked for legality. (A legal expression is said to be **Well Formed).** The procedure for this check is simple to perform but must be carefully prepared.

Steps.

a. 'Rank' value is assigned as shown and is used solely for this check.

Reverse Polish String Member	Rank Value
Variable or Constant	1
Unary operator eg ∿	0
Other (binary) operators	–1

b. The Reverse Polish symbol string is constructed, Rank values assigned and then Rank Value subtotals are evaluated as shown here.

For the expression AB + CD – * (The letters h to m are annotations)

Symbol String	Rank Value		Rank Value Subtotal		Comment
*	–1	h	–1	h	subtotal ⩽ 0
–	–1	i	–2	h + i	subtotal ⩽ 0
D	1	j	–1	h + i + j	subtotal ⩽ 0
C	1	k	0	h + i + j + k	subtotal ⩽ 0
+	–1	l	–1	h + i + j + k + l	subtotal ⩽ 0
B	1	m	0	h + i + j + k + l + m	subtotal ⩽ 0
A	1	n	1 = (Total of all) (Rank values)		total = 1

e. The Reverse Polish string is well formed IF and ONLY IF

i. Each subtotal is ⩽ 0
ii. The total of all Rank values = 1

35. Code Generation and Reverse Polish String Evaluation. The details of code generation are beyond the scope of this book but if you can see how to write a set of machine instructions for the following example of string evaluation you will have grasped the basic principles.

36. Evaluating a Reverse Polish String.
To illustrate the method we will assume that successive symbols in the string are stored in a table as shown below. The expression can be thought of as being in successive memory locations if you wish. (Numerical values are also shown to aid understanding). For Reverse Polish expression AB + CD – *

LOCATION	CONTENT
1	A = 10
2	B = 14
3	+
4	C = 18
5	D = 15
6	—
7	*

Assume we can use a stack to store location values. The procedure is as follows.

a. Work through the table one location at a time.

b. If the contents are an operand place its address on top of the stack.

c. If the contents are an operator then

i. Remove addresses of the required number of operands from the stack. (Usually two, one in the case of unary minus).

ii. Perform the operation and replace the operator by the result.

iii. Place the address of the result on top of the stack.

On completing the first scan the expression will be calculated. The table below shows successive contents of locations and stack when following the above procedure. The stack could be used to hold the operands rather than their addresses.

LOCATIONS							STACK (Top at right)
1	2	3	4	5	6	7	
A=10	B=14	+	C=18	D=15	—	*	1,
							1, 2
		(A + B)=24					3
							3, 4
							3, 4, 5
					(C–D)=3		3, 6
						(A+B)*(C–D) =72	7

Note. The final entry in the stack gives the location of the result.

TREE REPRESENTATION.

37. A procedure for constructing the tree representation of a Reverse Polish String is as follows:–

Start at the **righthand** end of the expression and work right to left thus:

a. Take the symbols in turn. For each symbol form a new right node, place the symbol in the node and traverse to that node. When the node which has just been created contains an operand start step b. Nodes containing operands are terminal nodes.

b. Traverse backwards up the tree until a left node is required. Fill this with the next symbol in the Reverse Polish string.

c. i. If the symbol filled in in b. is an operand continue with b.

ii. If the symbol filled in in b. is an operator return to step a.

The tree representation of AB + CD – * is shown here.

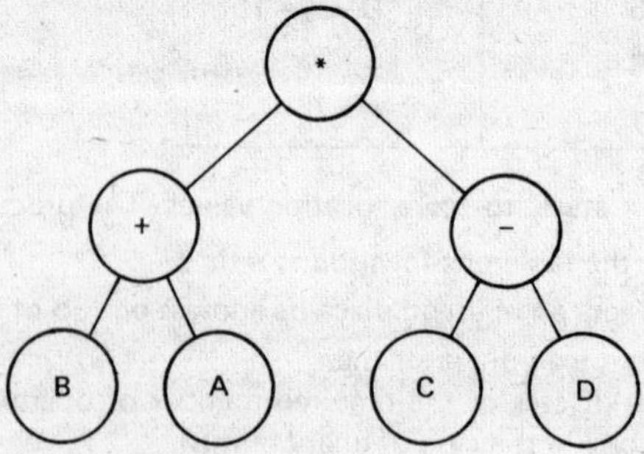

SUMMARY.

38. a. The two main topics discussed were:

i. Language Definition.

ii. Reverse Polish Notation.

b. Languages may be defined by **generative schemes** or **recognitive schemes.** BNF is a useful generative classification or meta-language.

c. Computer languages require unambiguous definition.

d. Parsing is the process of defining the **productions** which when applied by recursion result in the given legal sentence or expression.

e. Reverse Polish (postfix) notation places operands and operators in a more usable order than that found in infix notation.

POINTS TO NOTE.

39. a. The emphasis in this chapter has been on techniques. You should however notice that the techniques apply to:–

i. the assembly process

ii. Compilation, both in terms of checking correct lexis and syntax and in the ordering of operations during code generation.

iii. Interpretive routines.

b. Reverse Polish can equally well be applied to Boolean operations. A possible precedence rule is:–

Operator	Precedence.
=	0
(	1
+)	2
. –	3

c. Although Reverse Polish notation provides a more useful order of presentation of expressions, further improvement can be made to the methods described which lead to more efficient ways of using machine instructions to perform operations.

d. You should be aware of this alternative terminology.

i. **Syntactic elements** are also called **terminal symbols.**

ii. **Syntactic variables** are also called **non-terminal symbols** or **meta-components.**

iii. **Unary operators** such as the unary minus are also called **monadic prefix operators** (fixed in front of an operand).

iv. **Binary operators** (ie they have two operands) are also called **dyadic infix operators** (fixed between two operands).

STUDENT SELF TEST QUESTIONS.

(Answers on page 739)

1. *A conditional jump statement in a simple programming language contains one expression which has two single letter operands separated by one of the operators =, ≠ , AND, or OR. Write productions which will generate legal expressions. The complete statement consists of a 3 digit line number followed by "IF", followed by the expression just described, followed by "THEN", followed by another 3 digit line number. Write the remaining production needed to generate whole statements. The line number is in the range 100 to 999 inclusive.*

2. *Write a set of productions which will generate from* < date > *all possible dates conforming to this description:–*

A 'date' consists of a day letter (eg M for Monday) followed by a month letter (eg F for February) followed by one of 31 day numbers for the month. Exceptions to the code are two letter codes introduced when the day or month letter is not unique, eg TH = Thursday TU = Tuesday. The three components of the date are separated by a space for which you may use the symbol ∇ . Outline amendments necessary to exclude non dates like M∇F∇31.

3. *Parse this expression using the language definition given in paragraph 16.*

*W / X + Z * Y*   *(Backtracking will be needed).*

4. *Convert the expression W / X + Z * Y into Reverse Polish. Then check that your answer is well formed.*

5. Convert these expressions to Reverse Polish. Draw a tree for each expression.

a. A = (–X + C ↑ E) * Y

b. Y = (X + B) / (W – Z)

QUESTIONS WITHOUT ANSWERS.

6. A first attempt to define a portion of the syntax of a programming language dealing with expressions involving only variables is made as follows,

<expression> → <variable> | <expression><op><expression>
<op> → + | * | ↑
<variable> → A | B | C | D

Show that this is unsatisfactory, by drawing two different syntax trees for the expression

A * B + C ↑ D .

Subsequently, this inherent ambiguity is removed by replacing the definitions above by,

<expression> → <term> | <expression> + <term>
<term> → <factor> | <term> * <factor>
<factor> → <primary> | <factor> ↑ <primary>
<primary> → <variable>
<variable> → A | B | C | D.

i. Using a tree derived from the revised syntax rules, express

A * B + C ↑ D

in Reverse Polish (postfix) notation.

ii. What change would you make to the definition of <primary> to allow for bracketed expressions in this language?

(London 1976)

7. Arithmetic expressions are often represented in a computer either in Reverse Polish form, in which each operator is preceded by its operands, or by means of a binary tree structure. For example (A + B) * C has Reverse Polish form AB + C * and may be represented by the tree.

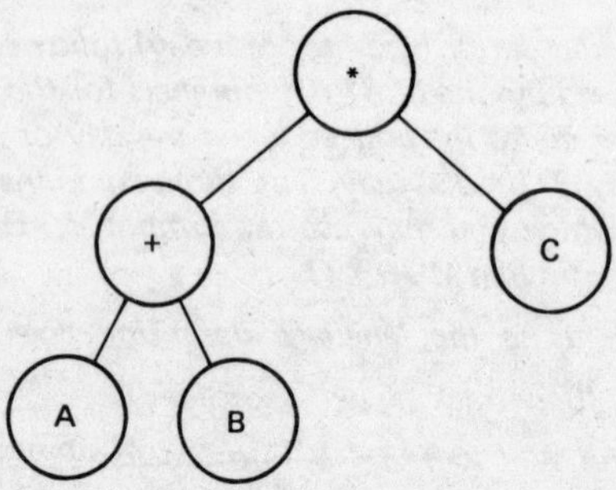

Why are these representations important?

Convert each of the following expressions to Reverse Polish form and draw an equivalent binary tree.

a. *(X + Y) * (X – Z)*

b. *2 * (3 * X + 1) ↑ 3*

c. *(A + B – 3 * (F – G)/H) – K * (F – G)*

Describe in outline the steps involved in generating the Reverse Polish form of an expression from its binary tree representation.

(London Specimen Paper)

8. Programs written in a high level programming language may be run on a particular computer using either a compiler or an interpreter. In each case the first part of the process is the same; as the program is entered a check is made for syntax errors, a symbol table is created, and the program is translated into reverse polish form. For the compiler the second part of the process is to translate the reverse polish form of the program into machine code which can subsequently be loaded and run. For the interpreter the second part of the process consists of interpreting the reverse polish form of the program and executing it, step by step.

a. *Explain what a symbol table is and how it is used.*

b. *Describe, with the aid of examples, what reverse polish form is. Why is it often used in the translation of high level programming languages?*

c. *Comment on the differences between the compiler and the interpreter. What particular advantages and disadvantages does each method have?*

(Cambridge 1982)

The Input-Output Subsystem

1. In this Part we see how various methods have been devised to overcome the problem of the wide range of speeds associated with different peripheral devices to endeavour to run the peripherals at, or near to, full speed with the minimum sacrifice of central processor time.

34 How Computers Handle Input and Output

INTRODUCTION.

1. This chapter discusses the general methods of computer input and output (I/O for short). It first introduces terminology and I/O problems. It then develops a discussion of the methods of I/O and shows how the various problems are overcome. The main methods discussed include the use of buffers, multiplexors, data channels, and, perhaps the most important, Interrupts.

2. An overall view of a **Typical Input-Output** (I/O) system is provided by Fig. 34.1. Reference to this diagram may be made throughout this chapter, but we will first define some terminology to be used.

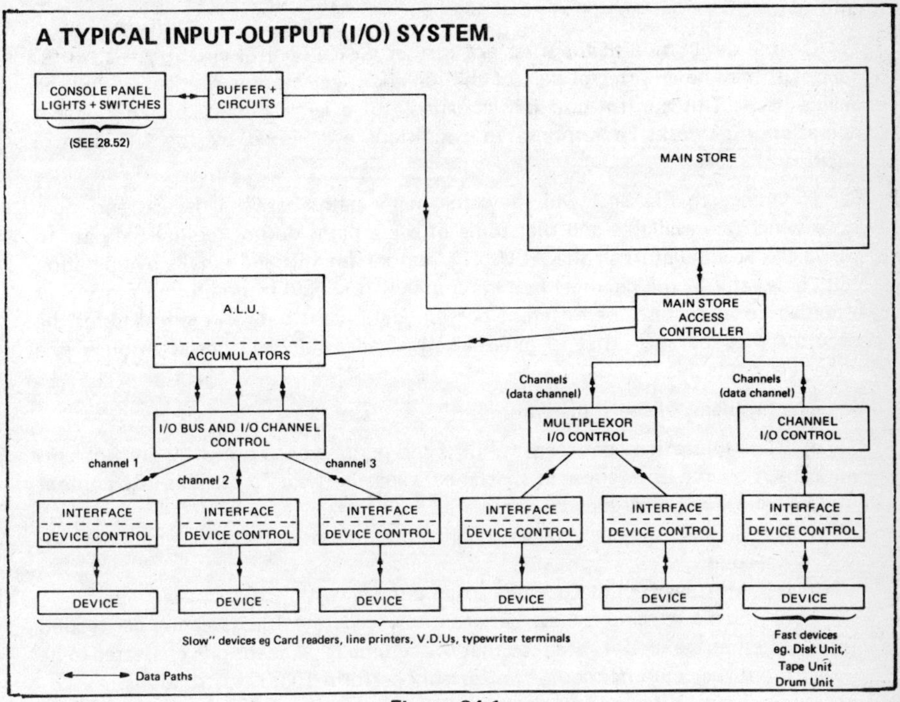

Figure 34.1.

3. A **buffer** is a temporary storage area which holds data during different stages of input or output. A buffer may be one of the following types:—

a. **Internal buffer area.** This is an area of main store set aside to hold data awaiting output or data recently input but not yet processed.

b. **Buffer registers.** These registers are located at various positions along the data path between the I/O devices and the CPU. They hold characters or groups of characters in the process of being transferred.

4. A **channel** is a path along which I/O data signals flow. Control signals follow a similar path to regulate the data flow. The peripheral end of the channel may be called a **port.**

5. A **bus** (also known as a **highway)** is an item of hardware within the CPU through which data signals pass from any one of a choice of sources to any one of a choice of destinations. On one side are connections to the channels for various devices, on the other are connections to accumulators in the ALU.

6. An **Interface** is an item of hardware located on each channel adjacent to the CPU. It converts control and data signals from the CPU, which are in a **standard form,** to forms usable by the device connected to the interface. It also turns all peripheral input to **one standard form** for the CPU.

The I/O control signals received by the interface from the CPU are usually generated by **I/O control circuitry** which itself is under the control of the **main control unit.**

7. On the device side of the interface further **device control circuitry** is at work. Part of it may be an integral part of the interface, yet more is resident within the device itself. This **control circuitry** is capable of a large amount of **autonomous operation** but works in response to conditions established by the **I/O control circuitry.**

8. Reference to Fig 34.1 will show the many paths between devices and main store which are available and that some of these paths do not require the data to go via the accumulators in the ALU. The reasons for this and details of operation will come later in the chapter. For the moment it should be noted that Fig 34.1 is intended to emphasise the different possible data paths but in practical terms the circuitry may be such that to external appearances all data passes through one rather elaborate bus.

9. The Problems of speed differences.

a. Communications between the CPU and peripherals is fraught with problems caused by the differences in speeds between the two. To put this into context the following points may be considered.

i. A memory cycle takes roughly one microsecond ie one millionth of a second.

ii. Most instructions can be carried out well within 10 microseconds.

ii. Some terminal typewriters can only generate 10 characters per second when at maximum speed, so that in the time it takes for one character to be input the computer could comfortably perform 10,000 instructions.

iv. Even faster devices such as chain printers or optical paper tape reader make transfers of data at rates which correspond to dozens or hundreds of instructions. Compared to the CPU they are slow.

v. Only for devices like magnetic disk, tape, or drum units which can transfer data at the rate of hundreds of thousands of characters per second can the speeds be considered as compatible with the CPU.

b. The differences in speed lead to a variety of techniques of I/O transfer.

10. Simple method of I/O (A typical arrangement is described).
We will consider the simplest method of transferring a single character from a peripheral and use the terminal typewriter for our example. First we must know of three special registers present in the interface card.

a. **Data buffer or Data buffer register.**
This holds one character either received from the device or to be sent to the device.

b. **'Busy' register or Control bit register.**
This is a **single bit register** solely under the control of the I/O control ie not influenced by the device. It is set to 1 when the channel is opened thereby starting a transfer and set to 0 if the channel is not to be used.

c. **'Done' register or Device status register.**
This is a **single bit register** normally set to zero as the Busy bit is set to 1. This register is set to one when a signal is received from the device, as it completes the transfer between itself and the data buffer register. A single bit register of this type is often called a FLAG.

This diagram summarises the arrangements. (It is not intended to give a complete picture).

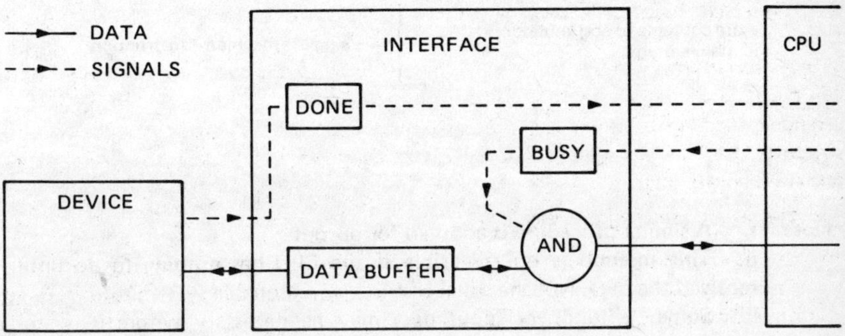

11. Crude Inefficient method of I/O (because the partial autonomy of the device is not used).
The following anotated pseudocode shows the types of machine instructions used in the various stages of input.

Notation B : value of Busy register
D : value of Flag in Done register.

Begin

Start input on specified device	The control circuitry will set B to 1 and send signals which will initiate the transfer of a character from the device to the data buffer register. It will also set D to zero. The peripheral then operates autonomously.
while D < > 1 **endwhile**	Repeated checks to see if the device has set the device status register to zero thereby indicating the completed transfer of data to the buffer. [This is a "listen loop". The CPU would waste time repeating this loop thousands of times]
transfer data from data buffer to accumulator	A single machine instruction.
store contents of accumulator in main storage	A single machine instruction.

end

Note. i. A similar procedure is adopted for output.

ii. This method is only sensible if the CPU has nothing to do until it received the data. Not the usual case in any reasonable system.

iii. Some "editing" of input data may be necessary before it is stored eg parity bits may be stripped off or one code form changed to another eg BCD to pure binary.

12. Simple I/O with other devices.

In principle many devices can operate in the manner just described with slight variations. Some examples are:—

a. **Optical Paper Tape Reader.**

Separate instructions are used for stopping or starting the tape motion. Once the tape is in motion each character may be read by starting a read action and then checking for a flag. The difference in speeds between the CPU and the device allows time for a check to be made to see if further characters are needed. If so, then another read action is started; if not there is still time to stop the tape before it reaches the next character code on the tape.

b. **Card Reader and Document Readers.**
Extra instructions are needed for non read actions such as removing the card from the hopper. The device status register is not just a single flag register as before, but hold codes giving information on such things as when the card is under the read station, when no cards are left, or when a card is jammed. Again each separate character is read in much the same way as described before.

c. **Line Printer.**
The **data buffer** register will hold a number of characters corresponding to a section of a line or a whole line. Characters are loaded into this buffer one after another and once the register is full a single print action is started by a suitable instruction.

d. **Graph Plotter** (See Fig. 6.5).
All drawing actions can be reduced to instructions such as:—

i. Raise or lower pen
ii. Move pen one unit across in ± Y direction
iii. Move pen (or drum) one unit side to side in ± X direction.

The instruction operand contains a control code for the appropriate movement. The instruction starts the device action which when terminated results in a flag being set.

Note. d.ii. and d.iii. may be combined to give 8 possible moves.

```
Begin
  place data in buffers for output

  repeat                                                      { Not those
    Start devices for which input or output is required ---{ already started
                                                              { of course.

    repeat                                                    { Devices are
      process available data for a while                 ---{ autonomous
                                                              { during this
                                                              { time.

                                                              { Flags are
                                                              { checked
    until any device has completed data transfer          --{ in turn
                                                              { for the
                                                              { queue of
                                                              { Devices

    transfer any data from buffer to main store      }       { Use would be
    place data in buffers for output                 }----{ made of an Internal
  until no input or output is required               }       { Buffer area
end                                                           { in Main Store.
```

Figure 34.2.

13. Where the program needs to make use of **several devices** for input and output and has processing to do at the ame time the following technique may be adopted. The method makes slightly better use of the processor's time but *'listening'* still forms part of the method.

BUFFERING.

14. Buffering. The technique just described is a simple example of **buffering.** Buffering is the name given to the technique of transferring data into temporary storage prior to processing or output, thus enabling the simultaneous operation of devices. This can only be achieved because of the autonomous operation of peripherals, which leaves the CPU **free for other work.**

15. Example. Suppose 2000 documents need to be input and the details on the document printed out on a line printer (one print line being used for each document read). The document reader operates at 1000 documents per minute and the printer at 500 lines per minute. The processing cycle and time required, would be as illustrated at Fig. 34.3.

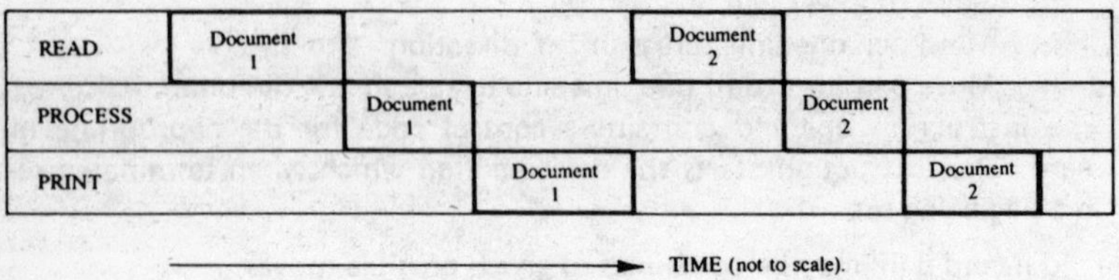

Figure 34.3.

Total time required:-

READ =	$2000 \times \frac{1}{1000}$	=	2 MINUTES
PROCESS	NEGLIGIBLE		–
PRINT	$2000 \times \frac{1}{500}$	=	4 MINUTES
		TOTAL	6 MINUTES

16. It should be recognised that whilst a document is being *processed,* both the document reader, and printer, are idle. Similarly, when a document is being read, the processor and printer are idle, and when a line is being printed, the processor and reader are idle.

17. Solution. Buffering is the name given to the technique of transferring data into temporary storage, prior to *processing* or *output.* This enables the *simultaneous operation of devices* as illustrated at Fig. 34.4.

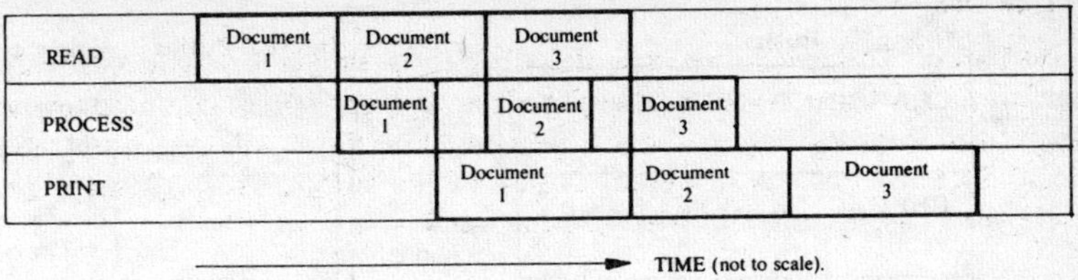

Figure 34.4.

Total time required:- After reading the first document all subsequent reading, processing and printing can be overlapped. Thus the total time required is a little over the speed of the slowest device ie. just over *4* minutes.

MULTIPLEXING.

18. Buffering is one way of overcoming differences in speeds of hardware devices and the CPU. Another way is by the use of **multiplexors.**

19. Multiplexing. This involves the transmission of character codes from a number of devices along **one** channel. The hardware device which performs this task is called a **multiplexor.** (Alternative spelling: multiplexer).

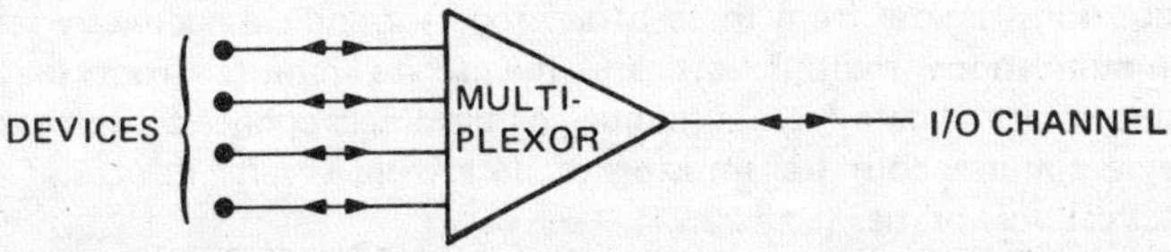

20. How it works. The multiplexor has its own buffer register used to receive characters from the various devices to which it is connected. These characters may be transmitted directly to a buffer area in main store as they arrive in the multiplexor buffer or they may be transmitted in a block at regular intervals. Either way a number of control signals are sent to and fro in order to identify the source of data so as to reorder it when received in main store. (See Fig 34.5). Multiplexors may act **synchronously** (ie transfer data at a regular timed frequency) or **asynchronously** ie transfer data as it is ready. Devices 1, 2 and 3 are inputting the strings ABC, PQR and XYZ respectively.

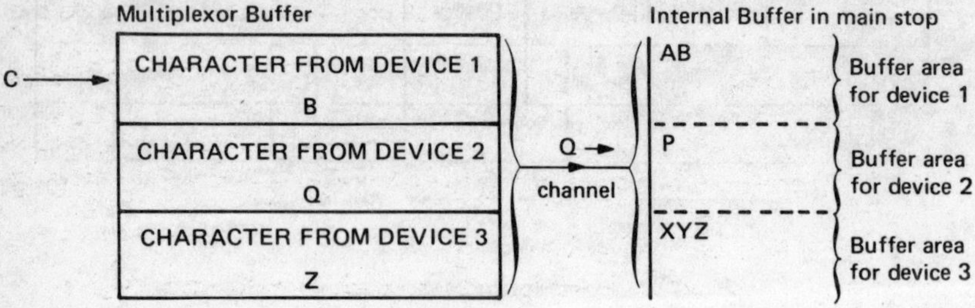

Figure 34.5.

Note. i. B has been transmitted and is about to be replaced by C in the multiplexor buffer.

ii. Q has just been received in the multiplexor buffer and is being transmitted.

iii. Z has been transmitted.

iv. Synchronous operation would involve a regular scan and clearing of the buffer.

21. Communications multiplexors.
Multiplexors are particularly useful in handling data from a number of terminals placed at positions remote from the central processor and connected by telephone links. **Communications multiplexors** are themselves remote from the central processor and transmit data from a number of terminals connected to them. They often provide simultaneous transmission of data from several devices. There are various practical possibilities (See 22.21).

DATA CHANNELS.

22. You will see from Fig 34.1 that the transfer of data between main store and devices such as disk or drum units is through a direct channel often called a **data channel.** Once the necessary conditions have been established by software, the transfers are entirely under the control of hardware. The data channel "steals" memory cycles from the instruction currently being performed in order to do the transfer. Since only one memory access can be handled at a time (through the main store access controller), the access by a data channel slows down the rate of program memory accesses. Once started the device has **autonomous operation.** (This technique is known as **DMA** (Direct Memory Access).

23. Example. The method is discussed with reference to magnetic tape and disc. We take the *magnetic tape case first.* You may wish to refresh your memory about the physical features of these units, and the blocking of records (5.26 and 16.11) before you read on.

a. Before the transfer can take place, machine instructions must be used to do the following:—

i. The tape is wound forward from the header label so as to bring the read/write heads over the IBG which lies in front of the first block of records on the tape file. (When writing *all* previous blocks and gaps are overwritten).

ii. Data from the tape will be read into an Internal buffer area, (or data will be written from this area to the tape). The address of the first location in this buffer will be placed into a special **memory address counter register.**

iii. The number of records or blocks to be read (or written) will be placed in another register.

iv. The tape read instruction is then issued.

b. The hardware now takes over, as follows (ie **autonomous operation**).

i. The tape is brought up to speed (if necessary).

ii. Magnetic coded marks on the tape indicate the start of the tape block to be read.

iii. When these marks are detected by the read heads a control signal is issued by the tape drive I/O control.

iv. When the control unit receives the control signal from the tape it automatically uses the next available memory cycle to transfer the first character between the tape block and the address specified in the memory address counter register.

v. The memory address counter register is increased by one, and the counter of number of records transferred adjusted.

vi. The hardware continues automatically to steal memory cycles (perhaps taking every other one) until the counter indicates that the transfer of all characters is complete).

vii. A 'Done' flag is then set by the I/O control unit.

24. Using data channels with magnetic disk units.

a. The principles are very similar to those used with magnetic tape:–

i. Setting **a memory address counter register** to specify the first location of the internal buffer area.

ii. The hardware 'steals' memory cycles as it transfers blocks of data.

b. With moving head disk units additional instructions are needed to do such things as:–

i. Select the surface read/write head.

ii. Move the heads over the appropriate tracks.

c. The unit detects data block positions by code marks on the disk. Timing tracks enable the I/O control to maintain accurate rotational speeds.

SYSTEM CONTROLS.

25. The I/O methods described so far have been described in terms of a single program handling the data transfers. To fully appreciate our next method you need to know these points about the **operating system** which handles it. (Operating systems are described in detail in chapter 39).

a. An operating system is a suite of programs which takes control over the operation of the computer.

b. A minimum operating system, and centre of a large one, is an 'Executive' or 'Supervisor' program which controls and schedules the use of hardware.

c. A program requiring to input or output data does so via the operating system in all but the simplest machines. The next method will be described in terms of such an arrangement.

INTERRUPTS.

26. An **interrupt** is a break into the normal automatic sequential control, so that instead of fetching the next instruction as part of the fetch execute cycle, the control unit fetches the first instruction of another program (the supervisor), or an instruction from another part of the same program. Details will be given in the next few paragraphs.

27. Use of Interrupts in I/O. (Practical implementations vary; this example is simplified but typical). For ease of explanation we start with a device which has *completed* a data transfer and therefore requires service.

a. The device attempts an interrupt request by setting the 'Done' flag to '1'. If the device's *interrupt status* is also '1' (ie Busy = 1) a '1' will also be loaded into a device status register thus making an interrupt request.

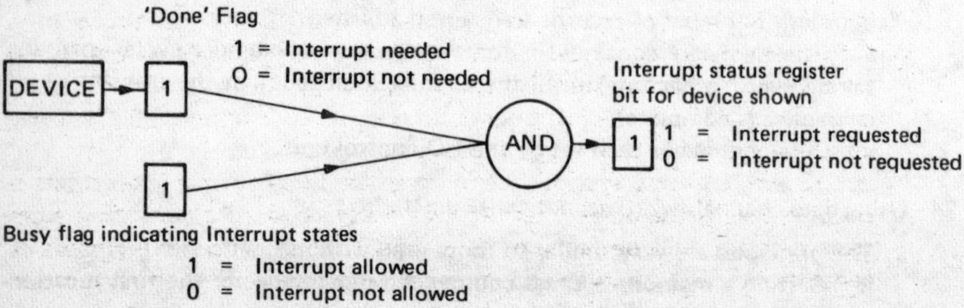

b. Just prior to **fetching** the next instruction, during the normal sequence of instructions, a check is made automatically by the CPU hardware to see if there are any **interrupt requests** (Interrupt Bit 1). If there are requests then there is a break in the normal sequence of instructions and the interrupt requests are dealt with. Control is then returned to the original interrupted program.

c. The checks for interrupts are only done if the interrupt system (hardware) is activated, so instructions usually exist for turning the interrupt system on or off. (An interrupt ON/OFF Flag is used).

d. Since more than one device may request an interrupt at any given time a position of priority is assigned to each device, eg by the position of the devices bit in the interrupt register.

e. A program which wishes to output data can request an interrupt in a similar way to a device. One way is to use an instruction which sets a special interrupt bit to '1'. The resultant interrupt causes an immediate exit from the program to the supervisor. On some systems the interrupt request is generated by the program attempting an I/O instruction. The hardware 'traps' the instruction and causes an interrupt.

28. The role of the supervisor. After an interrupt the supervisor is entered as follows:—

a. One particular location is used to hold the address of the first instruction in the supervisory program, eg location zero may be used, we will assume it is.

b. An interrupt request causes the CPU hardware to instigate an unconditional jump to the instruction whose address is specified in location zero. In this way the supervisory program is entered.

Provision is made for the supervisory program to save the link in order to return to the main program, eg the interrupt may place the contents of the SCR in a specified accumulator register.

c. On being entered the supervisor has these tasks to do:—

i. The link for return to the main program must be saved.

ii. The contents of all the accumulators must be saved so they may be replaced before returning to the main program.

iii. If an interrupt occurred during execution of a routine which was itself handling I/O from a device it could cause the loss of data by that routine. In such cases the routine usually switches off the interrupt system until it has completed its task and then switches it on again. While the interrupt system is switched off no interrupt can take place. (An interrupt ON/OFF flag 1 = ON 0 = OFF shows the interrupt system status).

iv. If the interrupt system is left on while handling one interrupt it is possible that yet another interrupt will occur. If this happens then again steps i. and ii. will be repeated. It is usual to store links and accumulator contents in LIFO stacks so that they can be obtained in the reverse order.

NB. A stack may be used for i and ii in a similar manner to that shown in 29.30.

Handling a Single Interrupt.

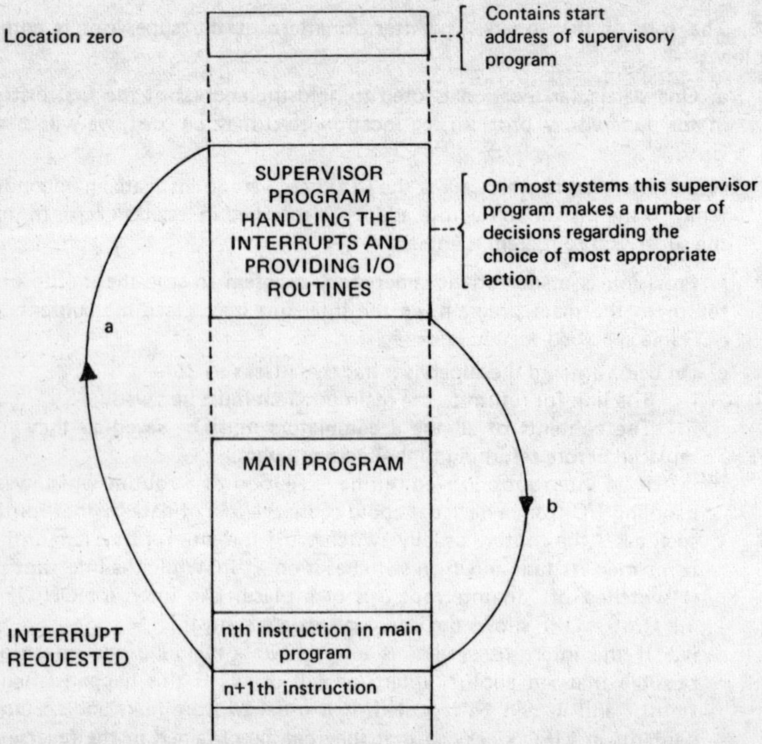

Note. i. The jump 'a' caused by the interrupt uses the contents of location zero to get the address of the supervisory program.

ii. Jump 'a' is done by CPU hardware, it is **not** a program instruction.

iii. For jump 'b' to occur the link (return address) must have been saved at the time of the original interrupt, eg. by being pushed onto a stack.

iv. I/O transfers are done in the same way as usual, eg buffer to accumulator. The necessary instruction must either be provided within the supervisory program or at a point in the main program known to the supervisory program.

Figure 34.5.

29. Using interrupts for input and output provides two main advantages over the 'look for flag/listen loop' method described earlier.

a. The interrupt occurs as soon as the device requires service, not when the program gets around to checking for the flag. The device can more easily be kept working at its maximum speed using interrupts.

b. It is essential with some devices that a check for the flag is made soon enough or data will have time to pass beneath the read/write heads or read stations. Interrupts allow these checks to be done as soon as possible before data is lost.

30. Assigning priority. (A more general discussion will follow later, chapter 39). The I/O channels usually have a priority assigned to them and the positioning of the devices along the I/O bus will therefore affect their priority. There are usually ways of overriding these basic hardware priorities and we will consider them shortly. First we will consider the way device speed affects priority.

31. Device speed. Low priority devices tend to wait a longer time for service (see device 3 in Fig 34.6). A slow device if given low priority might eventually hold up all processing activity by not having input sufficient data. As a general rule therefore low speed devices are given higher priority.

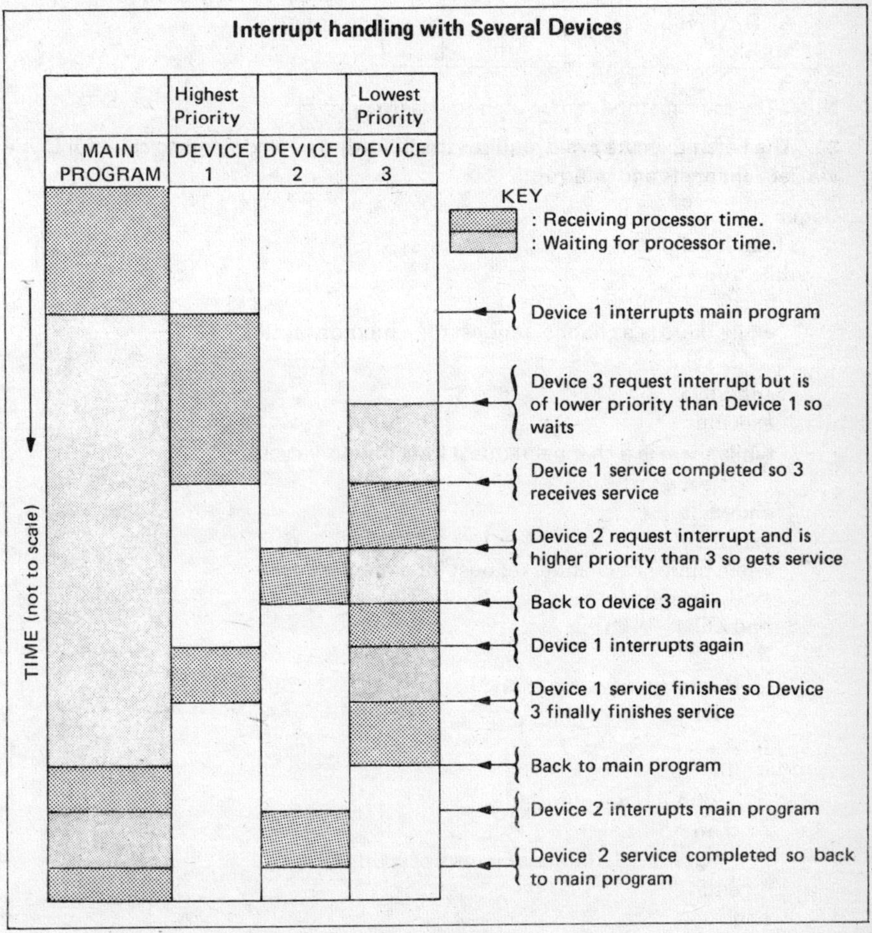

Figure 34.6.

32. Masking out low priority devices. The supervisor routine may need to prevent interrupts from low priority devices while it handles I/O from a high priority device. This can be done by a simple AND operation as shown here:—

DEVICE	1	2	3	4	
INITIAL INTERRUPT STATUS	1	1	1	1	All devices requesting interrupts.
MASK	1	0	0	0	
INTERRUPT STATUS AFTER AND WITH MASK	1	0	0	0	Only device 1 allowed to interrupt

Note. The same method can be used to change priority.

33. The Fetch-Execute cycle requires the following amendments to cater for DMA via data channels and interrupts.

```
Begin
  (* loop indefinitely *)
  while true
    fetch
    while there is a channel request for a memory cycle
          set it up
    endwhile
    execute
    while there is a channel request for a memory cycle
          set it up
    endwhile
    execute
    while there is a channel request for a memory cycle
          set it up
    endwhile
    if
       (* interrupt system is on *)
       interrupt_flag = 1
    then
       if
          there is an interrupt
       then
          SCR := (address of interrupt routine)
       endif
    endif
  endwhile
end
```

SUMMARY.

34. The main techniques are summarised in this table:

TECHNIQUE	DEVICE USED	CPU INVOLVEMENT	SOFTWARE/ HARDWARE ORIENTATION	COMMENTS	COMPLEXITY
'Listen loop' or program/ listen combined	Slow devices eg Terminal typewriter	Total	S	Only used in single program environment	Minimum
Autonomous Peripheral transfer	Fast devices eg Disk, Tape	Minimal—setting up and closing down hardware used	H	Processing speeds are affected because of stolen memory cycles during Fetch-Execute.	More complex hardware
Interrupts	Maximum advantage with slow devices. Used in set up or close down autonomous peripherals	CPU free between interrupts but has some extra work handling interrupts	S/H	Necessary when handling more than one program	Extra hardware needed

POINTS TO NOTE.

35. a. Take care to distinguish between the two types of buffer.

b. Note that when hardware "steals" memory cycles it does **not** change the normal sequence of instructions it merely slows things down a little.

c. Although described separately within the chapter all the methods are usually in use on a given system.

d. It is unusual and not desirable to use some devices without an interrupt system. Most devices which are in constant motion during data transfer run more smoothly and give faster rates of transfer if operated using interrupts.

e. The use of interrupts extends beyond input and output but the principle of working is the same. (Further discussion follows in chapter 39).

f. The handling of data in internal buffers often involves the use of queues, stacks, strings and lists. (chapter 31).

g. Buffering may be improved by **double buffering** in which one buffer is filled by the program as another is emptied by the device. The two swap over at a convenient stage.

STUDENT SELF TEST QUESTIONS.

(Answers on page 740)

1. *What are the problems of speed differences between the CPU and its peripherals?*

2. What is DMA? How does DMA work?

QUESTIONS WITHOUT ANSWERS.

3. Suggest possible ways in which VDU I/O could be handled on a system in which multiple VDUs are in use.

4. What is meant by the following terms?

a. channel
b. port
c. interface
d. autonomous operation.

File Processing

1. The processing of files is very important in Computer Science. This Part discusses the subject in detail.

2. In order to understand file processing it is necessary to first have some prior knowledge of both storage devices and media, and programming which is why the subject matter of this Part could not be introduced earlier in this book.

3. Chapter 35 describes traditional sequential file processing and makes particular reference to batch processing and magnetic tape.

4. Chapter 36 describes non-sequential file processing with particular reference to magnetic disk. It describes more advanced batch processing methods and introduces the ideas of transaction processing.

5. The methods of chapters 35 and 36 may be described as *conventional file processing.* In chapter 37 some problems of conventional file processing methods are identified and possible solutions are presented in the form of data bases and integrated systems.

35 Sequential File Processing

INTRODUCTION.

1. The main purpose of this chapter is to apply the basic ideas concerning storage media and processing requirements to sequential file processing. In order to place the subject matter in context, though, we also consider some factors affecting the choice of methods for file organisation and access. Methods associated with sequential file processing will be discussed too.

2. Sequential file processing is an important feature of the simpler and long established methods of batch processing. Such methods were established when magnetic tape was the main file processing medium. Today, the same methods continue to be used but with magnetic disk as the usual choice of storage medium.

3. The chapter contains two examples. The first is used to explain how a sequential master file is updated. The second example is more general and typifies sequential file processing using magnetic tape. The example is followed by a discussion of the advantages and limitations of magnetic tape as a file storage medium.

CHOICE OF FILE ORGANISATION AND ACCESS METHODS.

4. Factors affecting choice:–

a. **Size.**

i. Very large files are stored more economically on magnetic tape. Small files can use disk space well if blocks are suitably sized, but may be troublesome to access if strung along magnetic tape.

ii. The percentage of additions or deletions in file maintenance if low may allow satisfactory organisation of Indexed or Random files, but if high will make sequential organisation more attractive.

iii. If a file is likely to increase in size then the design of an Indexed or Random file must allow for it.

b. **Reference and Enquiry.** If quick reference is essential then Indexed or Random files will be needed. If the file is only used for quick one-off reference then a Random organisation will be best.

c. **Hit Rate** (15.18). This relates to b., in that low hit rates are suited by Indexed or Random files, and high hit rates are suited by sequential files. Putting together batches of enquiries to form a transaction file can raise hit rates.

d. **Security and Backup.** The 'Father-Son' concept (Fig. 16.2) is an aid to security when using sequential files. Indexed and Random files are overwritten *during processing* so they may need to be dumped onto tape or another disk *between processing,* as well as keeping a copy of all transactions between dumps.

FILE HANDLING TECHNIQUES.

5. The techniques discussed in this chapter apply to the following file handling activities.

a. **File creation.** The creation of transaction files **after** the validation stage will be considered

b. **File updating** (amendment)

c. **File maintenance**

The techniques described in this chapter apply mainly to sequential and Index Sequential file handling. During Random file handling each record is handled separately, and so techniques used with sequential transaction files may either apply to single records or be irrelevant.

6. Prior to any sequential file update or maintenance it is necessary to get the transaction file into a suitable form. This usually involves:

a. **file conversion** ie. converting from the input medium (diskette say) to storage medium. (magnetic tape say).

b. **Sorting** ie. the transaction file must be sorted into the sequence of the master file before processing can take place. The key fields of the transaction file may be sorted into either **numerical sequence** or **alphabetic sequence** according to the method used on the master file.

7. File conversion was discussed in chapters 5 and 19 and needs no further mention. Sorting was discussed in an earlier chapter but needs further discussion here.

SORTING.

8. The **number of records to be sorted** and **limitations of main storage** do not normally allow the sorting to be done in one attempt, so the sort is usually split into two stages:—

a. **String generation phase.** Manageable groups of records from the unsorted file are read into main storage. These groups are sorted into sequence and written as sequenced groups or **strings** onto other output tapes/disks.

b. **String merging phase** during which strings are read into main storage, **merged** into larger groups (records are in sequence within groups) and written out to disk or tape. The process is repeated until the whole file is in one sequence.

Each repetition of the string merging phase is called a **pass.**

9. **Internal Sorting.** This is sorting within main storage and is the type of sorting done during the **String generation phase.** Two basic types of method are

a. methods which swap whole records each time.

b. methods which swap keys and pointers.

The difference is illustrated by this diagram.

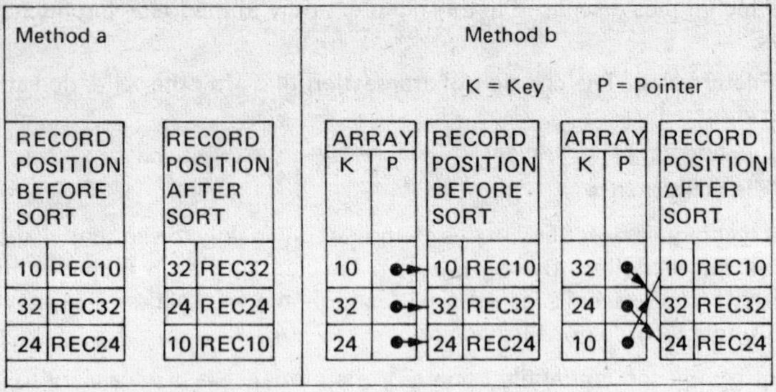

10. Sort Examples. A detailed example of sorting was given in 12.20. Some further methods are outlined here. The first two examples sort the data into descending sequence which is less common than sorting into ascending sequence. The reader is invited to rework them as ascending sequences as an exercise.

a. **Sort Example 1.** This is just one of the many possible methods.
Suppose that 10 numbers in an array are to be sorted. The following method could be used.

Procedure

i. Find largest number
ii. Swap it with 1st number
iii. Find next largest (ie largest between 2nd and last)
iv. Swap with 2nd number
v. Find next largest (ie largest between 3rd and last)
vi. Swap with 3rd number.

etc. (see below).

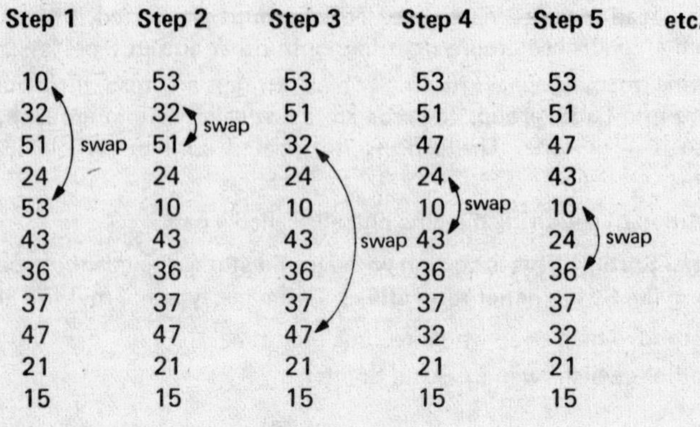

b. **Sort Example 2. (Bubble Sort).**
The previous example shows a method which takes no account of the initial order of the data. The bubble sort is quicker if the data is partially sorted.

Procedure.

i. Work down from the top to find the first number out of sequence

ii. Move the number up until its correct position is found moving other numbers down as you go. (The number rises like a bubble in liquid)

ii. Repeat as long as necessary.

Step 1		**Step 2**		**Step 3**		**Step 4**	**Step 5**	**etc.**
10		32		51		51	53	53
32	raise 32	10		32		32	51	51
51	lower 10	51		10		24	32	43
24		24	raise 51	24		10	24	32
53		53	lower 10	53	raise 24	53	10	24
43		43	and 32	43	lower 10	43	43	10
36		36		36		36	36	36
37		37		37		37	37	37
47		47		47		47	47	47
21		21		21		21	21	21
15		15		15		15	15	15

c. **Quicksort Example.** This method is one of the most efficient methods of internal sorting but is rather more complicated. The method is recursive and is applied to smaller and smaller sub-divisions of the array to be sorted. In this example we will consider a sort into ascending sequence.

Procedure.

i. Use the first value as **pivot** value (ideally the pivot will be a middle value in terms of magnitude).

ii. Permute the remaining values so that for a given subscript (the partition subscript) all values with this and lower subscripts are lower in value than the pivot and all values with higher subscripts are larger than or equal to the pivot. To permute the values perform a set of swaps in which successive high values in the lower part of the array are swapped with successive low values in the upper part.

iii. Swap the pivot value with the value at the partition subscript.

iv. Re-apply the procedure to the part of the array above the partition subscript and to the part below the partition subscript.

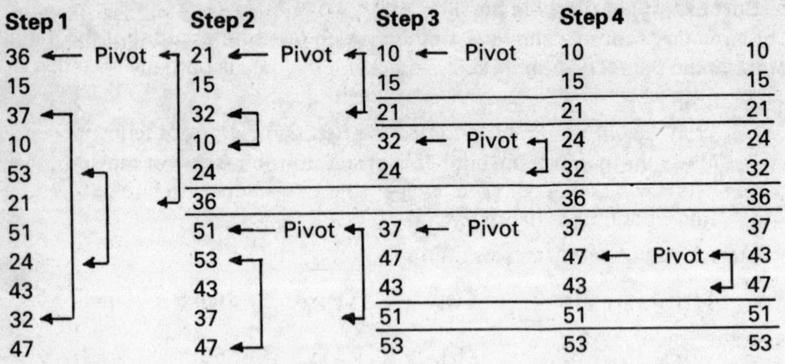

NB. The pivot is pointed to in those parts of the array in which sorting is incomplete.

STRING MERGING. (NB. These are strings of records **not** character strings).

11. The merge sort. This works as follows:–

a. Sequenced strings are placed alternately on two magnetic tapes. (Disk could be used but the 'classical' method uses tapes). Call the tapes A and B.

b. The 1st string from A is merged with the 1st string from B and this new sequence string is written onto a third tape C. (If possible these strings are placed alternately on two tapes C and D).

c. The process is repeated until **just one** string exists. This is the transaction file ready for use.

Note. The tape pairs AB and CD can be used alternately as input and output tapes as shown in this diagram.

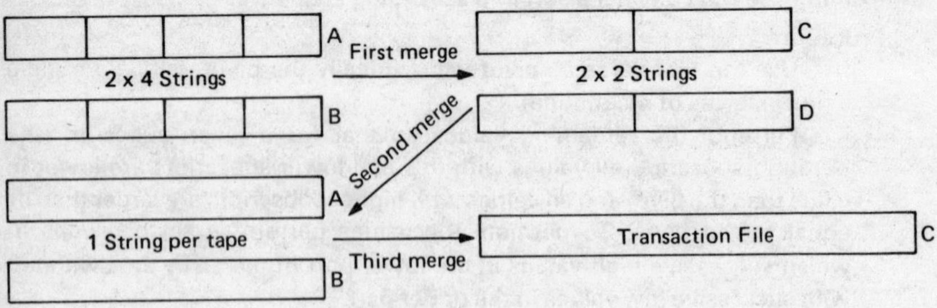

12. The procedure for merging the strings is given in the following pseudocode. The pseudocode shows the logic of merging one pair of strings rather than the practical details.

```
Begin
  if
      there is a record left in both string A and string B
  then
      if
          Key of string A > Key of string B
      then
          place the A record onto C
      else
          place the B record onto C
      endif
  endif
  place the remaining records onto C
end
```

13. Three tape merge using the Fibonacci sequence.
The Fibonacci sequence starts, 1, 1, 2, 3, 5, 8, 13, 21 . . . . and successive terms are the sum of the previous two eg 21 = 8 + 13. Strings are distributed on two of the three tapes in proportion to two suitable successive terms in the Fibonacci sequence eg 8 strings would be distributed 5, 3. The following diagram outlines the method. (Details of tape copies and records are omitted for the sake of clarity).

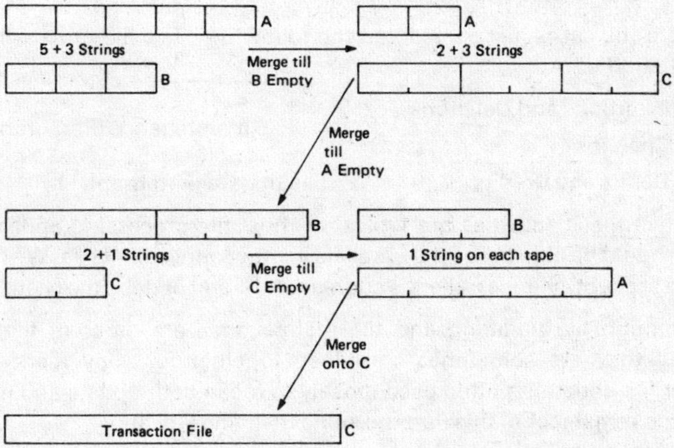

14. Final sequencing.
A final check may be made to ensure that all records on the transaction file do lie in sequence.

15. Collating.

a. The merging of punched card files is called collating.

b. An offline device able to do this task is called a **collator**.

c. Collating can also involve merging and matching eg a transaction file is merged with a master file and unpaired records are removed thus leaving only those records needed for updating.

APPLICATION EXAMPLE.

16. In order to illustrate file processing activities we will now consider a simple stock control system. This example will be used both in this chapter and again in the next one.

17. Details about individual stock items may be stored as logical records in a stock master file. ie. a stock item is an "entity" (15.7). One "attribute" (15.7) of the stock item entity will be the number of items in stock.

18. Events taking place in the organisation will change the actual stock. The master file must be made to reflect these changes so that the required information about stock can be produced from it.

19. Events such as the introduction of new stock items, or the discontinuation of existing items, correspond to the *insertion* or *deletion* of entities in the master file.

20. Events such as the delivery of items as they are sold, correspond to *"Debiting"* or *"Crediting"* the attribute value of the number of items in stock.

21. Events such as price increases to stock items correspond to *changing* the attribute value of stock item price.

22. From the cases just considered the following basic file processing activities can be identified:-

a. Insertions and Deletions
b. Changes } File maintenance (Paragraph 5c)

c. Debits and Credits } File update (Paragraph 5b)

In fact these activities are typical of most file processing applications. The reader should be able to see the parallels in other applications eg. We may open or close an account, change a client's address and credit or debit the client's account.

23. Although file updating and file maintenance are different file processing activities they are sometimes combined together for convenience. The term "master file update" is often used loosely to mean both update and maintenance and in the remainder of this Part the same meaning will apply.

24. Transactions. Relevant details of events need to be recorded and input to provide the data needed to update the master file. Since data is recorded about the events, the events are entities too. In traditional file terminology these entities are called transactions.

PROCESSING STRATEGIES.

25. There are two basic strategies for processing transactions against the master file:-

a. **Transaction processing** – ie. processing each transaction as it occurs.

b. **Batch processing** – ie. collecting transactions together over some interval of time and then processing the whole batch.

26. One method of processing is no better than the other. It is a matter of "horses for courses". Details of the different methods of file processing will be discussed in the chapter following this one. The relative advantages and disadvantages of the different methods will be included in the discussion.

27. Transaction processing will be considered in the next chapter. Batch processing is most commonly achieved by sequential file processing so batch processing will now be explained before we continue with an example of sequential file processing.

28. The majority of commercial computer applications are involved in batch processing. Transactions are accumulated into batches of suitable sizes, then each batch is sorted and processed. The concept is not new, in fact it is *also* adopted in most manual and mechanised systems of data processing. By its very nature a batch processing system will involve a degree of "delay". Generally, the result of processing a particular *item* of data will not be known until the results of the *batch* are known.

EXAMPLE 1 – UPDATING A SEQUENTIAL MASTER FILE.

29. This example illustrates the basic principles involved in the update of a sequential master file, by dealing with the update of a simple stock master file.

30. Each item of stock is an entity about which data is recorded in one logical record. Each logical record is identified by its own unique key (its stock number). At any one time only some of the set of available keys will be *allocated* to stock items. eg. if an account number is a key some account numbers are not allocated.

31. It will aid a clearer understanding of the master file update if we think of the master file as the *complete* sequence of available keys, although only some keys will be allocated to stock items at any one time. The *status* of a key, ie. allocated or not allocated, is signified by the fact that only allocated keys have records physically present within the master file.

32. Processing operations. There are different types of transactions, and each transaction corresponds to a particular operation on a master file record. The status of the key will determine whether or not the operation is a valid one in a particular situation. The possible combinations of valid and invalid operations are shown in the following table:-

		TRANSACTION TYPE				
		INSERT NEW RECORD	DELETE EXISTING RECORD	CHANGE EXISTING RECORD	CREDIT EXISTING RECORD	DEBIT EXISTING RECORD
Key Status Prior To Processing The Transaction	Allocated	×	√	√	√	√
	Not Allocated	√	×	×	×	×

Key: / : a valid operation.
× : an invalid operation.

eg. "Insert new record" is **not** a valid transaction if the key is already allocated ie. present. Similarly "Delete existing record" is **not** valid if the key is not allocated.

Figure 35.1.

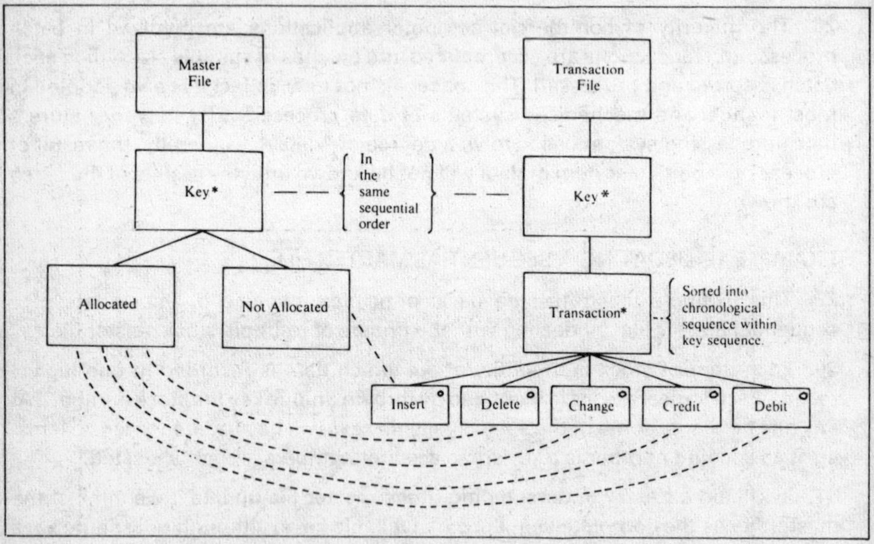

NB. ----- indicates valid operations.
Note: Some master keys may not have any corresponding transactions.

Figure 35.2. Structure Diagrams for the Two Files used in the Update.

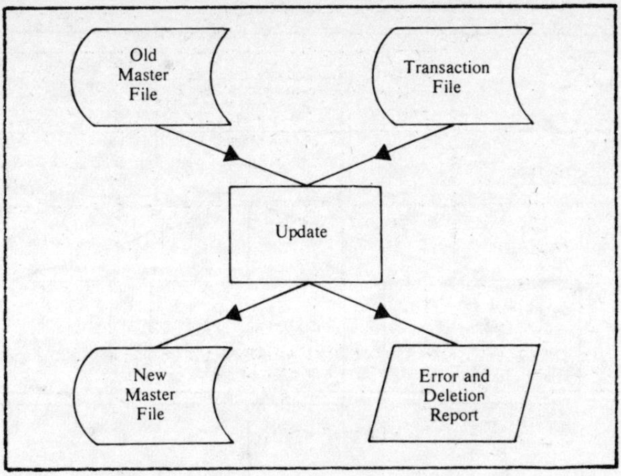

Figure 35.3. Sequential Master File Update – System Flowchart.

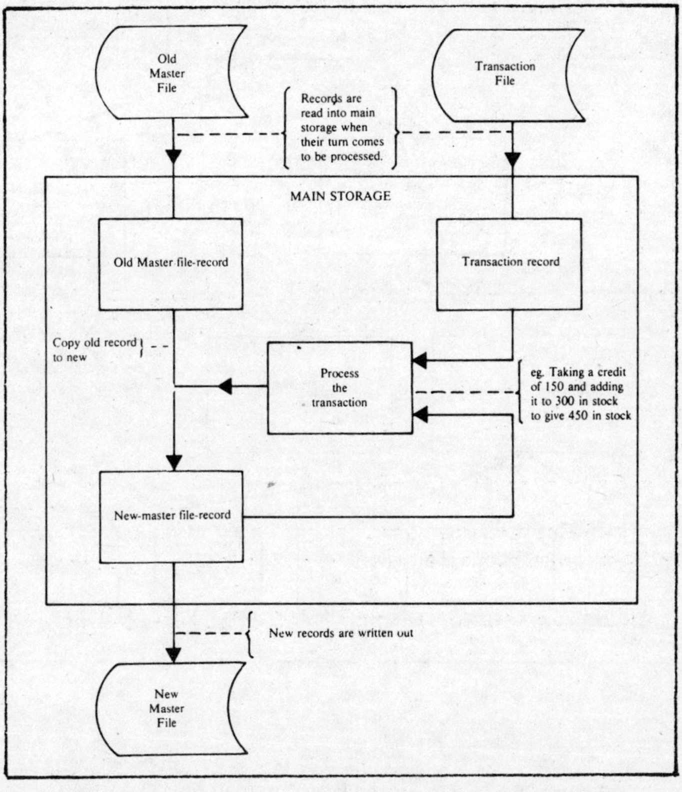

Figure 35.4. The Flow of Data during a Sequential File Update.

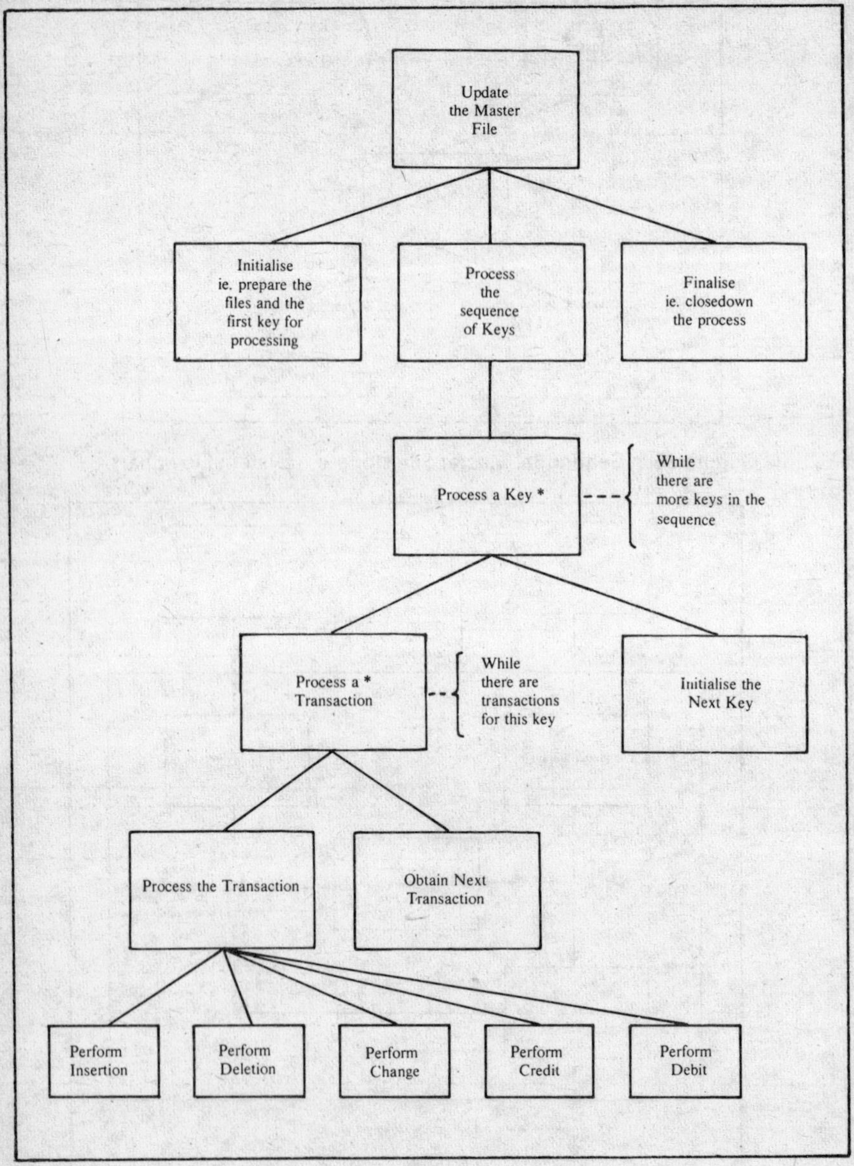

Figure 35.5. A Structured Diagram giving an Overview of the Master File Processing.

Key	Old Master File Records			Transaction File Records			New Master File Records			Comment
	Key	Item Price	Number in Stock	Key	Type	Value	Key	Item Price	Number in Stock	
1000	1000	15	300	1000 1000 1000	Credit Credit Debit	150 200 300	1000	15	350	The number in stock takes the successive values 300, 450, 650, 350, as credits and debits are made
1001	1001	25	450				1001	25	450	No transaction, so master record is unchanged
1002										Key not allocated
1003	1003	20	0	1003	Delete					Master record is deleted by not writing to new master
1004										Key not allocated
1005				1005 1005	Insert Credit	30 250	1005	30	250	A new master record is created with an item price of 30 and zero stock. Stock is then credited with 250 items
1006										Key not allocated
1007	1007	15	300	1007	Change	20	1007	20	300	Assume for simplicity that change applies to price only
1008	1008	30	350	1008	Insert	35	1008	30	350	An invalid transaction – cannot insert existing record
1009	1009	25	400				1009	25	400	No transaction, so master record is unchanged.
1010				1010	Debit	200				An invalid transaction – cannot debit non existent stock.
1011										Key not allocated
1012				1012	Delete					An invalid transaction – can only delete existing record
1013	1013	30	200				1013	30	200	No transaction, so master record is unchanged.
............etc............And so on............										

Figure 35.6. Detailed example showing how the File Data is processed.

```
Program Master_file_update
constants
        sentinel = 99999
variables
        the_key_to_process          : integer
        key_is_allocated            : boolean
        old_master_record       : record
                                        Key                 : integer
                                        item_price          : real
                                        number_in_stock     : integer
                                  endrecord
        new_master_record       : record
                                        key                 : integer
                                        item_price          : real
                                        number_in_stock     : integer
                                  endrecord
        transaction_record      : record
                                        key                 : integer
                                        transaction_type    : string
                                        item_value          : real
                                        stock_value         : integer
                                  endrecord
```

```
Begin
    (* open files *)
    open old_master_file for sequential input
    open new_master_file for sequential output
    open transaction_file for sequential input
        (* initialise records and keys *)
    call read (old_master_file, old_master_record)
    call read (transaction_file, transaction_record)
    the_key_to_process : = min (old_master_record.key,
                                transaction_record.key)
    call initialise_the_key_to_process (the_key_to_process,
                                        old_master_record,
                                        new_master_record,
                                        key_is_allocated)
    (* process all keys *)
    while (* there is a key to process *)
            the_key_to_process < > sentinel
        while (* there is a transaction for this key *)
                the_key_to_process = transaction_record.key
            call process_the_transaction (new_master_record,
                                          transaction_record,
                                          key_is_allocated)
            call read (transaction_file, transaction_record)
        endwhile
        if
            key_is_allocated
        then
            call write (new_master_file, new_master_record)
        endif
        the_key_to_process : = min (old_master_record.key,
                                    transaction_record.key)
        call initialise_the_key_to_process (the_key_to_process,
                                            old_master_record
                                            new_master_record,
                                            key_is_allocated)
    endwhile
    (* close files *)
    close old_master_file
    close new_master_file
    close transaction_file
end
```

```
procedure read (  IN    file_name        : string
                  OUT   record_name      : record )
        (* If there are more records in the named file yet to be read this
           procedure reads the next record from the file into the named record.
           Otherwise, the procedure assigns the value of the sentinel to the
           named record's key.
           NB. In this case the sentinel is a value higher than any key value.
        *)
procedure write ( IN    file_name        : string
                  OUT   record_name      : record)
        (* This procedure writes the value of the named record out to the
           named file.
        *)
function min (first_key, second_key, : integer ): integer
        (* This function returns the smaller value of its two arguments.
        *)
        Begin
              if
                 first_key < second_key
              then
                 min : = first_key
              else
                 min : = second_key
              endif
        end
```

```
procedure initialise_the_key_to_process(
            IN       the_key_to_process     : integer
            IN-OUT   old_master_record,
                     new_master_record      : record
                     key_is_allocated       : boolean)
      (* Provided there are still records to be processed this procedure sets
         key_is_allocated to the appropriate state and sets up a new_master_
         record if one is required.
      *)
      Begin
          if
              (* there are still records to process*)
              the_key_to_process < > sentinel
          then
              if
                  the_key_to_process = old_master_record.key
              then
                  key_is_allocated : = true
                  new_master_record : = old_master_record
                  read(old_master_file, old_master_record)
              else
                  key_is_allocated : = false
              endif
          endif
      end
```

```
procedure process_the_transactions (    IN-OUT   new_master_record
                                        IN       transaction_record
                                        IN-OUT   key_is_allocated )
        (* This procedure processes the five types of transactions.
        *)
        Begin
            selectcase transaction_type
              case insert
                    if
                      NOT Key_is_allocated
                    then
                      (* copy details from transaction
                         to new_master_record
                      *)
                      key_is_allocated : = true
                    else
                      output ("ERROR – record already exists")
                    endif
              case delete
                    if
                      key_is_allocated
                    then
                      key_is_allocated : = false
                      (* output to deletion report *)
                    else
                      output ("ERROR – record does not exist ")
                    endif
              case change
                    if
                      key_is_allocated
                    then
                      (* make_changes to new_master_record *)
                    else
                      output ("ERROR – record does not exist ")
                    endif
              case credit
                    if
                      key_is_allocated
                    then
                      (* add transaction value to new master value *)
                    else
                      output ("ERROR – record does not exist")
                    endif
```

```
        case debit
                if
                    key_allocated
                then
                    (* subtract transaction value
                        from new master value *)
                else
                    output ("ERROR – record does not exist ")
                endif
        case else
                (* the transaction is of an invalid type
                    and should be reported *)
        endselectcase
end
```

33. Batched Transactions. Batches of transactions of different types are accumulated together into a transaction file. The means by which these transactions are entered into the system have been covered in earlier chapters.

34. In the case of a sequential master file update, the transaction file is *sorted* into the same key sequence as the master file prior to processing. This enables the processing to be carried out in an orderly and efficient manner.

35. Within one transaction file there are likely to be multiple transaction records with particular key values eg. several debits from the same stock item. The sequence in which these transactions are processed should correspond to the chronological sequence of events which created them eg. new stock must be introduced before it is removed, and similarly a key must be allocated before stock is debited from its record.

36. The way in which transaction file and master file are related by key sequence is shown in Fig. 35.2.

37. The update. An overview of the update is provided by Fig. 35.3. Fig. 35.4 gives a further level of detail by showing how only one key is processed at a time, so that only a limited number of records need be present in main storage at any one time.

38. The procedure is given in outline in the structure diagram (Fig. 35.5) and in greater detail, in pseudocode, in Fig. 35.7. The procedure shown in these two diagrams may be easier to understand if read in conjunction with Fig. 35.6.

EXAMPLE 2 – MULTIPLE FILE UPDATES.

39. This example, which deals with order processing, shows batch processing involving the update of two master files. The method typifies batch processing using magnetic tape. The reasons why *magnetic disk is normally used in preference to magnetic tape* will be given later.

40. The following Systems Flowcharts should be studied in conjunction with the notes that follow them.

FILE UPDATES USING MAGNETIC TAPE.

This chart illustrates the computer runs necessary to update the stock and customer files and to produce invoices. Orders are entered at a VDU and the stock file (held in stock number sequence) and customer file (held in customer number sequence) are stored on magnetic tape.

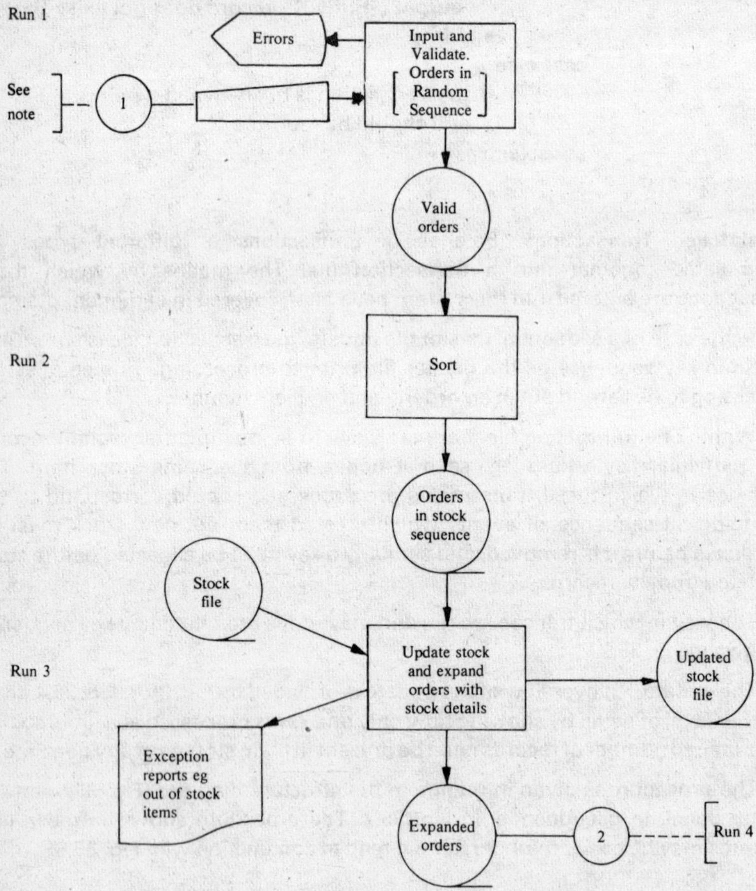

Note:

Connector symbol 1 shows the link between this part of the systems flowchart and another part of the chart which contains the clerical procedures involved in preparing the documents for input.

Figure 35.8.

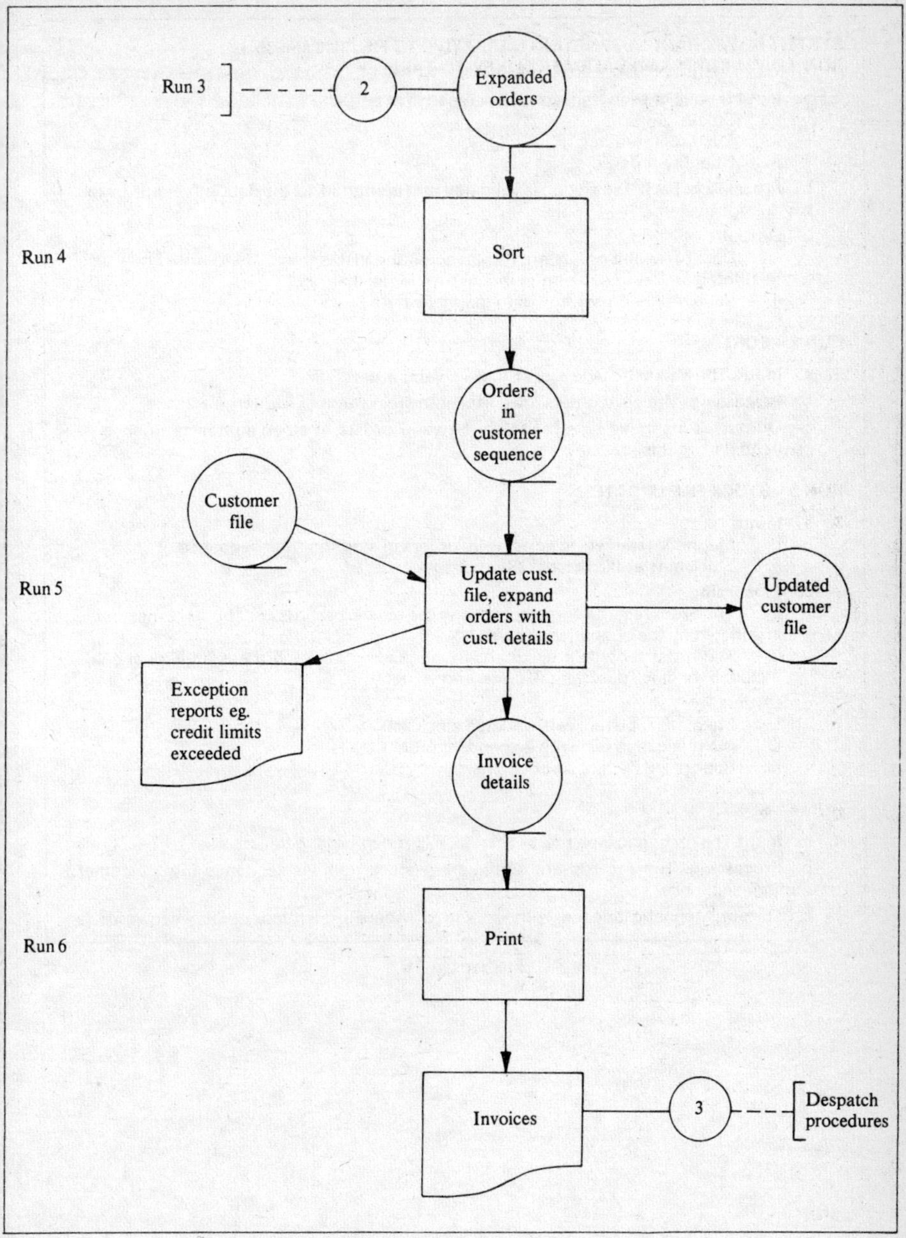
Run 3
2
Expanded orders
Run 4
Sort
Orders in customer sequence
Customer file
Run 5
Update cust. file, expand orders with cust. details
Updated customer file
Exception reports eg. credit limits exceeded
Invoice details
Run 6
Print
Invoices
3
Despatch procedures

Figure 35.9.

SYSTEM FLOWCHART SUPPORTING NARRATIVE TO FIG. 35.8 and 35.9.
RUN 1 DATA INPUT AND VALIDATION (KEY-TO-TAPE).

1. a. **Input** Details of each transaction are typed in at a VDU:–
i. Stock number.
ii. Customer number.
iii. Quantity ordered.

b. **Processing.** Each transaction is validated as it is entered. ie. the data is "vetted" by the key-to-tape system.

c. **Output**
i. Data of invalid orders are displayed on the VDU screen. These errors may also be printed on low speed printer (not shown in the diagram).
ii. Valid orders are written onto *magnetic tape.*

RUN 2 – SORT.

2. a. **Input.** The magnetic tape reel at 1c.ii. ie. valid orders.

b. **Processing.** The valid orders are sorted into stock number sequence.

c. **Output.** A magnetic tape reel with the valid orders in stock number sequence ie. *sequentially* organised.

RUN 3 – STOCK FILE UPDATE.

3. a. **Input.**
i. Magnetic tape reel at 2c. ie. valid orders in stock number sequence.
ii. Stock master file in stock number sequence.

b. **Processing.**
i. The order records are matched with the master records and the stock master file is updated by the quantities of items.
ii. The order records are 'expanded', ie. each order record has additional fields included for stock description, price, and value.

c. **Output.**
i. Magnetic tape reel with updated stock file.
ii. Magnetic tape reel with 'expanded' order details.
iii. Reports on "out of stock" items.

RUN 4 – SORT.

4. a. **Input** The magnetic tape reel at 3c.ii., ie. expanded order details:

b. **Processing.** The records are sorted from stock number sequence into customer number sequence.

c. **Output.** Magnetic tape reel with 'expanded' orders in *customer number* sequence.

Figure 35.10.

RUN 5 – CUSTOMER FILE UPDATE.

5. a. **Input.**
- i. the magnetic tape reel at 4c.
- ii. Customer master file in customer number sequence.

b. **Processing.**
- i. The order records are matched with the customer master records and the invoice amount calculated. The customer master records are updated by the value of the invoices.
- ii. Name and address details are extracted from master records.

c. **Output.**
- i. Magnetic tape reel with updated customer file.
- ii. Magnetic tape reel with invoice details.
- iii. Reports on credit limits being exceeded (etc.)

RUN 6 – PRINT OUTPUT.

6. a. **Input.** The magnetic tape reel at 5c.ii. ie. invoice details.

b. **Processing.** The invoices are printed.

c. **Output.** Printed invoices on the line printer.

Notes:

1. The use of tape as the storage medium requires that each transaction file and appropriate master *must* be in the same sequence in order to carry out processing.

2. Consequently there is need for much sorting and re-sorting of the transaction file.

3. Two updating runs were required (ie. Updating the stock file and the customer file) and a sort was necessary before each.

4. Not all the information required could be obtained in one RUN and thus 6 separate runs were necessary to produce the final output.

5. a. If an order is found to be unacceptable on Run 5 (for reasons of "credit" for instance) then the stock file shows a false position. The order will have been recorded during Run 3, thus reducing the balance of the particular produce. Notice that all subsequent orders for that product on Run 4 will be processed in the light of the stock having been depleted by the amount involved; a situation which in fact does not exist as Run 5 shows.

b. The stock file is "put right" on the next run by means of a "receipt" transaction (ie. an adjustment voucher).

Figure 35.11.

MAGNETIC TAPE.

41. Having just considered an example in which magnetic tape was shown in use for file processing, this is an appropriate point for us to discuss the advantages and limitations of tape as a storage medium.

42. Advantages of tape.

a. It is relatively cheap. (eg. approx' £10 per reel vs approx £250 per disk pack).

b. It has high capacity enabling it to store the largest files.

c. The data transfer speed is fairly high.

d. It requires no complicated systems software for its operation.

e. Industrial standards govern the way data is normally recorded on tape. This ensures compatibility between different computers and therefore allows bulk off-line data transfers between systems.

43. Limitations of tape.

a. The major limitation of tape lies in the fact that it is a *serial* non-addressable medium and many of the other limitations spring from this.

b. As tape is a serial medium all transaction files must be in the sequence of the appropriate master file. This involves a great deal of *unproductive* time spent in sorting and re-sorting input data.

c. Updating a master tape file involves reading and writing the complete file however small the transaction file may be. Notice that when the batches are very small (ie. the hit-rate (15.18) is low) – this will involve a high proportion of *redundant processing* (ie. the reading and writing of the inactive records).

d. Because tape is a non-addressable medium a particular record cannot be accessed directly. Information required from a particular record is *not available* until the whole batch has been processed.

e. Several runs are required to produce output and this may result in some files not reflecting a *true up to date position* at a given moment (Fig. 35.11 Note 5).

44. These limitations have caused the steady decline of tape as an on-line storage medium, although tape is still of major importance for off-line storage eg. backup and data entry. Magnetic tape is still used in some applications where there is a high hit-rate, where "delay" as such is of no consequence, and where a direct access facility is not required. Examples of such applications are payroll which requires processing only once a week and files of historical data which are only required periodically.

SUMMARY.

45. a. The factors affecting choice of file processing method were discussed:
- i. Size.
- ii. Reference and Enquiry.
- iii. Hit Rate.
- iv. Security and Backup.

b. File handling techniques applicable to sequential files were discussed.

c. Sequencing and sorting are common techniques required to get transaction tapes in the sequence of the master file.

d. The sorting of files usually has to be done in two stages:–
- i. String generation phase, done internally.
- ii. String merging phase, using backing store.

e. Choice of sorting methods affected by:–
- i. File size – whether or not two stages are necessary.
- ii. Main store size – whether or not two stages are necessary.
- iii. Degree of pre-ordering – the bubble sort is quicker.
- iv. Record size – whether the whole record or just the key is moved.
- v. For final sequencing a serial check is sufficient.

f. Batch processing was explained.

g. A detailed example of the updating of a sequential master file was given.

h. Multiple file updates were explained by example.

i. The advantages and limitations of tape as a file processing medium were explained.

POINTS TO NOTE.

46. a. Internal sorting is sometimes called **in-core storting** a term left over from the days when main storage was made from cores.

b. The time taken to perform an internal sort increases with the number of records. If n records are to be sorted then the time taken will be in proportion to n^2 for all the methods described, with the exception of quicksort. In average conditions quicksort will take a time in proportion to n log n which means that quicksort is normally much quicker than the other methods when n is large.

c. We say that the records are **sorted** but the file is **sequenced.**

d. The merge using the Fibonacci sequence is more efficient than the classical merge sort.

e. The example of file updating and maintenance shows a common method of combining maintenance with updating thereby saving a separate run with low hit rate.

f. Tape is no longer an important on-line storage medium because it is a serial access medium.

g. Tape is very important as a low cost high volume off-line storage medium.

STUDENT SELF TEST QUESTIONS.

(Answers on page 740)

1. *Describe a sorting method that would be suitable for records held*

   a. on magnetic tape,

   b. in immediate access store.

   State two factors, other than the storage media, that would influence your choice of sorting method.

   (A.E.B. 1977)

2. *How does the hit rate influence the choice of file processing method?*

3. *Describe the stages involved in preparing a batch of transactions for a sequential file update.*

4. *Identify the basic file processing activities.*

QUESTIONS WITHOUT ANSWERS.

5. *In 35.10 you were invited to rework the sorting examples so that the results were in ascending order. If you have not yet done so do so now.*

6. *With reference to 35.13 show how a file of 21 sorted sequences of records can be split up and successively merged into one sorted file.*

7. *Distinguish between batch processing and transaction processing.*

8. *Explain what is meant by a check digit and give an example of its use.*

By use of a chart or otherwise, indicate how an ordered master file can be updated using a similarly ordered transaction file if one allows deletions, insertions and amendments of the records.

How can you protect this process against hardware or software failures?

(15 marks)

(London 1983)

9. *A supermarket uses a computer to keep a daily check on its stock levels. Information regarding the sale and delivery of goods is recorded, resulting in a transaction file containing records which consist of the following three fields:*

Item number: Quantity; Marker.

For goods sold the marker is S, for goods received it is R. At the end of each day this file is used to update the master file, the records of which consist of the following fields:

Item number; Description; Quantity-in-stock; Re-order-Level.

Both of the above files are sorted into ascending item number sequence.

Construct a flowchart or an appropriate pseudocode description for a program to update the master file with the stock movements from the transaction file and to produce a report of all those items where the updated quantity in stock is less than the re-order level on one printer and an error report on another.

You may assume that each file is terminated by a dummy record containing a 'high value' item number. *(20 marks)*

(AEB 1983)

36 Non-Sequential File Processing

INTRODUCTION.

1. The previous chapter introduced sequential file processing by the use of examples which explained the basic methods and which typified the use of magnetic tape. In this chapter we will see how the advantages of magnetic disk over magnetic tape make it possible to use disk for a wide variety of file processing activities including more sophisticated forms of batch processing. Several examples are used to illustrate the points that are made.

MAGNETIC DISK.

2. Disk is a direct access storage medium and therefore overcomes the major limitation of tape. This gives it a very real advantage over tape in this respect. Disk does require the use of systems software, although this is not a serious problem with the current range of computers. It has a higher data transfer speed than most models of tape and effectively has a greater storage capacity. The cost of disk is much higher than that of tape but it is a cost users seem willing to pay for the benefits of its use.

3. Not all the limitations of tape are overcome by the use of disk. However, the facility of direct access will help to solve some of the problems and help to alleviate others. We will now reconsider the limitations of tape in the same order as previously outlined (35.43) and see how the use of disk helps overcome them.

a. The question of access has been covered already and disk does overcome this limitation completely.

b. Despite the fact that disk provides a direct access facility it is often expedient to sort a transaction file into the sequence of the master file. For example an Indexed Sequential File processed Selective Sequentially makes use of direct access while involving the access mechanism in *no* back-tracking provided no other use is made of the disk by the other users while the file is being processed. If the same file were processed in a random manner (ie. using an unsorted transaction file) a great deal more time would be spent by the access mechanism in moving to and fro across the face of the disk. The first method involves sorting time and seek time, the second involves no sorting but considerably more seek time. Individual circumstances will indicate the method to be used.

c. If a very large file with a low hit-rate is stored on disk then the direct access capability makes it possible to access *only* those records requiring updating, thus eliminating the redundant processing which occurs with tape.

d. Requests for information can be answered quickly. File Enquiry (as it is called) is accomplished by linking a terminal (possibly a Visual Display Unit – VDU) to the CPU. A request for information can be answered by displaying the contents of a particular record on the VDU. This could be done while the enquirer (a customer) is waiting at the other end of a telephone. Notice that using a multiprogrammed computer (ie. one that runs more than one program at a time), file enquiries can be answered during the running of another program eg. an updating program. (An example will be given later).

e. In the example in Fig. 36.1 the use of disk storage solves the problem of a file not reflecting a true situation. The stock file is stored on disk and access is made to it at the *same time* as the customer file. Thus the two runs are combined and all the data required is available at the same time. The underlying principle is important because it represents a significant advance on tape processing.

Notice that the "delay" problem is *still* present, because it is inherent in the batch processing system itself.

4. Most small system use either floppy disks or small hard disks and can exploit the direct access capabilities of disks. However, few small systems can provide simultaneous file access by multiple programs as just described in d. although it is becoming more common on 16 bit micro-computers.

FILE UPDATES USING MAGNETIC DISK.

This chart shows the computer runs necessary to update the stock and customer files and to produce invoices. Orders are entered at a VDU and the stock file (held in stock number sequence) and customer files (held in customer number sequence) are stored on magnetic disk.

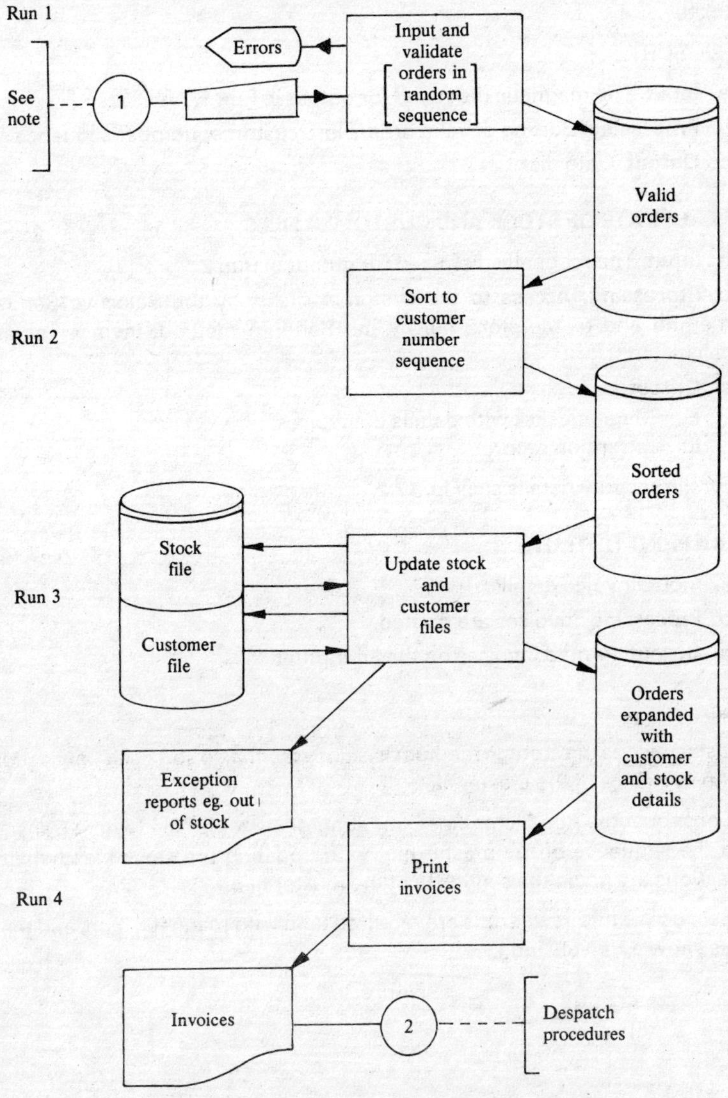

Figure 36.1.

SYSTEMS FLOWCHART DISK PROCESSING – SUPPORTING NARRATIVE.

RUN 1 – DATA VALIDATION.

a. **Input.** See Fig. 35.10 para 1a.

b. **Processing.** See Fig. 35.10 para 1b.

c. **Output.** Onto disk instead of tape, otherwise the same as shown in Fig. 35.10.

RUN 2 – SORT.

a. **Input.** The magnetic disk used for output in Run 1.

b. **Processing.** Sorting of valid orders into customer number sequence.

c. **Output.** Onto disk.

RUN 3 – UPDATE OF STOCK AND CUSTOMER FILES.

a. **Input.** The magnetic disk used for output in Run 2.

b. **Processing.** Access to the customer file is by the Selective Sequential method and to the stock file by the Random method. Invoice values are calculated.

c. **Output.**

i. Magnetic disk with details of invoices.

ii. Exception reports.

NB. For file security details see Fig. 17.2.

RUN 4 – PRINT OUTPUT.

a. **Input.** Invoice details.

b. **Processing.** Invoices are printed.

c. **Output.** Printed invoices on the lineprinter.

Notes:

1. Using disk as the storage medium it is not *essential* to sort each transaction file into the sequence of the master file.

2. Consequently, Run 3 combines updating of customer file (where transaction *are* in the sequence of the master file) with updating the stock files (where the transactions are *not* in the sequence of the master file).

3. Because of this, fewer runs are required than with magnetic tape, and the files always show a *true* position.

Figure 36.2.

MULTI-USER SIMULTANEOUS FILE PROCESSING.

This chart shows the simultaneous processing of two files and file enquiry in a multi-user, multi-programming system.

1. It is a multi-programming system because more than one program is running. In this example one program is the update program (as in Fig. 36.1 run 3), another is the file enquiry program.

2. The stock file and customer file are each being processed by both programs so simultaneous file processing is taking place.

NB. Careful controls on file access are necessary in order to deal with situations where two different programs try to access the same record at the same time. One method, called **record locking,** enables the first program accessing the record to prevent access by the other programs until the first program has completed processing the record.

3. This requires direct access storage and a file organisation method which supports random access.

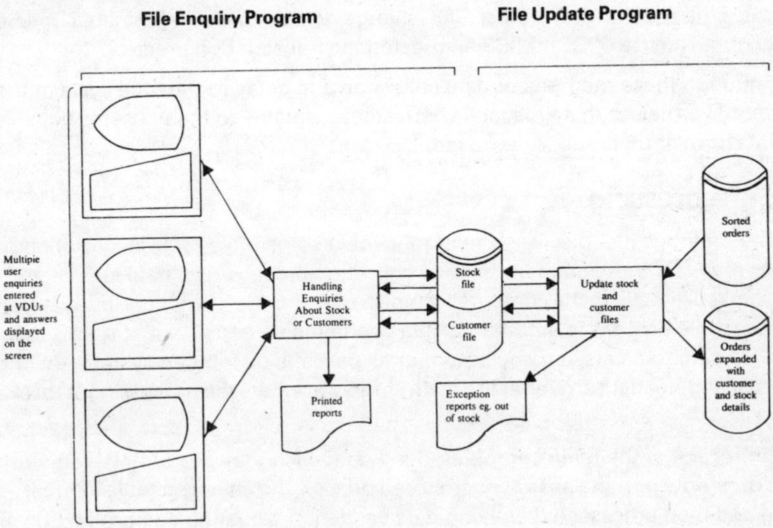

Figure 36.3.

PROCESSING APPLICATIONS USING DISK STORAGE.

5. a. **File enquiry.** This has been mentioned already. The information required must be stored on a DAS medium. Random access would be necessary in this particular application in order to be able to deal with any enquiry as it arose.

b. **Random access.** Building Societies and Insurance Companies have extremely large files with a very low hit-rate. Random access is used in view of the small size batches, thus saving the vast amount of redundant processing of inactive records which would be required with tape. Such files stored on tape can take some six hours to process completely, which will give you an idea of the problem.

c. **Simultaneous processing of files.** A customer file and stock file can be processed together provided the stock file is on a DAS medium.

6. So far we have considered the concept of batch processing purely in terms of computer processing and have seen how the use of disk storage can overcome many of the limitations of tape. We now want to extend our considerations to include the link with data collection so that we can see a more complete picture.

LINK WITH DATA COLLECTION.

7. For many years the delay spoken of earlier in terms of batch processing was *aggravated* by the time it took for data to pass through all the stages of data collection (18.3) prior to processing. Newer methods of data collection have helped to reduce data collection times. The change to key-to-disk eliminated media conversion. The use of OCR/MICR eliminated the transcription process.

8. Although these methods of data collection add delay to the time cycle of the system, nevertheless this time lag is perfectly acceptable to many users, which is why this form of DP is still widely used.

ON-LINE PROCESSING.

9. The methods just discussed tend to involve some *physical* transportation of data or *manual intervention* in the data collection process. The data source itself can be linked directly to the computer in which case there is no manual intervention and the whole process is automatic. This "on-line data entry" may take place by means of data transmission equipment or as part of a distributed system. By one means or another data arrives at the main computer where the processing is to take place.

10. On receipt at the main computer, the data (which may be coming from hundreds of remote terminals), is at once stored on disk and after a suitable interval, is sorted and then processed (involving data validation, updating and production of output). Notice that in essence all we have done is to dramatically speed up the process of data collection. The batch processing concept *still applies.*

11. The advantage of "on-line" processing is that data is less out of date when it arrives in the computer. As a result, files reflect a much more up to date, a much more *real* picture of a particular set of circumstances. Furthermore, the results of processing are available more quickly as they can be fed back to the same terminal if need be. Additionally the remote terminal can also be used for enquiries which arise at the source.

12. The major Clearing Banks have an on-line system of processing coupled with File Enquiry. This is a good example to quote in an examination answer.

13. It should be realised that on-line systems of batch processing are much more costly than the conventional method involving transporting the data by post. However the advantages lie in the time saved and the availability of more up to date information.

TRANSACTION PROCESSING.

14. We have just seen how the time lag in batch processing systems can be reduced by the use of various data collection techniques and more especially by the use of the techniques of on-line processing (coupled with the use of DAS). Most businesses *do not* require their files of data to be right "up to date" at all times and gear their activities to a time-cycle which is acceptable.

15. There are situations, however, which require any data that arises to be immediately processed and the relevant file updated because any action taken must be based on the *true current* circumstances. Such a processing system is said to be working in REAL-TIME. Real-time processing is the processing of data so quickly that the results are available to influence the activity currently taking place. Decisions are continually being made on the very latest information available because files are kept permanently up to date.

16. You could say that a single transaction becomes the batch, which is processed *on demand.* Thus the process of input, validation, updating and output must be gone through just as with batch processing but for *each* transaction as and when it occurs. This real-time processing of individual transactions is known as **"Transaction Processing"**.

17. Transaction processing is just one kind of real-time processing. Other kinds of real-time processing are those concerned with the control of physical systems such as chemical plants or power stations.

18. Further details of transaction processing and its applications will be given in later chapters.

SIMPLE PRACTICAL EXAMPLE.

19. The following examples shows Random access to a disk file to display and view **or** display, view and update records singly. Old records are overwritten by updated records. Each record is identified by its key which is keyed in at a terminal.

System Run Diagram.

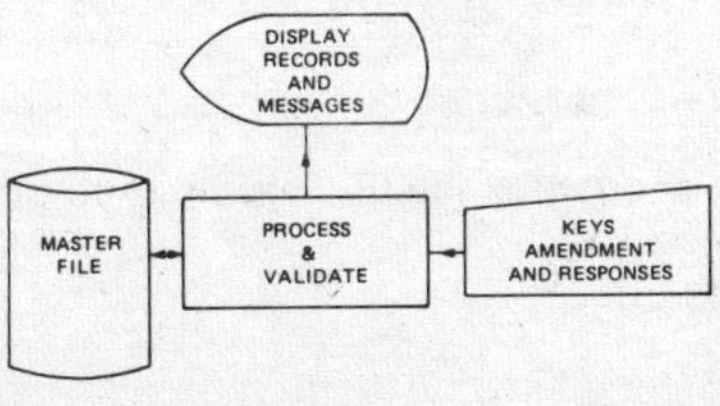

19. The following pseudocode outlines how the main processing is performed. Assume that

a. The file has been opened for random input and output.

b. "Key" is an integer, reply and response are strings, record-valid is boolean and master-record is a record containing a key.

c. The function **key-allocated** returns **true** when its argument has a record with that value in the file.

d. The procedure **get** has **key** as an IN parameter and **master_record** as an OUT parameter. It reads and returns the master_record with the specified key from the file.

e. The procedure **put** has **key** and **master_record** as IN parameters. It writes the master_record to the appropriate position on the disk.

```
Repeat
    (* get a key value from the program user *)
    output (" Which key ? ")
    input ( key )
    if
        key_allocated (key)
    then
        call get (key, master_record)
        output (master_record)
        output ("Any changes? (yes or no)")
        input (reply)
        if
            reply = "yes"
        then
            repeat
                    (* input record amendments *)
                    (* validate amendments *)
                    (* displaying errors messages where necessary *)
            until record_valid
            call put (key, master_record)
        endif
    else
        output ("there is no record with this key")
    endif
    output ("Any more records? (yes or no)")
    input (response)
until response < > "yes"
```

SUMMARY.

20. a. The various non-sequential file processing methods have been illustrated by example.

b. A direct access storage device such as disk is essential for these processing methods.

c. *On-line processing of batches* and *transaction processing* have been explained.

POINTS TO NOTE.

21. a. Note how DAS makes possible file enquiry and on-line systems.

STUDENT SELF TEST QUESTIONS.

(Answers on page 741).

1. What are the limitations to file processing using magnetic tapes and how can the use of magnetic disks help to overcome them?

2. Distinguish between on-line processing and real-time processing.

QUESTIONS WITHOUT ANSWERS.

3. This question is concerned with a file of student records with the following fields:

student number	*4 numeric characters*
surname	*20 characters*
forenames	*20 characters*
address	*40 characters*
date of birth (YYMMDD)	*6 characters*
course code	*4 numeric characters*
subject details – a group of three items where each consists of –	
subject studied	*3 characters*
total mark to date	*integer*
number of items marked	*integer*

Each student may be studying up to three subjects, the subjects studied are coded so that each subject has a standard abbreviation e.g. STA – statistics, MAT – maths, ACC – accounts, etc. In the questions which follow invent your own abbreviations if you find it necessary.

a. Write a program which reads the student records for those students studying a particular subject, typed in by the user, into a table. Then for that group compute the average mark achieved so far in that subject and output a list of those students whose own average is below the group average.

b. Write a program to update the student file with transactions of the form:

student number	*4 numeric characters*
subject code	*3 characters*
mark for one piece of work	*integer*

Assume both files are sequential files sorted into ascending order of student number. Your algorithm should cater for a number of transactions for the same student – including several marks for the same subject and marks for a number of subjects; also check for errors such as student numbers not matching and students having marks for subjects they do not apparently study.

c. Design an algorithm to validate a file of transactions for the maintenance of the student file detailed above. The format for the transactions will be the same as the master file except for the addition of an extra field of one character which denotes the record type – A for amendment, I for insertion, D for deletion.

Transactions indicating a deletion will consist of the record type and the student number, the rest of the record will be spaces. Transactions indicating an insertion will have all fields present but the total marks and the number of pieces of work must be zero. Transactions for amendments will have the record type, the student number and any fields to be changed, other fields will be left blank.

The output will be a file of valid transactions and an error report containing the invalid transactions and an indication of the errors in each record. You must choose a suitable method for this.

4. Write an algorithm to produce invoices given data in the following files: an orders file and a customer reference file; both are sequenced on customer number. There may be several order records for each customer but each order record gives rise to a separate invoice.

The customer reference records consist of the following fields:

customer number
name
address

The orders records consist of the following fields:

customer number
stock number of item ordered
date of order (YYMMDD)
number of items ordered.

The invoices consist of:

customer number
name
address
date of order
stock number of item ordered
number of items ordered
price per item
total price of items ordered
VAT at 15% of total price
total cost (total price + VAT)

You may choose the layout of the invoices.

The prices of the items are found from a table which is read into an array at the beginning of the program. There are 100 stock items. Each entry in the table consists of the stock number and its price per item, these are stored in sequential order of stock number. Hence given the stock number you need to search the table to find the price.

37 Data Bases and Integrated Systems

INTRODUCTION.

1. When organisations first began to use computers, they naturally adopted a piece-meal approach. One system at a time was studied, re-designed and transferred to the computer. This approach was necessitated by the difficulties experienced in using a new and powerful management tool. It had the drawback, however, of producing a number of separate systems, each with its own program suite, its own files, and its own inputs and outputs. The main criticisms of this approach are that:

a. The computer-based systems, being self-contained, do not represent the way in which the organisation really works – ie. as a complex set of interlocking and inter-dependent systems.

b. Systems communicate with each other outside the computer. This proliferates inputs and outputs and creates delays. For example, input of a customer order to an order processing system might create an output of an invoice set fig. 35.9. This in turn would have to be converted back into input for activating the sales accounting system. Similarly, if the order reduced stock levels to the re-order level (ie. the level at which they must be re-ordered so that ordered stock arrives before existing stock runs out) another output would be created which would then have to be input to the production control and/or the purchasing system.

c. Information obtained from a series of separate files is less valuable because it does not give the complete picture. For example, the sales manager reviewing outstanding orders from customers has to get information about stocks from another file.

d. Data may be duplicated in two or more files, creating unnecessary maintenance and the risk of inconsistency.

INTEGRATED FILE SYSTEMS.

2. Integrated files systems represent an approach to solving the problems just described, by conventional means. In an integrated file system the data is pooled into a set of inter-locking and inter-dependent files which are accessible by a number of different users.

3. When a transaction enters an integrated file system *all* the appropriate files are updated. The features of an integrated system are shown in Fig. 37.1.

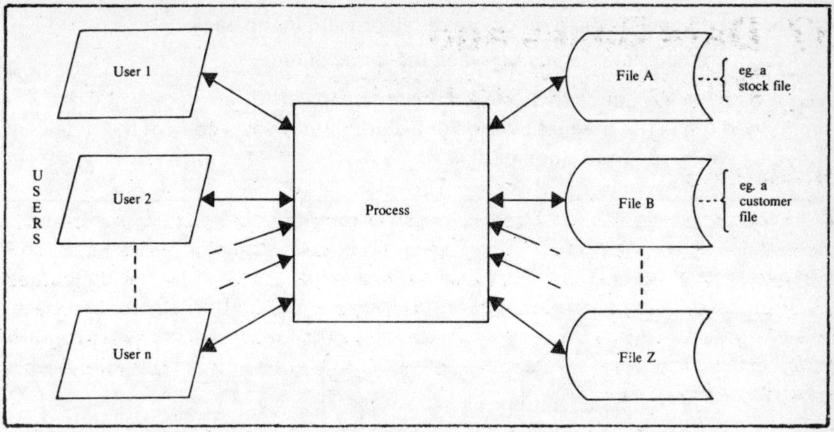

Figure 37.1. An Integrated File System.

4. A large number of integrated file systems are in use today. Many of them have been tailor made to meet the requirements of particular organisations.

5. Integrated file systems do not provide a satisfactory answer to all the criticisms mentioned in paragraph 1, however. They tend to suffer from the problems caused by *data duplication* (1d) and from the fact that the task of maintaining the data is shared between the programs which access and maintain the data and therefore lacks proper central control.

NB. The idea of integrating the *processing functions.* will be returned to later in this chapter.

DATA BASES.

6. Data bases represent a radically different approach to solving the problems discussed so far in this chapter.

7. Data Base Definition. A data base is a single organised collection of structured data, stored with a minimum of duplication of data items so as to provide a consistent and controlled pool of data. This data is common to all users of the system but is independent of programs which use the data.

8. The independence of the data base and programs using it means that one can be changed without changing the other.

9. The users of a data base may find it convenient to imagine that they are using an integrated file system like the one shown in Fig. 37.1. In reality the data base is organised as in Fig. 37.2.

10. Data bases are normally set up in order to meet the information needs of major parts of an organisation.

11. It is not possible to construct a data base in one single operation, it is usually built up section by section. During this process, it is possible to:-

a. add new "files" of data.

b. to add new fields to records already present in the base.

c. to create relationships between the items of data.

12. A data base requires to be stored on large-capacity direct-access devices. The usual medium is the magnetic disk. For security purposes a copy of the data base may be held on magnetic tape or disk.

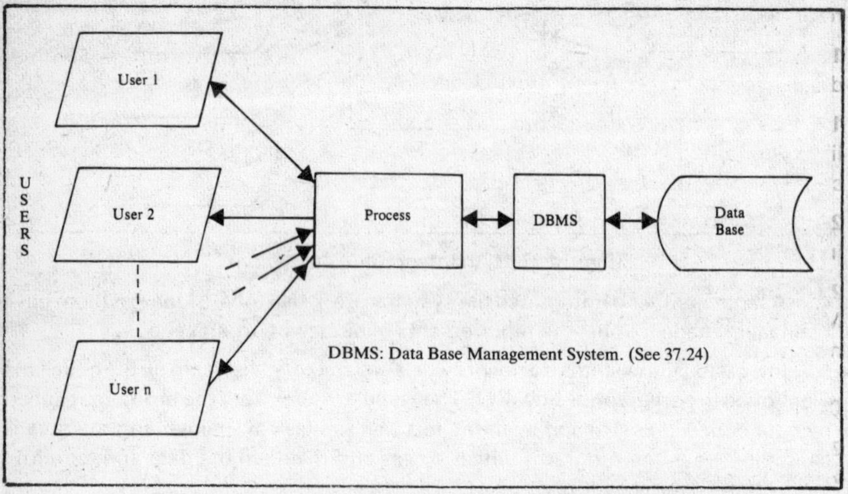

Figure 37.2. An Outline View of a Data Base System.

13. It is often *wrongly stated* that there is no duplication of data in a data base. Data may be duplicated, but it is important to realise that duplications are minimised and controlled. This is referred to as *"controlled redundancy"*.

14. Although, to the user, the data base may appear as a collection of files, the data in the data base is organised in a more complex way than the data in conventional files.

15. Data bases may be classified according to the approaches taken to data base organisation. The classes are:

a. Relational.

b. Network.

c. Hierarchical.

d. File inversions.

The last two are more basic, have a number of practical limitations and do not merit further discussion here.

16. Relational data bases use types of tables called **relations**. The terminology is initially confusing because of the use of the name "relation" for a table and because relations are not the same as relationships. However, relational data bases were developed from mathematically sound ideas, have an elegant simplicity and are likely to be increasingly important in the future.

17. **Network data bases** have been around in several forms for a number of years. TOTAL Is a well established example. In recent years the network approach has been developed by the work of CODASYL (30.13). Network data bases are based upon ideas similar to those used for linked lists. The links are used to express relationships between different items of data.

18. When new sets of data are added, it is often found that some of the required data is already stored for other purposes.

19. The data base is maintained by a 'single input'. This means that just as there is little duplication of data, there is also no duplication of inputs. One transaction will cause all the necessary changes to be made to the data.

20. As the base is expanded, or as user requirements change, the links or relations in the data base can be changed and new relationships can be established.

21. The user is unaware of the structure of the data base. The Data Base Management System (see paragraph 24) provides the user with the services needed and handles the technicalities of maintaining and using the data.

COMMUNICATING WITH THE DATA BASE.

22. Some data bases have their own computer languages associated with them which allow the user to access and retrieve data at a terminal. Other data bases are only accessed via languages such as COBOL, to which extra facilities have been added for this purpose.

23. Data descriptions must be standardised. For this reason, a **Data Description Language (DDL)** is provided which *must* be used to specify the data in the base. Similarly, a **Data Manipulation Language (DML)** is provided which must be used to access the data. The function of these two languages may be compared to the Data and Procedure Divisions of a COBOL program, although their scope is wider and the degree of standardisation much higher. As indicated by the previous paragraph DDLs and DMLs may be either free standing or embedded in another language.

THE DATA BASE MANAGEMENT SYSTEMS (DBMS).

24. The Data Base Management System is a *complex software system* which constructs, expands and maintains the data base. It also provides the interface between the user and the data in the base.

The DBMS allocates storage to data. It maintains indices so that any required data can be retrieved, and so that separate items of data in the base can be cross-referenced. As mentioned above, the structure of a data base is dynamic and can be changed as needed.

25. The DBMS maintains the data in the base by:-

a. adding new records,

b. deleting 'dead' records,

c. amending records.

In addition to these functions (which are performed by any file maintenance program) it can expand the base by adding new sets of records or new data to existing records.

26. The DBMS provides an interface with user programs. These may be written in a number of different programming languages. However, the programmer need not be familiar with the structure of the base because the data his program requires is retrieved by the DBMS.

27. The DBMS provides facilities for different types of file processing. It can:–

a. process a complete file (serially or sequentially)

b. process required records (selective sequential or random)

c. retrieve individual records.

It can also, as has been explained above, retrieve related records or related data within records.

28. The DBMS also has the function of providing security for the data in the base. The main aspects of this are:-

a. protecting data against unauthorised access

b. safeguarding data against corruption

c. providing recovery and restart facilities after a hardware or software failure.

The DBMS keeps statistics of the use made of the data in the base. This allows redundant data to be removed. It also allows data which is frequently used to be kept in a readily accessible form so that time is saved.

29. Data Dictionary. The DBMS makes use of descriptions of data items provided by the DDL. This "data about data" is called a **data dictionary.**

30. Clearly, something so complex as a DBMS needs to be organised in a logical way and this logical organisation is achieved by having a number of distinct levels within the DBMS. At the top level, data is expressed in a form compatible with the view of individual users (as applications files, say). At the middle level the data is expressed in global terms applicable to all applications. At the bottom level the data is expressed in forms which relate to the way the data is actually stored. The DBMS transforms data as it moves it from level to level.

THE DATA BASE ADMINISTRATOR (DBA).

31. The importance of a data base is such that a special manager is often appointed, sometimes with a staff. His functions are described below.

The DBA must have a sound knowledge of the structure of the data base and of the DMBS. The DBA must also be thoroughly conversant with the organisation, its systems, and the information needs of the managers.

32. The DBA is responsible for ensuring that:-

a. the data in the base meets the information needs of the organisation.

b. that the facilities for retrieving data and for structuring reports are appropriate to the needs of the organisation.

33. The DBA is responsible for the following documentation:-

a. The data dictionary.

b. Manuals for users describing the facilities the data base offers and how to make use of these facilities.

34. Another function is to supervise the addition of new data. For this purpose, the DBA will have to liaise with the managers who use the data, and the systems analysts and programmers who develop the systems.

35. Security of the data base is also the responsibility of the DBA, and in the future, requirements of privacy.

36. The DBA is also responsible for periodic appraisal of the data held in the base to ensure that it is complete, accurate and not duplicated.

EXAMPLE OF A DATA BASE.

37. There are at present few organisations who have a really comprehensive data base. An example is given here of a data base used by a major computer manufacturer.

38. The data base comprises:-

a. Records of customers who have purchased or rent the manufacturers computer equipment.

b. Records of the different items of equipment ie. processors, peripherals and other devices.

c. Records of spare parts showing the location where they are stored and the quantity held.

d. Records of customer engineers responsible for maintenance and repairs.

39. The uses made of the data base are too numerous to list completely, but a selection does give some idea of the facilities which a data base can provide:-

a. **Accounting.** Customers are billed for maintenance and rental charges. Any change in configuration automatically causes the customer charges to be amended (the 'single input' principle).

b. **Spares.** The data base is used to control stocks of spares. It can also be used to find the location of a spare part nearest to the installation which requires it.

c. **Modifications.** If a modification to a particular item of equipment is needed, all installations in which it is present can be quickly identified.

d. **Engineering Services.** The data base shows which customers are served by which engineer (an example of the 'linking' or cross-referencing of records). Engineers can be allocated to cover absence or sickness or to assist at an installation which is in trouble. The records show which types of equipment the engineers are qualified to service.

ADVANTAGES OF A DATA BASE.

40. The following are the advantages of a data base:-

a. Information supplied to managers is more valuable because it is based on a comprehensive collection of data instead of files which contain only the data needed for one application.

b. As well as routine reports, it is possible to obtain *ad hoc* reports to meet particular requirements.

c. There is an obvious economic advantage in not duplicating data. In addition, errors due to discrepancies between two files are eliminated.

d. The amount of input preparation needed is minimised by the 'single input' principle.

e. A great deal of programming time is saved because the DBMS handles the construction and processing of files and the retrieval of data.

f. The use of integrated systems is greatly facilitated.

INTEGRATED SYSTEMS.

41. The data base represents the integration of the data/information of an organisation. Associated with this concept is the integration of the systems which use the data. As has been seen, the development of separate systems increases the amount of external communication (inputs and outputs) between systems and is also likely to duplicate programming effort.

42. The concept is best illustrated by an example of three systems which are often integrated: order processing, sales accounting and stock control.

a. The basic input to the system is that of a customer order.

b. On input, the order is validated in the normal way. It is then

i. checked against the customer record to ensure that the credit position is satisfactory, and

ii. checked against the stock file to ensure that the stock is available.

c. After the order has passed these checks, the files are updated. The stock level is reduced by the amount ordered. An invoice is generated, and the customer record is updated.

d. The documentation is distributed as necessary; eg. the invoice is sent to the customer and the copies for despatch procedures sent to the warehouse.

e. If the supply of the order causes the stock level to fall below the re-order level, a report is printed indicating that replenishment of stock is necessary.

f. Subsequently, the monthly statement for the customer would be produced.

43. This example obviously represents only a small part of the total activities of the company. Possible future developments would be:

a. In a manufacturing organisation, input of a customer order would generate the necessary works order. This would be the 'input' to the production scheduling system, which would in turn generate the Bill of Materials.

b. The Bill of Materials would be 'input' to the Stock Control system. The necessary stocks would be allocated. If purchases were necessary, an input to the Purchasing system would be generated.

c. Subsequent receipt of the invoice from the supplier would cause another input to the Purchase Accounting system, resulting in checking of the invoice, notification of queries and eventual payment of the suppliers.

d. The Production Scheduling system would allocate the necessary machines and labour, using and updating Plant and Personnel files.

e. At the due date, the Production Scheduling system would activate the Production Control system. Progress of the job through the factory would be controlled and actual inputs from the factory floor would be received to monitor progress.

On completion of the order, the documentation would be produced and the Customer file updated with details of the invoice.

44. It will be realised of course that a number of new files would have to be added to the data base to make this possible – resource files of plant and labour, supplier file, work-in-progress etc.

At the time of writing the above is somewhat futuristic, as very few organisations have constructed a *comprehensive* data base and *fully* integrated their systems. A gradual approach, building up the data base section by section and adding new systems one at a time is obviously desirable. There is really nothing difficult to understand in the concept; the approach is simply to move into the computer *all* the files, *all* the systems and *all* the communications between them, instead of using the computer for only the more straightforward work and linking the computer-based systems externally.

FILE MANAGEMENT SYSTEMS.

45. A number of software products have appeared on the market in recent years which appear to offer *some* of the features of data bases on even the smaller computers. These products, some of which claim to be "data base packages" are usually more correctly called "File Management Systems".

46. Typical file management systems usually have rudimentary DDLs and DMLs which allow the user to set up and maintain a few files with a minimum of programming effort or skill. Facilities are often included which allow limited but extremely useful data retrieval functions such as sorting and selecting.

47. A file management system may therefore be thought of rather loosely as a "computerised filing cabinet".

SUMMARY.

48. a. The development of separate systems with their own files is simple but does not make the best use of resources. Integrated files, data bases, and integrated systems are more difficult to instal, but have many advantages.

b. A data base is a comprehensive, consistent, controlled and coordinated collection of structured data items.

c. A **Data Base Management System (DBMS)** is a software system which constructs, maintains and processes a data base.

d. Communication with the data base is via the **Data Description Language (DDL)** and **Data Manipulation Language (DML).**

e. The **data dictionery** holds "data about data" in the data base.

f. A **Data Base Administrator (DBA)** is the manager responsible for that data base.

g. Integrated systems are a natural corollary to data bases.

POINTS TO NOTE.

49. a. Another term you may come across is 'data bank'. This has a slightly different meaning to 'data base'. An organisation constructing a data base will put into it only data that it expects to use – for obvious reasons of economy. A 'data bank' on the other hand is designed to contain any data that *may* be required – just as a librarian has to keep stocks of books, *some* of which may never be referred to. An example of a data bank is a file of legal cases; they all have to be there because enquiries cannot be predicted, but some may never be inspected.

b. The integrated system extends data base to include *all* information flows in a business and automates as many 'decisions' as possible to produce a comprehensive management information system.

c. The computer is being increasingly used as the centre of a *communications network.* Many organisations are replacing the traditional, centralised methods of data collection with terminal devices linked to a central machine. The flows of data (inwards) and information (outwards) are greatly accelerated, and there is considerable improvement in communication and control.

d. Integrated file systems are integrated systems without the use of data bases.

STUDENT SELF TEST QUESTIONS.

(Answers on page 741)

1. *Distinguish between a data base and a file management system.*
2. *Explain the terms:*
   a. *DDL.*
   b. *DML.*
   c. *DBMS.*
   d. *DBA.*

Software

1. Definition. Software is the term used (in contrast to *hardware*) to describe *all* programs which are used in a particular computer installation. The term is often used to mean not only the programs themselves but their associated documentation.

2. There are numerous types of software, so the whole of chapter 38 is used to provide a detailed classification of the different types and a description of each type.

3. Operating systems are such an important type of software that the whole of chapter 39 is used to provide a discussion of them.

38 Software Types

INTRODUCTION.

1. This chapter explains the differences between the various types of software and describes each type.

TYPES OF SOFTWARE.

2. The two basic types of software are:-

a. System software.

b. Applications software.

3. **System Software.** The user of a computer has at his or her disposal a large amount of software provided by the manufacturer. Much of this software will be programs which contribute to the control and performance of the computer system. Such programs are given the collective name **system software.** Any one of these programs is a **systems program,** eg. compilers (32.18) and DBMs (37.24) are systems programs.

4. **Applications Software.** Applications programs may be provided by the computer manufacturer or supplier but in many cases the users produces their own applications programs called **user programs.** (eg. payroll programs, stock control programs etc.) A single applications program is often called a **job.** Sometimes a job may be divided into smaller units called **tasks.** A job may comprise program + data. Most applications programs can only work if used in conjunction with the appropriate systems programs.

5. **Further sub-division.** A more detailed sub-division of 2a and 2b is as follows:-

a. Operating systems and control programs b. Translators c. Utilities and service programs d. Data Base Management Systems (DBMSs)	System Software
e. User applications programs f. Applications packages.	Applications Software

6. The remainder of this chapter discusses software under headings which correspond to this classification.

OPERATING SYSTEMS AND CONTROL PROGRAMS.

7. Computers are required to give efficient and reliable service without the need for continual intervention by the user. This requirement suggests that computers should monitor and control their own operation where possible. **Control programs** are the means by which this is achieved. A control program controls the way in which hardware is used.

8. Under many circumstances at least two programs are within main storage. One may be an applications program the other will be a control program which monitors, aids and controls the applications program.

9. On small computer systems such as microcomputers the control program may also accept commands typed in by the user. Such a control program is often called a **monitor.**

10. On larger computer systems it is common for only part of the monitor to remain in main storage. Other parts of the monitor are brought into memory when required ie. there are "resident" and "transient" parts to the monitor.

11. The resident part of the monitor on large systems is often called the **Executive** or **Supervisor Program.**

12. The executive is one of a suite of control programs which are able to allow a number of applications programs to run concurrently and in sequence without the intervention of the user. Such a suite of control programs is called an operating system, but a more precise definition is now given.

13. An **operating system** is a suite of programs which takes over the operation of the computer to the extent of being able to allow a number of programs to be run on the computer without human intervention by an operator.

14. The reader should now be aware of what operating systems and control programs are, and how they relate to other software. Further details are left for discussion in the next chapter.

TRANSLATORS.

15. These were described in chapter 32 and need no further discussion.

UTILITIES AND SERVICE PROGRAMS.

16. Utilities, also called service programs, are systems programs which provide a useful service to the user of the computer by providing facilities for performing common tasks of a routine nature.

17. Common types of utility programs are:-

a. Sort.

b. Editors.

c. File copying.

d. Dump.

e. File maintenance.

f. Tracing and debugging.

18. Sort. This is a program designed to arrange records into a predetermined sequence. A good example of the requirement for this service program is the need for sorting transaction files into the sequence of the master file before carrying out updating. Sorting is done by reference to a record key.

a. **Parameters required.** It is a *generalised* program which must be *"specialised"* as it were, before use; this is accomplished by supplying the program with parameters which will be different for each application. Such parameters are:-

i. Key – size and number (if more than one).

ii. Record size (length).

iii. Peripheral units available for the sorting process, ie. number of tape units, disk units, etc. which can be made available to the program.

iv. Required sequence (ascending order of numeric or alphabetic keys etc).

b. **How accomplished.** Sorting methods were discussed in 35.8–35.15.

19. Editors are used at a terminal and provide facilities for the creation or amendment of programs. The editing may be done by the use of a series of commands or special edit keys on the keyboard. If, for example, a source program needs correction because it has failed to compile properly, an editor may be used to make the necessary changes.

20. File copying. (also called media conversion) This is a program which simply copies data from one medium to another, eg. from disk to tape.

21. Dump. The term 'dump' means "copy the contents of main storage onto an output device". This program is useful when an error occurs during the running of application programs. The printed "picture" of main storage will contain information helpful to the programmer when trying to locate the error. It is also used in conjunction with a CHECKPOINT/RESTART program. This program stops at various intervals during the running of an application program and dumps the contents of main storage. If required, the Checkpoint/Restart program can get the application program back to the last checkpoint and restart it with the conditions exactly as they were at the time.

NB. "Dump" is sometimes used to mean "copy the contents of on-line storage onto an off-line medium" eg. dumping magnetic disk onto magnetic tape for backup purposes.

22. File maintenance. A program designed to carry out the process of insertion/deletion of records in any files. It can also make amendments to the standing data contained in records. File maintenance may also include such tasks as the reorganisation of index sequential files on disk.

23. Tracing and debugging. Used in conjunction with the debugging and testing of application programs on the computer. Tracing involves dumping internal storage after obeying specified instructions so that the cycle of operations can be traced and errors located. Debugging is the term given to the process of locating and eliminating errors from a program.

NB. Well written and tested programs will tend to be more reliable and will therefore require less debugging than badly written programs.

DATA BASE MANAGEMENT SYSTEMS (DBMSs).

24. These were described in the previous chapter and need no further discussion.

USER APPLICATIONS PROGRAMS.

25. User applications programs are programs written by the user in order to perform specific jobs for the user. Such programs are written in a variety of programming languages according to circumstances, but all should be written in a systematic way such as that indicated in the Part on programming.

26. For many applications it is necessary to produce sets of programs which are used in conjunction with one another and which may also be used in conjunction with service programs such as sort utilities.

27. For some applications it may be necessary to compare available software or hardware before writing the applications software. For example, the user may wish to compare the performance of two different COBOL compilers. Such a comparison may be made using a bench mark.

28. Benchmarks. A benchmark is a standard program, or assembly of programs used to evaluate hardware or software. For example, a benchmark might be used to:

a. compare the performance of two or more different computers on identical tasks.

b. ascertain if the configuration provided by a manufacturer performs according to his claims.

c. assess the comparative performance of two Operating Systems.

APPLICATION PACKAGES.

29. These are similar in concept to service programs except that application packages are generalised programs for solving applications problems as opposed to programs for carrying out computer systems tasks.

30. Many users have the same type of problem to put onto a computer and thus manufacturers and specialist software writers have written standard programs to solve these problems and sell them to the many users who want them. Examples are Stock Control, Sales Invoicing, Network Analysis.

31. Applications packages are of major importance to small computer system users who do not have the necessary resources or expertise to produce their own software.

32. Advantages of packages.

a. The main advantage is the saving of programming effort and expense on the part of the user. Development costs are effectively shared between the users.

b. The user gets a well tried and tested program which he is able to use with confidence.

c. Relatively quick implementation results from the use of packages.

33. Practical considerations.

a. Many users' systems will differ in some detailed area especially if there is a relationship between applications, as there is for example between labour cost analysis and payroll.

b. A solution would be for the user to modify his system to suit the package but this has its problems.

c. Some users may decide arbitrarily to design a system to suit the package.

d. Some software houses built packages on the *modular* principle and thus are able to combine the various modules to suit a particular user's requirement.

e. The question of cost must not be ignored and will be reflected in the service provided by the supplier of the package.

f. A number of Trade Associations etc. have sponsored the writing of packages for particular industries. The Motor Manufacturers Association have set up packages for their dealers.

g. Thorough research should be made into the reliability of the package and the particular software house offering it for sale. It is a good idea to ask current users of the package about their experience.

h. A program maintenance agreement should be sought where changes to the package are likely, eg. a payroll package could be affected by government legislation.

34. How the package is supplied. A package normally consists of:

a. A program (or suite of programs) actually written onto a suitable medium eg. magnetic tape, disk or floppy disk.

b. Documentation which specifies:

i. how to set up the package
ii. how to use the package
iii. necessary technical details.

35. Any software which the user buys is likely to be supplied in a similar form to that just described. Suppliers tend to provide no more than the necessary technical detail in order to protect their trade secrets.

SUMMARY.

36. a. Software falls into two main categories:-

i. System software.
ii. Applications software.

b. A further sub-division of software is as follows:-

i. Operating system and control programs which ensure efficient hardware use with a minimum of human intervention.
ii. Translators which translate from one language to another.

iii. Utilities and service programs which perform routine tasks for the user.

iv. Data Base Management Systems which maintain data bases.

v. User applications programs which are written by the user for a specific purpose.

vi. Applications packages which are purchased by the user for a particular application.

POINTS TO NOTE.

37. a. Time spent in running systems software is really non-productive from an organisational stand point.

b. The operating system (especially the executive part) can be regarded as a "Program which controls Programs".

STUDENT SELF TEST QUESTIONS.

(Answers on page 741)

1. Distinguish between systems software and applications software and give further sub-classifications of each.

2. What is an editor and how might an editor be used?

3. When might the user of a computer consider using an applications package instead of writing programs from scratch?

How would they be able to decide which package to use from among those available?

QUESTIONS WITHOUT ANSWERS.

4. Find out about the various kinds of software available on the computer system which you use.

39 Operating Systems

INTRODUCTION.

1. The concept and basic purpose of an operating system was introduced in the previous chapter (38.7). This chapter explains the purposes, facilities and functions of operating systems and also describes various types of operating system.

WHY OPERATING SYSTEMS WERE ORIGINALLY DEVELOPED.

2. Over many years the increased processing speed of the *central processing unit* and its massive problem-solving capability brought about the need for more sophisticated means of *operating* computers. *Problems* encountered on the early generations were:–

a. **Set-up time.** Required as each job was put onto the machine and during which time the computer was completely *idle.* For example, changing tape reels on tape units, changing stationery on a printer, etc.

b. **Manual intervention.** This was necessary in order to investigate error conditions and to initiate corrective action. Again the machine would lie idle while this was being done.

c. **Imbalance between CPU and peripherals.** This meant that the central processor was lying idle for "long" periods of time during the operation of peripheral units.

3. When analysed it can be seen that in a computer system comprising *many* units only a *small part* is "in action" performing a specific task at any *one* point in time. What is required is a "super controller" to ensure that the vast facilities are used to optimum advantage. It became clear that the job could only be undertaken by some form of *internally stored program.* This became known as an *operating system.*

DEFINITION

4. An operating system is a *suite* of programs which has taken over many of the functions once performed by human operators. The sophistication and speeds of modern computers is beyond the capability of human operators to control without the aid of an operating system.

5. For a more precise definition of an operating system see 38.13.

BASIC ORGANISATION

6. It can be seen from what has been said so far that the operating system controls the way software uses hardware. This control ensures that the computer not only operates in the way intended by the user but does so in a systematic, reliable and efficient manner. This "view" of the operating system is shown in Figure 39.1.

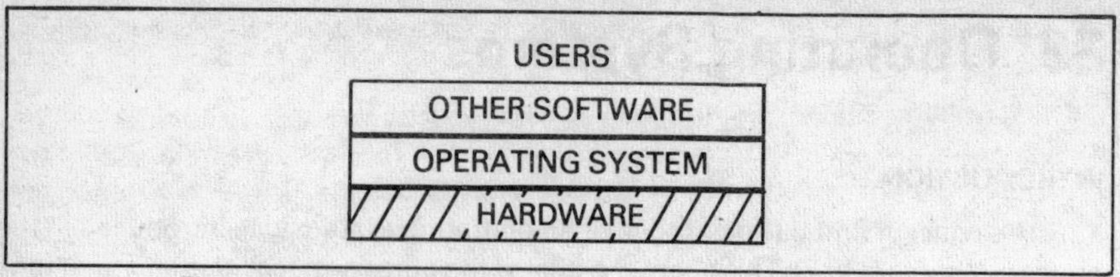

Figure 39.1. An overview of the organisation of a system showing the position of the operating system

BASIC ORGANISATION

7. Part of the operating system remains in main storage *permanently* during the running of the computer. This part is called the EXECUTIVE (or Supervisor) and as the name suggests is the "controlling" part of the operating system. It controls the running of all other programs. The remainder of the operating system programs are stored on a direct access storage device (preferably) from which any particular one will be "called" into main storage by the Executive when required.

8. On small computers the operating system takes the form of a rudimentary control program normally called a **monitor**.

9. On many very small microcomputers the monitor is stored permanently in ROM and starts execution the moment the computer is turned on. A message is usually displayed on the VDU screen by the monitor to signify it is ready to accept commands which the user may type in at a keyboard.

10. On most other modern computers the monitor or executive is not in main storage when the machine is switched on. The system must be "booted up". This often involves pressing special "boot buttons" or switches which cause the hardware to load the monitor or executive into main storage from a predetermined position on a disk.

THE FUNCTIONS OF AN OPERATING SYSTEM

11. The functions may include:

a. The scheduling and loading of programs, or subprograms, in order to provide a continuous sequence of processing or to provide appropriate responses to events.

b. Control over hardware resources eg. control over the selection and operation of devices used for input, output or storage.

c. Protecting hardware, software and data from improper use.

d. Calling into main storage of programs and sub-routines as and when required.

e. Passing of control from one job (program) to another under a system of priority when more than one application program occupies main storage.

f. Provision of error correction routines.

g. Furnishing a complete record of all that happens during processing (usually in the form of a typewritten log).

h. Communication with the computer operator usually by means of the console typewriter. The operator communicates with the operating system by means of a JCL (Job Control Language) which is translated and executed by an interactive command interpreter.

METHODS OF OPERATION AND MODES OF ACCESS.

12. Operating systems are often described in terms of the methods by which they *operate the system* and the modes of system access they provide. The common alternatives are introduced here. More detail will be given in the following paragraphs where necessary.

a. **Multiprocessing.** This is the name for the situation which occurs if two or more CPUs are present in a computer system and sharing some or all of the same memory. In such cases two programs may be processed at the same instant. In the remainder of this discussion assume just one processor is used unless otherwise stated.

b. **Multiprogramming.** This occurs when more than one program in main storage is being processed **apparently** at the same time. This is accomplished by the programs taking turns at short bursts of processing time.

c. **Batch processing.** The job (program + data) is not processed until fully input. The jobs are entered and stored on a disk in a **batch queue** and then run one or more at a time under the control of the operating system. A job may wait in a batch queue for minutes or hours depending on the work load. No amendments are possible during processing.

d. **Remote job entry** refers to batch processing where jobs are entered at a terminal remote from the computer, and transmitted in to the computer.

e. **Interactive Computing.** This occurs if the computer and terminal user may communicate with each other.

f. **Conversational mode.** This is Interactive computer operation where the response to the users message is immediate.

g. **Multi-access.** This occurs if the computer allows interactive facilities to more than one user at a time.

h. **Time-sharing.** Processor time is divided into small units called **time slices** and shared in turn between users to provide multi-access.

i. **Real-time system.** A real time system is a computer system which is capable of processing data so quickly that the results are available to influence the activity currently taking place. There is often a need for multiprocessing and a front end processor in these systems.

CHOICE OF OPERATING SYSTEM

13. Choice of Operating System. The applications for which a computer is needed largely determine the choice of hardware and accompanying software. The operating system supplier will need to consider these factors.

a. The hardware provision and basic design of the computer.

b. The applications intended for the computer.

c. The method of communication with the computer, eg many or few peripherals.

d. The method of operating the computer.

TYPES OF OPERATING SYSTEM

14. Single program systems. The majority of small micro-computer based systems have **monitors** which allow a single user to operate the machine in an interactive conversational mode but normally only allow one user program to be in main storage and processed at a time. ie. there is no multi-programming of user programs.

15. There are a number of well established operating systems which fall into this category. Apart from those operating systems which are specific to particular manufacturers' machines there are some which are available on a wide variety of different machines. Examples: CP/M (Control Program for Microcomputers) produced by Digital Research and MSDOS produced by Microsoft.

16. Simple Batch Systems. These are systems which provide multi-programming of batch programs but have few facilites for interaction or multi-access. Many commercial computer systems in use during the 60's and early 70's were of this type.

17. Multi-access and Time-sharing Systems. The majority of operating systems fall into this category, but there is a wide range of complexity in such systems.

18. On the larger micro-computers and smaller minicomputers there are a number of operating systems which are available for use on a variety of machines produced by different manufacturers. One such operating system which is gaining in popularity is UNIX which was developed by Bell Laboratories in the USA.

19. On large minicomputers and main frames, operating systems are normally specific to the particular machine and manufacturer.

20. Real-Time Systems. The operating system has to cater for the type of real-time system being used. The three types are given here in order of increasingly fast response time.

a. A more complex multi-access time sharing system where each user has a largely independent choice of system facilities eg. each using a different language.

b. Commercial Real-time systems in which there is essentially one job such as handling booking and the multi-access user has a clerical rather than programming function. These systems often make use of extensive data bases.

c. **Process Control Systems** eg. a system to control the operation of a chemical factory plant. Response to changes must be as fast as possible and reliability is essential. Real-time process control systems vary greatly in size.

The big systems like the one just mentioned are at one extreme. At the other extreme are the embedded Real-time control systems used in micro-processor based instruments and monitoring devices, eg. the control system in a service station petrol pump.

OPERATING SYSTEM LANGUAGES

21. The three types of language to be considered here are:

a. Command languages
b. Job Control Languages
c. Languages in which to write operating system software.

22. Command language. A programming language used for communications with the operating system is called a command language. Most statements (commands) in the language are directives requiring immediate execution and are handled by **command interpreters**. Some command languages provide no more than a set of single line commands which may be keyed in by a user, eg. individual commands to print, compile, load, execute copy or delete a named file. Other command languages also provide control structures so that commands may be selected or repeated according to specified conditions. An example of the latter is the **shell** language on the UNIX operating system (39.18).

23. Job Control Language (JCL). This is a special command language which is used to identify jobs and state their requirements to the operating system. JCLs are of particular importance in batch processing. An example of a fictitious JCL now follows.

24. Example. The **JCL program** shown here is a user's fictitious JCL program. Assume that it is to be loaded by the operating system and then executed under the action of a JCL interpreter which forms part of the monitor.
A JCL program called ABC.JCL.

```
* USER 12345
* COPY XYZ.CBL (DISK 1) FROM XYZ.CBL (TAPE 1)
* COMPILE XYZ.CBL (DISK 1)
* LOAD XYZ.OBJ (DISK 1)
* RUN
* ENDJOB
```

Notes.

i. The first JCL command identifies the user to the operating system. The operating system can check that the users number ie. 12345, is valid and then book charges to the user's account.

ii. The copy command causes the operating system to copy COBOL source program "XYZ.CBL" from a magnetic tape input device onto disk. The copy is given the same name.

iii. The third JCL command causes the program XYZ.CBL to be compiled.

Assume that the "COBOL" compiler is to be used. The compiler produced an object program XYZ.OBJ.

iv. The fourth JCL command causes the program XYZ.OBJ to be loaded into main storage.

v. The fifth JCL command causes the program in main storage to be executed.

vi. The sixth JCL command indicates the end of the JCL program.

25. Languages in which to write operating system software vary considerably. It is common to find some parts of the operating system's software written in assembly language because of the machine orientated nature of the software or for reasons of efficiency. However, in order to aid operating system portability and improve system programmer productivity a number of higher level languages are used. These are often variations on high level languages or are special purpose languages. For example, there are system programming languages based upon PL/I such as PL/M, which was used in the creation of CP/M (39.15), and there are special purpose languages such as "C" which is used on the UNIX system.

PROCESSES

26. A concept fundamental to the understanding of how an operating system works is that of a **process**.

27. A process may be thought of as *the execution of a program* and clearly the process will be carried out by a processor. However, there is rather more to the idea of a process than that because it is seldom the case that there is just one program assigned to a given processor for execution.

28. At this point it may help to use a simple analogy. Let us compare a processor executing a program with a student reading a book borrowed from the library. It will help if we think of the *process* of "reading the book" as starting once the book is borrowed and ending when the book is returned. The student (processor) will have other things to do than just carry out the process of reading the book and so at any one time the book may be waiting for the reader to start or continue reading it, or have the student in the act of reading it. Whenever the student sets the book to one side in order to do something else it will be necessary for the student to remember the point reached in the text and to remember any facts needed in order to be able to read on later. This is very like the case when a processor executes a program. The process may be in a state where it is waiting for the processor to continue execution or it may be in the running state. If running is suspended it will be necessary to save details of the point reached in the program and the state of variables, registers etc.

29. Example. Consider the execution of the JCL program given in paragraph 39.24. The whole job is a process and stages in the job involve other processes. The process begins when the system gets the job and identifies it and the user. The process ends with the system recording the final details of the user's use of the computer. The stages in the job are:

```
Begin
      Copy     XYZ.CBL
      Compile  XYZ.CBL
      Load     XYZ.OBJ
      Execute  XYZ.OBJ
end
```

30. Each of these four stages is a process. The first three processes involve executing system programs and the last one involves executing an applications program. The job process has its execution suspended each time it requires one of these processes to be created and run. Its execution resumes after each of these processes is completed until eventually the job process is completed. There are some complications to this situation, however. First, if an error arises during the execution of a process which is detected by the operating system then the process will be suspended and should the error be one which the operating system cannot overcome (a **"fatal"** error) the process will be aborted. (Examples of such errors will be given later). Secondly, if multiprogramming is taking place processes will be suspended and resumed as they take turns at using the processor. We will now pursue these ideas further by examining multiprogramming in batch.

MULTIPROGRAMMING IN BATCH

31. The operating system will try to optimise the use of hardware by jobs currently available to it using the following methods.

32. Job priority. It is also advantageous to assign a priority to the job before it is submitted. The two factors influencing this are:–

a. The relative proportion of I/O operation and processing.

i. A job requiring a **large amount of I/O operation** will be given **high priority** because such a program will allow other programs more opportunity to use processor time.

ii. A job requiring a large amount of processor time would be given **low priority** because if given high priority it would prevent I/O programs from obtaining the small amount of processor time they needed.

b. A secondary factor is the urgency with which the program must respond to peripherals since data can be lost if some devices such as magnetic tape units are not serviced in time.

Note. The **priority** of a job is **not** the same as its **importance.**

33. a. Jobs requiring a large amount of peripheral time are called **peripheral bound or I/O bound.**

b. Jobs requiring a large amount of processing time and little I/O are called **CPU bound** or **processor bound.**

34. Scheduling. There are two types of scheduling in a batch operating system.

a. **Job schedule.** This system software routine works out a 'priority index' for each job based on such factors as:

i. Processor time required by the job

ii. I/O time required by the job
iii. Resources available on-line eg free memory and free I/O devices
iv. The deadline by which the job must be completed.

b. **Processor schedule.** This system software routine is entered frequently to decide "WHAT TO DO NEXT". It works out the hardware resources currently demanded by each job and checks what resources are available. It then gives processor time to the most appropriate job according to a **scheduling strategy** such as : "Process the highest priority job which can use available resources". The job given processor time will run until

i. It has ended, or
ii. an interrupt occurs, eg I/O request, operator break in or run time error, or
iii. an interrupt is requested by the job, eg for output.

35. Passing control from one job to another under a scheduling scheme.
This transfer of control is handled by the executive as follows:–

a. The cause of an interrupt may be:–
i. **External** eg an input device requesting service, or
ii. **Internal** eg a programming error which causes an exit from the compiler.
In either case control is transferred to the executive.

b. In the case of an external interrupt the executive might transfer control to a routine to handle data input, taking it from a **processor bound** program.

c. In the case of an internal interrupt the executive might terminate the job and pass control to the most suitable program under the given scheduling scheme.

THE GENERAL WORK OF OPERATING SYSTEMS.

36. Before examining examples of operating systems in more detail we will find it helpful at this stage to look through the general work common to most operating systems. The main headings are:–

a. I/O control
b. Interrupt handling
c. Error Correction
d. Device Allocation
e. File security and management
f. Log of events and operator communication
g. Loading programs and subroutines
h. Storage Management.

37. I/O Control. This will consist of a set of programs for controlling the input from and output to the various devices. These programs form part of the executive and are entered via the executive when an interrupt occurs, eg one such program might set up and read blocks from a tape.

38. Interrupt handling. This is one function of the executive. When an interrupt occurs, control is passed to the executive which determines the cause of the interrupt and transfers control to the most appropriate program. Sources of interrupts are listed here.

a. **An interrupt caused by power failure.** This usually has highest priority. The executive saves vital information using the dying power supply so that it can be restarted when power is returned.

b. **Arithmetic or Logic errors.** When the arithmetic and logic unit detects that an error has taken place it generates a signal which causes an interrupt, eg overflow or underflow may cause an error signal, or output may be requested to a non existant device. Control is transferred to the executive which initiates the appropriate error routines. Control will be returned to the program once corrective action has been taken and error messages printed, or in the case of a fatal error which cannot be corrected the program will be suspended permanently.

c. **Hardware Malfunction** (eg. Parity errors). The I/O control for each device and its associated hardware normally takes care of parity checking. If a parity error is detected the executive is notified by an interrupt, and so on.

d. A clock, often called a real time clock, can generate interrupts at regular time intervals, by treating this clock as an input device. This facility provides the means by which **time sharing** can take place.

e. I/O interrupts (34.26).

f. **External interrupts** caused by events such as the operator pressing an interrupt key in the console or caused by signals from other processes in a multiprocessor machine.

39. Provision of error correction routines.

Little can be done about errors in jobs which are the result of programming faults, apart from providing information as to the type of fault. The operating system should be able to handle errors which occur as part of the normal operating activity however. For example, if data is lost during transfer because of late service of an interrupt, a routine should be available to recover the data by setting up the read process again.

40. Allocation of devices.

Several jobs may request the same output media. If more than one output device is available for that media then some programs will be allocated one device and other programs another device. If subsequently the queue for one device is longer than for another then reallocations are made. To do this track must be kept of the allocations made.

Example.

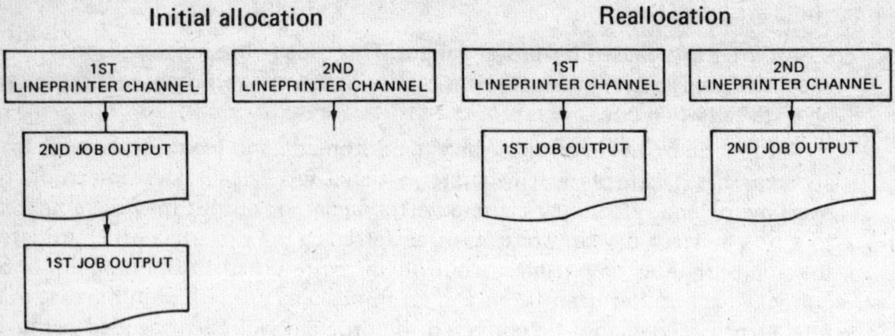

41. File security and management.

This involves these main activities:—

a. Preventing illegal access or amendments to user or system files.

b. 'Dumping' the contents of files from time to time in case of future loss eg Disk files may be transferred to tape and then stored offline.

c. Keeping track of file descriptions and locations.

42. Furnishing a Log of Events.

a. Most of the information will be presented to the console typewriter and provided by a **Monitor program** which keeps track of job execution and hardware use. These may also or alternatively be written to a tape file or disc file called the journal.

b. Information may also be furnished as part of the user's job output either as a result of errors or because of job control card requests. Further contributions to the console log come from communication with the operator.

43. Communication with the operator.

This is usually via the console keyboard. Apart from the operator's job of loading and unloading peripherals mentioned earlier the operator also has the responsibility of dealing with errors missed by the operating system and in the event of operating system failure the operator must re-establish it. The operator can key in responses to prompts from the system and also key in commands available in the command language (paragraph 22). Routine activities include:—

a. Operator activities such as:—

i. Using the command language to load jobs or other software.

ii. Using the command language to call in routines for tracing faults.

iii. Using the command language to terminate a job eg in the case where a program starts printing out page after page of garbage.

b. System messages such as:—

i. Reporting the completed run of a job.

ii. Reporting detail of job usage eg time it ran and CPU time used.

iii. Reporting program suspension caused by error conditions such as lack of input data or device not connected.

iv. Requests for operator action eg loading unloading and connecting peripherals.

44. Loading Programs and Subroutines.
Main storage is not usually able to hold all the software which is being used so transfers between main storage and direct access storage are frequently being made. The following transfers are handled.

a. Loading system software into main store as required eg a compiler.

b. Swapping applications programs or part of the programs between main storage and direct access storage as part of the multiprogramming activity.

c. Bringing into main store and linking together the applications or systems subroutines to be used in conjunction with particular jobs.

STORAGE MANAGEMENT.

45. The operating system may organise main storage into blocks of convenient size called **partitions.** It can then allocate storage space by partitions rather than by piecemeal allocation by individual locations.

a. In order to place jobs in whatever partition of main storage is available the programs must be **relocatable** (see 28.55). Their **absolute (hardware) address** is set by the executive when it adds the base address of the partition to the relative address of each instruction.

b. The executive may be able to change continually the allocation of programs by repeated reapplications of the process described in a. This is called **dynamic allocation** of main storage.

46. Tasking and segmenting.

a. A job may be broken down into stages called tasks. It may be possible to treat these tasks as separate programs to the extent that they may be multiprogrammed with each other. This is called **tasking.**

b. The job may be divided up into convenient storage units called **segments.** (A segment may well correspond to a task) and these segments may be organised so that only those segments currently requiring processing are held in main storage. The rest are held on direct access storage. This is known as **segmenting.** As each new segment is brought into main store it is said to **overlay** the segment it replaces. When segments of different programs are multiprogrammed the method is called **interleaving.**

47. Virtual Storage.
A combination of segmenting and dynamic allocation of main storage can make it possible for the programmer to write a program in segments with little regard to the main storage available. The segments of his program will be brought into main storage from direct access storage and dynamically allocated a unit of main storage (a partition). This is known as virtual storage since main storage can be regarded as larger than its real size. Very complex executives are needed to handle such systems.

AN EXAMPLE OF MULTIPROGRAMMING.

48. This example is intended to illustrate multiprogramming under a batch operating system.

In this example we suppose that the main storage not occupied by system software has been **partitioned** into three areas each being used for one job. The jobs considered in the example are:–

a. Job A. Which is initially of highest priority during its input stage and is receiving data from a 'slow' peripheral.

b. Job B. Which is also periphal bound but assigned a lower priority than A and which is receiving data from a device which needs prompt servicing.

c. Job. C. Which is processor bound and therefore given lowest priority.

d. Job D. Which is much the same as B but which is in the queue of jobs awaiting service and currently on backing store.

Multiprogramming Three Programs.

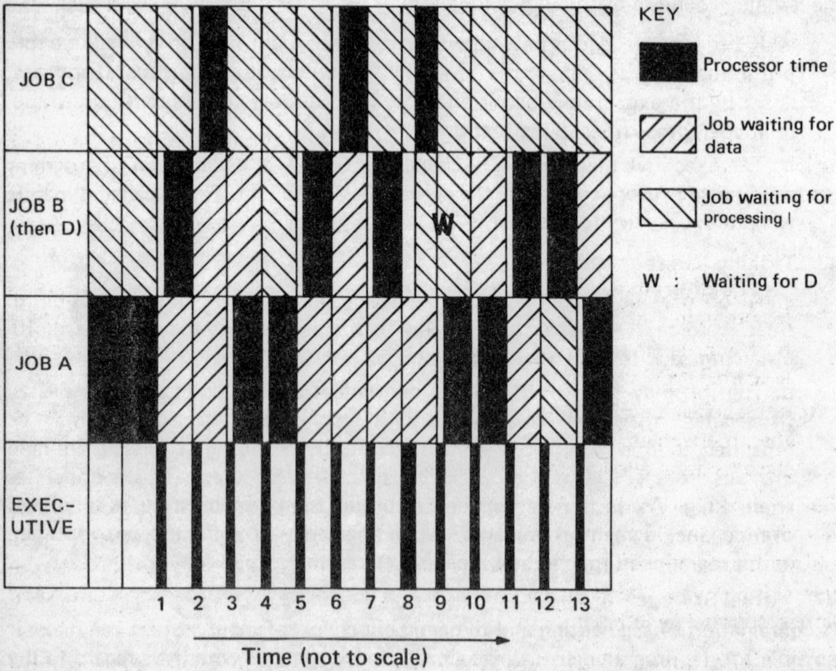

Fig. 39.2

Explanatory notes (see numbers on diagram).

1. A requests data. Executive uses I/O control then transfers control to B.

2. B requests data. Executive uses I/O control then transfers control to C.

3. Interrupt from A's peripheral. Input handled by executive and control passed to A.

4. Interrupt from B's peripheral. Input handled but control returned to A because of higher priority.

5. A requests data. Executive passes control to B.

6. As for 2.

7. Interrupt from B's peripheral. Executive handles input and hands control to B.

8. Internal interrupt caused by error in B. Operator informed. Loading of D started. Executive passes control to C.

9. As for 3.

10. Interrupt caused by completed load of D. Executive leaves control with A.

11. As for 1.

12. Interrupt from A's peripheral. Input stage of A now over so higher priority given to D and control passed back to D.

13. D requests data. Executive uses I/O control and transfers control to A.

49. Time Sharing Operating Systems.

Time sharing was defined in paragraph 12.h. Although time sharing can occur as a method of multi-access to a single program it is often used as a strategy for multiprogramming. The smaller multi-access, multiprogramming systems may be restricted to one language at a given time, eg multi-user BASIC. Larger systems allow multiprogramming in different languages.

The following facilities are usually made available by a time sharing operating system.

a. The programmer is informed of errors in his source program or execution of his program immediately.

b. The programmer is able to make corrections to his source program on-line, ie editing is possible.

c. Debugging (ie removing the faults (bugs) from a program). This is done by the programmer being able to have variable values printed at various points in the execution and by amending values at the same time.

50. In time sharing the division of processor time into 'time-slices' is provided by a 'real-time clock' which generates pulses at regular and frequent intervals. These pulses cause interrupts just as input devices do. Time slices are shared between the users in a way which gives each user a fair share of processor time and conversational facilities.

51. A typical time-slice lasts less than one hundredth of one second. At each pulse of the clock the user program currently being executed has its execution suspended. (The user will probably not be aware of this because time-slices happen so frequently that within a second execution is likely to be resumed). Then the operating system checks the status of each user, in strict sequence, to see whether the user requires processor time. Some may not. For example, they may have paused during typing for some reason. Once the operating system finds a user requiring processor time, that user's program is allowed to continue execution for the duration of the time-slice.

52. When the end of the sequence of users is reached, the operating system returns to the start of the sequence and repeats the sequence again. This is known as **polling** in a **round-robin.**

53. The operating system has greater demands made on it than in a batch multiprogramming system. For example:–

a. Process scheduling must take account of fair waiting time and time-slice length.
b. Frequent interrupts demand more frequent transfers of control between programs and greater movement of programs or program segments between main storage and backing store.
c. With frequent changes a single source statement under time sharing may require all the control given to a whole batch job.

54. Real time systems. The systems described so far are **single program systems** ie the use of one processor means that only one program is active at any one instant in time. Real time systems often have more than one processor and a front end processor with its own executive is often used. The front end processor takes care of I/O control communications with peripherals and some aspects of scheduling. The main processor (processors) handle the time shared multiprogramming required. The multiprogramming of system software is common on these systems. Details of real-time operating systems are beyond the scope of this book.

OFF-LINING AND SPOOLING.

55. These are methods of getting around the I/O bottleneck and are used in various multiprogramming environments.

a. **OFF-LINING.** A job which requires to output data, to a line printer for example, places the output data onto backing store instead, and is therefore able to complete processing quickly. Later, either

i. the tape or disk is physically moved to a separate processor which outputs the data onto a line printer, or
ii. the tape drive or disk drive is reassigned to another front end communications processor which outputs the data to a line printer.

b. **PSEUDO OFF-LINING.** This happens when the output data is transferred from backing storage onto the appropriate output device by the main processor at some later more convenient stage.

c. **SPOOLING.** (**S**imultaneous **P**eripheral **O**peration **O**n **L**ine). This uses the same principle as OFF-LINING. The term can refer to pseudo off-lining using disk. (Simultaneous operation is 'apparently' possible because of the autonomous peripheral operation as data is placed onto the disk). Alternatively spooling can form part of a multiprocessing system. The program which transfers data from the disk to the output device is called a despooling program. See Fig. 39.3.

Job and Data Flow in OFF-LINING AND SPOOLING.

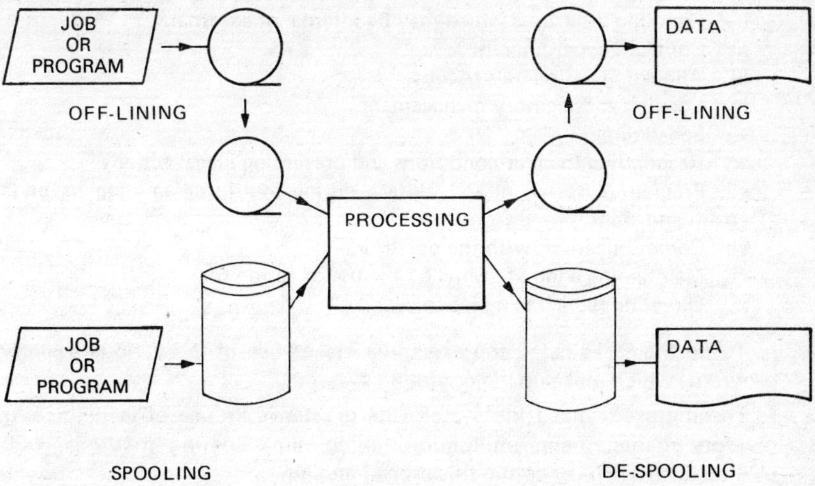

SUMMARY

56. a. The operating system is a suite of programs which takes control over the operation of the computer.

b. The operating system handles the flow of jobs through the systems. Its functions were listed in paragraph 11.

c. We considered features of operation and communication of:–

i. Multiprocessing.
ii. Multiprogramming.
iii. Batch processing.
iv. Multi-access.
v. Time sharing.
vi. Real-time.

d. We considered systems which used:–

i. Single program operation.
ii. Batch operation.
iii. Time sharing operation.
iv. Real-time operation.

e. These operating system languages were discussed:–

i. Command Languages
ii. Job Control Languages (JCLs)
iii. Languages in which to write operating system software.

f. The concept of a process was introduced.

g. The executive or supervisor program is the basic control program at the centre of the operating system. We have considered these functions which it has:–

i. Handling interrupts which may be internal or external.
ii. Controlling peripherals.
iii. Allocating peripherals to jobs.
iv. Loading and memory management.
v. Scheduling.
vi. Responding to error conditions and preventing illegal actions.
vii. Program suspension and restart during multiprogramming or under error conditions.
viii. Communications with the operator.
ix. Maintaining a log of events by the use of a monitor.
x. Directing fault tracing facilities.

h. To do the tasks listed the executive makes use of the various systems programs which make up the operating system.

i. The more advanced the system the greater is its use of techniques of memory management, multiprogramming, time sharing methods, OFF-LINING, SPOOLING or communications handling.

POINTS TO NOTE

57. a. The terms **foreground** and **background** are sometimes used to distinguish between, in the first case programs which make use of multi-access interactive activities and in the second case those running on the same system which are being handled in batch mode.

b. On very small computer systems the so called 'operating system' is usually a subset of what we have discussed as the executive. The intervention of an operator may be very frequent in such cases.

c. Small scale interactive time sharing systems may be referred to as pseudo-real-time systems.

d. Terminology is far from universal when it comes to naming what we have called the Executive. Other commonly used terms are **Kernel, Nucleus** and **Core**. Each operating system has its own version of an Executive too, so what we are considering is typical cases.

STUDENT SELF TEST QUESTIONS.

(Answers on page 742)

1. a. Explain what is meant by the term interrupt *and give two examples of an interrupt, with a brief explanation of the purpose of each.*

b. Explain the meaning of the term priority *as used in connection with multi-programming.*

Three programs are submitted for processing within a single multiprogramming run, as follows:–

Program A is a card listing program which reads and prints out the contents of punched cards;

Program B is a program to calculate stresses in boiler shells and involves the solution of equations by numerical techniques;

Program C is a payroll program which produces payslips.

Place these programes in order of priority giving your reasons.

c. List five functions of an executive or control program.

(AEB 1976)

2. What do you understand by the terms "spooling" and "off-lining" when applied to computer input and output? How do they affect the way in which hardware may be used?

Outline briefly the main hardware and software requirements for implementation of these facilities.

(B.C.S. Part 1 1976)

3. a.

*Distinguish between **multi-programming** and **multi-access**. Outline the methods by which each is achieved by an operating system and indicate the effects on the user.* [8]

*b. Give **four** examples of **interrupts**.* [6]

*c. Give **two** examples of **utilities** that are provided with a modern operating system and show how a programmer could take advantage of them.* [6]

(Welsh 1983)

QUESTIONS WITHOUT ANSWERS.

4. An operating system carries out several functions which ensure the efficient operation of a computer system. Three such functions are

i. optimising use of the CPU,
ii. memory management and
iii. management of files and peripherals.

Describe techniques which can be used to implement these functions. 16

(JMB 1983)

5. Explain the differences between the ways in which an unbuffered printer (eg. a teletypewriter) and a buffered printer (eg. a line printer) are driven from the central processing unit of a computer system.

(Cambridge 1983)

*6. a. Briefly describe **four** functions of an operating system that encourage efficient utilisation of the hardware.* (8 marks)

b. On one particular multi-access computer, two versions of the operating system are available:

Version A allocates a fixed time period, 50 milliseconds, to each user terminal regardless of tasks in hand. At the end of the period, control is passed to the next terminal in sequence.

Version B allows a particular terminal's program to run until delayed waiting for an input or output transfer. When a delay occurs, control is passed to the next terminal in sequence.

i Compare the effectiveness of versions A and B of the operating system when each manages the following combination of jobs:.

Job 1. A slow teletypewriter interactively running a game of noughts and crosses.

Job 2. A visual display unit where a long mathematical calculation has been initiated and no further input-output activity is expected until the end of the computation.

Job 3. A teletypewriter printing a long list of names and addresses.

(8 marks)

*ii. Suggest **two** methods of improving one of the above versions of the operating system. (4 marks)*

(AEB 1983)

7. *a. Explain what is meant by the term **multiprogramming** and describe briefly how it works and why it is useful.*

b. Two programs which run in a multiprogramming system both direct output to a line printer during their execution.

There is only one line printer available.

*Explain carefully how **spooling** makes it possible for the two programs to run concurrently. State the main reasons why such a system uses spooling.*

(Cambridge 1983)

Systems Analysis

1. System Analysis may be defined as the methods of determining how best to use computers, with other resources, to perform tasks which meet the information needs of an organisation.

2. The use of the word "analysis" in the term is therefore misleading because "analysing" is only *one* of the activities which are generally regarded as coming under the heading "Systems Analysis".

3. Systems Analysis consists of a series of stages forming part of what is often called the "System Life Cycle".

Life Cycle Stages:-

a. Preliminary Survey/Study.
b. Feasibility Study.
c. Investigation and Fact Recording.
d. Analysis.
e. Design.
f. Implementation.
g. Maintenance and Review.

(c.–g.: Main Stages in Systems Analysis and the work of the "Systems Analyst")

4. An overview of the system life cycle is given in chapter 40.

5. The subsequent chapters in this Part deal with the details of the stages in Systems Analysis.

ORGANISATION OF SYSTEMS ANALYSIS.

6. The requirements of people engaged in systems analysis, ie wide *technical knowledge, business knowledge,* and *experience,* are not normally found in one individual. Thus teams of analysts are generally formed and operate on specified assignments. Specialisation within the team will result in junior analysts doing the fact finding and recording, with more senior analysts designing and implementing. The way they may fit into the organisation structure of a business is shown in the figure below.

(See 13.23–13.27)

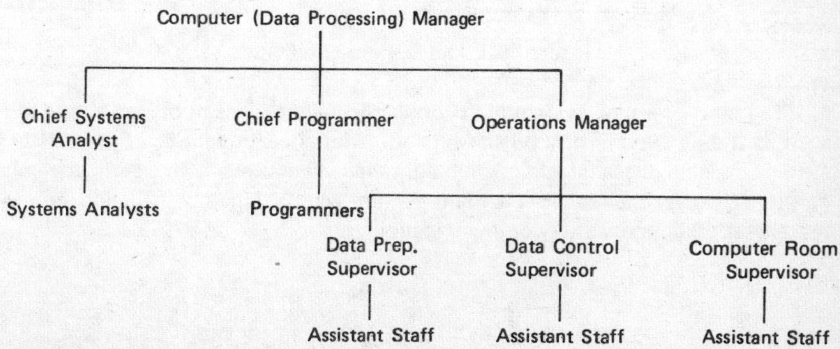

40 The System Life Cycle

INTRODUCTION.

1. New computer systems frequently replace existing manual systems, and the new systems may themselves be replaced after some time. The process of replacing the old system by the new happens in a series of stages and the whole process is called the **"system life cycle".**

2. This chapter provides an overview of the system life cycle. The individual stages in the life cycle are described in detail in subsequent chapters.

THE LIFE CYCLE IN OUTLINE.

3. Fig. 40.1 shows the major stages in the system life cycle.

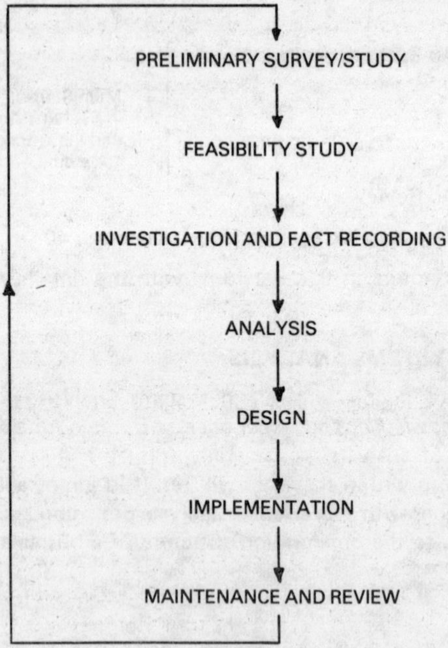

Figure 40.1. The System Life Cycle.

4. The start of a new system life cycle is normally the result of some *"trigger"* such as the perception of a business need, failures or limitations of the existing system causing dissatisfaction, or heightened awareness of modern developments. Whatever the reason it is management who will initiate the selection of a project for preliminary study or investigation.

5. **Preliminary Survey/Study.** The purpose of this survey is to establish whether there is a need for a new system and if so to specify the objectives of the system.

6. **Feasibility Study.** The purpose of the feasibility study is to investigate the project in sufficient depth to be able to provide information which either justifies the development of the new system or shows why the project should not continue.

7. The findings of the feasibility study are presented to management in the form of a report which will make appropriate recommendation. If the report finds in favour of the project then senior management may decide to move to the next stage.

8. **Investigation and Fact Recording.** At this stage in the life cycle a detailed study is conducted. This study is far more detailed and comprehensive than the feasibility study. The purpose of this study is fully to understand the existing system and to identify the basic information requirements.

9. **Analysis.** Analysis of the full description of the existing system *and* of the objectives of the proposed system should lead to a **full specification of the user's requirements.** This **Requirements Specification** can be examined and approved before system design is embarked upon. In recent years greater emphasis has been placed upon this stage because of former expensive and frustrating experiences of designs which failed to meet requirement. The earlier in the system life cycle that a mistake is discovered the less costly it is to correct.

10. **Design.** The analysis may lead to a number of possible alternative designs. For example different combinations of manual and computerised elements may be considered. Once one alternative has been selected the purpose of the design stage is to work from the requirements specification to produce a **System Specification.** The system specification will be a detailed set of documents which provide details of all features of the system.

11. **Implementation.** Implementation involves following the detail set out in the system specification. Two particularly important tasks are programming and staff training. It is worth observing in passing that the programming task has its own "life cycle" in the form of the various stages in programming ie. analysis and design occur at many different levels.

12. **Maintenance and Review.** Once a system is implemented and in full operation it is examined to see if it has met the objectives set out in the original specification. Unforseen problems may need to be overcome and that may involve returning to earlier stages in the cycle to take corrective action. From time to time the requirements of the organisation will change and the system will have to be examined to see if it can cope with the changes. At some stage the system life cycle will be repeated again and yet again.

AREAS OF RESPONSIBILITY.

13. Different types of staff are responsible for different stages in the life cycle. For example, the early stages will have a significant involvement by senior manage-

ment, the middle stages will be the responsibility of "Systems Analysts" and a stage such as implementation will give major responsibility to programmers.

14. In the remainder of this Part those activities which are primarily the responsibility of the system analyst will be discussed. The responsibilities of programmers have already been discussed in earlier chapters.

SUMMARY.

15. a. The system life cycle is the series of stages involved in replacing an old system by a new one.

b. The life cycle stages are:
- i. Preliminary Survey/Study – initiated by management.
- ii. Feasibility Study.
- iii. Investigation and fact recording.
- iv. Analysis.
- v. Design.
- vi. Implementation.
- vii. Maintenance and Review.

c. Some form of documentation accompanies all stages in the cycle. The following documentation is of particular importance:-
- i. Feasibility study report.
- ii. User requirements specification.
- iii. System specification.

POINTS TO NOTE.

16. a. "System Analysis" takes place at all stages in the life cycle not just the analysis stage.

STUDENT SELF TEST QUESTIONS.

(Answers on page 742)

1. *What is a System Specification?*
2. *What is the purpose of a feasibility study?*

41 Investigation and Analysis

INTRODUCTION.

1. The items to be covered in this chapter are the confirmation of the terms of reference, the fact finding and recording, and the analysis of the recorded facts to produce a requirements specification.

TERMS OF REFERENCE.

2. It is of the utmost importance that clear objectives are laid down by management. If analysts are allowed to set their own objectives, then these may not accord with the overall company objectives. Before the analyst begins his or her task, he or she should, therefore, confirm the terms of reference. The *number of analysts required,* and the *length* and *breadth* of the assignment will depend, to a great extent, upon the objectives set. For example if the objective were "to reduce the turn-round time for orders from one *week* to a *day*" a completely new system would perhaps need to be designed requiring many analysts, taking a long time and having wide effects on the organisation. Conversely, the objective "to reduce the number of clerks in the accounts department" may require a straight transfer of existing procedures to a visible record computer or magnetic tape computer involving fewer analysts, shorter time and little organisational disruption.

FACT FINDING.

3. It is essential to gather all the facts about a current system to ensure that all *strengths* and *weaknesses* are discovered. Thus, when a new system is designed, as many of the weaknesses as possible are eliminated, whilst retaining the strengths.

4. There are four main techniques available, those used depending upon the particular circumstances:-

a. **Interviewing.** This is probably the most widely used technique and the most productive. Interviewing is an art not readily acquired. During interviews facts about what is happening come to light, together with the opinions of the interviewee regarding weaknesses in the system. The personal contacts are important in getting the cooperation of the people involved, and in giving them the feeling of having made a substantial contribution towards the design of the new procedure. It is vital to gain the confidence of the individuals concerned at this stage in order for all the facts to be gathered.

b. **Questionnaires.** The second technique is the use of questionnaires. They save the time of the interviewer but are difficult to design and are generally considered irksome to complete. They are particularly useful when a little information is required from a great number of people. Moreover when the study involves many different geographical locations they may be the only practicable method of gathering facts.

c. **Observation.** This is best employed in conjunction with other techniques and carried out after the observer has an understanding of the procedures involved. Only then will he be able to spot irregularities and generally apply a "seeing" eye to the job.

d. **Record inspection.** The study of organisation charts, procedure manuals and statistics, can reveal much useful information about a procedure. However, a close study of the forms currently being used should give the best guide to current practice which may, or may not, accord with the original requirements.

FACT RECORDING.

5. Fact recording. During the fact finding stage, unless the investigator has formulated a plan for the keeping of notes of the facts, he will end up with a mass of notes on all areas, which will be difficult to examine.

6. A good practice is to sectionalise notes into *areas* of investigation (eg. by *department* or *operation*) or by *type* of information (eg. organisation charts, interviews, forms, etc). Use should be made of *procedure flow charts* and *work charts,* examples of which are shown in Fig. 41.1. In addition use will be made of decision tables and flowcharts. The flowcharts will reflect the varying degree of detail required. These two forms of recording are particularly suited because of the "YES/NO" type situation met in solving computer problems.

7. Note that at this stage no attempt is made at analysis or design since the existing system must be fully understood first.

ANALYSIS.

8. At this point, the analyst has gathered all the facts which are relative to the objectives set and has grouped them into a form suitable for analysis. The analysis stage is an important intermediate stage between investigation and design. The analyst must examine all the facts he or she has gathered in order to make a proper assessment of the existing system. He or she must resist the temptation to include ideas in the new system which have not been fully worked out. The aim of this stage is to ensure that *all* feasible alternatives are eventually produced. The present system must be criticised against the Principles of Procedure (see below), after which the strengths and weaknesses of the system should be apparent.

9. Principles of procedure. The present system may be criticised against the principles of procedure:-

a. **Purpose.** Are the purposes being satisfied? Are they still *necessary?* Could they be achieved in *any other way?*

b. **Economical.** Is it economical? Benefits should be related to the cost of producing them. Are there more economical methods?

c. **Work flow.** Are the work flows satisfactory?

Charts are used to give a pictorial representation of a procedure, departments' or operators' work etc, to aid analysis. There are no *standard* work charts, but the following are examples of those used.

1. **Movement chart (or string diagram).** This is used to show the movement of clerks or documents and is constructed by lines drawn, or string pinned, on a planned layout of the work area.

2. **Process chart.** This is used to portray the *operations* to be carried out, the *flow of work,* and the *distance between points of operation.*

It is constructed by listing the operations (filing, copying, sorting etc.) down the left hand side and *standard symbols* used to pictorially represent those operations (eg □ = filed; '0' = operation).

3. **Operation chart.** This shows what is done and gives a comparative record of productive and idle time of an operator and machine:-

OPERATION	TIME	OPERATOR	TYPEWRITER
Making tea	0915	/	×
Typing	1000	/	/
Idle	1030	×	×
Taking dictation	1100	/	×

4. **Procedure flowchart.** This shows the flow of multiple copy forms:-

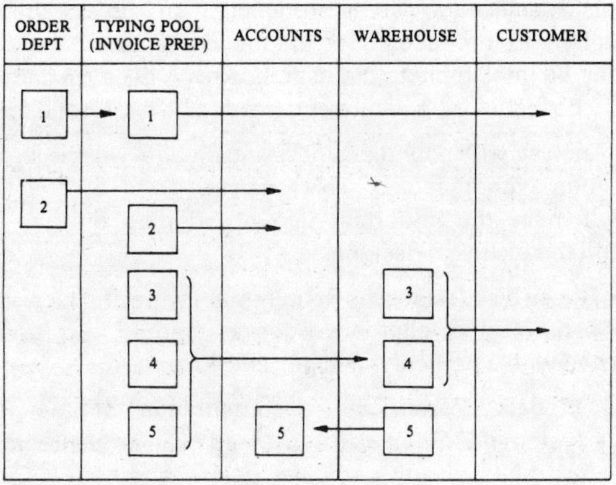

Figure 41.1. Work Charts.

d. **Specialisation/simplification/standardisation.** Are the three S's being practised? Is the work capable of being carried out by machine? Can the complex procedures be simplified? Are standard practices observed?

e. **Flexibility.** Is the system flexible? What will be the effect on the system of a big increase or decrease in the volumes to be processed?

f. **Exception principle.** Is the principle of exception being observed? Factors requiring action should be highlighted and not submerged in a mass of routine detail.

g. **Reliability.** How reliable is the procedure? What provision is there for such events as staff sickness, machine breakdown? Could more up to date equipment be justified?

h. **Form.** Is the information being produced in the form best suited to the recipient? Is there a need for a hard copy?

i. **Existing system.** If a change is made, what equipment and other facilities currently being used could be incorporated in the new procedure?

j. **Continuous control.** What types of errors are occurring? Are the controls satisfactory? What other types of controls could be used?

k. **Time.** Is the information being produced in time for meaningful action to be taken?

10. Requirement Specification. An important aim of the analysis is to produce a **Requirements Specification.** In recent years methods have been developed so that the Requirements Specification can be produced in an *implementation free* form which is intelligible to the user. Not all the contents of the Requirements Specification may be intelligible to the user, however, because some parts of the requirement may be technical in nature and need to be expressed formally.

11. A Systems Analyst, with sound business knowledge, will discuss the Requirements Specification with the user. This analyst, aided by the Requirements Specification, will have the important task of bridging the gap between the business user and the technical designer.

12. At the end of these discussions the Requirements Specification should be in an accepted form, estimates for alternative designs should be prepared, and the decision to proceed with a particular design can be made.

13. Conceptual Models. Within the documentation of the Requirements Specification is a **system definition** also expressed in an *implementation free* way ie. free of the constraints of any particular design alternative. Such a system definition is called a **"conceptual model"**, a term originally used in data base design.

14. Don't be put off by the name because a conceptual model has three very natural components:-

a. a *data model* which defines the data requirements in terms of entities, attributes and relationships. (eg. an entity such as an order contains attributes such as quantities required and has a relationship with other entities such as customers).

b. a *process model* which defines the processing requirements in terms of events and operations. (eg. the event of an order arriving gives rise to operations such as the update of stock data and production of invoices).

c. a *system model* which defines functional areas and their interrelationship (eg. one functional area may deal with the reception of an order and then pass it to another functional area which processes the order).

15. The methods for constructing the conceptual model are too specialised for inclusion in this book although the models themselves are easy to understand.

SUMMARY.

16. The terms of reference of an assignment must be clearly laid down.

17. Fact finding, recording, and examination, are necessary to discover the strengths and weaknesses of the area under investigation.

18. The analysis stage is important because of the need to ensure that

a. the requirements are *fully* understood and correctly specified.

b. *all* feasible design alternatives are contemplated.

It is an important breathing space between investigation and design.

19. There is a tendency, in practice, for some analysts to neglect the analysis stage and to go ahead with the design of a new system based on a pre-conceived notion that he or she has held from the beginning. In this way the system produced may be neither what is required nor the most feasible alternative. The mandatory production of a Requirements Specification guards against such bad practices.

POINTS TO NOTE.

20. a. Methods of analysis have been developed greatly over recent years. It is not necessary for you to learn these methods but you should be aware of their importance in improving the quality and effectiveness of Systems Analysis.

b. Improvements to the analysis stage have an impact on the design stage. The designer starts from a much stronger position if he or she has a Requirements Specification.

STUDENT SELF TEST QUESTIONS.

(Answers on page 743)

1. Even if the objectives of an assignment indicate the need for a completely new system, it is still important to critically examine the present system. Why do you think this is so?

42 Systems Design

INTRODUCTION.

1. It is during the design stage that the systems analyst is called upon to use his or her creative abilities. The implementation-free nature of the Requirements Specification means that *all* feasible alternative designs are open to consideration. By applying judgement, skill and knowledge the analyst can interpret the requirement specification to create one or more **System Specifications** (or **System Definitions**). A System Specification provides *detailed* documentation of the new system ie. it gives the detail of a particular implementation, unlike the Requirements Specification which is implementation-free. A System Specification requires acceptance by management just as the Requirements Specification does.

2. This chapter deals with the elements of design and the sequence in which they might be carried out. Design criteria are then dealt with and are followed by a description of a System Specification.

DESIGN ELEMENTS.

3. The design of a new system can be conveniently divided into the following elements:-

a. Outputs.

b. Inputs.

c. Files.

d. Procedures.

4. **Outputs.** It is necessary to consider what is required from the system before deciding how to set about producing it. These requirements will have become clear as the project progressed. The analyst will need to consider form, types, volumes, and frequency of reports and documents. Choice of output media will also have to be made.

5. **Inputs.** Consideration of input will be influenced greatly by the needs of output, eg. the necessity for quick response from the system would determine the need for an on-line type of input. Consideration would be given to:-

a. Data collection methods, and validation.

b. Types of input media available.

c. Volumes of input documents.

d. Design of input layouts.

6. **Files.** This element is very much linked to input and output. Input is processed against the files to produce the necessary output. Considerations involved in designing files are:-

a. Storage media.

b. Method of file organisation and access.

c. File security.

d. Record layouts.

7. Procedures. Procedures are the steps which unify the whole process, which link everything together to produce the desired output. These will involve both computer and clerical procedures. They will start with the origination of the source document and end with the output document being distributed. The design of the computer programs will constitute a major task in itself.

8. Because of their importance in the design of a new procedure the aspects of form design and internal check are dealt with in some little detail.

9. Forms design.

a. **Introduction.** The design of forms and the design of procedures are very much linked. The completion of a form may be the first operation of a procedure (eg. compilation of an order form); a by-product of an operation within a procedure (eg. a receipt, as a by-product of posting to the cash book, in machine accounting); the end product of a procedure (eg. reports to management); or the form may be completed at various stages within a procedure (eg. invoice sets).

Whether the requirements of the form dictate the procedure, or the steps in the procedure dictate the design of the form, is determined by individual circumstances. Very often, the justification of expensive machines brings in its wake the need for redesign of forms to fit the procedure.

b. **Aim.** The aim is to keep forms to the minimum consistent with serving the needs of the system.

c. **Features of design.**

i. **Sizes.** The use of *standard* size forms should be used, as it is more economic to do so, and *handling, filing,* and *copying* are simplified.

ii. **Types of paper.** The quality of paper used should be appropriate to requirements. Consideration should be given to such things as frequency of handling, storage needs, conditions under which forms are completed, and prestige requirements.

iii. **Identification.** There should be a brief, self explanatory title; copies should be identified by different colours or bold symbols; serial numbering may be required for internal check purposes.

iv. **Common information.** If two forms are used in conjunction with each other, the common information should be in the same sequence and position.

v. **Vertical spacing.** There should be adequate space for each item of entry (eg. an invoice should have enough spaces to cover the normal number of items ordered). If a typewriter is being used in recording data on a form, consideration must be given to the normal vertical spacing requirements of the machine.

vi. **Columns.** The length of column headings should be tailored to the width required by the information to be entered in the column.

vii. **Pre-printing.** As much as possible of the common detail should be pre-printed, leaving only variable data to be entered.

viii. **Clarity.** There should be overall simplicity of instructions. Material of a similar nature should be grouped together. A logical sequence for completion should be followed and unambiguous wording should be used. The size of the print should make for ease of reading.

ix. **Miscellaneous.** There may be a requirement for perforation for subsequent bursting or pre-punched holes for subsequent filing.

x. **Multi part sets.** Where more than one document is to be raised at the same time, consideration should be given to the method employed in carrying the image through all copies eg. carbon; no carbon required paper; carbon patches, etc.

10. Internal check.

a. **Definition.** The arrangement of procedures and systems, and the *allocation of duties* so that there is an automatic check on what is being done.

b. **Principle.** No one person should be placed in the position of having responsibility for *all aspects* of a business transaction. Thus the work flow is so arranged that the work of one person, or section, is independently checked by some other person or section.

c. **Purposes achieved.**

i. The possibility of fraud and error is reduced.
ii. The responsibility for errors is determinable.
iii. Supervision is assisted (because of the built-in checks).
iv. The work of internal and external auditors is reduced.

d. **Examples of the operation of internal check.**

i. The serial numbering of forms.
ii. The requirement for two signatures on cheques.
iii. The use of control accounts.

DESIGN METHOD AND DESIGN SEQUENCE.

11. Over the last ten years or so a number of design methods have become established, each with its own set of dedicated supporters.

12. The advocates of each of these methods naturally proclaim the advantages of their methods over the alternatives. Terms such as "structured", "hierarchical", "top-down", and others are used to label the different approaches to design.

13. What all these design methods have in common is a recognition that large problems, such as those found in design, can only be tackled effectively if they are broken down into smaller, more manageable tasks in some systematic way. The same ideas were first put into practice with considerable success in program writing, where terms such as "Structured" and "Top-down" suffer less ambiguity.

14. Without going into unnecessary detail about any particular method it is still possible to identify the following design sequence:

a. The system is described at a logical level in terms of *what* it will do in the context of a particular design. ie. a combination of design elements (para 3) will be put together in a way which can meet the requirements in general terms.

b. The "logical model" is refined in a series of steps in which successive detail is added. Some steps may be re-traced as the emerging design is evaluated. Considerations of physical details are postponed as long as possible, because, for example, it is senseless to design a report document before it is decided exactly what the report should contain.

c. Finally the physically detail is added to the logical detail so that the design shows not only *what* the system should do but also exactly *how* it should do it.

CRITERIA FOR DESIGN.

15. Purpose. The purpose must be to meet the demands of the Requirements Specification, and for that matter, the objectives which were agreed at the beginning of the project. At one time, and still in some organisations, a Requirements Specification was not produced at the end of the analysis stage and so the System Specification had to serve both purposes.

16. Some of the criteria outlined in the following paragraphs may be applied to the Requirements Specification. Where the criteria do apply it is a clear indication of the economic benefits of the Requirement Specification in catching errors earlier and saving inappropriate design effort and costs.

17. Economical. The costs and benefits of the new system should be compared with those of the existing system. This is not easy to do because of the difficulty of quantifying benefits such as "better or more" information. It is important however that the attempt be made.

18. Work flows. The best work flows must be attained. This includes methods of transmitting data to and from the computer, the number of runs required, file organisation, the requirements of internal check, and the link with clerical procedures.

19. Specialisation, simplification and standardisation. The benefits to be derived from the practice of the "three S's" are well known. The analyst will have them in mind throughout the design stage.

20. Flexibility. Points to be considered here are:-

a. **Integration of procedures.** Systems should be designed with possible integration of procedures in mind. This is particularly important as the centralised nature of computer processing makes possible the integration of many procedures carried out independently under conventional methods.

b. **Modularity of hardware.** It is important when choosing the hardware to ensure that it is capable of being expanded (units added) when the need arises.

c. **Peak periods/treatment of exceptions.** The system can be designed to cope with peak period processing; an alternative arrangement is to use a bureau for the unusually high loads. Similarly, exceptional items (ie. those not recurring frequently) could be designed into the system but it may be more convenient to have them dealt with separately by conventional methods.

21. **Exception principle.** The principle of exception should be incorporated in the design of the new system, so that only deviations from plan are reported for management's attention. In a stock control system, for example, warnings would be given of slow moving stocks. The analyst must ensure that only *necessary* output is produced.

22. **Reliability.** The reliability of all the hardware and software must be considered. The analyst must ensure that facilities required for the new system have a proven record of reliability. Maintenance requirements, the expected life of the hardware, and the back up facilities (in case of breakdown) must be considered.

23. **Form.** Data must be presented to the computer in a machine sensible form. The analyst must consider all the methods of input and try to reduce the steps necessary between origination of data and its input. If output from one run is used as the input to another, the ideal medium for the subsequent input should be used. When output is required in a humanly legible form, choice of method of presentation is important. Methods available are visual display, printed copy, graphical, etc, and the needs of the person receiving the output will determine which one is appropriate.

24. **Existing system.** Consideration must be given to the existing staff, procedures, equipment, forms, etc, in the design of any new system. For example, if punched card input is currently being operated, the procedures already exist for transferring the source data into a machine sensible form although it may well not be incorporated into the design of a new computer system.

25. **Continuous control.** As the majority of steps are carried out automatically, there is an even greater need for care in internal check. Audit trails (ie. documentary records of various stages in processing which can be used to check that procedures have been carried out correctly) must be laid to the satisfaction of the auditors. Controls such as those described in Chapter 21 should be incorporated.

26. **Time.** The analyst must design the system to satisfy time requirements. Speeds of equipment, modes of access and processing methods must be considered. The length of the processing cycle is a most important consideration. The presentation of source data to the computer and the production of output documents will be subject to strict time constraints.

SYSTEMS SPECIFICATION (OR DEFINITION).

27. The Systems Specification is the detailed documentation of the proposed new system. It serves two main purposes:-

a. **Communication.** It serves as a means of communicating all that is required to be known to all interested parties; as follows:-

i. **Management** for final approval.

ii. **Programmers** to enable them to write the programs necessary for implementation.

iii. **Operating staff,** detailing all necessary operating procedures.

iv. **Users,** as they will ultimately be responsible for running the new system. They must therefore be fully aware of the contents of the Specification and their agreement is essential.

b. **Record.** A permanent record of the system in detail is necessary for control. It will be used for evaluations, modification, and training purposes.

It is of particular importance to have the system well documented as those analysts who took part in its design go on to other projects, or perhaps change employment.

28. Different persons require to know only *parts* of the whole specification (eg. programmers need to know the runs required and the file layouts, but will not need to know the timings for data preparation or numbers of staff required etc.) The specification is also produced at different stages of design ie. *in outline* for top management, *in detail* for lowest levels. The specification is sectionalised to enable only the appropriate parts to be sent to the interested parties.

29. Contents. The following are the main items to be found in a Systems Specification.

a. **Preliminary information.** This comprises contents, lists, names of recipients of particular sections, names of those having authority to change files, programs, etc.

b. **Objectives of the system.** A brief statement is given of the aims indicating the departments and the main procedures involved. The benefits arising from implementation are also stated.

c. **Systems description.** This will detail all procedures both clerical and computer using flowcharts where applicable.

d. **Detailed specification** of:-

i. Input files.
ii. Output files.
iii. Master files.
} with specimen layouts.

iv. Source documents.
v. Output documents.
} with specimen copies of each document.

Supporting narrative would accompany each item. Methods of file organisation and modes of access are detailed.

e. **Program specification.** This contains:

i. Details of inputs, outputs and processes for each program run.
ii. Test data and expected results.
iii. Stop/start, file checking, error checking procedures.
iv. Controls.
v. Relationship between procedures and computer runs.

f. **Implementation procedures.**

i. Detailed timetable (using networks or other scientific aids).

ii. Details of conversion procedures.
iii. Change-over procedures, including systems testing.

g. **Equipment.** All equipment including ancillary equipment necessary and maintenance arrangements.

h. **User department instructions.** These relate to the input to the system (ie. times for forwarding source documents) the output from the system (ie. dealing with documents, and control totals etc).

SUMMARY.

30. The design stage is the creative stage in systems analysis, all feasible design alternatives should be considered.

31. The systems analyst can use the Requirement Specification as the criteria against which to judge his or her designs.

32. The Systems Specification is important as a means of communication and a record of the detailed design.

POINTS TO NOTE.

33. a. Terminology is not universal. For example a "System Specification" may also be called a "Requirement Specification". This is seldom a practical difficulty because the context normally prevents any ambiguity.

b. The terms *'specification'* and *'definition'* are used synonomously.

c. The Systems Specification acts as the *acceptance* of the design of the new system by all levels of management.

d. In reading this chapter on design, students should realise that much of the detail involved has been described under the appropriate headings eg. data collection, computer files, etc.

STUDENT SELF TEST QUESTIONS.

(Answers on page 743)

1. *What are the factors which govern choice of output media and device?*
2. *Describe the contents of a System Specification.*

43 Implementation and Review

INTRODUCTION.

1. Implementation follows on from the detailed design stage. This involves the co-ordination of the efforts of the *user* department and the data processing department in getting the new system into operation. A Co-ordinating Committee is sometimes formed for this purpose, having as its members the managers of the departments concerned and a representative from the computer department. The analyst responsible for the design of the new system will be an important member because of his thorough knowledge of the system.

2. Planning for the implementation will have begun early in the design stage. Details will have been stipulated in the Systems Specification.

They would cover the following:-

a. Training of staff.

b. Programming.

c. System testing.

d. Master File conversion.

e. Changeover procedures.

f. Review and Maintenance.

TRAINING OF STAFF.

3. The amount of training required for various categories of personnel will depend upon the complexity of the system and the skills presently available. The systems analyst would be required to ensure that all persons involved with the new system were capable of making it an operational success. The following aids would be used, as appropriate:-

a. **Handbooks.** These will be produced as part of, or development from, the Systems Specification.

b. **Courses.** Either full-time or part-time courses, often run by the computer manufacturers.

c. **Lectures.** General background knowledge, or knowledge of specific areas, could be covered by means of lecture.

PROGRAMMING.

4. The programmer must design programs which conform to the requirements set out in the system specification (42.29). The stages in programming have already been discussed in 13.13.

5. The work of the programmer has already been discussed in chapter 13. Program implementation can pose problems of management in large computer departments where the programmers might specialise in certain areas of programming. These specialisms may be:

a. **Applications.** Applications programmers are the people who write the initial programs for each application.

b. **Maintenance.** Once the programs written by the Applications programmer are operational they are handed over to a Maintenance programmer, whose job it will be to carry out any amendments or improvements that may be necessary. The Applications programmer then moves on to fresh fields.

c. **Systems software.** This programmer will specialise in writing "non-application" programs ie. systems software. These programs will supplement those supplied by the manufacturer.

6. In smaller installations, of course, a smaller team of programmers will have to turn their hands to any task that comes along.

SYSTEM TESTING.

7. There is a need to ensure both that the individual programs have been written *correctly* and that the *system* as a whole will work, ie. the link between the programs in a suite. There must also be co-ordination with *clerical* procedures involved. To this end the systems analyst must provide the necessary test data as follows:-

a. **Program testing.** The systems analyst will need to supply test data designed to ensure that all possible contingencies (as specified in the Systems Specification) have in fact been catered for by the programmer. *Expected results* of the test must be worked out beforehand for comparison purposes.

b. **Procedure testing.** The aim of procedure testing will be to ensure that the *whole system* fits together as planned. This will involve the clerical procedures which precede input; the actual machine processes themselves; and the output procedures which follow. Overall timings and the ability of staff to handle the anticipated volumes will all be under scrutiny.

MASTER FILE CONVERSION.

8. It is necessary to convert the existing master files into a magnetic form. The *stages* of file conversion will depend on the method currently used for keeping the files (eg. manually; in box files) but are likely to be:-

a. Production of control totals, by adding machine.

b. Transcription of all 'standing' data (such as account number, address etc). to a special input document designed for ease of data entry.

c. Insertion of all *new* data required onto input document eg. account numbers where none were used previously.

d. Transcription of data from documents to magnetic media. This can be a major task in the case of a large manual system. Extra staff may need to be drafted in.

e. Verification of transcribed data.

f. Data is then used as input to a 'file creation run'. A specially written computer program produces the master records in the required format.

g. Printing out of files for comparison with old files.

h. Printing out of control totals for agreement with pre-lists.

i. At a date immediately prior to changeover, variable data is inserted in master files. (eg. *balance* on accounts).

CHANGEOVER PROCEDURES.

9. There are two *basic* methods of changing over to a new system:-

a. **Parallel.**

b. **Direct.**

10. Parallel. The old and new systems are run concurrently, using the same inputs. The outputs are compared and reasons for differences resolved. Outputs from the old system continue to be distributed until the new system has proved satisfactory. At this point the old system is discontinued and the new one takes its place.

11. Direct. The old system is discontinued altogether and the new system becomes operational immediately.

A variation of *either* of the two basic methods is the so-called 'pilot' changeover.

A 'pilot' changeover would involve the changing over of *part* of the system, either in *parallel* or *directly.*

12. The features of the various methods of changeover are:-

a. **Parallel.**

i. It is a costly method because of the amount of duplication involved.

ii. This method would mean the employment of extra staff or overtime working for existing staff. This can create difficulties over the period of the changeover.

iii. It is only possible where the outputs from old and new systems are easy to reconcile, and where the systems are similar.

iv. Its use does give management the facility of fully testing the new system whilst still retaining the existing system.

b. **Direct.**

i. If the new system bears no resemblance to the old then a direct changeover is probably inevitable.

ii. There must be complete confidence in the new system's reliability and accuracy before the method is used.

c. **Pilot.**

i. Use of the variation of the two main methods is possible when part of the system can be treated as a separate entity, eg. a department or branch might be computerised before the undertaking as a whole.

REVIEW AND MAINTENANCE.

13. Once the system has become operational it will need to be examined to see if it has met its objectives. For example the costs and benefits will be compared with the estimates produced at the systems inception. This particular activity is often known as *"post audit"*.

14. The system will also need to be reviewed and maintained periodically for the following reasons:-

a. To deal with unforeseen problems arising in operation. eg. programs may need to be modified to deal with unforseen circumstances.

b. To confirm that the planned objectives are being met and to take action if they are not.

c. To ensure that the system is able to cope with the changing requirements of business.

15. The results of a systems review would be used in future systems analysis assignments.

OPERATIONS AFTER IMPLEMENTATION.

16. The day to day operations of the computer system rely upon a number of specialist staff including the following:

a. **Operations Manager.** He or she is responsible to the Computer Manager for operation of the computer and ancillary equipment. Also under his control will be:–

- i. Data control section.
- ii. Data preparation.
- iii. Tape and disk library/ies.

b. **Computer Operator** handles and operates the hardware in the computer room. He or she handles the input and output media (eg. placing tapes onto tape drives), communicates with the operating system and tries to keep the installation running smoothly by stepping in when things go wrong to correct them immediately.

c. The layout of a typical computer room for a large installation requiring several operators is shown in fig. 43.1.

This diagram shows the lay-out of a typical Computer Room. There is a separate room for the assembly of incoming work which contains a number of storage cabinets for stationery etc. and a guillotine/decollator for handling output stationery.

Inside the computer room, the various input/output devices face the console to minimise movement by the operators and to allow the senior operator to see what is going on. The CPU, which the operators never touch, is out of the way at one end. In this example, the library of magnetic tapes and disks is kept in the computer room with a desk for the librarian.

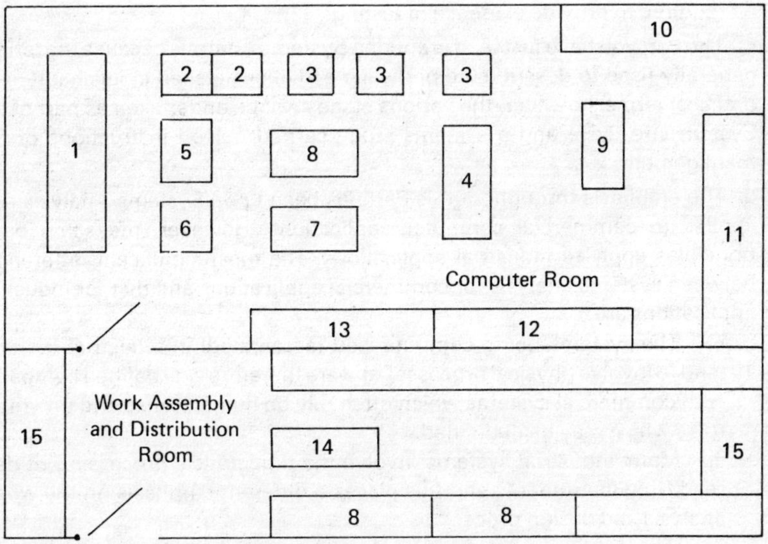

KEY.

1. CPU.
2. Magnetic Tape Drives.
3. Magnetic Disk Drives.
4. Line Printer.
5. Diskette Drives.
6. PABX.
7. Console.
8. Work Tables.
9. Librarian's Desk.
10. Magnetic Disk Cabinet.
11. Magnetic Tape Racks.
12. Diskette Cabinets.
13. Operators' and Engineers' Manuals.
14. Guillotine/Decollator.
15. Stationery Cupboards.

Figure 43.1. Layout of a Computer Room.

SUMMARY.

17. a. Implementation is concerned with the *co-ordinating* and *controlling* of the activities necessary to put the new system into operation.

b. *Staff training, programming, testing, file conversion, changeover,* review and maintenance are the stages in implementation.

c. The systems analyst is needed at this stage because of his knowledge of the designed system and its implications.

POINTS TO NOTE.

18. a. Note the difference between program testing and procedure testing.

b. The responsibility for program testing lies with the programmers who will be required to provide evidence of testing.

c. The Part you have just read is entitled Systems Analysis because the term is generally used to describe the particular activities detailed in its chapters. In practical terms, however, the various stages will be undertaken as part of the System Life Cycle and a systems study carried out on instructions of top management.

d. The emphasis throughout this Part has been upon Systems Analysis as it applies to commercial computer applications. However, the same basic principles apply to industrial applications. The most significant differences between systems analysis for commercial applications and that for industrial applications are:

i. The systems being computerised (automated) in industrial systems tend to involve physical processes and are therefore well defined compared with commercial systems which often rely on human sense and unwritten rules which may be ill-defined.

ii. Many industrial systems involve the time critical processing of data read from instruments and this places a different emphasis on the whole analysis and design process.

STUDENT SELF TEST QUESTIONS.

(Answers on page 744)

1. *What are the features of the various methods of changeover?*

2. *If a manual system is scheduled for future computerisation what steps could be taken to alter the existing documents and procedures in order to make master file conversion more straightforward? (Hint: Apply your knowledge of methods of data entry.)*

Applications

1. This Part brings together the areas you have studied by discussing specific applications areas in which complete computer systems are used.

44 Application Areas

INTRODUCTION.

1. The purpose of this chapter is to focus attention on the areas where computers are employed. In doing so we will concentrate on the underlying principles rather than the details of the procedures themselves many of which have been dealt with elsewhere in the manual. First of all, however, we will consider the criteria for using computers.

CRITERIA FOR USING COMPUTERS.

2. The following are the criteria by which to judge an application's possible suitability to the use of computers:–

a. **Volume.** The computer is particularly suited to handling large amounts of data.

b. **Accuracy.** The need for a high degree of accuracy is satisfied by the computer and its consistency can be relied upon.

c. **Repetitiveness.** Processing cycles that repeat themselves over and over again are ideally suited to computers. Once programmed the computer happily goes on and on automatically performing as many cycles as required.

d. **Complexity.** The computer can perform the most complex calculations. As long as the application can be programmed then the computer can provide the answers required.

e. **Speed.** Computers work at phenomenal speeds. This, combined with the ability to access records directly and from remote locations, enables them to respond very quickly to a given situation.

f. **Common data.** One item of input data can effect several *different* procedures. For example a customer's order for a particular stock could involve production of an invoice, updating of the customer's record, updating the stock record, and initiating a reorder for the stock item. The many files involved can all be stored in one physical location and accessed together so that a decision is made in the light of all the information. Contrast a manual system where the item of data will go through many separate independent procedures.

3. It is usually the combination of two or more of the criteria listed which will indicate the suitability of an application to computer use. The criteria that have been described will be used by those who carry out the Preliminary Survey (40.5) in order to judge the suitability of applications for computerisation.

4. Technological innovations over the last ten years or so have not only increased the range of technically feasible applications, they have reduced costs so that computers provide a cost effective solution to a far wider range of problems than they did before.

5. If the general criteria for using a computer suggest that a particular application may be suitable for computerisation, then there are a number of questions which will require satisfactory answers before any decision to computerise is taken. The main questions will be:–

a. Is the use of a computer for this application **technically feasible?** ie. can it be done with the computer technology currently available?

b. Would the use of a computer be **cost effective?** ie. would the computer pay for itself in terms of the benefits it would provide?

c. Would the use of a computer be **socially acceptable?** ie. would the impact of the computer on people's work, jobs or general lifestyle be acceptable?

MAIN AREAS OF APPLICATION

6. Two main areas of computer application may be identified:–

a. **Commercial applications.** This covers the use of computers for clerical, administrative and business uses, in private and public organisations, ie. the emphasis is on data processing.

b. **Scientific, Engineering and Research Applications.** This covers the use of computers for complex calculations, the design, analysis and control of physical systems, and the analysis of experimental data or results, ie. the emphasis is on Scientific Processing.

There are other minor areas which do not fall into either of the two main categories eg. "Personal Computing" ie. computing done as a hobby. One could argue that it falls into either category.

7. Many organisations use computers for a variety of applications. For example, a manufacturer may use computers for data processing, scientific research and engineering development work.

8. Further benefits can be obtained by integrating different applications eg. linking the payroll system to the labour or production control system.

MAIN COMMERCIAL APPLICATIONS AREAS

9. In general terms one can consider the commercial application areas under two headings:–

a. Routine administrative, or clerical.

b. Management.

The earliest computers concentrated on the clerical applications such as payroll and order processing, but today there is an awareness of the power of the computer in many other areas notably management information and office automation.

ROUTINE APPLICATIONS.

10. Some of these you will have already met elsewhere in the manual:–

11. a. **Payroll.** This was invariably one of the first applications to be put onto the computer by a user. It is a well defined procedure sometimes involving complex piece rate and bonus calculations. Much of the data could also be used for labour cost control.

b. **Order processing.** This can satisfy nearly all the criteria. Notice the data common to stock recording, sales ledger, and invoicing.

12. Although these and similar applications may be considered as routine tasks a great deal of the data is of use in aiding planning and control. Also there is a definite link between production, purchasing, sales, etc, and the computer applications should reflect this link. For this reason the routine and the control applications would ideally be part of an *integrated* system.

13. Many organisations have taken the levels of computerisation of routine tasks to very advanced states, thereby increasing their efficiency and expanding their spheres of activity. The clearing banks are a notable example. They first computerised cheque clearing in the late 1950s. Now they have extended banking concepts with the aid of computers to create on-line cash dispensers and credit transfer facilities which may lead to a distant goal of the "cashless society".

14. The price paid for such advances is total reliance on computer systems.

15. **Office Automation.** Office automation involves the substantial use of computers, in conjunction with other electronic equipment, to automate the basic secretarial and clerical task of the office. It is the *routine* nature of a large amount of office work that makes office automation a likely candidate for automation, and reduced equipment costs now make it cost effective.

16. Basic office automation consists of Word Processors connected to one another and to a corporate computer by means of a local network (22.26).

17. **Word Processing.** The term 'Word Processing' has developed from the use of micro or mini computing equipment to produce documents such as standard letters, accounts, contracts, estimates etc. Special purpose software enables a document to be displayed on the VDU as it is typed in at the keyboard. A completed document can be transferred to the printer any number of times and/or recorded on disk for future use. Some basic typing functions, eg. carriage return, are taken over to speed up the process and wide range of additional keyboard functions make it possible to edit and re-edit documents simply – thus removing the need for correcting fluids and/or re-typing. Other facilities include machine generated page numbers, indexes etc. or generating a list of individually headed letters using standard paragraphs and a list of names and addresses stored on disk. Whilst the name *'Word Processor'* has been given to a machine dedicated to this type of work, which usually requires a quality printer, increasingly the smaller office uses a micro computer for *all* data processing work, including word processing.

MANAGEMENT.

18. A company needs information on which to base decisions concerning the current operations and future plans. It requires this information to be timely and

The new IBM System/23 incorporates a separate display that can be tilted, rotated, and easily adjusted up and down, a separate height adjustable keyboard (with palm rest), and a processor. Picture and details courtesy of IBM.

accurate. Examples of the use of computers in the area of **management control** are now given:–

a. **Stock control**. The computer is able to process data quickly, making available information on stock levels, slow moving items or trends in demand. A central computer can link together widely separated warehouses, thus treating them as one vast stockholding. Customer orders can be satisfied from an alternative warehouse should an item not be available in the local area. Used in this way the computer enables stockholdings to be kept to a minimum, thus releasing cash for other purposes.

b. **Production control.** This is an extremely complex area especially in batch production factories. Production must be able to respond quickly to changes in demand and other circumstances. To do so requires the provision of up to date information which is accurate and timely. On-line systems such as Plastic Badges help to get the data from the shop floor quickly enough to influence current events. Machine loading, materials control, batch size calculation, and machine utilisation are all things which a computer can make more efficient because of its ability to make complex calculations and sift vast amounts of data speedily and accurately. Sophisticated computerised control systems must be capable of assessing the effect on production of the continuing happenings which are the everyday lot of the production manager.

c. **Labour control.** Much of the information used in the control of labour can be obtained from the payroll and personnel records applications. Ideally they will all be part of an integrated system. An analysis of labour hours into various categories such as idle time, sickness, and absence, can aid forecasting future requirements. Departmental and sectional summaries help to highlight these problems on a wider basis. Actual performance is measured against budgeted performance. Daily reports for the shop floor manager aid control of routine operations. Reports of a more general nature will aid overall manpower utilisation.

d. **Network Analysis.** This technique is used for the planning and control of large complex projects. Examples are the building of a factory, the installation of new plant and the manufacture of an aircraft or ship. The model (which requires the careful preparation of large amounts of base data) shows each stage in the project and its dependence on other stages. For example, when new plant is being installed, it cannot be moved in until the site has been prepared, and this in turn cannot take place until the old machines have been removed. When the necessary data has been supplied, the program produces a plan which management can use. A great advantage of the technique is that the plan can be quickly modified by the program in the light of actual progress, and revised plans produced at short notice to allow for delays. The program also indicates the *critical path,* ie. the series of interdependent activities which will take longest to complete and which, if delayed, will hold up the whole project. Resources can then be concentrated on these activities.

e. **Linear Programming.** This technique is used to find the optimum solution (ie. that which maximises profits or minimise costs) from a large number of possible alternatives. Examples are the optimisation of product mix and the minimisation of transport costs. Again, a considerable amount of accurate base data has to be supplied to construct a model. The methods used are not dealt with in detail here; the key point to note is that the computer has the storage capacity and the speed to calculate and evaluate *every* feasible solution and thus to find the best one. The manager, if dependent on human resources, cannot possibly do this; the timing required to make the necessary calculations would be prohibitive. He would have to depend on his experience and perhaps instinct.

f. **Financial Modelling.** A model is constructed of the companies finances – its resources, its income and its expenditure. It is possible by using the model to *simulate* the effects of different policies. For example, the likely results of different investment policies can be forecast, and external factors such as the national growth rate and the trend in national incomes can be introduced to see what effects they will have. It is possible by a series of computer runs, with variations of the basic assumptions on each one, to obtain a forecast of the likely effects of alternative policies. The usefulness of the computer lies in its high speed, which enables it to simulate in a few hours events which will actually occur over many years. The technique is of great use to the manager in enabling the evaluation of the results of different decisions which can be made.

19. Intelligent Knowledge Based Systems (IKBS). These systems have appeared on the market in the last few years. They are intended to provide an expert consultative service to management and are sometimes called **"expert systems"**.

20. A typical system contains a large data base containing details of a particular discipline eg. Company Law or medical diagnosis. The system is also programmed with a decision making strategy which has been developed by careful consultation with people who are experts in the field. The third component is an interactive facility built into the system. The user sits at a terminal and takes part in a question and answer session in which data about the problem is typed in. At the end of the session the system makes an assessment of the problem and suggests actions to be taken.

21. Current systems are limited in scope, but can be very effective.

CHANGES IN THE SPREAD OF APPLICATIONS.

22. Computers have been successfully applied to many new areas of work in the last few years. Notable examples are:-

a. Office automation (see paragraph 15).

b. The use of micro-computer based systems in small firms and offices.

c. CAD/CAM (Computer Aided Design/Computer Aided Manufacture). (Details later).

23. The advent of micro-computer based system has meant that applications such as payroll and stock control, which could only be economically computerised in organisations of some size, can now be usefully introduced into very small firms.

PARTICULAR APPLICATIONS AREAS.

24. In this section a number of particular applications areas are described because of their importance and interest.

25. Applications exploiting the full computational power of computers. Many of these applications have a scientific bias. They include:–

a. **Weather forecasting systems.** Reliable weather forecasting demands vast computational powers. This is an area for the **super computers** such as those described in 9.67–9.70.

b. **Mathematical and Statistical Analysis.** This includes large calculations and the solution of mathematical problems. The applications requiring this include research in physics, chemistry, geology, archaeology, medicine, astronomy etc. Some commercial problems also have a mathematical bias eg. those that require mathematical analysis to determine the optimum use of resources.

c. **Design work.** Computers can be exploited as a design tool in engineering and other disciplines. **CAD** (Computer Aided Design) is growing in importance in Electronic, Electrical, Mechanical and Aeronautical Engineering and in Architecture. This application often also exploits **computer graphics.**

26. Medical Applications. There are numerous applications of computers in medicine. Here are some examples:–

a. Computers can be used as an aid to medical research by analysing data produced from experiments eg. in the trial of drugs.

b. Computers can be used to aid diagnosis. The computer acts as a large bank of data about known medical conditions. Once the computer system has been set up by medical experts an ordinary doctor can be taken through a question and answer session by the computer until a correct diagnosis is made. This is an example of an IKBS (paragraph 19).

c. Computers can be used to hold details of dentists' or GPs' patients. Small computer systems have been used for this purpose in increasing numbers since the late 70's.

d. Computerised childrens' health records for immunisation have been used by local health authorities for a number of years. These records are used by medical officers, health visitors etc.

27. Education. Computers are not only used extensively as part of specialist study in Computer Science, they are used as an extremely versatile way of aiding the understanding of a wide variety of other subjects. The computer can guide a user through a course of instruction at a VDU. The computer can provide instructions and ask questions of the user. This kind of activity is called **CAL** (Computer Aided Learning) or CAI (Computer Aided Instruction).

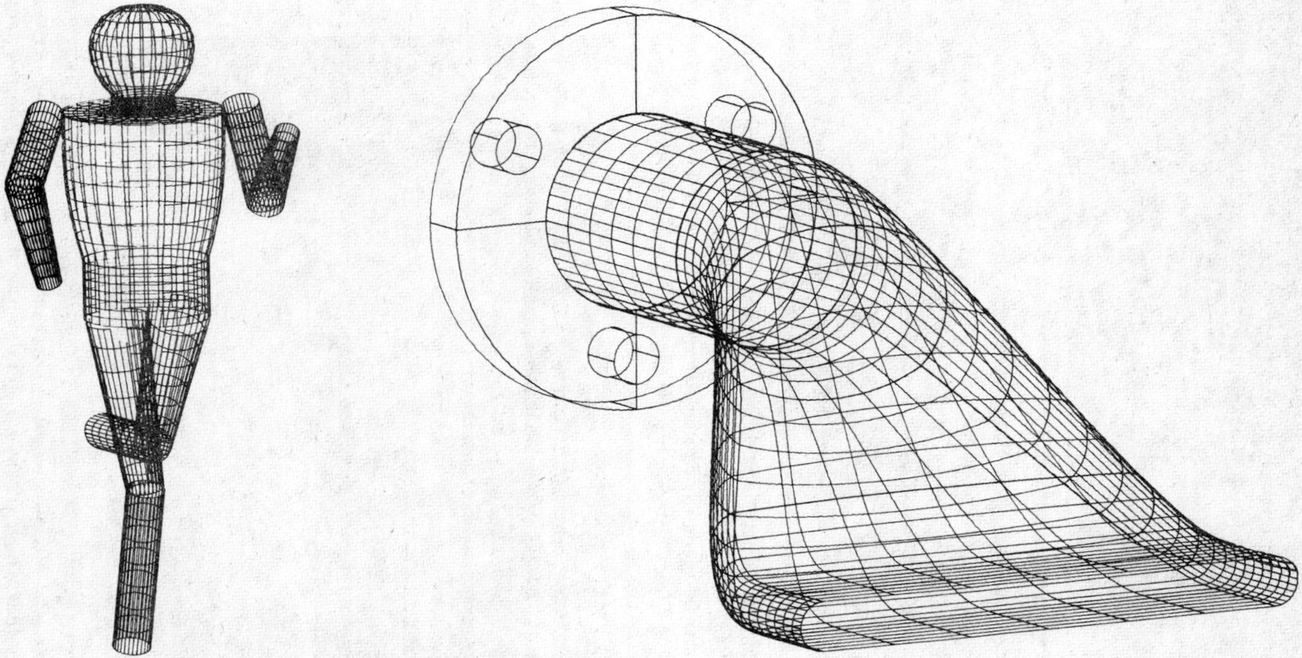

Two graph plotter outputs produced by an applications package in CAD, called SPIDER which uses a library of routines called BEZLIB.
The package can be used to design complex surfaces such as those used for vehicle bodywork castings etc.
(Courtesy J. Beasley The Hatfield Polytechnic)

A large-scale, high accuracy flatbed pen plotter from CalComp which can use other ballpoint or liquid ink pens to plot at very high speeds (up to 42 ins/sec.) on standard drafting media or can be fitted with special tools for scribing or cutting strippable film. Photograph with caption by courtesy of CalComp Ltd.

The beltbed pen plotter is a unique CalComp design in which the drafting medium, in this case any size up to A00, is taped to a continuous belt of stable polyester film which moves up and down in the x axis while the pens move back and forth along the y. Photograph with caption courtesy of CalComp Ltd.

28. Computers are also used for a number of other applications in Education eg. the marking of multiple choice examination papers and processing examination results for many examinations boards.

29. Manufacturing. Some aspects of computer use in manufacturing have already been covered eg. stock and production control, and engineering design. The design, manufacturing and testing processes are all becoming increasingly computerised, hence the terms **CAD** (Computer Aided Design), **CAM** (Computer Aided Manufacture) and CADMAT (Computer Aided Design Manufacture and Testing).

30. Robots. The word "Robot" comes from a Czech word meaning "to labour" and first appeared in a play written by Karel Capek in 1920. For many years the term "robot" was associated with science fiction rather than science fact. That association is now changing. Even so, modern industrial robots do not resemble people! (see figure 44.1).

31. The main difference between modern industrial robots and other automated machines is that a robot can be programmed to carry out a complex task and then reprogrammed to carry out another complex task. Each complex task is a series of actions involving multi way mechanical manipulation.

32. The majority of robots in current use, eg. in car assembly lines, are "blind" and lack a "sense of touch". The next generation of robots will probably be able to find and locate objects or detect their presence by touch and a light sense mechanism.

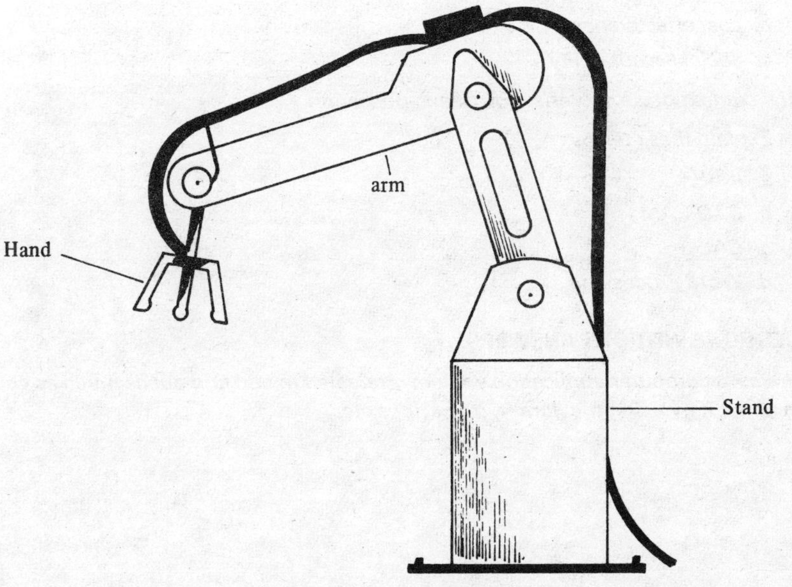

Figure 44.1. An Industrial Robot.

CONCLUSION.

33. Many of the procedures, and techniques are possible without a computer but it is the speed and accuracy with which the computer carries them out that makes it such an invaluable tool of management.

SUMMARY.

34. a. The criteria for using a computer are, volume, accuracy, repetitiveness, complexity, speed, and the use of common data.

b. Computers can be applied successfully to administrative tasks and to the production of management control information.

POINTS TO NOTE.

35. a. Not all applications have been dealt with – other applications will be dealt with elsewhere. eg. analog and hybrid computing is covered in chapter 48.

STUDENT SELF TEST QUESTIONS.

(Answers on page 744)

1. *Explain the terms:*

   a. *technical feasibility,*

   b. *cost effectiveness,*

   c. *social acceptability*

in the context of computerisation of an application.

2. *Explain these terms:*

   a. *IKBS*

   b. *CAD/CAM*

   c. *CAL*

   d. *Word Processing.*

QUESTIONS WITHOUT ANSWERS.

3. *Pick a computer application you are interested in and find out as much as you can about it by using the library, magazines etc.*

45 Application Organisation

INTRODUCTION.

1. Whatever applications computers are used for it is important to ensure that they are used effectively and not abused. This chapter deals with the issues involved.

BASIS OF ORGANISATION.

2. The development and operation of a computer system requires careful organisation of the individuals involved and those individuals need to be suitably trained in the correct practices to follow.

3. The nature of several types of specialist work have been covered previously and do not merit repeating here:

a. Systems Analysis (13.23).

b. Programming (13.25 and 43.5).

c. Operating (43.16).

Details of the work of other specialist staff are given in the following paragraphs.

THE COMPUTER MANAGER (DP MANAGER IN COMMERCIAL ORGANISATIONS).

4. The Computer Manager is a key figure in the organisation. His or her job is to ensure that the computer department functions efficiently in the *service* of the company. He or she is responsible for ensuring that the computer needs of the organisation are met within the policy guide lines laid down.

5. He or she must be a good administrator as well as having a sound business knowledge. He or she must also have the knowledge and expertise necessary to enable him or her to control his teams of specialists in the various computing fields.

6. **Status.** It is important that his or her status be clearly defined especially with regard to his right of access to the board.

7. Ideally one would like someone who has previous experience of installing successful systems and the appointment should be made very early on in the planning cycle to enable the company to get the benefit of his or her specialist knowledge and experience. If not recruited from outside the potential computer manager could be found in the Management Services Division.

DATA CONTROL STAFF IN A DP DEPARTMENT.

8. These staff are responsible for the co-ordination of all machine processing operations and for ensuring a smooth flow of work through the operations department. In order to explain their work we will trace a particular job through from beginning to end.

9. a. **Source documents** accompanied by control totals are received from the clerical function (outside the DP department) and vetted visually.

b. **Control totals** are agreed and documents passed under this control to the Data Preparation Section.

c. **The data preparation** section prepares floppy disks or other media for source documents.

d. Source documents are returned to the clerical function and the floppy disks now represent the input for a particular run (job) eg. "invoice run".

e. **The job assembly** section 'make up' the run and prepare a Run Authorisation document. This will detail the various tapes/disks required and how the output is to be disposed of. This is then passed to the computer room supervisor.

f. **Tape/disk library.** The librarian will provide all the tape reels and disk packs required for the particular job and will pass them to the computer room itself for the computer to process.

g. On completion of the computer run/s the tapes/disks etc. go back to the library and all the documentation to the Data Control section.

10. **The control section** now scrutinises the control log to ensure all action has been taken correctly and to initiate any possible corrective action indicated. Control totals will be reconciled. These will now include totals of items rejected on the run/s but all totals will need to be reconciled back to those compiled at the beginning of the job.

11. The output is dealt with; invoices for example will be despatched to customers and warehouses etc.

12. All necessary information will be fed back to the user department eg. copies of all output despatched, error lists, control totals.

DATA PREPARATION STAFF.

13. These staff are responsible for:-

a. Preparing floppy disks from source documents or preparation by other means eg. key-to-disk etc.

b. Operation of ancillary machines such as floppy disk units, paper bursters etc.

TAPE/DISK LIBRARIAN.

14. All tape reels and disk packs used in the installation are stored in a library adjacent to the computer room. The librarian issues tapes/disks to the computer room as per a Run Authorisation document from Data Control.

15. The librarian will maintain a register of all tapes and disks noting the particular generations required for current use. Maximum security is observed and access is strictly limited.

COMPUTER ROOM SUPERVISOR.

16. The computer room is under the day-to-day control of a supervisor. Only authorised personnel are allowed entry. It is essential that anyone who has participated in the writing of the programs is forbidden for security and audit reasons to interfere with the operational running of those programs.

THE CONTROL OF COMPUTING ACTIVITIES.

17. The use of computers imposes certain disciplines on those who work with them. Work has to be carried out in a uniform and orderly manner in the most efficient way. Staff and equipment will be well regarded if work is completed quickly and with the minimum of error or interruption. Well defined standards allow the control of these activities to happen naturally.

18. Factors which aid control are:–

a. **Organisation.** ie. all staff should know what their duties are and where they fit in the general picture (See Systems Analysis Part introduction).

b. **Staff training.**

c. **Supervision and working to plans.**

d. **The use of documentation** to guide and assist work.

e. **Clear procedures** for individuals to follow.

DATA SECURITY.

19. One important aspect of control is the control of data to prevent its loss, misuse or disclosure. This type of control is called "data security".

20. Data security is the protection of data. In some situations data security will be concerned with preventing the loss of data eg. in the file security method used during updates. In other situations data security will be concerned with preventing the misuse or unwanted modification of data eg. due to access by unauthorised persons. A third situation is the prevention of disclosure of data to unauthorised persons eg. where the data is important to national security.

21. Various measures can be taken to ensure all three types of security. Here are some common methods.

a. The use of backup copies of tapes or disks eg. in conjunction with generations of files (Figure 16.2).

b. Physical prevention eg.

i. Write permit rings (Figure 5.5) and similar devices.

ii. Restricting the access of personnel.

iii. Keeping data under lock and key.

c. The use of passwords to prevent unauthorised use of computer terminals or unauthorised access to on-line files.

d. Constant checks of security.

22. People often demand higher standards of security from computer systems than they demand from manual systems. The reader might consider which is most secure, a folder of printed documents or a floppy disk holding the same information. A floppy disk can easily be damaged by dust or scratches so that its data is lost. On the other hand specialist equipment and software will be needed to read its data, thus the data is more secure from those not trained in its use.

SUMMARY.

23. a. Careful organisation is needed to ensure that computers are used effectively and properly.

b. The work of various specialist staff was described.

c. The control of specialist work was discussed.

d. Data security was defined and methods of data security were described.

POINTS TO NOTE.

24. The more dependent people or organisations are upon computers the more important becomes the need for careful control and organisation of how the computer application systems are developed and the way they are operated.

STUDENT SELF TEST QUESTIONS.

(Answers on page 744)

1. *Define the term "data security" and identify three types of data security.*

46 Micro-computers and Mini-computers

INTRODUCTION.

1. The basic hardware features of micro-computers and mini-computers were described in chapter 9 (9.51–9.53). This chapter considers the use of these computers and examines where they fit in the overall picture of computer applications.

MICRO-COMPUTERS.

2. Microprocessors are now to be found in a wide variety of devices from petrol pump to wrist watches. Such devices are highly specialised and the computer systems within them are called **embedded systems.** In this chapter we are primarily concerned with general purpose computer systems rather than those just described.

3. The processing capability of the larger micro-computers is comparable to that of many main frames of the 1960s. This fact should emphasise the major role which these small machines can play if properly utilised.

4. **Software.** The system software available on these systems may be rather limited but this limitation is more than compensated for by the wide range of software packages which are available.

5. System Software usually comprises a simple interactive monitor and a limited choice of programming languages eg. BASIC, PASCAL, CIS-COBOL (A portable version of COBOL produced by Microfocus) and assemblers.

6. Software Packages are available for a wide range of applications including:-

a. payroll
b. stock control
c. order processing invoicing and sales ledger
d. production control
e. job costing
f. information storage and retrieval
g. word processing
etc.

7. A number of well established software suppliers produce software packages which can be made to run on a wide variety of machines produced by different manufactures eg. Micropro's WORDSTAR package for word processing and Visicorp's VISICALC package for financial modelling.

An Apple II 8-bit microcomputer based system.

8. **Dual-purpose.** Many micro-computers are able to meet a dual purpose:

a. They may be used as "stand-alone" machines. ie. working autonomously for a particular purpose.

b. They may be used as "intelligent terminals" within a distributed data processing system.

This enables such machines to deal not only with data processing which is only of 'local' interest but also with corporate data processing.

9. Advantages of a microcomputer include:-

a. A full configuration costs less than £4,000.

b. Cheap software packages arising out of the large volume sales.

c. Just plugs into the nearest mains socket.

d. User-friendly "menu-driven" programs mean that there is no need to employ specialist staff, the computer can be operated by general clerical staff.

e. Brings E.D.P. within the budget of even the very smallest organisations.

f. Allows a large organisation to implement distributed processing with each department possessing its own independent processing facilities.

10. Disadvantages include:-

a. Limited file store and memory capacity.

b. Smaller systems often lack languages other than BASIC.

c. Purchased software is often of a poor quality.

d. Too often purchased by non-specialists who are too easily convinced by salesmen.

e. Can lead to several departments duplicating the same procedures.

NB. 16 bit micro-computers with hard disks overcome 9a, and 9b is a problem of hobbyist machines rather than small business machines.

MINI-COMPUTERS.

11. The hardware of a typical mini-computer system was described in 9.53.

12. Whereas the typical micro-computer is designed as a single user system (eg. with 1 VDU) the larger micro-computers and typical mini-computers are multi-user systems.

13. A user with an apparent need for multiple micro-computers at one particular location may be able to meet the same need with the single mini-computer.

14. **Software.** There is far more system software available on most mini-computers than there is on the typical micro-computer, but perhaps surprisingly there is not always such a good choice of applications software.

15. System Software on mini-computers has been developed over many years and had its origins in the fast key-to-disk system. Many single-user systems are in use but the typical mini-computer has a time-sharing operating system plus some

communications facilities. The latter reflect the fact that mini-computers frequently form part of a distributed system.

16. The choice of programming languages on mini-computers is usually better than that available on micro-computers and is very similar to that available on most main frames.

17. Software package are available for use on most mini-computers but they do not have the same importance that they have with micro-computers. The reasons are simply that the production of applications software for mini-computers has tended to take place using the same methods as those used for mainframe computers. That is, software is often written *by the user or for the user* in order to meet specific requirements rather than to meet the needs of some general market.

18. This situation is changing, however, as many packages first written for micro-computers have since been converted and extended to run on larger systems.

19. The applications dealt with by mini-computers include all those listed earlier under the heading of micro-computers but also include such things as:-

a. Retailing eg. Point-of-Sales systems.

b. Banking.

c. Life assurance.

d. Stock Exchange dealing.

etc.

20. Multi-purpose. Mini-computers may be used for several different purposes:-

a. As "stand alone" machines (often multi-user).

b. As the central host computer in a small distributed system eg. with a number of micro-computers acting as "intelligent terminals".

c. As the second tier in a larger scale distributed system eg. acting as a local host to a number of micro-computers but also connected to some central corporate mainframe.

21. Relative advantages and disadvantages of mini-computers compared with other computers.

a. They are more expensive than a typical microcomputer but much less expensive than a main frame.

b. They have system software which is broadly comparable to that found on main frames but they do not always have the same wide choice of applications packages found on micro-computers.

c. They have greater file storage and memory capacities than most micro-computers and can cope with all but the largest data processing problems.

d. Their multi-user and communications facilities make them well suited to the integration of local data processing activities and the provision of distributed processing facilities.

GENERAL CONSIDERATIONS.

22. System Support. Generally speaking, smaller organisations buying micro and mini-computers will not be able to economically justify the employment of the DP specialists required in main frame installations. The supplier must therefore either be able to offer suitable applications packages or be willing to get more involved in program writing for the user. The latter is seldom an economic alternative in the case of micro-computers because the full development cost must be borne by the one user. The supplier will also be expected to provide considerable support for the user.

23. To understand the market situation, it is important to realise that many micros and minis are sold in what is called the OEM market, ie. Original Equipment Manufacturer. That is to say, they are sold not to the eventual user but to another manufacturer who incorporates them into a larger system. Many manufacturers of micros and minis are wholly or partly dependent on this type of business. It was the decision of some of them to provide peripherals and software and to sell direct to the end user that created the recent explosion in 'mini' and now 'micro' sales.

SUMMARY.

24. a. There is no difference in principle between a 'micro' or 'mini' and the larger computer.

b. Machines described as 'micros' or 'minis' vary widely in specification and price.

c. Essentially, the 'micro' or 'mini' is a smaller, cheaper, slower machine which is, however, acquiring an increasing degree of sophistication.

d. Although the typical micro-computer is noticeably different from the typical mini-computer, the larger micro-computers and smaller minis are indistinguishable for most practical purposes. In answering examination questions, concentrate on typical features first and then mention any overlap.

e. 'Micros' and 'minis' play an important part in computer networks.

f. Software is usually supplied by the manufacturer as part of a complete system.

g. Applications cover a very wide range, and include all conventional accounting tasks.

h. The micro-computer is even smaller and cheaper than the 'mini'.

POINTS TO NOTE.

25. a. Single user micro-computers are often called "Personal Computers" because of their use by individuals either at work, or at home as a hobby.

STUDENT SELF TEST QUESTIONS.

(Answers on page 745)

1. *What are the advantages and disadvantages of micro-computers for small commercial applications?*

QUESTIONS WITHOUT ANSWERS.

2. *Describe a typical micro-computer and a typical mini-computer. Why is the distinction between a micro-computer and a mini-computer hard to make in some cases?*

3. *The widespread adoption of micro computer systems by commerce and industry has led to a large increase in the use of general application packages.*
   a. *What is an application package?* ***(5 marks]***
   b. *Discuss the advantages and disadvantages for the user of general application packages compared with user produced software.* ***[10 marks]***
   c. *Describe the documentation which you would expect to obtain with an application package.* ***[5 marks]***

(AEB 1982)

47 Large Computer Systems

INTRODUCTION.

1. This chapter illustrates the use of large computer systems by providing a discussion of three applications:-

a. an airline booking system (a Real-time system).

b. a commercial time-sharing system (and alternatives).

c. a system used by a large corporate organisation.

2. The first two applications are specialised whereas the third application considers the typical general purpose large system. Refer back to Real-time systems before you continue (39.20).

APPLICATION 1.

3. Airline booking system. Records of seat availability on all its planes will be kept by an airline on a central computer. The computer is linked via terminals to a world-wide system of agents. Each agent can gain access to the flight records and within seconds make a reservation in respect of a particular flight. This reservation is recorded *immediately* so that the next enquiry for that flight (following even microseconds after the previous reservation) finds that particular seat or seats reserved. Notice the computer records reflect an accurate picture of the airline's seating load at all times because there is no time lag worth mentioning. The computer would then output information for the production of the customer's ticket and flight instructions, on confirmation on the booking by the customer. (see Fig. 47.1).

4. Each booking is a separate transaction which is processed immediately ie. not batched. This is therefore a *transaction processing system.*

FEATURES OF REAL-TIME.

5. Response time. The service given by a real-time processing system can be measured in terms of *response time.* This is the time taken by the system to respond to an input, eg. the time interval between the pressing of the last key by the operator of a VDU and the display of the required (updated) information.

6. "Traffic" pattern. An important feature of real-time is the 'traffic' pattern, ie. the *volumes* of data being input, the *times* at which they are input, the *types* of input and the *places* at which they are input.

7. Reliability. Because real-time systems operate automatically an extremely high standard of system reliability is required.

a. **Program protection.** Many programs will occupy main storage simultaneously and the integrity of each program must be protected.

b. **File security.** Duplicate files will probably need to be kept and in addition their contents will be dumped at intervals. These measures will aid reconstruction should the need arise. (Note the duplicate database in Fig. 47.1).

c. **Stand-by machinery.** In the airline application two CPUs would be required, one of which is operational and the other a stand-by machine. In the event of failure the stand-by machine would automatically come into use. (Again refer to Fig. 47.1)

d. **Security.** Confidentiality of information held on magnetic storage is achieved by the use of special code numbers allowing access to certain files only by certain people.

HARDWARE, SOFTWARE CONSIDERATIONS.

8. Implicit in the operation of real-time systems described are:

a. A large main storage requirement to accommodate systems software and application programs. Also required will be an area to use as buffers for queueing of messages.

b. Direct access storage of large capacity as backing storage.

c. A sophisticated operating system to handle the many different operations being handled simultaneously.

d. A data communication system linking the many terminals with the CPU.

COST.

9. Real-time systems are usually specially designed for a particular application and are extremely costly. Cost will vary with the service one wishes the system to provide. The better the service (ie. the shorter the response time generally) then the more costly it becomes in terms of hardware and software etc.

APPLICATION 2.

10. Commercial Time-sharing. These systems have many features in common with the Real-time systems used for transaction processing but their fast response capability is used to serve a large number of different users at the same time.

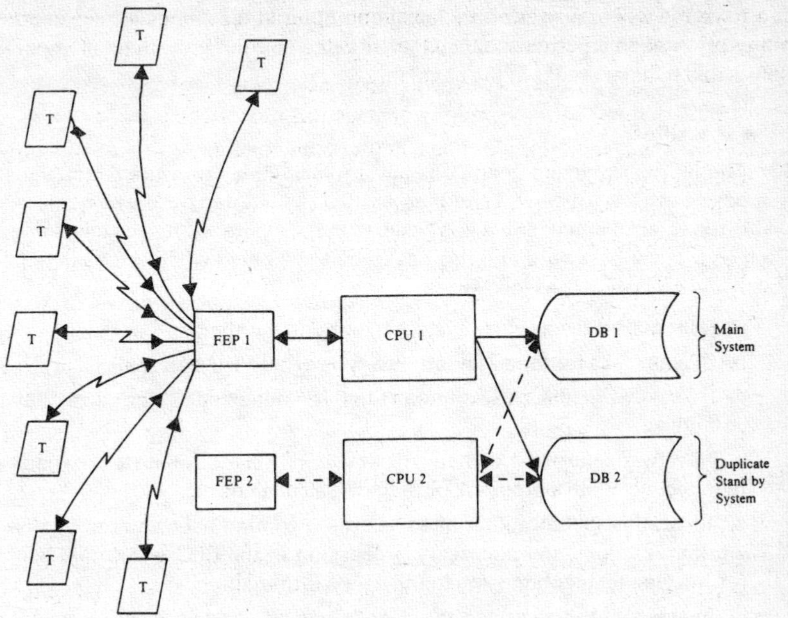

Key: CPU 1, CPU 2 — Central Processing Units (Two main frames)
FEP 1, FEP 2: — Front End Processors. (Computers Handling Communications with the main frames)
DB 1, DB 2: — Bookings Database: (Held on disks)
T: — Terminals at remote location used by booking agents (VDUs)

Figure 47.1. A Real-Time Airline Booking System.

THE NEED.

11. There are many people who would like to use a computer but cannot afford to buy or lease one. Or they may be able to afford a microcomputer but the micro would not be large enough or powerful enough to handle their processing requirements. There are also many people who need the power of the computer, but want it at odd times, not regularly; for them it would be decidedly uneconomic to acquire one. One answer would be to send the data to a bureau for processing but this may not be convenient especially if you are an engineer making hundreds of calculations each one conditioned by the previous one. In this case, as with most others, the engineer wants the computer when it is convenient to *him* and thus he has to put up with the tedium of a slide rule or desk calculator.

THE SOLUTION.

12. The answer to the problem posed is for a terminal to be installed at the place of work of the engineer which is linked to a time-sharing computer system. In this way, through the medium of a simple typewriter terminal or VDU and telephone he can have the whole power of the latest computer at his disposal. And of course, many other people perhaps 200 share the same computer system, all apparently being able to have access at the *same time.*

HOW IT WORKS.

13. The number of users of any one system is limited, to ensure a high speed of response. Each has a typewriter terminal or VDU installed (anywhere he or she wishes within the establishment) and this is linked to the computer system by telephone line. Each user has a password and this has to be transmitted when access is required. Briefly the procedure is as follows:-

a. User dials the computer system telephone number.

b. System asks for the password (via typewriter VDU terminal).

c. User keys in the code number and is connected ("signed on") to the computer.

d. Now by means of the keyboard he or she will get the system to do whatever is required, eg. write a program, or perform calculations etc.

e. To do this the computer allocates the incoming user an area on disk (ie. work area), does any necessary processing in the CPU and sends back the results via the telephone line to the user's terminal.

f. At the end of his session the user "signs off" and replaces the telephone receiver. It is as easy as that!

14. Remember, as many as 200 users could be wanting access at once but each has the impression that they are *alone* in using the computer because there is no apparent delay in getting the necessary output. This is achieved by *queueing* all incoming requests and allocating each in turn, a "slice" of the CPU. Such is the speed of response of the CPU compared with the slowness of the data link and of the human user, that the computer is able to cope with a large number of requests at once. Typically, while one user is getting output eg. a program listing, or results of engineering calculations, the CPU is able to carry out the computing requirement for many others.

USES.

15. Because of the constraints of the data link, time-sharing is, generally speaking, suited to applications with little input/output and large amounts of complex processing. However, there have been moves towards extending the use of time-sharing to include volume data processing such as invoicing, payroll etc.

16. Remote batch processing. Processing of high volumes of data needs a more sophisticated terminal, with special facilities for rapid input and output (costing thousands as opposed to hundreds of pounds for the ordinary teletype). Data is batched in the normal way and input to the computer over a data link. Data may be processed overnight (off peak) and results sent back next day via the terminal, or output could be printed by the bureau and sent back by post or courier. It will all depend on the terms of the contract drawn up with the bureau. This type of processing is called remote batch processing and not all time-sharing systems have such a facility. This particular use of time-sharing can of course be extended to include line-printers and even magnetic tape units on the user's premises. In this way output from the computer can be transmitted over the data link directly onto magnetic tape and then printed "off-line" later.

SECURITY.

17. In time-sharing computer systems the problem of security must always be considered. Because many users have access to one computer system strict measures are necessary to ensure the privacy of stored information.

COMPUTER SERVICE BUREAUX.

18. These are the alternative to a time-sharing terminal for people not wishing to lease or buy their own computer.

19. Services offered. They exist to carry out computer work on behalf of their customers. The services offered may include:–

a. Aid in data preparation and transcription.

b. Ad hoc hardware renting.

c. Complete service providing system analysis, programs, hardware etc.

d. Consultancy. Providing ad hoc advice.

e. Selling specialist software.

20. The services listed in paragraph 19 indicate that a variety of people use bureaux for a variety of reasons.

APPLICATION 3.

21. Systems used by large corporate organisations. Such systems are required to meet the diverse information needs within the organisations.

22. Depending upon the type of organisation any number of the following functions of the organisation may be supported by the computer system:–

a. Top level management.

b. Finance and accounting.

c. Manufacturing.

d. Marketing.

e. Purchasing, stocking and distributing (ie. logistics).

f. Personnel.

g. Administration.

23. Levels of computer support vary from function to function but particularly distinctive levels are:-

a. Automation of basic clerical procedures such as those found in ordering, invoicing, payroll production and bookings. Batch or transaction processing will be used as appropriate.

b. Office automation and communications to support the administrative functions eg. by the use of word processors and electronic mail.

c. Automation of management control operations such as the control of stock, production, materials distribution, accounts and personnel.

d. Automated aids to strategic planning such as financial modelling, linear programming and other analysis methods.

FEATURES OF THESE SYSTEMS.

24. In order to support the processing needs outlined in the previous two paragraphs these systems must be large, versatile, reliable and efficiently organised.

25. Specific features may include:-

a. **Distributed facilities.** For example there may be a mainframe computer at head office acting as host to smaller computers at divisional offices. A divisional office could deal with marketing or production say. A lower level of the distributed system might handle office automation by means of word processors linked to the main computers.

b. **Integrated Files or Databases.** The advantages of integrated file processing or databases can be exploited so that, for example, the receipt of orders may *automatically* give rise to, the ordering of materials, the movement of stock, the scheduling of production, the control of production and the distribution of manufactured goods.

c. **Combinations of different processing methods.** Run of the mill stock control and payroll production may take place by batch processing while enquiries, orders, bookings etc. are being handled by transaction processing. Additional processing loads, such as those used for financial modelling, will also be placed upon the system from time to time.

26. The hardware and software features of these systems have comparable complexity to those of the real-time systems mentioned earlier in the chapter. The principal differences are:

a. The distribution of processing, communications and data.

b. The use of many different types of software to support the varied processing needs.

SUMMARY.

27. The three applications described in this chapter all use large amounts of hardware. The first two systems must have fast response times in order to satisfy the needs of the users. The third system must strike a balance between response and processing throughput. The airline booking system has essentially one large job to handle but the other two systems have many different jobs to handle.

28. Real-time involves the processing of data as it arises thus providing records which are permanently up-to-date.

29. Response time, traffic pattern and reliability are major features.

30. The hardware and software requirements are complex.

31. A commercial time-sharing system operates in a way in which *each* of the concurrent users is unaware of others using it:-

a. Users are independent of one another.

b. Requests from users are *queued* and dealt with in order, but the user is hardly ever aware of any delay.

c. Each user is allocated a fixed period of processing time, ie. *time-slice.*

d. The CPU has a very fast speed compared with extremely slow human response time.

32. The system in a large corporate organisation will:-

a. have distributed processing, communications and data.

b. use many different types of software.

c. exploit integrated files or databases.

d. use a variety of processing methods.

POINTS TO NOTE.

33. In the case of a transaction processing system such as the one used by the airline the following points apply:-

a. The accurate assessment of response time and traffic pattern is very difficult but of vital importance, as errors can be very costly in terms of size of CPU, sophistication of software and transmission line capacity. (Unlike batch processing, where overtime or an additional shift might be possible, real-time processing depends upon the system being able to cope at the time required).

b. Because of the difficulties of accurate assessment, applications are normally implemented on a 'pilot' basis (eg. with the airlines reservations system – no pun intended – a few branch offices would have access initially).

c. The essence of a real-time system is that it should provide an up-to-date (real) picture of events as they occur. Therefore a retrieval system is generally associated with it. It is possibly for this reason that students give undue prominence in examination answers to this latter function, forgetting that they are dealing witha system of *processing* just as they were with batch systems.

34. Other areas where real-time applications of computers are applied are automated process control and production control.

35. There are various interpretations of the term real-time. A system where the time factor is critical is properly called a real-time system.

36. The following points apply to the commercial time-sharing system.

a. The feature of such systems is the use of remote terminals.

b. Note the extension here of the technique of the sharing of the CPU by many programs, to one of sharing the computer by many *users.*

c. You must appreciate that a time-sharing computer system requires a large sophisticated operating system. A typical system using say an IBM 370/168 computer could have up to 8,092K main store, of which 384K would be occupied by the operating system. It would also have about 480 million bytes of disk storage on-line.

d. The use of multi-programming is inherent in a time-sharing system.

e. The difference between the "immediate" response type of system and the remote batch type. The former is described as a conversational system whereas of course the latter is batch mode and involves delay which could be hours, days, etc. according to the terms of the contract.

f. **Cost**. User pays to the bureau:-

i. Connect time – which is the total time the user is connected to the computer.

ii. CPU time – the amount of time the CPU is actually in use for that particular user.

iii. Storage – a charge is made per so many characters per period.

The user also rents a terminal and ancillary equipment for about £500 per annum. The telephone charges are normal STD. Rental charges for a remote batch system would however be considerably more.

g. A time-sharing system is an example of a *multi-access* system, thus described because many users are on-line to the same computer, each operating independently.

37. Many smaller computers have time-sharing operating systems but they do not necessarily maintain the immediate response at all times as is expected of the commercial time-sharing systems described in this chapter.

38. Most large scale organisations are now totally reliant upon systems like the one described in the third example in the chapter.

STUDENT SELF TEST QUESTIONS.

(Answers on page 745)

1. What are the advantages of time-sharing? When might a bureau be used instead of a time-sharing system.

2. Name seven functions within a large organisation which could be supported by a computer system.

3. State the main factors that must be considered by a systems analyst before designing a system for implementation on a computer.

4. If the company does not own a computer, state two alternatives to purchasing one, giving one advantage and one disadvantage in each case.

QUESTIONS WITHOUT ANSWERS.

5. *Discuss the use of a computer system for airline bookings, including in your answer:*

  a. *the nature of the equipment at the point of sale and the way in which it is used;* *[4, 4]*

  b. *the equipment required to hold the files and process the transactions;* *[6]*

  c. *why it is necessary that the software should ensure rapid response, and how it can be designed to prevent confusion when multiple demands are made on the same file;* *[2, 4]*

  d. *the effects of employing computers in this application and the reasons why they are not in general use in this way for other forms of transport.* *[5]*

(OLE)

6. *A robot is required for the following task. Pick up a part which is lying at any place on a tray, but in a fixed orientation. Set it right way up and place it on an upright cone that is in a known place. The part has a socket in its base to fit the cone.*

  a. *Describe:*

    i. *the arm of the robot which would transfer the part and the way in which it would need to be linked to the computer controlling it;* *[8]*

    ii. *the procedure by which the part could be collected, set upright, and placed on the cone;* *[6]*

    iii. *a convenient way of setting up or programming the robot to follow this procedure.* *[5]*

  b. *What would be considered in order to decide whether to use such a robot?* *[6]*

(OLE)

Analog and Hybrid Computers

1. This Part is different from the rest of this text in that we are not primarily concerned with digital computers and their uses. Instead, we consider the specialist subject of analog and hybrid computers.

48 Analog and Hybrid Computers

INTRODUCTION.

1. Analog and Hybrid computers were defined in (1.8). This chapter deals with their advantages, uses and limitations. It also deals with Analog/Digital conversion and a special application called 'Process Control'.

2. Uses. The various elements of an analog computer have electronic properties which makes their behaviour **analogous** to a variety of known physical phenomena. For example the variation in output current with changing input voltage may be comparable to the variation in water flow in a given physical system when subjected to changing pressures.

In such a situation the analog computer could be used to study the physical systems by **simulating** it at less expense. Common areas of use are **simulation** of

a. Mechanical system eg the suspension system of a truck.

b. Hydraulic system eg irrigation.

c. Aircraft and missile flight.

d. Chemical systems eg chemical production in a factory.

e. Electrical systems eg grid supply.

Many of these systems can be described in terms of differential equations and so analog computers are of general use in the mathematical modelling and solving of differential equations.

3. Time Scaling. The time scales on which analog computers simulate phenomena can be adjusted to suit the applications. Examples:–

a. Simulating the movement of a glacier would require a contracted time scale to speed up the simulation in order that observations could be made in reasonable time.

b. At the other extreme the movement of a camera shutter would need a dilated time scale to slow down the simulation.

4. Real Time operation is operation on a unit time scale ie on the same time scale as the simulated events. In many of the applications mentioned so far in this chapter an analog computer can work effectively in real time where a digital computer would be hopelessly slow. When working in real time an analog computer can continuously monitor the behaviour of the system it simulates, thereby giving the chance to immediately detect faults within the real system. The method can be extended to give a **feedback** system ie. the output from the real system can be examined by the analog computer which will 'feed back' appropriate controls to correct system performance. One example is on board missile flight control, another is an automated chemical process.

5. Limitations. The two main limitations of analog devices are:–

a. It can take a considerable time to prepare the computer to do a task because many components have to be physically moved or reconnected ie the **set up** time is long.

b. Very accurate numerical values are hard to obtain without prohibitive expense being incurred.

BASIC ELEMENTS.

6. The basic elements used in analog computers are illustrated below. Their physical structure is beyond the scope of this book. (The scale is not part of the circuit but used to illustrate the action of the device).

a. **Summers.** (perform addition).

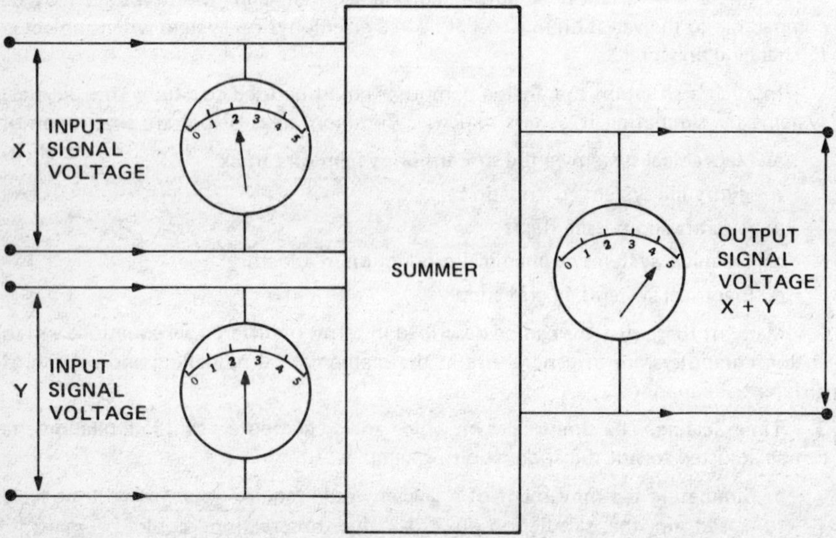

b. **Multiplier.** (amplifies signals by a constant factor).

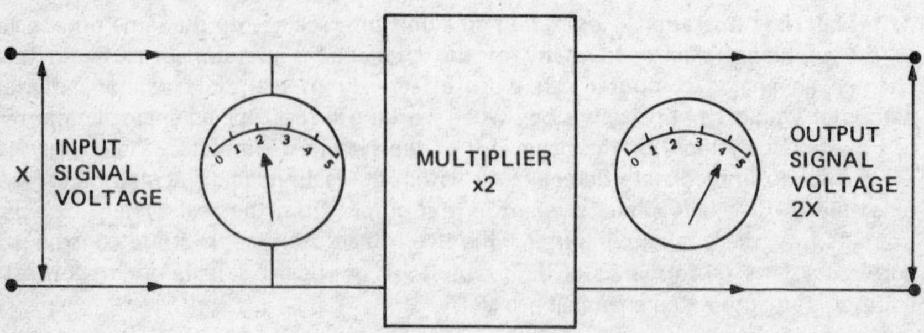

c. **Potentiometers.** (corresponds to division or multiplicating by a fraction)

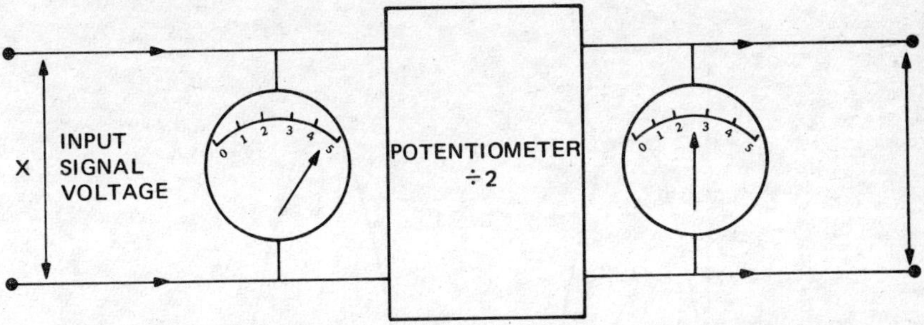

d. **Integrator.** Corresponds to the mathematical operation of integration. If you are unfamiliar with **integration** then an everyday example is given by the speedometer of a car. **Integration** would correspond to calculating the distance gone from the speed readings.

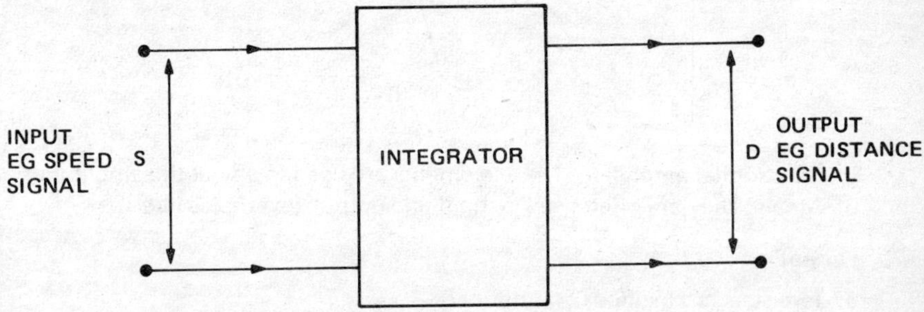

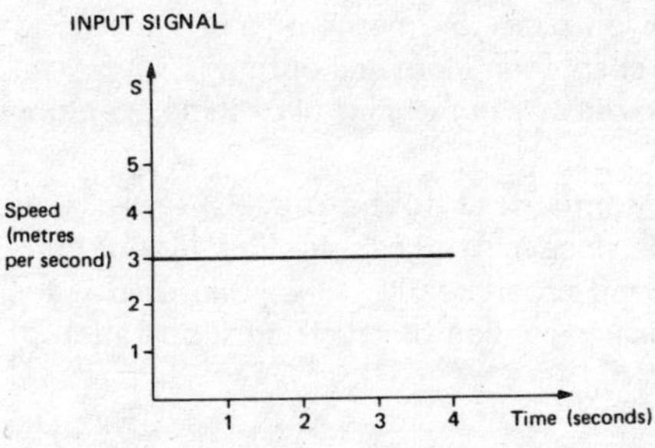

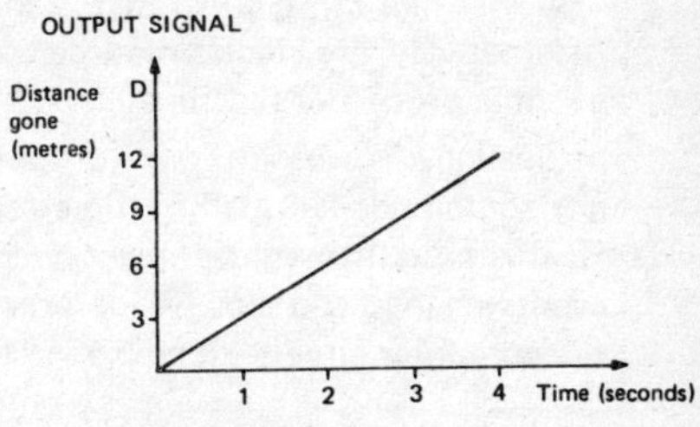

e. **Special function generation.** These are elements which generate signals whose magnitude is time dependent in some way, eg:–

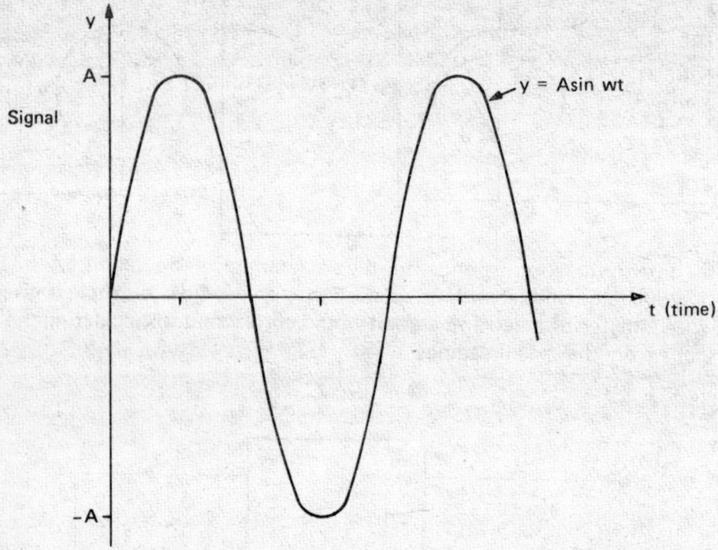

g. **Operational amplifiers.** These elements are used to adjust the amplitudes of signals. They are often used in input and output. (examples later).

7. **Output.**

a. Two standard methods of output are:–

i. Generating a trace on a cathode ray tube which is a general name for electronic display tube of which the TV tube is perhaps the best known.

ii. Producing a permanent trace on paper by means of a pen plotter: a device like those illustrated in the chapter on input and output.

Alternatively the signals may be used directly in the control of some operation of some process or machine.

b. **Scaling.** To be of use, output forms need to be suitably scaled. The horizontal axis is usually a time scale since most signals are functions of time. Real time is sometimes abandoned and an alternative time scale used if the events change too slowly for practical recording or satisfactory operation of the computer circuits. (See paragraph 3).

HYBRID COMPUTERS.

8. A hybrid system can be achieved by the direct interconnection (using suitable interfacing) of a digital computer to an analog computer. A purpose built hybrid computer would have the analog and digital elements combined within the same CPU and would probably be built for a specific task.

9. Advantages.

a. The hybrid computer combines the analog advantages of continuous real time response and immediate mathematical operation with digital advantages of storage capacity, easy programming and accuracy.

b. The digital computer can store an instruction repertoire for controlling the analog device thus avoiding analog programming using a **plug-in** technique. The analog device can interrupt digital operation at the appropriate time when a response is needed eg when the process under control needs action.

c. The digital device can edit analog output or use it as a starting point to obtain a more accurate result.

ANALOG/DIGITAL CONVERSION.

10. Any hybrid system requires units to convert analog output signals into digital representation, and units to convert digital codes into analog settings. A device which converts analog signals to digital codes is called a **digitizer.** The units' names are often abbreviated to D/A converter and A/D converter (digitizer).

NB. Digital computers may also use A/D and D/A conversion for some types of input and output, so these conversions are not only important for analog and hybrid computing .

11. Accuracy and Resolution. Accuracy indicates the closeness of the converted value to the true value whilst resolution is the size of the steps between converted values eg a signal of 100mV measured with accuracy to within 1% could give rise to readings of 99.5mV, 100mV or 100.5mV if the resolution was in units of 0.5mV.

12. Input and Output arrangements:–

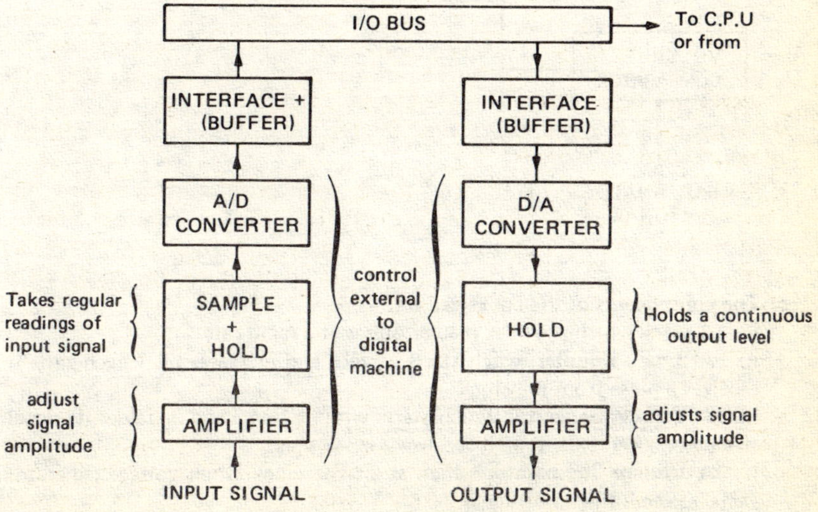

13. An Analog/Digital converter (Digitizer). This process can be repeated rapidly to give frequent conversion readings.

a. **Conversion Table.**

Analog Signals (eg Volts)	Binary Code
0 –	0 0 0
1 –	0 0 1
2 –	0 1 0
3 –	0 1 1
4 –	1 0 0
5 –	1 0 1
6 –	1 1 0
7 – 8	1 1 1

b. **Main Features.**

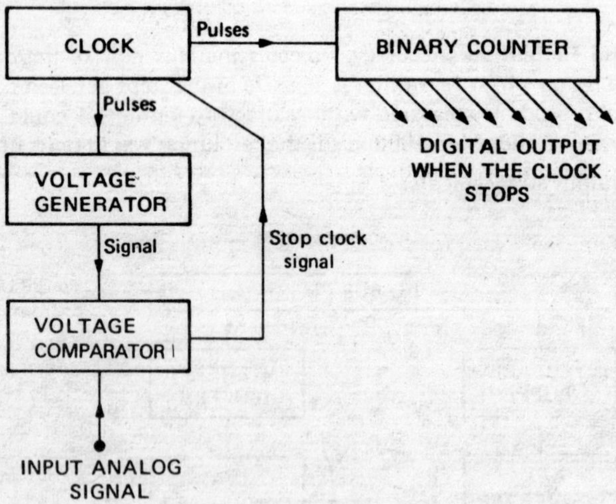

c. The components of the converter are:–

i. **A clock** which provides regular pulses at a rapid rate.

ii. **A Binary Counter** which starts at zero and increases by 1 each time it receives a pulse from the clock.

iii. **A Voltage Generator** which starts with no signal and increases its signal size by one unit each time it receives a clock pulse.

iv. **A Voltage Comparator** which stops the clock when voltage generator signal exceeds the input signal.

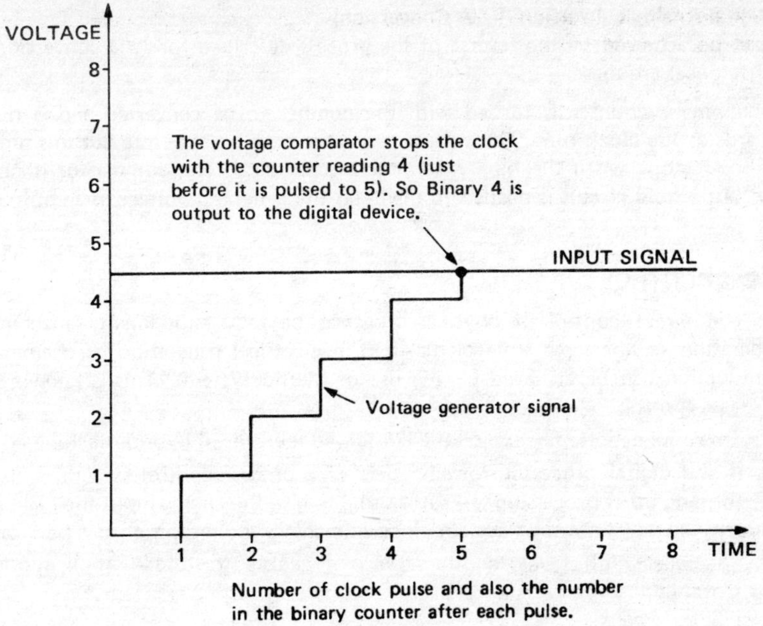

14. Optical Method.
Example. The rotational speed of a shaft (perhaps on a disc drive) may be measured by coding zones on an optical disc using light and dark areas. A photo sensor is then used to read the code.

Grays code is normally used for coding the optical disc. (23.37).

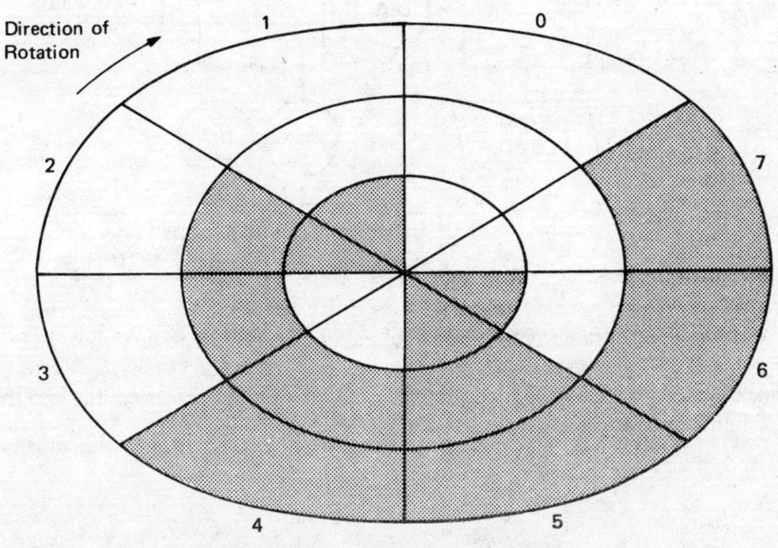

15. Digital Analog conversion. (D/A Conversion).
This can be achieved by the reverse of the process described for A/D conversion. The differences are these:—

The binary counter is loaded with the number to be converted and is run backwards as the clock runs. The voltage generator steps up as before but this time the process stops when the binary counter reaches zero. The **comparitor** is not needed but a **hold circuit** is needed to maintain the generator voltage as an output signal.

PROCESS CONTROL.

16. a. The direct control of physical processes be they experiments, machine operation or the large scale plants used in electrical generation or chemical production can be achieved by the use of hybrid systems. This is known as **process control**.

b. This application may exploit the combined features of hybrid machines.

c. If the digital processor forming part of a process control system is also performing other processing tasks it is usual to give the analog input the highest priority in any interrupt system since immediacy or response may be vital.

d. Specialist high level languages are available for these applications eg. Coral-66.

17. Simplified Example of a Working Arrangements.

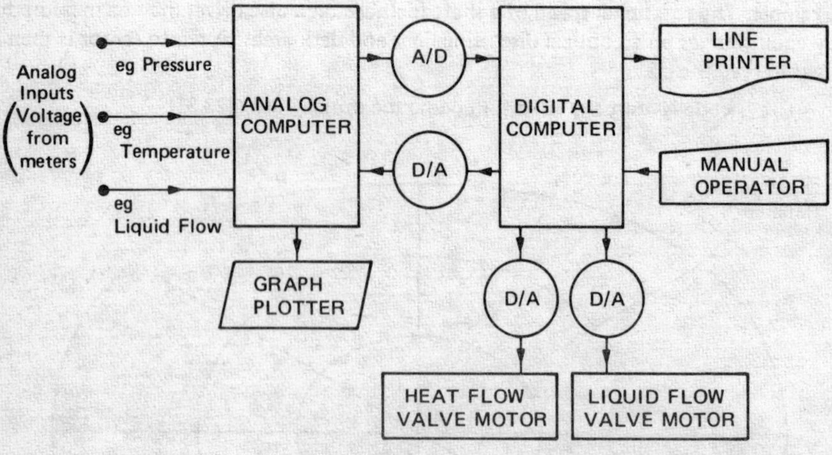

18. Process control need not necessarily involve the use of an analog or hybrid computer. In many cases digital computers are used but in such cases there may be extensive use of D/A and A/D converters between the digital computer and the instruments or controls to which it is connected.

SUMMARY.

19. a. The three types of computer are:
- i. Digital
- ii. Analog
- iii. Hybrid (a combination of the other two).

b. Analog computers are useful in simulating, modelling and solving problems concerned with physical phenomena which are describable in terms of systems of differential equations.

c. Analog computers provide real-time operation and fast solutions to some analytical problems but suffer from limitations in memory, set up time and accuracy.

d. Standard elements in an analog computer are:–
- i. Summers
- ii. Multipliers
- iii. Potentiometer
- iv. Integrators
- v. Special function generators.

e. Hybrid computers combine the features of analog and digital devices. They are often purpose built and interconnection of the analog and digital units requires A/D or D/A converters plus suitable interfacing.

POINTS TO NOTE.

20. a. Most examinations are concerned with comparative features of analog and digital devices in relation to applications, and often require details of A/D, D/A conversion.

b. **Array Processors** are extra fast processing units which can perform high precision arithmetic at speed by performing an array of 'sequential' arithmetic operations in parallel. In the future they may be able to compete favourably with analog computers in many real time applications.

STUDENT SELF TEST QUESTIONS.

(Answers on page 746)

1. a. Describe, with numerical illustrations, each of the following codes, stating one advantage of each code:–
- *i. Excess-three code*
- *ii. Gray (or Cyclic) code.*

b. Explain how an analog computer represents and displays numerical information and state two advantages of using an analog computer to simulate physical problems.

c. What is hybrid *computing? Briefly describe an application of this form of computing.*

(AEB 1976)

2. What is another name for an analog to digital converter? Explain how such a converter works.

Computational Methods

1. This Part deals with computer applications and methods of a mathematical or statistical nature.

2. The material contrasts sharply with that in the part entitled "applications" which had a data processing bias and therefore helps to provide a broader view of the applications for which computers may be used.

3. In some examinations for which this text is a preparation the material within this Part is optional. As a broad guide, students with post O level Mathematics often show a preference for this material whilst students who are less mathematically inclined can usually afford to avoid the material if they so wish. However, even the non-mathematical reader is recommended to read the introductory material in each chapter in this Part in order to gain a general impression of the basic ideas covered.

4. Chapter 49 defines what is meant by **"iteration"** in Computer Science and explains basic iterative methods.

5. Chapters 50 and 51 deal with different aspects of Statistics in Computer Science.

6. The links between Statistics and Computer Science are in these main areas.

a. The basic rules and methods of statistics can be usefully applied to a large number of computer applications in which output data has to be summarised and presented in the most meaningful way.

b. In more advanced study, statistics can be applied to such problems as the design and organisation of computer files, and optimising computer system operation.

c. The ability of computers to handle large quantities of data at speed make them invaluable tools to the statistician. One important application in this area is 'simulation' a last resort technique used to study problems too difficult for normal mathematical analysis.

7. Chapter 50 deals with some basic methods of handling statistical data.

8. Chapter 51 deals with the basic methods of statistical simulation. You may recall that simulation has been referred to elsewhere in this book in different contexts. eg. 48.4.

49 Iteration

INTRODUCTION.

1. This chapter uses post O level Mathematics in places and some readers may wish to omit some sections. The concept of **iteration** is an important one in numerical computing. **In an iterative process** for the solution of a problem, newer approximations are obtained from earlier ones by the repeated application of some formula or procedure. We say that the result has been obtained by **iteration.**

2. Exact Methods. Iterative methods are different from **exact methods.** If an **exact method** is used to solve an equation then the true (exact) value of the solution is obtained directly, usually by the use of a formula such as

$$x = [-b \pm \sqrt{b^2 - 4ac}]/2a$$

3. Starting and Stopping. To start the iterative process, a first approximation is needed and sometimes more than one approximation is needed. These first approximations are called **starting values.** Starting values may be obtained by

a. guessing
b. prior knowledge
c. inspection
d. graph.

An iterative process is stopped when the required accuracy is reached. Rounding of intermediate results does not affect the final accuracy.

4. Example. To find the cube root of 19 by an iterative method.
The root must be between 1 and 19 so we will use these as **starting values.** This method uses **two** approximations at each stage, one which is too low, called "low", and one which is too high, called "high". The approximate value of the cube root at each stage of iteration is called "approx".

The basic method is shown in the following pseudocode. The reader should be able to see how to adapt this example so as to construct a function which finds the cube root of any real number.

```
variables
      low,
      high,
      approx
      cube_of_approx : real

Begin
      (* initialise variables *)
      low                    : = 1
      high                   : = 19
      approx                 : = (low + high) / 2
      cube_of_approx         : = approx ↑ 3
      while  cube_of_approx < > 19
            if
                        cube_of_approx > 19
            then
                        high : = approx
            else
                        low : = approx
            endif
            approx : = (low + high)/2
            cube_of_approx : = approx ↑ 3
      endwhile
      output ("The cube root of 19 is ", approx)
end
```

The following table shows the first few steps using this pseudocode.

low	high	approx	cube_of_approx	Comment
1	19	10	1000	**approx** too high, replaces **high**
1	10	5.5	166.375	**approx** still too high, replaces **high**
1	5.5	3.25	34.33 (2D)	**approx** still too high, replaces **high**
1	3.25	2.125	9.596 (3D)	**approx** too low, replaces **low**
2.125	3.25	2.6875	19.41 (2D)	**approx** too high, replaces **high**
	etc.			

$\sqrt[3]{19}$ is 2.66840 correct to six figures.

Note. The process could appear to go on for ever since $\sqrt[3]{19}$ is irrational and therefore not expressible exactly as a decimal fraction. In practice an iterative process will reach a practical limit when the value is correct to the limits of accuracy of the computer on which it is run.

USES.

5. Iterative methods are used in the following situations.

a. When no exact method is known.

b. When an exact method proves difficult in practice eg by accumulating errors.

c. When it is the most convenient method.

The repetitive nature of iteration makes the method very suitable for computer applications.

CONVERGENCE.

6. We will define convergence more rigorously later. The main ideas are as follows.

If an **iterative process** gives approximations which get **nearer** and **nearer** to the **true value** then the iterative process **converges,** otherwise it **diverges.** One process is of a **higher order of convergence** than another if it converges more quickly.

The method of iteration in the example in 4. converged because A gave better approximation to $\sqrt[3]{19}$ at each stage, but it was a **low order method** since many steps were needed to get a good approximation.

THE GENERAL PROBLEM.

7. Most problems we wish to deal with can be expressed in the form $f(x) = 0$ where $f(x)$ is a function of x, eg $f(x) = ax^2 + bx + c = 0$ (Quadratic equation)
or $f(x) = x^3 - 19 = 0$ (Cube root of 19)

8. **Notation.** We will represent the true value of the solution by α and the successive approximations by $x_0, x_1, x_2, x_3, \ldots x_n$ when x_0 is usually the starting value.

Note. $f(\alpha) = 0$ and if the process converges then
$x_n \triangleq \alpha$ and $f(x_n) \triangleq 0$

ITERATIVE METHODS.

9. **Bisection or Binary Split.** This is the method used in the example given earlier. It is "slow" but simple.

x_0 and x_1 are starting values, they correspond to L and H.

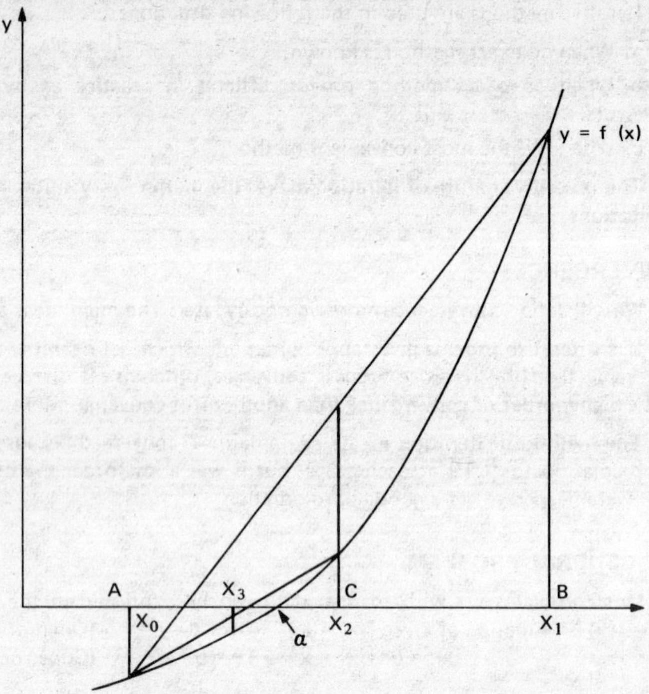

Note.

a. Starting values x_0 and x_1 are those for which f(x) has opposite sign.

b. The next approximation is the **mid-point** eg C is the mid-point of AB.

c. Points for which f(x) has opposite sign are chosen for next step eg x_0 and x_3 are used to obtain x_4.

10. Method of false position. Starting values are selected in the same way as for bisection. Successive approximations are the x co-ordinates for points where the chord cuts the x-axis.

See the following diagram.

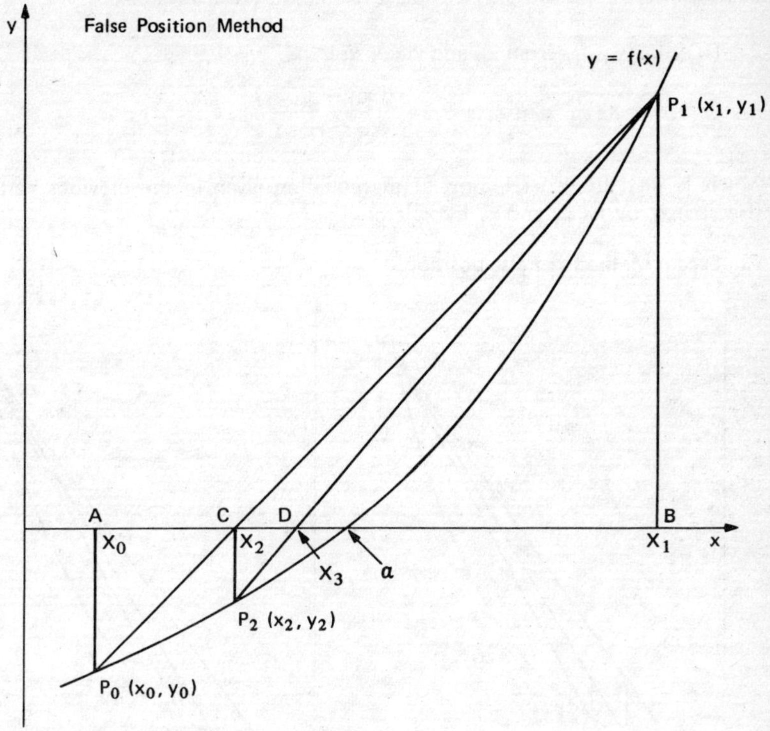

Note.

a. X_2 is the x co-ordinate of the point C where chord $P_0\ P_1$ cuts the x-axis.

b. The process is repeated using the latest pair of points **with opposite f(x) sign.** So x_1 and x_2 give x_3.

11. Derivation of formula.

To find x_2 from x_0 and x_1.

Equation of chord $P_0\ P_1$ is $$\frac{y - y_0}{x - x_0} = \frac{y_1 - y_0}{x_1 - x_0}$$

If y = 0 then this rearranges to give

$$x = x_0 - \frac{y_0(x_1 - x_0)}{y_1 - y_0}$$

x will be the next approximation ie x_2.

12. Secant Method. Very similar to the method of false position but **instead** of taking points of opposite sign the latest two points are always taken.

To obtain x_{n+1} from x_n and x_{n-1} use

$$x_{n+1} = x_{n-1} - y_{n-1}\frac{(x_n - x_{n-1})}{y_n - y_{n-1}}$$

which is just the general form of the equation given in the previous paragraph. (Replace x_0 by x_{n-1} and x_1 by x_n etc).

13. Secant Method vs False position.

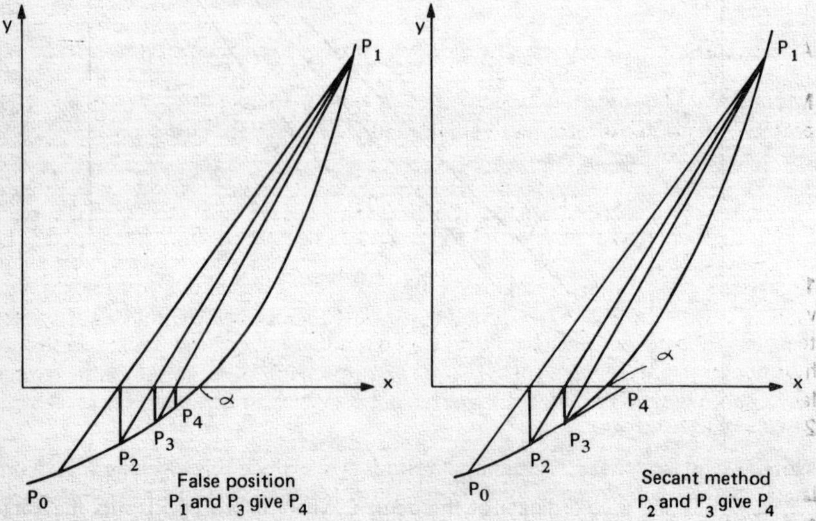

False position
P_1 and P_3 give P_4

Secant method
P_2 and P_3 give P_4

The secant method is **simpler** than the method of false position **but** there is a risk of divergence with the secant method.

14. Example. To solve $x^3 - 19 = 0$ using the false position method.
Suitable starting values are $x_0 = 2$ and $x_1 = 3$

since $y_0 = f(2) = 2^3 - 19 = -11$ and $y_1 = f(3) = 3^3 - 19 = +8$ (one positive, one negative)

We will use $x_2 = x_0 - \dfrac{y_0(x_1 - x_0)}{(y_1 - y_0)}$ and **working to 3 decimal places.**

substituting gives $x_2 = 2 - \dfrac{-11(3-2)}{8-(-11)} = 2 + \dfrac{11}{19} = 2.579$ (3D)

$y_2 = f(x_2) = 2.579^3 - 19 = -1.846$ (3D)

Use $x_3 = x_1 - \dfrac{y_1(x_2 - x_1)}{y_2 - y_1}$ (Using x_1 and x_2 because y_2 was negative)

substituting gives $x_3 = 3 - \dfrac{8(2.579-3)}{(-1.846-8)} = 3 - \dfrac{8 \times (0.421)}{9.846} = 2.658$ (3D)

$y_3 = f(x_3) = 2.658^3 - 19 = 18.779 - 19 = -0.221$ (3D)

Use $x_4 = x_1 - \dfrac{y_1(x_3 - x_1)}{y_3 - y_1} = 2.667$ (Using x_1 and x_3 because y_3 was negative)

AND SO ON. You may wish to continue further for practice.

Note. If we had used the secant method in this example then we would have proceeded in much the same way **but** we would have obtained x_4 from

$$x_4 = x_2 - \frac{y_2(x_3 - x_2)}{y_3 - y_2} = 2.669$$

15. Accuracy of Results. In the previous example the absolute error was absolute value – true value ≏ 2.667 – 2.66840 = 0.00140 so we can see that x_4 is correct to at least 2 places of decimal. Since we do not know the true value in practice we have to use an alternative check. A convenient check is to use absolute error = latest approximation – previous approximation which in this case is = $x_4 - x_3$ = 2.667 – 2.658 = 0.009.

The digit in the third decimal position is 9 and since this is greater than 5 our latest approximation cannot be relied upon as being accurate to 2 decimal places and a further iteration is advisable.

Note. Although we may sometimes do more iterations than necessary when using this estimate of the error we can be confident of the accuracy of our result.

16. The Method of Rearrangement of Formula (for successive substitution).
In practice some trial and error may be needed in this method in order to get a suitable formula which converges. We will deal with systematically checking for convergence later.

Example. To solve $x^3 - 19 = 0$ (i). We rearrange this to get a formula of the form $x = F(x)$, then use the iterative formula

$$\boxed{x_{n+1} = F(x_n)}$$

The simplest way to rearrange (i) is as

$x = \dfrac{19}{x^2}$ and we may try to use $x_{n+1} = \dfrac{19}{x_n^2}$

However if we try this formula it fails to give convergence, eg starting with $x_0 = 3$ we get, working to 3 decimal places:–

Using $x_{n+1} = 19/x_n^2$ $\quad x_1 = 19/3^2 = 2.111 \quad x_2 = 19/2.111^2 = 4.264$

$x_3 = 19/4.264^2 = 1.045 \quad x_4 = 19/1.045^2 = 17.399$

which is diverging away from the required value 2.66840 (6s)

17. If the simplest rearrangement fails to converge then a simple averaging may produce a formula which will converge. We had earlier

$x = \frac{19}{x^2}$ also $x = x$. Take away the average ie $x = \frac{1}{2}(\frac{19}{x^2} + x)$

We will try the formula $x_{n+1} = \frac{1}{2}(\frac{19}{x_n^2} + x_n)$ again taking $x_0 = 3$.

Working to 3 decimal places.

$$x_1 = \frac{1}{2}(\frac{19}{3^2} + 3) = 2.556$$

$$x_2 = \frac{1}{2}(\frac{19}{2.556^2} + 2.556) = 2.732$$

$$x_3 = \frac{1}{2}(\frac{19}{2.732^2} + 2.732) = 2.639$$

$$x_4 = \frac{1}{2}(\frac{19}{2.639^2} + 2.639) = 2.684$$

$$x_5 = \frac{1}{2}(\frac{19}{2.684^2} + 2.684) = 2.661$$

$$x_6 = \frac{1}{2}(\frac{19}{2.661^2} + 2.661) = 2.672$$

$$x_7 = \frac{1}{2}(\frac{19}{2.672^2} + 2.672) = 2.666$$

The method is slowly converging to 2.66840 (6S)

18. Newton-Raphson Method. (Sometimes just called Newton's method). This method gives good convergence.

Informal Explanation. The intention is to start with a value x_0 and from it obtain a value x_1 which is nearer to α than x_0.

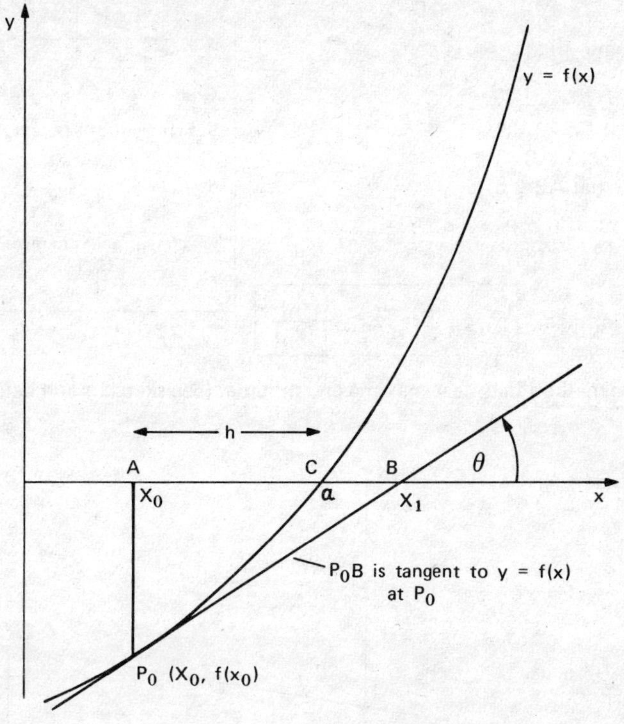

$$\tan\theta = \text{Gradient of curve at } P_0$$
$$= \text{derivative of curve at } x_0$$
$$= f'(x_0) \qquad \text{(i)}$$

But

$$\tan\theta = \frac{P_0A}{AB} = -\frac{f(x_0)}{AB} \qquad \text{(ii)}$$

From (i) and (ii)

$$AB = \frac{-f(x_0)}{f'(x_0)}$$

Take $x_1 = x_0 + AB$
(We hope that $AB \triangleq h$)

$$x_1 = x_0 \frac{-f(x_0)}{f'(x_0)}$$

General Formula

$$\boxed{x_{n+1} = x_n - \frac{f(x_n)}{f'(x_n)}}$$

AN ALTERNATIVE APPROACH

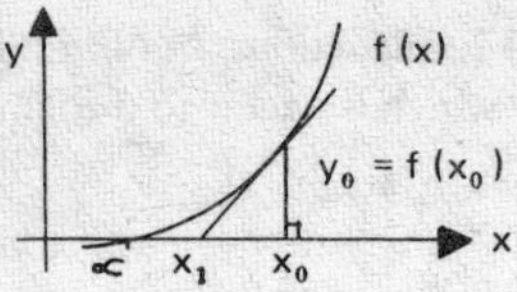

Gradient of f (x) at $x_0 = f'(x_0)$

but gradient of f (x) at $x_0 = \frac{y_0}{x_0 - x_1}$

So $f'(x_0) = \frac{y_0}{x_0 - x_1}$

which rearranges to give

$$x_1 = x_0 - \frac{f(x_0)}{f'(x_0)}$$

Note. The method fails near maxima and minima. (See sketch graph below).

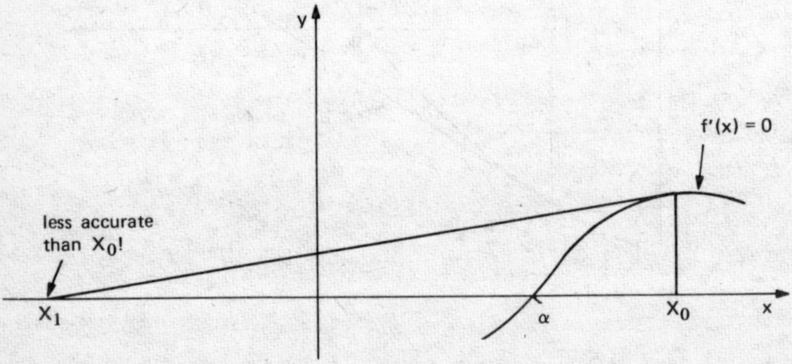

19. Example. To solve $x^3 - 19 = 0$ using the Newton-Raphson method. $f(x) = x^3 - 19$ which differentiates to give $f'(x) = 3x^2$

$$\text{Using } x_{n+1} = x_n - \frac{f(x_n)}{f'(x_n)}$$

$$= x_n - \frac{x_n^3 - 19}{3x_n^2} \qquad \text{which simplifies to:—}$$

$$x_{n+1} = \frac{1}{3}\left(2x_n + \frac{19}{x_n^2}\right)$$

Taking $x_0 = 3$ and working to 3 decimal places

$$x_1 = \frac{1}{3}(2 \times 3 + \frac{19}{3^2}) = 2.704$$

$$x_2 = \frac{1}{3}(2 \times 2.704 + \frac{19}{2.704^2}) = 2.669$$

$$x_3 = \frac{1}{3}(2 \times 2.669 + \frac{19}{2.669^2}) = 2.668$$

Then, $x_4 = 2.668$. The approximation is repeating so we have reached a value correct to 3 decimal places.

Note. By considering $x_{n+1} = x_n - \frac{f(x_n)}{f'(x_n)}$ we can see that $\frac{f(x_n)}{f'(x_n)}$ gives an approximate value for the absolute error in the nth iteration and so may be used as a check for accuracy.

$$\text{eg} \quad \frac{f(2.668)}{f'(2.668)} = \frac{2.668^3 - 19}{3 \times 2.668^2} = -0.000401$$

showing accuracy to at least three decimal places.

20. A more formal derivation of Newton's Method which makes use of Taylor's Theorem. By Taylor's Theorem (See A level Mathematics Texts), we have

$$f(\alpha) = f(x_n) + (\alpha - x_n)\, f'(x_n) + \frac{1}{2}(x - \alpha_n)^2\, f''(x_n) + \ldots\ldots \text{(a)}$$

We note that $\alpha - x_0$ is small since $x_0 \triangleq \alpha$, the true value, so we will ignore the term in $(\alpha - x_n)^2$ and higher order terms.

Thus $f(\alpha) \triangleq f(x_n) + (\alpha - x_n)\, f'(x_n)$

but $f(\alpha) = 0$ (by definition) so rearranging we have

$$\alpha \triangleq x_n - \frac{f(x_n)}{f'(xn)}$$

(b) This suggest that we take

$$x_{n+1} = x_n - \frac{f(x_n)}{f'(x_n)}$$

which is the same formula as before (18.).

21. The error in the nth iteration. The absolute error in the nth iteration is denoted by e_n, thus $e_n = x_n - \alpha$ and $e_{n+1} = x_{n+1} - \alpha$. For an iterative process to converge these errors must get smaller ie we require $|e_{n+1}| < |e_n|$. Before we investigate this condition further we require a useful form for our iterative formulae which is now introduced.

22. The General Form of the Iterative Formula. Most iterative formulae we are using can be expressed in the form $x_{n+1} = F(x_n)$. The rearrange 'successive substitution' formula (16.) is already in this form. The secant method cannot be put into this form because *two previous* values occur in the formula but for Newton's Method $x_{n+1} = F(x_n)$, where

$$F(x_n) = x_n - \frac{f(x_n)}{f'(x_n)}$$

23. Form of the general solution. The solution corresponds to the point α at which $f(x) = 0$. In terms of the general iterative formula this is the solution of the equation $x = F(x)$ with solution $\alpha = F(\alpha)$.

24. The graphical representation of this solution is illustrated here by the iteration in (19.) $x_{n+1} = F(x_n)$ where

$$F(x_n) = \frac{1}{3}\left(2x_n + \frac{19}{x_n^2}\right)$$

The graph shows that the solution occurs at the point where the lines $y = x$ and $y = F(x)$ intersect. This is the point at which $\alpha = F(\alpha)$.

AN ITERATIVE SOLUTION OF $X^3 - 19 = 0$

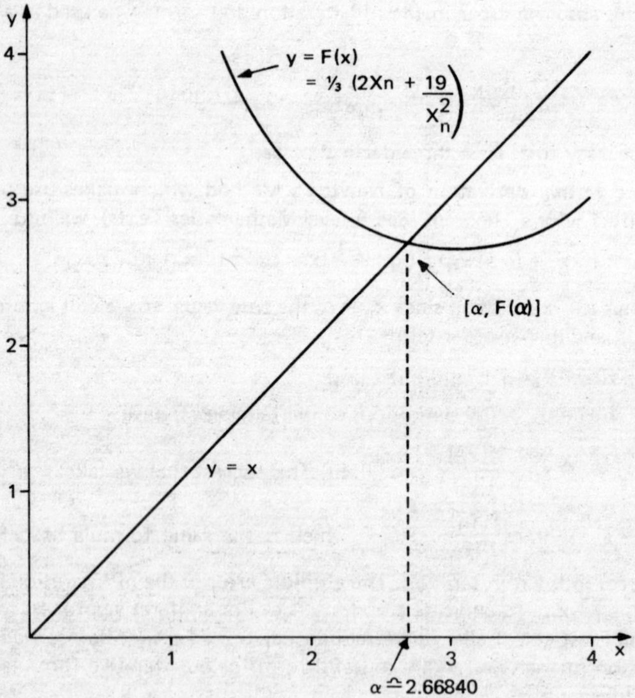

25. Conditions of Convergence. The iterative processes $x_{n+1} = F(x_n)$ only converges to a solution if the gradient of $F(x)$ near the root is sufficiently small. We will state this more formally presently. First we look at an illustration, then we look at a proof.

Example. Consider an iterative solution of $2x^2 - x - 1 = 0$, which has an exact solution $x = -0.5$ or $x = 1$. Suppose that we rearrange $2x^2 - x - 1 = 0$ to give

$$x = \frac{1}{2x - 1}$$

and attempt to use the iterative formula $x_{n+1} = F(x_n)$ where

$$F(x_n) = \frac{1}{2x_n - 1}$$

We may attempt to find both solutions by iteration thus:—

a. Taking a starting value of −1.5, the process converges to x = −0.5 where the gradient is −0.5

b. Taking a 'good' starting value 1.1 the process diverges away from the root x = 1.0, where the gradient is 2.

The following graph illustrates both iterative attempts. In general a process will converge if the modulus of the gradient of F(x) is less than 1 near the root. This is proved in the next section.

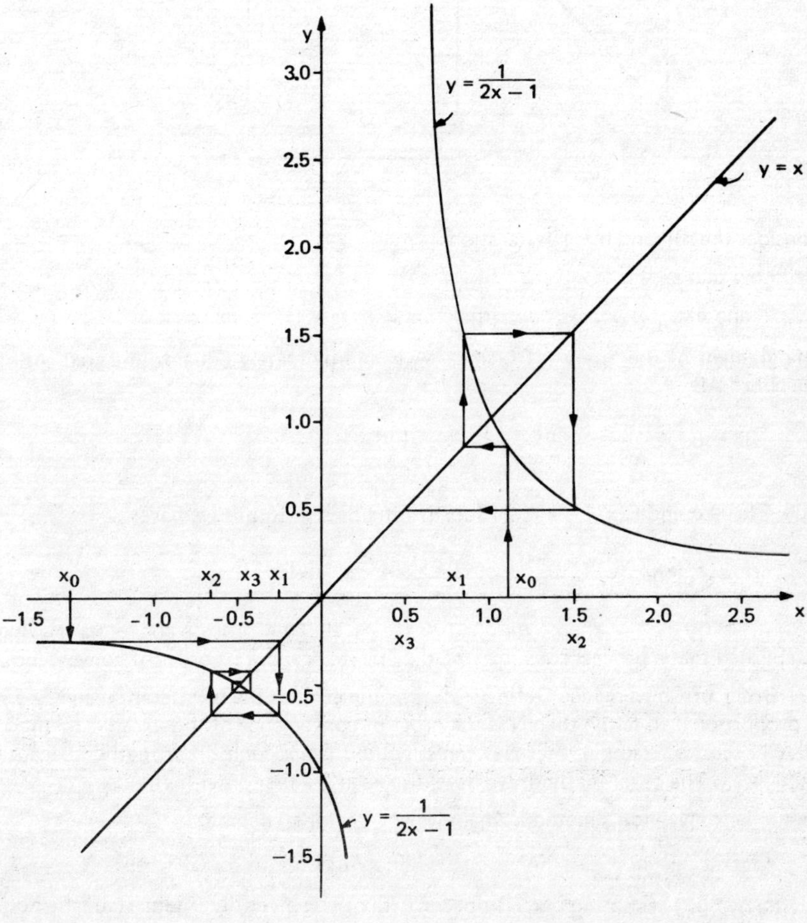

26. Conditions for convergence. The iterative formula $x_{n+1} = F(x_n)$ converges to a solution of $x = F(x)$ if $|F'(x)| < |$ in the neighbourhood of the solution, and x_0 is sufficiently near the solution ie within the neighbourhood.

The reason for this result is explained with the aid of the following diagram.

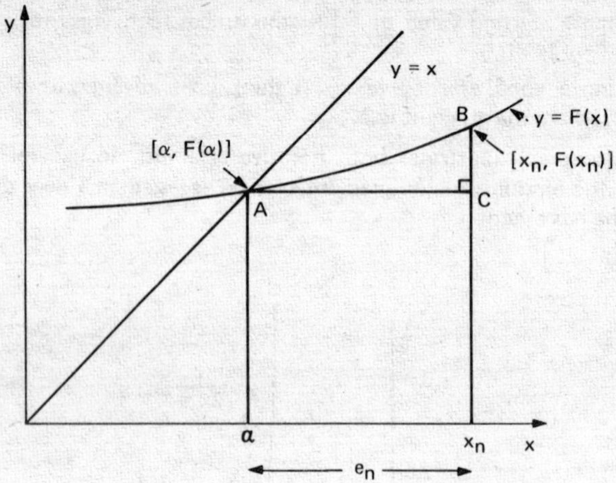

Consider the nth and $n+1^{th}$ iterations

We know that $e_n = \alpha - x_n$ (i)

and $e_{n+1} = \alpha - x_{n+1}$ (ii)

The gradient of the line $y = F(x)$ near A is approximately equal to the gradient of the chord AB

$$\text{ie } F'(x) \simeq \frac{CB}{AC} = \frac{F(x_n) - F(\alpha)}{e_n} \qquad \text{(iii)}$$

Now $F(\alpha) = \alpha$ and $F(x_n) = x_{n+1}$. Substituting these into (iii) we have

$$F'(x_n) \simeq \frac{x_{n+1} - \alpha}{e_n} = \frac{e_{n+1}}{e_n} \qquad \text{(iv)}$$

Now if $|F'(x)| < 1$ then $|e_{n+1}| < |e_n|$ and the process converges. Having established that a process converges we may next ask about its order of convergence.

27. Order of Convergence Defined. If e_n is the error in the nth iteration and e_{n+1} is proportional to $(e_n)^N$ then N is the order of convergence of the iterative method. We will see for example, that Newton's method is a *second order* method because $e_{n+1} \propto e_n^2$. The other methods we have discussed are first order methods.

Example for Newton's method. Again we use Taylor's Theorem.

$$0 = f(\alpha) = f(x_n) + (\alpha - x_n) f'(x_n) + \tfrac{1}{2}(\alpha - x_n)^2 f''(x_n) + \ldots.$$

Divide by $f'(x_n)$ assuming $f'(x_n)$ is not zero. ($f'(x_n) = 0$ gives divergence (see the note in paragraph 18.)

$$0 = \frac{f(x_n)}{f'(x_n)} + (\alpha - x_n) + \tfrac{1}{2}(\alpha - x_n)^2 \frac{f''(x_n)}{f'(x_n)} + \ldots$$

This rearranges to give $x_n - \dfrac{f(x_n)}{f'(x_n)} - \alpha = \tfrac{1}{2}(\alpha - x_n)^2 \dfrac{f''(x_n)}{f'(x_n)} + \ldots$

ie $$F(x_n) - \alpha \doteq \tfrac{1}{2}(\alpha - x_n)^2 \frac{f''(x_n)}{f'(x_n)}$$

ie $$x_{n+1} - \alpha \doteq \tfrac{1}{2}(\alpha - x_n)^2 \frac{f''(x_n)}{f'(x_n)}$$

ie $$e_{n+1} \doteq \tfrac{1}{2}\, e_n^2 \frac{f''(x_n)}{f'(x_n)}$$

The small changes in x allow us to regard $\dfrac{f''(x_n)}{f'(x_n)}$ as a constant,

so $e_{n+1} \propto e_n^2$ **(Second order convergence)**

In practical terms the second order convergence of Newton's method means that the number of significant digits is roughly **doubled** at each iteration.

28. The case of $F'(x) = 0$ (Not to be confused with $f'(x) = 0$ in (18)).

From equation (iv) paragraph 26. we have $F'(x) \doteq \dfrac{e_{n+1}}{e_n}$ if e_n is small. Suppose $F'(x)$ is also small so that $|F'(x)| \doteq |e_n|$. Then we have $e_n \doteq F'(x) \doteq e_{n+1}/e_n$ ie $e_n^2 \doteq e_{n+1}$. This means that for $F'(x)$ close to zero the process will be **quadratically** convergent ie roughly order 2 convergence. If $|e_n| > |F'(x)|$ the process will clearly be **at least** quadratically convergent, perhaps better.

SUMMARY.

29. a. Iterative methods lend themselves to computer application because of their repetitive nature and they avoid problems with rounding errors met in some exact methods.

b. Iterative processes need starting values and their order of convergence determines the rate at which errors decrease.

c. Methods discussed were:—

- i. Bisection or Binary split
- ii. False position
- iii Secant method
- iv. Rearrangement of formula.
- v. Newton-Raphson method — a second order method.

d. The order of convergence of Newton's method was established.

e. Conditions for convergence were discussed.

POINTS TO NOTE.

30. a. Those derivations given in the text may be asked for in examinations.

b. The conditions for convergence stated in paragraph 26 are sufficient for convergence to take place but are not necessary, ie convergence may sometimes take place even when these conditions are not satisfied.

STUDENT SELF TEST QUESTIONS.

(Answers on page 746)

1. *Given the function $y = f(x) = x^3 - 3x^2 + 15x - 30$*

   a. Show that the equation $x^3 - 3x^2 + 15x - 30 = 0$ has a root between $x = 2$ and $x = 3$

   b. Use the Newton-Raphson method to find the value of the root correct to 4 decimal places. Use a starting value $x_0 = 2$.

   c. Use an iterative formula formed by rearrangement of the formula to again find the root to 4 decimal places using starting value $x_0 = 2$.

   d. Use the secant method to find the same root. Use starting value $x_0 = 3$, $x_1 = 2$.

2. *Discuss the conditions under which an iterative formula of the form*

$$x_{n+1} = f(x_n)$$

will converge.

3. *a. Show that the eq:ation $5x^3 + 7x^2 - 14x - 16 = 0$ has a root between $x = 1$ and $x = 2$.*

   b. Use the Newton-Raphson method to find the root. Take a starting value $x_0 = 1$.

   c. i. Show that one iterative formula formed by rearranging the intial equation is

$$x_{n+1} = \frac{16}{5x_n^2 + 7x_n - 14}$$

   but that is does not satisfy the conditions for convergence at $x = 1.6$.

   ii. Show that the conditions of convergence are satisfied when using starting value $x_0 = 0$ and using this starting value find another root of the original equation.

4. *Explain what is meant by order of convergence and show that the Newton-Raphson iterative process has, in general, order of convergence 2.*

By sketching a graph, or otherwise, show that the cubic equation

$$4x^3 + 4x^2 - 4x - 1 = 0$$

has one positive root.

Prepare a flowchart to show how this root could be calculated to 5 decimal places using the Newton-Raphson method. You should incorporate a suitable starting value.

(AEB 1976)

50 Simple Statistics

INTRODUCTION.

1. The two main areas of statistical activity are:

a. From a mass of data a few descriptive values (statistics) are extracted or the data is presented in more intelligible diagrammatic representation.

b. From a few items of data attempts are made either to make generalised inferences or to test the reasonableness of general assumptions. This chapter deals mainly with a.

BASIC STATISTICAL CONCEPTS.

2. Population. The statistical meaning of the term population is not restricted to the normal meaning of the word. A population is the whole set of items under consideration. In mathematical language it is the **universal set.** It is possible to have a population of light bulbs, nuts and bolts, cars and of course people. More frequently the population is a population of **either** measurements (eg lifetimes of light bulbs, lengths of bolts, prices of cars or wages of people) **or** attributes like shapes of light bulbs colours of cars, etc).

3. Samples. A sample is a **subset** of the population, ie a collection of items taken from the population.

Sampling and Testing. Many statistical methods involve sampling (ie taking samples from a population) and then using the results obtained from the sample to either infer properties of the population or to test the creditworthyness of some prior claim or assumption about the population.

As was suggested in the introduction to this chapter we will restrict ourselves to looking at some simple methods of reducing sample data to intelligible forms which may be used to throw light on the population.

4. Variables. The numerical characteristics of population members are called **variables** since they vary from one member to another. Examples are lengths, weights, sizes, ages, etc.

5. Discrete and Continuous Variables.

a. Variables are either **discrete** or **continuous:**–

i. Discrete variables take only certain values eg shoe size, number of peas in a pod.

ii. Continuous variables take any values within set intervals, eg heights and weights of people, lifetimes of light bulbs.

b. Populations may be defined by stating which variable values occur and with what frequency. This may be done by:–

i. Listing all population members and the frequency with which they occur.

ii. Providing a formula which provides the required information.

ORGANISING DATA.

6. Reducing Raw Data. Raw data is data in its collected form and prior to any processing. It may subsequently be organised into the following forms:–

a. Tables
b. Charts
c. Graphs
d. Maps.

The purpose is to simplify interpretation and highlight relevant features. Further simplification may be achieved by summarising the data by a numerical value such as an average.

7. Example. Arrange the following raw data into a table and represent it by a histogram and cumulative frequency curve.

Data. (Length of assorted bolts in mm)

3.6	3.2	3.1	3.3	3.3
3.4	3.5	3.3	3.4	3.5
3.4	3.3	3.6	3.3	3.3
3.2	3.4	3.5	3.2	3.4

8. Table.

Bolt length (mm)	3.1	3.2	3.3	3.4	3.5	3.6
Frequency of bolts with given length	1	3	6	5	3	2
Cumulative Frequency	1	4	10	15	18	20

9. Histogram

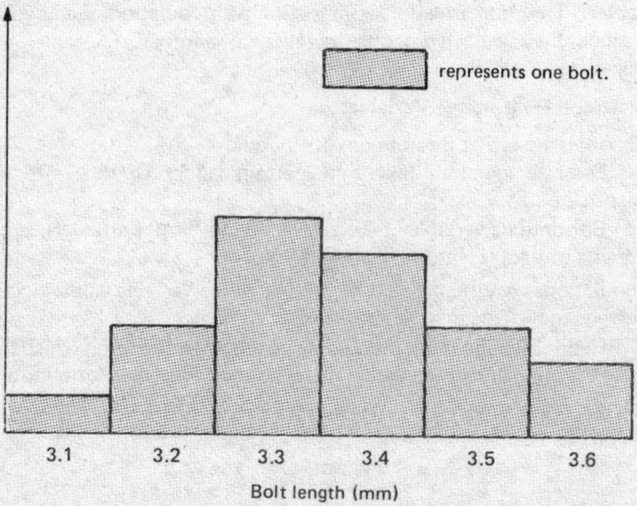

10. Cumulative Frequency Curve. (Sometimes called an **Ogive**)

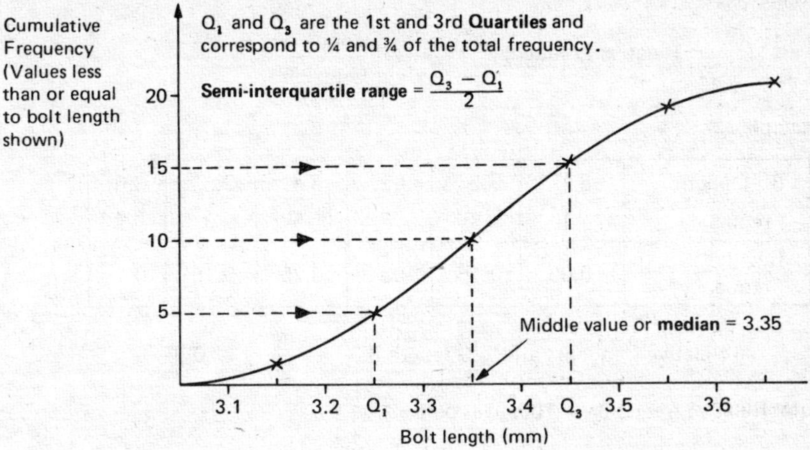

11. Frequency Distribution. The **frequency distribution** of a variable is formed by classifying the **variable** in terms of the number of items possessing the same value. eg The table of bolt lengths given in the previous example shows the **frequency distribution** of the **variable** bolt length.

12. Histogram. We have seen that a frequency distribution may be conveniently represented by a histogram. Note that on a histogram AREA represents FREQUENCY. If HEIGHT Is used to represent frequency the graph is called a **bar chart**.

13. Example. The histogram below shows the same frequency distribution as before, only the values for 3.1 and 3.2 have been combined. The area remains the same but heights are different.

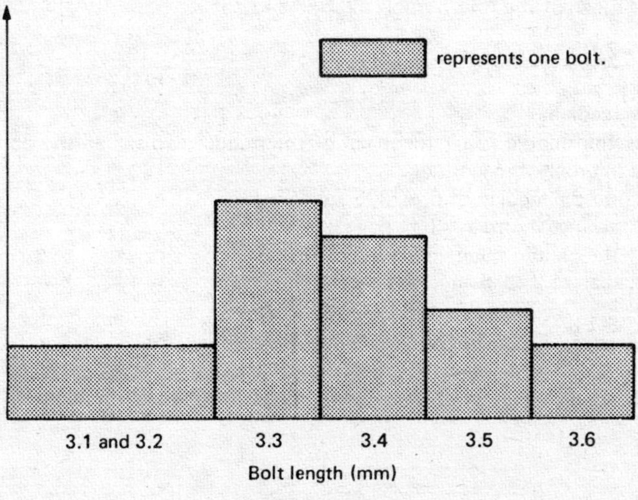

14. Relative Frequency. Sometimes relative frequencies are more useful than frequencies.

$$\text{Relative Frequency} = \frac{\text{Frequency}}{\text{Total Frequency}}$$

Example.

Bolt length	3.1	3.2	3.3	3.4	3.5	3.6
Frequency	1	3	6	5	3	2
Relative Frequency	0.05	0.15	0.3	0.25	0.15	0.1

eg Relative frequency of Bolts length 3.3 $= \frac{6}{20} = 0.3$

Note. Relative frequency x 100 gives percentage.

STATISTICAL MEASURES.

15. Measures of Location. A measure of location is a single number which in some way summarises a set of numbers. The three common examples are:

a. The arithmetic mean, or simple average.

b. The median.

c. The mode.

16. Details of Averages.

a. **The arithmetic mean (or mean for short).**
This is often referred to as the average. It is the total, divided by the number of numbers making the total.

eg The mean of the **four** numbers 2, 3, 6 and 7 is

$$\frac{2+3+6+7}{4} = 4.5$$

b. **The median.**
This is the middle value (or mean of the middle two) when the numbers are placed in order of magnitude.
eg To find the median of 6, 9, 3, 5 and 7

i. arrange in order 3, 5, 6, 7, 9.

ii. the middle value "6" is the median.

The median of 2, 3, 6 and 7 is

$$\frac{3+6}{2} = 4.5 \text{ ie the average of the middle two.}$$

In this case the same as the mean. (Also see paragraph 10).

c. **The mode.**
The mode is the most frequently occurring value if such a value exists.
eg The mode of 3, 3, 5, 6, 7, 5, 5, and 4 is 5 because it occurs more frequently than any of the other numbers.

17. Dispersion or spread. Often an **average value** for a set of data will tell us all we need to know if we are only interested in typical or likely values. If we also wish to know how variable the data is then the average will not help us.

Example. Consider these two samples each of three bolts.

a. Lengths of bolts of type A mm 3.4, 3.5, 3.6

b. Lengths of bolts of type B mm 1.4, 3.5 5.6

Both types have the **same** average (mean) length of 3.5mm but type B appears to be far more variable. If the bolts we required had to be of a minimum length of 3.3mm say, this fact would be of interest to us. Certain measures of this variability, spread, or dispersion can be used.

18. Measures of spread. We will consider just two measures of spread, they are:—

a. **The range.** This is simply the difference between the largest and smallest value. (A superior alternative is the semi-interquartile range (43.10)).
eg Range of sample a above = 3.6 – 3.4 = 0.2
Range of sample b above = 5.6 – 1.4 = 4.2

b. **The Standard deviation.** (The square of the standard deviation is called the variance). For a sample we use S, for a population we use σ (small sigma) For a sample of n values of x we use this formula which is explained shortly.

$$\text{Standard deviation} \quad S = \sqrt{\frac{\Sigma (x - \bar{x})^2}{n}}$$

NB. There is an alternative formula with divisor (n – 1) which is used when the population variance is to be estimated from the sample variance.

19. Notation and Formulae.

a. The mean of a sample of values of a variable x is often represented by $\bar{x}$ pronounced "x bar".

b. The mean of a **population** of the same variable is represented by μ_x or μ.

c. The symbol Σ, capital sigma means "sum of" so Σx means "sum of x values".

d. If there are n items in a sample each with a given x value then the mean can be expressed in the formula

$$\text{mean} = \bar{x} = \frac{\Sigma x}{n}$$

In the case of a **frequency distribution** where items have frequency f an equivalent formula for the mean is

$$\text{mean} = \frac{\Sigma fx}{\Sigma f}$$

e. An example of using the standard deviation formula is given in paragraph 21.

20. Example. (Using previous data in paragraph 8.)

	Bolt length (mm) x	frequency f	f.x
	3.1	1	3.1
	3.2	3	9.6
Mode►	3.3	6	19.8
	3.4	5	17.0
	3.5	3	10.5
	3.6	2	7.2
	Totals	$\Sigma f = 20$	$\Sigma fx = 67.2$

Mean Bolt length

$$= \bar{x} \qquad \frac{\Sigma fx}{\Sigma f} = \frac{67.2}{20} = 3.36\text{mm}$$

21. Example. (Calculating the standard deviation for the data in paragraph 17).

a. i. For bolts of types A with mean $\bar{x} = 3.5$

$$S = \sqrt{\frac{(3.4 - 3.5)^2 + (3.5 - 3.5)^2 + (3.6 - 3.5)^2}{3}} = \sqrt{\frac{0.02}{3}} \triangleq 0.082$$

ii. For bolts of type B also with mean $\bar{x} = 3.5$

$$S = \sqrt{\frac{(1.4 - 3.5)^2 + (3.5 - 3.5)^2 + (5.6 - 3.5)^2}{3}} = \sqrt{\frac{8.82}{3}} \triangleq 1.71$$

The second sample is more variable and has a larger standard deviation.

b. To calculate the standard deviation of a frequency distribution the formula

$$S = \sqrt{\frac{\Sigma f(x - \bar{x})^2}{\Sigma f}}$$ may be used.

Example. (Using previous data on bolts) $\bar{x} = 3.36$

x	f	$x - \bar{x}$	$(x - \bar{x})^2$	$f(x - \bar{x})^2$
3.1	1	–0.26	0.0676	0.0676
3.2	3	–0.16	0.0256	0.0768
3.3	6	–0.06	0.0036	0.0216
3.4	5	0.04	0.0016	0.0080
3.5	3	0.14	0.0196	0.0588
3.6	2	0.24	0.0576	0.1152
Totals	$\Sigma f = 20$			0.3480

$$S = \sqrt{\frac{\Sigma f(x - \bar{x})^2}{\Sigma f}} = \sqrt{\frac{0.3480}{20}} = 0.132$$

22. Errors in using formulae. An alternative formulae for the **manual** calculation of standard deviations is

$$S = \sqrt{\frac{\Sigma x^2}{n} - \bar{x}^2}$$

It is NOT suitable for calculation by computer because of error accumulation and loss of accuracy. For example it is common to get situations such as:—

$$\frac{\Sigma x^2}{n} = 36872592 \quad (8S)$$

$$\bar{x} = \sqrt{36872576} \quad (8S)$$

$$\text{giving } S = \sqrt{36872592 - 36872576} = \sqrt{16} = 4 \qquad (1S)$$

where almost all accuracy is lost in the rounding errors of the calculation.

23. A most efficient method for calculating the standard deviation by computer is the Box-Hunter method. Pseudocode for this method is shown below. The method is efficient and free of large error accumulation.

```
variables
        n: integer          (* Number of observations  *)
        m,                  (* mean                    *)
        ss,                 (* Sum of Squares          *)
        sd,                 (* Standard Deviation      *)
        x: real             (* Input value             *)

Begin
    Output ("Input values. Key in 999 to terminate.")
    input (x)
    while x <> 999 (* 999 is a sentinel *)
        n : = n + 1
        s : = ss + (x – m) * (x – m) * (1 – 1/n)
        m : = m + (x – m)/m
        output ("next value = ?")
        input (x)
    endwhile
    sd : sqrt (ss/n)
end
```

NB. Short variable names have been used here because in mathematical formulae long variable names can be counter productive in the pursuit of clarity.

CHANCE AND PROBABILITY.

24. Chance affects many events which occur in our lives, some trivial, some important. The mathematical concept of **probability** may be used to deal with problems involving chance. Examples of questions requiring an answer in terms of probabilities are:—

a. What are the chances of rain today?
b. If I fly in this aircraft will it crash?
c. If I am vaccinated can I still contract the disease?
d. If I plant these seeds will they germinate?

25. Scale of Probability. The scale of possible value for the **probability** of an **event** is shown below.

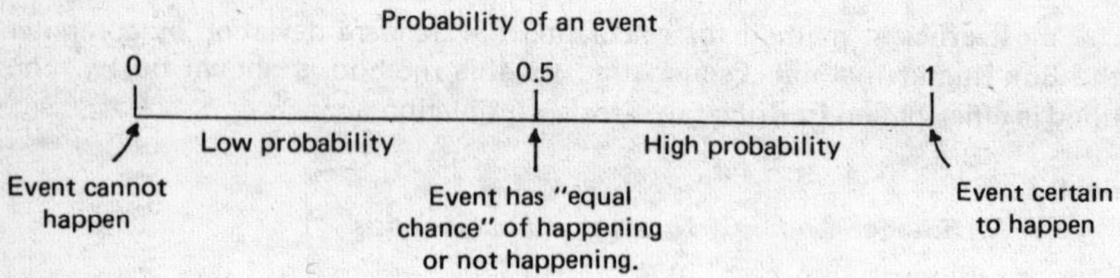

Events with probabilities close to zero have little chance of happening whilst those with probabilities close to one have a good chance of happening. So we would hope that the event "Aircraft crash" will have a probability close to zero and the event "seeds germinate" will have a probability nearer to one than zero.

26. Definitions of Probability. No definition proves adequate in all cases, but two definitions frequently used are:—

a. The probability of an event = $\dfrac{\text{Number of ways events can happen}}{\text{Total number of possible outcomes.}}$

Examples.

i. To find the probability of a head when tossing a "fair" coin.
The event is "a head" and it can happen in just one way. There are **two** possible outcomes because we may get head or tail.
So Probability of a head = ½ = 0.5.

ii. Find the probability of an ace if a card is chosen from a pack. The event is "an ace" and there are four aces in a pack. There are 52 possible outcomes since there are 52 cards in the pack.

$$\text{Probability of an ace} = \frac{4}{52} = \frac{1}{13}$$

b. **Relative frequency definition.** In a.i. we considered a "fair" coin but the only way of testing the fairness of the coin would be to toss it very many times to see if "in the long run" we get an equal number of heads and tails. The **relative frequency definition** of probability uses "long run" values.

$$\text{Relative frequency of event} = \frac{\text{Number of times event has happened}}{\text{Total number of trials}}$$

Probability of event = value of relative frequency after all possible trials.

$\triangleq$ value of relative frequency after a large number of trials.

27. Examples.

a. A biased coin has been tossed 1000 times and 200 heads observed.

$$\text{Probability of 'a head'} = \frac{200}{1000} = 0.2$$

b. If experiments show that 95% of seeds of a particular type germinate then for a single seed

$$\text{Probability of seed germinating} = \frac{95}{100} = 0.95$$

Note. The first definition is simple but tends to apply only to artificial problems the second definition is more troublesome but is easier to apply to practical problems.

DISTRIBUTIONS.

28. Earlier in paragraph 11 we saw that like values of a variable could be collected together so as to form a **frequency distribution.** A **relative frequency distribution** may also be formed in the same way.

If sufficient members of the population are included in a sample then the **relative frequency distribution** of the sample will approximate to **relative frequency distribution** of the whole population. From our definitions of probability we can see that the relative frequency distribution of the population is in fact a **probability distribution.** We often refer to this probability distribution as the **distribution of values of the variable.**

29. Types of Distribution. There are two main types of distributions, they are:—

a. **Discrete distributions,** ie distributions of discrete variables.

b. **Continuous distributions,** ie distribution of continuous variable.

30. Discrete distribution example. This graph shows the distribution of a variable x where x is the value on the side of a 'fair' die.

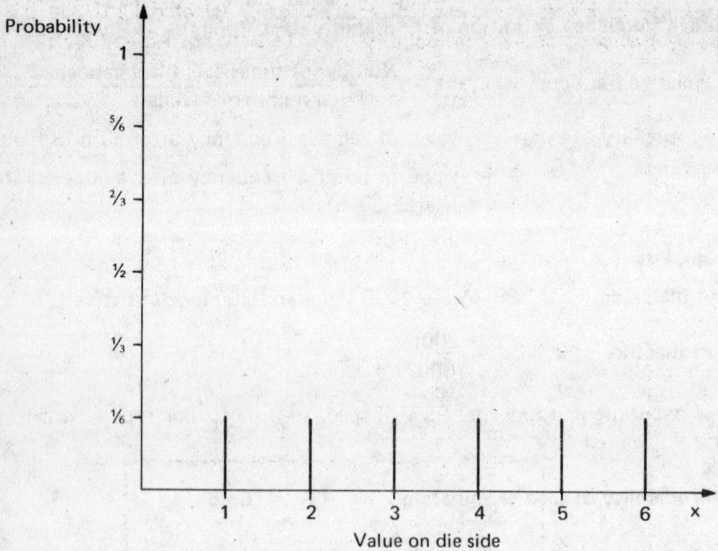

Note. a. A histogram has **not** been used because the variable x is discrete.

b. In this case heights of lines represent probabilities. So the probability of each x value is ⅙.

31. Continuous Distribution Example. The graph below shows the **rectangular distribution** of the variable x. An application will follow later.

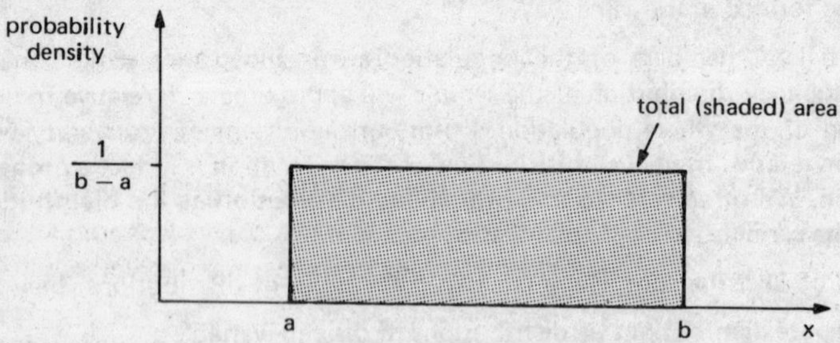

Note. i. Area represents probability.

ii. The total area is one unit (ie x must lie between a and b).

iii. The height represents probability density.

iv. **Any** value between a and b can occur.

32. Finding Probabilities.

Example. Consider a rectangular distribution with a = 1 and b = 5. To find the probability of a value between 1.5 and 2.2 being selected (ie if you select a value by chance what is the probability it will be between 1.5 and 2.2).

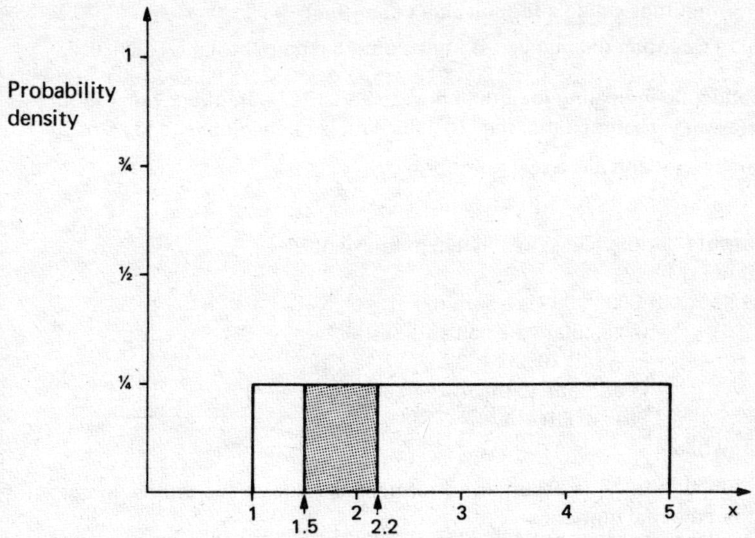

The Probability that a selected value lies between 1.5 and 2.2 is represented by shaded area.

$$\text{Shaded area} = \frac{2.2 - 1.5}{4} = 0.175$$

So Probability that a selected value will lie between 1.5 and 2.2 = 0.175.

CONSTRUCTING HISTOGRAMS BY COMPUTER.

33. This is a common task and will be required in the next chapter.

a. **Constructing the frequency distribution.** The **raw data** is first grouped into a frequency distribution and then a printout or further calculations may follow. Frequency may be conveniently stored in an array.

b. **Example.** To construct the frequency distribution given below *from* the raw data given in paragraph 7. When *completed* the frequencies will be stored in an array 'F' as indicated.

Bolt length (mm)	3.1	3.2	3.3	3.4	3.5	3.6
Frequency	1	3	6	5	3	2
Stored as	F(1)=1	F(2)=3	F(3)=6	F(4)=5	F(5)=3	F(6)=2

c. In this case the x values are equally spaced so the elements of the frequency array 'F' can be calculated from x using i = 10(x – 3.0). eg When x = 3.2, i = 2 and so frequency for x = 3.2 will be stored in F(2).

The input of data is usually terminated by either

i. Checking for a terminator ie a number not belonging to the data. (Sometimes called a **rogue value or sentinel**)

ii. Counting the number of inputs until a required total is reached.

34. Pseudocode indicating in outline how to construct a frequency distribution is given below. It is assumed that the F(i) values have been initialised to zero.

NB. i is an integer and **x** is a real number.

```
Begin
    output ("Input values. Key in 999 to terminate.")
    input (x)
    while x <> 999 (* 999 is a sentinel *)
            (* calculate the cell address *)
            i : = int (10 * (x – 3.0))
            (* add one to the frequency in the cell *)
            F(i) : = F(i) + 1
    endwhile
```

NB. The function int(y) is assumed to return the value of the largest integer not greater than the real number y.

35. Grouped data. In the previous example each frequency corresponded to a single x value but more often x values are grouped together into cells.

Example.

Data. Service times at a checkout measured to the nearest second.

Service time x seconds	Frequency f
20 – 24	2
25 – 29	3
30 – 34	4
35 – 39	4
40 – 44	7
45 – 49	8
50 – 54	6
55 – 59	5
60 – 64	1

Note. i. The **class interval** shown as 25 – 29 will include values between 24.5 and 29.5 because measurement is to the nearest second.

ii. 24.5 and 29.5 are called the **class boundaries.**

iii. To calculate the mean or standard deviation use the mid-values

$$\text{eg } \frac{24.5 + 29.5}{2} = 27$$

36. Constructing the frequency distribution. (With equal classes).
Suppose that F(1) stores frequencies in the class interval 20 – 24, F(2) stores frequencies in the class interval 25 – 29 etc. The class intervals are equal, so a similar method to that used in the previous example is appropriate. In fact the only modification is to the calculation of i.

In this case we use $i = 1 + \text{int } [(x - 20)/5]$

eg when x = 36 $i = 1 + \text{int } [(36 - 20)/5]$

$= 1 + \text{int } [3\tfrac{1}{5}]$

$= 1 + 3$

$= 4$ for the **fourth** class interval frequency.

Note. i. We subtracted 20 because that was the lowest class value.

ii. We divided by 5 because we wanted to divide the total range 45 into 9 equal parts for the 9 class intervals.

37. Constructing the frequency distribution (With unequal classes).
Suppose the previous data was regrouped as follows:—

Service time x seconds	Frequency f
20 – 29	5
30 – 34	4
35 – 39	4
40 – 44	7
45 – 49	8
50 – 54	6
55 – 64	6

The classes are unequal, so to form a frequency table by computer a different approach is required.

38. Methods of construction. Two possible uses are:—

a. **A linear search** ie looking through the class intervals from start to finish until the data value matches the class interval, eg x = 56 would be checked against each interval starting with 20 – 29 until a match at 55 – 64 was found. This is inefficient since on average half the intervals will be searched for each match.

b. **A binary search.** This is better than the linear search. The appropriate half, quarter, eighth etc. of the cells is checked until the appropriate class interval is found. An example follows.

39. Binary Search Example. In this example F(1), F(2) . . . . . F(7) store the frequencies of their respective class intervals.

A second array C( ) is used to hold the **lowest value** in each class, so

	C(1)	=	20
	C(2)	=	30
	C(3)	=	35
	C(4)	=	40
	C(5)	=	45
	C(6)	=	50
	C(7)	=	55
and	C(8)	=	65

Note. C(8) is used as the **upper limit** of the 7th class.

In the following flowchart other notation used is

L for Lower cell number
H for Higher cell number
W for Working value.

40. Flowchart. A method of constructing the frequency distribution.

NB. The pseudocode representation is set as an exercise at the end of this chapter.

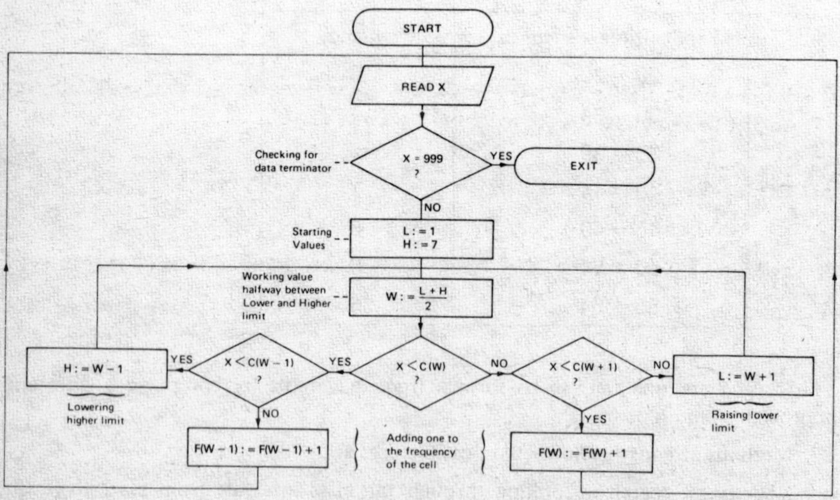

The table below shows successive values when x = 33 is read.

X	L	H	W
33	1	7	4
		3	2

Note. The higher limit is lowered because 33 is in the lower half.

41. **Printout.** It is relatively simple to produce a computer printout of the histogram for a given frequency distribution. The following principles are applied.

a. The frequencies of values are stored in an array.

b. The maximum frequency is used to determine a suitable scale for the output media. (The number of characters per line will be relevant to this).

c. The program will go through a loop in which it prints a number of characters across the page proportional to the cell frequency.

d. Axes and labels will be incorporated as appropriate, eg elements of the vertical axis will be printed within each loop.

SUMMARY.

42. a. The basic terminology – population, sample, discrete or continuous variable, frequency distribution, relative frequency, mean, median, mode etc was introduced.

b. Presentation of data in graphical forms and by numerical measures was demonstrated.

c. Probability was defined and types of distributions discussed. In particular the rectangular distribution (of use to us in the next chapter) was described.

d. Computer methods for constructing histograms were described.

POINTS TO NOTE.

43. a. The work covered was of an introductory nature only. The techniques described are to be used in chapter 51.

b. The computer techniques described have wider uses but you should expect to just be examined on the techniques themselves.

STUDENT SELF TEST QUESTIONS.

(Answers on page 750)

1. *Find the mean, median, range and standard deviation for each of these sets of data.*

a. 49, 13, 56, 26

b. 22, 30, 19, 44, 15

QUESTIONS WITHOUT ANSWERS.

2. *Show that the sequence of numbers 1, 2, 3, 4, 5, 6, 7 has a mean of value 4 and a standard deviation of value 2.*

3. *Write a pseudocode representation of the method given in paragraph 40.*

51 Statistical Simulation

INTRODUCTION.

1. This chapter deals with simulation, which is the mimicking of real-life situations in order to study them. The varied practical applications of simulation make it a popular choice for students' examination projects. This chapter is intended to give the student both a theoretical and practical guide. We start by defining the terms to be used.

2. **Systems.** The **systems** we will consider now are not necessarily computer systems. In this context a **system** will be **any** complex set of interrelated **entities.**

Examples.

a. The traffic system in a town or city where the entitites will be the roadways, traffic lights, queues of cars etc.

b. The system making up a habitat for various animals where the entities will be the animals, plants, geographical features etc.

c. An Industrial complex system in which the entities will be the various plants within the complex and items produced during manufacture.

Other examples of systems could be drawn from modern business, economics, psychological or social systems, and military organisations.

3. **System studies.** To study how a system will perform under different policies or strategies it is obviously not often possible to try out the policy on the real-life system because, apart from the considerable expense, the consequences could be dangerous or even disastrous. The method adopted is that of building and testing a **model.**

4. **Models** are working analogies. A model will not necessarily be a **physical model,** but something which acts like the real system for the properties under investigation. If a policy creates the same results with the model that it does with the real system then the model is a **valid model.**

Example. The game monopoly is certainly a model of the property market system, but clearly not a valid one, otherwise some readers of this book might now own Mayfair!

5. **Choice of Model.** Two basic types of model are:—

a. **The Mathematical model** in which the behaviour of the system can be adequately described in terms of suitable mathematical formulae, equations etc. The various policies can be tried out by substituting suitable values into these equations. (An analog simulation might apply in the case of differential equations 48.2).

b. **The Simulation** model in which the mathematical analysis is too troublesome or impossible and results are obtained by observing the behaviour of the model in particular circumstances. Simulation is often **very costly** and is a **last resort technique.** Even so it is frequently used.

6. Types of Simulation model.

a. **Analog simulation** is used for systems which change continuously with time and which can be expressed in terms of sets of differential equations. We will not discuss them further here (see chapter 48).

b. **Digital Simulation** is used for systems which can be considered to undergo **discrete changes** at various points in time. eg The number of cars in a queue is a whole number which may increase or decrease at a moment in time as a car leaves or arrives.

7. Elements of the Model. The elements of the model can be compared with the features of a board game. These are:—

a. Rules for changes in the **state** of the system which are like the rules of the game which concern the changes in fortune of the players.

b. Book-keeping which corresponds to keeping a score.

c. Sampling from a distribution which corresponds to throwing the dice to determine the next move.

d. Time advance. Not usually having a counterpart in the game but used to keep a track of the time on an imaginary clock recording the real time of events which change the state of the system.

SAMPLING FROM A DISTRIBUTION.

8. Random Sampling. A **random sample** is one chosen in such a way that each member of the population has an equal chance of being selected. The **method of selecting** the sample is thus free of bias.

A standard method of **random sampling** is by the use of **random numbers.**

9. Random Numbers. Random numbers should possess two characteristics:—

a. They should all occur with equal probability.

b. They should be independent of each other.

10. Example. Rolling a die will generate a stream of random numbers with the values 1, 2, 3, 4, 5 and 6. If in the long run all six numbers did not appear to occur with equal frequency then the numbers would **not** be random. They would also **not** be random if there was some pattern to their order which allowed predictions of future values, eg if 4 often followed 6.

11. Pseudo Random Numbers. In simulation experiments it is often required to use exactly the same set of random numbers a second time. This repetition of the **same** random numbers means that in one sense they are not random and they are therefore called **pseudo random numbers.**

The repetition of the same random number stream allows the model to be tested under exactly the same conditions each time.

12. Pseudo random number distributions. The most common distribution used in computer applications is the rectangular distribution (50.31) distributed over the interval from 0 to 1. This is shown below, the pseudo random number is R.

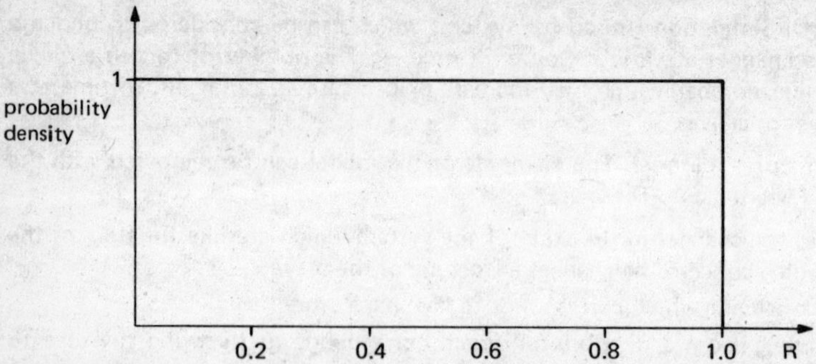

Note. Finite word length results in the variable R not being truly continuous and also in the range being limited to $0 \leqslant R < 1$ or $0 < R < 1$.

13. Generating random variables from random numbers.

a. The method used here is called the **inversion method.** The **cumulative probability** of the random variable is used as a random number value and the corresponding variable value is found. Effectively an **inverse function** is obtained. (Strictly speaking the term inversion should only be used when an actual function and inverse exist).

b. **Example.** R is a random number stream which has rectangular distribution. $0 \leqslant R < 1$. Suppose we wish to simulate a die. The method is illustrated below.

Die value d	1	2	3	4	5	6
Probability	⅙	⅙	⅙	⅙	⅙	⅙
Cumulative probability R	⅙	⅓	½	⅔	⅚	1

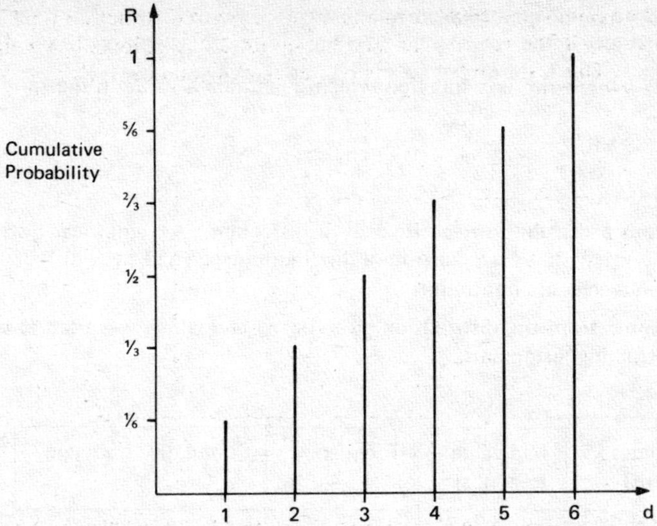

c. **Procedure.**

i. The rectangular distribution of R is sampled.

ii. The corresponding 'd' value is obtained from the graph by drawing a horizontal line across to the vertical line passing the 'd' value.

iii. The 'd' value is then used.

eg A value of R **greater than or equal to** ⅙ but **less than** ⅓ will generate the 'd' value 2.

14. Generating random variables by computer.

The procedure given in the example on simulating a die can be expressed as a function ie d = 1 + int (6 * R)

Examples.

When $R = \frac{1}{12}$ (between 0 and $\frac{1}{6}$)

$$d = 1 + INT\ (6 * \frac{1}{12})$$

$$= 1 + INT\ (\frac{1}{2}) = 1 + 0 = 1$$

When $R = \frac{1}{6}$

$$d = 1 + INT\ (6 * \frac{1}{6})$$

$$= 1 + INT\ (1) = 1 + 1 = 2$$

When $R = 0.9$

$$d = 1 + INT\ (6 * 0.9)$$

$$= 1 + INT\ (5.4) = 1 + 5 = 6$$

15. A die value, d, may be generated as follows:

```
Begin
    R : = rnd (* Where rnd is a function which generates a value in the range
                                                                    0 ≤ R < 1 *)
    d : = 1 + int (6 * R)
end
```

16. Sampling from a distribution specified by a histogram. (An empirical distribution). Suppose we wish to sample from a distribution specified by a histogram for which cell frequencies are not uniform.

Example. To sample from the distribution given below and which was used as an example of constructing histograms.

Service times x (seconds)	Mid value (seconds)	Frequency	Cumulative frequency
20 – 29	24.5	5	5
30 – 34	32	4	9
35 – 39	37	4	13
40 – 44	42	7	20
45 – 49	47	8	28
50 – 54	52	6	34
55 – 64	59.5	6	40

A binary search can be used to obtain x mid-values by comparing an appropriately scaled R value with the cumulative frequency.

17. Pseudocode to sample from a histogram.

Notation. The array 'M' stores mid-values eg M(1) = 24.5. y is a scaled R value for frequency range 0 to 40. x is a mid-value generated by the subroutine.

"low" and "high" are lower and higher cell numbers. The boolean variable is-found is used.

"w" is a working value used in the binary search.

The array 'F' stores lowest cumulative frequency values:–

F(1) = 0   F(2) = 5   F(3) = 9   F(4) = 13
F(5) = 20   F(6) = 28   F(7) = 34   F(8) = 40

The table below shows successive values when R = 0.9

y	low	high	w
36	I	7	4
	5		6
	7		

(* **NB.** R, y and F( ) values are real. low, high and w are integers *)

```
Begin
    (* generate R value *)
    R : = rnd
    (* rescale R value to frequency range *)
    y : = 40 * R
    (* initialise search *)
    low : = 1
    high : = 7
    is_found : = false
    repeat
        w : = (low + high)/2
        if
            y < F(w)
        then
            if
                y < F(w - 1)
            then
                high : = w - 1
            else
                x : = M(w - 1)
                is_found : = true
            endif
        else
            if
                y < F(w + 1)
            then
                x : = M(w)
                is_found : = true
            else
                low : = w + 1
            endif
        endif
    until is_found
end
```

SOURCES OF PSEUDO RANDOM NUMBERS.

18. So far we have assumed that a generator of pseudo random numbers in the range $0 \leqslant R < 1$ is available. We will now consider ways of generating pseudo random numbers.

19. Mid-square Method. (Simple but has faults). Successive numbers are obtained by squaring and extracting the middle digits.

Example using 4 digit numbers. Division by 10,000 gives R values.
Take Starting value x_0 = 4317 and successive values as x_1, x_2, x_3, etc.

x_i	x_i^2
4317	18636489
6364	40500496
5004	25040016
0400	00160000
1600	02560000
5600	31360000
3600	12960000
9600	92160000
1600	02560000

Note that 1600 occurs a second time and the numbers will repeat themselves in the same **cycle** again and again from now on.

The numbers are repeating themselves in a short cycle (ie every fourth number is the same) so they are neither uniformly distributed nor independent.

The method tends to result in one of these faults:

i. short cycles
ii. a greater frequency of low numbers
iii. degeneration to the same number or zero.

20. Mid-Product Method. This tends to give longer cycles and less bias to low numbers. Instead of squaring each x_i value the product $x_{i-1} \cdot x_i$ is used. Two starting values are used.

Example using 4 digit numbers

Take starting values $x_0 = 4317$, $x_1 = 9265$

x_{i-1}		x_i	Product
4317	x	9265	39997005
9265	x	9970	92372050
9970	x	3720	37088400
3720	x	0884	03288480
0884	x	2884	02549456
2884	x	5494	15844696
5494		8446	etc

21. Congruence Methods. Any pseudo random sequence will be cyclic. Congruence methods were devised to achieve pseudo random numbers with long cycles. They tend to produce sufficiently uniform distributions if correctly used and are frequently used in practice.

22. Multiplicative Congruence formula.

The formula is $x_{n+1} = a\ x_n \text{ (Mod b)}$ (See appendix 2.4)

but the constants a and b must be carefully chosen, as must the starting value or "seed" x_0.

Example with **arbitrary** values $a = 5$, $b = 100$, $x_0 = 3$

$$x_{n+1} = 5\ x_n \quad \text{(mod 100)}$$

$$x_0 = 3$$

$$x_1 = 5 \times 3 \quad \text{(mod 100)}$$

$$= 15$$

$$x_2 = 5 \times 15 \quad \text{(mod 100)}$$

$$= 75$$

$$\left.\begin{aligned} x_3 &= 5 \times 75 \quad \text{(mod 100)} \\ &= 375 \quad \text{(mod 100)} \\ &= 75 \end{aligned}\right\} \text{The sequence has degenerated to a constant.}$$

23. Choice of constants. The following points must be considered.

a. The maximum cycle length is never greater than b. So the value b = 100 was too small.

b. To make the division in calculating the modules easy b is chosen as a power of the number base used and so as to have a large cycle the maximum practical value is often used as follows.

i. Using binary arithmetic a suitable choice is $b = 2^w$ where w is the number of bits available eg word length.

ii. Using decimal arithmetic a suitable choice is $b = 10^w$ where w is the number of significant figures used.

c. x_0 should be chosen **relatively prime** to b, ie the only common factor is 1.

d. a should be chosen so that:—

i. $a = 8p \pm 3$ where p is a positive integer. (This improves cycle length).

ii. a is close to $2^{\frac{w}{2}}$ (This prevents successive values being too closely related).

The reasons behind c. and d. are beyond the scope of this book and are drawn from number theory. You may wish to try out these rules by experiment.

24. Setting up and running the model. The following are main points which need to be considered.

a. What information is the model expected to provide?

b. What features must be included in the model to obtain the information?

c. Initial starting values of any simulation run must be realistic eg it may not be reasonable to start with a queue of zero length.

d. Successive states of the system are often closely related, eg long queues **gradually** get shorter. This means that simulation runs often have to be very long in order to provide reasonable estimates of values obtained, such as average queue length.

e. The model requires validation on existing policies before trying new ones.

f. Cost — is it worth the expense to get the information?

SPECIMEN SIMULATION.

25. Passengers enter a station of the "Metro-Dustrap Steam Railway" by queuing at the barrier kiosk for a ticket. It is proposed that automatic barriers be introduced to reduce queues at the kiosk. The barrier will allow entry (to *prepaid* ticket holders) in negligible time. The effect on waiting times under different selling policies is to be investigated by simulation. These selling policies correspond to different distributions of tickets eg existing distribution is 100% manual, another policy might be 80% manual, 20% automatic. The following example shows a first model which might be tried.

26. Plan of Model.

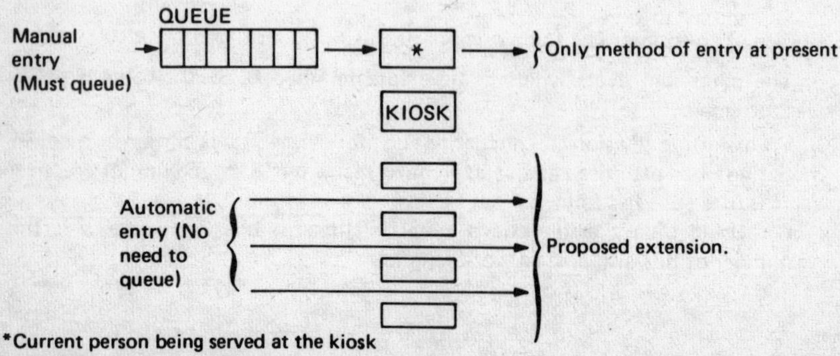

*Current person being served at the kiosk and NOT part of the queue.

27. Figure 51.1 gives an outline program written in pseudocode which carries out the simulation. During the simulation various times are sampled from suitable distributions. For example, the kiosk-service-time, which represents the time till the current person at the kiosk ('*' in the plan model) receives a ticket, is sampled using the function sam-kiosk. The remaining details are given in Fig. 51.1.

```
Program   simulation
          (* This program conducts a simulation of
             the railway described in paragraph 25 *)
variables
          number-entering,            (* ie. number of people entering *)
          queue_length                : integer
          clock_time,                 (* in minutes *)
          arrival-time,               (* ie. time till next passenger arrives to
                                         either queue or enter automatically *)
          kiosk-service-time,         (* goes negative when queue is empty *)
          waiting_time,               (* till next event ie. till passenger
                                         arrival kiosk service completed *)
          total_waiting_time          : real
function  same_arrival: real
          (* samples an arrival_time from the distribution of arrival times *)
function  sam_kiosk : real
          (* samples a kiosk_service_time from the distribution of kiosk service
             times *)
function  sam_entry-automatic : boolean
          (* samples from the distribution of entry methods.
             true represents automatic, false represents manual
             (to be altered for each run) *)
function  min (a, b : real) : real
          (* this function returns the smaller value of a and
             b discounting negative b *)

Begin
            (* initialise variables *)
            clock_time           : = 0
            total_waiting_time   : = 0
            number_entering      : = 0
                  (* NB the arrival_time, kiosk_service_time and queue_length
                        must be set to suitable values using prior knowledge.
                  *)
```

```
        (* carry out a 180 minute simulation run *)
    while clock_time < = 180
            (* find waiting_time till next event *)
            waiting_time : = min (arrival_time, kiosk_service time)
            (* update times *)
            clock_time              : = clock_time             + waiting_time
            arrival_time            : = arrival_time           - waiting_time
            kiosk_service_time      : = kiosk_service_time     - waiting_time
            if
                (* passenger has arrived *)
                arrival–time = 0
            then
                if
                    sam_entry_automatic
                then
                    number_entering : = number_entering + 1
                else
                    (* add new arrival to the queue *)
                    queue_length : = queue_length + 1
                endif
                arrival_time : = sam_arrival
            endif
            if
                (* service to a passenger at the kiosk has ended *)
                kiosk_service_time = 0
            then
                number_entering : = number_entering + 1
            endif
            if
                (* kiosk is free to serve *)
                   kiosk_service_time < = 0
                AND
                (* there is a queue *)
                   queue_length > 0
            then
                (* send one person from the queue to the kiosk *)
                queue_length : = queue_length - 1
                kiosk_service_time : = sam-kiosk
            endif
    endwhile
    (* calculate the averages and output results
       NB. full details of the code are not given here but note that the
       average waiting time is the total_time divided by number_entering
    *)
end
```

Figure 15.1. Outline Program for the Simulation.

MONTE-CARLO METHODS.

28. Definition. A monte-carlo method is any method of solving a problem which makes use of random numbers. The simulation methods met so far are monte-carlo methods.

A more restricted definition requires that the problem be deterministic, ie the answer is an exact ascertainable quantity such as the solution of an equation. We will use the restricted definition.

29. Hit and Miss Monte-Carlo Method.

a. **Example.** Finding the area under the curve $y = x^3 - 2x^2 + x$ between $x = 0$ and $x = 1$. The curve is sketched in the diagram.

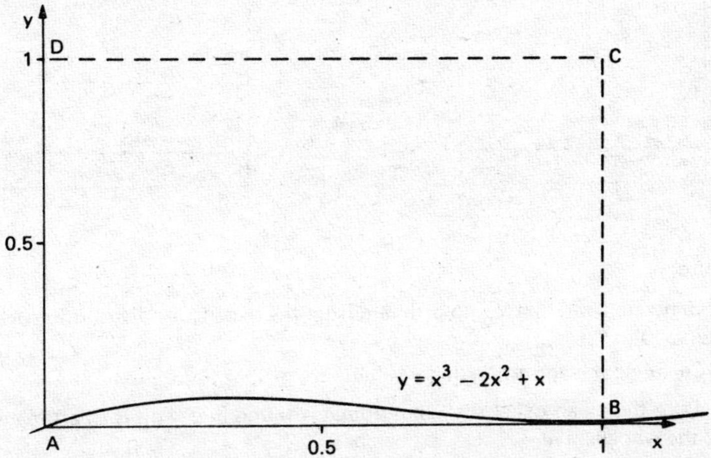

b. **Procedure.**

i. Random points within the square ABCD are obtained by using two random numbers drawn from a rectangular distribution with interval from 0 to 1.

ii. If the point lies above the curve it is a MISS if it lies below or on the curve it is a HIT.

iii. The proportion of HITS is used as an estimate of the area, ie

$$\text{Estimation of area} = \frac{\text{Number of Hits}}{\text{Number of Hits and Misses.}}$$

c. Suppose the first random number obtained is 0.5 and we use it as the x–co-ordinate. The curve will pass through a y value given by

$$\begin{aligned} y &= 0.5^3 - 2 \times 0.5^2 + 0.5 \\ &= 0.125 \end{aligned}$$

If the next random number which is the y co-ordinate is greater than 0.125 it is a MISS.

Note. In this particular case it can easily be shown by calculus that the area is ¼ and so the method is not appropriate. You may however use this result to see the kind of accuracy you can get using the method.

30. "Crude" Monte-Carlo Method. It is more accurate than 'HIT and MISS' because the estimate is based on less variable values.

Example. To calculate the same area as before. We use the fact that

(Area under curve) = (Average (mean) height of curve) x (Base length of curve)

and take a sample of curve heights to *estimate* the average height ($\bar{y}$).

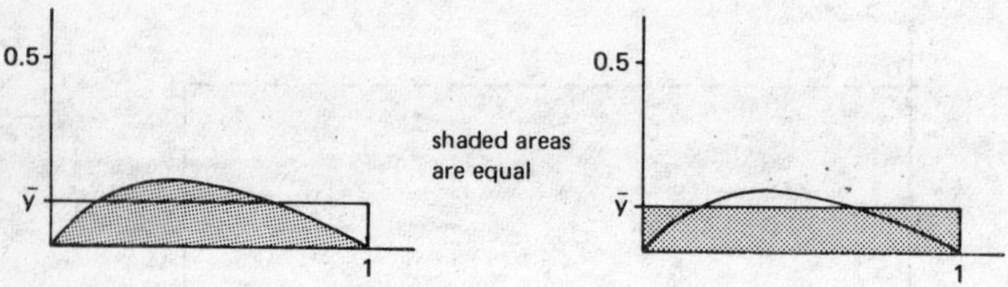

Procedure.

a. Generate a random x– co-ordinate from the rectangular distribution over the interval 0 to 1.

b. Calculate the corresponding y value.

c. Take the mean of all the y co-ordinates found in b. This is an estimate of $\bar{y}$ for the whole curve.

d. Area estimate = (Estimated height) x (base length)
= $\bar{y}$ estimate x 1 = $\bar{y}$ estimate.

SUMMARY.

31. a. We restricted our attention to digital simulation of systems which could be considered to undergo discrete changes.

b. Random number and Pseudo Random numbers were discussed in terms of their use in sampling from distributions.

c. Generation of random variable by computer was illustrated, as was sampling from a histogram.

d. The following methods of generating pseudo-random numbers were described:—

i. Mid-square method.
ii. Mid-produce method.
iii. Congruence Methods.

e. A specimen simulation was provided.

POINTS TO NOTE.

32. a. Many high level languages provide random number generator functions often a rectangular distribution which can be used to generate other distributions eg those specified by a histogram.

b. Several special purpose simulation languages are available eg C.S.L. They usually provide a choice of random number generators and have features which aid the procedures of **state changes** and **time advance.**

c. The presentation of simulation results requires the use of methods described in the previous chapter eg producing histograms and finding averages. These aid interpretation of results.

d. This topic can provide a number of opportunities for examination course work but care should be taken to handle the work in thorough fashion even if there are limitations to its validity.

e. The methods of pseudo random number generation can often be employed for **address generation algorithms** when using random access files.

STUDENT SELF TEST QUESTIONS.

(Answers on page 750)

1. *Describe a method for a subroutine for a digital computer to generate pseudo-random numbers uniformly distributed in the range (0, 1).*

Describe how this subroutine would be used in a program for simulating a system in which it is required to generate pseudo random numbers between 0 and 5 corresponding to the distribution given by the following histogram.

Range	*(0, 1)*	*(1, 2)*	*(2, 3)*	*(3, 4)*	*(4, 5)*
Frequency	*2*	*6*	*10*	*8*	*4*

(A.E.B. Specimen paper)

Computers in Context

1. In this Part we take a broader view of computers in terms of their general setting historically and in society.

2. Throughout the rest of this manual every effort has been made to present the reader with a modern view of computers. The reader's understanding will be increased by also seeing how computing took place in the past and why it changed to what it is today. For that reason an account of the evolution of computer systems is provided in the following chapter.

3. In chapter 53 we look at the role of computers in society and consider issues which affect individuals and the organisations in which individuals use computers.

52 The Evolution of Computer Systems

INTRODUCTION.

1. Most modern computers are based upon general design principles which were established during the 1940s and which have not changed greatly since then. In striking contrast, changes in technology have revolutionised the ways in which computers are made.

2. In this chapter we consider not only those changes which led to the creation of the first true computers in the 1940s but we also consider the changes which have taken place since then.

THE ORIGINS.

3. In looking for the origins of computers it is useful first to consider the origins of the methods of representating and storing data.

4. In ancient times herdsmen devised rudimentary methods of counting in which the number of pebbles, sticks or scratches on stone corresponded to the number of animals in their care. At a latter date the use of those simple scratches led to the idea of using stylized pictures or symbols to represent objects, numbers and ultimately languages. Such representations provided a means of storing information for subsequent retrieval and use. The use of inventories and libraries exemplify two aspects of the use of such data.

5. Modern computers provide sophisticated ways of providing these long established facilities.

THE DEVELOPMENT OF CALCULATING DEVICES.

6. Simple calculating devices were already in use over two thousand years ago. A notable example of such a device is the **abacus** which is a mechanised pebble counter in which beads are strung on wires or strings held in a frame. (See Fig. 52.1). The beads are slid along the wires when counting, adding etc.

A Simple Abacus

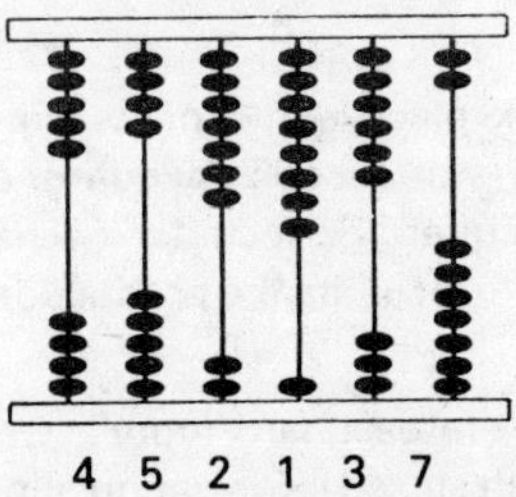

Figure 52.1. A simple form of abacus.

The abacus is still used today in parts of Asia.

7. The seventeenth century was the time for many significant developments:

a. In 1614 **John Napier,** a Scottish mathematician, invented logarithms. Logarithms aid manual multiplication and division.

b. In 1617 Napier devised a set of rods for use as multiplication aids. The rods were carved from bone and often called **"Napier's bones".**

c. In 1620 **William Oughtred,** an English parson, invented the **slide rule,** an **analog** calculating device which uses the principles of logarithms. (Fig. 52.2).

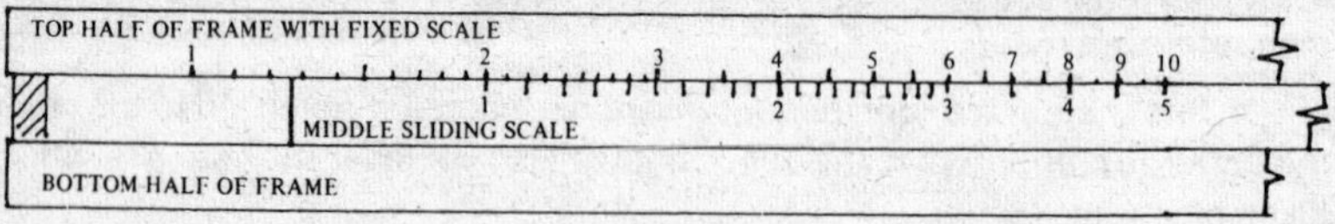

The middle scale has been positioned with the '1' against the '2' of the top scale so that multiples of 2 can be read off along the scale. Alternatively the scale shows divisions giving quotients of 2.

Figure 52.2. A section of a simple slide rule.

d. In 1623 **Francis Bacon** made the first known use of binary codes for number representation.

e. In 1642 the French mathematician **Blaise Pascal** devised **the first true calculating machine.** It consisted of a series of six numbered dials and a ratchet "carry" mechanism. Addition and subtraction were straighforward but multiplication and division were slow and laborious. Pascal's contribution to computing was given a mark of recognition in the later 1960s when Professor **Niklaus Wirth** of Zurich named his new programming language **"Pascal".**

f. In 1671 the German mathematician **Gottfried von Leibniz** invented a calculating machine capable of true multiplication and division. The machine was a development of Pascal's idea. The new feature was a **shift mechanism.** Pascal had already devised a method of number complements for use in subtraction.

AUTOMATION.

8. A major advance took place early in the nineteenth century through the brilliantly imaginative efforts of **Joseph Jacquard,** a french textile manufacturer. Between 1802 and 1804 Jacquard perfected a mechanical means of automatically controlling weaving looms to facilitate the production of woven cloth with complex patterns.

9. The machine, called "the Jacquard loom", was programmed by means of special punched cards which stored information about the required patterns in the cloth. These punched cards were strung tightly together side by side in a long

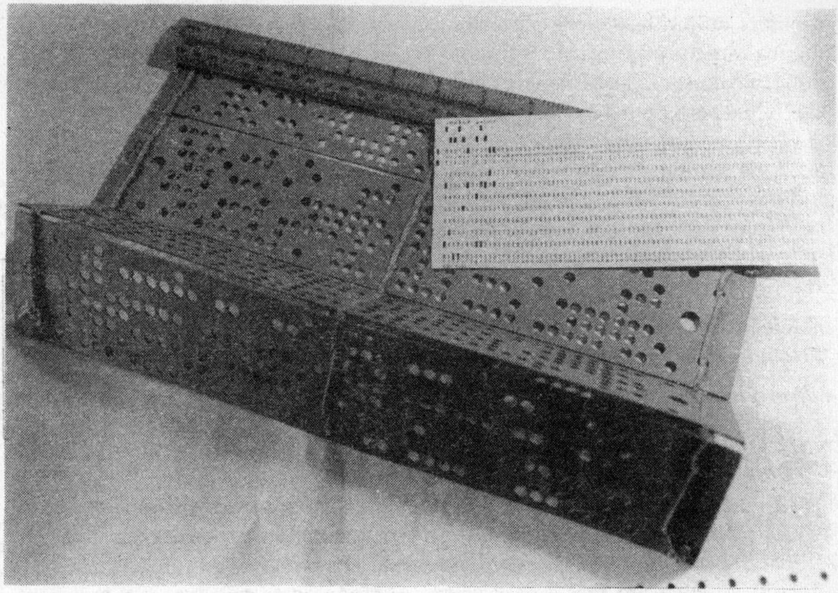

An 80 column punched card on top of Loom Cards of the same type as those used by Joseph Jacquard.

continuous strip. They were automatically fed through a loom mechanism in sequence with the purpose of controlling the loom's weaving action. The pattern in woven cloth is produced by raising particular selections of warp thread (those fixed to the frame) each time the shuttle is passed across the frame. In the Jacquard loom each warp could be raised by an individual hook unless a sprung pin deflected the hook. If the sprung pin aligned with a hole in a punched card, one end of the pin would pass through the hole so that the other end of the pin failed to deflect the hook. Before each pass of the shuttle the next card was moved close to the pins. Then, as the mechanism operated, each warp was either raised, or not raised according to the rule:

Hole in card – warp thread raised.
No hole in Card – warp thread raised.

10. The binary nature of the representation should be apparent to the reader.

11. Jacquard's loom was the start of a chain of developments which has lead to the robot operated factory production lines of today.

12. The automation of calculations was attempted within a few years of Jacquard's invention by **Charles Babbage** a Professor of Mathematics at Cambridge University. In 1822 Babbage demonstrated a small working model of his **"Difference Engine"** to the Royal Society. The demonstration won government backing for Babbage who wished to produce a larger machine able to generate reliable astronomical and mathematical tables containing values accurate to 20 decimal places. The machine was never completed because of mechanical difficulties. However, Babbage's researches led him to develop the concept of an **"Analytic Engine"**, essentially a general purpose automatic calculator, which he designed in 1834. Its design owed much to Jacquard's invention and incorporated many features present in modern computers:–

a. Data and program instructions fed in a via a device using a suitable medium (punched cards).
b. Storage facilities for data and instructions.
c. A mechanised unit for calculation – a "mill".
d. A suitable output device.

13. Lady Ada Lovelace, an amateur mathematician and friend of Babbage produced supporting material for the analytic engine in the form of programs and explanatory documentation. It may be argued that Lady Lovelace was the first programmer. The programming language "Ada" has been named after her.

14. Computer Logic. An important theoretical development occurred between 1847 and 1854 as **George Boole,** an English Logician, devised an algebraic system, now called "Boolean Algebra", for representing and manipulating logical expressions. The full significance of these developments was not realised at the time.

15. Hermann Hollerith. Dr. Hermann Hollerith was a census statistician at the U.S. census bureau in the mid 1880's. At that time the bureau was still trying to count results from the 1880 census and saw little prospect of completing the count before the next census which was scheduled for 1890. Hollerith proposed a mechanised solution to the problem which was based upon equipment handling punched cards. His idea was to 'code' the data by representing it by punched hole combinations on the cards. Some equipment was used to punch holes in the card. Other equipment was able to process the data by detecting holes in the cards. Electrical contacts brushed the cards and made contact through holes in the cards as the cards passed through the device. These devices were called **tabulators.** Tabulators were also used for the semi-automatic selection and sorting of cards.

16. The impact of Hollerith's methods was very striking. Whereas the census of 1880 on 50 million citizens had taken over 7 years to complete, the census of 1890 on 63 million citizens took only 3 years to complete.

17. These ideas were exploited further by the development of devices rather like difference engines fed with cards which could perform calculations like those designed by Babbage. Other developments continued in the commercial application of these machines.

18. Hollerith set up his own company, "The Computing Tabulating Recording Company" which later became the International Business Machine Corporation **(IBM)** which today is by far the largest computer manufacturer in the world.

THE DEVELOPMENT OF ELECTRICAL AND ELECTRONIC METHODS.

19. Recording Devices, Valves & Switching Circuits. In 1900 **Valdemar Poulson** was developing recording devices which used media consisting of tapes and drums coated with thin films of magnetic material. These were the fore runners of a host of modern devices, including domestic audio tape records, cassette recorders, Video cassette recorders, and of particular interest, computer data storage devices, including several versions also using magnetic tape. An even more significant technological advance took place in 1906 when **Lee de Forest** invented the **thermionic valve.** A valve resembles a squat cylindrical light bulb glowing dimly, into which has been inserted a number of additional wires and metalic plates. Valves are able to amplify or switch electrical signals electronically, ie. without the movement of electrical or mechanical parts. **Electronic Switching** is a vital feature within modern digital computers, and valves were the first devices to be employed for that purpose. Valves have since been superseded by newer and better alternatives.

20. The use of Electronic Switching Circuits in computers is largely due to the fact that such circuits can be employed to perform logic and arithmetic. This fact was established in 1938 by **Claude Shannon,** an electrical engineer. Shannon showed how the hitherto theoreticaly Boolean Algebra could be applied to practical problems of circuit design.

21. Another important theoretical step took place one year before Shannon's discovery when in 1937 **Alan Turing,** A British Mathematician, showed how *any* problem having a logical solution can be reduced to a solution based upon a small set of simple instructions. Modern computers are therefore able to solve very complex problems by the rapid application of a relatively small set of inbuilt operations.

22. From Electrical Machines to Electronic Machines.

a. **The Automatic Sequence Controlled Calculator (ASCC)** – Also called the **Harvard Mark 1.**

The ASCC was a fully automatic electrically driven machine. Its development was started at Harvard University USA in 1937 by Professor **Howard Aiken** in conjunction with IBM.

Hollerith cards containing data or instructions were fed into the machine a few at a time and results were output onto punched cards or an electric typewriter. Aiken also developed punched paper tape as an input medium. The machine was completed in 1944 and was used until 1959.

b. **Early special purpose electronic machines.**

i. During the second world war electronic valve based calculating machines called Z3 and Z4, were produced in Germany by **Konrad Zuse.** They are known to have been used for a time in 1941, and to have used stored programs to perform calculations, but they were later destroyed by Allied Bombing.

ii. In Britain at the same time another valve based machine called **COLOSSUS** was produced at the British Intelligence Establishment at Bletchley Park. **Alan Turing** was a member of staff on the project. The machine was used in 1943 to break a top secret German code called ENIGMA.

c. **Electronic Numerical Integrator and Calculator (ENIAC).** This machine was developed by **J. Presper Eckert** and **John Mauchly** at Pennsylvania University and was completed by 1946. It was the electronic equivalent of the ASCC and contained some 18,000 valves. It could perform 5000 additions per second, an astonishing feat at the time, but consumed 150 kilowatts of power, which would be enough to heat a mansion, and needed to be water cooled.

23. The Von Neumann Report. In what is now an historic report **John Von Neumann** in 1946 set out a summary of the design requirements for the modern computer. The main points were:–

a. Binary codes should be used for the representation of Data and Instructions in a way which would make no distinction between them, and allows them to be stored together and share the same storage space within the computer.

b. The computer should be able to process both data and instructions. This includes the modification of programs by programs.

These two principles contain within them the possibilities for the controlled modification and manipulation of data and instructions under one automatic process.

COMPUTER GENERATIONS WITH CHANGING TECHNOLOGY.

25. The First Generation. The "first generation" computers were valve based machines based upon Von Neumann's design principles. Starting with the first they included:–

a. **Electronic Delay Storage Automatic Computer (EDSAC).** This machine was built at Cambridge University by **M.V. Wilkes** and first ran in May 1949.

b. **Electronic Discrete Variable Automatic Computer (EDVAC).** This machine was built at Pennsylvania University, the home of ENIAC, and was completed in 1950.

c. **Automatic Computer Engine (ACE).** This was built at the National Physics laboratory in 1951.

d. **Lyons Electronic Office (LEO).** This was the *first commercial computer* and it was produced in 1951 by **M.V. Wilkes.**

e. **UNIVAC–1.** This machine was produced by UNIVAC (Universal Accounting Company) in 1951. The company was set up by Eckert and Maunchly.

26. The Transistor was invented in 1948 by a team of scientists headed by **William Shockley** at the Bell Laboratories in America. Transistors are made from materials called **semiconductors** principally silicon (the main element in sand and rock), and germanium. A transistor is produced by 'doping' layers of crystal with impurities which drastically alter the electrical properties of each layer.

27. Transistors are able to perform similar operations to valves eg. amplification or switching, but they are simpler to manufacture less prone to failure, cheaper, smaller, consume less power and have a longer life. They have replaced valves in all but a few specialist applications. Transistors and developments from them are often called **solid-state devices.**

28. Simple transistor circuits called **bistables** (two stable states) or **flip-flops** are of particular importance. They can be built to flip from one state to the other and back again in a clock like fashion, or built to hold either state until switched to the other by a single electrical pulse. These bistable states suggest the possibilities for using them for storing binary coded data.

29. The Second Generation. "Second generation" computers used transistors instead of valves. The use of transistors reduced size, manufacturing costs and running cost, and improved reliability and processing power. Early second generation models were the IBM 7000 series and LEO mark III. In 1962 Manchester University completed what was probably the best known second generation machine, the **ATLAS.** ATLAS used **magnetic disk storage** and exploited the features of disk storage very well.

30. During the second generation manufacturers moved towards making computers of **modular construction.** A suitable combination of processing, storage, input and output units could be assembled from a range of possible modules in order to meet the particular needs of each customer.

31. Also at that time there were major advances in computer languages away from codes directly usable by the machine (ie. machine languages) and towards the 'natural' languages of English and Mathematics. The first of the **"high level languages"** called **FORTRAN** (FORmula TRANslation) was released in 1957. Over the next few years many other new languages appeared. (See chapter 30).

32. Integrated Circuits. After the invention of the transistor it was realised that the properties of semiconductors would allow the production of entire electronic circuits within single crystals. The name **Integrated Cricuit (IC)** was adopted for such units. The first IC was patented by **Harwick Johnson** of RCA in 1953 although the inventor is said to be **Jack Kilby** of the USA. Later developments resulted from;

a. the application of photo engraving to IC manufacture,

b. the use of layers of silicon oxide insulation in order to build up multiple layers of crystal circuitry.

The latter of these two methods is often referred to as **MOS technology (Metal-Oxide- Semiconductor).**

33. The Third Generation. "Third generation" computers using integrated circuits were first released onto the market in 1964. Two of the successful first series of third generation computers were the IBM 360 series and the ICL 1900 series.

34. LSI and VLSI have been discussed in several earlier chapters and therefore do not require further detailed discussion here. One important LSI development which does deserve another mention here is the microprocessor. The first microprocessor was the model 4004 produced by the Intel corporation in 1972.

THE PRESENT AND THE FUTURE.

35. Technological advances continue to make an even greater number of applications cost effective to computerise. For example, office automation has increased dramatically over recent years.

36. Magnetic media costs have fallen relative to paper costs so that computerised filing system are cheaper than conventional systems for many applications. Some predictions imply that magnetic media will be cheaper than paper for all but a few applications within eight years.

37. The developments in distributed systems and networks, together with advances in data bases have placed the computer systems of today into a position to play a far greater role within the organisations they serve. At the same time we see computers being successfully employed for many new applications all the time.

38. There are still many problems to be faced, however. Greater reliance on computers calls for greater reliability. More applications areas means the need for more software. The more widespread use of computers means the need for systems which are easy for almost anyone to use.

39. Although hardware costs have fallen, software development costs continue to rise. Modern methods of analysis, design and programming attempt to tackle the problem of software cost and produce systems which meet the user's requirements to a high standard of reliability.

40. Even more radical approaches to solving these problems are being taken, such as the design of new machine architectures (9.67) and new types of programming languages (30.30).

41. Considerably more effort will need to be made in solving such problems as those of human/machine communication, the so called "man machine interface".

42. Clearly, computers have come a long way in the last forty years and who can say what state of development they may be at in another forty years? It is not inconceivable that the changes may be even greater than in the past. However, the really major questions concerning computers and the future are not technical ones but questions about how people, organisations and society at large will use them and regard them.

SUMMARY.

43. a. This chapter has traced the origins of modern computers.

b. The work of a number of computer pioneers was described. Here is a checklist of names:– John Napier, William Oughtred, Blaise Pascal, Niklaus Wirth, Gottfried Von Leibnitz, Joseph Jacquard, Francis Bacon, Charles Babbage, Ada Lovelace, George Boole, Hermann Hollerith, Valdermar Poulson, Lee de Forest, Claude Shannon, Alan Turing, Howard Aiken, Konrad Zuse, J. Presper Eckert, John Mauchly, John Von Neuman, William Shockley, Harwick Johnson, Jack Kilby and M.V. Wilkes.

c. Technical innovations, followed by advances in manufacturing methods, have made the use of computers in many situations not only technically feasible but also cost effective. The range of cost effective applications is broadening all the time.

53 The Social Aspects

INTRODUCTION.

1. The role of computers in society is a large subject to consider and this chapter merely highlights some important issues. Computers are just one example of automation although they have many special features. In a society which relies heavily on all forms of automation and on the automated handling of information, computers are bound to be very important. Issues related to jobs and privacy are particularly siginificant.

COMPUTERS IN INFORMATION TECHNOLOGY.

2. It is generally recognised that we live in an industrial society in which the efficency of production of wealth depends heavily on various kinds of automation. Computers are special in that they *automate many methods of processing information.* Computers are also playing an ever increasing role in many other forms of automation.

3. Computers, telecommunications equipment, and other technologies associated with automation, come under the general heading of **Information Technology (IT)**. Information Technology is having an impact on individuals, organisations and society. Various aspects of this impact will be discussed in the remainder of this chapter. Particular reference will be made to computers, and some key issues, notably privacy and employment.

THE GENERAL BACKGROUND.

4. Prior to industrialisation approximately 90% of the labour force was engaged in agriculture, ie. society was agrarian. Methods of communication were limited and a very small proportion of the labour force was involved with the processing, storage and retrieval of information, which in any case merely involved manual paper based methods or word of mouth.

Industrialisation produced a major shift in the labour force, with the proportion involved in agriculture falling below 10% in the UK. With industrialisation came the beginning of Information Technology and the start of a series of IT developments taking us right up to the present day:- Telegraph, Telephone, Radio/TV, Computers, Microelectronics etc.

5. These new forms of IT, and other developments, produced new forms of work. The larger scale of organisations has given rise to large administrative structures in which there are large numbers of clerical workers and people with technical and managerial skills collectively known as "white collar workers". Computerisation has mainly affected white collar work so far.

6. In addition to changes in the type of work there has been an increase in the number of organisations involved in activities other than manufacture. Some such organisations, for example those in the power industries, contribute to manufacturing and provide a general service. As a result of this change only 25%

of the labour force remained in organisations directly involved in the manufacture of goods. For a number of reasons, not particularly related to IT, that 25% has fallen to 20% in the last few years and levels of unemployment have risen.

7. The fact that so few remain in manufacture, although manufacturing continues to generate most wealth, has lead to society today being called "Post Industrial Society".

8. Looking at the whole of the national and international community, and at the way organisations are run, highlights the fact that modern society is heavily dependent on the communication, processing and storage of information. It is claimed by some, that we are moving towards an "Information Society" in which the majority of the labour force will be engaged in Information Processing and the use of "Information Technology".

9. It is a mistake to imagine that technological innovation is what causes such changes. Such changes are the collective result of actions taken by those people able to control and influence the use and distribution of resources, within their own organisations, or within society at large. The uses of resources are determined by the goals which are being pursued. The next section looks at these issues.

ORGANISATIONS.

10. The uses of computers in various kinds of organisations have been discussed in a number of earlier chapters. The term "organisation" was used fairly informally. However, it is possible to be more formal in defining what an organisation is and doing so highlight some significant points.

11. An organisation is a human group which has been deliberately constructed with the aim of seeking specific goals. An organisation will be reconstructed, from time to time, so that it can continue to seek its goals effectively.

12. The goals sought will depend on the organisation.

Examples:

a. The owners of commercial organisations may have profit as their goal with themselves as the main beneficiaries eg. in private or public companies.

b. The goals of many organisations are to provide *"services"* to their clients or the general public eg. medical services, schools and colleges.

c. Other organisations have the mutual benefits of their members as goals eg. clubs or trade unions.

13. Any organisation needs to be controlled and coordinated and to be able to plan ahead. To do so it will need information and facilities to communicate.

14. In most organisations, and particularly in large ones, Information Technology can aid in the processing of information and thereby help the organisation to meet its goals. Whether or not an organisation uses such technology will depend on its evaluation of the technology in relation to its own goals.

EVALUATION OF INFORMATION SYSTEMS.

15. There are many methods of evaluating new methods and technologies. In the area of computerisation the main methods are those used in Systems Analysis (chapters 40-43). A proposed computer system is evaluated in terms of how well it can meet objectives which will enable the organisation to meet goals such as profit, service or optimum use of resources.

16. The results of such evaluations determine whether organisations invest in computers. This in turn promotes or limits technological developments.

17. Large organisations such as government bodies or large corporations can have a major influence in this way. For example the US government attached a high importance to micro-electronics and silicon chip technology because of the goals of providing national defence. That depended on having miniaturised electronic circuitry in rockets, planes etc. The necessary research and development costs were provided from the defence budget.

COMPUTERISATION AND WORK.

18. When computers are introduced into organisations because of the benefits they can provide, it usually affects the work of staff within the organisation. Some jobs are changed, some may be created and some may be lost. This creates a demand for training and retraining.

19. Any loss of jobs due to computerisation can give rise to alarm particularly at a time of high unemployment. However, such job "losses" probably signify yet another shift in the work of the general labour force as has happended many times in the past.

20. Only a very small proportion of the current level of unemployment is directly attributable to new technology. In certain particular applications jobs are likely to be lost, notably:

a. Some office jobs eg. caused by Word Processing.

b. Factory production where industrial robots may replace production line workers.

21. Whether these job losses will result in permanent unemployment is another matter. It depends on the process of redeployment of labour and labour retraining. It may help to consider an example at this stage.

22. In the USA in the early 1970s there were proposals to introduce bar coded PoS equipment into supermarkets. This appeared to be an attractive proposition because a saving of $100 million could be achieved if such equipment was introduced into 5000 stores.

23. Initially there was alarm from the trade unions who predicted 20% job losses by 1975, the date at which implementation was due to be completed.

24. These fears were unfounded for two reasons. First, the rate at which the new technology was introduced was much slower which allows staffing changes to be dealt with by redeployment and natural wastage. By 1979 only 803 stores had equipment installed. Very different from the predicted 5000 by 1975. The trade unions were also able to negotiate an automation deal with their employers. This protected their jobs. The store owners were still able to make large savings by the introduction of the equipment, and to redeploy staff in ventures which improved and extended company activities. (In Britain the banks have also used automation to allow them to redeploy staff in broader and better services).

25. Since these early difficulties were overcome the introduction of the equipment has continued smoothly in the USA and at an increasing rate. In Britain this kind of supermarket automation is only just under way.

PRIVACY.

26. Another consequence of higher levels of computerisation is the increase in the use of computer based equipment to store large quantities of data about individuals. Some of this data is of a particularly personal or private nature and there is a natural concern that it should not be misused. There is also concern that individuals may have personal information stored about them without their knowledge or control, and that it may be hard or impossible to find out whether such information is accurate.

27. In 1975 a government white paper considered this issue and in 1976 a committee was set up chaired by Sir Norman Lindop. The idea was that systems dealing with records containing personal details should be controlled.

28. The Lindop report appeared about two years later and was well received. It established a number of principles eg. that stored data should only be used for the purpose for which its use was originally authorised and intended. The report suggested that a **Data Protection Authority (DPA),** should be set up which would enforce codes of conduct for different types of systems.

29. At about the same time, the Council of Europe set up a "Convention for the Protection of Individuals with regard to Automatic Processing of Personal Data". Each country signs twice, once to agree to legislate and the second time when it has legislated. Britain had only signed once by early 1984 and computer organisations such as the BCS (British Computer Society) and CSA (Computer Services Association) have expressed fears that delays could cost the UK dearly in terms of lost international contracts through failure to introduce legislation.

30. Such legislation is the primary responsibility of the Home Office, itself an important user of computer data banks of an unusual kind, eg. those concerned with police records like those held on the Police National Computer at Hendon (North London).

31. A further government white paper appeared early in 1982. It only covered some aspects of data protection. In April 1983 a bill began its passage through Parliament but ran into initial trouble over the issue of confidentiality. The bill was lost when the general election was called. It was reintroduced, in a slightly modified form, in 1984.

THE FUTURE.

32. The current rapid rate of computerisation and technical innovation has lead some people to talk of a "micro electronics revolution". To others these changes are merely viewed as another phase in the process of automation which started with the industrial revolution. Either way it seems reasonable to expect change and yet more change in the future.

33. The "fifth generation" supercomputers may well be here by the end of this century if current research and development programmers keep to schedule. Who can say whether these computers will cause delight or dismay? The answers do not rest in the technology.

SUMMARY.

34. a. The place of computers in Information Technology was discussed.

b. The general background to the current state of computerisation in society was given.

c. Organisations were defined and their role in computerisation was discussed.

d. Computerisation and its impact on employment was discussed.

e. Privacy and recent development in data protection were discussed.

f. The future was considered briefly.

POINTS TO NOTE.

35. a. Computerisation is not just a matter of technological innovation and development. It is a process which involves individuals, organisations and society in general.

Revision Test Questions

1. What is understood by the terms *high-level* and *low-level* when applied to programming languages? Write down **three** major factors that influence the decision to write a program in a low-level language rather than a high-level language.

Describe, with the aid of a flow diagram or its equivalent, how the number of binary ones in a computer word could be counted using an assembly language.

[11]

(Welsh 1983)

2. a. Explain what is meant by an arithmetic shift, making particular reference to what happens at each end of a word when this shift is applied.

Show the result of applying a 2-bit arithmetic left shift and a 2-bit arithmetic right shift on each of the following signed integers, where the first bit is a sign bit (twos-complement convention).

0011110
and 1101110

State the decimal equivalent of each number in your working.

b. Given that x = 1010101 and y = 1100011 evaluate the result of x AND y, x OR y, and x NOT-EQUIVALENT y.

Write down a briefly worded set of instructions to show how the partial sum *s* and the carry bits *c* can be obtained when adding two numbers by using the NOT-EQUIVALENT operation and the AND operation combined with a left shift.

c. Show how a 24-bit word can be arranged to store from left to right a decimal integer in the range −100 to +100, a decimal integer in the range 0 to 1023 and a 6-bit character. Show how each of these groups of bits can be extracted and placed at the right hand end of separate registers.

(AEB 1977)

3. Read the following description of an (imaginary) compiler and explain briefly the meaning, in this context, of each italicised term.

"This is a load-and-go compiler, reading *source code* from a deck of punched cards and writing *object code* directly into core storage. After a successful *compilation* control is passed to the user program which uses the compiler's workspace for variable storage. During compilation, this workspace contains the *'name-table'* of variable names and corresponding locations. Mathematical routines are used either as *open subroutines* in the user program or as *closed subroutines* in the compiler library, which remains in core during *execution.*"

(LONDON 1977)

4. Describe briefly what is meant by **three** of the following:

i. multiprogramming
ii. hybrid computation
iii. virtual storage
iv. optical character recognition
v. interactive computing.

(BCS Part 1 1975)

5. a. Explain what is meant by an **executive routine** (supervisor or director routine) in an operating system.

b. Discuss:

i. **three** aspects of a **job** which can be taken into account by an operating system to decide whether a job should be started in a multiprogramming situation and explain why each aspect is significant;

ii. the actions which need to be taken by an operating system, and why they are necessary, where a job is terminated;

iii. **three** of the functions of the executive routine (other than those relating to job starting and termination).

(OLE 1976)

[Author's note: For 'executive routine' read 'executive.]

6. What is meant by batch processing?

Describe a typical example of the application of this technique which involves the sorting and sequencing of a transaction tape and the updating of a master file.

(AEB Specimen paper)

7. a. Four binary input signals are denoted by a, b, c, d where abc represents an octal integer and d is a control signal. An output signal x is required where x = 1 if d = 1 and abc represents 2,3,6 or 7, and x = 1 if d = 0 and abc represents 2 or 3, otherwise x = 0. Draw up a table to represent the above system of signals and sketch an equivalent logic diagram using AND, OR and NOT elements. **(12)**

b. What is an analog device? Briefly discuss, with the aid of an example, how such a device may be used in conjunction with a digital computer. **(8)**

(AEB 1979)

8. a. Explain the difference between an *operand* and an *operand address* as used with reference to an assembly language. State **four** ways in which the address part of a machine level instruction may be used and give an example of each. **(6)**

b. Describe **one** method of representing alphanumeric characters for storage in a fixed word length of 24 bits. State **two** machine code operations which are desirable for the internal manipulation of such characters. **(3)**

c. Describe, with the aid of a diagram, **one** method of storing data items based on the principle of *last in—first out*. Draw flow diagrams to show how an item of data can be removed from the store you have described and how an item of data can be input, incorporating tests to examine whether the store is full or empty as necessary. **(11)**

(AEB 1979)

9. a. Explain, with the aid of a block diagram, how the major functional units of a simple computer are interrelated with respect to the flow of information (ie instructions and data) and the flow of control commands.
Note: *Use firm lines to show the information flow and dotted lines to show flow of control commands.* **(7)**

b. Draw a flow diagram to represent the basic process of the *fetch-execute* cycle in the control unit of a typical computer, naming and stating the functions of any special registers involved. Your diagram should show how the cycle takes account of jumps, address modification and indirect addressing.
Note: *You are not required to discuss or represent the electronic circuitry of the control unit.* **(13)**

(AEB 1979)

10. Explain the functions of the following personnel in a computer installation and outline how their jobs inter-relate.

a. Computer Manager, **(4)**
b. Systems Analyst, **(6)**
c. Programmer, **(5)**
d. Computer Operator. **(5)**

(AEB 1978)

11. a. What is meant by *multiprocessing, networks, message switching* and *terminals?* [3, 3, 3, 3]

b. Backing storage for a network can be distributed, or concentrated at a point, or both. Discuss the advantages of these arrangements in relation to the type of work to be done. [8]

c. A network can be provided with intelligent terminals (terminals with processing power). Describe an application for this and explain why it would be an advantage. [5]

(OLE 1983)

12. a. Explain the term *subroutine* and describe the purpose of subroutines. (3 marks)

b. How do *open* subroutines differ from *closed* subroutines? What advantage does the closed subroutine offer over the open variety? (5 marks)

c. A subroutine is stored from locations 1199 to 1250 inclusive. It will be called from location 499 and from location 699 in the main program. Using these store locations:

i. explain the problem of subroutine linkage – the problem of organising return addresses when calling a subroutine from different points in a main program.
ii. describe **two** methods of solving the linkage problem. (8 marks)

d. The subroutine in (c) evaluates a result (R) given a parameter (X).

Explain:

i. how the value of parameter X might be passed from the main program to the subroutine.

ii. how the value of result R might be returned to the main program on completion of the subroutine. (4 marks)

(AEB 1980)

13. i. Convert the following BASIC expression into a Reverse Polish form in which the variables appear in the same order as in the original expression:

A * (B + C) – (D/E)

(2 marks)

ii. Why is the Reverse Polish form of an expression such as this particularly convenient for processing during the execution of a program? (2 marks)

iii. Describe an algorithm, making use of a stack, that converts an expression such as that given in (i) into a Reverse Polish form. You should give a table indicating the priority of your operators. (6 marks)

iv. Trace the algorithm you have given in (iii), using as input the expression in (i), by listing the contents of the stack, whenever these contents change. (5 marks)

(London 1982)

14. a. The array T has numeric elements T(I) held in ascending order, where I ranges from 1 to 1000. Describe in either flowchart or pseudocode form a program to locate which, if any, element has the value N using the method known as binary search (binary chop). (10 marks)

b. Given below is a subset of the statements available in a particular assembly language. Write a program in this assembly language to load into the accumulator the element in the Ith row and Jth column of an array A which has 14 rows and 10 columns. Include the statement to allocate space to this array assuming that each array element occupies one storage location.

The assembly language subset:

FRED:	DEF	n	reserves n storage locations naming the first FRED
	LDA	var	load the contents of the location called var into the accumulator
	LDA	(var)	load the address of var into the accumulator
	ADD	var	add the contents of var to the accumulator contents
	MUL	n	multiply the accumulator contents by the value n
	LDI	var	load into the accumulator the contents of the location whose address is in var
	STA	var	store the accumulator contents in var
	SUB	n	subtract the value n from the accumulator contents

(10 marks)

(AEB 1983)

15. A real-time system is to be introduced by a newspaper to enable reporters to prepare articles using a video screen and keyboard terminal. The reporters would collect information and rearrange the text over a number of days, and then produce a finished article of a specified size. Indicate what the objectives of such a system would be.

Discuss the main features of the software required for this task and indicate how this software might incorporate facilities for the inclusion of photographs.

(15 marks)

(London 1983)

16. A firm of consultants is brought in by a company to advise it on the present manual invoicing system. A systems analyst is seconded to the company to study the system and prepare a report.

State three ways in which he can obtain information about the system, and outline the factors that must be considered before any recommendation can be made. (12 marks)

Assuming a computerised system is proposed, describe the tasks that would be delegated to the programmers, and how the analyst would ensure that the program suite produced would satisfy the system requirement.

State how the new system could be brought into use, giving one advantage and one disadvantage of your method of changeover. (8 marks)

(AEB 1980)

17. Answer any *three* of the following five questions.

a. Explain briefly what is meant by a *protocol* for a computer network, and explain why a protocol is necessary.

b. Explain briefly why a *systematic method of program development* is desirable, and describe one example of such a method.

c. Explain briefly the need for *recovery procedures* in an information-retrieval system and describe one example of such a procedure.

d. Explain briefly what is meant by a *feasibility study* study system design and describe what might happen if such a study were not carried out.

e. Explain briefly what is meant by the *privacy* of data, and give examples of how privacy could be protected by legislation. (12 marks)

(London 1983)

18. Write notes on **two** of the following:

a. Data Base Management Systems and their objectives. [10 marks]

b. Computers and privacy. [10 marks]

c. Distributed Processing Systems. [10 marks]

d. Structured Program Design techniques. [10 marks]

(AEB 1982)

19. a. Magnetic tape remains an important form of backing store despite the faster access time of magnetic disk.

i. Suggest, with reasons, one use in which tape is preferable to disk as a backing store medium.

ii. Discuss the factors which influence the time required to read a file from magnetic tape.

iii. Describe methods of reducing the likelihood of errors when either writing to tape or reading from tape. (10 marks)

b. A small microcomputer system is employed to collect and print meteorological information. Part of the system records wind direction as indicated by a weathervane.

i. With a labelled diagram, show how wind direction might be sensed and converted to binary form. (Illustrate the principle of the device and ignore practical complexities such as weather-proofing.)

ii. With an explanation, state the absolute accuracy of your design.

iii. Discuss the factors which influence the frequency with which the wind direction should be monitored and the occasions when it should be printed by the computer. (10 marks)

(AEB 1982)

20. a. With the aid of an example, explain the term *single-address instruction format* as applied to binary machine code instructions. (4 marks)

b. The assembly language instructions for addition, ADN 27, ADD 27 and ADI 27 will be executed in different ways because of their different modes of addressing (*immediate, direct* and *indirect,* respectively).

i. Distinguish between these three modes, showing the effect of the instruction in each case. (6 marks)

ii. Explain how the processor would distinguish between each mode of addressing when executing the machine code instructions. Relate the explanation to the individual instruction format and to the appropriate steps in the execution cycle. (10 marks)

(AEB 1983)

21. a. Describe **two** methods of addressing immediate access store. Explain why each of the methods is useful, and indicate any disadvantages. 8

b. Most computers having backing store such as disks and/or magnetic tapes as well as immediate access store. Give **two** advantages and **one** disadvantage of having both kinds of store in a system. 6

c. Give **one** application for which backing store is essential, saying why. For this application describe why and when transfer occurs between the two stores. 6 = 20

(JMB 1982)

22. A certain computer which has 16 bit words uses the following instruction format.

function code	mode	n	
6	2	8	(number of bits)

The mode bits are interpreted as follows:

00 immediate – n is the operand, an 8 bit signed value (in two's complement notation);
01 direct – n is the word address of the operand;
10 indirect – the content of word address n is the word address of the operand;
11 indexed – n plus the content of the index register is the word address of the operand.

Describe the steps in the machine instruction fetch and execute cycle for this computer, using the instruction LOAD (load the accumulator with the operand value) for illustration.

(Cambridge 1981)

23. Explain what is meant by a recursive routine in a program and how a stack may be used in its implementation. To illustrate your answer, show what happens for the function call **fib(4)** where the function **fib** has a single non-negative integer parameter **n** and has the value **fibval** given by

if n < 2 then fibval := n
else fibval := fib(n−1) + fib(n−2)

Show the order in which the calls to the function are made, the order in which the returns are made, and the data that are stacked at each call. Use diagrams wherever possible in your answer.

(Cambridge 1982)

24. a. Explain the difference between the terms "privacy of information" and "security of information". 4

b. Briefly describe **two** developments in computing which might increase public concern about privacy of information. 6

c. Briefly discuss and justify **two** steps which might be taken by government to alleviate such public concern. 6 = 16

(JMB 1982)

25.

This diagram is a very simplified illustration of a part of a computer. An active program initiates a read operation for a particular block from the disk; after a certain interval the read operation has been completed and the program may proceed to process the data which has been read.

Describe the activities which take place in the central processing unit, in the disk drive and in the interface between them during the disk read operation.

(Cambridge 1982)

26. A function PRN is available which takes a single integer value as its argument. The function uses a pseudo-random number generator in such a way that a series of calls PRN (J) will return a series of pseudo-random integers uniformly distributed over the range 0, 1, 2 . . . J.

A program is required to simulate the throwing of a die many times, until three consecutive sixes are thrown, to perform this task several times, and to print the average number of throws required to achieve three consecutive sixes.

Either write such a program, clearly annotated, in a programming language of your choice, **or** describe in detail an algorithm for such a program.

(Cambridge 1982)

Appendix 1

This appendix contains answers to student self test questions set at the end of chapters followed by answers to revision test questions. The answers given either give references to chapters and paragraphs which provide the information required for the answer or they outline the points to be included in an answer. In the case of Examination questions slightly more detail is given where necessary. Remember that in an examination you score marks for the **number of relevant points you make not for the number of pages you fill.**

Chapter 1

Answer 1.

1.1 and 1.5.

Answer 2.

1.14, 1.15 and Fig. 1.1.

Chapter 2

Answer 1.

a. Even

b.

CHARACTER	BINARY	OCTAL	CHARACTER	BINARY	OCTAL	CHARACTER	BINARY	OCTAL
0	001 010	12	C	110 011	63	O	100 110	46
1	000 001	01	D	110 100	64	P	100 111	47
2	000 010	02	E	110 101	65	Q	101 000	50
3	000 011	03	F	110 110	66	R	101 001	51
4	000 100	04	G	110 111	67	S	010 010	22
5	000 101	05	H	111 000	70	T	010 011	23
6	000 110	06	I	111 001	71	U	010 100	24
7	000 111	07	J	100 001	41	V	010 101	25
8	001 000	10	K	100 010	42	W	010 110	26
9	001 001	11	L	100 011	43	X	010 111	27
A	110 001	61	M	100 100	44	Y	011 000	30
B	110 010	62	N	100 101	45	Z	011 001	31

Answer 2.

2.9, 2.11 and 2.12.

The start and stop bits are needed in asynchronous transmission to inform the device that a transmission is about to take place. Data is sent at fixed intervals of time in synchronous transmission so there is no need to inform the receiver when transmission is to begin.

Answer 3.

a. Add a 0.

b. Add a 1.

Chapter 3

a. i. 26
 ii. 32
 iii. 37
 iv. 46
 v. 54
 vi. 65
 vii. 72
 viii. 135
 ix. 1357
 x. 2655

b. i. 10 110
 ii. 11 010
 iii. 11 111
 iv. 100 110
 v. 101 100
 vi. 110 101
 vii. 111 010
 viii. 1 011 101
 ix. 1 011 101 111
 x. 10 110 101 101

c. i. 16
 ii. 1A
 iii. 1F
 iv. 26
 v. 2C
 vi. 35
 vii. 3A
 viii. 5D
 ix. 2EF
 x. 5AD

Answer 2.

a. i. 59
   ii. 231
   iii. 849
   iv. 1260
   v. 2011

b. i. 3B
   ii. E7
   iii. 351
   iv. 4EC
   v. 7DB

c. i. 0011 1011
   ii. 1110 0111
   iii. 0011 0101 0001
   iv. 0100 1110 1100
   v. 0111 1101 1011

Answer 3.

i. 106
ii. 239
iii. 712
iv. 839
v. 1754

Answer 4.

3352653 octal and DD5AB Hex.

Chapter 4

Answer 1.

4.11.

Answer 2.

4.25.

Answer 3.

4.31.

Answer 4.

4.38, 4.39 and 4.40.

Chapter 5

Answer 1.

5.3d.

Answer 2.

5.27 and 5.29.

Chapter 6

No questions.

Chapter 7

Answer 1.

Note R is 0101 0010
A is 0100 0001
M is 0100 1101

a. 8-bit micro computer.

01010010	R
01000001	A
01001101	M

b. 16-bit micro-computer.

R	A
01010010	01000001
01001101	00000000
M	

Chapter 8

No questions.

Chapter 9

Answer 1.

a. 9.18.

b. 9.19 – 9.21.

Answer 2.

a. 9.23c.

b. 9.26. Also called the sequence control register.

c. 9.23b, 9.25 and 9.26.

d. 9.23.

Answer 3.

a. 1.6 and 9.2.

b. 9.44 and 9.14.

c. 1.6 and 9.2.

d. 7.22.

e. 7.21.

f. 7.23.

Answer 4.

a. 9.55 and 9.56.

b. 9.72c, 9.60, 9.59, 9.61.

c. 9.59, 9.62 – 9.64.

Answer 5.

a.

LOCATION NO.	301
CONTENTS	0000 1001 0111 0011

b.

LOCATION NO.	301	302	303
CONTENTS	001001	000111	000011

c.

LOCATION NO.	301	302
CONTENTS	0000 1001	0111 0011

Answer 6.

a.

LOCATION NO.	401	402
CONTENTS	FIRST INSTRUCTION	SECOND INSTRUCTION

b.

LOCATION NO.	401	402	403	404	405	406	407	408
CONTENTS								
COMMENT	Locations occupied by First Instruction				Locations occupied by Second Instruction			

Answer 7.

a. Possible reasons:

i. Economical in terms of no paper consumed.

ii. Fast display compared with similarly priced printers.

iii. The user can interact with the image because of cursor positioning ability.

iv. Quieter than most printers.

v. Very reliable: no moving parts or consumable components.

Possible disadvantages:

i. No hard copy.

ii. Screen size limits size of output.

iii. Not pleasant to read for long intervals.

b. The key depression causes a signal which causes the VDU to generate and store the appropriate character code in its own memory. It transmits this character code to the CPU where it is initially stored in the accumulator and then saved in main store.

Author's note. The reader should be able to give a more thorough answer having read some later chapters in this text.

c. 5.3g.

Further facilities might include:

i. Editing of text on the screen.

ii. Programming simple processing functions.

Answer 8.

a. 7.2–7.3, 8.1–8.2.

Author's note. You should compare both features and uses of both.

b. **Access speed** is usually expressed in terms of the access time, ie. the time between the CPU requesting data from a device and the time the CPU receives it. eg. disk access time involves finding the track, waiting for a sector and reading the data into memory.

Capacity. The amount of data a device can store is called its capacity and is usually measured in bytes or characters.

Cost per bit. In order to obtain the cost per bit we need the cost of the device and to divide this by the capacity in bytes. Then we divide by 8 (8 bits/byte) to give the cost per bit.

Generally speaking the cost per bit is greater for devices with high access speeds. These devices also tend to have lower capacities. At the other extreme devices with large capacities and low access speeds tend to have lower costs per bit, and so on.

c. Magnetic media are relatively cheap and can store data almost indefinitely if kept in controlled conditions. The read/write heads for such media can deal with data recorded at high densities but are expensive to produce. Therefore, the devices all adopt a method of moving the media under a limited number of read/write heads rather than having read/write heads for each section of the medium. High access speeds can therefore only be achieved by moving the medium quickly beneath the read/write heads or by increasing recording density. The high speeds and high precision required makes these devices liable to mechanical failure. Devices with no moving parts would not suffer from these problems.

Answer 9.

a. Fig. 8.2, 8.13.

b. i. The track number.
   ii. The sector number.

Both these values would be recorded as a stream of bits together with synchronisation data.

It is normally possible to store each number as a single byte.

Chapter 10

Answer 1.

a.

0000	0000	0111	1001
0	0	7	9

b. (See fig. 2.5 for codes).

0000	000111	001001
	7	9

c.

10110111	00111001
7	9

d. 0000 0000 0100 1111

79

Answer 2.

10.2.

Answer 3.

10.62, 10.63 – 10.66.

Answer 4.

a. The operands are of different types.
   Suitable correction: either "15" < "26"
   or 15 < 26

b. Types are being mixed in this expression.
   Possible correct: (5 < 10) OR (5 < 19) but this simplifies to 5 < 19.

Answer 5.

a. – 384
b. True.
c. True.

Answer 6.

a. 49 + 51 = 100
b. "CAT"
c. "Z"

Chapter 11

Answer 1.

11.7 – 11.8.

Answer 2.

11.22 – 11.23.

Answer 3.

Key in an integer.
6
Key in another integer.
8
The result is 7

Answer 4.

```
Procedure discount (IN total_value : real OUT discount : real)

    Begin
      if
        total_value > 100
      then
        discount : = total_value / 10
      else
        if
          total_value > 20
        then
          discount : = total_value / 20
        else
          discount : = 0
        endif
      endif
    end
```

NB. This procedure could also be written as a function.

Answer 5.

11.69 and 11.74.

Chapter 12

Answer 1.
M(2, 3), M(2, 2), M(1, 1), M(1, 2), M(2, 1), M(1,3)

Answer 2.

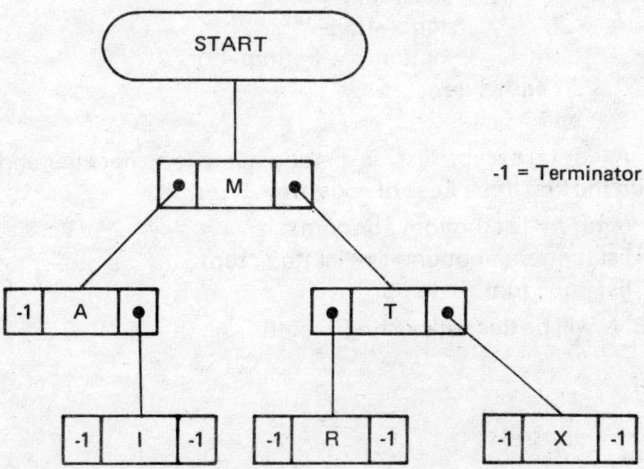

Answer 3.

Outline solution:

```
function below_average (number_of_marks, mark, average_mark): integer
        variables
                i : integer
        Begin
                below_average : = 0
                for  i : = 1 to number_of_marks
                     if
                          mark (i) < average_mark
                     then
                          below_average : = below_average + 1
                     endif
                endfor
        end
```

Answer 4.

Outline solution:

a. **procedure** reverse_list (**IN-OUT** list : **array** [1 . . N] **of integer**)

```
    variables
            bottom,
            top,
            temp : integer
    Begin
        bottom   : = 1
        top      : = N
        while    bottom < top
                 temp : = list (bottom)
                 list (bottom) : = list (top)
                 list (top) : = temp
                 top : = top – 1
                 bottom : = bottom + 1
        endwhile
    end
```

b. As for (a) except "list" is a string, temp is a character and within the while loop the first three lines of code are:

```
temp : = list (bottom : bottom)
list (bottom : bottom) : = list (top : top)
list (top : top) : = temp
```

NB. N will be this list's string length.

Answer 5.

A two dimensional array may be used. The array will have 100 rows, one for each stock item, and 20 columns, one for each location.

NB. Other possible solutions to this question could be based upon arrays of records.

Chapter 13

Answer 1.

13.6; reasons 13.3 – 13.5.

Answer 2.

13.7.

Answer 3.

a. No! It is not user-friendly. It is supposed to treat 999 as a sentinel but it treats 999 as data and produces a wrong value for t.
The program does not meet its specification.

b. (See a)
The program is badly set out, data names lack meaning and comments are missing.

c.
```
program calculate_total
    variables
        number,
        total : real
    Begin
      total : = 0
      output ("Key in a data value or key in 999 to stop.")
      input (number)
      while number < > 999
          total : = total + number
          output ("Key in a data value or key in 999 to stop.")
          input (number)
      endwhile
      output ("The total of all numbers input is", total)
    end
```

NB. Comments are omitted here in order to save space.

Answer 4.

13.22.

Answer 5.

13.23 – 13.27.

Answer 6. Outline solution:

```
Program rectangle
constants
        star = "*"
variables
        height,
        width,
        row,
        column : integer
Begin
        (* get a valid height *)
        repeat
            output ("Key in rectangle height, NB at least 1")
            input (height)
        until height > = 1
        (* get a valid width *)
        repeat
            output ("Key in rectangle width NB at least 1")
            input (width)
        until width > = 1
        for row : = 1 to height
            (* output a row of stars *)
            for column : = 1 to width
                out (star)
            endfor
            (* generate a new line *)
            output
        endfor
end
```

NB. Assume "output" by itself generates a new line.

Chapter 14

Answer 1.

a. Outline solution:

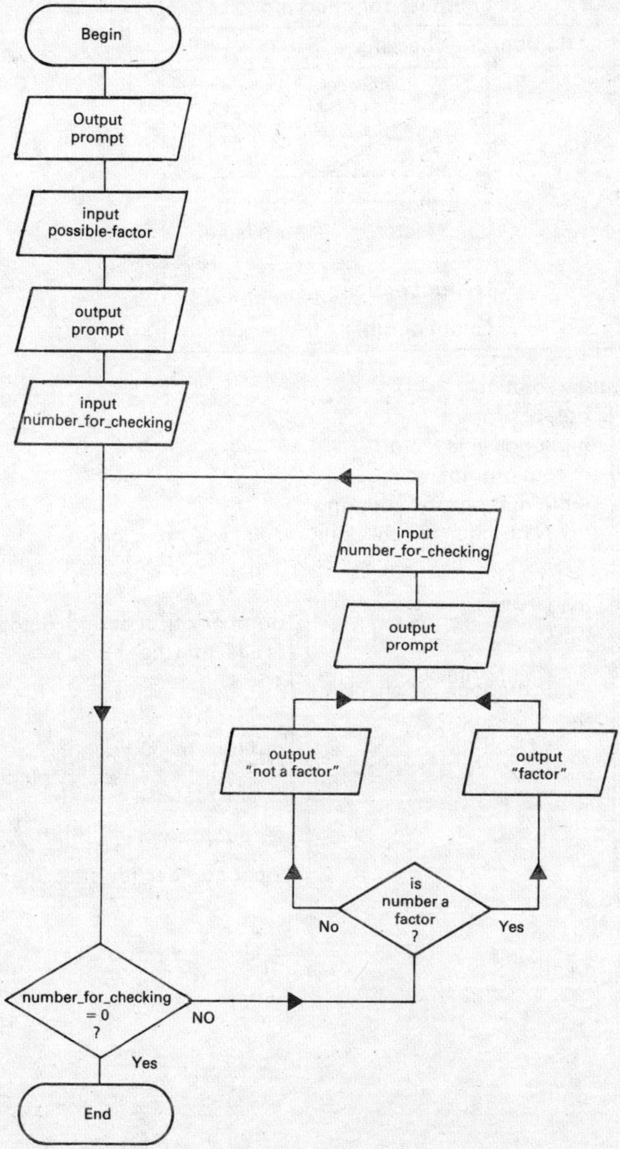

b. Outline solution.

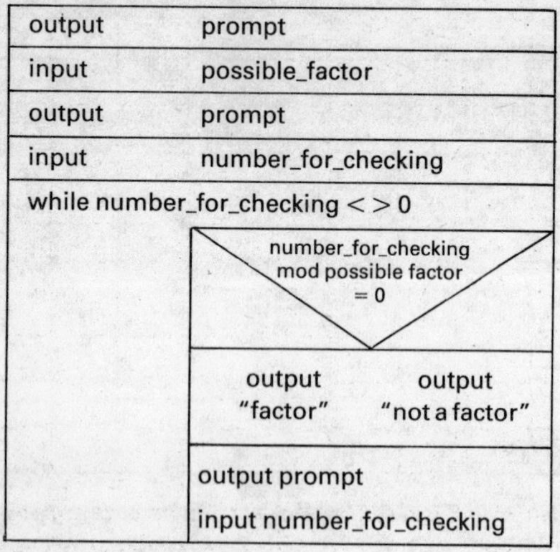

c. Outline solution

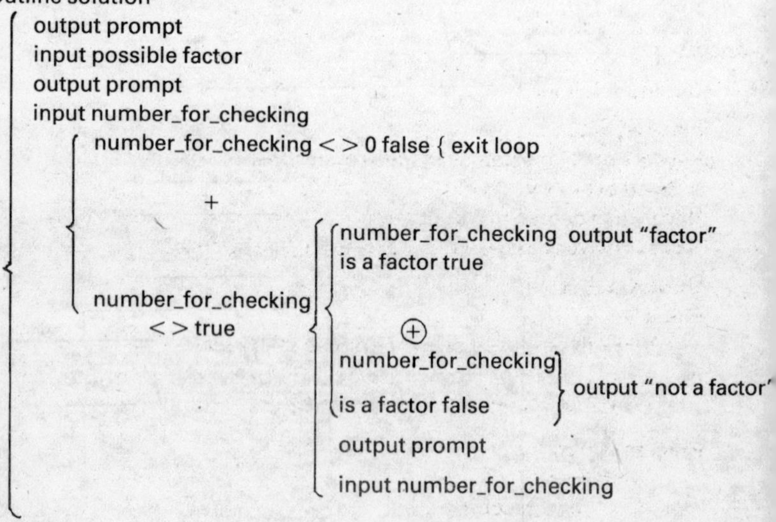

Answer 2.

14.17 – 14.18.

Answer 3.

	Rules							
Conditions	1	2	3	4	5	6	7	8
age > 25	Y	Y	Y	Y	N	N	N	N
degree in computing	Y	Y	N	N	Y	Y	N	N
3 years programming experience	Y	N	Y	N	Y	N	Y	N
Actions								
Point 1 on salary scale						X	X	
Point 2 on salary scale		X	X		X			
Point 3 on salary scale	X							
Reject				X				X

Note Three conditions implies $2^3 = 8$ rules. Therefore the table is complete. The table can be reduced by one rule because rules 4 and 8 can be combined with a dash for age > 25.

Answer 4.

Outline solution.

Input layout
Key in Y or N in response to these questions.
Are you over 25 years old?
Have you a degree in computing?
Have you over three years programming experience?

Output layout
Either
 You will be placed at point _ on the salary scale.
or
 Your application has been rejected.

```
Program salary
    variables
        age_response,
        degree_response,
        exper_response : character
```

```
Begin
    (* prompt and get input – see layout *)
    if
        age_response = "Y"
    then
        if
            degree_response = "Y"
        then
            if
                exper_response = "Y"
            then
                output ("You will be placed at point 3 on the salary scale")
            else
                output ("You will be placed at point 2 on the salary scale")
            endif
        else
            if
                exper_response = "Y"
            then
                output ("You will be placed at point 2 on the salary scale")
            else
                output ("Your application has been rejected")
            endif
        endif
    else
        if
            degree_response = "Y"
        then
            if
                exper_response = "Y"
            then
                output ("You will be placed at point 2 on the salary scale")
            else
                output ("You will be placed at point 1 on the salary scale")
            endif
        else
            if
                exper_response = "Y"
            then
                output ("You will be placed at point 1 on the salary scale")
            else
                output ("Your application has been rejected")
            endif
        endif
    endif
end
```

Chapter 15

Answer 1.

Possible entities: Members, Accounts, transactions.

The member entity might have attributes such as members name, members address, members department etc.

The Account entity might have attributes such as account number, account holder, current balance etc.

The transaction entity might have attributes such as account number, date, amount, type of transaction (credit or debit) etc.

Answer 2.

Key field 15.10.

a. May not be unique so not suitable.

b. Unique and usable but might be unnecessarily long.

c. Unique and usable. Specially designed for the job.

Answer 3.

hit rate 15.18.
volatility 15.19.
volatility is also used in connection with memory devices.

Chapter 16

Answer 1

16.2 and 16.11.

Answer 2.

16.6.

Answer 3.

a. Each record takes $\frac{250}{1600}$ inches plus ½" for the IRG.

Therefore, the file is $15{,}000 \left(\frac{25 + 80}{160}\right)$ inches long

$= 9843.75'' \triangleq 820$ feet

$$\text{Time taken} = 10 + \frac{250 \times 1000}{75 \times 1600} + 10 \times 15000 \text{ ms}$$

$$331250 \text{ ms} \quad \triangleq 5\tfrac{1}{2} \text{ minutes}$$

With 5 records per block.

Each block takes $\frac{250 \times 5}{1600} + \frac{1}{2}''$ for the IBG

Therefore the file occupies $3000 \left(\frac{125 + 80}{160}\right)$ inches.

$$= 3843.75'' \triangleq 320 \text{ feet}$$

$$\text{Time Taken} \left(10 + \frac{1250 \times 1000}{75 \times 1600} + 10\right) 3000 \text{ ms}$$

$$= 91250 \text{ ms} \triangleq 1\tfrac{1}{2} \text{ minutes}$$

Note the savings provided by blocking the records.

Double buffering (16.15) may reduce these times.

Chapter 17

Answer 1.

The main types of storage are:—

(IAS)	Immediate access storage	eg core, RAM
(DAS)	Direct access storage	eg drum, disk and magnetic card.
(SAS)	Serial access storage	eg magnetic tape, punched paper tape and punched card.

The tasks that they are best suited to carry out are:—

a. **Immediate access.** Because of its unique electronic properties giving extremely quick access to stored data this type of storage is used as the computer's *main storage.* Access to individual characters/bytes is completely independent of their position in store. It is in main storage that the programs are held during processing so that their instructions can be executed swiftly. Also the particular data currently being worked on is held in main storage. Ideally, IAS would be used for storage of all data because it is fast in operation. This is not practicable because of cost and its use therefore is limited to main storage. Thus some alternative form must be found for storing the file and data which are not immediately required by the program.

b. **Direct access.** One such alternative is DAS. Storage capacity can vary from thousands to hundreds of millions of characters. DAS has the important facility of allowing direct access, that is records can be accessed independently of each other. It is thus suitable for files being processed in a selective manner, also for storing programs and systems software which are required to be called into main storage at any time during the running of an application program. It is an essential requirement for on-line processing or where file-interrogation facilities are needed. Drum storage has a very much faster access time than disk but considerably less storage capacity.

c. **Serial access.** If bulky auxiliary storage is required and the need for random access is not present then the choice may well fall on SAS the most common form of which is magnetic tape. It is also cheaper than main memory, disk or drum. Because of its inherent serial nature, access to a record on tape is a function of its position on the tape. Therefore every preceding record on a master file must be read (and written out onto the new tape) before the required record can be located. Nevertheless millions of characters can be stored very cheaply.

Conclusion.
IAS is the ideal storage medium but is very expensive. If bulk storage is required combined with facility for random access then the less expensive DAS is indicated. If the limitations of Serial Access are no serious hindrance then the cheapest form of store ie SAS can be used.

Answer 2.

a. 16.4 and 16.5. For magnetic tape labels see 16.9.

b. 17.20, 17.21 and Fig. 17.3. For magnetic disk files labels see 17.28 and 17.29.

Answer 3.

For the first part see 17.33 and 17.34.

a. **Flowchart. Note** that in recent years alternatives to flowcharts have also been accepted in the examinations.

There are many possible solutions to this problem. A reasonable solution might

i. input the key, generate a block address and read in that block into an array.

ii. Scan the array looking at each record until either the record was found or the end of the block was reached.

iii. In performing this scan the key for each record must be selected. The record must be scanned until a "?" is reached and if after a "?" a "/" occurs the end of the block has been reached. This suggests a nested loop structure for the scans.

b. The terminator / used in the question could be altered in an overflow situation to allow for a pointer to be provided. The pointer would have to provide the block address of the overflow records.

Procedure in obtaining record from overflow.

i. Obtain block from overflow pointer.

ii. Read overflow block into string array.

iii. Repeat previously described search for record key.

Answer 4.

See references for question 2.

Answer 5.

17.15– 17.17.

Answer 6.

17.25.

Answer 7.

a. If N is 1000 or more we may merely subtract 2500 from the key. If N is smaller some rescaling will be needed too.

b. Each entry in the index will be a record consisting of a key and a record number. The index will itself have to be stored.

NB. These methods will be more complicated if as is quite likely, the physical records and logical records differ in size. For example, in case (a) if there are 10 logical records per physical record then the method may involve the formula.

$$\text{address} = \text{int}\left(\frac{\text{key} - 2500}{10}\right)$$

where the function int returns an integer value.

Answer 8.

a. 4 records per sector.

b. 50%

c.

$$\text{Total time} \doteq \left[\begin{matrix}\text{seek}\\ \text{time}\end{matrix} + \left[\begin{matrix}\text{latency + data transfer}\\ \text{time}\end{matrix}\right] \times \begin{matrix}\text{Number of}\\ \text{sectors per}\\ \text{cylinder}\end{matrix}\right] \times \begin{matrix}\text{Number of}\\ \text{cylinders}\\ \text{per file}\end{matrix}$$

$$= [20 + [12 + 2] \times 48] \times 100 \text{ ms}$$

$$= 69.2 \text{ seconds}$$

ie. just over one minute.

d.

$$\text{Total time} \doteq \left[\begin{matrix}\text{seek}\\ \text{time}\end{matrix} + \begin{matrix}\text{latency + data transfer}\\ \text{time}\end{matrix}\right] \times \begin{matrix}\text{Number of}\\ \text{records}\end{matrix}$$

$$= [40 + 12 + 2] \times 19200 \text{ ms}$$

$$\doteq 17\tfrac{1}{2} \text{ minutes}$$

In case (d) each block (containing 4 records), will be read four times, once for each record, whereas in case (c) each block will be read just once because of the sequential order.

In case (d) the seek time and the number of seeks required are each greater than in case (c).

Answer 9.

a. 16.7 – 16.8.

b. Index file : 17.20 – 17.21.

The block size of 2400 characters suggests the storage of 8 records per block. Initially, not all 8 record positions would be used so that each block could accept insertions without the creation of overflow.

The index could be organised as a table of highest keys in each block plus the block address with records in ascending order by key.

To find a record:

i. Search the index for the first key higher than the key given in order to find the required block.

ii. Read the block into main storage.

iii. Search the block for the required record which can be identified by its key.

Chapter 18

Answer 1.

All – see 18.3.

Answer 2.

Human sensible – can be understood by a human.

Machine sensible – can be read by a machine.

Examples: eg. MICR, OCR.

Chapter 19

Answer 1.

The call-over method can be adapted if a hard copy of the data on disk can be obtained or if verification from the screen is possible.

The two-tape method can be implemented via a program which compares results of two separate key entries.

19.12.

Answer 2.

19.15 – 19.16.

Answer 3.

Control systems and monitoring systems could be used as examples.

Answer 4.

a, i. 19.24.
ii. 19.17.
iii. 19.18 and 19.26e.

b. i. Payroll. Most, or all, records require access.
ii. Stock file. Updates to stock may require sequential processing but enquiries will require random access.
iii. An on-line enquiring or booking system. Each enquiry will require very fast access.

Chapter 20

Answer 1.

INTRODUCTION.

1. It *must* be noted that advantages and disadvantages are relative. Also in many cases a user will disregard certain disadvantages of being of no consequences, or will be obliged to adopt a method *despite* its disadvantages. Finally, as has already been pointed out in the text, some methods will be better suited for certain applications than others.

PUNCHED CARDS.

2. Possible advantages.

a. Can be sorted off-line (by using a mechanical sorter).

b. Cards can be easily inserted/removed.

c. Can be used as dual purpose media ie. as source document and data collection media. Also used as a turnaround document.

d. Punched data can be interpreted (ie. printed on the card).

3. Possible disadvantages.

a. Handling problems – bulky.

b. Slow input speed.

c. Need to be kept in controlled environment.

d. Low utilisation of card capacity.

NB. This is an obsolete medium.

PAPER TAPE.

4. Possible advantages.

a. Easier and cheaper to produce as by-product (than card).

b. Less bulky than cards.

c. Variable length records easy to accommodate.

d. Suitable for transmission purposes.

e. No environmental problems.

5. Possible disadvantages.

a. Insertions/deletions generally entail preparation of a new tape.

b. Cannot be sorted off-line.

c. Slow input speed.

NB. This is an obsolete medium.

KEY-TO-DISK (Key Processing).

6. Possible advantages.

a. Data is keyed onto magnetic tape which is a fast input medium.

b. A certain amount of validation can be done off-line (to the main computer).

c. Incorporates control totals.

d. There are no cards etc. to be handled by operators (nor tapes for that matter).

e. Error correction is more easily accomplished than with punched cards.

f. Quieter and cleaner (no card dust) than card machine (it is electronic).

g. Only one tape reel involved (compare key-to-tape). Fewer operators may be required than for punched cards or paper tape.

h. Once data has been keyed onto disk verification can be carried out from any of the key-stations.

7. Possible disadvantages.

a. All key stations are linked to *one* processor – if the processor breaks down all key-processing ceases.

b. A relatively high capital outlay needs large volumes of data to justify it.

KEY-TO-TAPE (ENCODING).

8. Possible advantages.

a. Data is encoded direct onto magnetic tape.

b. There is no card handling involved.

c. Error correction is easier than with punched cards.

9. Possible disadvantages.

a. Tapes have to be re-loaded to verify (not with key-to-disk).

b. Tapes have to be pooled before input (not with key-to-disk).

c. Not so flexible as key-to-disk in terms of program capability.

MAGNETIC TAPE CASSETTE.

10. Possible Advantages.

a. Can be prepared as a by-product.

b. Inexpensive.

c. Easily transportable.

11. Possible disadvantages.

a. Slower input than ½" tape.

b. Smaller capacity of cassette.

KEY-TO-DISKETTE.

12. Possible advantages.

a. Data is encoded directly onto the diskette.

b. There is no card handling involved.

c. Error correction is easy.

d. Diskettes are easily transportable.

13. Possible disadvantages.

a. Diskette needs careful handling.

OCR.

14. Possible advantages.

a. No transcription is required, thus there are no errors in the data preparation stage.

b. Characters are both human and machine-sensible.

c. Documents prepared in OC are suitable for use as turnaround documents.

15. Possible disadvantages.

a. A high standard printing of optical characters is required.

b. High document standards are needed to keep down error rejections.

c. The cost of readers/scanners is relatively high, especially those used on-line to the computer.

MICR.

16. Advantages and disadvantages as for OCR except that print tolerances are much stricter.

Possible disadvantages.

a. Very high degree of accurancy required in forming characters.

PUNCHED TAGS.

17. Possible advantages.

a. Data is captured at source.

b. Data collection is done mainly by machine (handling excluded).

c. Sales attendant's job is simplified as data is already recorded.

18. Possible disadvantages.

a. There are limits to the amount of data which can be stored in tags.

b. Problems arise if (in retailing) goods are marked down in price.

c. Tags are small and present handling problems.

PLASTIC BADGES.

19. Possible advantages.

a. Plastic badges are able to withstand much handling and are suitable for shop floor systems and ordinary employees can operate the machines.

b. The collection system is mechanised.

c. The data recording machines can be linked directly to the computer.

20. Possible disadvantages.

a. Limited scope.

b. The recording machines are operated by the workers themselves.

ON-LINE SYSTEMS.

21. Possible advantages.

a. Transcription can be eliminated.

b. Speeds up entry of data to the computer and return of processed information.

c. Cuts down delays in dealing with error rejections.

22. Possible disadvantage.

a. Cost is considerable.

AUTHOR'S NOTE.

There is a tendency for candidates in examinations to write down what they know about the subject of a question rather than answer the specific question. Beware of this danger!

To illustrate this point, suppose that rather than ask about the advantages and disadvantages of the methods and media for data collection the question had asked for a summary of these methods and asked what were the problems of data capture and their possible solution. The answer, although on the same subject matter, would need to be very different:–

A. Data has to be presented to the computer in a form which is acceptable as input (so called machine-sensible form). This *capturing* of data can be accomplished in many ways, using different input media. A summary of the main methods and media is given below:

NO.	METHOD OF DATA CAPTURE	MEDIA USED
1	On-line (to computer)	Data transmission terminals, plastic badges, etc.
2	Character recognition	Source documents using OCR; MICR or OMR.
3	Manual key punching	Punched card or paper tape.
4	Manual encoding	Magnetic tape (using encoders).
5	Key processing	Magnetic tape via disc (using Computer-controlled Data Entry Systems).
6	By-product	Paper tape, tally rolls with cash registers, typewriters, etc.

Answer 2.

BASIC PROBLEMS.

B. a. **Accuracy and validity** of data when finally input to computer.

b. **Form of source data** which in many cases means a clerically produced document and indifferent document standards.

c. **Cost** of machinery, operators and buildings etc which sometimes equals that of the computer system itself.

d. **Time.** Many of the methods outlined are cumbersome and very time consuming.

e. **Volumes of data.** Increasing volumes of data, indicating the need for more sophisticated methods of data capture.

f. **Movement of data** (in raw or transcribed form) to the central processing point present problems of packaging, delay, loss, etc.

g. **Control.** With so many stages involved with some methods the problem of controlling and co-ordinating the whole is far from easy.

DISCUSSION OF PROBLEMS AND SOLUTIONS. (Methods referred to are those given in answer B)

C. a. **Accuracy.** This problem is most acute with method 3 which requires *verification* to reduce errors made by punch operators. Even so errors will creep through and there is a necessity for a computer check of input. Limited *validity* checking can be carried out by the *computer.* Methods 4 and 5 (especially 5) claim increased accuracy and certain validity checks can be done *off-line.*

b. **Form of source data.** On-line systems can do away with source document, which is the ideal solution. Method 2 (character recognition) avoids the need for transcription especially with the use of the *"turn around"* document. Method 6 (By-product) also enables the source data to be produced in a machine-sensible form. (Example – Cash Registers equipped with Paper Tape rolls which capture data as sale is entered). Kimball tags also obviate the need for manually scribed document.

c. **Cost.** Each method is going to cost a great deal but Computer-controlled Data Entry is probably more cost effective in large installations than its predecessor – Manual Key punching (fewer operators, but higher machine costs).

d. **Time.** Method 1 gets over this problem by capturing data at source and putting it *directly* into computer. The methods which employ more machinery and fewer humans are likely to be more efficient in this respect.

e. **Volumes.** Similarly increased volumes point to the choice of on-line systems, Character Recognition, or Computer-controlled Data Entry as appropriate.

f. **Movement.** The solution is the use of on-line system or something approaching it.

g. **Control.** The methods which eliminate the most stages in data capture will be the answer. This points again to on-line systems and to a lesser degree Character Recognition, and Computer-controlled Data Entry (and possibly By-product).

CONCLUSION.

D. The capture of raw data for use within a computer system is a time-consuming and costly affair. The basic underlying problem is the interface of the slow human with the high speed computer.

The ultimate solution must be to capture data at its point of origin in a machine-sensible form, thus eliminating the many stages involved at present in getting it into such a form.

However it is as well to appreciate that very often *cost* and the *appropriateness* of a method of data capture to a particular application will be very important factors influencing choice.

Answer 2.

Relative Advantages.

VDU	Printer Terminal
No stationery costs Faster maximum speed Quieter than most printers Very reliable: no moving parts except the keyboard Parts of an output layout can be changed without re displaying the whole screen.	Produces permanent copies Not limited to length of screen when viewing Nicer to read than a VDU screen.

Answer 3.

Appropriateness – the need for a hard copy. Multiple copies would prompt the use of an inpact printer. A quiet environment would prompt the use of a non-impact printer, etc.

Cost – High speeds and extras raise the price.

Time – High speed printers may be needed if there is little time to produce output.

Accuracy – Printer accuracy in positioning characters varies greatly. Impact line printers often produce slightly smudged and uneven lines of characters whereas daisywheel printers and good quality matrix printers product clear and accurate print.

Volume – Total volume of output in a given time is limited by printer speed.

Confidence – Well proven printer types such as line and matrix printers tend to be favoured.

Chapter 21

Answer 1.

21.7 – 21.8. Both verification and validation involve checking. Verification is the checking for transcription errors, validation is checking that data conforms to rules which apply to it.

Answer 2.

21.9.

Answer 3.

a. i. Date can be checked to ensure that each part of the date is valid eg. if the month is given as a number it should be in the range 1 . . 12.

ii. The account holders name can be cross checked with the name assigned to the account number.

iii. The account number can be checked for character type (numeric say), format and range. A check digit check may also be used.

iv. Amounts in pounds should be numeric.

v. Signatures can be checked manually against a given copy.

NB. One day pattern recognition techniques may allow this check to be computerised.

b. eg.

BATCH CONTROL SLIP

Date – – / – – / – –
dd mm yy

Number of documents in this batch

Total of all amounts in this batch

Total of all account numbers (hash total)

Sent by ______________

Received by ____________

c.

Field Number	Field Contents	Field Description
1	Account Number	A six digit number, say.
2	Transaction Type	"P" for payment "W" for withdrawals, say.
3	Date	A 6 digit number in the form YYMMDD*.
4	Account holders name	Twenty character spaces, say.
5	Amount	A number between 0.00 and 999.99, say.

* eg. 3rd April 1985 will have the form 850403

Chapter 22

Answer 1.

a. 22.8.
b. 22.22.
c. 22.13.
d. 22.15 and 22.21d.
e. 22.13 and 22.14.
f. 22.47.
g. 22.34.
h. 22.45.

Answer 2.

22.17.

Answer 3.

22.21.

Acoustic coupler.

Answer 4.

22.25.

Answer 5.

22.34.

Chapter 23

Answer 1.

a. 10110_2
b. 1011101_2
c. 110000_2
d. 110011_2

Answer 2.

a. 102_8
b. 743_8

Answer 3.

a. $120B_{16}$
b. $19ED_{16}$

Answer 4.

Self checking since the results are the same as for decimal.

Answer 5.

a. ones is 11101010, twos is 11101011

b. ones is 11011000, twos is 11011001

Answer 6.

7	**0111**	ADD
–4	1100	
3	[1]0011	

Answer 7.

i. 0.75
ii. 0.8125
iii. 0.4375
iv. 2.625
v. 5.375

Answer 8.

i. 0.0101
ii. 0.1111
iii. 110.0011
iv. 0.10001
v. 0.0011 0011 Note. The last 4 bits recur.

Answer 9.

a. i. 0.011 110
ii. 0.110 101
iii. 0.111 100 010

b. i. 0.0010 1011
ii 0.0011 1100 1111
iii. 0.0101 1011 1001

Answer 10.

11 decimal is 1011
3 decimal is 11 (twos complement is 1101).

Multiply.

```
000000          1   1
000000   <------┘   |
------              |
  1011              |
------              |
  1011              |
 10110   <----------┘
  1011
------
100001          1011 x 11 = 100 001
------
```

Divide.

```
01011
10100
-----
11111        0
01100
-----
01011
-----
10110        shift
10100
-----
01010        0 1
-----
10100        shift
10100
-----
01000        0 1 1 .      (Result 3 remainder 2)
-----
    ↖
    point
```

Chapter 24

Answer 1.

a. Most positive $2^{11}-1$, Least positive 1
Least negative -1, Most negative -2^{11}

b. Most positive $1-½^{11}$, Least positive $½^{11}$
Least negative $-½^{11}$, Most negative -1

Answer 2.

i. 0.36×10^{2}
ii. 0.159×10^{3}
iii. -0.276×10^{3}
iv. -0.56724×10^{5}
v. 0.37692×10^{3}
vi. 0.365×10^{4}
vii. -0.498×10^{2}
viii. 0.9824×10^{-2}
ix. -0.1562×10^{-3}
x. -0.26×10^{-7}

Answer 3.

a.

i.	0	1	0	1	0	0	0	0	0	0	1	1
ii.	1	0	1	1	0	0	0	0	0	0	1	1
iii.	0	1	0	0	0	0	0	0	0	0	0	0
iv.	1	0	0	0	0	0	0	0	1	1	1	1
v.	0	1	0	0	0	1	1	0	0	1	1	0
vi.	1	0	1	1	1	0	1	0	0	1	1	0
vii.	0	1	1	1	0	0	0	0	0	0	1	0
viii.	1	0	0	1	0	0	0	0	0	0	1	0
ix.	0	1	0	0	0	0	0	0	1	1	1	0
x.	1	0	0	0	0	0	0	0	1	1	0	1

b. i. $(1 - \frac{1}{2^7}) \times 2^7 = 127$

ii. $\frac{1}{2} \times 2^{-8} = \frac{1}{2^9} = \frac{1}{512}$

iii. $-(\frac{1}{2} - \frac{1}{2^7}) \times 2^{-8} = -\frac{1}{2^9} + \frac{1}{2^{15}}$

iv. $-1 \times 2^7 = -128$

Answer 4.

a. **Advantages of floating point representation over fixed point representation.**
   i. Wider range for given word length.
   ii. Automatic scaling.
   iii. Both fractional and integer representation
   iv. Convenience to programmer.

b. **Disadvantages of floating point representation with respect fo fixed point representation.**
   i. Slower.
   ii. Extra expense if done by hardware because of hardware cost.
   iii. Loss of precision for given word length.
   iv. More troublesome conversion to other codes.
   v. Less control over accuracy.

Answer 5.

a. The three possible methods are:
   i. Twos complement method.
   ii. Ones complement method.
   iii. Explicit sign.

They are given in the order in which arithmetic can be most efficiently performed and reverse order of simplicity of representation. The advantage of i. makes it the most common.

b. i. +0.101 is +0.625, Decimal, +.5 Octal, +.A Hex.
   ii. Decimal –91 is –133 Octal, 1 011 011 Binary, 5B Hex.
   iii. +237 Octal is + 010 011 111 Binary, +9F Hex and 159 Decimal.
   iv. +E8 Hex is +1110 1000 Binary +350 Octal and +232 Decimal.

Answer 6.

a. 0111 1111_2 ie. $2^7 - 1$ or 127

b. Representations are normalised in order to keep numbers in a standard form which allows control to be maintained over range, scale and accuracy.

NB. The University of London University Entrance and Schools Examination Council require this disclaimer be printed by all persons given permission to reproduce questions from their past examination papers:

"The University of London University Entrance and Schools Examination Council accepts no responsibility whatsoever for the accuracy or methods of working in the answers given."

Chapter 25

Answer 1.

a. 25.2, 25.4a, 25.4b.

b. 25.5

Answer 2.

a. i. 0.5
 ii. 0.00625

b. i. 0.0005
 ii. 0.004

c. i. 5
 ii. 0.0142857

d. i. 0.005
 ii. 0.0008

Answer 3.

a. 25.5

b. Word length, method of rounding.

c. 25.23

Answer 4.

a. 0.0005

b. 5924 ± 2.962

Answer 5.

Using the floating point error formula on each formula gives a result

$$uv - u.w + 2u(v - w)\in$$

in the case of $u(v - w)$ and a result of

$$uv - u.w + 2(\pm uv \pm uw)\in$$

in the case of $uv - uw$, so there is a smaller maximum error for the first formula when $u \triangleq v$.

Answer 6.

a. i.

16^2	16	1
3	F	2

convert to decimal

3 x 256	768	
15 x 16	240	
2 x 1	2	Add
	1010	decimal value

1	0	1	0	decimal
0001	0000	0001	0000	BCD code by inspection.

ii. Use the fact that the representation abc represents the number a x 100 + b x 10 + c

Procedure:–

i. a x 10
ii. (a x 10) + b
iii. (a x 10 + b) x 10
iv. [(a x 10 + b) x 10] + c

The procedure is used when doing conversion often during input or output.

For the BCD number 0111 0110 0101

a b c

10 Decimal is 1010 Binary.

(Author's note: Refer to 23.33 for details).

Working (Manual method)

```
  0111 x 1010
  -----
  0000
 01110
  0000
 11100
 ------
100010
```

Procedure

Step		
i.	0111 x 1010	1000110
ii.	+ 0110	0110
		1001100
iii.	x 1010	1011111000
iv.	+ 0101	0101
		1011111101
		binary form

```
   1001100 x 1010
   -------
  10011000
1001100000
----------
1011111000
```

Binary form of the number 1011111101

b. (Replace 7 by 'n' in 24.13b). We assume the point is between the first and second leftmost bits.

The A product is double the length if both numbers multiplied are the same length the sum of their lengths in general.

The result could be wrong by one whole bit in the 24th place the maximum loss of accuracy is therefore.

$$\frac{1}{2^{24}}$$

c. 35 ÷ 5

35 decimal = 43 octal = 0100011 binary
5 decimal = 0101 binary : Twos complement 1011
0100011 Dividend
0101000 Shifted divisor (3 shifts needed)

		Dividend		Quotient
		0100011		0000000
restore (add back)		1011000	Add complement (Subtract)	
		1111111	negative result	
		0100011		
		1000110	shift	
lost		1011000	Add complement	
	1	0011110	positive result	0000001
		0111100	shift	
		1011000	Add complement	
	1	0010100	positive result	0000011
		0101000	shift	
lost		1011000	Add complement	
	1	0000000	no remainder	0000111

Quotient = 0000111_2

Answer 7.

a = 1, b = –100.1, c = 0.05

$$x = \frac{100.1 \pm \sqrt{(-100.1)^2 - 4 \times 1 \times 0.05}}{2}$$

$$x = \frac{100.1 \pm \sqrt{10020 - 0.2}}{2}$$ Working to 5 Figure accuracy

$$x = \frac{100.1 \pm \sqrt{10020}}{2}$$ Working to 5 Figure accuracy

$$x = \frac{100.1 \pm 100.1}{2}$$ Working to 5 Figure accuracy

So x = 100.1 or x = 0. The error occurred in x = 0 because the difference between terms was of the same order of magnitude as the error. The error in x = 0 can be reduced using this method.

$$x = \frac{c}{\alpha a} = \frac{0.05}{100.1 \times 1} = 0.0004995$$

So x = 100.1 or x = 0.0004995

b. (25.34)

$$100x + 100y = 200 \quad \text{I}$$

$$Kx + 101y = 201 \quad \text{II}$$

I & II yield $y = \dfrac{20100 - 200K}{10100 - 100K}$ (III) and $x = 2 - y$ (IV)

Using the nominal value K = 100 III and IV give x = 1, y = 1

i. With K = 99.25 III & IV yield $x = \frac{4}{7}, y = 1\frac{3}{7}$

With K = 100.75 III & IV yield x = 4, y = –2

$-2 \leqslant y \leqslant 1\frac{3}{7}$ and $\frac{4}{7} \leqslant x \leqslant 4$

ii. With a 2% error in K, K can take the value 101. This is the case of parallel lines and no solution.

Taking extreme values

With K = 98 III & IV yield $x = \frac{1}{3}, y = 1\frac{2}{3}$

With K = 102 III & IV yield x = –1, y = 3

Range of x values $x \leqslant 1$ or $\frac{1}{3} \leqslant x$

Range of y values $y \geqslant 3$ or $y \leqslant 1\frac{2}{3}$

Author's Note. It would be worth drawing a sketch when doing this problem for your own sake. The ones below illustrate the problem.

Case i.

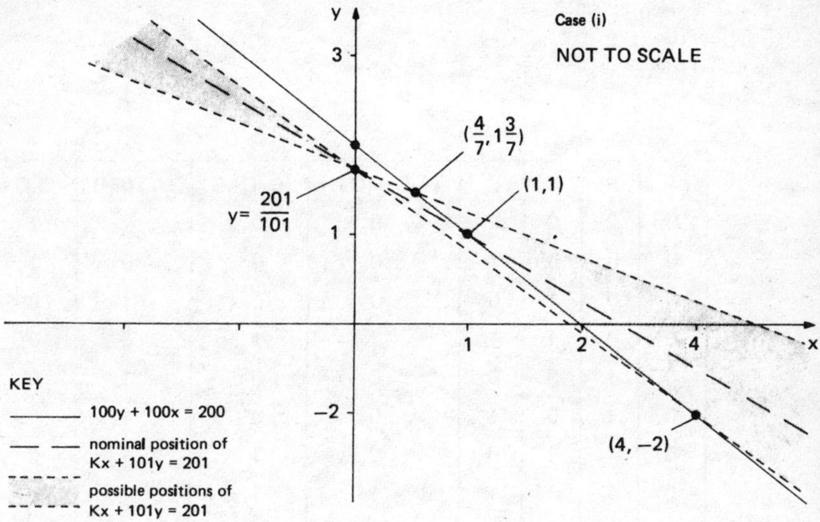

Case ii.

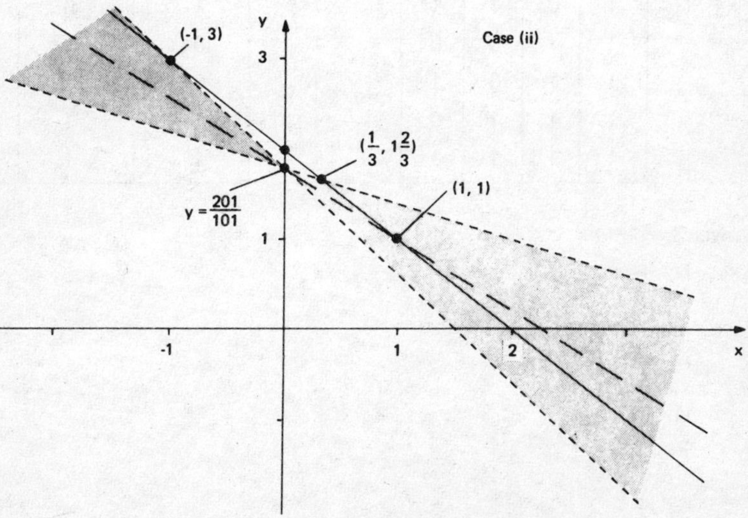

Chapter 26

Answer 1.

i. True
ii. True
iii. False
iv. True
v. True

Answer 2.

A	B	C	D	(A.B)+(C.D)	(B+D).C	$(\bar{A}.\bar{D})+B$	$\bar{B}.\bar{C}$
0	0	0	0	0	0	1	1
0	0	0	1	0	0	0	1
0	0	1	0	0	0	1	0
0	0	1	1	1	1	0	0
0	1	0	0	0	0	1	0
0	1	0	1	0	0	1	0
0	1	1	0	0	1	1	0
0	1	1	1	1	1	1	0
1	0	0	0	0	0	0	1
1	0	0	1	0	0	0	1
1	0	1	0	0	0	0	0
1	0	1	1	1	1	0	0
1	1	0	0	1	0	1	0
1	1	0	1	1	0	1	0
1	1	1	0	1	1	1	0
1	1	1	1	1	1	1	0

Answer 3.

i. $\bar{B}$
ii. $B + \bar{A}$
iii. $A + \bar{B}.\bar{C} + D$
iv. $X + Y + VW$
v. XY
vi. $\overline{U.V.W.X}$

Answer 4.

i. $\overline{B}$
ii. $B + \overline{A}$
iii. $X + Y + VW$
iv. $\overline{A}.\overline{B} + AB\overline{C}$

Answer 5.

i. $\overline{A.C}$
ii. $B.\overline{D}$
iii. XY

Answer 6.
The dual is $(A.B.C) + (A.B.\overline{C}) + (A.\overline{B}.C) + (\overline{A}.B.\overline{C})$
It simplifies to $(A.C + B\overline{C})$ which has the dual $(A + C) . (B + \overline{C})$

Chapter 27

Answer 1.

X	Y	$\overline{X}$	$\overline{Y}$	$\overline{X}.Y$	$X+(\overline{X}.Y)$	$X+Y$	$X.Y$	$X.\overline{Y}$	$(X.Y)+(X.\overline{Y})$
0	0	1	1	0	0	0	0	0	0
0	1	1	0	1	1	1	0	0	0
1	0	0	1	0	1	1	0	1	1
1	1	0	0	0	1	1	1	0	1

Truth Table.

A	B	C	D
0	0	0	0
0	0	1	0
0	1	0	1
0	1	1	1
1	0	0	0
1	0	1	1
1	1	0	1
1	1	1	1

By Algebraic manipulation

$$
\begin{aligned}
D &= \bar{A}B\bar{C} + \bar{A}BC + A\bar{B}C + AB\bar{C} + ABC \\
&= B(\bar{A}.\bar{C} + \bar{A}.C + A\bar{C} + AC) + A\bar{B}C \\
&= B[\bar{A}(\bar{C} + C) + A(C + \bar{C})] + A\bar{B}C \\
&= B(\bar{A} + A) + A\bar{B}C \\
&= B + A\bar{B}C \\
&= B + AC
\end{aligned}
$$

By Karnaugh map

	A	$\bar{A}$	
B	1	1	C
$\bar{B}$	1	0	C
$\bar{B}$	0	0	$\bar{C}$
B	1	1	$\bar{C}$

For diagram

$$
\begin{aligned}
B + AC &= \overline{\overline{B}\,.\,\overline{\overline{A.C}}} = \overline{\bar{B}\,.\,(\bar{A} + \bar{C})} = \overline{\bar{A}.\bar{B} + \bar{B}.\bar{C}} \\
&= \overline{\overline{A + B} + \overline{B + C}} \qquad \text{(De Morgan)}
\end{aligned}
$$

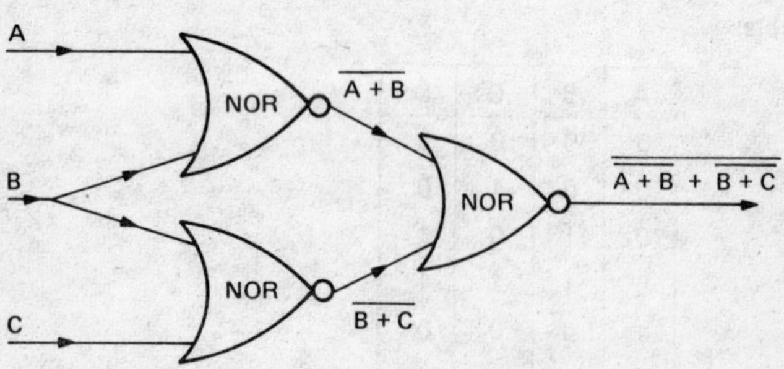

Answer 2.

Not ((not A) or (not B)) is $(\overline{\bar{A} + \bar{B}}) = A.B$ (by De Morgan's rule) so the expression is simply **A and B.**

Venn diagram

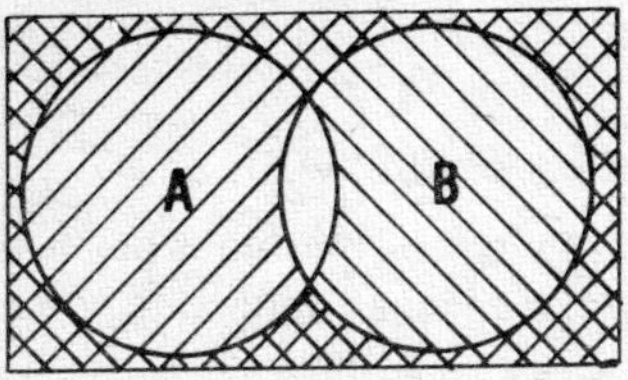

/// **is not B**

\\\ is not A

Total shaded area is (not A) or (not B)

remaining area is not ((not A) or (not B)) and also **A and B**

The whole of the lefthand circle is A.
The whole of the righthand circle is B.

Generalised result $\overline{(\bar{A} + \bar{B} + \bar{C} + \bar{D} + \ldots)} = A.B.C.D.....$

Table of Values N is the number represented in decimal.

a	b	c	d	N	
0	0	0	0	0	reduces to $\bar{a}$ (by inspection)
0	0	0	1	1	
0	0	1	0	2	
0	0	1	1	3	
0	1	0	0	4	
0	1	0	1	5	
0	1	1	0	6	
0	1	1	1	7	
1	0	0	0	8	$a.\bar{b}.\bar{c}.\bar{d}$
1	0	0	1	9	$a.\bar{b}.\bar{c}.d$
1	0	1	0	10	not allowed
1	0	1	1	11	
1	1	0	0	12	
1	1	0	1	13	
1	1	1	0	14	
1	1	1	1	15	

Required function is

$$\bar{a} + a.\bar{b}.\bar{c}.\bar{d} + a.\bar{b}.\bar{c}.d$$
$$= \bar{a} + a.\bar{b}.\bar{c}.(\bar{d} + d)$$
$$= \bar{a} + a.\bar{b}.\bar{c}$$

Answer 3.

Intergrated circuits were the basis of third generation machines in the form of SSI, and later, MSI. The first of these machines date from the 1960s.

Computers built since the mid 1970s, ie. fourth generation computers, have been largely based on LSI, although some components may still be SSI or MSI. These computers include the microcomputers.

The fifth generation computers will probably be based upon VLSI.

NB. Generation numbers are convenient labels to use for typical machines but, like many systems of classification, are difficult to decide upon when applied to some specific examples.

Answer 4.

27.14 – 27.17.

Answer 5.

27.50.

Answer 6.

27.37.

Answer 7.

27.40.

a. combinational in basic form. (A full serial adder is sequential).
b. combinational.
c. sequential.
d. combinational.

Answer 8.

a.

A	B	C	D	E	F
0	0	0	0	0	0
0	0	0	1	0	1
0	0	1	0	0	0
0	0	1	1	0	1
0	1	0	0	0	0
0	1	0	1	0	1
0	1	1	0	0	0
0	1	1	1	0	1
1	0	0	0	0	0
1	0	0	1	0	0
1	0	1	0	0	1
1	0	1	1	0	1
1	1	0	0	1	0
1	1	0	1	1	0
1	1	1	0	1	1
1	1	1	1	1	1

NB. A simplified version of this truth table could be given as an alternative answer.

b. $E = A.B.\overline{C}.D + A.B.\overline{C}.D + A.B.C.\overline{D} + A.B.C.D$

$F = \overline{A}.\overline{B}.\overline{C}.D + \overline{A}.\overline{B}.C.D + \overline{A}.B.\overline{C}.D + \overline{A}.B.C.D$
$+ A.\overline{B}.C.\overline{D} + A.\overline{B}.C.D + A.B.C.\overline{D} + A.B.C.D$

c. **NB.** With practice you may be able to omit (b) and write (c) directly from the truth table.

$E = A.B$

$F = A.C + \overline{A}.D$

d.

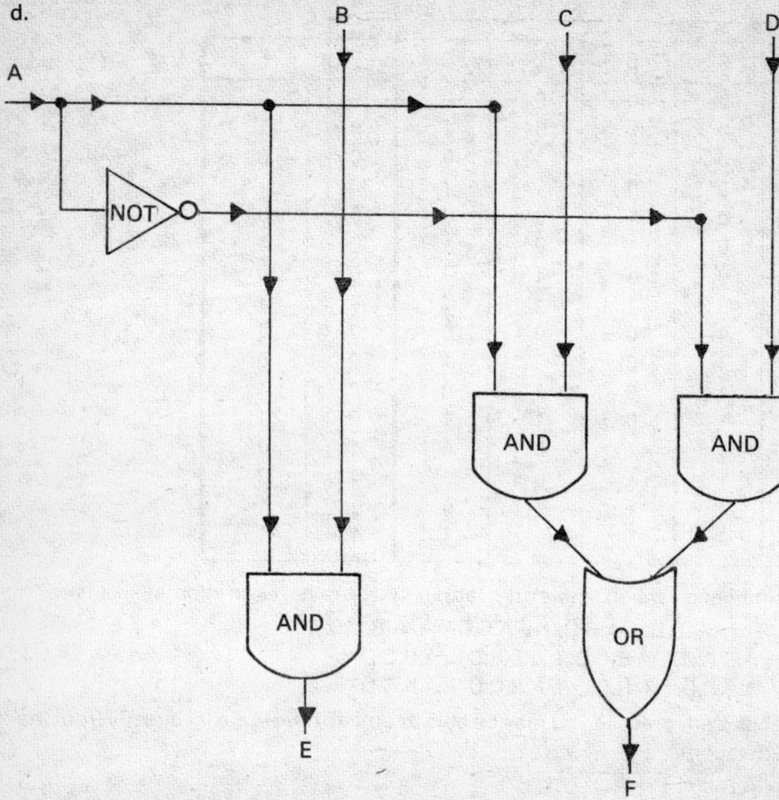

e. This implementation uses 5 gates. Implementations with NOR or NAND would use more gates.

Answer 9.

a.

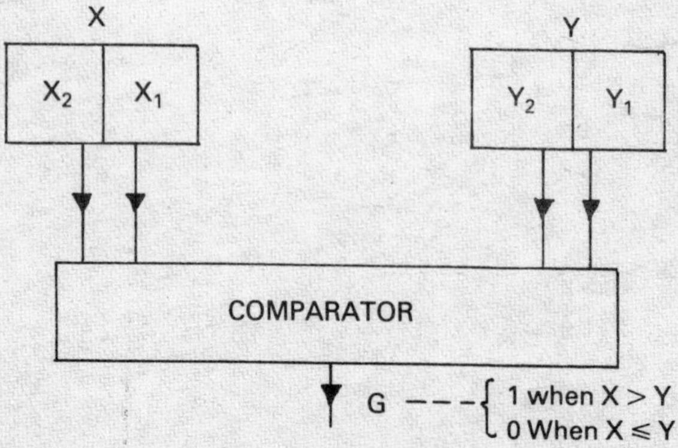

b.

X		Y		X>Y
X_2	X_1	Y_2	Y_1	G
0	0	0	0	0
0	1	0	0	1
1	0	0	0	1
1	1	0	0	1
0	0	0	1	0
0	1	0	1	0
1	0	0	1	1
1	1	0	1	1
0	0	1	0	0
0	1	1	0	0
1	0	1	0	0
1	1	1	0	1
0	0	1	1	0
0	1	1	1	0
1	0	1	1	0
1	1	1	1	0

c. $G = X_2 \,.\, \overline{Y}_2 + X_1 \,.\, \overline{Y}_1 \,.\, (X_2 + \overline{Y}_2)$

d.

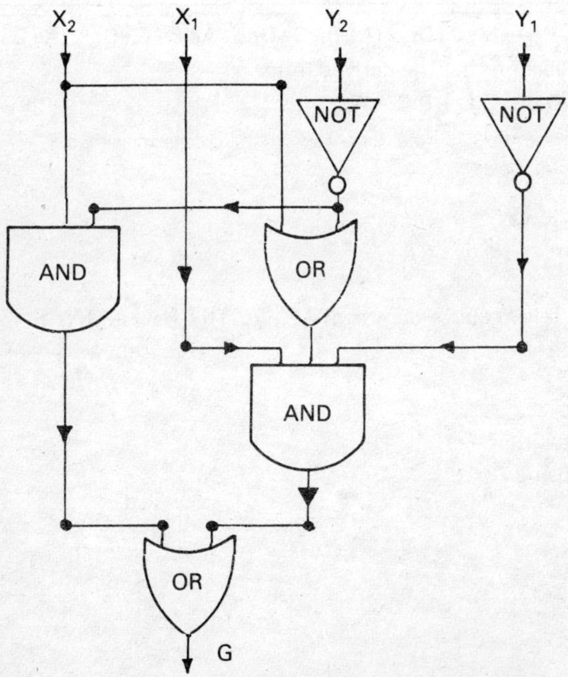

NB. Alternative solutions are possible with NAND and NOR.

Answer 10.

a. 27.22.

b.

A	B	C	$\overline{A+B}$	W = $\overline{\overline{A+B}+C}$	$\overline{B+C}$	X = $\overline{A+\overline{B+C}}$	$\overline{C+A}$	Y = $\overline{B+\overline{C+A}}$	$\overline{A+B+C}$
0	0	0	1	0	1	0	1	0	1
0	0	1	1	0	0	1	0	1	0
0	1	0	0	1	0	1	1	0	0
0	1	1	0	0	0	1	0	0	0
1	0	0	0	1	1	0	0	1	0
1	0	1	0	0	0	0	0	1	0
1	1	0	0	1	0	0	0	0	0
1	1	1	0	0	0	0	0	0	0

c. $(\bar{A}.\bar{B}.\bar{C}) + (A.B.C) = \overline{(A+B+C)} + (A.B.C)$

$= W + X + Y$

d. Let the four bits of the input be A, B, C and D working left to right in the bit pattern.

The output is

$\overline{(\bar{A}.\bar{B}.\bar{C}.\bar{D}) + (\bar{A}.\bar{B}.\bar{C}.D) + (\bar{A}.\bar{B}.C.\bar{D}) + (\bar{A}.B.\bar{C}.\bar{D}) + (A.\bar{B}.\bar{C}.\bar{D})}$

which may be expressed as

$\overline{\overline{(A+B+C+D)} + \overline{(A+B+C+\bar{D})} + \overline{(A+B+\bar{C}+D)} + \overline{(A+\bar{B}+C+D)} + \overline{(\bar{A}+B+C+D)}}$

Further simplications may be derived from

A.B. + A.C + D.B + D.C + B.C + A.D

Chapter 28

Answer 1.

Addressing 4096 cells requires the use of 12 bits. This leaves 6 bits to implement 64 distinct op. codes.

Answer 2.

a. 28.51 – 28.55.

b. 9.23 – 9.26 and 28.21.

Notation used in the flowchart

SCR	Sequence Control Register
CIR	Current Instruction Register
MAR	Memory Address Register
L	Location specified in MAR
MDR	Memory Data Register
ACC	Accumulator
( )	Contents of eg (SCR) means contents of the SCR
F	Function to be performed.
OP	Operand part of CIR

Flowchart.

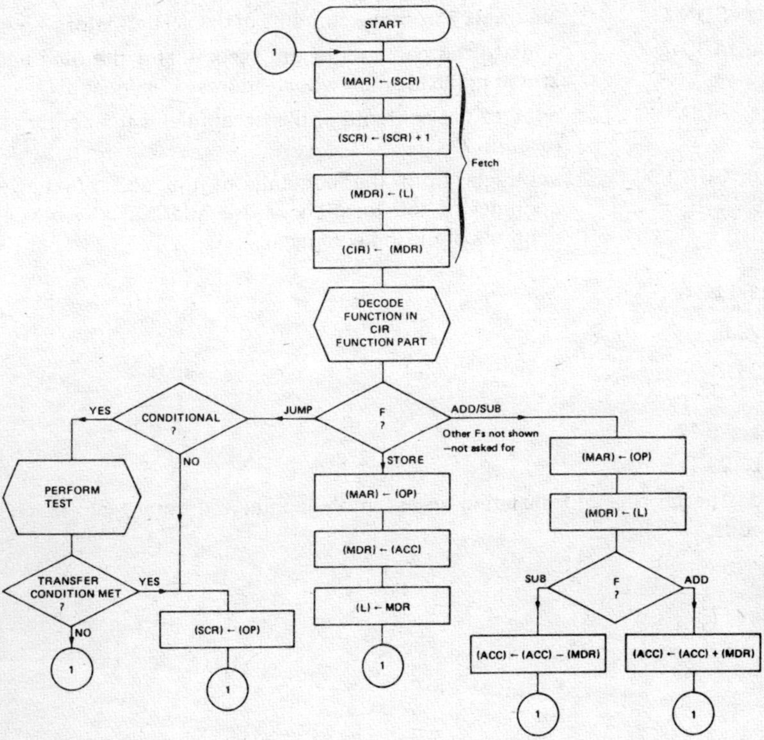

Answer 3.

28.7.

a. 28.28 – 28.29.

b. 28.38.

c. 28.34.

d. 28.39.

Answer 4.

28.12 – 28.3.

a. i. 0000 1101
   ii. 1111 0101

b. i. 0000 1101
   ii. 0011 0101

Chapter 29

Answer 1.

a. SUN 7	subtracts 7 from the contents of the accumulators
b. ADD @ 7	adds to the contents of the accumulator the data value stored in the location whose address is in location 7.
c. ADD 7	adds to the contents of the accumulator the contents of location 7.
d. SUB 7, X	subtracts from the contents of the accumulator the contents of the location whose address is 7 plus the contents of the index register.

Answer 2.

29.8.

Answer 3.

a. 29.12.

b. 29.12.

c. The process of translating an assembly language program into machine code.

Answer 4.

```
                                 (* NB. no_stars and i are integers *)
         .START                  Begin
         LDN  1     }
         STA  NOST  }----            no_stars : = 1
OLOP:    LDN  4     }
         SUB  NOST  }----            while (* there is a line to be printed *)
         JAL  FIN   }                      no_stars < = 4
                                       (* print a line *)
         LDN  0     }
         STA  I     }----              i : = 0
ILOP:    LDA  NOST  }                  while (* there are more asterisks
         SUB  I     }----                    to output on this line *)
         JAZ  LINE  }                        i < = no_stars
         LDA  52    }                      (* output an asterisk *)
         IO   2     }---                   out ("*")
         LDA  1     }
         ADN  1     }----                  i : = 1 + 1
         STA  1     }
         JPU  ILOP                     endwhile
LINE:    LDA  CR    }                  (* generate a new line *)
         IO   2     }----              output
         LDA  LF    }
         IO   2     }
         LDA  NOST  }
         ADN  1     }----              no_stars : = no_stars + 1
         STA  NOST  }
         JPU  OLOP                   endwhile
FIN:     STOP                    end
         .END
```

Answer 5.

(Author's comment. There is a wide variety of possible answers for part a., test yours works).

a. i. **Indirect Addressing.**

LOCATION	CONTENTS
1	LN 0
2	ST 99
3	LN 100
4	ST 98
5	ILA 98
6	AD 99
7	ST 99
8	LA 98
9	SN 149
10	JZ 14
11	AN 150
12	ST 98
13	JM 5
14	STOP

Test Data

LOCATION	CONTENTS
100	3
101	2
102	6

ii. **Address Modification**

LOCATION	CONTENTS
1	LN 0
2	ST 99
3	SN 50
4	ST 98
5	LA 150/98
6	AD 99
7	ST 99
8	LA 98
9	AN 1
10	ST 98
11	JZ 12
12	JM 5
13	STOP

Notes on i.
Location 98 holds the address of the next location whose contents have to be added to the total in 99. It is increased by 1 each time through the loop. The end is checked for by subtracting 150.

Notes on ii.
Location 98 contains a negative modifier (assuming this is allowed). It is incremented by one each time through the loop until it is zero. This is achieved by indexing since the accumulator is loaded with the number in location address (150 plus contents of 98).

Test on i.

Successive Contents

98	99	Accumulator
100	0	0
101	3	3
	5	100
		–49
		101
		2
		5
		101

Test on ii.

Successive Contents

98	99	Accumulator
–50	0	0
–49	3	–50
	5	3
		–50
		–49
		2
		5
		49
		–48

b. i.

LOCATION	CONTENTS	
198	LN 201	Saves return address 201 in 499
199	ST 499	
200	JM 500	← jumps to subroutine
201		← Instruction returned to

ii. **Address Modification.**
Use JM 0,499
Jump to location 0 + (499) ie jumps to 201

Indirect address
IJM 499
Jumps to location given at 499 ie jumps to 201

Chapter 30

Answer 1.

The advantages and disadvantages of high level languages are:–

Advantages.

a. Program writing easier because of vocabulary which is relatively simple to learn.

b. Program writing takes less time so programmers are utilised more efficiently.

c. Amendments during program writing are easily incorporated and subsequent revision is also easier.

d. Extensive use of macros and subroutines (both those of the manufacturer and the user) is permitted.

e. High level languages are largely independent of the machine and orientated towards the problem.

f. Source programs may be understood by people other than the person who wrote them.

Disadvantages.

a. Require translation unlike machine code. (This is not a too significant disadvantage since low level symbolic languages have the same problem.)

b. A large number of rules must be adhered to.

c. The object programs tend to be less efficient in terms of storage utilisation and running time because of general constraints of the language which may conflict with the best method of solution.

Answer 2.

30.5 and 30.6.

Answer 3.

Different manufacturers provide different dialects of BASIC.

They can attempt to solve their problem by attempting to define a common subset of each language which they can both use to write programs.

In general there is a need for language standards. They could both have born this point in mind when buying their computers in the first place.

Chapter 31

Answer 1.

Advantages of the List.

a. A more flexible method of storage, allowing deletion and insertion without moving existing data. This reduces the amount of data movement within store.

b. The size of a block of data may not be known before it is placed in store. With tables or strings a block of core might be set aside and then part of it might be left unused thereby wasting storage. Enough storage might not be set aside and the table would have to be reorganised in a larger block. Using lists avoids these problems by placing data in the next available space.

c. Lists do not waste storage space by leaving gaps where deletions have occurred as happens with tables and strings.

d. Using lists avoids rigid structures which can create difficulties when organising storage allocation.

e. When tables or strings have to be broken down into units of manageable size lists form an efficient method of connecting units.

Answer 2.

a. Look up table (31.31) slow access, saves space.

b. Direct access table (31.32) fast access, can waste space.

c. Hash table (31.34) compromise between a. and b.

The differences lie in the *methods* of storage and access and *use* of storage.

Answer 3.

a. i. 12.50 and 12.61f.

ii. **Example.**

LOCATION	10	11	12	13	14	15	16	17	18	19
CONTENTS	B	L	D	R	T	B	L	D	R	T
COMMENT	First node entered in tree					Second node entered in tree				

Notation. L : Left descendant of pointer.
R : Right descendant pointer
B : Back pointer
T : Trace pointer
D : Datum.

The pointers would give addresses of data in other nodes **or** would write in a terminator. Some pointers shown may not be present in some cases.

Note. An array representation could be shown.

b. The tree below illustrates one way in which competitor 7 might win. The number of the competitor winning a round becomes the datum of the parent node.

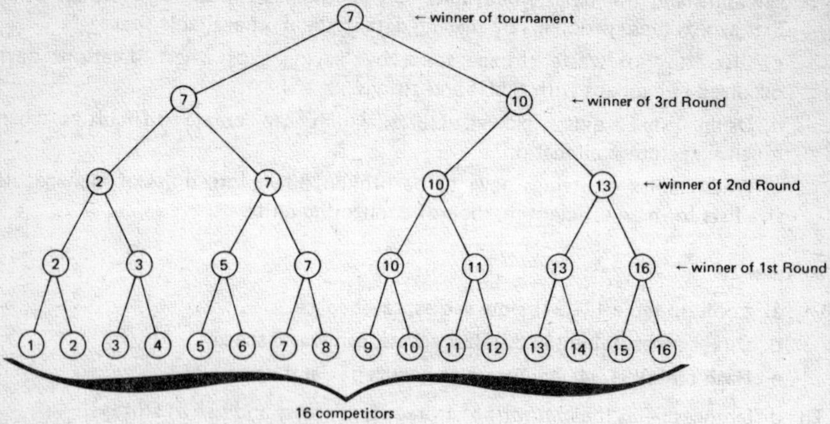

Author's Comment. The procedure to find these competitors will work as follows.

i. Start with root node (winner).

ii. Check datum in right or left descendant.

iii. If the datum is not the winner's number print it then go to other node and repeat step ii.

iv. If the datum is the winner's number print datum in other node but stay at node and repeat step (ii).

v. When a terminator is discovered in the pointers all the competitors are found.

Continuing with part b. We assume the data is in array as follows:—

	L	R	D
1			
N values 2			
3			

L Lefthand pointer

R Righthand pointer

D Datum (winners' numbers)

N Present node position

So A(N,1) is Lefthand pointer at node N
A(N,2) is Righthand pointer at node N
A(N,3) is Datum at node N
let W be the winners number.

Assume for convenience that the root node is Node 1. Also assume that the terminator is 99.

Flowchart.

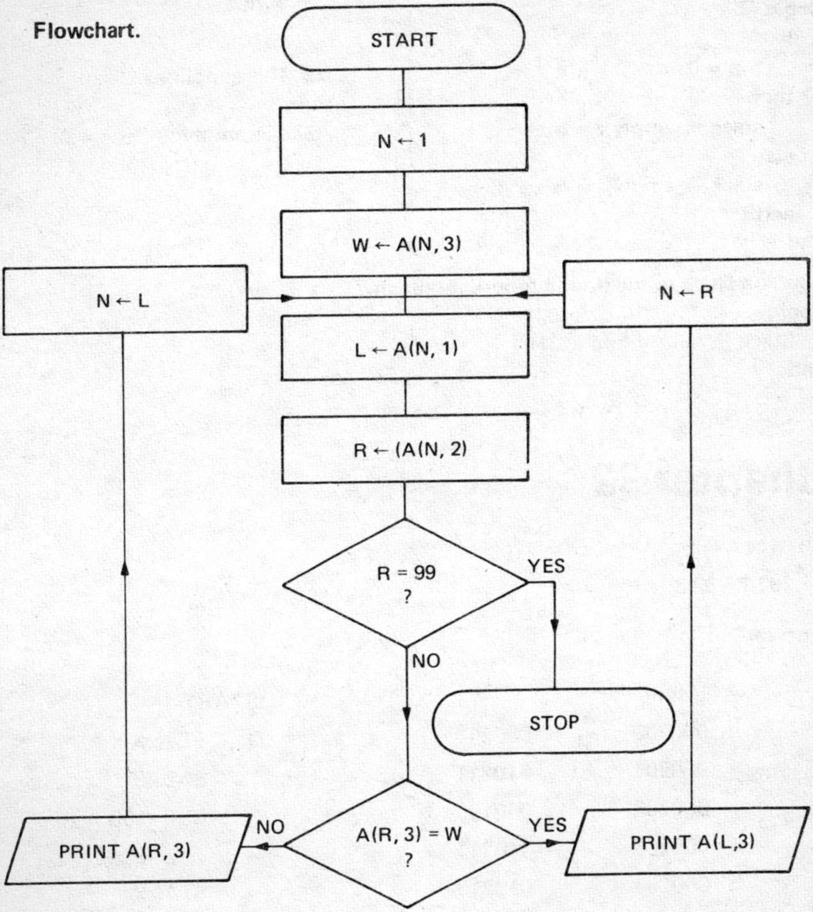

Answer 4.

```
function stack_is_empty (top : integer): boolean
Begin
   if
      top = 0
   then
      stack_is_empty : = true
   else
      stack_is_empty : = false
   endif
end
```

NB. This simplifies to:
stack_is_empty : = (top = 0)

```
function stack_is_full (top: integer) : boolean
Begin
   Stack_is_full : = (top = 21)
end
```

Chapter 32

Answer 1.

32.2 – 32.3.

Answer 2.

Listing			
		.START	
000200	000213	D:	LDA X
000201	010211		JAZ E
000202	040100		SUB 100
000203	140211		JAL E
000204	010213		STA X
000205	000212		LDA Q
000206	050001		ADN 1
000207	010212		STA Q
000210	120200		JPU D
000211	170000	E:	STOP
000212	000000	Q:	0
000213	000060	X:	60
		.END	

The program divides 'X' by the number in location 100. The quotient is stored in Q and the number left in 'X' is the remainder.

Answer 3.

a. **Author's Comments.** You should make it clear in your answer that 'internal machine instruction' refers to a machine code (28.3) whereas "external symbolic machine instruction' refers to a low level assembly language type instruction. (29.12).

The two should be contrasted in terms of these features:—

	Internal machine code	External symbolic machine code
Representation	Binary Code	Symbols and Mnemonics
Entry	Direct by 'keying in', more often by loading using standard software.	Must first be assembled, then loaded.
Execution	Immediate once in store.	Requires translation to machine code.
Addressing	Binary code interpreted by hardware to give absolute address.	Mostly symbolic for programmer convenience but requires assembly and conversion to machine address.
Correspondence to machine function set	one-one correspondence.	one-one correspondence except for macros.

b. i. **Assembly phase** (Refer to 32.9 to 32.16).

Assuming a two pass assembler actions in the **first pass** would include:—

a. Checks of legality in instruction format
eg Is ADD a legal operation
Is COST a legal symbol
Is modifier 3 in the allowed range.

b. Checks if the operation is a pseudo op in this case no.

c. Checks to see if the operand COST is symbolic — it is. It would be checked against a symbol table and entered if absent eg:—

	Symbol	Address	
entered →	COST		← not yet known.

d. Error listings eg missing symbols and errors in the above checks.

On the second pass.

a. The object form of each instruction would be built up in binary (machine code) using a special register. This would include:—

i. Entering the binary code corresponding to ADD

ii. Entering the binary address corresponding to COST using the symbol table.

iii. Making suitable adjustments to instruction format and codes to set address modification details.

b. Output of a listing showing machine code and corresponding mnemonic.

c. Output of object program onto required media.

ii. **The execution phase.** The execution of this instruction requires a full fetch execute cycle. In outline it involves:–

a. Fetching the instruction (now in machine code) into the Current Instruction Register.

b. Interpreting from the instruction both the type of instruction – ADD and the address type – address modification.

c. The **absolute address** must be obtained by hardware by adding the contents of the modifier register to the binary code for COST.

d. The instruction ADD would then be performed obtaining the operand from main store using its absolute address and then adding it to the contents of the accumulator.

e. Any error conditions created during execution (eg arithmetic error or addition) would generate an error signal.

Answer 4.

i. a, b, c 32.21 – 32.25.

ii. **Advantages.** This restriction aids translation. In particular, it means that simple and compact symbol tables (32.22) can be used which saves storage and improves the efficiency of the translation process.

Disadvantages. The disadvantages are that when a programmer uses longer variable identifiers in order to improve program readability there is a chance that an ambiguity will arise. If the programmer tries to avoid that problem by keeping identifiers to two characters program readability suffers.

iii. Advantages include:

a. It allows access to hardware facilities not directly accessible to the high level language.

b. It enables optimisation of critical sections of code.

c. It allows extra functions and facilities to be incorporated into the language.

iv. There are two probable reasons.

a. A good optimising compiler may detect that the loop is redundant and therefore miss it out of the object code.

b. It the loop is translated into object code by the compiler its execution will be very much faster than when it is interpreted and therefore no longer satisfactory.

NB. The University of London University Entrance and Schools Examination Council require this disclaimer be printed by all persons given permission to reproduce questions from their past examination papers:

"The University of London University Entrance and Schools Examination Council accepts no responsibility whatsoever for the accuracy or method of working in the answers given."

Chapter 33

Answer 1.

< expression > → < operand >< operator >< operand >
< operand > → A | B | C | D | E | F | G | H | I | J | K | L | M | N | O | P | Q | R | S | T | U | V | W | X | Y | Z
< operator > → = | ≠ | AND | OR
< statement > → < line number > IF < expression > THEN < line number >
< line number > → < digit >< symbol >< symbol >
< digit > → 1 | 2 | 3 | 4 | 5 | 6 | 7 | 8 | 9
< symbol > → < digit > | < zero >
< zero > → 0

Answer 2.

< date > → < day > ∇ < month > ∇ < day number >
< day > → M | TU | W | TH | F | SA | SU
< month > → JA | F | MA | AP | MY | JU | JY | AU | S | O | N | D
< day number > → 1 | 2 | 3 | 4 | 5 | 6 | 7 | 8 | 9 | 10 | 11 | 12 | 13 | 14 | 15 | 16 | 17 | 18 | 19 | 20 | 21 | 22 | 23 | 24 | 25 | 26 | 27 | 28 | 29 | 30 | 31

Possible amendments

< date > → < day > ∇ < month detail >
< day number > → 1 | 2 | 3 | 4 | 5 | 6 | 7 | 8 | 9 | 10 | 11 | 12 | 13 | 14 | 15 | 16 | 17 | 18 | 19 | 20 | 21 | 22 | 23 | 24 | 25 | 26 | 27 | 28 | 29

< month detail > → < jan > | < feb > | < mar > | < apr > | . . . . etc
< jan > → JA ∇ < day number > | JA ∇ 30 | JA ∇ 31
< feb > → F ∇ < day number >
< mar > → MA ∇ < day number > | MA ∇ 30 | MA ∇ 31
etc

Answer 3.

[3, 2, 3, 2, 1, 3, 2, 3, 2, 1] Two back tracks are necessary.

Answer 4.

W X / Z Y * + **Note.** In table below the working is from *right to left.*

Symbol String	W	X	/	Z	Y	*	+
Rank Value	1	1	–1	1	1	–1	–1
Subtotal	1	0	–1	0	–1	–2	–1

The expression is "Well Formed".

Answer 5.

a. A X ∿ C E ↑ + Y * =

b. Y X B + W Z – / =

Tree a.

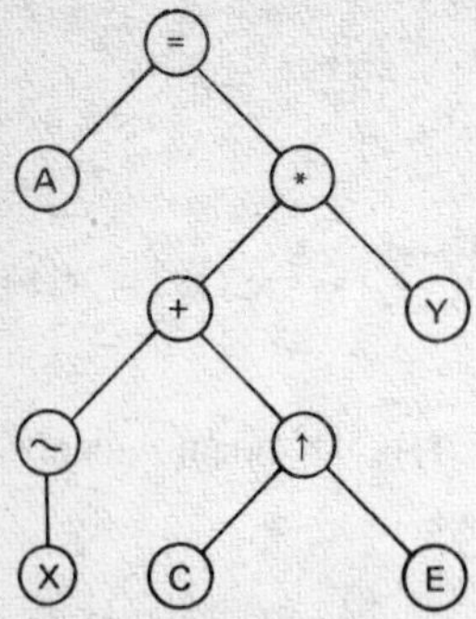

Tree b.

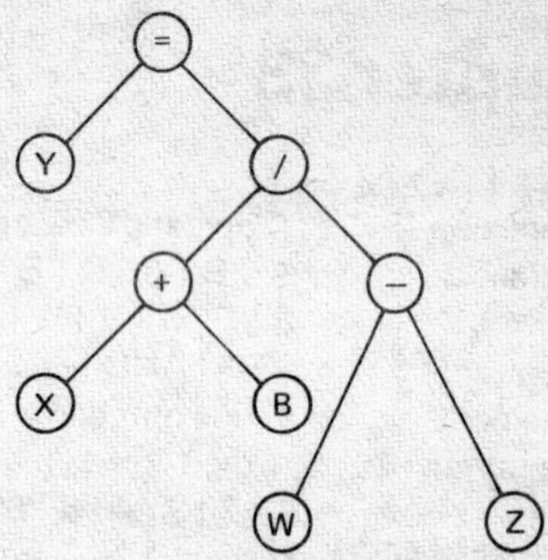

Chapter 34

Answer 1.

34.9.

Answer 2.

34.22 – 34.23.

Chapter 35

Answer 1.

a. 35.11 – 35.14.

b. 35.10.

Choice of method.

Factors:
- i. Extent of pre-ordering.
- ii. Number of records.
- iii. Size of records (For large records sort key and position).

Answer 2.

35.3c.

Answer 3.

35.6.

Answer 4.

35.22.

Chapter 36

Answer 1.

36.3.

Answer 2.

36.9–13 and 36.14–36.15.

The critical distinction is that real-time processing requires a response within a small enough time period to affect events in the real world as they happen.

Chapter 37

Answer 1.

37.7 and 37.45.

Answer 2.

a. 37.23.
b. 37.23.
c. 37.24 – 37.30.
d. 37.31 – 37.36

Chapter 38

Answer 1.

38.3 – 38.5.

Answer 2.

38.19.

Answer 3.

38.32 – 38.33.

Chapter 39

Answer 1.

a. 34.26, 39.35, 39.38, 39.40. The general purpose of each of these interrupts is to allow *significant events* to be dealt with as they occur.

b. 34.30, 39.34. The correct order of priority is ACB because the program with most input or output must have highest priority and the one with most processing time (and least output) must have least priority. (39.52)..

c. 39.7 and 39.11.

Answer 2.
39.55.

Hardware requirements.
Adequate main storage, additional on-line backing store units, small processor for off lining output jobs used in conjunction with its own tape unit and printer. Key-to-tape and key-to-disc input unit are an advantage.

Software requirements.
An operating system which includes multiprogramming features and foreground/background operation.

Answer 3.

a. 39.12, 39.31–39.35, 39.47–39.51.

The effects on the user of multi-programming are faster turnaround of jobs. Multi-access may enable alternative methods of use or even interaction with the program by the user.

b. i. Peripheral requires attention.
ii. End of time-slice.
iii. Hardware error/power failure.
iv. Program error eg. overflow.
(See 39.36).

c. 38.17 and 38.18–38.23.

Chapter 40

Answer 1.

40.10.

Answer 2.

40.6.

Chapter 41

Answer 1.

A critical examination is needed because there are reasons for carrying out each step in the present system. These reasons must be discovered and questioned to see if they *need* to be incorporated in the new system.

Chapter 42

Answer 1.

Basically the choice of output depends on its subsequent use, or the type of application.

CHOICE ACCORDING TO SUBSEQUENT USE.

1. Output can be produced for use by humans or for use by machines:–

a. **Use by humans.** Output for use by humans must be in a form understood by humans so we have the following:–

i. **Printed output.** Either on pre-printed stationery or plain paper and in various formats.

ii. **Visual display.** Output in the form of script or graphs etc, displayed on a screen.

iii. **Microfilm.** Output required for storage and subsequent reference.

b. **Further use by machines.** Output for use by machines will be prepared in a machine-sensible form. The following are examples:–

i. **For subsequent re-input into computer.** Such output can be prepared on magnetic tape, disc etc as appropriate. For example, output which goes directly to another run as input.

ii. **Output converted off-line to another medium.** Magnetic tape may be used for output from an updating run which is subsequently printed as an off-line operation.

iii. **Transmission of output.** Output to be transmitted over communication lines will need to be in a form acceptable to the transmission device.

CHOICE ACCORDING TO TYPE OF APPLICATION.

2. Choice of output will vary with applications, one type of output being more appropriate to one application than another:–

a. **Batch processing.** Output will be on magnetic tape or disc if spooling techniques are used.

b. **Real-time processing.** The use of data communication devices is essential so that output can be transmitted immediately to the control point (a terminal).

c. **Interrogation or enquiry.** A visual display or terminal is the choice where immediate response to enquiries for information held on master files is required. These can be located locally or at a remote point.

d. **Turnaround document.** Used where output subsequently re-enters the computer system without there being any intermediate off-line coding process. To achieve this, output documents can be prepared in optical characters. Such documents can also be read by humans.

Note. There is an obvious overlapping between 1 and 2.

Chapter 43

Answer 1.

43.9–43.12.

Answer 2.

The process of 43.8 can be made simpler if, well in advance, the manual documents are re-designed so that when the time for conversion comes they will be easy to transcribe. Better still, they will have been designed to exploit document reading methods such as OMR or OCR.

Chapter 44

Answer 1.

44.5.

Answer 2.

a. 44.19 and 44.26b.
b. 44.29.
c. 44.27.
d. 44.17.

Chapter 45

Answer 1.

45.19 – 45.21.

Chapter 46

Answer 1.

Advantages 46.9, disadvantages 46.10.

Chapter 47

Answer 1.

Advantages of time sharing are:–

a. No major capital investment is required.

b. It is possible to have instant access to a computer.

c. A user gets a fast response in his own office.

d. A large variety of standard programs is available to the user.

e. The user has a relatively low operating cost.

f. The user gets the benefits of all the latest program techniques.

g. Users have access to the latest generation computer hardware.

Bureaux 47.18 – 47.20.

Answer 2.

47.22.

Answer 3.

Main factors considered

a. Terms of reference must be laid down and objectives set.

b. Investigation and fact finding. The present system must be studied in terms of:–

i. Costs
ii. Staffing
iii. Equipment
iv. Procedures
v. Controls
vi. Data handled, volume, variety
vii. Data collection.

c. Analysis of facts with reference to the objectives laid down in the terms of reference and using principles of procedure (41.9).

Alternatives to Purchase.

a. Renting time sharing facilities (47.12).

Disadvantages

i. Computer staff must be employed even if volume of work does not merit it.

ii. Equipment must be purchased or rented and accommodated.

b. Using a Bureau (47.18).
Disadvantages
- i. Slow 'turn-around time'.
- ii. Less controls are possible over an external organisation.

Chapter 48

Answer 1.

a. i. 23.23.
 ii. 23.37.

b. Numerical information (values) are represented by physical quantities such as voltages and current magnitudes.

These values are represented generating a trace in a cathode ray tube or producing a graphical plot on paper.

Advantages (Two from the following).
- i. Cheaper than using the real thing.
- ii. Faster results than with a digital machine in some cases.
- iii. Suitable timescaling gives information earlier than with the real system.
- iv. No extra material costs.
- v. Safer in some cases.

c. (48.8). Application 48.16 and 48.17.

Answer 2.

Digitiser.
48.10 – 48.14.

Chapter 49

Answer 1.

a. $f(x) = x^3 - 3x^2 + 15x - 30$

$f(2) = -4$ and $f(3) = 15$. So $f(x)$ changes sign, and is therefore zero, at a point between $x = 2$ and $x = 3$.

b. $f'(x) = 3x^2 - 6x + 15 = 3(x^2 - 2x + 5)$

Newton Raphson formula is

$$x_{n+1} = x_n - \frac{f(x_n)}{f'(x_n)}$$

In this case $$x_{n+1} = x_n - \frac{x_n^3 - 3x_n^2 + 15x_n - 30}{3(x_n^2 - 2x_n + 5)}$$

Working to 6 figures using a calculator we get

$$x_0 = 2, x_1 = 2.26667, x_2 = 2.25285, x_3 = 2.25281$$

The solution is 2.2528 4D

c. Given $x^3 - 3x^2 + 15x - 30 = 0$

$$x(x^2 - 3x^2 + 15) = 30$$

$$x = \frac{30}{x^2 - 3x + 15}$$

Using $$x_{n+1} = \frac{30}{x_n^2 - 3x_n + 15}$$

Working to 6 figures using a calculator we get

$$x_0 = 2, x_1 = 2.30769, x_2 = 2.23841, x_3 = 2.25644$$
$$x_4 = 2.25188, x_5 = 2.25304, x_6 = 2.25275$$
$$x_7 = 2.25282, x_8 = 2.2528, x_9 = 2.25281$$

We get the same solution of course but in more steps.

d. Using $$x_{n+1} = x_{n-1} - \frac{y_{n-1}(x_n - x_{n-1})}{y_n - y_{n-1}}$$

Working to 6 figures we get

$$x_0 = 3, x_1 = 2, x_3 = 2.21053, x_4 = 2.25517$$
$$x_5 = 2.25278, x_6 = 2.25281$$

Answer 2.
(42.26)

Answer 3.

a. $f(x) = 5x^3 + 7x^2 - 14x - 16$

$f(1) = 5 + 7 - 14 - 16 = -18$ } sign change

$f(2) = 40 + 28 - 28 - 16 = 24$

b. $f'(x) = 15x^2 + 14x - 14$

Use $$x_{n+1} = x_n - \frac{(5x^3 + 7x^2 - 14x - 16)}{(15x^2 + 14x - 14)}$$

$$x_0 = 1, x_1 = 2.2, x_2 = 1.74899, x_3 = 1.61279$$
$$x_4 = 1.60011, x_5 = 1.6$$

c. $$5x^3 + 7x^2 - 14x - 16 = 0$$

i. so $x(5x^2 + 7x - 14) = 16$

or $$x = \frac{16}{5x^2 + 7x - 14}$$

So we may form an iterative formula

$$x_n \quad = \quad \frac{16}{5x_n^2 + 7x_n - 14}$$

This formula is of the form $x_{n+1} = f(x_n)$

To test for convergence

$$f'(x) \quad = \quad \frac{-16(10x+7)}{(5x^2 + 7x_n - 14)^2}$$

$$f'(1.6) = 3.68$$

The condition for convergence is not satisfied since $|\,f'(x)\,| > |$

ii. $\quad f'(0) \quad = \quad -\frac{4}{7} \triangleq -0.57$

So $\quad |\,f'(0)\,| < | \quad$ and we may expect convergence to a root.

We obtain another root $x = -1$

Answer 4.
(49.27).

Let $\quad f(x) \quad = \quad 4x^3 + 4x^2 - 4x - 1$

then $\quad f'(x) \quad = \quad 12x^2 + 8x - 4$

To sketch the graph we note that $f(0) = -1$

Turning points occur for $f'(x) = 0$, ie

$$4(3x^2 + 2x - 1) \quad = \quad 0$$

$$4(3x - 1)(x + 1) \quad = \quad 0$$

Turning points at $x = \frac{1}{3}$ and $x = -1$

$f(-1) \quad = \quad -4 + 4 + 4 - 1 \quad = \quad 3$

$f(1) \quad = \quad 4 + 4 - 4 - 1 \quad = \quad 3$

We have enough to sketch the graph.

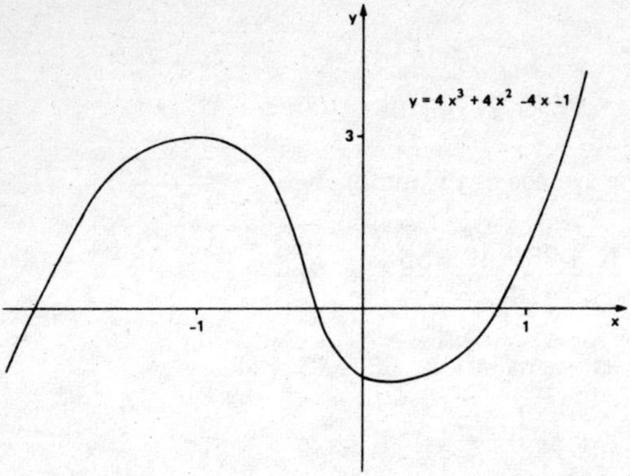

Newton's formula is $x_{n+1} = x_n - \dfrac{f(x_n)}{f'(x_n)}$

Flowchart.

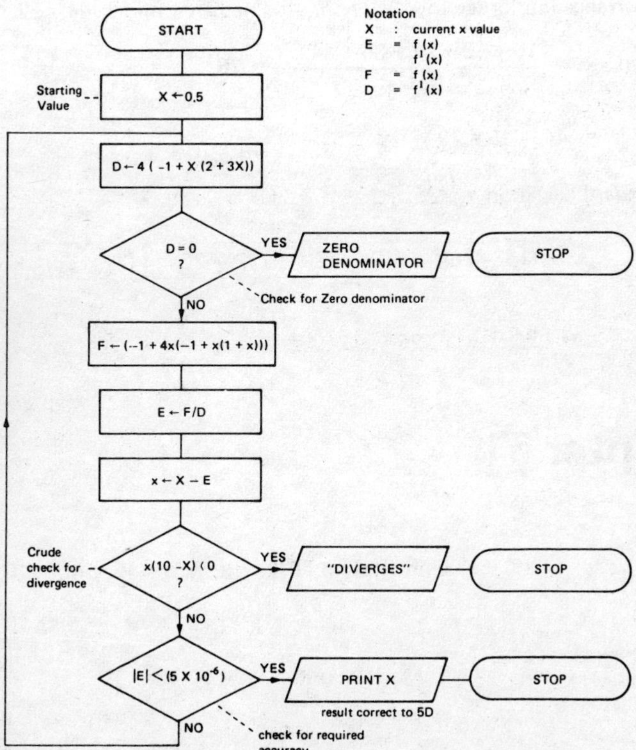

Chapter 50

Answer 1.

a. Arrange into order 13, 26, 49, 56

The median is the average of the middle two $= \dfrac{26+49}{2} = 37.5$

The mean $\bar{x} = \dfrac{13+26+49+56}{4} = 36$

The range is largest – smallest = 56 – 13 = 43

$$\text{Standard deviation} = \sqrt{\frac{\Sigma(x-\bar{x})^2}{n}}$$

$$= \sqrt{\frac{(13-36)^2 + (26-36)^2 + (49-36)^2 + (56-36)^2}{4}}$$

$$= \sqrt{\frac{1198}{4}} = \sqrt{299.5} \triangleq 17.3$$

b. Arrange into order 15, 19, 22, 30, 44. Median is mid value = 22.

Mean $\bar{x} = \dfrac{15+19+22+30+44}{5} = 26$

Range = 44 – 15 = 29

$$\text{Standard deviation} = \sqrt{\frac{\Sigma(x-\bar{x})^2}{n}}$$

$$= \sqrt{\frac{(15-26)^2 + (19-26)^2 + (22-26)^2 + (30-26)^2 + (44-26)^2}{5}}$$

$$= \sqrt{\frac{526}{5}} \triangleq 10.26$$

Chapter 51

Answer 1.
(51.22).
Routine as in (51.19) but with F(1) = 2, F(2) = 8, F(3) = 18, F(4) = 26, F(5) = 30.

Revision Test Answers

Answer 1.

High level language 30.3.

Low level language 29.8.

Factors in the choice of low level languages.

i. Efficiency in use of time or storage.

ii. The problem is specific to the hardware and not suited to high level programming.

iii. The required facility is not available in the high level languages provided for the system.

There are many possible solutions to the last part of this question. This method performs an AND operation between the word and a 1 in each bit position and counts the 1s which are encountered. The mask is shifted along after each test.

Outline method:

Begin
    Store zero in total
    Store 1 in mask
    Store wordlength in length
    Store 1 in position.
    While position < = length
        load mask
        AND with word
        ADD 1 to total of result is not zero
        Load mask shift left one place and store
        ADD 1 to position
    endwhile
end

Answer 2.

(23.30, 23.31, 24.13).

```
          0 0 1 1 1 1 0    =  36 Octal   =  30 Decimal
convert   1 1 0 1 1 1 0
          0 0 1 0 0 0 1
                      1
          -------------
          0 0 1 0 0 1 0    –22 Octal     =  18 Decimal
```

	0 0 1 1 1 1 0		
	0 1 1 1 1 0 0	1 shift left	
change	1 1 1 1 0 0 0	2 shifts left	**overflow**

	0 0 1 1 1 1 0		
	0 0 0 1 1 1 1	1 shift right	
	0 0 0 0 1 1 1	2 shifts right	7 Decimal

	1 1 0 1 1 1 0		
	1 1 1 0 1 1 1	1 shift right	
	1 1 1 1 0 1 1	2 shifts right	–5 Decimal
convert	0 0 0 0 1 0 0		
	1		

	1 1 0 1 1 1 0		
	1 0 1 1 1 0 0	1 shift left	
change	0 1 1 1 0 0 0	2 shifts left	**overflow**

b.

x	1 0 1 0 1 0 1
y	1 1 0 0 0 1 1
x.y	1 0 0 0 0 0 1

x	1 0 1 0 1 0 1
y	1 1 0 0 0 1 1
x+y	1 1 1 0 1 1 1

	1 0 1 0 1 0 1
	1 1 0 0 0 1 1
x≢y	0 1 1 0 1 1 0

The partial sum is the not-equivalent operation ie sum without carry.

Procedure for partial sum, using x and y as above.

i. Load x into the accumulator
ii. Do a x ≢ y operation.
iii. Store the contents of the accumulator (This is s)
iv. Reload x.
v. Do a x.y operation (produces 1 s to be carried)
vi. Do a left shift (this is the carry bit in position)
vii. Store the contents of the accumulator (This is c.)

c. We assume pure binary representation of decimal quantities. It is easier to **work** from right to left. $1023 = 2^{10} - 1$ and requires 10 bits with no sign.

Signed integer		+ve Decimal integer	Character
Sign bit	7 bits	10 bits	6 bits

Last part. Use an AND mask (28.13).

Answer 3.

source code	32.1
object code	32.1
compilation	The task carried out by a compiler (32.3).
"name table"	ie. a symbol table (32.22)
open subroutine	29.33.
closed subroutine	29.33.
execution	Performing a set of program instruction on a computer

NB. The University of London University Entrance and Schools Examination Council require this disclaimer be printed by all persons given permission to reproduce questions from their past examination papers:

"The University of London University Entrance and Schools Examination Council accepts no responsibility whatsoever for the accuracy or method of working in the answers given."

Answer 4.

i. 39.12b.
ii. 48.8 – 48.9.
iii. 39.47.
iv. Optical character recognition.
v. 39.12e.

Answer 5.

a. The executive or supervisor program is the basic control program at the centre of the operating system. The executive remains permanently in main store while other parts of the operating system may at times be held on direct access media. Its primary task is to control and schedule the jobs' use of hardware.

b. i. Aspects to be considered
a. Priority
b. I/O device requirements
c. Storage requirements

d. Software requirements. (ch. 39).

ii. Consider termination by error and termination by completion. (Ch. 39).

iii. See (a).

Functions. eg. Storage management,
Peripheral management,
Resource allocation.

Answer 6.

35.25 – 35.28.

Answer 7.

a.

d	2^2 c	2^1 b	2^0 a	x
0	0	0	0	0
0	0	0	1	0
0	0	1	0	1
0	0	1	1	1
0	1	0	0	0
0	1	0	1	0
0	1	1	0	0
0	1	1	1	0
1	0	0	0	0
1	0	0	1	0
1	0	1	0	1
1	0	1	1	1
1	1	0	0	0
1	1	0	1	0
1	1	1	0	1
1	1	1	1	1

$x = b(\bar{c} + d)$

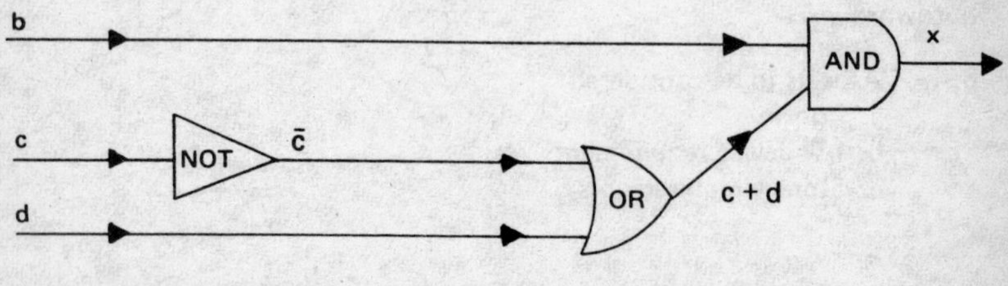

b. 1.8b 48.8 – 48.10.

Answer 8.

a. 28.7 and Four ways: (28.7 – 28.39).

b. Answers could include

i. Using four 6 bit character codes eg 6 bit BCD

ii. Using three 8 bit bytes, eg ASCII with parity

1st	2nd	3rd	4th
6 bit code	6 bit code	6 bit code	6 bit code

Manipulation:– Mask, shifts, swaps (28.13).

c. (31.14 – 31.17).

Answer 9.

a. 1.14 – 1.16

Appendix 2.2, (28.21) (Also see answer 2 chapter 28).

Answer 10.

a. 45.4.

b. 13.23.

c. 13.25 and 43.5.

d. 43.16.

NB. Answers to the remaining questions are given in the supplement for teachers and lecturers except where the publication of answers is not permitted by the examining board concerned.

Appendix 2

Appendix 2.1. Core Storage

1. a. A core is a tiny ring of magnetic material. In every location of core storage each bit is represented by its own individual core. Cores are arranged in horizontal planes so that cores belonging to the same location are situated vertically one above another as shown in this diagram.

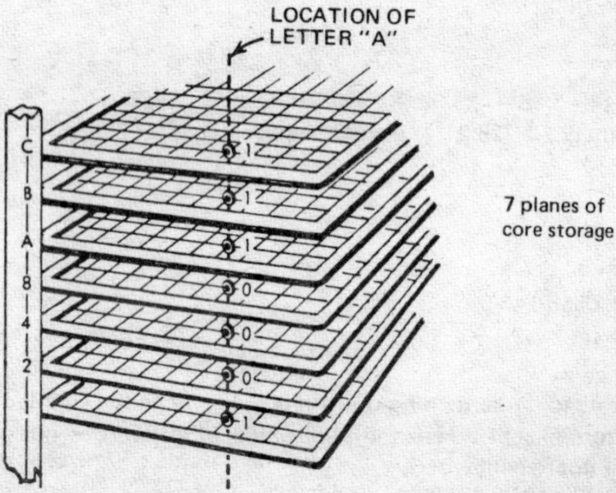

b. The cores each have two stable and distinguishable states into which they can be individually magnetised. The two states are used to represent '0' and '1'. The 'X' and 'Y' wires, on which the cores are threaded, are used in pairs rather like map references.

c. **Writing to core.** When a selected core is to be magnetised, currents are passed through both the X and Y wires at the same time. Only the core referenced by both wires will be affected by the currents.

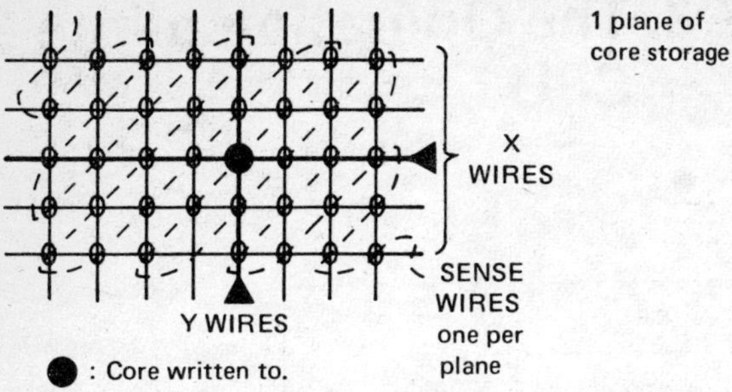

The directions of the currents along the X–Y lines to produce a '0' bit or a '1' bit are shown below.

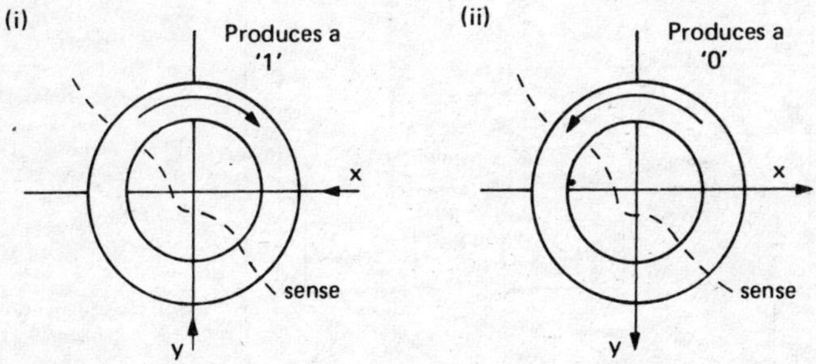

Note: The sense wires are not used in writing.

d. **Reading from a core.** To read from a core, the currents are passed along the X–Y wires as shown in (i) above. If the core holds a '1' no change is detected by the 'sense wire'. If the core holds a '0' a change is detected by the 'sense wire' because the change creates an (induced) current in the wire, *and also produces a '1'.* To correct for any changes made, the core is returned to its original state by the appropriate write action (c.i. or c.ii.). This complete process, including the final write, is known as reading from core.

e. Core storage is *non-volatile* because of the magnetically stable states of the cores.

Appendix 2.2. The Operation of the CPU

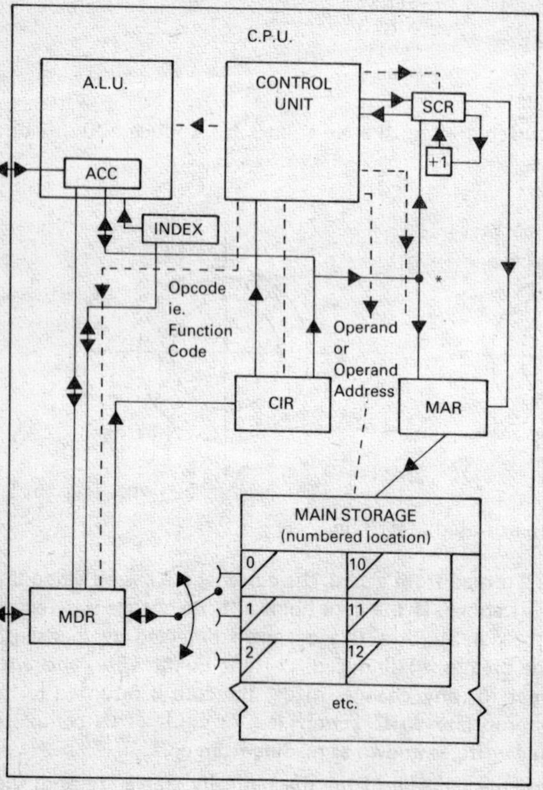

KEY

→ : Path of data or instructions

- - → : Path of command signals

ACC : Accumulators [9.23d]

MDR : Memory Data Register [9.24a]

CIR : Current Instruction Register [9.24b]

SCR : Sequence Control Register [9.27]

MAR : Memory Address Register [9.27b]

INDEX : Index Register [28.31]

I/O : Input and Output of data [9.24]

* : Selectable data path [9.29]

Appendix 2.3. Flowcharts

1. SYSTEMS FLOWCHART SYMBOLS.

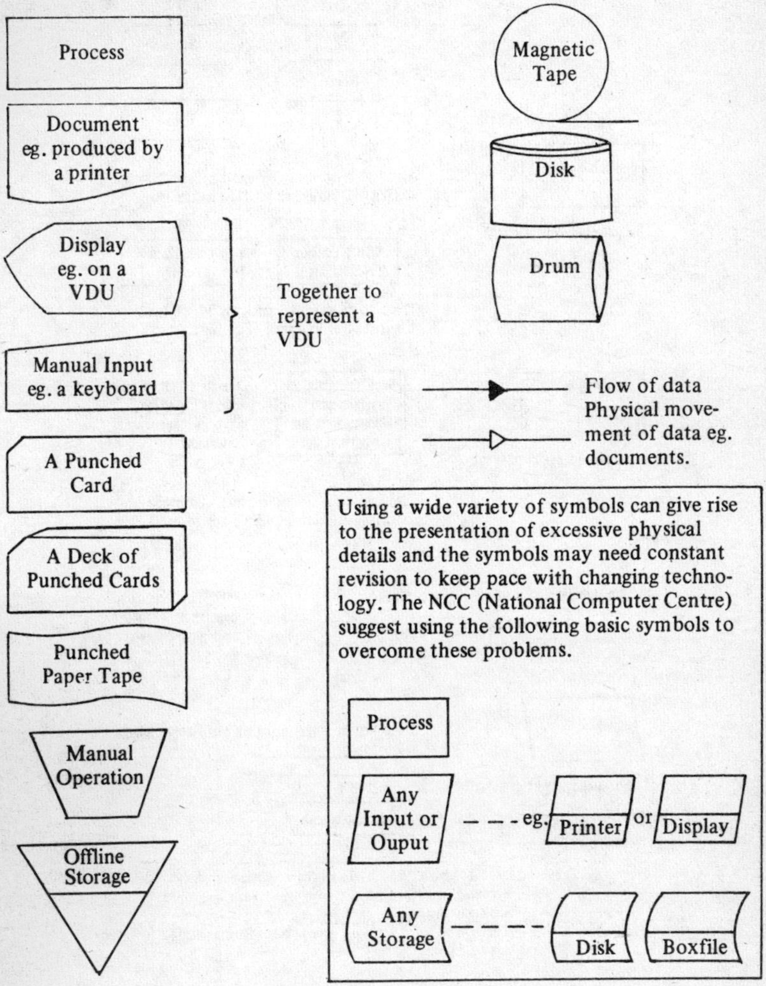

(Consult your examination regulations to see which symbols you should use in your examination).

NB. A system flowchart may show what the data processing procedures are, and how the procedures are arranged into sequences, but it will *not* show how the procedures are carried out.

2. PROGRAM FLOWCHART SYMBOLS.

The **terminal** symbol

Used as the first or last symbol in a program or separately drawn program module.

eg.

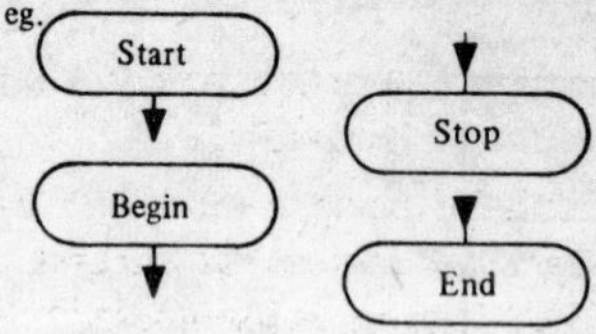

The **process** symbol

Used to represent any kind of processing activity. Details are written in the box.

eg.

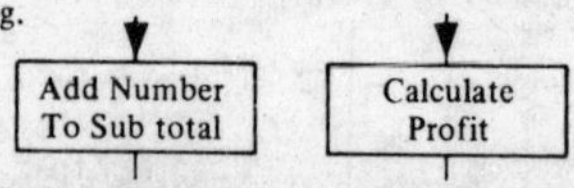

A **pre-defined process** symbol

Used to represent a process which has been set out in detail elsewhere.

eg.

Details of "Sort transactions" may be given in a separate flowchart.

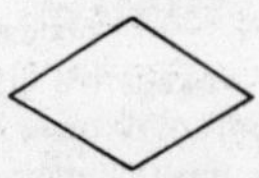

The **decision** symbol

Used where a decision has to be made in selecting the subsequent path to be followed.

eg.

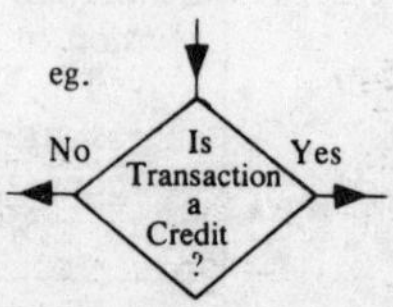

NB. There is only one entry point and at least two exits.

The **input/output** symbol

Used where data input or output is to be performed.

eg.

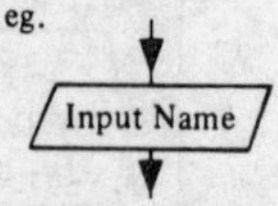

Used to show the flow/path of a sequence of symbols. Vertical lines without arrow heads are assumed to flow top to bottom.
Horizontal lines without arrow heads are assumed to flow left to right.

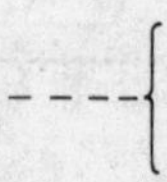

Used to add explanatory notes or descriptions.

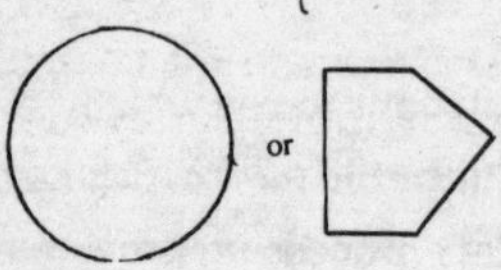

Exit to, or entry from, another part of the chart. (Connector symbol).

(Also see 14.29).

Appendix 2.4. Modulo Numbers and Check Digits

INTRODUCTION.

1. a. A check digit is a means of ensuring that a number (eg a customer account number) maintains its validity.

b. It is calculated using a modulus. Various moduli are used in practice and each has varying degrees of success at preventing certain types of errors. MODULUS 11 (eleven) is used here.

2. Modulus notation. Two numbers are **congruent** in a given modulus if both yield the same remainder when divided by the modulus

eg $8 \equiv 3 \pmod 5$

$\uparrow$

means congruent to

ie 8 has remainder 3 if divided by 5, and so does 3.

3. Finding modulus 11 check digits requires the division by 11 to find a remainder eg $15 \equiv 4 \pmod{11}$.

4. Check digits are calculated by a computer in the first place and are generally used in conjunction with fixed data (ie customers' numbers etc). As a result of a test done on Modulus 11 it was discovered that it detected all transcription and transposition errors and 91% of random errors.

5. Calculating the check digit.

a. Original code number 4214

b. Multiply each digit by the yield 5432

c. Product = (4 x 5) = 20
(2 x 4) = 8
(1 x 3) = 3
(4 x 2) = 8

d. Sum of products = 39

e. Division by 11 = 3, remainder 6, ie $39 \equiv 6 \pmod{11}$

f. Subtract remainder from modulus (ie 11 – 6) = 5

g. 5 is the check digit.

h. Code number now becomes 42145.

i. If the number yields a check digit greater than 9 it may be discarded or the check digit replaced by some other value.

6. Checking numbers. When the code number is input to the computer precisely the same calculation can be carried out (using weight of 1 for the rightmost digit) and the resultant remainder should be 0. If not then the number is incorrect.

$42145 = (4 \times 5) + (2 \times 4) + (1 \times 3) + (4 \times 2) + (5 \times 1) = 44$

Divide by 11; remainder = 0

7. This check can be carried out off-line by a machine called a CHECK DIGIT VERIFIER.

8. You would find this a useful programming exercise and it may also be worth including in an examination project in which account numbers or similar keys were used.

Appendix 3 Course Work Projects and Study

Course Work. Most of the examinations for which this book is a preparation require students to undertake a considerable amount of practical programming work throughout the course and include a project as part of the final examination.

Approaching Coursework. You may find the following ideas useful.

a. Try to relate your practical work to the theory you have covered so far, (ie turn principle into practice).

b. You can often build on earlier work or experience so look for:

i. A pattern in a problem

ii. Similarities and differences between the present problem and those done earlier. (This helps you to build up a set of general programming skills).

c. Keep your work in a suitable folder and in sufficient order that you can understand it later eg keep a diary or log.

Projects. (If possible choose *real* problems with *real* data).

a. Plan ahead and keep to deadlines as you prepare it.

b. It is easier to develop a project which has been clearly defined in terms of objectives at each stage and an overall aim.

c. Don't get sidetracked into trivial work which may make your program look nice, when you should be tackling programming problems. The examiner will not be fooled by pages of printout which hide a lack of substance in the work.

d. The examiner has to be able to understand your project when he reads it. He can only mark what you give him, and may miss some of what you have submitted if it is not clearly presented.

e. The required contents of a project are usually specified for each examination. Make sure you include every section. In particular, projects should make sense to possible other users.

Other Study.

1. Visits to installations near your home can give you an insight into current practice.

2. Reading occasional articles in weekly computer magazines can give you details of modern ideas and developments and sometimes provide case studies which act as a framework for examination answers.

Index